2007–2008
SUNDAY SCHOOL
COMMENTARY

Eighty-seventh Edition

Sunday School Publishing Board
National Baptist Convention, USA, Inc.

TOWNSEND**PRESS**
KJV • NRSV

BASED ON THE INTERNATIONAL LESSON SERIES

Writers: Dr. William Burwell, Dr. Geoffrey V. Guns; *Editors:* Dr. Gideon Olaleye; Rev. Olivia M. Cloud, Rev. Wellington A. Johnson, Sr.; *Copy Editors:* Yalemzewd Worku, Tanae McKnight, Lucinda Anderson, Tanya Savory; *Layout Designer:* Royetta Davis.

ISBN: 9781932972597

CONTENTS

CYCLE OF 2007-2010

Arrangement of Quarters According to the Church School Year,
September Through August

	Fall	Winter	Spring	Summer
2007–2008	God Created a People (Genesis) Theme: Creation	God's Call to the Christian Community (Luke) Theme: Call	God, the People, and the Covenant (1 and 2 Chronicles, Daniel, Haggai, Nehemiah) Theme: Covenant	Images of Christ (Hebrews, Gospels) Theme: Christ
2008–2009	New Testament Survey Theme: Community	Human Commitment (Luke, Old Testament) Theme: Commitment	Christ and Creation (Ezekiel, Luke, Acts, Ephesians) Theme: Creation	Call of God's Covenant Community (Exodus, Leviticus, Numbers, Deuteronomy) Theme: Call
2009–2010	Covenant Communities (Joshua, Judges, Ezra, Nehemiah, Mark, 1 and 2 Peter) Theme: Covenant	Christ the Fulfillment (Matthew) Theme: Christ	Teachings on Community (John, Ruth, New Testament) Theme: Community	Christian Commitment in Today's World (1 and 2 Thessalonians, Philippians) Theme: Commitment

LIST OF PRINTED TEXTS—2007-2008

The Printed Scriptural Texts used in the *2007-2008 Townsend Press School Commentary* are arranged here in the order in which they appear in the Bible. Opposite each reference is the page number on which Scriptures appear in this edition of the *Commentary*.

PREFACE

The *Townsend Press Commentary*, based on the International Lesson Series, is a production of the Sunday School Publishing Board, National Baptist Convention, USA, Incorporated. These lessons were developed consistent with the curriculum guidelines of the Committee on the Uniform Series, Education Leadership Ministries Commission, National Council of the Churches of Christ in the United States of America. Selected Christian scholars and theologians—who themselves embrace the precepts, doctrines, and positions on biblical interpretation that we have come to believe—are contributors to this publication. By participating in Scripture selection and the development of the matrices for the Guidelines for Lesson Development with the Committee on Uniform Series, this presentation reflects the historic faith that we share within a rich heritage of worship and witness.

The format of the *Townsend Press Commentary* consists of: unit title, general subject with age-level topics, printed text from the *King James Version* of the Bible, Objectives of the Lesson, Unifying Lesson Principle, Points to Be Emphasized, Topical Outline of the Lesson—with the Biblical Background of the Lesson, Exposition and Application of the Scripture, and Concluding Reflections (designed to focus on the salient points of the lesson), Word Power and the Home Daily Bible Readings. Each lesson concludes with a prayer.

The 2007-2008 *Commentary* features a Glossary of Terms to help readers better understand specific theological terms and biblical issues.

The *Townsend Press Commentary* is designed as an instructional aid for persons involved in the ministry of Christian education. While the autonomy of the individual soul before God is affirmed, we believe that biblical truths find their highest expression within the community of believers whose corporate experiences serve as monitors to preserve the integrity of the Christian faith. As such, the Word of God must not only be understood, it must also be embodied in the concrete realities of daily life. This serves to allow the Word of God to intersect in a meaningful way with those realities of life.

The presentation of the lessons anticipates the fact that some concepts and Scripture references do not lend themselves to meaningful comprehension by children. Hence, when this occurs, alternative passages of Scripture are used along with appropriate content emphases that are designed to assist children in their spiritual growth. There will, however, remain a consistent connection between the children, youth, and adult lessons through the Unifying Principle developed for each session.

We stand firm in our commitment to Christian growth, to the end that lives will become transformed through personal and group interaction with the Word of God. The challenge issued by the apostle Paul continues to find relevance for our faith journey: "Do your best to present yourself to God as one approved by him, a worker who has no need to be ashamed, rightly explaining the word of truth" *(2 Timothy 2:15, NRSV)*.

ACKNOWLEDGEMENTS

The *Townsend Press Commentary* is recognized as the centerpiece of a family of church school literature designed especially to assist teachers in their presentation of the lessons as well as to broaden the knowledge base of students from the biblical perspective. Our mission has been and will always be to provide religious educational experiences and spiritual resources for our constituency throughout this nation as well as many foreign countries. To achieve this end, the collaborative efforts of many people provide the needed expertise in the various areas of the production process. Although under the employ of the Sunday School Publishing Board, personnel too numerous to list approach their respective tasks with the dedication and devotion of those who serve God by serving His people. This *Commentary* is presented with gratitude to God for all those who desire a more comprehensive treatment of the selected Scriptures than is provided in the church school quarterlies, and it is intended to be a complementary resource thereto.

Our gratitude is hereby expressed to Dr. Geoffrey V. Guns, expositor for the Fall and Winter Quarters, and to Dr. William Burwell, expositor for the Spring and Summer Quarters, for their devotion in the development of the respective lessons. These two writers bring diversity and a broad spectrum of ministerial and educational experience to bear on the exposition and application of the Scripture.

The Sunday School Publishing Board consists of employees with expertise in their assigned areas whose self-understanding is that of "workers together with God" and partners with those who labor in the vineyard of teaching the Word of God in order to make disciples and nurture others toward a mature faith.

Special appreciation is appropriately accorded to the late Dr. E. L. Thomas, Executive Director of the Sunday School Publishing Board, for his insightful and inspiring leadership and motivation over the past eleven years. The determination he exhibited in seeking to meet the needs of our constituency by providing top-quality curriculum materials is not only reflected in this publication, but it also pervades all of the other educational resources that are produced for the enrichment and enhancement of the people of God. It is a credit to his leadership that the employees continue to embrace the mission of the Sunday School Publishing Board with a self-perspective that enhance their personal commitment to the cause of Christ as they interact with one another and intersect with the greater community of faith.

The task we are all involved in would be meaningless and fruitless were it not for the many readers for whom this publication has been so diligently prepared. The faithfulness of our constituency has been enduring for over a century, and we consider ourselves blessed to be their servants in the ministry of the printed Word exalting the living Word, our Lord and Savior Jesus Christ. We pray that God's grace will complement our efforts so that lives will be transformed within and beyond the confines of classroom interaction as the Spirit of God manifests Himself through the intersection of teaching and learning. It is our prayer that God may grant each of us the power to live for Him and be witness to the saving grace of the One who died for us, even Jesus Christ, our Lord and Savior.

Wellington A. Johnson, Sr.
Managing Editor

IN TRIBUTE
to
The Reverend Dr. E. L. Thomas

Executive Director
SUNDAY SCHOOL PUBLISHING BOARD

Since 1996, and each year thereafter that the *Townsend Press Sunday School Commentary* has been printed, Dr. E. L. Thomas has been recognized in the Acknowledgment section for his visionary leadership of this august organization. This year is different, however. Dr. Thomas passed from labor to reward on April 30, 2007. This edition is printed in tribute to him.

Dr. Thomas has served as Executive Director of the Sunday School Publishing Board since September 1996. He represented the Sunday School Publishing Board to the constituents of the National Baptist Convention, USA, Inc. and the world, serving as its chief ambassador.

Dr. Thomas' devotion to Jesus Christ, his deep commitment to the mission of the Sunday School Publishing Board, his love for Christian education, his fervor for preaching and his intellectual gifts, along with his professional accomplishments, provided a rich foundation through which he played a significant role in the Publishing Board and Convention at large. It was his visionary leadership and astute management style that enabled this publication to be one of the premier commentaries in our nation.

It is a credit to Dr. Thomas' leadership that the Sunday School Publishing Board stands today as a viable, vibrant organization. The entire staff of the Sunday School Publishing Board will truly miss Dr. Thomas, particularly the Publishing Division, where he untiringly demonstrated his gift of writing to edify God's people.

As our Executive Director may the work he has done speak for him!

Know Yor Writers

Dr. Geoffrey V. Guns ▼
Fall and Winter Quarters

Dr. Geoffrey V. Guns is a native of Newport, Rhode Island. He is the son of a retired Baptist pastor and co-pastor. Dr. Guns received his elementary and secondary education in the Norfolk public school system. He earned his B.S. degree in Business Administration from Norfolk State University in 1972.

In 1981, he earned his Masters of Divinity degree from the School of Theology, Virginia Union University, graduating *summa cum laude*. He earned his Doctor of Ministry degree from the School of Religion, Howard University in Washington, D.C. in 1985.

Dr. Guns is the senior pastor of the Second Calvary Baptist Church in Norfolk, Virginia, where he has served for the past twenty-three years. He is active in his denomination, the National Baptist Convention, USA, Inc. Dr. Guns served as the president of the Virginia Baptist State Convention (VBSC) from 1997 to 2001 and is currently the moderator for the Tidewater Peninsula Baptist Association (TPBA).

He has written articles for the *Christian Education Informer* of the Department of Christian Education of the Sunday School Publishing Board. Dr. Guns serves as vice chairman of the Council of Christian Education for the Department of Christian Education of the Sunday School Publishing Board of the NBC. He works with the Home Mission Board of the NBC and serves as the regional representative for the Southeast region.

He is the author of two books: *Church Financial Management* (1997), which is published by Providence House Publishers; and *Spiritual Leadership: A Practical Guide to Developing Spiritual Leaders in the Church* (2000), published by Orman Press, Inc.

He is married to the former Rosetta Harding of Richmond, Virginia. Mrs. Guns is a licensed social worker and works as a school social worker for the City of Chesapeake public schools. They are the parents of two daughters, Kimberly Michelle Cummings and Nicole Patrice. Dr. and Mrs. Guns have one granddaughter, Kennedy Nicole Cummings.

Dr. William Burwell ▼
Spring and Summer Quarters

The Reverend Dr. William Burwell comes to us with a rich background of education and experience. He holds several graduate and post-graduate degrees, including the Master of Divinity from Talbot Theological Seminary and the Doctor of Philosophy from the University of Southern California.

Dr. Burwell is a teacher of preachers and a regular lecturer at the National Baptist Convention USA's National Conference of Christian Educators. Through this conference, Dr. Burwell has utilized his insight and inspiration to guide those in attendance to effectively confront problems and explore possibilities in their local congregations. Because he is a renowned preacher, revivalist, lecturer, consultant and worship coordinator, Dr. Burwell has been a featured guest at ministers' conferences across the nation and in Germany, including the Oakcliff Baptist Ministers' Conference of Dallas, Texas; the Illinois Baptist Congress; and the Baptist Ministers' Conference of Oklahoma City, Oklahoma.

In addition to serving as Director of Christian Education at the Bethany Baptist Church in West Los Angeles, CA from 1979 to 1981, Dr. Burwell organized the First Berean Christian Church of Los Angeles in 1983. In just eight years, that congregation grew from 12 members to over 350 congregants. Since 1991, Dr. Burwell has been a full-time teacher, evangelist, and CEO of Burwell Ministries.

God Created a People

GENERAL INTRODUCTION

The study for this quarter surveys the theme of God's creative activity as seen from an Old Testament perspective. The three units in this quarter trace the story of God's creative power from the creation of the universe through human creation to the creation of a covenant people. When the people were threatened with starvation and death, God preserved their lives and continued to bless them.

Unit I, *God Created a People,* is a five-lesson unit that examines Israel's earliest stories. Lesson 1 raises the following question: "How Is Creation Possible?" The Genesis 1 account shows us how God chose to create life where none had existed and how God provided means of support for that life. Lesson 2 asks a pertinent question: "Why Are We Here?" The Bible states in Genesis that God created male and female in His own image and entrusted them with the stewardship of all creation. In Lesson 3, we learn about "Our Place in the Family." The Abraham, Sarah, and Isaac story helps us to recognize our place in our human family and in God's family. Lesson 4 highlights the issue of "Dealing with Dissension in the Family." We see how dissension in the family escalates with Sarah and Hagar. Lesson 5 deals with the topic, "Recognizing the Right Woman," and provides an example of God at work through human choices.

Unit II, *God's People Increased,* follows the development of the family of promise through Jacob and his twin, Esau. Lesson 6 reveals the rivalry between these two that began at birth. This rivalry of Esau and Jacob was exacerbated by their parents' favoritism. The seventh lesson on the topic "Understanding Our Dreams," focuses on the story of Jacob at Bethel. A dream reassured Jacob of God's continuing covenant with him as he fled from his enraged brother, who wanted to kill him. The eighth lesson looks at how the family of promise would develop through Jacob. Jacob dearly loved Rachel but unexpectedly found, after seven years of work, that he must first marry her older sister, Leah, and then work seven more years for the woman of his heart. With Lesson 9, the unit concludes with the reconciliation of the two estranged brothers, Esau and Jacob. Esau, who had been wronged by his brother, willingly greeted Jacob and offered him hospitality and signs of reconciliation.

Unit III, *God's People Re-created,* begins in Lesson 10 with Joseph, Jacob's beloved son by Rachel, dreaming about his future power. We see how Joseph announced his dreams of greatness to his family and how, understandably, he was met with anger and jealousy—a jealousy that led to Joseph's being sold into slavery and being taken to Egypt. In Lesson 11, "A Dream Unfolds," Joseph's boyhood dream begins to come true when he interprets a dream for Pharaoh. God gave Joseph the ability to interpret Pharaoh's dream. Pharaoh responded by elevating Joseph to a position of power, just as Joseph himself had dreamed. Lesson 12, titled "Negative Actions, Positive Results," spotlights Joseph's self-revelation to his brothers. Joseph tells his brothers that God had sent him to Egypt to preserve a remnant of the family of promise. The unit concludes in Lesson 13, "Leaving a Legacy," with Jacob moving to Egypt and living out his last days. He blessed his grandsons, assured that they would continue to grow into a multitude just as God had promised Abraham and Sarah.

IN THE BEGINNING...

Then God reached out and took the light in his hands,
And God rolled the light around in his hands
Until he made the sun;
And he set that sun a-blazing in the heavens.
And the light that was left from making the sun
God gathered it up in a shining ball
And flung it against the darkness,
Spangling the night with the moon and stars.
Then down between
The darkness and the light
He hurled the world;
And God said: That's good!

LESSON 1   **September 2, 2007**

GOD CREATED THE HEAVENS AND THE EARTH

DEVOTIONAL READING: **Psalm 8**
PRINT PASSAGE: **Genesis 1:1-6, 8, 10, 12-15, 19-20, 22-23, 25**

BACKGROUND SCRIPTURE: **Genesis 1:1-25**
KEY VERSES: **Genesis 1:1-2**

Genesis 1:1-6, 8, 10, 12-15, 19-20, 22-23, 25—KJV

IN THE beginning God created the heaven and the earth.

2 And the earth was without form, and void; and darkness was upon the face of the deep. And the Spirit of God moved upon the face of the waters.

3 And God said, Let there be light: and there was light.

4 And God saw the light, that it was good: and God divided the light from the darkness.

5 And God called the light Day, and the darkness he called Night. And the evening and the morning were the first day.

6 And God said, Let there be a firmament in the midst of the waters, and let it divide the waters from the waters.

.....

8 And God called the firmament Heaven. And the evening and the morning were the second day.

.....

10 And God called the dry land Earth; and the gathering together of the waters called he Seas: and God saw that it was good.

.....

12 And the earth brought forth grass, and herb yielding seed after his kind, and the tree yielding fruit, whose seed was in itself, after his kind: and God saw that it was good.

13 And the evening and the morning were the third day.

14 And God said, Let there be lights in the firmament of the heaven to divide the day from the night; and let them be for signs, and for seasons, and for days, and years:

Genesis 1:1-6, 8, 10, 12-15, 19-20, 22-23, 25—NRSV

IN THE beginning when God created the heavens and the earth,

2 the earth was a formless void and darkness covered the face of the deep, while a wind from God swept over the face of the waters.

3 Then God said, "Let there be light"; and there was light.

4 And God saw that the light was good; and God separated the light from the darkness.

5 God called the light Day, and the darkness he called Night. And there was evening and there was morning, the first day.

6 And God said, "Let there be a dome in the midst of the waters, and let it separate the waters from the waters."

.....

8 God called the dome Sky. And there was evening and there was morning, the second day.

.....

10 God called the dry land Earth, and the waters that were gathered together he called Seas. And God saw that it was good.

.....

12 The earth brought forth vegetation: plants yielding seed of every kind, and trees of every kind bearing fruit with the seed in it. And God saw that it was good.

13 And there was evening and there was morning, the third day.

14 And God said, "Let there be lights in the dome of the sky to separate the day from the night; and let them be for signs and for seasons and for days and years,

Without the earth and its ecosystems, human life would not be possible. How did creation come into being? In the Genesis 1 account, we learn that God chose to create life where none had existed and God provided means of support for that life.

15 And let them be for lights in the firmament of the heaven to give light upon the earth: and it was so.

.….

19 And the evening and the morning were the fourth day.
20 And God said, Let the waters bring forth abundantly the moving creature that hath life, and fowl that may fly above the earth in the open firmament of heaven.

.….

22 And God blessed them, saying, Be fruitful, and multiply, and fill the waters in the seas, and let fowl multiply in the earth.
23 And the evening and the morning were the fifth day.

.….

25 And God made the beast of the earth after his kind, and cattle after their kind, and every thing that creepeth upon the earth after his kind: and God saw that it was good.

15 and let them be lights in the dome of the sky to give light upon the earth." And it was so.

.….

19 And there was evening and there was morning, the fourth day.
20 And God said, "Let the waters bring forth swarms of living creatures, and let birds fly above the earth across the dome of the sky."

.….

22 God blessed them, saying, "Be fruitful and multiply and fill the waters in the seas, and let birds multiply on the earth."
23 And there was evening and there was morning, the fifth day.

.….

25 God made the wild animals of the earth of every kind, and the cattle of every kind, and everything that creeps upon the ground of every kind. And God saw that it was good.

TOPICAL OUTLINE OF THE LESSON

I. **Introduction**
  A. The Creation Story
  B. Biblical Background

II. **Exposition and Application of the Scripture**
  A. In the Beginning, God! (Genesis 1:1-5)
  B. God Creates the Heavens (Genesis 1:6, 8)
  C. God Creates Plant Life (Genesis 1:10, 12-13)
  D. God Creates the Sun and the Moon (Genesis 1:14-15, 19)
  E. God Creates the Beasts of the Field and Blesses Creation (Genesis 1:20, 22-23, 25)

III. **Concluding Reflections**

LESSON OBJECTIVES
Upon completion of this lesson, the students will know that:
1. God is truly the creator of heaven and earth, as opposed to the evolutionist idea of creation;
2. God is a God of order who systematically creates in orderly fashion; and,
3. God's creatures are subservient to Him.

POINTS TO BE EMPHASIZED
ADULT/YOUTH
Adult Topic: How Is Creation Possible?
Youth Topic: Starting Line
Adult/Youth Key Verses: Genesis 1:1-2
Print Passage: Genesis 1:1-6, 8, 10, 12-15, 19-20, 22-23, 25
—The original audience members were Semitic nomadic herders.
—Why would this poetic account have been so precious to them?

—What does this account say about creation?

—God is the One who creates.

—Everything that exists finds its source in God.

—In the Scriptures, the day begins at dusk and so a new day begins with rest. Note in Scripture it consistently says it was evening and it was morning.

—God calls creation "good."

CHILDREN

Children Topic: God Created the World

Key Verse: Genesis 1:10

Print Passage: Genesis 1:1-6, 8-11, 13, 16, 19, 21, 23

—The pre-existence of God "in the beginning" (verse 1) is assumed.

—At each step in the creation process, God announced what was to be created.

—God was totally responsible for the creation of the world, and when each "day" was complete, God surveyed it and pronounced it "good."

—In the first five "days," God created things in a very orderly progression.

—The physical world received God's blessings.

I. INTRODUCTION

A. The Creation Story

The creation of the heavens and the earth is one of God's most remarkable achievements. Throughout the ages, scientists and philosophers have speculated about the origin of the universe. There have been many theories about how the universe came to be in its present form; however, none of those theories has been proven to be true. Christians believe that the account of the Creation, as written in the Bible, is a fact that we accept by faith. Both Christians and Jews believe that the account of the origin of the universe is found in the book of Genesis. The writer of Hebrews 11:3 wrote, "Through faith we understand that the worlds were framed by the word of God, so that things which are seen were not made of things which do appear."

Today's lesson affirms that God is the creator of heaven and earth. This includes everything that is part of the world in which we live. Everything that exists finds its source and sustenance in God. In this lesson, we will study the first five days of Creation and what God brought into being during that time.

B. Biblical Background

Genesis is the first book in both the Hebrew and Christian Scriptures. It is a part of the portion of the Old Testament that we call the Pentateuch (first five books of the Bible). There have been a variety of positions set forth as to who might have written and compiled this marvelous work detailing God's creative activity. The question of authorship has been at the center of many disagreements between conservative and liberal scholars. Many liberal scholars believe that Genesis, along with the other four books of the Law, reflects the writing of four different Hebrew writers that they call: J (Jahwist), E (Elohist), P (Priestly), and D (Deuteronomic). Bible scholars call these fancy names the "Four Source Hypothesis." The brain behind this hypothesis was J. Julius Wellhausen.

However, the majority of Christians, who take a more conservative stand on the Scriptures, affirm the authorship of Moses, because it is attested to within the Scriptures (see Exodus 24:1-4; Deuteronomy 31:9; Joshua 23:6; 2 Chronicles 25:4). The ancient Hebrew and Jewish scribes and rabbis never raised a question about the authorship of the Torah. They affirmed the authorship of Moses. Jesus also affirmed the authorship of Moses and his authority as a lawgiver (see Mark 1:44; 7:10; 10:3; 12:26; Luke 5:12; 16:31; 24:44; John 4:56).

Genesis is called the "book of beginnings" (Hebrew—*bereshith*) because it is our primary source for knowledge about the beginning of Creation, the origin of the human race, the cause and result of human disobedience, which is sin, and because it details the early history of the ancient Hebrew people.

II. EXPOSITION AND APPLICATION OF THE SCRIPTURE

A. In the Beginning, God!
(Genesis 1:1-5)

IN THE beginning God created the heaven and the earth. And the earth was without form, and void; and darkness was upon the face of the deep. And the Spirit of God moved upon the face of the waters. And God said, Let there be light: and there was light. And God saw the light, that it was good: and God divided the light from the darkness. And God called the light Day, and the darkness he called Night. And the evening and the morning were the first day.

Genesis begins with the most basic of theological affirmations—"In the beginning...." The very first question that we must answer has to do with how we understand the "beginning." Primarily, it does not refer to the beginning of God, because God has always been. He is the One who has neither origin nor ending (see John 1:1-4). He is infinite—that is, without an ending (see Isaiah 41:4; Revelation 1:8). Therefore, the beginning here refers to the beginning of the Creation as it is outlined in this first chapter, since what follows the introductory verse is the account of God's daily activity in creating the heavens and the earth. Anything that had been said about how God came to be, and when He first existed, would be mere speculation. We can never know because the Bible does not address the question of God's beginning.

A second affirmation refers to the existence and being of God. In other ancient creation stories, such as the Babylonian creation myth, other beings participate in this creative process. The Bible affirms that God is the creator. This is the most basic affirmation of our faith. Here we have a picture of the mighty God who stands over and above creation, yet He is active within the very creation that He made. He is the One who is before all things (see Colossians 1:17). The word created comes from a Hebrew word, *bara,* which means "to fashion," or "to cause to be." Verse 2 begins, "And the earth was without form...." Was the substance of the earth here before God began creating? The answer is *no!* First, the Creation out of nothing was followed by order out of chaos. The Hebrew word for "without form" is *tohuw* (to-hoo) meaning "unreality—confusion and disorder." Hence, there was nothing present when God began to create.

The telling of how the "Spirit of God," *ru_ah Elohim,* moved across the face of the deep is a way of capturing in words the creative energy of God. Here we have a picture of what could well be the Trinity (the Father, Son, and Holy Spirit) involved in the Creation process. The Hebrew word for God *(Elohim)* is plural and refers to more than one. The text does not mention that there were three persons involved in the Creation, although some have implied it. The point of the passage is that everything we see in the world and in the heavens above has its origin in God. God is the one who brings order out of chaos. In these two verses, we see several of the attributes of God. That He is all-powerful speaks to us of His omnipotence. He has no beginning nor ending; this speaks to us of His eternality. Here we take comfort in knowing that God is more than capable of handling any problem or crisis we face.

Creation was a reflection of the omnipotence of God and the wisdom of God. "And God said...." He spoke and order came out of chaos. His Word was both powerful and creative at the same time. God said, "Let there be light," and light came into existence. The next thing God did was to divide the light from the darkness. Why would God create light first? We can only speculate. Some have suggested that He did it for the purpose of being able to see His creation. But such thinking and reasoning is unsound, because God can see in the darkness; hence, He did not need to create light to see what He had made (see Psalm 139:12).

God separated the light from the darkness. Moreover, God named what He did. He called the light *day,* and He called the darkness *night.* And the evening and the morning were the first day. The separation of darkness and light created time. God created time, but He does not live in time. He stands over and above time, yet He can step into our days and nights.

What are the lessons for us? First, we see that God's Word produces life. In the New Testament, the Word of God came to be associated with Jesus Christ, who is the living Word of God made flesh (see John 1:14). Second, it is through the preaching of God's Word that we experience the power of God to save the lost (see Romans 1:16-17; 1 Corinthians 1:18). Finally, it is interesting to note that when someone comes to saving faith, that person is said to come from the darkness into the light of life (see 2 Corinthians 4:6; Ephesians 5:8).

B. God Creates the Heavens (Genesis 1:6, 8)

And God said, Let there be a firmament in the midst of the waters, and let it divide the waters from the waters. ...And God called the firmament Heaven. And the evening and the morning were the second day.

The second day of God's creative activity began like the first. The Scriptures note that, "And God said..." God created a *firmament,* a word that means "expanse" or "curtain." In ancient Hebrew belief, this was thought of as a flat, solid-like curtain that held the atmosphere in place. This was not a physical surface, but rather one that served the purpose of keeping the atmosphere or sky in place. God divided the waters of the earth (vapors) from the clouds. He called the firmament *heaven.* And the evening and morning were the second day.

C. God Creates Plant Life (Genesis 1:10, 12-13)

And God called the dry land Earth; and the gathering together of the waters called he Seas: and God saw that it was good. ...And the earth brought forth grass, and herb yielding seed after his kind, and the tree yielding fruit, whose seed was in itself, after his kind: and God saw that it was good. And the evening and the morning were the third day.

On the third day of Creation, God gathered the waters below the heavens into one place and He called them the *seas.* He caused the dry land to appear and called it the *earth* (verse 10). The earth was commanded to produce vegetation and various plant life. "And the earth brought forth grass, and herb yielding seed after his kind..." (verse 12). Interpreters have debated as to whether God created the seed first or the actual plant. What is certain is that the earth began to blossom with beauty and pageantry. The grass was given the power to produce its own offspring without further interference by God.

In these verses, we learn to appreciate the beauty of God's creation and we must sense the need to be more concerned about its preservation. The world of plants was created by God with the ability to reproduce itself and sustain itself from generation to generation.

You and I are the product of the seed of the incorruptible Word of God (1 Peter 1:23). Jesus Christ has commanded the church to go and make disciples of all nations and to reproduce in others what Jesus Christ has produced in us. Are you good seed or bad?

D. God Creates the Sun and the Moon (Genesis 1:14-15, 19)

And God said, Let there be lights in the firmament of the heaven to divide the day from the night; and let them be for signs, and for seasons, and for days, and years: And let them be for lights in the firmament of the heaven to give light upon the earth: and it was so. ... And the evening and the morning were the fourth day.

On the fourth day, God created the sun, moon, and stars. There is no mention of the sun and moon, but clearly this is what was meant. They are not mentioned by name, quite possibly because the pagans who lived around Israel worshiped the sun and moon and named their own gods after them. They were called the "greater lights" and the "lesser lights" because that is what they were (verse 16). The greater light ruled by day and the lesser lights of the moon and stars ruled by night. These lights still serve very specific purposes in the plan of God. They were set up in the heavens to give light to the earth. On a clear night when the moon is full and bright, the illumination it gives can be startling. God intended that these lights would serve His purpose in the Creation.

First, these lights divided the day from the night. We cannot be sure whether or not this was a twenty-four hour period. Second, they were signs (Hebrew—*owth,* pronounced "oth") of God's creative intentions. The signs pointed beyond themselves to the seasons, days, and years. Signs are very important in the Scriptures because they point to something or someone greater than themselves (see Exodus 7:3; 10:1; Deuteronomy 6:22; Joshua 24:17; Isaiah 8:18; Jeremiah 32:20). Third, and finally, the signs determined the seasons, days, and years. They were and are the dividing markers that indicate when new seasons begin.

E. God Creates the Beasts of the Field and Blesses Creation (Genesis 1:20, 22-23, 25)

And God said, Let the waters bring forth abundantly the moving creature that hath life, and fowl that may fly above the earth in the open firmament of heaven. ... And God blessed them, saying, Be fruitful, and multiply, and fill the waters in the seas, and let fowl multiply in the earth. And the evening and the morning were the fifth day. ... And God made the beast of the earth after his kind, and cattle after their kind, and every thing that creepeth upon the earth after his kind: and God saw that it was good.

In this section, we take up the activity of God on the fifth day and a portion of the sixth day. Again, God spoke and things began to happen. He called for the waters to bring forth an abundance of sea creatures and birds. The Hebrew word for *abundantly* means "swarms of fish" or "sea creatures." Further, the creatures that are mentioned were not the wild animals. The word refers to creeping and crawling creatures. They were all blessed and told to recreate themselves in abundance. "Be fruitful, and multiply, and fill the waters in the seas, and let fowl multiply in the earth." Fruitfulness is a sign of fertility and blessing. God blessed the animals, which was the reason why they were fruitful and why they multiplied. For the first time, we see living creatures upon the earth and in the skies above the earth. This was the end of the fifth day.

During the sixth day, God created the beasts of the earth, and like everything else, they were created to reproduce their own kind. Cattle would produce cattle and creeping creatures would produce creeping creatures. When it was all said and done, God looked at what He had done and saw that it was all good. In the next lesson, we will take up the other things that God did on the sixth day.

III. CONCLUDING REFLECTIONS

Genesis is perhaps the most important book in the canon of Scripture. There are several reasons why: First, it teaches us the history of the origin of the world and all that is contained therein. Second, we see the awesome power of God who is able to speak and bring things into existence. Third, we see the power of God that is limitless and boundless. There is nothing that God cannot do. Fourth, we see that it is God's will for everyone in the human race to be blessed and in a position to be fruitful and multiply.

PRAYER

Lord God almighty, teach us to appreciate the gift of the earth that You have so graciously given to each of us. May we live in such a way that we will bring joy to Your heart as we seek to be better stewards of the planet and its vast wealth. In Jesus' name, we pray. Amen.

WORD POWER

Form and Void (Hebrew: *tohuw* and *bohuw*)—*void* carries the idea of confusion and disorder, and no distinction of parts. *Void* also means "undistinguishable ruin." However, out of this came order when God spoke to it. We will not be able to comprehend how formless the materials looked. One thing we know is that God brought order out of disorder.

HOME DAILY BIBLE READINGS
(August 27—September 2, 2007)

God Created the Heavens and the Earth
MONDAY, August 27: "God the Creator" (Psalm 8)
TUESDAY, August 28: "The First Day" (Genesis 1:1-5)
WEDNESDAY, August 29: "The Sky" (Genesis 1:6-8)
THURSDAY, August 30: "The First Harvest" (Genesis 1:9-13)
FRIDAY, August 31: "The Sun and Moon" (Genesis 1:14-19)
SATURDAY, September 1: "The Birds and Sea Creatures" (Genesis 1:20-23)
SUNDAY, September 2: "The Animals" (Genesis 1:24-25)

LESSON 2   September 9, 2007

GOD CREATED HUMANKIND

DEVOTIONAL READING: **Isaiah 40:25-31**
PRINT PASSAGE: **Genesis 1:26-30**

BACKGROUND SCRIPTURE: **Genesis 1:26–2:3**
KEY VERSE: **Genesis 1:26**

Genesis 1:26-30—KJV

26 And God said, Let us make man in our image, after our likeness: and let them have dominion over the fish of the sea, and over the fowl of the air, and over the cattle, and over all the earth, and over every creeping thing that creepeth upon the earth.

27 So God created man in his own image, in the image of God created he him; male and female created he them.

28 And God blessed them, and God said unto them, Be fruitful, and multiply, and replenish the earth, and subdue it: and have dominion over the fish of the sea, and over the fowl of the air, and over every living thing that moveth upon the earth.

29 And God said, Behold, I have given you every herb bearing seed, which is upon the face of all the earth, and every tree, in the which is the fruit of a tree yielding seed; to you it shall be for meat.

30 And to every beast of the earth, and to every fowl of the air, and to every thing that creepeth upon the earth, wherein there is life, I have given every green herb for meat: and it was so.

Genesis 1:26-30—NRSV

26 Then God said, "Let us make humankind in our image, according to our likeness; and let them have dominion over the fish of the sea, and over the birds of the air, and over the cattle, and over all the wild animals of the earth, and over every creeping thing that creeps upon the earth."

27 So God created humankind in his image, in the image of God he created them; male and female he created them.

28 God blessed them, and God said to them, "Be fruitful and multiply, and fill the earth and subdue it; and have dominion over the fish of the sea and over the birds of the air and over every living thing that moves upon the earth."

29 God said, "See, I have given you every plant yielding seed that is upon the face of all the earth, and every tree with seed in its fruit; you shall have them for food.

30 And to every beast of the earth, and to every bird of the air, and to everything that creeps on the earth, everything that has the breath of life, I have given every green plant for food." And it was so.

BIBLE FACT

The book of Genesis explains the beginning of many important realities. The writer asserts that God created in the beginning: the universe, the earth, and humankind. But Adam and Eve were created in His own image. They were special to God. He gave them a home in the beautiful, luscious Garden of Eden. God gave them choices, but they disobeyed Him when they chose not to follow His order. In a nutshell, they sinned. Because of God's love He made a promise, which we call covenant. God is a promise keeper and He keeps them now. He promises to love, accept, and forgive us.

UNIFYING LESSON PRINCIPLE

Human beings are amazing creatures, sharing much with other forms of life and yet remaining distinctly different. Why was humanity created and placed on the earth? The Israelites believed, as the Bible states in Genesis, that God created male and female in God's own image and entrusted them with the stewardship of all creation.

TOPICAL OUTLINE OF THE LESSON

I. **Introduction**
   A. Fulfilling God's Purpose
   B. Biblical Background

II. **Exposition and Application of the Scripture**
   A. Invitation to Create (Genesis 1:26)
   B. Male and Female Created with Responsibility (Genesis 1:27-28)
   C. Created to Have Dominion (Genesis 1:29-30)

III. **Concluding Reflections**

LESSON OBJECTIVES

Upon completion of this lesson, the students will know that:

1. God created us as His masterpiece;
2. We are created to love God and have dominion; and,
3. God created us as male and female to replenish the earth.

POINTS TO BE EMPHASIZED

ADULT/YOUTH

Adult Topic: Why Are We Here?
Youth Topic: In Whose Image?
Adult Key Verse: Genesis 1:26
Youth Key Verse: Genesis 1:27
Print Passage: Genesis 1:26-30

—What does it mean to be "created in the image of God"?
—God entrusted human beings with "dominion" over other created beings.
—What does the command to "be fruitful and multiply" mean in the world today?
—God created human beings and gave them oversight of creation.
—Scripture emphasizes God's abundance, whereas human systems introduce the notion of scarcity.
—On the seventh day, God rested. Working seven days demonstrates human arrogance and lack of trust in God's benevolence.

CHILDREN

Children Topic: God Created People
Key Verse: Genesis 1:27
Print Passage: Genesis 1:24-31; 2:2

—God created human beings in His image.
—God made human beings stewards over all He had created.
—As part of God's creative acts, the creation of human beings served as a climax to the creative process.
—God surveyed all creation and found it "very good."
—God demonstrated the need for both work and rest.

I. INTRODUCTION

A. Fulfilling God's Purpose

Every human being upon the face of the earth has a God-given calling that only he or she can fulfill. I have come to believe that every major problem plaguing the human race is intended for resolution by someone who has been born or who is yet to be born. Yet there are many people who go through life failing to discover and discern God's purpose for their lives. God's will for your life is not a secret that has to be endlessly pursued in order to be discovered. Every Christian has been given an assignment from God.

In the previous lesson, we learned that God created the heavens and the earth and that everything in the created order was created for a purpose (see Genesis 1:1-25). The moon was created to serve as the lesser light of the night and the sun was created to heat the planet and serve as the source of daylight.

In this lesson, we will examine the events that concluded the sixth and final day of God's creative activity. Second, we will discover the original intentions and purposes of God when He created the human race. Third, we will examine the meaning of the expression, "the image of God" *(imago dei)*. Fourth, we will come to appreciate our uniqueness as males and females created in God's image.

B. Biblical Background

Today, we take up the study of the creation of the human race. Within the field of theology, this particular area would be classified as "Biblical Anthropology." Anthropology is the study of the origin, culture, and social behavior of the human race. Biblical anthropology is the study of the origins and the destiny of the human race.

The origin of the human race has been a question of serious concern for thousands of years. Every major civilization has developed some concept or belief about the origin of the human race. In recent years, the question of human origins has returned to the forefront of public debate and is one of the most contentious social, religious, and scientific issues of our day. Those who embrace a purely scientific perspective contend that the origin of the human race is the result of millions of years of evolution. Creationists, on the other hand, teach that the Bible is the source of our understanding regarding the origin of the human race. The preponderance of teachings in the Bible that declare that God is the creator of heaven and earth is overwhelming. It is a consistent thread of teachings that begins in Genesis and concludes with Revelation. We simply must understand and be able to intelligently express our beliefs regarding the creation of the world and the origin of the human race. This lesson today will help ground our understanding of human origins in the Word of God. *Genesis* is the appropriate name for this book, for it is the "book of beginnings."

II. EXPOSITION AND APPLICATION OF THE SCRIPTURE

A. Invitation to Create
(Genesis 1:26)

And God said, Let us make man in our image, after our likeness: and let them have dominion over the fish of the sea, and over the fowl of the air, and over the cattle, and over all the earth, and over every creeping thing that creepeth upon the earth.

In His previous creative acts (Genesis 1:1-25), God spoke and things came into existence. He spoke and said "Let there be light," and it was so. He ordered the earth to bring forth living creatures, and it was so. Now we come to God's crowning achievement, the creation of human beings. God said, "Let us make man in our image..." (Genesis 1:26). *Man* comes from the Hebrew word *'adam* and it literally means "human being" or "humankind." It does not just refer to man, but to both men and women.

There are two theological issues in this verse that have been widely discussed and debated for hundreds of years. The first concerns the use of "let us" and the second concerns the use of "image of God." Old Testament interpreters, from the earliest times, have debated the question of exactly who was referred to in the use of the plural, "let us." Some interpreters have suggested that God consulted with the angels of heaven when He decided to make man. There are some who suggest that this may be a reference to the adoption of some of the polytheistic beliefs of the nations that surrounded Israel. But there is nothing in any of the ancient writings of the Jewish rabbis or the Jewish oral tradition that would lend support to either of these arguments.

The traditional Christian interpretation states that in this verse we see the first glimpse of the Trinity, all participating together to form a human being from the dust of the earth (John 1:1-3). The second question concerns the meaning of the phrase, "image of God." Neither the Old Testament nor the New Testaments offers a clear definition of what is meant by "image of God." *Image* comes from the Hebrew word *tselem* which means "resemblance, likeness." Man was not created to take the place of God, but to represent the interests of God on the earth. Man represents God's interests by taking responsibility for ruling everything upon the earth.

What are the lessons that we learn from this important verse? First, we learn that human beings were created. We are creatures who have been given glory, will, honor, and dignity. This implies that all people are important in the eyes of God. Second, there is within all human beings the capacity to seek and desire true communion with our Creator. It is in Him that "we live, and move, and have our being" (Acts 17:28).

Third, the image of God can be destroyed or distorted by sin and disobedience. Sin is the result of human beings' attempts to step outside of the boundaries established by God. As creatures, we can never be on the same level as God. If we want to know what it means to live in the image of God today, all we need to do is look at Jesus Christ. Jesus was the visible image of the invisible God on the earth (John 14:7-10; 2 Corinthians 4:4; Colossians 1:15). How do we regain the lost image of God? We must confess our sins to God, forsake them, and then receive the gift of the Holy Spirit in our lives.

B. Male and Female Created with Responsibility (Genesis 1:27-28)

So God created man in his own image, in the image of God created he him; male and female created he them. And God blessed them, and God said unto them, Be fruitful, and multiply, and replenish the earth, and subdue it: and have dominion over the fish of the sea, and over the fowl of the air, and over every living thing that moveth upon the earth.

Verse 27 begins with a restatement of what God has already done. Now we come to what may be one of the most divisive current debates of the twenty-first century. How do we understand human sexuality? Was it God's original intention that men and women could become confused about their genders? First, we are told that God created man in His own image. Second, we are told that it was in the image of God that He created humankind, or "man" (singular). Third, we are told that God created male and female (plural). How are we to understand this language?

First, there are limits that God placed upon us as human beings from the very foundation of the world. We were not created to live forever. There is nothing in the creation story that supports a belief that we are infinite. We are finite. We will live for a fixed number of days and will return to the dust from whence we came.

Second, humankind as the crowning achievement of God's creative genius has been given a rational mind which distinguishes us from all other creatures on the earth. We possess the ability to know, do, and act upon rational thoughts. Human beings can dream and envision their futures, something that other living animals cannot do. This places us in a position of greater responsibility before God. We are fully capable of being in relationship with God.

Third, both men and women are created in the image of God. This does not make God feminine in any way. It does mean that men and women are equally important in the eyes of God. This also reinforces the truth that men are not greater than women in any way; they simply were created with different functions in the divine plan of Creation.

Fourth, we see the creation of sexual identity. We are not free to redefine our sexual identity. We are not to justify sexual deviancy by claiming that we were born with desires to be attracted to the same sex. One of the primary reasons that Sodom was destroyed by fire and brimstone had to do with the unholy desires of the men and boys in that city (see Genesis 19:4-11). The Bible strongly condemns homosexuality and calls it an abomination before the Lord. Leviticus 18:22 says, "Thou shalt not lie with mankind, as with womankind: it is abomination" (see also Leviticus 20:13; Judges 19:22ff; Romans 1:27). An abomination is something that God finds to be despicable and abhorrent. God created male and female, distinct, different, yet capable of being in holy fellowship with God and each other.

There are people who argue that human sexuality has nothing to do with whether one is a male or female, as far as sexual desires and preferences. Those who wish to give support to same-sex marriage would like to use the distorted belief that they were born with desires for the same sex. However, such logic and thinking is totally foreign to the teachings of Scripture. To make such a presumptuous claim is to state that God made a mistake. Such a claim then means that God is less than perfect and that creation was not good. When God finished everything that He had made He pronounced that it was very good, which included the male and female that He had made. Deviant sexual behavior is more a matter of choice than it is a reflection of God's divine plan.

Fifth, God created male and female to live in harmony and relationship with each other. God ordained marriage by the mere fact of the creation of a single species with different sexual identities. God has so made us that we desire each other's presence and companionship.

C. Created to Have Dominion
(Genesis 1:29-30)

And God said, Behold, I have given you every herb bearing seed, which is upon the face of all the earth, and every tree, in the which is the fruit of a tree yielding seed; to you it shall be for meat. And to every beast of the earth, and to every fowl of the air, and to every thing that creepeth upon the earth, wherein there is life, I have given every green herb for meat: and it was so.

Immediately after creating human beings, God blessed them. To bless is to bestow favor upon someone. God did not just bless the male—He blessed both male and female together. The act of God's blessing is a trait of His divine character and it is seen throughout the Scriptures. One of the central pronouncements of blessing was made to Abraham that through his seed all of the families of the earth would be blessed (Genesis 12:1-3). God can bless in such a way that we cannot outrun all of the blessings that He can bestow upon us (Deuteronomy 28:1-14). However, blessings come because of one's obedience and faithfulness to God.

The very first clause in Genesis 1:28 states, "Be fruitful, and multiply, and replenish the earth, and subdue it and have dominion … over every living thing that moveth upon the earth." What are we to make of these commands? Fruitfulness implies health and the presence of life. The command to be fruitful was a command to live in such a way that they could continually reproduce themselves. Here

we come face-to-face with the principal reason for the different sexes. Only a male and a female can come together to reproduce another human being.

Multiply means to become great, and *replenish* gives the notion that life will fade, but the male and female have the potential for living forever through new generations that are reproduced from their seed. These verses force us to look at some rather common beliefs that are held among some Christians that the first man and woman were created to live forever. The Old Testament says nothing of the kind.

God gave the first people everything that they needed to succeed and prosper. The first man and woman were told to subdue the earth—that is, to bring it under their control and then take dominion over it. At no time was man given dominion over the woman. When we look at the sad state of affairs in the world today, we see numerous instances where people are being viciously dominated by others, such as in Darfur in Sudan, Burma, and throughout the Middle East. These stories are the same.

Clearly, human beings bear a serious responsibility for the ecological damage that they have done to the earth. I have traveled on several occasions to Nigeria, West Africa. Nigeria is the world's sixth largest exporter of petroleum. But it is also one of the most polluted countries in the world and is an environmental disaster. The oil companies have polluted the rivers, lakes, and soil while the government has looked in another direction. What will God require at the hands of those who presided over such a shameful policy of destruction? The Creation narrative points out our responsibility and accountability before God. We are blessed to take dominion over all other creatures, but to cause ecological disaster when the locals are powerless is a sin against the Creator. Equally, any domination of any human being anywhere in the world is a sin against the almighty God.

III. CONCLUDING REFLECTIONS

This lesson is critically important because Genesis is the book of beginnings. It is this understanding about the origins of life and the world that should guide our thinking about life and our responsibilities in God's world. The title for today's topic is: "Why Are We Here?" Every individual who participates in this lesson should know that we are here for God's sake. That being the case, we are to seek ways which please God, our Creator. In the beginning, He created all things at the command of His voice. Nothing came into existence outside of the will of God. Finally, He created us to enjoy life. However, we have turned our backs on Him. Augustine, one of the early church fathers, said, "Thou have created us for Thy self and our hearts are restless until they find their rest in Thee."

Here are several points to ponder:

- God created human beings as male and female;
- God created people to live in partnership and harmony together;
- God created the male and female with clear and distinct sexual identities;
- God created man and woman with a clear and distinct purpose; and,
- God blessed them and gave them all that they needed to be prosperous and successful.

PRAYER

Dear Lord, our heavenly Father, teach us to love everyone and everything that You love. May we recognize the dignity and glory given to all human beings. Heavenly Father, Your Word reminds us that You are the Creator of all things. We thank You that everything we need has been so graciously provided for us. In the name of Jesus, we pray. Amen.

WORD POWER

Dominion (Hebrew: *rahdah- raw-daw*)—the word *dominion* means "to tread, trample down, subjugate, prevail, or to be in absolute control." This is a delegated authority which God gave to the human race. The reason He gave us this is because we are created in the image of God and are placed here to do His will. All things are subjected to the control of the human race. Read Psalm 8:6-8 as a supportive text.

HOME DAILY BIBLE READINGS
(September 3-9, 2007)
God Created Humankind

MONDAY, September 3: "The Creator of All" (Isaiah 40:25-31)

TUESDAY, September 4: "Created in God's Image" (Genesis 1:26-27)

WEDNESDAY, September 5: "God Provides" (Genesis 1:28-31)

THURSDAY, September 6: "A Hallowed Day" (Genesis 2:1-3)

FRIDAY, September 7: "God's Glory in Creation" (Psalm 19:1-6)

SATURDAY, September 8: "Thanksgiving for God's Greatness" (Psalm 103:1-14)

SUNDAY, September 9: "Remember God's Commandments" (Psalm 103:15-22)

LESSON 3   September 16, 2007

ABRAHAM, SARAH, AND ISAAC

DEVOTIONAL READING: **Isaiah 51:1-5**
PRINT PASSAGE: **Genesis 15:5-6;**
18:11-14a; 21:1-8

BACKGROUND SCRIPTURE: **Genesis 15:1-6;**
18:1-15; 21:1-8
KEY VERSE: **Genesis 18:14a**

Genesis 15:5-6; 18:11-14a; 21:1-8—KJV

5 And he brought him forth abroad, and said, Look now toward heaven, and tell the stars, if thou be able to number them: and he said unto him, So shall thy seed be.

6 And he believed in the LORD; and he counted it to him for righteousness.

.....

11 Now Abraham and Sarah were old and well stricken in age; and it ceased to be with Sarah after the manner of women.

12 Therefore Sarah laughed within herself, saying, After I am waxed old shall I have pleasure, my lord being old also?

13 And the LORD said unto Abraham, Wherefore did Sarah laugh, saying, Shall I of a surety bear a child, which am old?

14 Is any thing too hard for the LORD?

.....

AND THE LORD visited Sarah as he had said, and the LORD did unto Sarah as he had spoken.

2 For Sarah conceived, and bare Abraham a son in his old age, at the set time of which God had spoken to him.

3 And Abraham called the name of his son that was born unto him, whom Sarah bare to him, Isaac.

4 And Abraham circumcised his son Isaac being eight days old, as God had commanded him.

5 And Abraham was an hundred years old, when his son Isaac was born unto him.

6 And Sarah said, God hath made me to laugh, so that all that hear will laugh with me.

7 And she said, Who would have said unto Abraham, that Sarah should have given children suck? for I have born him a son in his old age.

8 And the child grew, and was weaned: and Abraham made a great feast the same day that Isaac was weaned.

Genesis 15:5-6; 18:11-14a; 21:1-8—NRSV

5 He brought him outside and said, "Look toward heaven and count the stars, if you are able to count them." Then he said to him, "So shall your descendants be."

6 And he believed the LORD; and the LORD reckoned it to him as righteousness.

.....

11 Now Abraham and Sarah were old, advanced in age; it had ceased to be with Sarah after the manner of women.

12 So Sarah laughed to herself, saying, "After I have grown old, and my husband is old, shall I have pleasure?"

13 The LORD said to Abraham, "Why did Sarah laugh, and say, 'Shall I indeed bear a child, now that I am old?'

14 Is anything too wonderful for the LORD?

.....

THE LORD dealt with Sarah as he had said, and the LORD did for Sarah as he had promised.

2 Sarah conceived and bore Abraham a son in his old age, at the time of which God had spoken to him.

3 Abraham gave the name Isaac to his son whom Sarah bore him.

4 And Abraham circumcised his son Isaac when he was eight days old, as God had commanded him.

5 Abraham was a hundred years old when his son Isaac was born to him.

6 Now Sarah said, "God has brought laughter for me; everyone who hears will laugh with me."

7 And she said, "Who would ever have said to Abraham that Sarah would nurse children? Yet I have borne him a son in his old age."

8 The child grew, and was weaned; and Abraham made a great feast on the day that Isaac was weaned.

TOPICAL OUTLINE
OF THE LESSON

I. **Introduction**
   A. The Story of Abraham
   B. Biblical Background

II. **Exposition and Application of the Scripture**
   A. God's Promise, Abram's Response (Genesis 15:5-6)
   B. Is Anything Too Hard for the Lord? (Genesis 18:11-14a)
   C. God Fulfilled His Promise (Genesis 21:1-8)

III. **Concluding Reflections**

LESSON OBJECTIVES

Upon completion of this lesson, the students will know that:

1. Absolutely nothing is too difficult for God to do;
2. Because we are Abraham's children by faith, we can emulate his faith in God; and,
3. With faith in God and patience on our part, the promises of God will be fulfilled.

POINTS TO BE EMPHASIZED

ADULT/YOUTH

Adult Topic: Our Place in the Family
Youth Topic: Child of Promise
Adult Key Verse: Genesis 18:14a
Youth Key Verse: Genesis 21:3
Print Passage: Genesis 15:5-6; 18:11-14a; 21:1-8

—Sarah's barrenness posed a serious threat to the continuation of the line promised to her and Abraham, but God's intervention allowed the line to continue.

—God's promises are sure despite apparent obstacles such as Abraham's and Sarah's advanced ages and continuing childlessness.

—What was God's covenant with Abraham and Sarah? How is it fulfilled in this story?

—God was at work in establishing a covenant people.

—God promised to bless not only the descendants of Abraham, but also all the nations of the earth (Genesis 12:3).

—Sarah's initial "laughter" wasn't from joy or happiness; it was from skepticism that later became laughter from happiness.

CHILDREN

Children Topic: God Gave Abraham and Sarah a Baby
Key Verse: Genesis 21:2
Print Passage: Genesis 18:1-8, 10-14; 21:1-3

—Abraham recognized the presence of God when the three visitors appeared at his tent.

—Overhearing the prediction of the visitors, Sarah laughed.

—Abraham and Sarah knew that through them and their son Isaac, God promised to create a covenant people.

—Abraham believed God, even when God's promises seemed unlikely to come true.

—This story teaches that God keeps promises.

I. INTRODUCTION

A. The Story of Abraham

The story of Abraham begins in Genesis 11:26 where we learn of his early family background. Abraham's family originated in Ur of the Chaldees, which is modern-day southern Iraq. This area is also referred to as Mesopotamia or the Fertile Crescent. Abram's other two brothers were Nahor and Haran. Haran died at an early age in Ur (Genesis 11:28). This period, referred to as the Patriarchal Period, begins sometime around 2000 B.C.E.

At some point, the family, under the leadership of Terah, set out for Canaan, but traveled as far as Haran and settled there. We are not sure how long they lived there—only that while they were there, Terah died at the ripe old age of 205 (Genesis 11:32). Sometime after his father's death, Abram received a vision and was called to leave Haran and go to a land that God would show him. This is the first mention of the covenant between God and Abram (Genesis 12:1-3).

In today's lesson, we see the fulfillment of God's original promise to Abram coming to pass with the birth of Isaac, and we will learn about the importance of absolute faith in God when the circumstances around us tempt us to turn away from God.

B. Biblical Background

Abram became a very wealthy man, just as God had promised (see Genesis 13:2). He had everything that his heart could have desired, except a son who would become his heir. One day in a vision Abram heard the voice of God speaking to him about his future. God told Abram not to live in fear because He would be a shield for him, and He was going to give him a great reward. God told Abram these things because of his faithfulness to the plan and promise of God to make of him a great nation. Also, Abram needed this assurance, because he had just defeated Chedorlaomaer and its kings who were with him (see Genesis 14:1-3, 13-14).

In the midst of joy mixed with sorrow, Abram asked God for an heir. In Genesis 15:2, we read, "And Abram said, Lord GOD, what wilt thou give me, seeing I go childless, and the steward of my house is this Eliezer of Damascus?" He was concerned that he would have no heir. Ancient Near Eastern customs allowed a man to adopt a servant and name that servant as his heir if he had no sons. The servant of the house would become the heir of the property of his master upon the master's death. One is not sure that Abram was as much concerned about the property as he was about continuing the family bloodlines. God answered Abram's concern by reassuring him that in His own due time, He would honor His Word to Abram, and Sarai would bear a son.

II. EXPOSITION AND APPLICATION OF THE SCRIPTURE

A. God's Promise, Abram's Response
(Genesis 15:5-6)

And he brought him forth abroad, and said, Look now toward heaven, and tell the stars, if thou be able to number them: and he said unto him, So shall thy seed be. And he believed in the LORD; and he counted it to him for righteousness.

There are times in life when we wonder about some of the promises that we have received from God. Sometimes delay can lead us to doubt God. In the life of Abram, we see one whose faith was challenged, but who continued to trust in the God who made the promise.

Abram must have been pondering when Sarai would conceive and bear him a son. One night, Abram had a vision. God told him that just as he could not count the number of stars in the heaven, so he would not be able to count the number of his descendants. Is it significant that this dream occurred at night? At night, Abram could see tens of thousands of stars and still not see all that were in the universe. As far as his eyes could see on the night sky's horizon, there were stars. This must have been a reassuring revelation to Abram, that God had not forgotten him and Sarai.

Verse 6 is one of the most important verses in the Old Testament. "And he believed in the LORD...." Abram was not worshiping an idol. He believed in the Lord, YAWEH, the one true and living God. This verse does not indicate that it was at that moment that Abram first truly believed God. His faith came to life when he heard the initial call of God to leave Haran and follow God wherever He would lead. "Believed" points to a past act of faith that continued to manifest itself in the present. The fact that one may, from time to time, raise questions with God is in no way to be construed as doubt or mistrust. Even in the Garden of Gethsemane, Jesus raised a question with His Father as to whether or not there was another way for His eternal will to be realized (see Luke 22:39-42). Abram believed in the Lord.

Abram believed and God counted it to him for righteousness. It was Abram's faith in the God who made the promise that certified him as righteous before God. This righteousness was not the result of any works of the law that he had done, but was based purely on his faith in God. What does the word *righteousness* mean in this instance? The word *righteousness* occurs more than three hundred times in the Bible with a variety of meanings. The most prominent meaning involves the idea of justice and equity. In some instances, it is used to refer to a standard of conduct or behavior that is based upon the standards set by God. It denotes obedience to godly standards.

In the New Testament, Abraham's faith is held up as the standard for all who would receive God's salvation. Verse 6 became the foundation for Paul's teachings about justification by faith (see also Habakkuk 2:4). In the teachings of the apostle Paul, righteousness is not the result of something we do; it is the result of what God bestows upon us. It is a gift of God's grace that comes through our faith in the Lord Jesus Christ (Ephesians 2:8-10). God in Christ makes us righteous because of our faith in Him (Romans 4:1-25; Galatians 3:6-14). It is faith in the resurrection of Jesus Christ that makes us truly the children of God. Paul's argument was centered on having a complete confidence in the finished work of Jesus Christ at Calvary (Romans 10:9-13). Here, we see that salvation was based purely upon faith in Jesus Christ, and not in church membership or participation in religious activities (John 3:16-17).

Abraham is called the "father of the faithful." In that great chapter on faith found in the book of Hebrews, more is said about Abraham and Sarah than about any other Old Testament personalities (see Hebrews 11:8-18). Abraham lived at a time when there was no Mosaic Law or sacrificial system. God counted on him to be righteous purely on the grounds of his faith in the promise. When one looks back through the Old Testament, there is no one whom God called righteous, except Abraham.

B. Is Anything Too Hard for the Lord? (Genesis 18:11-14a)

Now Abraham and Sarah were old and well stricken in age; and it ceased to be with Sarah after the manner of women. Therefore Sarah laughed within herself, saying, After I am waxed old shall I have pleasure, my lord being old also? And the Lord said unto Abraham, Wherefore did Sarah laugh, saying, Shall I of a surety bear a child, which am old? Is any thing too hard for the Lord?

A lot happens between Genesis chapters 15 and 18. Ten years after arriving in Canaan, Sarai gave up hope of ever bearing a child. She pleaded with Abram to go in to Hagar, her handmaid of Egyptian origin. From this unholy union, a son was born and Abraham named the child Ishmael (Genesis 16:4, 15-16). Thirteen years later, God reappeared to Abram and reaffirmed His promise and covenant with him. At that time, God changed the names of Abram and Sarai. Abram (exalted father) was no longer going to be called Abram; instead, he was to be called Abraham (father of many nations—Genesis 17:5). Sarai (my princess) would be called Sarah (mother of many nations—Genesis 17:15). God reaffirmed His covenant with Abraham and established circumcision as the sign of the covenant between Himself and the descendants of Abraham (Genesis 17:10-13). All of these things occurred one year before the birth of Isaac. Abraham thought it was absolutely impossible that at one hundred years old he would become a father, while his wife would become a mother at ninety.

One afternoon, three men appeared at the tent of Abraham while he was living by the oaks of Mamre (Genesis 18:1). Abraham did not know who these men were or where they had come from. Here he was, sitting in the heat of the day, and the Lord appeared out of nowhere. This should not surprise us, because there are other recorded instances where angels or heavenly beings suddenly appeared in person or in dreams and visions (see Exodus 3:2; Judges 6:12; 13:3; Matthew 1:20). Following the customs of that day, Abraham had his servants wash the men's feet and prepare a meal for them (verses 3-8). He hurried into the tent and asked Sarah to prepare some bread cakes, and he went out and found the best, most tender calf in his flock, and prepared it for his guests (verses 6-7). The men asked where Sarah was. This was the final appearance of the Lord to Abraham before the birth of Isaac. God shows up when He is about to do something miraculous in the lives of His people. The Lord said to Abraham, "I will certainly return unto thee according to the time of life; and, lo, Sarah thy wife shall have a son" (verse 10). Sarah, who was standing in the doorway of the tent, overheard the conversation between Abraham and the three men. She probably could not believe her ears.

The faithful couple had waited patiently for the promise of God to be fulfilled, and then they got word that they were finally going to have a son. At this point they had become very old. Upon hearing this pronouncement, Sarah laughed within herself. Surely, she thought, this must be some kind of joke. How could she possibly have children when she was well past the age at which one would expect her to have sexual desire, let alone children? The Lord heard the laughter and asked Abraham why Sarah would laugh as though it were impossible for the promise to be realized.

The Lord asked, "Is any thing too hard for the LORD?" (verse 14). The Lord announced that at the appointed time, He would return and Sarah would have a son. It is possible that the announcement of the divine visitation was just as much for Sarah's faith as it was for Abraham's. After all, she had been just as much a patient participant in the plan of God for herself and Abraham.

C. God Fulfilled His Promise
   (Genesis 21:1-8)

AND THE LORD visited Sarah as he had said, and the LORD did unto Sarah as he had spoken. For Sarah conceived, and bare Abraham a son in his old age, at the set time of which God had spoken to him. And Abraham called the name of his son that was born unto him, whom Sarah bare to him, Isaac. And Abraham circumcised his son Isaac being eight days old, as God had commanded him. And Abraham was an hundred years old, when his son Isaac was born unto him. And Sarah said, God hath made me to laugh, so that all that hear will laugh with me. And she said, Who would have said unto Abraham, that Sarah should have given children suck? for I have born him a son in his old age. And the child grew, and was weaned: and Abraham made a great feast the same day that Isaac was weaned.

Twenty-five years after God first spoke to Abraham in Ur of the Chaldees and gave him the promise of a son, Isaac was born. In verses 1-2, there are three affirmations: "… The LORD visited Sarah….The LORD did unto Sarah.… Sarah conceived…at the set time of which God had spoken to him." What God had said and promised, He did. He visited Sarah (verse 1a). We are not told any of the details surrounding the pregnancy. However, we can only imagine the joy and excitement that enveloped the camp of Abraham when the news began to spread that Sarah had finally conceived. Might this have been a reason for the faith of the entire household of Abraham to trust God even more? And the Lord did to Sarah just as He promised (verse 1b). The Lord is faithful and keeps His promises, then and now.

Women are often told that at a certain age, a pregnancy can become a very risky venture. Either something could happen to the child at birth or the mother might not be able to carry the baby to full term. Is it possible that God showed up the day that Isaac was born to make sure that the delivery went smoothly and without a hitch? Remember, in ancient times there were no hospitals, sterile delivery rooms, or medical technology.

It is interesting to note that the only person who did any talking in this passage was Sarah. She said that God had brought laughter to her heart. At the announcement of the future birth of Isaac she laughed out of scorn, but at the birth of Isaac, her scorn and sadness were turned into joy and excitement. Sarah remained astonished that such a thing had happened. And she said, "Who would have said unto Abraham, that Sarah should have given children suck…?" (verse 7).

Isaac reached an important milestone in his young life when he was weaned. He may have been either two or three years of age. He had survived the harsh conditions of the nomadic life. "The child grew…." (verse 8). The word *grew* means to make powerful or to magnify. Here we have a testimony to the health and strength of Isaac. God was blessing him and ensuring that he would live a long life and see the fulfillment of the promise made to his father. Abraham celebrated the occasion by making a great feast the same day that Isaac was weaned (verse 8). There was no time to wait. God had granted him another blessing, and he needed to commemorate the moment.

III. CONCLUDING REFLECTIONS

At the heart of this passage is the underlying question of our own faith in God. Can God be trusted? Some people will answer *no* because they have prayed, trusted, and hoped against hope, and things in their lives still seemed to falter. Here we learn a valuable lesson about patiently waiting on God to act in His own time. Abraham and Sarah learned that God is the One who keeps His promises in His own way. Even when Abraham and Sarah decided to take the matter into their own hands, God never ceased to honor His Word or promise. Christians believe that God is able to do exceedingly abundantly above everything that we can think, hope, or believe (see Ephesians 3:20). Do you trust God enough to wait upon Him regardless of the current circumstances you face?

Adverse circumstances in our lives are to be looked upon as stepping stones. Winners don't quit. Standing in faith honors God. Abraham faltered, but God did not remove His promise. This is not to encourage faltering; rather, it is to let us know that, "Weeping may endure for a night, but joy cometh in the morning" (Psalm 30:5). Our Key Verse states, "Is any thing too hard for the LORD?" (Genesis 18:14a). Of course the answer is *no*. All we need is to be patient under extreme conditions.

PRAYER

Lord, teach us how to trust You completely. Father, we know that You honor Your every Word. Thank You for honoring Your Word by giving us the greatest gift when You gave Jesus Christ for our sins. In His name, we pray. Amen.

WORD POWER

"Is any thing too hard for the Lord?"—This could also be translated as: "Shall a word or thing be too wonderful for the Lord?" The obvious answer is no. This question reveals much about God. Make it a habit to insert your specific needs into the questions: Is this day in my life too hard for the Lord? Is this problem too hard for the Lord to solve?

HOME DAILY BIBLE READINGS
(September 10-16, 2007)

Abraham, Sarah, and Isaac

MONDAY, September 10: "Listen!" (Isaiah 51:1-5)
TUESDAY, September 11: "Abraham Believed" (Genesis 15:1-6)
WEDNESDAY, September 12: "Abraham Doubted" (Genesis 17:15-22)
THURSDAY, September 13: "Abraham the Host" (Genesis 18:1-8)
FRIDAY, September 14: "Sarah's Laughter" (Genesis 18:9-15)
SATURDAY, September 15: "Sarah's Joy" (Genesis 21:1-8)
SUNDAY, September 16: "The Faith of Abraham" (Hebrews 11:8-12)

LESSON 4   September 23, 2007

ABRAHAM, HAGAR, AND ISHMAEL

DEVOTIONAL READING: **Genesis 16**
PRINT PASSAGE: **Genesis 21:9-21**

BACKGROUND SCRIPTURE: **Genesis 21:9-21**
KEY VERSE: **Genesis 21:13**

Genesis 21:9-21—KJV

9 And Sarah saw the son of Hagar the Egyptian, which she had born unto Abraham, mocking.

10 Wherefore she said unto Abraham, Cast out this bondwoman and her son: for the son of this bond-woman shall not be heir with my son, even with Isaac.

11 And the thing was very grievous in Abraham's sight because of his son.

12 And God said unto Abraham, Let it not be griev-ous in thy sight because of the lad, and because of thy bondwoman; in all that Sarah hath said unto thee, hearken unto her voice; for in Isaac shall thy seed be called.

13 And also of the son of the bondwoman will I make a nation, because he is thy seed.

14 And Abraham rose up early in the morning, and took bread, and a bottle of water, and gave it unto Hagar, putting it on her shoulder, and the child, and sent her away: and she departed, and wandered in the wilderness of Beer-sheba.

15 And the water was spent in the bottle, and she cast the child under one of the shrubs.

16 And she went, and sat her down over against him a good way off, as it were a bowshot: for she said, Let me not see the death of the child. And she sat over against him, and lift up her voice, and wept.

17 And God heard the voice of the lad; and the angel of God called to Hagar out of heaven, and said unto her, What aileth thee, Hagar? fear not; for God hath heard the voice of the lad where he is.

18 Arise, lift up the lad, and hold him in thine hand; for I will make him a great nation.

19 And God opened her eyes, and she saw a well of water; and she went, and filled the bottle with water, and gave the lad drink.

20 And God was with the lad; and he grew, and dwelt in the wilderness, and became an archer.

21 And he dwelt in the wilderness of Paran: and his mother took him a wife out of the land of Egypt.

Genesis 21:9-21—NRSV

9 But Sarah saw the son of Hagar the Egyptian, whom she had borne to Abraham, playing with her son Isaac.

10 So she said to Abraham, "Cast out this slave woman with her son; for the son of this slave woman shall not inherit along with my son Isaac."

11 The matter was very distressing to Abraham on account of his son.

12 But God said to Abraham, "Do not be distressed because of the boy and because of your slave woman; whatever Sarah says to you, do as she tells you, for it is through Isaac that offspring shall be named for you.

13 As for the son of the slave woman, I will make a nation of him also, because he is your offspring."

14 So Abraham rose early in the morning, and took bread and a skin of water, and gave it to Hagar, put-ting it on her shoulder, along with the child, and sent her away. And she departed, and wandered about in the wilderness of Beer-sheba.

15 When the water in the skin was gone, she cast the child under one of the bushes.

16 Then she went and sat down opposite him a good way off, about the distance of a bowshot; for she said, "Do not let me look on the death of the child." And as she sat opposite him, she lifted up her voice and wept.

17 And God heard the voice of the boy; and the angel of God called to Hagar from heaven, and said to her, "What troubles you, Hagar? Do not be afraid; for God has heard the voice of the boy where he is.

18 Come, lift up the boy and hold him fast with your hand, for I will make a great nation of him."

19 Then God opened her eyes and she saw a well of water. She went, and filled the skin with water, and gave the boy a drink.

20 God was with the boy, and he grew up; he lived in the wilderness, and became an expert with the bow.

21 He lived in the wilderness of Paran; and his mother got a wife for him from the land of Egypt.

Seeds of dissension often continue to bear fruit long after the seeds have been sown. What contemporary examples can we find of long-standing dissension? The seeds of dissension begun in the Genesis story continue today between Muslims, who claim Ishmael as their ancestor, and Jews, who claim Isaac as their ancestor.

TOPICAL OUTLINE OF THE LESSON

I. **Introduction**
   A. Dealing with Family Dissension
   B. Biblical Background

II. **Exposition and Application of the Scripture**
   A. Sarah's Concern and Abraham's Grief (Genesis 21:9-11)
   B. God Comforts Abraham (Genesis 21:12-13)
   C. Hagar and Ishmael in Crisis (Genesis 21:14-16)
   D. God's Promise to Ishmael (Genesis 21:17-21)

III. **Concluding Reflections**

LESSON OBJECTIVES

Upon completion of this lesson, the students will know that:

1. Impatience could lead to future crises in our lives;
2. In spite of our impatience, God remains faithful to His promises; and,
3. God works out His plans, even though we mess up in the beginning.

POINTS TO BE EMPHASIZED

ADULT/YOUTH
Adult Topic: **Dealing with Dissension in the Family**
Youth Topic: **A Great Nation**
Adult/Youth Key Verse: **Genesis 21:13**
Print Passage: **Genesis 21:9-21**

—Sarah's and Hagar's behaviors sowed seeds of dissension between Isaac and Ishmael.
—What was Abraham's responsibility in the dissension?
—God's choice to bless the descendants of Ishmael demonstrates that God's love is not restricted to Isaac's descendants.
—God's care extends to Hagar in the wilderness.
—Dissension in the family escalates with Sarah and Hagar.
—God works redemptively in the midst of family dissension (Genesis 16:13).

CHILDREN
Children Topic: **God Promised to Care for Ishmael**
Key Verse: **Genesis 21:18**
Print Passage: **Genesis 21:9-21**

—Because of Sarah's partiality to her son Isaac, she demanded that Hagar and Ishmael be sent away.
—Abraham experienced distress over the conflict of loyalties between his two sons.
—God had a promise and a place for Ishmael.
—Hagar was concerned about the well-being of her son.
—God cared for both Ishmael and Hagar.

I. INTRODUCTION
A. Dealing with Family Dissension

Divorce is increasing at an alarming rate in America and throughout the world. Even in Africa, divorce has become a major social issue. What causes divorce? There are as many reasons for divorce as there are people who are divorcing. However, the leading causes of divorce are: (1) not waiting on God for guidance; (2) failure to seek godly counsel at the time of choosing one's mate; (3) unresolved marital tension; and (4) family conflict. The rise in divorce has led to a significant shift in household demographics. For the first time in American history, there are more single households than married households. This statistic will have a huge impact on how congregations design and structure their ministries. What do we need to do to stem this tide of divorce? There is a need for a greater emphasis to be placed upon building healthy families and strengthening marriages both in the church and in the larger community.

In today's lesson, we see how blended families can also suffer from the inability of couples to reconcile their differences. In the previous lesson, Abraham and Sarah were promised that they would be the parents of a son within twelve months. Sarah finally conceived and bore Abraham a son, and he called him Isaac. The birth of Isaac was the end of one crisis, which was the barrenness of Sarah, and the beginning of a new one for Abraham. The new crisis would be Sarah's persistence that Hagar and Ishmael be expelled from the house of Abraham. In Sarah's heart and mind, there was neither a role nor a place for Ishmael within the family structure. This caused a great deal of personal anguish for Abraham. But in spite of the difficulty, God's will was ultimately achieved.

B. Biblical Background

At some point, Abraham and Sarah became impatient with God's delayed fulfillment of His initial promise of an heir and many descendants for Abraham (see Genesis 12:1-3). Ten years had elapsed between God's first announcement and Genesis 16, and still nothing had happened (see Genesis 16:3; compare with Genesis 12:4 and 16:16). Abraham asked God, "…what wilt thou give me…?" (Genesis15:2). Abraham feared that Eliezer, his chief steward, could become his sole heir. Sarah decided that she had waited long enough, and that something needed to be done. After all, she and Abraham were not getting any younger and she was already well past child-bearing age (Genesis 16:1). Sarah strongly suggested to Abraham that he should go in to her maid, Hagar, and let her give Abraham a son (Genesis 16:2). Here was an attempt to help God's plan come to fulfillment, as though God needed help. When Hagar conceived and bore Abraham a son, the situation in the house took a different turn. Sarah finally gave birth, as the Lord promised. Ishmael and Isaac did not get along well. Sarah became quite jealous, despising Hagar and setting off a chain of events that would eventually lead to the expulsion of Hagar and her son (Genesis 16:4).

II. EXPOSITION AND APPLICATION OF THE SCRIPTURE

A. Sarah's Concern and Abraham's Grief
(Genesis 21:9-11)

And Sarah saw the son of Hagar the Egyptian, which she had born unto Abraham, mocking. Wherefore she said unto Abraham, Cast out this bondwoman and her son: for the son of this bondwoman shall not be heir with my son, even with Isaac. And the thing was very grievous in Abraham's sight because of his son.

Sarah's joy over the birth of Isaac turned to hostility toward the son of Hagar. We are not told the ages of either of the boys. Isaac was more than likely about three years old and Ishmael was between thirteen and fourteen years of age. This incident took place during or shortly after the feast given in recognition of Isaac having been weaned (see Genesis 21:8). Sarah became concerned when she saw the son of Hagar mocking or playing with Isaac. *Mocking* in Hebrew can refer to either "playing, making fun of someone, or laughter." In Galatians 4:29, the apostle Paul referred to this incident as Ishmael's persecution of Isaac. Was it playfulness or scorn? Whatever it was, Sarah approached Abraham to discuss the matter.

Sarah realized that if Hagar and her son remained in the clan, Hagar's son could inherit all of Abraham's wealth. She went to Abraham and demanded that he *cast out* (Hebrew—"drive away," "divorce," "thrust out," "expel") Hagar and her son. Hagar was never called by her name. She was referred to by her status as a slave woman. Sarah was insistent that the son of Hagar would never be heir with her son, nor would he receive anything from the wealth of Abraham.

Was Sarah wrong for her reaction toward Hagar and her son? African-Americans know all too well what it means to be mistreated based purely upon the color of one's skin.

The request caught Abraham completely by surprise. We are not told whether there were prior conversations between Abraham and Sarah about Hagar and Ishmael. This situation was very *grievous* (Hebrew—"tremble," "quiver") to Abraham. Abraham did not lose faith in the promise of God, but he saw nothing bad in his sons growing up together. He did not know what to do or how to respond to Sarah's demand. Although Ishmael was the son of a slave, he was still Abraham's firstborn. Like Isaac, Ishmael had been born in Abraham's old age and had, no doubt, brought him much joy until the birth of Isaac.

B. God Comforts Abraham
(Genesis 21:12-13)

And God said unto Abraham, Let it not be grievous in thy sight because of the lad, and because of thy bondwoman; in all that Sarah hath said unto thee, hearken unto her voice; for in Isaac shall thy seed be called. And also of the son of the bondwoman will I make a nation, because he is thy seed.

God reassured Abraham that even in this situation of deep pain, His will would be done (see Romans 8:28). During major turning points in his life, God always spoke personally and directly to Abraham (see Genesis 12:1-3; 15:1-5; 17:1-2; 18:1; 22:1). If we, too, care to listen and are sensitive enough, God still speaks to us in our situations. God spoke a word of comfort to Abraham. He assured him that Hagar would be taken care of, along with her son. She was the mother of his firstborn son. How could he put his firstborn son out of the camp? God told Abraham to listen to the voice of Sarah. This too was all in the will of God. It was not God's plan that Abraham lie with Hagar; that was Sarah's plan. God's will and purposes will never be thwarted by human efforts. Believers must continually pray for patience (see Isaiah 40:31; Galatians 6:10).

C. Hagar and Ishmael in Crisis (Genesis 21:14-16)

And Abraham rose up early in the morning, and took bread, and a bottle of water, and gave it unto Hagar, putting it on her shoulder, and the child, and sent her away: and she departed, and wandered in the wilderness of Beer-sheba. And the water was spent in the bottle, and she cast the child under one of the shrubs. And she went, and sat her down over against him a good way off, as it were a bowshot: for she said, Let me not see the death of the child. And she sat over against him, and lift up her voice, and wept.

We do not know how much time elapsed between Sarah's initial request and Abraham's response, but his actions probably took place the very next day. He rose early in the morning, probably just after sunrise; this would enable him to move without attracting a lot of attention. There is no mention of a conversation taking place between Abraham and Sarah, nor between Abraham and Hagar. We are not told anything about an emotional response from any of the people in the narrative. We can only assume how Abraham and the others must have felt.

Abraham showed compassion and care for Hagar and Ishmael. He gave them bread and water. Food and water would surely be needed in the harsh environs of the desert surrounding Beer-sheba. Hagar departed and wandered in the wilderness of Beer-sheba. She had nowhere to go and no one to help her. She and Ishmael were alone and isolated. Fear, heartbreak, and feelings of abandonment probably describe Hagar's frame of mind.

What lessons can we learn from Abraham's actions? First, he was willing to work for peace in his home. Second, he was sensitive to the concerns of his wife. Third, he continued to obey God in spite of the personal pain and heartache that resulted from sending Hagar and Ishmael away. Fourth, Abraham knew that God would be faithful to His promises. We too can rest assured that the mercy of the Lord is inexhaustible.

After a few days of wandering under the rays of the searing sun, Hagar's and Ishmael's water ran out (verse 15). They could possibly survive for a few days longer without food, but without water they could only live briefly. Hagar and Ishmael would quickly face dehydration and death without water. There was nothing Hagar could do and no one she could call upon. She was completely and utterly helpless and probably felt hopeless. Her actions describe someone who has resigned himself or herself to a tragic end. The word *cast* does not mean that she threw her son under a bush but that she gently placed him there to rest and shield him from their ordeal and the rays of the sun.

Verse 16 describes how Hagar could not bear the agony of seeing her firstborn and only child suffer a slow, agonizing death. She went and sat down in the midst of the desert, the distance that a master bowman could shoot an arrow, which was a distance of several hundred feet. Why? She did not want to see the approach of death nor hear the cries of her son as he languished in the desert sun. And it could be that she wanted to spare him the pain of watching his mother die a helpless death as well. We are told that she sat down and wept profusely. Hagar could no longer contain her brokenness and all of the pain that had invaded her life within the past few days.

D. God's Promise to Ishmael
(Genesis 21:17-21)

And God heard the voice of the lad; and the angel of God called to Hagar out of heaven, and said unto her, What aileth thee, Hagar? fear not; for God hath heard the voice of the lad where he is. Arise, lift up the lad, and hold him in thine hand; for I will make him a great nation. And God opened her eyes, and she saw a well of water; and she went, and filled the bottle with water, and gave the lad drink. And God was with the lad; and he grew, and dwelt in the wilderness, and became an archer. And he dwelt in the wilderness of Paran: and his mother took him a wife out of the land of Egypt.

God heard Hagar's cries, but He responded to the voice of Ishmael. Some of the most reassuring promises of the Scriptures state that God hears the cries of the righteous and is attentive to their prayers (see Exodus 3:7; 22:23; 2 Kings 13:4; Psalms 34:4-6; 50:12; 62; 91:15). God had an angel, a divine messenger, speak to Hagar. God used angels on various occasions to deliver messages of comfort and to offer hope to His people during desperate times (see Genesis 16:9, 11; Numbers 22:22-27; Judges 6:22; 13:3; 1 Kings 19:7; 2 Kings 1:30; Psalm 34:7; Zechariah 1:11-12; Matthew 2:13; Acts 1:11; 5:19).

The angel asked Hagar what was ailing her. This was not an insensitive question, for surely God knew all that there was to know about this situation in the same way He knows all about us (see Psalm 139:1-9). The angel of the Lord appeared to Hagar a second time (Genesis 21:17), the first being the announcement regarding the birth of Ishmael in Genesis 16:9, 11. The angel said, "…fear not; for God hath heard the voice of the lad where he is" (verse 17). Hagar needed to hear this reassuring statement from the angel. She was in an unknown territory with all kinds of ferocious animals. When we are within the will of God, His purpose and promise will always come to pass in our lives. God had made a promise that He would make of Ishmael a great nation, and no desert was going to stand in the way of that.

Hagar was told to arise and lift the lad to his feet and hold him by the hand (verse 18). Here we see the reaffirmation of the promise made to Abraham that Ishmael would be a great nation. The same God who promised to bless Isaac would bless Ishmael as well.

When Hagar obeyed the voice of God, He opened her eyes and she saw a well of water. Had the well been there all along? Quite probably, but because she was in a panicked condition and had not turned completely to God for help, she could not see it. For the first time, she was not being blinded by her circumstances. She saw hope for herself and Ishmael. Hagar went to the well and filled their water bottles and then gave the boy a drink.

Time passed and Ishmael grew and the Lord was with him. In verse 20, we have both promise and fulfillment. "And God was with the lad." God's presence with us is always a solid guarantee of support and success. Joseph, who was one of the descendants of Abraham, was blessed even though he was in prison in Egypt (see Genesis 39:2-3; Joshua 1:5; Judges 1:19; 1 Samuel 18:12-14; 2 Samuel 5:10; 2 Chronicles 17:3; Matthew 28:19-20; Acts 1:11; 2 Timothy 4:17).

The word *grew* has a double meaning. First, it means that Ishmael grew in age and stature. Second, it means that he also increased in wealth and power. God had promised to make his father Abraham great as well as all of his descendants. Ishmael's life prospered not because of anything that he did, but because he was the seed of Abraham.

He lived permanently in the wilderness of

Paran, which is located in the south central portion of the Sinai Peninsula, between Sinai and Canaan. As Abraham did for Isaac, Hagar arranged for Ishmael to marry a woman from among her own people. We have no details of the location, date, time, or any other matters surrounding the marriage. We know that in one of the harshest environments on the earth, Ishmael strived and increased in wealth. God blessed him in the wilderness of Paran.

III. CONCLUDING REFLECTIONS

This lesson teaches us that God is the source of our salvation and blessings. Even in the midst of what would appear to be dire and deadly circumstances, God made a way of escape for Hagar and Ishmael. Further, we see how the breakup of a family can lead to anguish and pain. Single mothers, who are often forced to rear their children without the benefit of a father's help, can take solace in knowing that God is able to help them, so that they can rear their children according to His will.

PRAYER

Lord, teach us to trust You completely. May we learn to live in the world without fear of the circumstances that we face. Thank You for all of Your provision and help. In the name of Jesus Christ, we pray. Amen.

WORD POWER

Seed (Hebrew: *Zar-kaa-Zer`-rah*)—this means "a seed sown in the ground." God recognized Ishmael as the son of Abraham even though he was not the promised son. God's promise to Ishmael calmed the stress Abraham felt when Sarah insisted that he should cut off Hagar and Ishmael from Isaac and the rest of the camp. We will not completely understand the mystery of this story while we are here on earth.

HOME DAILY BIBLE READINGS
(September 17-23, 2007)

Abraham, Hagar, and Ishmael

MONDAY, September 17: "Sarah Deals Harshly with Hagar" (Genesis 16:1-6)
TUESDAY, September 18: "God Protects Hagar" (Genesis 16:7-16)
WEDNESDAY, September 19: "Abraham's Offspring" (Genesis 21:9-13)
THURSDAY, September 20: "Waiting for Death" (Genesis 21:14-16)
FRIDAY, September 21: "Water from God" (Genesis 21:17-19)
SATURDAY, September 22: "Ishmael Grows Up" (Genesis 21:20-21)
SUNDAY, September 23: "Ishmael's Descendants" (Genesis 25:12-18)

LESSON 5   September 30, 2007

ISAAC AND REBEKAH

DEVOTIONAL READING: **Psalm 100**
PRINT PASSAGE: **Genesis 24:34-40, 42-45, 48**

BACKGROUND SCRIPTURE: **Genesis 24**
KEY VERSE: **Genesis 24:48**

Genesis 24:34-40, 42-45, 48—KJV

34 And he said, I am Abraham's servant.

35 And the LORD hath blessed my master greatly; and he is become great: and he hath given him flocks, and herds, and silver, and gold, and menservants, and maidservants, and camels, and asses.

36 And Sarah my master's wife bare a son to my master when she was old: and unto him hath he given all that he hath.

37 And my master made me swear, saying, Thou shalt not take a wife to my son of the daughters of the Canaanites, in whose land I dwell:

38 But thou shalt go unto my father's house, and to my kindred, and take a wife unto my son.

39 And I said unto my master, Peradventure the woman will not follow me.

40 And he said unto me, The LORD, before whom I walk, will send his angel with thee, and prosper thy way; and thou shalt take a wife for my son of my kindred, and of my father's house.

.....

42 And I came this day unto the well, and said, O LORD God of my master Abraham, if now thou do prosper my way which I go:

43 Behold, I stand by the well of water; and it shall come to pass, that when the virgin cometh forth to draw water, and I say to her, Give me, I pray thee, a little water of thy pitcher to drink;

44 And she say to me, Both drink thou, and I will also draw for thy camels: let the same be the woman whom the LORD hath appointed out for my master's son.

45 And before I had done speaking in mine heart, behold, Rebekah came forth with her pitcher on her shoulder; and she went down unto the well, and drew water: and I said unto her, Let me drink, I pray thee.

.....

48 And I bowed down my head, and worshipped the LORD, and blessed the LORD God of my master Abraham, which had led me in the right way to take my master's brother's daughter unto his son.

Genesis 24:34-40, 42-45, 48—NRSV

34 So he said, "I am Abraham's servant.

35 The LORD has greatly blessed my master, and he has become wealthy; he has given him flocks and herds, silver and gold, male and female slaves, camels and donkeys.

36 And Sarah my master's wife bore a son to my master when she was old; and he has given him all that he has.

37 My master made me swear, saying, 'You shall not take a wife for my son from the daughters of the Canaanites, in whose land I live;

38 but you shall go to my father's house, to my kindred, and get a wife for my son.'

39 I said to my master, 'Perhaps the woman will not follow me.'

40 But he said to me, 'The LORD, before whom I walk, will send his angel with you and make your way successful. You shall get a wife for my son from my kindred, from my father's house.

.....

42 "I came today to the spring, and said, 'O LORD, the God of my master Abraham, if now you will only make successful the way I am going!

43 I am standing here by the spring of water; let the young woman who comes out to draw, to whom I shall say, "Please give me a little water from your jar to drink,"

44 and who will say to me, "Drink, and I will draw for your camels also"—let her be the woman whom the LORD has appointed for my master's son.'

45 "Before I had finished speaking in my heart, there was Rebekah coming out with her water jar on her shoulder; and she went down to the spring, and drew. I said to her, 'Please let me drink.'

.....

48 Then I bowed my head and worshiped the LORD, and blessed the LORD, the God of my master Abraham, who had led me by the right way to obtain the daughter of my master's kinsman for his son.

TOPICAL OUTLINE OF THE LESSON

I. **Introduction**
   A. Arranged Marriage
   B. Biblical Background

II. **Exposition and Application of the Scripture**
   A. Abraham's Servant Reveals His Mission (Genesis 24:34-40)
   B. Abraham's Servant Prays for Guidance (Genesis 24:42-45)
   C. Abraham's Servant Praises God for Success (Genesis 24:48)

III. **Concluding Reflections**

LESSON OBJECTIVES

Upon completion of this lesson, the students will know that:

1. God should be involved in choosing a life partner;
2. Godly counseling is an integral part of choosing a life partner;
3. Advice from parents should not be discounted in choosing a life partner; and,
4. Prayer and waiting on the Lord are essential.

POINTS TO BE EMPHASIZED

ADULT/YOUTH

Adult Topic: **Recognizing the Right Woman**
Youth Topic: **Here Comes the Bride**
Adult Key Verse: **Genesis 24:48**
Youth Key Verse: **Genesis 24:40**
Print Passage: **Genesis 24:34-40, 42-45, 48**

—Abraham's servant knew Rebekah was to be Isaac's wife because she was the woman who had shown kindness to him, just as he had prayed.
—The story of Isaac and Rebekah's courtship brings with it the hope of continuing God's promised line of covenant people.
—God can act in ordinary situations, such as helping someone find a suitable mate.
—Arranging the marriage of Isaac and Rebekah is an example of God at work through human choices.
—God makes a way for Abraham's family line to continue.
—Rebekah makes the choice to go with Abraham's servant (verses 58-59).

CHILDREN

Children Topic: **God Prepares to Bring Isaac and Rebekah Together**
Key Verse: **Genesis 24:67**
Print Passage: **Genesis 24:34-40, 42-45, 48**

—Abraham was determined that Isaac would marry a woman from among his extended family.
—Abraham sent his servant to Haran to find a wife for Isaac.
—The loyalty (24:9) and steadfast love (24:12) the servant had for his master, Abraham, caused him to take an oath to carry out his master's wishes.
—Both Abraham and his servant displayed total trust that God would guide the servant to the right woman.
—When his mission was successful, the servant's immediate response was to give thanks to God.

I. INTRODUCTION

A. Arranged Marriage

Most parents want their sons or daughters to make the right choice when it comes to choosing lifetime partners. God intended that the union between a man and a woman would be the foundation upon which healthy societies would be built. However, in recent years we have begun to see a change in societal norms regarding marriage and family. According to recent census data, nearly forty percent of all American-born males have never married, while slightly more than twenty-five percent of American females have never married. For African-American males and females, the numbers are much higher. In the United States, nearly six and a half out of ten marriages end in divorce within three years. Is this the way it was supposed to be? The answer is a resounding *no*. God intended that a man and a woman should live permanently together in harmony and peace, working to fulfill the purpose of God together (see Matthew 19:7-9). If parents had their way, they would choose their sons' or daughters' future partners. Pre-arranged marriages are not the custom in America, but there are some cultures where they do still occur and are even to be expected.

In our lesson today, we see Abraham's arrangements for the marriage of his son, Isaac. Is it God's will that every man and woman on the face of the earth have a specific lifetime partner? God's will for the fulfillment of the promise He made to Abraham resided not just in the hearts of the patriarchs alone, but also in their choices of wives for their offspring.

B. Biblical Background

Chapter twenty-four marks a decisive turning point in the patriarchs' narratives. Abraham was well advanced in years and had recently buried Sarah, his beloved wife (see Genesis 23:1, 19-20). God blessed Abraham to acquire great wealth and had blessed him in every way (Genesis 24:1). The only thing that remained for him to do before his own death was to arrange for the marriage of Isaac. One day, Abraham called his oldest and chief servant and gave him the assignment of going to Mesopotamia and finding a wife for Isaac. We are not told the name of the servant; it may have been Eliezer (see Genesis 15:2). Abraham had his servant make a vow that he would not bring a Canaanite woman back for Isaac to marry (Genesis 24:3). He had him place his hand on Abraham's inner thigh as a pledge that he would fulfill his assignment exactly as requested by Abraham (Genesis 24:2; see also 47:29). The inner thigh was believed to be the source of male strength and procreation.

After all of the arrangements for the trip had been completed, the servant, along with all of the provisions necessary for a long journey, set out for Mesopotamia to the city of Nahor (Genesis 24:10). The servant took a lot of gifts; this was known as a dowry. (This is still a common practice in Africa.) The journey from Canaan to Nahor took several months. Ancient Nahor quite possibly referred to Haran, the place Abraham left when he journeyed to Canaan (see Genesis 11:31-32). Once in Nahor, the servant went to the local well, where he prayed that God would give him favor and that he would meet the future wife of Isaac (Genesis 24:11). The chief of the servants asked for some signs which would enable him to make the right choice (see 24:13-18). Rebekah was the one who fulfilled the signs he requested from the Lord. Rebekah went and brought her brother, Laban, out of the city to meet the servant to hear his story (Genesis 24:17-33). At this point, we have not seen the last of Laban, who will figure prominently in the account of the life of Jacob.

II. EXPOSITION AND APPLICATION OF THE SCRIPTURE

A. Abraham's Servant Reveals His Mission
(Genesis 24:34-40)

And he said, I am Abraham's servant. And the Lord hath blessed my master greatly; and he is become great: and he hath given him flocks, and herds, and silver, and gold, and menservants, and maidservants, and camels, and asses. And Sarah my master's wife bare a son to my master when she was old: and unto him hath he given all that he hath. And my master made me swear, saying, Thou shalt not take a wife to my son of the daughters of the Canaanites, in whose land I dwell: But thou shalt go unto my father's house, and to my kindred, and take a wife unto my son. And I said unto my master, Peradventure the woman will not follow me. And he said unto me, The Lord, before whom I walk, will send his angel with thee, and prosper thy way; and thou shalt take a wife for my son of my kindred, and of my father's house.

Abraham's servant and the men who accompanied him were welcomed into the home of Rebekah and her brother, Laban. It was customary in that day for pilgrims and strangers to be invited into the home for overnight lodging and a meal. The urgency of the servant's business was demonstrated by his refusal to eat first. Before eating, he introduced himself to the family as the servant of Abraham (verse 34). This was totally unimportant and secondary to the assignment that he had been given. However, the servant established the fact that everything that he had in his possession belonged to his master.

The servant told how the Lord had greatly blessed Abraham (verse 35). The servant acknowledged that everything his master owned was given to him by the Lord. Abraham had not acquired his wealth independent of the Lord's favor. When he began his pilgrimage to Canaan, Abraham left with very few material possessions, but over time, God increased his wealth in many ways. In Canaan, he had become both rich and powerful. The magnitude of his wealth is enumerated by the things that he possessed. He had acquired flocks, herds of sheep and cattle, silver, gold, male and female servants, camels, and asses. Abraham left Haran empty but God had given him great wealth. Abraham was not a poor man, something that Laban may have quickly recognized.

The servant next shared more details about his master, Abraham. He told how in their latter years God had blessed Abraham with the son that he most desired. Abraham and Sarah had waited for almost a generation (a generation is twenty-five years) before God gave them Isaac. He told how Sarah had given birth to a son in her old age (verse 36). The mention of the name of Sarah as Abraham's wife indicated that this was not a son born of a concubine or slave, such as Ishmael, the son of Abraham and Hagar.

Abraham's true heir would be the recipient of a great inheritance. He would not be a poor man when he married. Whoever married Isaac would marry a man who would receive all of the wealth that had just been enumerated by the servant (verse 36b). What neither Rebekah nor her family knew about was the sterling promise of a future greatness made by God to Abraham and his descendants. Wealth, greatness, and the favor of God upon her life were all waiting for the woman chosen to marry Isaac.

The servant told the family of Rebekah of the oath that Abraham made him take. He was under strict obligation not to secure a wife for Isaac from among the Canaanite people, which is where Abraham was living (verse 37). We can be certain that Abraham told his servant the names of all of his relatives living in Mesopotamia. Further, we can assume that over the years there had been some contact with the family members, although that is not specifically mentioned in the story of Abraham.

Abraham gave specific instructions to the servant to go to the house of his father, among his own kindred, and there he would find a wife for Isaac. He could not have been more blessed in the assignment, for he ended up among the very family of Abraham (Genesis 24:27). Did the family of Rebekah have any reservations about her going with this strange man? If they did, they were relieved when they realized who was asking for her hand in marriage. She would not be living among strangers, but among her own people in Canaan.

Did the servant have reservations about the possible success of his assignment? It is clear from verse 39 that he may have had some reservations about whether or not he would be successful. Abraham assured him that God would go before him and that the Lord would send His angel with him. The angel of the Lord would guarantee that he would succeed in his assignment. Abraham had experienced God's faithfulness firsthand and he knew that the Lord stood behind every statement He made (see Joshua 1:1-10). There was an echo of confidence voiced to the servant by Abraham, "Thou shalt take a wife for my son of my kindred, and of my father's house" (verse 40).

B. Abraham's Servant Prays for Guidance (Genesis 24:42-45)

And I came this day unto the well, and said, O Lord God of my master Abraham, if now thou do prosper my way which I go: Behold, I stand by the well of water; and it shall come to pass, that when the virgin cometh forth to draw water, and I say to her, Give me, I pray thee, a little water of thy pitcher to drink; And she say to me, Both drink thou, and I will also draw for thy camels: let the same be the woman whom the Lord hath appointed out for my master's son. And before I had done speaking in mine heart, behold, Rebekah came forth with her pitcher on her shoulder; and she went down unto the well, and drew water: and I said unto her, Let me drink, I pray thee.

These verses are a recapitulation of verses 11-14 with some slight modifications, which can be expected when stories are retold. The servant continued to give his account of how he arrived in the home of Bethuel, Rebekah's father. Did he know that he was in the will of God? He and his companions had arrived safely in Nahor, which had to have been a sign that God's favor was upon them. God had blessed his going out and all that remained was for God to bless his arrival and going back into Canaan.

The servant told Bethuel and Laban that when he arrived at the well that very day, the first thing that he did was pray that God would continue to give him favor. The servant had been exposed to the God of Abraham. He knew that Abraham's God was faithful and that one could put her or his complete trust in Him. After all, he had seen the God of Abraham honor His Word by giving Abraham and Sarah the son that they longed to have. The life of Abraham affected the slaves in his house. The head of the slaves called on the God of his master to guide his steps. This is an indictment on modern Christians who choose life partners without asking God for guidance. This is the reason for the uncontrollable plague of divorce which is spreading like a prairie fire.

The servant's prayer was specific to his situation. He wanted God to make His will concerning the woman whom he would take back to Canaan to be so perfectly clear that he could not possibly err. There were probably several women who came to the well. We will never know. But what is known is that he wanted God's choice to be the woman who would respond to his request for a drink by giving his camels a drink as well. There is much that could be made about Rebekah's willingness to show such kindness to total strangers. Clearly, this demonstrated the spirit of a servant, which is what Isaac would eventually become in the eyes of the Lord. The woman whom he married must be willing to serve God by serving others.

He stated that while he was still praying, God answered his prayer. The servant stated that he was praying within himself when God answered. There are times when God's answer is immediate. The prophet Isaiah wrote, "And it shall come to pass, that before they call, I will answer; and while they are yet speaking, I will hear" (Isaiah 65:24; [see also 58:9; 2 Kings 20:1-11; Psalms 32:5; 50:15; 91:15; Daniel 9:20-23; Mark 11:24; Luke 15:18-20; Acts 10:30-32; 1 John 5:14-15]). Prayer should be spoken with confidence that God has heard and will answer our prayers. The servant received an immediate response with the arrival of Rebekah at the well.

Many Christian men and women who are looking for life partners should learn the godly way of choosing. There are matchmakers who specialize in psychoanalyzing men and women and making arrangements for marriages. This is a wrong approach to choosing a life partner. God is still on the throne, and His methods are not outdated. God has a personal relationship with His children and is interested in human affairs.

C. Abraham's Servant Praises God for Success (Genesis 24:48)

And I bowed down my head, and worshipped the LORD, and blessed the LORD God of my master Abraham, which had led me in the right way to take my master's brother's daughter unto his son.

In the praise of the servant, we have a retelling of his story found first in verses 26-27. God had led him all of the way from Canaan to Nahor, enabling him to successfully accomplish the assignment given to him by Abraham. Three actions describe his praise. First, he bowed his head, which was an act of humility. He bowed in humility to affirm that truly God was alive. Second, he worshiped, which showed reverence to the One who had led him safely and successfully. It is one thing to bow, and it is another thing to worship the almighty God. This unidentified slave worshiped God for leading him to an unknown place. God is in the business of leading us if we truly seek Him. Third, he blessed or acknowledged that God was the source of his success. He praised God because the Lord had led him in the right way.

This is the desire of every disciple of the Lord Jesus Christ—that He leads us in the right way (see Exodus 18:20; Ezra 8:21; Psalms 32:8; 107:7; Proverbs 3:5-6; 4:11; Isaiah 48:17). There is one trait that characterized the servant that Abraham chose. He completely relied upon God for everything, especially guidance. He continually praised God in all things (see Psalm 34:1-2). Do you want to be led by God all the days of your life? The secret is found in the life of this servant who, by observation and experience, came to know the God of Abraham. He believed in the God of his master, and that God did not disappoint him.

ambitions, and wishes? First, God's will is not a mystery. His will can be known with clarity and certainty. We begin by reading and applying God's Word to our lives. As we read God's Word, walk in it daily, and faithfully and sincerely serve Him, we will find ourselves within the will of God. Abraham's servant merely did as he was told, without question or reservation, and God gave him good success. One of the basic ways of knowing and doing the will of God is found in Joshua 1:9-10, and Psalm 1:1-3. Paul says, "…He which hath begun a good work in you will perform it…" (Philippians 1:6).

III. CONCLUDING REFLECTIONS

God has a plan and purpose for each person born on the earth. Some people will never reach their destiny or achieve their life's ambitions because they will not obey God without reservation. How do you know when you are being led by God and not by your own desires,

PRAYER

Almighty and loving Father, teach us through Your Word to honor You in all things. Bless the Word that we have studied today, that it may take root in our hearts and grow, producing a bountiful harvest. In the name of Jesus Christ, we pray, Amen.

WORD POWER

Worship: (Hebrew: *shachah–shaw-khaw)*—this means to prostrate, to bow with the head touching the ground; to pay homage to royalty or to God. The servant of Abraham studied the ways his master worshiped God, and he did the same thing here. We may look at this as an archaic mode of worship, but whatever posture we assume, let it emanate from the heart.

HOME DAILY BIBLE READINGS
(September 24-30, 2007)
Isaac and Rebekah
   MONDAY, September 24: "Wanted: A Wife" (Genesis 24:1-9)
   TUESDAY, September 25: "A Drink for the Camels" (Genesis 24:10-21)
   WEDNESDAY, September 26: "The Daughter of Bethuel" (Genesis 24:22-27)
   THURSDAY, September 27: "A Show of Hospitality" (Genesis 24:28-32)
   FRIDAY, September 28: "The Errand" (Genesis 24:33-41)
   SATURDAY, September 29: "A Wife for Isaac" (Genesis 24:42-51)
   SUNDAY, September 30: "God's Steadfast Love" (Psalm 100)

LESSON 6   October 7, 2007

ESAU AND JACOB AS RIVALS

DEVOTIONAL READING: **1 Corinthians 1:26-31**
PRINT PASSAGE: **Genesis 25:19-34**

BACKGROUND SCRIPTURE: **Genesis 25:19-34**
KEY VERSE: **Genesis 25:23**

Genesis 25:19-34—KJV

19 And these are the generations of Isaac, Abraham's son: Abraham begat Isaac:

20 And Isaac was forty years old when he took Rebekah to wife, the daughter of Bethuel the Syrian of Padan-aram, the sister to Laban the Syrian.

21 And Isaac intreated the LORD for his wife, because she was barren: and the LORD was intreated of him, and Rebekah his wife conceived.

22 And the children struggled together within her; and she said, If it be so, why am I thus? And she went to inquire of the LORD.

23 And the LORD said unto her, Two nations are in thy womb, and two manner of people shall be separated from thy bowels; and the one people shall be stronger than the other people; and the elder shall serve the younger.

24 And when her days to be delivered were fulfilled, behold, there were twins in her womb.

25 And the first came out red, all over like an hairy garment; and they called his name Esau.

26 And after that came his brother out, and his hand took hold on Esau's heel; and his name was called Jacob: and Isaac was threescore years old when she bare them.

27 And the boys grew: and Esau was a cunning hunter, a man of the field; and Jacob was a plain man, dwelling in tents.

28 And Isaac loved Esau, because he did eat of his venison: but Rebekah loved Jacob.

29 And Jacob sod pottage: and Esau came from the field, and he was faint:

30 And Esau said to Jacob, Feed me, I pray thee, with that same red pottage; for I am faint: therefore was his name called Edom.

31 And Jacob said, Sell me this day thy birthright.

32 And Esau said, Behold, I am at the point to die: and what profit shall this birthright do to me?

33 And Jacob said, Swear to me this day; and he sware unto him: and he sold his birthright unto Jacob.

Genesis 25:19-34—NRSV

19 These are the descendants of Isaac, Abraham's son: Abraham was the father of Isaac,

20 and Isaac was forty years old when he married Rebekah, daughter of Bethuel the Aramean of Paddan-aram, sister of Laban the Aramean.

21 Isaac prayed to the LORD for his wife, because she was barren; and the LORD granted his prayer, and his wife Rebekah conceived.

22 The children struggled together within her; and she said, "If it is to be this way, why do I live?" So she went to inquire of the LORD.

23 And the LORD said to her, "Two nations are in your womb, and two peoples born of you shall be divided; the one shall be stronger than the other, the elder shall serve the younger."

24 When her time to give birth was at hand, there were twins in her womb.

25 The first came out red, all his body like a hairy mantle; so they named him Esau.

26 Afterward his brother came out, with his hand gripping Esau's heel; so he was named Jacob. Isaac was sixty years old when she bore them.

27 When the boys grew up, Esau was a skillful hunter, a man of the field, while Jacob was a quiet man, living in tents.

28 Isaac loved Esau, because he was fond of game; but Rebekah loved Jacob.

29 Once when Jacob was cooking a stew, Esau came in from the field, and he was famished.

30 Esau said to Jacob, "Let me eat some of that red stuff, for I am famished!" (Therefore he was called Edom.)

31 Jacob said, "First sell me your birthright."

32 Esau said, "I am about to die; of what use is a birthright to me?"

33 Jacob said, "Swear to me first." So he swore to him, and sold his birthright to Jacob.

UNIFYING LESSON PRINCIPLE

Siblings have clashed since the days of Cain and Abel. What are the roots of family conflict, especially hostility between brothers or sisters? The story of Jacob and Esau reveals that a rivalry begun at birth continued into their adult years as Jacob persuaded Esau to sell his birthright.

34 Then Jacob gave Esau bread and pottage of lentiles; and he did eat and drink, and rose up, and went his way: thus Esau despised his birthright.

34 Then Jacob gave Esau bread and lentil stew, and he ate and drank, and rose and went his way. Thus Esau despised his birthright.

TOPICAL OUTLINE OF THE LESSON

I. Introduction
A. Peace in the Family
B. Biblical Background

II. Exposition and Application of the Scripture
A. The Beginning of Isaac's Legacy (Genesis 25:19)
B. The Birth of Jacob and Esau (Genesis 25:20-26)
C. The Selling of a Birthright (Genesis 25:27-34)

III. Concluding Reflections

LESSON OBJECTIVES

Upon completion of this lesson, the students will know that:

1. Some parents are responsible for sibling rivalry;
2. There is a godly way of handling sibling rivalry; and,
3. The plan and purpose of God cannot be frustrated.

POINTS TO BE EMPHASIZED

ADULT/YOUTH
Adult Topic: **Sibling Rivalry**
Youth Topic: **Costly Stew**
Adult/Youth Key Verse: **Genesis 25:23**
Print Passage: **Genesis 25:19-34**

—Esau rashly sold his birthright as the elder son to Jacob, simply because he was hungry for a bowl of stew that Jacob was willing to trade for the birthright.
—Isaac prayed to God because Rebekah was barren. Again, the continuation of Abraham's promised line was threatened by the barrenness of the matriarch.
—God continues His plan despite human rules, traditions, or interventions.
—God's plans are not bound by human expectations.
—The origin of the Edomites is described in Genesis 25:30.
—The rivalry of Esau and Jacob was exacerbated by their parents' favoritism.

CHILDREN
Children Topic: **Jacob Played a Trick on Esau**
Key Verse: **Genesis 25:33**
Print Passage: **Genesis 25:20-34**

—God told Rebekah that her sons represented two nations.
—The competition between Esau and Jacob grew as they matured.
—Isaac and Rebekah showed favoritism in their relationships with Esau and Jacob.
—Esau saw very little value in the birthright.
—Jacob's strength was shown in his cunning.

I. INTRODUCTION

A. Peace in the Family

Nothing can be more heartbreaking than seeing families torn apart by strife. There are many families in America that are broken, not because of external problems, but because of their inability to resolve family conflicts and live in harmony. I have two adult daughters who are as different as night and day. When they were growing up, the younger daughter was more outgoing and loved to play outdoors. She loved the beach, crabbing, and just doing outdoors kinds of things. The older daughter was more of a homebody. She did not like being outdoors and certainly did not like the beach. She was always afraid that she would get saltwater in her hair or would be forced to deal with the heat. They also had their share of disagreements, and I just knew that as they grew older they would grow apart. But that has not been the case. They have become closer to each other and more willing to be there for one another during times of difficulty. My daughters represent what I believe is God's will for how brothers and sisters should live in harmony with each other. Our lesson today presents a picture that is just the opposite of the one I have described. The story of Jacob and Esau is one of the most enduring stories of all time. It teaches us the power of God's enduring promise and the details of the covenant that was first made to their grandfather, Abraham.

B. Biblical Background

In this lesson, we meet the second and third of the chief patriarchs of ancient Israel, Isaac and Jacob. We have already learned that Isaac was the only son born to Sarah and Abraham. After Sarah died, Abraham fathered other children besides Ishmael and Isaac (see Genesis 25:1-4). However, it was Isaac who received everything that Abraham had accumulated during his life (Genesis 25:5). Isaac was blessed with abundance from the day that he was born. There is no record of any personal contact between Isaac and Ishmael. However, they did come together to bury their father in the cave of Machpelah where Abraham had buried Sarah (Genesis 25:9-10).

Jacob was the younger son of Isaac and Rebekah. The Edomites descended from Esau. Jacob and Esau were as different as night and day. Jacob was loved by his mother, while Esau was more admired by his father, because of his hunting skills. Both parents showed favoritism, which turned out to be a source of great family conflict. God's Word clearly teaches against favoritism (see James 2:1-10). These two brothers were born heirs of the great wealth amassed by their grandfather, Abraham, and their father, Isaac. Yet it would be Jacob who would inherit the promise and covenant made first to Abraham and passed along to Isaac.

In their young adult years, the rivalry between Jacob and Esau would bring deep division and heartache into the life of Isaac. Eventually, Jacob would be forced to leave the family and journey to the ancestral home of his mother and grandfather in search of peace and security. Our study will lead us to see that man's ways and customs are not the ways of God. By giving the promise to Jacob, God exerted His sovereignty to choose whomever He willed. God's prerogatives exceed those of human beings. God revealed to Rebekah before her children were born that He had chosen Jacob, even though he was the younger of the two sons, to be the inheritor of the great promise (see Genesis 25:23).

II. EXPOSITION AND APPLICATION OF THE SCRIPTURE

A. The Beginning of Isaac's Legacy (Genesis 25:19)

And these are the generations of Isaac, Abraham's son: Abraham begat Isaac.

We do not know much about Isaac, because he lived a rather peaceful life. He spent many of his approximately 185 years or so living in Beer-sheba (see Genesis 26:23, 33; 28:10; 35:28). His life stands in stark contrast to the life of Abraham, whose days were filled with drama and excitement and various encounters with God. Isaac never fought any major battles, nor had any unforgettable encounters with heavenly beings. However, he was highly favored by the Lord. His wealth increased in flocks, herds, and resources. Genesis 26:13 reports that he became very wealthy, quite possibly surpassing the wealth of his father, Abraham. As He did with Isaac's father, the Lord appeared to him and reaffirmed His covenant relationship with Isaac, guaranteeing him the same promise that was given to his father (see Genesis 26:24-25).

Our passage begins with a simple genealogical statement concerning the life and family history of the descendants of Isaac. Moses made it known that this Isaac was the same Isaac who was the son of Abraham and Sarah.

B. The Birth of Jacob and Esau (Genesis 25:20-26)

And Isaac was forty years old when he took Rebekah to wife, the daughter of Bethuel the Syrian of Padan-aram, the sister to Laban the Syrian. And Isaac intreated the Lord for his wife, because she was barren: and the Lord was intreated of him, and Rebekah his wife conceived. And the children struggled together within her; and she said, If it be so, why am I thus? And she went to enquire of the Lord. And the Lord said unto her, Two nations are in thy womb, and two manner of people shall be separated from thy bowels; and the one people shall be stronger than the other people; and the elder shall serve the younger. And when her days to be delivered were fulfilled, behold, there were twins in her womb. And the first came out red, all over like an hairy garment; and they called his name Esau. And after that came his brother out, and his hand took hold on Esau's heel; and his name was called Jacob: and Isaac was threescore years old when she bare them.

Isaac's place as family patriarch began at the age of forty when he married Rebekah (Genesis 24:61-67). Both his mother and father were deceased by the time that the events in this lesson took place (Genesis 25:8). Again, we are given facts about the family tree of Rebekah. She was the daughter of Bethuel, and Milcah was her mother. Bethuel was the son of Nahor, Abraham's brother. Rebekah was the sister of Laban, who would figure prominently in the life of Jacob (Genesis 11:29). They were all from Padan-aram (Haran was a major city in northwest Mesopotamia). Family trees and connections were very important in the ancient world and still are in some cultures today, especially in many African cultures. Even today, who one is and where one comes from in many African cultures determines whether or not one will be readily accepted into the community.

Like Isaac's mother, Rebekah was unable to have children (verse 21). Unlike Isaac's parents, Isaac and Rebekah did not seek to usurp the plan of God by introducing a foreign woman into the family. Whether or not Isaac had received the promise of being the father of many descendants before the birth of his sons is not known. We do not read of the affirmation of the covenant relationship between God and Isaac until after the birth of Jacob and Esau (Genesis 26:2-6, 24). It is possible that Abraham may have shared God's covenant with him because a sign of the covenant was the circumcision of all male children on the eighth day (Genesis 17:1-14; 21:4).

Isaac was a man of deep faith and prayer. He prayed to God on behalf of his wife. He loved Rebekah so deeply that he could not bear the thought that God would close her womb permanently. We do know that the Lord heard and answered the prayer of Isaac because God opened her womb and Rebekah conceived (1 Samuel 1:11, 27; Psalms 34:4-6; 50:15; 65:2; 91:5; Isaiah 45:11; 58:9; 65:24). Rebekah was not blessed with just one child, but with two children—twins. This fits the pattern of how God had increased the blessings of Isaac's life. He acquired twice as much as his father Abraham. Instead of one son from his wife, God gave him two. This was nothing short of a miraculous occurrence.

As the sons grew in her womb, Rebekah felt a struggle going on between them. Apparently, the struggle was so intense that it produced more than just common discomfort associated with a normal pregnancy. The struggle within her was a foreshadowing of the struggle that would take place when her two sons would be born. Rebekah inquired of the Lord about this (verse 22). Here we see a side of Rebekah that we did not see in Sarah—the willingness to personally seek God in prayer.

Rebekah received a word from the Lord (verse 23). God's answer further confirmed the original promise made to Abraham concerning many nations coming from his seed. God told her four things about the children struggling in her womb. First, there were two nations living in her womb. Second, there would be two different types of people with different customs and lifestyles in each of her sons' lives. Third, the sons would not be equal in strength, for one would be stronger than the other. Fourth, the younger would be served by the older sibling. It was unheard of in the patriarchal society for the older son to be subservient to the younger (Genesis 29:26; Deuteronomy 21:15-17). We do not know how Rebekah responded, but clearly she pondered these things in her heart and held on to them.

When the pregnancy reached full term, Rebekah gave birth to twin boys (verse 24). The first came forth red and hairy and they called him Esau. He was followed by Jacob, who took hold of the heel of Esau as he was coming out of the womb. Jacob was born trying to supplant Esau. This would not be the last time that Jacob would seek to supplant his older brother Esau and take what was his by birthright. Like his father before him, Isaac had to wait twenty years for the birth of his sons. Isaac was sixty years old when Jacob and Esau were born.

C. The Selling of a Birthright
(Genesis 25:27-34)

And the boys grew: and Esau was a cunning hunter, a man of the field; and Jacob was a plain man, dwelling in tents. And Isaac loved Esau, because he did eat of his venison: but Rebekah loved Jacob. And Jacob sod pottage: and Esau came from the field, and he was faint: And Esau said to Jacob, Feed me, I pray thee, with that same red pottage; for I am faint: therefore was his name called Edom. And Jacob said, Sell me this day thy birthright. And Esau said, Behold, I am at the point to die: and what profit shall this birthright do to me? And Jacob said, Swear to me this day; and he sware unto him: and he sold his birthright unto Jacob. Then Jacob gave Esau bread and pottage of lentiles; and he did eat and drink, and rose up, and went his way: thus Esau despised his birthright.

Jacob and Esau grew and took on two distinct personalities and lifestyles (verse 27). Esau became a hunter; a man who lived a rugged life. He was quite skilled at hunting. He is described as "a man of the field." His brother was just the opposite. Jacob would be considered a homebody who loved hanging around the tent. He is described as a "plain man." The word *plain* denotes one who was complete in every way, possessing outstanding physical attributes and great mental abilities. All of these skills would serve him well in the days to come.

The favoritism shown by the parents laid the foundation for later friction between Jacob and Esau. Rebekah loved Jacob, probably because he was always around and available for his mother. Moreover, Rebekah also had access to information about the future of Jacob that he did not have. She knew that God had told her that the younger son would be served by the older. Apparently, this was not information given to Isaac. The father loved one son and the mother the other (verse 28). Isaac loved Esau because he was a hunter, and he brought Jacob venison, who prepared it just the way his father liked to eat it.

One day, Esau went out to hunt and came back empty-handed. When he arrived at the tent of his father, Jacob had prepared pottage, which is probably something he did rather frequently (verse 29). Esau was fainting with hunger; no doubt, he had not eaten anything in hours, and the walking and running had nearly sapped his strength. Esau pleaded with Jacob to give him some of the pottage he had cooked. "I am faint" was his plea (verse 30).

Jacob saw this as the moment to get the one thing that he wanted most—Esau's birthright. Jacob said to his older brother, "Sell me this day thy birthright." The birthright gave the oldest son the first right of inheritance of his father's wealth and possessions. In some instances, the firstborn son could receive double what all of the other children received (Deuteronomy 21:17). We are not told how Jacob came to possess any knowledge of the importance of the birthright or whether or not he had any prior knowledge of the promise God made to his father. It was highly unusual for a father to give any of his wealth to his children while he was living (Luke 15:11-24).

Esau pleaded with his brother, telling him he was at the point of death. He was so hungry that he simply asked what good a birthright would do him if he were dead. Jacob, the ever-shrewd and cunning thinker, would not relent and give Esau anything to eat. Here we see a man obsessed with the need to acquire the birthright of his older brother. Jacob made Esau take an oath that he would sell him his birthright and that he would not come back later to ask for it. This was going to be an irreversible transaction that would forever cement Jacob as the inheritor of all that his father owned. It would also put Jacob in line to become the head of the family upon the death of his father,

Isaac. Further, it would also put Jacob in a position of becoming the recipient and bearer of the covenant relationship with God. This was a promise which was first made to his grandfather and passed along to his father. Now we cannot and must not assume that Jacob stole the covenant promise from Esau. It was the will of God that Jacob would inherit the promise made to Abraham and Isaac (Romans 9:10-13). After Esau sold his birthright to Jacob and the deal had been consummated, Jacob gave Esau the pottage and he satisfied his hunger. We are told that he ate and drank and then left. The passage ends with a summary statement that simply says, "thus Esau despised his birthright" (verse 34).

III. CONCLUDING REFLECTIONS

God works His will and purpose through people. And many times the people that God chooses to use may be the least desirable with the greatest amount of personal baggage and hang-ups. Who would have thought that the eternal purpose of God would be worked out through a man like Jacob—a deceiver, liar, and cheater? In many ways Jacob reminds us of ourselves and how God has looked beyond all of our sins, brokenness, and hang-ups to call us into a greater and nobler work. Jacob was quite different from his father and grandfather. He was preoccupied with his own self-interests. At the other end of this family saga, we see Esau, a man who despised what was rightfully his and exchanged it for the personal gratification of his appetite.

PRAYER

Heavenly Father, we bless You for the privilege of living in families. May the homes where we live be places of peace, and may we know the joys of living according to Your will and purpose. In the name of Jesus Christ, we pray. Amen.

WORD POWER

Serve (Hebrew: `abad: aw-bad)—this means to be in bondage to another; it also carries the idea of compelling one to labor. This was a prophecy made to Rebekah when she asked God about the cause of the pain of her pregnancy; her older son would serve the younger. We will not be able to unravel the mystery of this verse. God and only God understands why He allowed this to happen.

HOME DAILY BIBLE READINGS
(October 1-7, 2007)

Esau and Jacob as Rivals

MONDAY, October 1: "God Chose the Least" (1 Corinthians 1:26-31)
TUESDAY, October 2: "Rebekah Agrees to Marry Isaac" (Genesis 24:50-61)
WEDNESDAY, October 3: "Isaac Takes Rebekah as His Wife" (Genesis 24:62-67)
THURSDAY, October 4: "Rebekah's Twins Struggle in the Womb" (Genesis 25:19-23)
FRIDAY, October 5: "The Birth of Jacob and Esau" (Genesis 25:24-28)
SATURDAY, October 6: "Esau Sells His Birthright" (Genesis 25:29-34)
SUNDAY, October 7: "Esau's Lost Blessing" (Genesis 27:30-40)

LESSON 7   October 14, 2007

JACOB'S DREAM AT BETHEL

DEVOTIONAL READING: **Psalm 105:1-11**   BACKGROUND SCRIPTURE: **Genesis 27:41–28:22**
PRINT PASSAGE: **Genesis 28:10-22**   KEY VERSE: **Genesis 28:15**

Genesis 28:10-22—KJV

10 And Jacob went out from Beer-sheba, and went toward Haran.

11 And he lighted upon a certain place, and tarried there all night, because the sun was set; and he took of the stones of that place, and put them for his pillows, and lay down in that place to sleep.

12 And he dreamed, and behold a ladder set up on the earth, and the top of it reached to heaven: and behold the angels of God ascending and descending on it.

13 And, behold, the LORD stood above it, and said, I am the LORD God of Abraham thy father, and the God of Isaac: the land whereon thou liest, to thee will I give it, and to thy seed;

14 And thy seed shall be as the dust of the earth, and thou shalt spread abroad to the west, and to the east, and to the north, and to the south: and in thee and in thy seed shall all the families of the earth be blessed.

15 And, behold, I am with thee, and will keep thee in all places whither thou goest, and will bring thee again into this land; for I will not leave thee, until I have done that which I have spoken to thee of.

16 And Jacob awaked out of his sleep, and he said, Surely the LORD is in this place; and I knew it not.

17 And he was afraid, and said, How dreadful is this place! this is none other but the house of God, and this is the gate of heaven.

18 And Jacob rose up early in the morning, and took the stone that he had put for his pillows, and set it up for a pillar, and poured oil upon the top of it.

19 And he called the name of that place Bethel: but the name of that city was called Luz at the first.

20 And Jacob vowed a vow, saying, If God will be with me, and will keep me in this way that I go, and will give me bread to eat, and raiment to put on,

21 So that I come again to my father's house in peace; then shall the LORD be my God:

22 And this stone, which I have set for a pillar, shall be God's house: and of all that thou shalt give me I will surely give the tenth unto thee.

Genesis 28:10-22—NRSV

10 Jacob left Beer-sheba and went toward Haran.

11 He came to a certain place and stayed there for the night, because the sun had set. Taking one of the stones of the place, he put it under his head and lay down in that place.

12 And he dreamed that there was a ladder set up on the earth, the top of it reaching to heaven; and the angels of God were ascending and descending on it.

13 And the LORD stood beside him and said, "I am the LORD, the God of Abraham your father and the God of Isaac; the land on which you lie I will give to you and to your offspring;

14 and your offspring shall be like the dust of the earth, and you shall spread abroad to the west and to the east and to the north and to the south; and all the families of the earth shall be blessed in you and in your offspring.

15 Know that I am with you and will keep you wherever you go, and will bring you back to this land; for I will not leave you until I have done what I have promised you."

16 Then Jacob woke from his sleep and said, "Surely the LORD is in this place—and I did not know it!"

17 And he was afraid, and said, "How awesome is this place! This is none other than the house of God, and this is the gate of heaven."

18 So Jacob rose early in the morning, and he took the stone that he had put under his head and set it up for a pillar and poured oil on the top of it.

19 He called that place Bethel; but the name of the city was Luz at the first.

20 Then Jacob made a vow, saying, "If God will be with me, and will keep me in this way that I go, and will give me bread to eat and clothing to wear,

21 so that I come again to my father's house in peace, then the LORD shall be my God,

22 and this stone, which I have set up for a pillar, shall be God's house; and of all that you give me I will surely give one tenth to you."

UNIFYING LESSON PRINCIPLE

Humans dream, though we do not always remember or understand our dreams. What is the purpose of a dream? In the story of Jacob at Bethel, a dream reassured Jacob of God's continuing covenant with him.

TOPICAL OUTLINE OF THE LESSON

I. **Introduction**
  A. Dreams
  B. Biblical Background

II. **Exposition and Application of the Scripture**
  A. Jacob's Departure and Dream (Genesis 28:10-12)
  B. The Abrahamic Covenant and Promise (Genesis 28:13-15)
  C. Jacob's Reaction to the Dream (Genesis 28:16-17)
  D. Jacob Established a Memorial at Bethel (Genesis 28:18-19)
  E. Jacob's Vow (Genesis 28:20-22)

III. **Concluding Reflections**

LESSON OBJECTIVES

Upon completion of this lesson, the students will know that:

1. God is forever faithful to His promises;
2. God still speaks to us through dreams; and,
3. Initially there may be some sort of confusion in understanding the plans of God, but when we wait on Him, He will make His purpose clear to us.

POINTS TO BE EMPHASIZED

ADULT/YOUTH

Adult Topic: **Understanding Our Dreams**
Youth Topic: **A Dream and a Promise**
Adult/Youth Key Verse: **Genesis 28:15**
Print Passage: **Genesis 28:10-22**

—Jacob's dream was about a ladder leading to heaven, with God at the top of the ladder.
—When Jacob recognized that his campground was a holy place, he responded by worshiping God and making a vow to God.
—Jacob deemed the spot a holy place because it was an entrance to God.
—Jacob's encounter with God in a dream had a major impact on the covenant people.
—What was Jacob's reason for travel, and what was his state of mind?
—God showed Jacob the future and confirmed to him the covenantal promise.
—Jacob did not ascend the ladder; God descended the ladder.

CHILDREN

Children Topic: **Jacob Had a Dream**
Key Verse: **Genesis 28:15**
Print Passage: **Genesis 27:41-43; 28:10-13, 15-18, 20-21**

—The animosity between Esau and Jacob escalated to the point that Esau plotted to kill Jacob.
—In order to save Jacob's life, Rebekah and Isaac sent Jacob to Haran.
—When Jacob awoke from his dream, he praised God for God's presence.
—Jacob made the stone pillar a memorial of his experience.
—In Jacob's dream, he saw angels ascending to and descending from heaven on a ladder.

I. INTRODUCTION

A. Dreams

The study and science of understanding dreams has been the subject of great debate for hundreds of years. In the modern era, psychologists are still no closer to reaching a consensus on how to interpret dreams. But the reality is that all of us have dreams. What is a dream? It is an extra-sensory experience that occurs in our subconscious minds during periods of sleep. How dreams form and what they reveal are all matters of debate. Although we do not know a lot about dreams, there is one thing we do know—God has often used dreams to reveal His will and purpose to His people. God used the interpretation of a dream to encourage Gideon to go up against the camp of the Midianites because He had given it into his hand (Judges 7:1-15). God told the Israelites that when He raised up a prophet among them, He would make His will and purpose known through visions and dreams (Numbers 12:6-7; 1 Kings 3:5-15).

Within the ancient world, the belief in dreams and visions was prevalent. Sometimes kings would base their decisions entirely on dreams. Hence, the interpretation of dreams and visions could be a very powerful tool for spiritual enrichment (Daniel 2:1-45; 4:1-27). Dreams are powerful, and we will see in this lesson how God used a dream to reveal to Jacob His promise for him and future generations.

B. Biblical Background

This lesson continues the story of Jacob and Esau. Isaac was advanced in age with poor sight and poor health. He was unwittingly deceived into blessing Jacob and giving to him the place of rank and family honor (Genesis 27:30-37). When Esau discovered how Jacob had cheated him out of his birthright, he began to hold a grudge against Jacob (Genesis 27:41). His plan was to kill Jacob, but he would wait until after their father Isaac had died and the period of mourning had passed. When Rebekah found out about Esau's plans, she summoned Jacob and told him to flee to her brother, Laban, who lived in Haran (Genesis 27:43). Jacob would stay with Laban a few days and then return after Esau's anger had subsided. In order to make Jacob's departure appear without suspicion, Rebekah went to Isaac and told him that she was fearful that Jacob would marry one of the Canaanite women (Genesis 27:46).

Isaac called Jacob to his bedside, blessed him, and charged him not to marry a woman from Canaan. Rather, Jacob was to go to Padan-aram, which was another name for Haran, and there find a wife among his mother's relatives (Genesis 28:1-2). Prior to leaving Beer-sheba, Jacob received the blessing of his father (Genesis 28:3-5).

II. EXPOSITION AND APPLICATION OF THE SCRIPTURE

A. Jacob's Departure and Dream
(Genesis 28:10-12)

And Jacob went out from Beer-sheba, and went toward Haran. And he lighted upon a certain place, and tarried there all night, because the sun was set; and he took of the stones of that place, and put them for his pillows, and lay down in that place to sleep. And he dreamed, and behold a ladder set up on the earth, and the top of it reached to heaven: and behold the angels of God ascending and descending on it.

The journey from Beer-sheba to Haran covered several hundred miles through some of the most desolate and difficult terrain in the ancient Near East. (Find a study Bible with maps at the back, and locate and look at a map of the land of Canaan and plot out the distance.) There is no record of anyone accompanying Jacob, which would make his journey all the more difficult. We are told in a very few words that Jacob departed and headed toward the ancestral home of his mother.

The events in verse 11 occurred after Jacob had been traveling nearly seven to ten days through the central highlands of Israel. We are told that he came upon a certain place. This was not some predetermined place along the route of travel, nor was it a normal resting place for people traveling from southern Negeb to the north and beyond. It was the end of another long day, and Jacob needed a place to rest and spend the night. Jacob found some stones, made a pillow, and lay down for a long night of restful sleep.

During the course of the night, he saw in a dream a ladder that was on the earth reaching up to heaven. On this ladder, there were angels going up and down. It is likely they were a sign to Jacob in his dream of something great that was about to take place in his life. These

angels brought assurance to Jacob of God's presence in his life.

B. The Abrahamic Covenant and Promise
(Genesis 28:13-15)

And, behold, the LORD stood above it, and said, I am the LORD God of Abraham thy father, and the God of Isaac: the land whereon thou liest, to thee will I give it, and to thy seed; And thy seed shall be as the dust of the earth, and thou shalt spread abroad to the west, and to the east, and to the north, and to the south: and in thee and in thy seed shall all the families of the earth be blessed. And, behold, I am with thee, and will keep thee in all places whither thou goest, and will bring thee again into this land; for I will not leave thee, until I have done that which I have spoken to thee of.

Jacob's dream reached a climax with the appearance of the Lord, who stood at the apex of the ladder. This was a theophany, or an appearance of a deity, namely, God. Here, Jacob met the Source (God) of all of his father's wealth and prosperity. God made a sterling promise and entered into covenant with Jacob just as He had done with his grandfather, Abraham, and his father, Isaac (Genesis 12:1-3; 15:1; 17:6-7; 26:24). It is critical that families take seriously the need to pass along their faith in God and in His promises to future generations.

There were several aspects of the promise God made to Jacob. First, God promised him the land that he was sleeping on. Not only would he receive it, but so would his children and future generations. Second, from his seed would come a multitude of people who would be as numerous as the dust of the earth.

Third, just as dust was carried about to many places, so his children would spread and reach the four corners of the earth: west, east, north, and south. What was most remarkable is that in the future, Jacob would be a blessing to others, as opposed to always looking to be blessed himself. There are many people inside and outside of churches who look for others to shower them with blessings; but here we learn that when we have been blessed, we should go and bless others.

Fourth, God promised to be with Jacob wherever he went and that God would keep him (Joshua 1:3-10; Psalms 41:10; 46:7, 10; 121:5-8; Isaiah 41:10; 48:16; Jeremiah 1:19; Matthew 18:20; 28:20; Romans 8:31-32).

Fifth, there was the guarantee from God that Jacob would arrive safely in Haran, and one day he would come back to his former destination. Here we have the ageless promise of God to protect those whom He has on assignment.

Sixth, Jacob could rest confidently in every word that God spoke that He was not going to leave Jacob until every word spoken had been accomplished in his life. God's Word is the basis of believers' hope (Psalm 119:74, 81, 114, 147).

C. Jacob's Reaction to the Dream (Genesis 28:16-17)

And Jacob awaked out of his sleep, and he said, Surely the LORD is in this place; and I knew it not. And he was afraid, and said, How dreadful is this place! this is none other but the house of God, and this is the gate of heaven.

Jacob woke up and realized that he had had a dream. This had not been a typical dream, for the things he saw and the voice he heard made it too real. He exclaimed in sheer excitement, "Surely the LORD is in this place; and I knew it not" (verse 16).

Jacob had experienced the awesomeness and majesty of the presence of the Lord (Exodus 15:11; Isaiah 6:1-8; Psalm 68:35). Is it possible that the Lord appears in many Sunday worship services, and there are people who do not recognize Him? Here we learn that God meets us in the most unlikely places and under the most unlikely circumstances. In these unlikely places, we can experience the wonder of God's grace.

Jacob came to experience God's redeeming grace. When he should have been cowering in fear, God told him not to be afraid. Where are some of the most unlikely places you have met the grandeur of God's presence and grace? Everything that he had seen in the life of his father, Isaac, and had heard about concerning his grandfather, Abraham, was about to burst forth in Jacob's life in even more dramatic ways.

Further, we learn that God never gives up on people, regardless of how wretched or treacherous their lives have been. Jacob was a schemer and a deceiver, but God chose him to be the bearer of the covenant of promise (Acts 9:1-9). Jacob declared the place of his experience to be the house of God and the gate of heaven.

D. Jacob Established a Memorial at Bethel (Genesis 28:18-19)

And Jacob rose up early in the morning, and took the stone that he had put for his pillows, and set it up for a pillar, and poured oil upon the top of it. And he called the name of that place Bethel: but the name of that city was called Luz at the first.

At daybreak, approximately 6:00 a.m. (by the Jewish reckoning of time), Jacob took the stone that he had used for a pillow and set it up as a memorial to the Lord. Early in the morning, Jacob began to worship the God of his fathers, Abraham and Isaac. Here the stone was referred to as a "pillar," which was the same thing done by his grandfather and father (Genesis 12:7; 13:18; 26:25). The earlier patriarchs built altars to offer sacrifices to God. The stone was not an idol, but it became a memorial for Jacob's encounter with God. Pillars served a useful purpose in the ancient world, especially in ancient Israelite practice. They were used at times to serve as symbols of the Lord's presence (Genesis 35:14). Pillars also served to witness between people (Genesis 31:45). When Rachel died, Jacob set up a pillar as a memorial to her life and to mark the place where she was buried (Genesis 35:20).

Jacob poured oil on the stone in an act of dedication and consecration of the place. Oil was used for anointing and dedication in ancient Israelite traditions. Moses was commanded by God to make a special, holy anointing oil that was to never be used on any humans except Aaron and his sons (Exodus 30:31; 31:11). The kings and the priests were also anointed with oil as a sign of consecration to God's service, and the fact that God had specifically chosen them to lead (1 Samuel 10:1). In many of the Levitical sacrifices, oil was used with the ritual of the sacrifices (Leviticus 2:1-7; 8:12; 21:10). In the New Testament church tradition, oil was used to anoint the sick for healing (James 5:14-15).

The use of oil in worship services has met with mixed reviews among African-American Christians. Some people are adamantly against the idea or the thought of anointing people with oil. Others see it as a biblical teaching, and therefore believe it to be within the boundaries of what is permissible in the church. During one of my mission trips to Nigeria, I carried a bottle of olive oil that I had purchased in Israel. Our mission team preached in one of the national prisons, and at the end of the service I stated that I was going to anoint all who wanted to be anointed with the oil that I brought back from the Holy Land. More than three hundred men and women lined up to be prayed for and anointed because they believed in the healing and forgiving power of Jesus Christ. Their faith in God was more important than the oil.

Jacob called the name of the place where he had the dream *Bethel* which means "house of God." Early in ancient Israelite tradition, Bethel was a very holy place because it was where Jacob met God and was blessed by Him.

E. Jacob's Vow
(Genesis 28:20-22)

And Jacob vowed a vow, saying, If God will be with me, and will keep me in this way that I go, and will give me bread to eat, and raiment to put on, So that I come again to my father's house in peace; then shall the Lord be my God: And this stone, which I have set for a pillar, shall be God's house: and of all that thou shalt give me I will surely give the tenth unto thee.

Jacob made a vow with God to make the Lord, the God of his fathers, his God as well. There were five conditions in Jacob's vow. First, he wanted God to be with him. Second, he wanted God to keep him. Third, Jacob wanted God to meet his need for food. Fourth, he wanted God to provide him with clothes. Fifth, Jacob wanted God to bring him back to his father's house in peace. Jacob established the stone as a pillar, which would symbolize God's house. Jacob vowed to give back to God the tenth of all that he had received. Abraham, his grandfather, gave God a tenth through the high priest Melchizedek (Genesis 14:20). What could more dramatically demonstrate Jacob's commitment to serve God, obey God, and follow God than to give a tenth? Tithing is never done out of legal requirements; it is an expression of our love for God, and it shows our appreciation for all that we have received from Him. Tithing acknowledges our gratitude to Him for His graciousness. Tithing demonstrates our desire to see the kingdom expand and expresses, more so than any other act, our true commitment to the kingdom (Luke 12:34).

III. CONCLUDING REFLECTIONS

Jacob left Beer-sheba as a man marked for death by his brother. Along the way, he met the God of his ancestors, who changed his life forever. After this encounter, Jacob's life took on a whole new dimension and direction. From this lesson, we have learned that God is gracious and often calls us to His service without regard to the failures and faults of our past. His will and plan for our lives is far greater than any sins we have committed. Jacob shows us how to commit ourselves to God. The most important thing we can give God, in addition to ourselves, is access to the abundance of things He has given to us. Material possessions are never a sign of favor, but how we use them can indicate the level of our gratitude for the favor we have received.

PRAYER

Heavenly Father, we bless You for Your boundless grace and abundant favor. May we be shining examples of how to trust You in every aspect of our lives. In Jesus' name, we pray. Amen.

WORD POWER

In all (Hebrew: *kol-kole*)—these words, in all, are only one word in Hebrew. It means "anywhere, in all places, at all times." This word is preceded by "I am." God overlooked Jacob's sins and made a promise to him. Jacob's mistakes could not frustrate the purpose of God. We may hurt ourselves by running ahead of God, but His purpose will prevail.

HOME DAILY BIBLE READINGS
(October 8-14, 2007)
Jacob's Dream at Bethel
MONDAY, October 8: "Remember God's Works" (Psalm 105:1-6)
TUESDAY, October 9: "An Everlasting Covenant" (Psalm 105:7-11)
WEDNESDAY, October 10: "The Conflict Deepens" (Genesis 27:41-45)
THURSDAY, October 11: "To Seek a Wife" (Genesis 27:46—28:5)
FRIDAY, October 12: "Esau Takes Another Wife" (Genesis 28:6-9)
SATURDAY, October 13: "God's Covenant with Jacob" (Genesis 28:10-17)
SUNDAY, October 14: "The Place Named Bethel" (Genesis 28:18-22)

LESSON 8   October 21, 2007

JACOB AND RACHEL

DEVOTIONAL READING: **Psalm 91**

PRINT PASSAGE: **Genesis 29:21-35**

BACKGROUND SCRIPTURE: **Genesis 29**

KEY VERSE: **Genesis 29:20**

Genesis 29:21-35—KJV

21 And Jacob said unto Laban, Give me my wife, for my days are fulfilled, that I may go in unto her.

22 And Laban gathered together all the men of the place, and made a feast.

23 And it came to pass in the evening, that he took Leah his daughter, and brought her to him; and he went in unto her.

24 And Laban gave unto his daughter Leah Zilpah his maid for an handmaid.

25 And it came to pass, that in the morning, behold, it was Leah: and he said to Laban, What is this thou hast done unto me? did not I serve with thee for Rachel? wherefore then hast thou beguiled me?

26 And Laban said, It must not be so done in our country, to give the younger before the firstborn.

27 Fulfil her week, and we will give thee this also for the service which thou shalt serve with me yet seven other years.

28 And Jacob did so, and fulfilled her week: and he gave him Rachel his daughter to wife also.

29 And Laban gave to Rachel his daughter Bilhah his handmaid to be her maid.

30 And he went in also unto Rachel, and he loved also Rachel more than Leah, and served with him yet seven other years.

31 And when the LORD saw that Leah was hated, he opened her womb: but Rachel was barren.

32 And Leah conceived, and bare a son, and she called his name Reuben: for she said, Surely the LORD hath looked upon my affliction; now therefore my husband will love me.

33 And she conceived again, and bare a son; and said, Because the LORD hath heard that I was hated, he hath therefore given me this son also: and she called his name Simeon.

34 And she conceived again, and bare a son; and said, Now this time will my husband be joined unto me, because I have born him three sons: therefore was his name called Levi.

35 And she conceived again, and bare a son: and she said, Now will I praise the LORD: therefore she called his name Judah; and left bearing.

Genesis 29:21-35—NRSV

21 Then Jacob said to Laban, "Give me my wife that I may go in to her, for my time is completed."

22 So Laban gathered together all the people of the place, and made a feast.

23 But in the evening he took his daughter Leah and brought her to Jacob; and he went in to her.

24 (Laban gave his maid Zilpah to his daughter Leah to be her maid.)

25 When morning came, it was Leah! And Jacob said to Laban, "What is this you have done to me? Did I not serve with you for Rachel? Why then have you deceived me?"

26 Laban said, "This is not done in our country—giving the younger before the firstborn.

27 Complete the week of this one, and we will give you the other also in return for serving me another seven years."

28 Jacob did so, and completed her week; then Laban gave him his daughter Rachel as a wife.

29 (Laban gave his maid Bilhah to his daughter Rachel to be her maid.)

30 So Jacob went in to Rachel also, and he loved Rachel more than Leah. He served Laban for another seven years.

31 When the LORD saw that Leah was unloved, he opened her womb; but Rachel was barren.

32 Leah conceived and bore a son, and she named him Reuben; for she said, "Because the LORD has looked on my affliction; surely now my husband will love me."

33 She conceived again and bore a son, and said, "Because the LORD has heard that I am hated, he has given me this son also"; and she named him Simeon.

34 Again she conceived and bore a son, and said, "Now this time my husband will be joined to me, because I have borne him three sons"; therefore he was named Levi.

35 She conceived again and bore a son, and said, "This time I will praise the LORD"; therefore she named him Judah; then she ceased bearing.

UNIFYING LESSON PRINCIPLE

Hopes are sometimes dashed or temporarily put on hold. How do we respond when our fondest wishes remain unfulfilled? Jacob dearly loved Rachel but unexpectedly found after seven years of work that he must first marry her older sister Leah and then work seven more years for the woman of his heart.

TOPICAL OUTLINE OF THE LESSON

I. **Introduction**
   A. Deception
   B. Biblical Background

II. **Exposition and Application of the Scripture**
   A. Jacob Meets His Match (Genesis 29:21-26)
   B. Jacob Makes Another Bargain for Rachel (Genesis 29:27-30)
   C. Jacob's Sons by Leah (Genesis 29:31-35)

III. **Concluding Reflections**

LESSON OBJECTIVES

Upon completion of this lesson, the students will know that:

1. When hope becomes weak, God is able to infuse energy to keep us going;
2. Reckoning on God's promises will help us when we are confused; and,
3. Delay is not denial; all that is required is to wait and see God at work.

POINTS TO BE EMPHASIZED
ADULT/YOUTH

Adult Topic: **Dashed Hopes and Fond Wishes**
Youth Topic: **Date and Switch**
Adult Key Verse: **Genesis 29:20**
Youth Key Verse: **Genesis 29:25**
Print Passage: **Genesis 29:21-35**

—God's promise of descendants to Abraham continues to be fulfilled in the marriages and births recorded in this passage.
—Deception is a prominent theme in the Jacob cycle of stories.
—Jacob's love for Rachel compelled him to work a total of fourteen years for her father, Laban.
—In the midst of disappointment and deceit, God's promise prevailed.
—Leah bore four sons, yet she did not receive Jacob's love.
—God's acts are redemptive, whereas human actions are questionable.

CHILDREN

Children Topic: **Jacob Loved Rachel**
Key Verse: **Genesis 29:18**
Print Passage: **Genesis 29:1-6, 9-14, 18-20**

—Jacob "the trickster" learned what it was like to be tricked.
—Jacob worked persistently toward his goal, even when things did not go as planned.
—Jacob's story teaches us about the nature of love.
—Leah's and Rachel's stories show that we are sometimes victimized by cultural customs.

I. INTRODUCTION

A. Deception

One of the underlying themes of today's lesson is the insidious nature of deception and its high costs. Every day, we experience deceit in one form or another. There are deceptions in church, in our work environments, between husbands and wives, between children and parents, and deceptions from Wall Street to Main Street. Millions of people have lost their livelihoods because an employer lied about the business prospects of his or her company. Most of us have experienced deceit in advertising when we find that the small print of a sales contract is not always clear, costing us hundreds or even thousands of dollars. Then there are people who live with the emotional trauma that comes from being in an intimate relationship where deceit has been practiced, and lies have been repeatedly told to cover up an illicit relationship.

Deceit is one of the most diabolical forms of lying. It is one of Satan's most powerful tools and he uses it with cunning accuracy. What is deceit? It is willfully giving out false information with the express intention of leading someone into a situation that they otherwise would not allow themselves to fall into.

B. Biblical Background

At Bethel, Jacob received a promise from God that He would provide for Jacob's needs, protecting him wherever he went. After this unforgettable experience at Bethel, Jacob continued his journey until he finally came into the region of Haran, where a well was located. This was a community well that was used exclusively for the watering of livestock (Genesis 29:3). About the time that Jacob was engaging in a conversation with the shepherds, Rachel showed up leading the sheep of her father, Laban. As Rachael drew near the well, Jacob rolled the heavy stone from above the well and watered Laban's sheep (Genesis 29:10). He told Rachel who he was and that he was the son of Rebekah, her father's sister (Genesis 29:12). At this point, we are told that Laban had two daughters. The older was named Leah and the younger one was named Rachel. It was Rachel who had stolen Jacob's heart with her beauty and grace. The text reports that Leah was weak around the eyes, an indication that she was delicate and soft. However, Jacob fell in love with Rachel, who was beautiful and well-favored. Jacob offered to serve Laban for seven years for the right to marry Rachel. The proposal pleased Laban and Jacob served him for seven years. The time went by like a flash in the night because of the great love that Jacob had for Rachel.

II. EXPOSITION AND APPLICATION OF THE SCRIPTURE

A. Jacob Meets His Match
(Genesis 29:21-26)

And Jacob said unto Laban, Give me my wife, for my days are fulfilled, that I may go in unto her. And Laban gathered together all the men of the place, and made a feast. And it came to pass in the evening, that he took Leah his daughter, and brought her to him; and he went in unto her. And Laban gave unto his daughter Leah Zilpah his maid for an handmaid. And it came to pass, that in the morning, behold, it was Leah: and he said to Laban, What is this thou hast done unto me? did not I serve with thee for Rachel? wherefore then hast thou beguiled me? And Laban said, It must not be so done in our country, to give the younger before the firstborn.

After working for seven years, Jacob found himself on a collision course with justice. He was sly and crafty, but now God was about to teach him a severe lesson about fairness. Seven years whisked by as a watch in the night and Jacob went to Laban and said, "Give me my wife, for my days are fulfilled..." (verse 21).

In an act befitting a proud father, Laban prepared a great feast and celebration for the marriage of his daughter. According to their custom, he gathered all of the men of the community together to celebrate his good fortune. After all, he had been blessed with a future son-in-law who loved his daughter so much that he was willing to work like a slave for seven years just to have her. In one night, Jacob would get a taste of the bitterness of deceit that he had forced his blood brother, Esau, to swallow.

Following the custom of that day, Laban presented his daughter to Jacob by bringing her to their wedding night tent. Jacob did not know that it was Leah and not Rachel that he would sleep with. How was Laban able to pull off this plot without Jacob being aware of it? There are several possible reasons that may explain the success of the father's plot. The bridal veil enveloped the whole person, so that it was virtually impossible to detect the fraud. Further, in the dark of the desert and within the enclosed and close confines of a Bedouin tent, how could he even recognize that his bride was Leah?

Here was Jacob, the one who was always trying to get over on people, being beaten at his own game. The hunter was captured by the game. Laban wanted to see both of his daughters married, and he did what he thought was necessary to see that it happened. No doubt he believed that Rachel would not have a problem meeting a suitable mate and getting married because of her beauty and youth. This was not the case with Leah.

At the first chance he had, Jacob confronted Laban and wanted to know why he had done this thing to him. What a strange and ironic twist of fate we see in this story! Jacob asked Laban, "...wherefore then hast thou beguiled me?" (verse 25). We see that the same Hebrew word *beguiled*, used by Jacob, was used to describe how the Serpent tricked Eve (see Genesis 3:13). Jacob had only received what he had given out to others.

Laban told Jacob that his wanting to marry Rachel was a complete violation of the customs of his country. In Haran, the older daughter had to be married before the younger. Here is another ironic twist of fate; Jacob had taken the birthright of his older brother without remorse. Now he was forced to take Leah in marriage, and Laban was not remorseful. In this act, we see Jacob's ignorance of the local customs, and also his blind love. It would appear that everyone knew about the plot but

Jacob. Clearly, the men who came to the feast must have had the expectation that it was Leah who was about to wed and not Rachel. Is it possible that everyone understood Leah to be the bride and not Rachel? If that was so, then the deception perpetrated against Jacob was far greater than anything he had done to others. The magnitude of the deception perpetrated by Laban was heightened by the fact that seven years before Jacob even began to work for Rachel, Laban knew what he was going to do. Was this a father's love for his daughters, or was it a man's selfish interests rising to the forefront? Laban led Jacob on for seven years, and there is no record of them ever having discussed Jacob's future marriage to Rachel.

God uses others sometimes to teach us discipline and respect for authority. Jacob would have never learned the importance of equity and fairness had he not met an uncle who was shrewder and more cunning than he.

B. Jacob Makes Another Bargain for Rachel (Genesis 29:27-30)

Fulfil her week, and we will give thee this also for the service which thou shalt serve with me yet seven other years. And Jacob did so, and fulfilled her week: and he gave him Rachel his daughter to wife also. And Laban gave to Rachel his daughter Bilhah his handmaid to be her maid. And he went in also unto Rachel, and he loved also Rachel more than Leah, and served with him yet seven other years.

Jacob revealed his unwavering love for Rachel by his willingness to serve his father-in-law again. Laban offered Jacob the opportunity to get what he really wanted—the hand of Rachel in marriage. But there was one condition: Jacob would have to serve Laban for another seven years (verse 27). Jacob willingly served Laban for seven more years to gain the hand of Rachel.

It is evident that Laban had no problems with one man being married to both of his daughters. They were not married to local men, but to a man who was from his own family, which was an accepted custom in that day. Jacob paid quite a price to be married to the woman of his dreams.

Here we are faced with the issue of polygamy. Evidently, it was an acceptable practice among the patriarchs and the people of that day. Within ancient Israel, it was permissible for a man to have more than one wife (see 1 Samuel 1:2; 25:43; 27:3; 30:3, 5; 2 Samuel 2:2; 5:13). Polygamy is still practiced in some places in the world today, without legal restraints. Once, while visiting the country of Jordan, I spoke to a man who told me he had four wives and dozens of children. I asked him how he was able to live with four women at one time. He said it was the custom of his village to have them all live in separate houses and for the man to stay with a different wife each night. Thus, he was able to keep them all happy. In some African cultures, it is still permissible to have multiple wives, especially among tribal chiefs. Therefore, while we may frown on the practice, it is still carried out today.

Laban gave Bilhah to Rachel to be her handmaid. We are told that Jacob went in to Rachel and that he loved Rachel more than Leah. Just as his parents had done with him and his brother, Jacob showed favoritism toward his wives. He spent more time with Rachel than he did with Leah. In this act, Jacob laid the foundation for future problems in his family.

C. Jacob's Sons by Leah (Genesis 29:31-35)

And when the LORD saw that Leah was hated, he opened her womb: but Rachel was barren. And Leah conceived,

and bare a son, and she called his name Reuben: for she said, Surely the Lᴏʀᴅ hath looked upon my affliction; now therefore my husband will love me. And she conceived again, and bare a son; and said, Because the Lᴏʀᴅ hath heard that I was hated, he hath therefore given me this son also: and she called his name Simeon. And she conceived again, and bare a son; and said, Now this time will my husband be joined unto me, because I have born him three sons: therefore was his name called Levi. And she conceived again, and bare a son: and she said, Now will I praise the Lᴏʀᴅ: therefore she called his name Judah; and left bearing.

The tension in the family of Jacob reached the very heart of God. Jacob never really accepted Leah as his wife. His heart and affections were always directed toward Rachel. Leah was simply an intrusion into what should have been a happy marriage. God knows the heart and the mind of everybody. He saw that Leah was hated and despised. This hatred was probably extended by both Jacob and Rachel. But God is sovereign and His power can overrule and conquer any heart and foe. He opened the womb of Leah and closed the womb of Rachel. Rachel lavished Jacob with plenty of love, companionship, and support, but she could not give him the one thing he desired most: children, especially sons. In this episode of the life of the patriarchs, there was no appearance by God to say when a child would be born; there was simply the act of God.

Two themes are at work in this story—barrenness and fruitfulness. On the one hand, the woman most loved was barren, and the one most despised was fruitful. God was clearly at work and continued to teach Jacob lessons about His sovereignty. Is it possible that Jacob remembered the promise of God that his seed would be as the dust of the earth, yet he had no children?

The passage introduces us to the foundational beginnings of ancient Israel and the founders of the twelve tribes of Israel. Leah was the fruitful of the two wives, indicating that she had found favor with the Lord (see Psalm 5:12; Proverbs 3:1-4). Leah conceived and gave birth to a son; she called him Reuben. In the ancient world, names meant a great deal. They either referred to some event in the lives of the parents, or to some place. Reuben's name meant, "Surely the Lᴏʀᴅ hath looked upon my affliction; now therefore my husband will love me" (Genesis 29:32).

Leah conceived a second time, and gave birth to another son, whom she named Simeon. His name also referred to the strained relationship that existed between Jacob and Leah. Simeon referred to the hatred that his mother experienced from his father. A third son was born, and his name was Levi. Finally, a fourth son was born, and he was given the name of Judah. Leah's fruitfulness may have occurred over a four-year period. Each of the sons was given a name that in some way reflected the tumultuous relationship between Jacob and Leah. In another ironic twist of divine justice, the first sons born became the leading tribes of Israel. It is possible that as the boys grew older, they came to know the significance of their names and what they meant.

III. CONCLUDING REFLECTIONS

Relationships are among our most prized possessions. But many people believe that if they can just earn enough money and acquire enough possessions, they will be able to live lives of absolute bliss. Jacob appears to have been like a lot of people today who will stop at nothing to get what they want, even if it means hurting the people closest to them.

This lesson clearly teaches about the sovereignty of God, whose power and will are able to overrule any plan or scheme we may hatch. Jacob believed that he had done the right thing in working faithfully for Rachel, only to be given Leah. Even in what Jacob considered a serious breach of trust, God worked out His divine plan for the future of Israel. From the womb of Leah came the tribe of Judah, which was one of the only two surviving tribes of ancient Israel; the other was Benjamin.

Finally, we learn the importance of faithfulness and service. Jacob may have been an unsavory person early in his life, but he had two qualities that are well worth emulating: faithfulness and determination. He never complained about what he was asked to do, nor did he shirk his duty. Fourteen years seems like a long time to work for the privilege of marrying someone. But Jacob proved that true love empowers us to wait, face, and overcome challenges that are thrown in our way.

PRAYER

Almighty, heavenly Father, teach us to live with honesty and integrity. We beseech Thee for Thy forgiveness and grace. We thank Thee for the privilege of being used by You for the fulfillment of Your purpose. In the name of Jesus Christ, we pray. Amen.

WORD POWER

Love (Hebrew: `*ahab ~ aw-hab)*—this word means "to have affection." This is a type of love that centers on external beauty. It is infatuation. This is the type of love which drove Jacob to be in bondage for Rachel's sake. He enslaved himself for fleeting beauty. This is a common phenomenon among youth today. Christian singles who are looking for life partners should concentrate more on inner character than external beauty.

HOME DAILY BIBLE READINGS
(October 15-21, 2007)

Jacob and Rachel

MONDAY, October 15: "Assurance of God's Protection" (Psalm 91)

TUESDAY, October 16: "The Kiss that Brought Tears" (Genesis 29:1-12)

WEDNESDAY, October 17: "Seven Years of Labor" (Genesis 29:13-20)

THURSDAY, October 18: "The Trickster Is Tricked" (Genesis 29:21-25a)

FRIDAY, October 19: "Seven More Years" (Genesis 29:25b-30)

SATURDAY, October 20: "Four Sons Born to Leah" (Genesis 29:31-35)

SUNDAY, October 21: "Rachel's Sons" (Genesis 30:22-24; 35:16-21)

LESSON 9   October 28, 2007

ESAU AND JACOB RECONCILED

DEVOTIONAL READING: **Psalm 133**
PRINT PASSAGE: **Genesis 33:1-11**

BACKGROUND SCRIPTURE: **Genesis 33**
KEY VERSE: **Genesis 33:4**

Genesis 33:1-11—KJV

AND JACOB lifted up his eyes, and looked, and, behold, Esau came, and with him four hundred men. And he divided the children unto Leah, and unto Rachel, and unto the two handmaids.

2 And he put the handmaids and their children foremost, and Leah and her children after, and Rachel and Joseph hindermost.

3 And he passed over before them, and bowed himself to the ground seven times, until he came near to his brother.

4 And Esau ran to meet him, and embraced him, and fell on his neck, and kissed him: and they wept.

5 And he lifted up his eyes, and saw the women and the children; and said, Who are those with thee? And he said, The children which God hath graciously given thy servant.

6 Then the handmaidens came near, they and their children, and they bowed themselves.

7 And Leah also with her children came near, and bowed themselves: and after came Joseph near and Rachel, and they bowed themselves.

8 And he said, What meanest thou by all this drove which I met? And he said, These are to find grace in the sight of my lord.

9 And Esau said, I have enough, my brother; keep that thou hast unto thyself.

10 And Jacob said, Nay, I pray thee, if now I have found grace in thy sight, then receive my present at my hand: for therefore I have seen thy face, as though I had seen the face of God, and thou wast pleased with me.

11 Take, I pray thee, my blessing that is brought to thee; because God hath dealt graciously with me, and because I have enough. And he urged him, and he took it.

Genesis 33:1-11—NRSV

NOW JACOB looked up and saw Esau coming, and four hundred men with him. So he divided the children among Leah and Rachel and the two maids.

2 He put the maids with their children in front, then Leah with her children, and Rachel and Joseph last of all.

3 He himself went on ahead of them, bowing himself to the ground seven times, until he came near his brother.

4 But Esau ran to meet him, and embraced him, and fell on his neck and kissed him, and they wept.

5 When Esau looked up and saw the women and children, he said, "Who are these with you?" Jacob said, "The children whom God has graciously given your servant."

6 Then the maids drew near, they and their children, and bowed down;

7 Leah likewise and her children drew near and bowed down; and finally Joseph and Rachel drew near, and they bowed down.

8 Esau said, "What do you mean by all this company that I met?" Jacob answered, "To find favor with my lord."

9 But Esau said, "I have enough, my brother; keep what you have for yourself."

10 Jacob said, "No, please; if I find favor with you, then accept my present from my hand; for truly to see your face is like seeing the face of God—since you have received me with such favor.

11 Please accept my gift that is brought to you, because God has dealt graciously with me, and because I have everything I want." So he urged him, and he took it.

UNIFYING LESSON PRINCIPLE

Relationships sometimes seem irreparably broken. What must happen for such damaged relationships to be restored? Esau, who had been wronged by his brother, willingly greeted Jacob and offered him hospitality and signs of reconciliation.

TOPICAL OUTLINE OF THE LESSON

I. Introduction
  A. Healing Broken Relationships
  B. Biblical Background

II. Exposition and Application of the Scripture
  A. Jacob Prepares to Meet Esau (Genesis 33:1-4)
  B. Jacob Introduces His Family to Esau (Genesis 33:5-7)
  C. Jacob Offers Presents to Esau (Genesis 33:8-11)

III. Concluding Reflections

LESSON OBJECTIVES

Upon completion of this lesson, the students will know that:

1. God has ways to heal broken relationships, if we are humble enough;
2. Prayer to God for help against one we have wronged can soften a hardened heart; and,
3. Tension is inevitable, but human beings have the capacity to live together in a peaceful environment.

POINTS TO BE EMPHASIZED

ADULT/YOUTH

Adult Topic: **Family Reunion**
Youth Topic: **Family Reunion**
Adult Key Verse: **Genesis 33:4**
Youth Key Verse: **Genesis 33:10**
Print Passage: **Genesis 33:1-11**

—The feuding twins, Jacob and Esau, finally meet and, to Jacob's surprise, embrace.

—Jacob's large family indicates that God continues to be faithful to the promise made to Abraham and Sarah that they would have numerous descendants.

—Although Esau had the motive and resources for revenge, he chose not to take revenge.

—Jacob is somewhat deceitful in his presentation to Esau (see verse 7).

—Esau is sincere in his attempt to reconcile with his brother.

—God seems to bless Jacob even though he is a scoundrel.

CHILDREN

Children Topic: **Two Brothers Reunite**
Key Verse: **Genesis 33:4**
Print Passage: **Genesis 33:1-11**

—Fear of Esau played a part in Jacob's reunion with his brother.

—Esau showed a forgiving attitude when he saw Jacob.

—Jacob offered a gift to Esau.

—Jacob saw God's favor in Esau's response to his return.

—Both Jacob and Esau had undergone positive changes.

I. INTRODUCTION

A. Healing Broken Relationships

Healing broken relationships is a formidable challenge for all leaders. Every day, we read stories about the rising tide of conflict and violence in Iraq, where Sunni and Shiite Muslims are pitted in a heated conflict over control. The inability of the people of the land of Abraham's birth to get along has left tens of thousands maimed, wounded, killed, or missing. We see images of fighting on the Horn of Africa between Ethiopia and Somalia because of unresolved conflicts. Within various Asian and African countries, there are endless conflicts that have gone unresolved for years. America is not immune to unresolved conflict. The racial divide still lingers after more than forty years of civil rights legislation and political change. This nation struggles in the chasm of a reemerging social and racial divide.

The Christian church is not a safe haven from conflict and broken relationships. One of the most thorny leadership challenges in the church is that of healing broken relationships. We live at a time when there are many fragile and easily offended believers who have mastered the art of holding and nurturing grudges. Resentment, open hostility toward pastors and lay leaders, unresolved conflict, and church fights and splits are all signs of spiritual immaturity within the body of Christ. I know of congregations where there is always something that brews into a major church fight and split. Why do these things happen? It is because believers may proclaim that they are following the teachings of Jesus regarding reconciliation and healing, but in reality they are not. Most denominations have covenants which state that members will respect one another and will do all they can to promote peace and harmony within the church; the question is, how well are those covenants being followed?

The story of Jacob and Esau is a model of how to be reconciled to a family member and even other believers. In spite of what Jacob had done to him, Esau did not hold it against his brother. He loved him with a deep love that healed the strains of their broken relationship.

B. Biblical Background

Jacob lived in Haran with his father-in-law, Laban, for twenty years (Genesis 31:38, 41). During that time, Jacob dealt with a man who was a master of deception and cunning. On ten separate occasions, Laban changed the wages of Jacob and manipulated him for his own benefit. Finally, the Lord appeared to Jacob and told him to return to his homeland. Jacob called his wives and children together, gathered all his possessions, and left without Laban's knowledge (Genesis 31:1-21). This caused quite a stir in Laban's household.

Prior to crossing the Jabbok River, Jacob sent word to his brother that he was returning (Genesis 32:2-8). Jacob sent messengers who were given specific instructions regarding how to approach and speak to Esau. As the time neared, Jacob was gripped by the worst possible case of fear and dread (Genesis 32:7). He prayed that God would protect him and honor His Word to make him a great nation. Jacob also prepared gifts to be presented to Esau and set out the order that they would follow in approaching Esau (Genesis 32:13-21). When they crossed the Jabbok River (located in modern-day Jordan) and headed toward Canaan, Jacob had no idea of what to expect (Genesis 32:22). During the hours leading up to the eventual meeting, Jacob wrestled with an angel of the Lord and his name was changed from Jacob to Israel (Genesis 32:28).

Jacob did not know whether he would find his father living, or what the condition of his family in Canaan would be. His biggest fear centered on meeting Esau for the first time in more than twenty years. How would his brother treat him? Would Esau be open to reconciliation? Would Jacob and his family be captured, enslaved, or even killed by Esau because of his anger? Jacob was in for a great surprise when he finally met his brother after such a long time. When the two brothers finally met, Jacob seemed to be humble and remorseful. Yet he never mentioned the birthright or Esau's stolen blessing. He offered his brother a gift, which Esau graciously refused. Esau offered to escort Jacob and his family to his home in Seir, providing protection and provisions. Jacob gave the impression that he would follow along and join him, but he had his own plans. He turned off the highway and headed toward the hill country of Succoth, eventually settling in Shechem (Genesis 33:19-20).

II. EXPOSITION AND APPLICATION OF THE SCRIPTURE

A. Jacob Prepares to Meet Esau (Genesis 33:1-4)

And Jacob lifted up his eyes, and looked, and, behold, Esau came, and with him four hundred men. And he divided the children unto Leah, and unto Rachel, and unto the two handmaids. And he put the handmaids and their children foremost, and Leah and her children after, and Rachel and Joseph hindermost. And he passed over before them, and bowed himself to the ground seven times, until he came near to his brother. And Esau ran to meet him, and embraced him, and fell on his neck, and kissed him: and they wept.

The meeting with Esau took place much more quickly than Jacob realized it would. While he was busy trying to organize the party, Esau appeared on the horizon with four hundred battle-tested men. Jacob was no match for him or his forces. He had only been a shepherd, and was not skilled in the methods of warfare. He hastily divided his family into four separate groups. He sent the children with each of their mothers, who could plead for their safety and lives, if it came down to that.

Ever the shrewd manipulator, Jacob would not put his beloved Rachel and Joseph near the front. The lineup consisted of the handmaids with their children leading the way, followed by Leah and her children, with Rachel and Joseph last of all (verse 2). In the previous chapter, Jacob was in the rear of the party. When he saw Esau coming, he took the lead and put himself out front. What produced this change in the heart of the man who had been a master schemer? Prior to crossing the Jabbok, Jacob had prayed and asked the Lord for protection and favor with his brother. God had promised that he would be with him and that he would bring him back to the land of his fathers. He knew that God was true to His Word because he had already experienced great prosperity and protection. What would make him think that God would fail him now? Jacob demonstrated courage by his willingness to lead the way rather than follow.

Jacob did not come with pride, pomp, or arrogance. After he passed over before his wives and children, he went out, bowing seven times until he came near to his brother. Seven is the number of completion; hence the seven bows were a sign of complete humility. This was a sign of respect for the ruler or the one who was the greater of the parties.

In some African and Asian countries today, people bow in respect for their elders or to people in authority. During one of my mission trips to Nigeria, we met with the Council of Chiefs in the Rivers State town of Buguma. First, one must bow in humble respect to the chief. It shows respect for the king and his office. Jacob bowed before Esau, which was a part of the custom of the people in that day.

When Esau saw his brother after an absence of twenty years, he ran to meet him. He did not wait until Jacob reached him; he reached out to Jacob because he had missed him and may have wanted desperately to be with him again. They were twins, and there is something in the DNA of twins that draws them to each other. Esau embraced Jacob and fell on his neck and kissed him and the two of them wept, openly and loudly. The evening before this historic meeting, Jacob had prayed for favor and protection. God heard his prayer and granted him the desires of his heart. Esau did not come with animosity, nor did he come holding a grudge. In this simple story of reconciliation, there are some powerful lessons that we can and must learn. We can learn from Jacob, who

demonstrated humility, and from Esau, who showed how to forgive and move on. Love is stronger than hatred. Esau was clearly the more gracious of the two brothers.

B. Jacob Introduces His Family to Esau (Genesis 33:5-7)

And he lifted up his eyes, and saw the women and the children; and said, Who are those with thee? And he said, The children which God hath graciously given thy servant. Then the handmaidens came near, they and their children, and they bowed themselves. And Leah also with her children came near, and bowed themselves: and after came Joseph near and Rachel, and they bowed themselves.

As Jacob and Esau continued to embrace, Jacob's family drew near. Esau lifted his eyes and asked, "Who are those with thee?" Esau never expected to see this sight. Jacob had left Beer-sheba with the clothes on his back and just enough resources to help him reach Haran. Esau had no idea that Jacob would become as wealthy as he had. He returned to Canaan accompanied by an entourage of women, children, flocks, and servants to help tend them.

Jacob replied to Esau's question by stating that these were the children that God had graciously given to him. The Hebrew word for "gracious" also has in it the idea of favor. Jacob acknowledged that God had shown him favor with the children that were coming and bowing before Esau. Jacob continued to pay homage and respect to his brother by referring to himself as Esau's servant (verse 5).

There was a deliberate order to the procession used by Jacob in presenting his family before Esau. Jacob was courageous enough to lead and face whatever consequences would befall him. Following him were the handmaids who came first, along with their children. Everyone continued to pay respect and homage to Esau by bowing. The handmaids were followed by Leah and her children, who also bowed as a sign of respect for Esau. The last people to come forth were Joseph and Rachel. It is interesting to note that the very last person that Jacob had come was Rachel, the one person he loved. This act showed that there was nothing that Jacob would not do to protect Rachel.

C. Jacob Offers Presents to Esau (Genesis 33:8-11)

And he said, What meanest thou by all this drove which I met? And he said, These are to find grace in the sight of my lord. And Esau said, I have enough, my brother; keep that thou hast unto thyself. And Jacob said, Nay, I pray thee, if now I have found grace in thy sight, then receive my present at my hand: for therefore I have seen thy face, as though I had seen the face of God, and thou wast pleased with me. Take, I pray thee, my blessing that is brought to thee; because God hath dealt graciously with me, and because I have enough. And he urged him, and he took it.

As the two brothers stood face-to-face, Jacob no doubt tried to overcome the awkwardness of the moment. He had not seen Esau in more than twenty years. What should he do? What should he say? Jacob had already prayed about the situation and thought through what he would do and say. He had already prepared a sizeable gift to be presented to Esau. He had even thought about how to present the gift and what words would be used by each of the presenters (Genesis 32:13-21). Would Esau accept his personal gift of appeasement? Esau asked Jacob the meaning of the droves of animals which he met. Jacob responded that they were a gift for Esau so that he (Jacob) might find favor in his sight.

Esau responded to his brother's overtures of kindness by telling him to keep what he had. This was a far cry from twenty years earlier.

Esau too was a son of the promise of God, and a recipient of the covenant of God's favor. He had been blessed and shown great favor by God. He need not accept anything from his brother, because he was not a poor man (verse 9). In Esau's statement we see something of the providential sovereignty of God, who is able to bless us in spite of attempts by others to harm us.

Jacob continued to plead with his brother to take the gift. If Esau would grant him favor and forgiveness, Jacob would feel better because the gifts would be a sign for him. The old Jacob would have been trying to get by with giving as little as possible; the new Jacob, who met God and wrestled with the angel of the Lord, had been changed. Jacob told Esau that when he looked into his face, it was as though he was seeing the very face of God. Esau's refusal to accept a gift as the grounds for reconciliation and forgiveness demonstrated how much he had grown and changed. God changed Esau's attitude toward his brother. Christians who have been estranged from others must always reckon that the power of God's love is greater than our bitterness and pain. God is able to heal our hurts and release us from the bondage and shackles of the past.

Is it possible that Isaac shared with Esau the nature of God's promise and covenant with his family? Is it possible that God appeared to Esau and told him about God's gracious favor upon the life of his brother? We will never know. We do know that something miraculous occurred in the life of Esau that healed his anger and cooled his bitterness toward Jacob. In Esau, Jacob saw the face of God, because he saw God's continuing favor.

The lesson concludes with Jacob acknowledging that God had been gracious to him and that God had given him everything he had. "God hath dealt graciously with me" (verse11) was how Jacob defined his life. In spite of how he had dealt with his brother, God had not done the same to him. In a twist of irony, Jacob continued to plead with Esau to take the gift. "Take, I pray thee, my blessing that is brought to thee..." (verse 11). Jacob took Esau's blessing when they were younger; now he himself offered Esau a blessing. We are not told what prompted Esau to finally take the gift from his brother, but he did. It may have been that Jacob was so sincere and the tears were so real that Esau was moved to believe that for the first time Jacob's heart was open to being a real brother to him.

III. CONCLUDING REFLECTIONS

There are many lessons that commend themselves to our prayerful consideration.

First, we are reminded of the grace and mercy of God, which is greater than our worst sins. Second, the lesson has taught us that family hurt and pain can be healed even though many years have gone by. Third, we have learned that in the worst situations of life where we have been sorely mistreated, God is able to bless us and increase us more abundantly than we can imagine. Fourth, when we have been blessed, we should seek to be a blessing to others. Jacob had been blessed with great wealth, and he was willing to share that abundance with others.

PRAYER

Almighty and gracious heavenly Father, we beseech Thee for mercy and favor. We thank Thee for what Thou hast already done in our lives. Look upon Your people with compassion and grant that we may increase, so that we may be a blessing to others. In the name of Jesus Christ, we pray. Amen.

WORD POWER

Wept (Hebrew: *bakah baw-kaw*)—this word means to weep profusely, to bemoan, or bewail. In the Key Verse, when Jacob met his brother, his action was described with four powerful verbs: embraced, fell, kissed, and wept. Thorough repentance that will bring quick resolution to a long-standing feud should include these elements. These elements are catharses that cleanse the soul and restore relationships.

HOME DAILY BIBLE READINGS

(October 22-28, 2007)

Esau and Jacob Reconciled

MONDAY, October 22: "Jacob's Prayer" (Genesis 32:3-12)

TUESDAY, October 23: "Jacob's Presents to Esau" (Genesis 32:13-21)

WEDNESDAY, October 24: "The Brothers Wept Together" (Genesis 33:1-4)

THURSDAY, October 25: "The Gift of Reconciliation" (Genesis 33:5-11)

FRIDAY, October 26: "Their Separate Ways" (Genesis 33:12-15)

SATURDAY, October 27: "An Altar to God" (Genesis 33:16-20)

SUNDAY, October 28: "The Blessedness of Unity" (Psalm 133)

LESSON 10   **November 4, 2007**

JOSEPH'S DREAM

DEVOTIONAL READING: **Psalm 70**

PRINT PASSAGE: **Genesis 37:5-11,**
19-21, 23-24a, 28

BACKGROUND SCRIPTURE: **Genesis 37**

KEY VERSE: **Genesis 37:5**

Genesis 37:5-11, 19-21, 23-24a, 28—KJV

5 And Joseph dreamed a dream, and he told it his brethren: and they hated him yet the more.

6 And he said unto them, Hear, I pray you, this dream which I have dreamed:

7 For, behold, we were binding sheaves in the field, and, lo, my sheaf arose, and also stood upright; and, behold, your sheaves stood round about, and made obeisance to my sheaf.

8 And his brethren said to him, Shalt thou indeed reign over us? or shalt thou indeed have dominion over us? And they hated him yet the more for his dreams, and for his words.

9 And he dreamed yet another dream, and told it his brethren, and said, Behold, I have dreamed a dream more; and, behold, the sun and the moon and the eleven stars made obeisance to me.

10 And he told it to his father, and to his brethren: and his father rebuked him, and said unto him, What is this dream that thou hast dreamed? Shall I and thy mother and thy brethren indeed come to bow down ourselves to thee to the earth?

11 And his brethren envied him; but his father observed the saying.

…..

19 And they said one to another, Behold, this dreamer cometh.

20 Come now therefore, and let us slay him, and cast him into some pit, and we will say, Some evil beast hath devoured him: and we shall see what will become of his dreams.

21 And Reuben heard it, and he delivered him out of their hands; and said, Let us not kill him.

…..

23 And it came to pass, when Joseph was come unto his brethren, that they stripped Joseph out of his coat, his coat of many colours that was on him;

24 And they took him, and cast him into a pit.

…..

Genesis 37:5-11, 19-21, 23-24a, 28—NRSV

5 Once Joseph had a dream, and when he told it to his brothers, they hated him even more.

6 He said to them, "Listen to this dream that I dreamed.

7 There we were, binding sheaves in the field. Suddenly my sheaf rose and stood upright; then your sheaves gathered around it, and bowed down to my sheaf."

8 His brothers said to him, "Are you indeed to reign over us? Are you indeed to have dominion over us?" So they hated him even more because of his dreams and his words.

9 He had another dream, and told it to his brothers, saying, "Look, I have had another dream: the sun, the moon, and eleven stars were bowing down to me."

10 But when he told it to his father and to his brothers, his father rebuked him, and said to him, "What kind of dream is this that you have had? Shall we indeed come, I and your mother and your brothers, and bow to the ground before you?"

11 So his brothers were jealous of him, but his father kept the matter in mind.

…..

19 They said to one another, "Here comes this dreamer.

20 Come now, let us kill him and throw him into one of the pits; then we shall say that a wild animal has devoured him, and we shall see what will become of his dreams."

21 But when Reuben heard it, he delivered him out of their hands, saying, "Let us not take his life."

…..

23 So when Joseph came to his brothers, they stripped him of his robe, the long robe with sleeves that he wore;

24 and they took him and threw him into a pit.

…..

28 Then there passed by Midianites merchantmen; and they drew and lifted up Joseph out of the pit, and sold Joseph to the Ishmeelites for twenty pieces of silver: and they brought Joseph into Egypt.

28 When some Midianite traders passed by, they drew Joseph up, lifting him out of the pit, and sold him to the Ishmaelites for twenty pieces of silver. And they took Joseph to Egypt.

TOPICAL OUTLINE OF THE LESSON

I. **Introduction**
   A. Calling
   B. Biblical Background

II. **Exposition and Application of the Scripture**
   A. Joseph's Prophetic Dreams (Genesis 37:5-11)
   B. The Plot to Kill Joseph (Genesis 37:19-21)
   C. Joseph Sold into Slavery (Genesis 37:23-24a, 28)

III. **Concluding Reflections**

LESSON OBJECTIVES

Upon completion of this lesson, the students will know that:

1. It is good sometimes to keep one's purpose in one's heart and be prayerful about it;
2. When we seek to fulfill our purpose, there will be opposition; and,
3. God will enable you to carry out your purpose in life.

POINTS TO BE EMPHASIZED

ADULT/YOUTH
Adult Topic: **Interpreting a Call**
Youth Topic: **Dreamer in the Pit**
Adult Key Verse: **Genesis 37:5**
Youth Key Verses: **Genesis 37:19-20**
Print Passage: **Genesis 37:5-11, 19-21, 23-24a, 28**

—Joseph dreamed that one day he would be elevated above his parents and siblings.
—Joseph's brothers set in motion a series of actions that cascaded in directions they could not possibly have imagined.
—In the Bible, dreams are often used as a mode of communication between humans and God.
—Joseph's brothers were jealous that he was his father's favorite son, so when Joseph told his brothers about his dreams, he was already in their disfavor.
—Joseph's dreams indicated God's calling early in his life.
—Many years elapsed before Joseph's dreams became reality.

CHILDREN
Children Topic: **From Son to Slave**
Key Verse: **Genesis 37:28**
Print Passage: **Genesis 37:3-8, 17, 18-21, 23-24, 28**

—The conflict between Joseph and his brothers kept his brothers from considering the truth of Joseph's dream.
—Although Jacob rebuked Joseph, he continued to think about the possibilities of Joseph's dream.
—Joseph's life was spared because of Reuben's influence, and his brothers sold him into slavery.
—Jacob and his sons found themselves in a hopeless situation.

I. INTRODUCTION

A. Calling

God often uses ordinary people in extraordinary ways. We have seen this throughout our study of the ancient Hebrew patriarchs. The call of Abraham and Sarah was a call to take an extraordinary step. Moses was called to lead the Hebrews out of bondage. God called Esther to protect the Jews from the plot of Haman.

What does it mean to be called by God? In our day, we refer to the call of God as a "call to preach." By this, we are thinking primarily of the ministry of the Word of God from the pulpit. However, the call of God is much greater and broader than just standing in a pulpit preaching a sermon. All believers are called and sent by Jesus Christ to be His witnesses in the world (Matthew 28:18-20; Acts 1:5-8; 9:1-9; 13:1-3). Some believers are called to fulltime congregational ministry, others to the mission field, and some may be called to institutional ministries. You may be called to be a volunteer in a homeless shelter or a nursing home. Whatever the case, all of us are called to witness to the great act of God's redemptive love.

In today's lesson, we are introduced to the life and times of Joseph and his tumultuous relationship with his brothers. Joseph was the first son born to Jacob and Rachel (Genesis 30:22-24).

B. Biblical Background

After being in Canaan for a few years, Jacob and his family eventually settled in Bethel, where he first encountered the Lord (Genesis 35:1). During their move from Shechem to Bethel, Rachel died after giving birth to her second child, and was buried in Ephrath, in a place that came to be called Bethlehem (Genesis 35:16-19). The story shifts from the main patriarchal characters to one of the sons: Joseph. It begins the narrative account of how Israel ended up in Egypt.

Joseph was seventeen when his life took a monumental turn. He used to tend the flock of his father with his other brothers, the sons of Bilhah and Zilpah (Genesis 37:2). From time to time, Joseph would give negative reports to his father about his brothers. They may have been reports of how the brothers acted in ways that might have brought shame upon the name of Jacob as they had done before (Genesis 34:27-30).

Jacob did not help the relationships between his sons, because he showed a great deal of favoritism toward Joseph. He loved Joseph more than he did his other sons, and he showed this by making a special robe of many colors for Joseph. This was a very expensive robe because dyes were hard to come by and when they could be found, they were quite expensive. Whenever Joseph wore the robe, it only confirmed to his brothers how their father felt about them compared to Joseph. They refused to speak kindly to Joseph. The brothers did not have a good relationship with Joseph. They plotted to kill Joseph at the first opportunity. However, there was disagreement among the brothers regarding how to go about getting rid of

Joseph. The day came when Joseph visited them in the fields; when they saw him far off, they conspired to kill him; however, they threw him into a pit at the suggestion of Reuben. Reuben was going to take him out of the pit later, but his plan was foiled. Ishmaelite traders came, and the brothers sold him for twenty pieces of silver. These merchants eventually sold Joseph to Potiphar (Genesis 37:36). One of the central lessons of the Joseph story is God's choice of an unlikely person for the purpose of fulfilling God's divine will.

II. EXPOSITION AND APPLICATION OF THE SCRIPTURE

A. Joseph's Prophetic Dreams
(Genesis 37:5-11)

And Joseph dreamed a dream, and he told it his brethren: and they hated him yet the more. And he said unto them, Hear, I pray you, this dream which I have dreamed: For, behold, we were binding sheaves in the field, and, lo, my sheaf arose, and also stood upright; and, behold, your sheaves stood round about, and made obeisance to my sheaf. And his brethren said to him, Shalt thou indeed reign over us? or shalt thou indeed have dominion over us? And they hated him yet the more for his dreams, and for his words. And he dreamed yet another dream, and told it his brethren, and said, Behold, I have dreamed a dream more; and, behold, the sun and the moon and the eleven stars made obeisance to me. And he told it to his father, and to his brethren: and his father rebuked him, and said unto him, What is this dream that thou hast dreamed? Shall I and thy mother and thy brethren indeed come to bow down ourselves to thee to the earth? And his brethren envied him; but his father observed the saying.

In the story of Joseph, we see the use of dreams as God's means for revealing His divine will and purpose. Joseph had no idea of the prophetic nature of his dreams. Dreams had previously played a significant role in the life of Jacob, who experienced the presence of God in a dream at Bethel (Genesis 28:12).

One night, Joseph had a dream that excited him to the point that he had to tell someone. He told his brothers his dream, and they hated him even more. Joseph might have been better off keeping his dreams to himself. It is not always a good thing to reveal too soon everything that God has put in one's heart.

Joseph's brothers already had disdain for him because of his status as his father's favorite son; the dream only intensified that hatred (verse 5).

When Joseph visited his brothers, he revealed to them his dream. In the dream, the brothers were all binding sheaves of grain, and a strange thing happened. Joseph's sheaf arose and stood upright and stood over and apart from the other sheaves. His sheaf was set apart for something special to do. The sheaves of his brothers, realizing that there was something superior about Joseph's sheaf, began to gather around and pay homage to his sheaf (verse 7). They bowed in subjection to the sheaf of Joseph.

The dream did not need interpreting, because the meaning was plain to all who heard it; Joseph was going to rule over his brothers. They asked him if he had plans to rule over them. They spoke in such a way that they questioned his intention, "Are you planning to rule over us and have dominion over us?" (verse 8). The question came in such a way as if to say, "Who do you think you are?" Joseph had no idea that he was revealing God's future plans for his family. Joseph was already hated, but he continued to deepen the hatred and bitterness of his brothers. They hated him for his dreams and the words that he used. Is it possible that Joseph told the dream in a manner that was condescending? We cannot gauge the tone of the conversation from the words written in the verse. In whatever way the words came out, they were met with total rejection and disgust.

Joseph was not done with his dreams. He had another dream, an even bigger dream, which he told to his brothers. In the second dream, the sun, the moon, and the eleven stars bowed down before him. The sun and moon were his parents and his brothers were the eleven stars. This was the final straw as far as his brothers were concerned. Joseph was not content to only tell his brothers; he told the dream to his father, Jacob, as well. His father rebuked him and wanted to know if Joseph really expected him and his mother to actually bow down before him. Since Rachel was already deceased by this time, which mother was Jacob referring to? He more than likely meant Leah, who had become Joseph's stepmother. Jacob may have been incensed by the very thought of bowing to Joseph. In the ancient world, a father would never bow to his son. Here was something completely out of the norm and customs of the people. Jacob had already bowed once to Esau in an act of humility, and it may be that there was no way that he would bow again, especially to his son (verse 10).

Jacob pondered and thought about the words he had heard from Joseph. It may be that Jacob pondered these things because of his own experience with dreams. God had revealed His will to Jacob in a dream. Was God now doing the same with Jacob's favorite son? Joseph did not gain any friends among his brothers—they only envied him more. However, his father pondered the matter in his heart.

Here we have the perennial challenge that faces those who would lead the people of God. Many people in congregations have difficulty appreciating and receiving visions from their leaders. Many times leaders must endure a wide range of negative reactions and emotions when they share God's vision and plans for the people. This negative energy can stifle the church and its progress and keep the congregation locked in the past.

Moreover, we see that God often chooses people who stand out from the crowd. Joseph was different from his brothers in several ways. He was not a violent person, nor was he dishonest. He had not joined in the massacre of the men of Shechem and brought shame to his father's name. His character was above reproach, unlike the characters of his brothers who were given to all types of unruly behavior.

B. The Plot to Kill Joseph (Genesis 37:19-21)

And they said one to another, Behold, this dreamer cometh. Come now therefore, and let us slay him, and cast him into some pit, and we will say, Some evil beast hath devoured him: and we shall see what will become of his dreams. And Reuben heard it, and he delivered him out of their hands; and said, Let us not kill him.

On one occasion, Jacob sent Joseph to Shechem to see how his other sons were doing. When Joseph arrived at Shechem, they had departed to Dothan. In Dothan, they would hatch their murderous and diabolical plot to get rid of their younger brother. As Joseph approached, the brothers began to sarcastically say to one another, "…Behold, this dreamer cometh" (verse 19). They encouraged each other to kill Joseph and throw his body in a pit. Then, they would tell their father that a wild beast ate Joseph (see verse 20). The purpose of the scheme was to kill the dream by killing the dreamer.

Rather than stand by and see Joseph killed, Reuben, who was Jacob's firstborn, spoke up (Genesis 29:32; 35:23). The text states that

Reuben delivered Joseph out of the hands of his brothers. How he did this, we do not know. He may have been able to do it through the art of diplomatic persuasion.

Why did Reuben want to save Joseph? There are three factors that could have come into play that influenced Reuben's decision to save Joseph from his brothers. First, as the oldest son, Reuben commanded more respect among his siblings. They would listen and give heed to what he had to say. Second, Reuben may have been trying to get back into the good graces of his father. Earlier, he had committed a cardinal offense against Jacob when he went in and slept with his father's concubine, Bilhah (Genesis 35:22). We are not told how Jacob responded to Reuben's indiscretion, but Reuben had shown absolute disrespect for his father. Third, Reuben understood how important Joseph was to his father. He may have understood, in ways his brothers did not, the devastation that would be heaped upon the heart of his father with Joseph's untimely death.

There are two types of people seen in this passage. The first is a person who despises another person's success and favor to the point that he or she will do anything to hurt the successful individual. In this type of person we see the epitome of jealousy and envy, which are both indicative of carnal and sinful hearts. The magnitude of the deed perpetrated against Joseph is dramatized even more when one considers that this was the brothers' blood relative. Joseph was not a neighbor or enemy—he was their brother. We see this kind of demonic spirit manifested often in churches, organizations, and families. Some members succeed, and hostility wells up against them.

The second type of person is the one who recognizes evil and seeks to respond in a godly manner. This is the person who will do what is right regardless of the personal cost. He or she always considers how others will be impacted by overt hostility. Reuben demonstrated the spirit of compassion and concern for his father and his younger brother.

C. Joseph Sold into Slavery (Genesis 37:23-24a, 28)

And it came to pass, when Joseph was come unto his brethren, that they stripped Joseph out of his coat, his coat of many colours that was on him; And they took him, and cast him into a pit. .... Then there passed by Midianites merchantmen; and they drew and lifted up Joseph out of the pit, and sold Joseph to the Ishmeelites for twenty pieces of silver: and they brought Joseph into Egypt.

When Joseph reached his brothers, they rushed upon him and overpowered him. They stripped him of his coat of many colors. It was this coat that served as a constant reminder of Joseph's favored status with their father. They then threw Joseph into a pit. The language of the text implies that they did not just gently lower him into the pit, but they violently threw him, without regard for how he would land or whether he would be hurt. The pit or cistern they threw him into was a dry one. However, cisterns were often used as holding tanks for storing water.

Cisterns can be as deep as 20-30 feet. Many of the rock formations of the area around Dothan consist of hard limestone. Once inside one of these cisterns, there would be no way to escape or even be heard once a stone top was placed over the opening. To be left in a cistern was a certain death sentence. Unless someone rescued him, Joseph would have died in that place.

The brothers had time to reassess their plan when a caravan of Midianite (Ishmaelite) merchants came upon their location. They pulled

Joseph up out of the pit and seized the chance to make a small profit for themselves. Joseph was sold for twenty pieces of silver, which was more than likely the sale price for male slaves in those days.

III. CONCLUDING REFLECTIONS

Unlike his father, grandfather, and great-grandfather, Joseph had no divine word from God regarding his future. All he had was a dream that he may not have fully understood. At such a young age, he did not know that he was on course for greatness in Egypt. He did not know what was happening or why. There is much that we can learn from the life of Joseph. First, Joseph feared God. Joseph's character was impeccable, and it came into play when he arrived in Egypt. Second, when we seek to do the right thing and live right before God, we are brought into conflict with others, who may not seek to live this way. Third, we must always be prepared for the possibility that the enemies of God will rise against us and seek to destroy us. Fourth, even when we have been surrounded by foes, God's will for our lives will ultimately prevail.

PRAYER

Heavenly Father, You have created us for Your own purpose. Grant that we will always have the courage to do that which is right and pleasing in Your sight. Keep us from committing acts of evil against other people. May our hearts be filled with love for others. In the name of Jesus Christ, we pray. Amen.

WORD POWER

Hated *(sane' saw-nay)*—this means to hate intensely, to make someone an object of derision. Jacob's favoritism for Joseph was the cause of family conflict. Parents should temper their admiration for their children so as not to cause chaos in the family. It is obvious that Joseph overcame all the odds against him, but we should not presume that a favored child or children will end up like Joseph.

HOME DAILY BIBLE READINGS
(October 29—November 4, 2007)
Joseph's Dream
   MONDAY, October 29: "The Favored Son" (Genesis 37:1-4)
   TUESDAY, October 30: "The Jealous Brothers" (Genesis 37:5-11)
   WEDNESDAY, October 31: "The Messenger" (Genesis 37:12-17)
   THURSDAY, November 1: "The Dreamer" (Genesis 37:18-24)
   FRIDAY, November 2: "Sold into Slavery" (Genesis 37:25-28)
   SATURDAY, November 3: "A Father's Distress" (Genesis 37:29-36)
   SUNDAY, November 4: "A Prayer for Deliverance" (Psalm 70)

LESSON 11   **November 11, 2007**

JOSEPH'S DREAM BEGAN TO COME TRUE

DEVOTIONAL READING: **Psalm 105:16-22**
PRINT PASSAGE: **Genesis 41:25-40**

BACKGROUND SCRIPTURE: **Genesis 41:25-45**
KEY VERSE: **Genesis 41:39**

Genesis 41:25-40—KJV

25 And Joseph said unto Pharaoh, The dream of Pharaoh is one: God hath shown Pharaoh what he is about to do.

26 The seven good kine are seven years; and the seven good ears are seven years: the dream is one.

27 And the seven thin and ill favoured kine that came up after them are seven years; and the seven empty ears blasted with the east wind shall be seven years of famine.

28 This is the thing which I have spoken unto Pharaoh: What God is about to do he showeth unto Pharaoh.

29 Behold, there come seven years of great plenty throughout all the land of Egypt:

30 And there shall arise after them seven years of famine; and all the plenty shall be forgotten in the land of Egypt; and the famine shall consume the land;

31 And the plenty shall not be known in the land by reason of that famine following; for it shall be very grievous.

32 And for that the dream was doubled unto Pharaoh twice; it is because the thing is established by God, and God will shortly bring it to pass.

33 Now therefore let Pharaoh look out a man discreet and wise, and set him over the land of Egypt.

34 Let Pharaoh do this, and let him appoint officers over the land, and take up the fifth part of the land of Egypt in the seven plenteous years.

35 And let them gather all the food of those good years that come, and lay up corn under the hand of Pharaoh, and let them keep food in the cities.

36 And that food shall be for store to the land against the seven years of famine, which shall be in the land of Egypt; that the land perish not through the famine.

Genesis 41:25-40—NRSV

25 Then Joseph said to Pharaoh, "Pharaoh's dreams are one and the same; God has revealed to Pharaoh what he is about to do.

26 The seven good cows are seven years, and the seven good ears are seven years; the dreams are one.

27 The seven lean and ugly cows that came up after them are seven years, as are the seven empty ears blighted by the east wind. They are seven years of famine.

28 It is as I told Pharaoh; God has shown to Pharaoh what he is about to do.

29 There will come seven years of great plenty throughout all the land of Egypt.

30 After them there will arise seven years of famine, and all the plenty will be forgotten in the land of Egypt; the famine will consume the land.

31 The plenty will no longer be known in the land because of the famine that will follow, for it will be very grievous.

32 And the doubling of Pharaoh's dream means that the thing is fixed by God, and God will shortly bring it about.

33 Now therefore let Pharaoh select a man who is discerning and wise, and set him over the land of Egypt.

34 Let Pharaoh proceed to appoint overseers over the land, and take one-fifth of the produce of the land of Egypt during the seven plenteous years.

35 Let them gather all the food of these good years that are coming, and lay up grain under the authority of Pharaoh for food in the cities, and let them keep it.

36 That food shall be a reserve for the land against the seven years of famine that are to befall the land of Egypt, so that the land may not perish through the famine."

37 And the thing was good in the eyes of Pharaoh, and in the eyes of all his servants.

38 And Pharaoh said unto his servants, Can we find such a one as this is, a man in whom the Spirit of God is?

39 And Pharaoh said unto Joseph, Forasmuch as God hath shown thee all this, there is none so discreet and wise as thou art:

40 Thou shalt be over my house, and according unto thy word shall all my people be ruled: only in the throne will I be greater than thou.

37 The proposal pleased Pharaoh and all his servants.

38 Pharaoh said to his servants, "Can we find anyone else like this—one in whom is the spirit of God?"

39 So Pharaoh said to Joseph, "Since God has shown you all this, there is no one so discerning and wise as you.

40 You shall be over my house, and all my people shall order themselves as you command; only with regard to the throne will I be greater than you."

TOPICAL OUTLINE OF THE LESSON

I. **Introduction**
   A. God's Way Is Mysterious
   B. Biblical Background

II. **Exposition and Application of the Scripture**
   A. Joseph Interprets Pharaoh's Dream
      (Genesis 41:25-32)
   B. Joseph Gives Guidance to Pharaoh
      (Genesis 41:33-37)
   C. Joseph Is Elevated
      (Genesis 41:38-40)

III. **Concluding Reflections**

LESSON OBJECTIVES

Upon completion of this lesson, the students will know that:

1. It is important to recognize their gifts;
2. Gifts are divine endowments that can bring one before royalty;
3. Using your gift may lead to liberating a generation; and,
4. Every child of God has a purpose in life.

POINTS TO BE EMPHASIZED
ADULT/YOUTH

Adult Topic: A Dream Unfolds
Youth Topic: A Dream Come True
Adult Key Verse: Genesis 41:39
Youth Key Verse: Genesis 41:25
Print Passage: Genesis 41:25-40

—Pharaoh had a puzzling dream that Joseph interpreted with God's guidance to mean that there would be seven years of abundance and seven years of scarcity.

—Joseph suggested that Pharaoh appoint someone with specific characteristics to oversee the land.

—Joseph's dreams began to come true as Pharaoh selected Joseph to be a leader in Egypt, second only to Pharaoh himself.

—Joseph had a solution ready to suggest to the king to meet the impending crisis.

—In the ancient world, to be ignorant of the meaning of one's dreams was to be deprived of vital knowledge about one's well-being.

—While the Hebrew people believed that dreams were a means of divine communication, they did not develop professional dream interpreters.

—There were striking parallels in the lives of Joseph and Daniel. Both disclaimed any innate ability to interpret dreams and gave credit to God.

CHILDREN

Children Topic: From Slave to Ruler

Key Verse: Genesis 41:25

Print Passage: Genesis 41:1-8, 15-16, 25, 29-31, 33, 41

—The two years Joseph waited in prison for his situation to change seemed like a long time.

—Pharaoh realized that the dreams that troubled his spirit held some important meaning.

—Joseph took a chance in confronting Pharaoh with his God, who gave Pharaoh instruction.

—Joseph left no doubt about the source of the interpretation or the dreams themselves.

—Joseph was "set over all the land of Egypt."

I. INTRODUCTION

A. God's Way Is Mysterious

God works in ways that are not always clearly discernible to human beings. When we walk in the Holy Spirit, we are able to discern the leading of God (Proverbs 3:5-6; 1 Corinthians 2:9-14). God never leaves us in doubt about His purpose for our lives. Believers must aspire to reach the fullness of the measure of the stature of Jesus Christ (Ephesians 4:14-16). As we follow God's simple commands, the revelation of what God wills for us will unfold with bold clarity. Joseph did not set out to become the second most important leader in Egypt; he simply lived each day respecting his father and walking in humble obedience to God's will. He had no Scriptures to read, nor did he have a teacher to show him the way—yet he did the right thing (Romans 2:12-13). Doing the right thing landed him in uncomfortable situations, but God kept him and raised him up. He feared God. When the temptation to fall into sin reached the highest peak, Joseph chose to obey God (see Genesis 39:9).

B. Biblical Background

Joseph was the inheritor of a covenant of promise from God that went back 220 years to the time of his great-grandfather, Abraham (Genesis 12:1-3). He would be blessed because everyone who had received the promise was blessed. Although his brothers hated him and sold him to some Ishmaelites, Joseph's life continued to take new turns. The Ishmaelites sold him to Potiphar, an officer of the army of the Pharaoh (Genesis 39:1). Even as a slave in the house of another man, Joseph prospered and was blessed (Genesis 39:2, 4). God gave him favor with his master, who placed everything under his control. Even his master was blessed because of Joseph's presence and favor with God.

Over the course of a few months, the plot took another twist. The wife of Potiphar lusted after Joseph and desired that he lie with her (Genesis 39:7-8). Joseph refused to betray the trust of his master by encroaching upon his wife and committing a terrible sin. Joseph made a strong statement when he refused her advances. He said, "…how then can I do this great wickedness, and sin against God?" (Genesis 39:9). As a result, Potiphar's wife falsely accused Joseph of attempted rape, so he went to prison. He went from being the favored servant of Potiphar to being a prisoner in Egypt. But even there God blessed him (Genesis 39:21-23). While in prison, Joseph met two men, one a butler and the other a cupbearer. One of these men would play a decisive role in his life (Genesis 40:1-23). God gave Joseph the ability to interpret dreams. The Word of God states, "A man's gift maketh room for him, and bringeth him before great men" (Proverbs 18:16). Joseph's ability to interpret dreams landed him an audience with the Pharaoh of Egypt. He went from being a slave to serving as the second-in-command of all of Egypt; only the Pharaoh was higher and had more authority.

II. EXPOSITION AND APPLICATION OF THE SCRIPTURE

A. Joseph Interprets Pharaoh's Dream (Genesis 41:25-32)

And Joseph said unto Pharaoh, The dream of Pharaoh is one: God hath shewed Pharaoh what he is about to do. The seven good kine are seven years; and the seven good ears are seven years: the dream is one. And the seven thin and ill favoured kine that came up after them are seven years; and the seven empty ears blasted with the east wind shall be seven years of famine. This is the thing which I have spoken unto Pharaoh: What God is about to do he sheweth unto Pharaoh. Behold, there come seven years of great plenty throughout all the land of Egypt: And there shall arise after them seven years of famine; and all the plenty shall be forgotten in the land of Egypt; and the famine shall consume the land; And the plenty shall not be known in the land by reason of that famine following; for it shall be very grievous. And for that the dream was doubled unto Pharaoh twice; it is because the thing is established by God, and God will shortly bring it to pass.

There was no one in all of Egypt who could interpret the Pharaoh's dreams (Genesis 41:8). The king's cupbearer remembered Joseph, who was brought to the palace to speak with the Pharaoh (Genesis 41:14-24). In his dreams, the Pharaoh saw seven fat cows come up out of the Nile River. Then he saw seven thin cows come up out of the same river. The seven thin cows ate up the seven fat cows. Then there appeared seven full ears of corn out of the river. They were followed by seven thin ears, driven by the east wind. The thin ears completely devoured the seven full ears.

Joseph told the Pharaoh that God had given him a single important message in two separate dreams. God had shown him what He was about to do (verses 25, 28). Egypt was going to have seven years of great economic and agricultural abundance. The Nile River, which was the primary source of Egypt's water, would enable the land to produce a bumper harvest for seven consecutive years. The fact that out of the Nile River would come both plenty and blight was quite disturbing to the Pharaoh. Seven years of plenty would be followed by severe famine. Seven is the number of perfection; hence the harvest would be beyond anything that the Egyptians had ever seen. Almost immediately after the years of abundance, there would follow unparalleled famine, which would last seven years (verse 27).

It was incumbent upon the Pharaoh that he should take the message in the dreams seriously and urgently act to avert a national disaster. The famine would be so severe that the people would completely forget that they had just come out of seven years of plenty (verse 31). Joseph encouraged the Pharaoh to act, because the matter had been firmly established by God. There was no question that what Pharaoh had seen in his dreams was going to happen (verse 32). God was going to bring the famine upon Egypt. Joseph clearly demonstrated his spiritual sensitivity by attributing everything to God, including the revelation and interpretation of the dreams.

One question that we are faced with in the text today is: Why would God use something as destructive as a famine to bring about His will in the lives of the patriarchs? There could be several reasons. First, there was the implied message to the Pharaoh that he was not in control of what happened with the Nile and the land. There are some matters that are beyond our control, and there is nothing that we can do to change or manipulate events for our benefit. God is the One who gives us the power to obtain wealth and who makes us prosperous.

Second, God used the famine as a means to elevate Joseph, so that he would be in a position to save his family and also the Egyptian people. What would have happened to the people of Egypt if Joseph had not been in place to interpret the dreams? What would have happened to Israel had Joseph not been in place to bring his family to Egypt to ride out the famine? Joseph's ability to interpret the dreams of the Pharaoh heightened his position as a man whose life had been touched by God. Third, God was and is sovereign, and hence He could and can do whatever He deems necessary to achieve His own purpose in the world. He did not and does not have to check with individuals or nations to execute His will. Fourth, in Joseph we see the perfect human vessel who allowed himself to be used by God.

B. Joseph Gives Guidance to Pharaoh (Genesis 41:33-37)

Now therefore let Pharaoh look out a man discreet and wise, and set him over the land of Egypt. Let Pharaoh do this, and let him appoint officers over the land, and take up the fifth part of the land of Egypt in the seven plenteous years. And let them gather all the food of those good years that come, and lay up corn under the hand of Pharaoh, and let them keep food in the cities. And that food shall be for store to the land against the seven years of famine, which shall be in the land of Egypt; that the land perish not through the famine. And the thing was good in the eyes of Pharaoh, and in the eyes of all his servants.

Joseph counseled the Pharaoh to act right away to avert this looming disaster. Although seven years seemed like a long time to prepare, the days would quickly go by. The Egyptians must take advantage of every planting and harvesting season. Nothing was to be lost or wasted. The king must find the right man for this awesome task. He must be smart and wise, understanding the nature and seriousness of the task (verse 33; 1 Chronicles 12:32). And he must have complete authority over all of the land of Egypt.

Joseph counseled the king to give the man whom he would appoint the right to choose officers and give him the power to appoint them to specific responsibilities. The officers would oversee the collection of one-fifth of every year's crop for seven years (verse 34). The corn collected would be under the hand of the Pharaoh so that people would know that it could not be touched or used without his direct authorization. Joseph urged that the food be kept in the cities. This would enable the swift movement of supplies to major population centers when the famine did come. The food would be for one purpose only—to "store to the land against the seven years of famine." The stored corn would be Egypt's salvation against the famine (verse 36). The matter seemed good to the Pharaoh and to all of his servants. Not one servant dissented or showed any signs of jealousy or envy toward Joseph.

The lessons of the passage are numerous and have a variety of leadership and stewardship applications. First, we see a king who was willing to take advice from someone who was a Hebrew slave and a prisoner. The Pharaoh recognized in Joseph something uniquely different about his demeanor and personality.

Second, there was total consensus and agreement among the leaders under the Pharaoh. They recognized, along with the king, that Joseph was telling the truth. Congregations and religious organizations will achieve greater success when leaders learn to agree on matters that promote the common good of the organization.

Third, Joseph conceived of a well-thought-out plan and organizational structure for the project. The proposal consisted of a short-term goal of getting the right people in place. These would be people who could carry out their assignments with discretion and wisdom. They would need to understand the gravity of the situation. The other goal involved setting up the right organizational structure that would enable them to achieve the goal and manage the process of food collection and storage. Joseph's plan would save Egypt, make the king look wise, and give God greater visibility in a land where idols, not the God of Israel, were worshiped.

Among the stewardship lessons is the practical need to take seriously our responsibility to develop sound financial plans for the future. It is important to talk with our children about the need to seriously think about how they earn, save, invest, and spend their money. They must become good stewards, remembering that tomorrow could bring financial strain for the entire nation. Our savings become a cushion when the economy takes a turn in a negative direction.

During the high moments of economic and financial prosperity, we must prepare for the days when economic disaster may strike. Thousands of people are forced into bankruptcy each year because they got into debt and were not prepared for economic downturns.

C. Joseph Is Elevated
(Genesis 41:38-40)

And Pharaoh said unto his servants, Can we find such a one as this is, a man in whom the Spirit of God is? And Pharaoh said unto Joseph, Forasmuch as God hath shewed thee all this, there is none so discreet and wise as thou art: Thou shalt be over my house, and according unto thy word shall all my people be ruled: only in the throne will I be greater than thou.

After receiving the counsel of Joseph, the Pharaoh would need to find someone who would fit the description that Joseph laid out. "Can we find such a one as this is, a man in whom the spirit of God is?" (verse 38). The nation would need a man with great wisdom and discretion. The Pharaoh looked at Joseph and decided that there was no one anywhere who was more suited for this job than Joseph. He was the one who gave the Pharaoh the plan of action that would avert disaster. The Pharaoh appointed Joseph to the position and gave him complete control and authority to execute the plan to enable the nation to survive the famine. Joseph would be able to rule the entire nation. Only Pharaoh himself held a higher office. Joseph went from being sold as a slave to being the second-in-charge of the whole country of Egypt. This shows how God can raise one up, such that one's family and friends will wonder how one reached such a lofty peak.

III. CONCLUDING REFLECTIONS

The life of Joseph teaches us how to walk in faith and leave the battles to God. There are times in life when God's purposes are not always going to be revealed quickly. The prophet Isaiah wrote that God's ways were not like the ways of men. His intellect was and is as high above the human intellect as heaven is above the earth (see Isaiah 55:8-9). One of the amazing things that we see in this lesson is how the providential will of God worked in the life of Joseph. Everywhere he went, God blessed Joseph with favor and prosperity. When people turned against him and forgot him, God was in control of Joseph's life. He had no idea that the dream he had told his brothers a few years earlier would actually be fulfilled. And not only would his dreams come to fulfillment, but God would give him the gift of interpreting the dreams of others. His brothers were correct when they called him "the great dreamer."

Believers must never limit themselves concerning what God is able to do in their lives. We must never assume that God has totally abandoned us just because things are not going according to *our* plans. What starts out as the worst situation in life can be the stepping stone to something greater and more fulfilling.

PRAYER

Lord God almighty, teach us how to honor You in all we do and say. May the revelation of Your will and purpose be crystal clear and may we be willing to follow, even when it takes us through uncharted territory. Grant Your servants peace and serenity. In the name of Jesus Christ, we pray. Amen.

WORD POWER

Dream *(chalom`-khal-ome`)*—this is a state of mind when images, pictures, and impressions pass through the mind at the moment when one is not conscious (Job 33:14-17). The purpose of dreams is often for encouragement (see Genesis 28:12) or for warning (see Genesis 31:24). God had a special purpose for Joseph, Jesus' earthly father, revealed in a dream (see Matthew 1:20). Pilate's wife received strong warnings about Jesus in a dream (see Matthew 27:19). God can still use dreams to communicate messages to us.

HOME DAILY BIBLE READINGS
(November 5-11, 2007)

Joseph's Dream Began to Come True

MONDAY, November 5: "In Potiphar's House" (Genesis 39:1-6a)
TUESDAY, November 6: "Joseph Refuses" (Genesis 39:6b-10)
WEDNESDAY, November 7: "Revenge" (Genesis 39:11-20)
THURSDAY, November 8: "Pharaoh's Dream" (Genesis 41:1-8)
FRIDAY, November 9: "Joseph the Interpreter" (Genesis 41:25-36)
SATURDAY, November 10: "Second-in-Command" (Genesis 41:37-45)
SUNDAY, November 11: "God's Wonderful Works" (Psalm 105:16-22)

LESSON 12   November 18, 2007

GOD PRESERVED A REMNANT

DEVOTIONAL READING: **Psalm 85**
PRINT PASSAGE: **Genesis 45:1-12**

BACKGROUND SCRIPTURE: **Genesis 43:1–45:15**
KEY VERSE: **Genesis 45:7**

Genesis 45:1-12—KJV

THEN JOSEPH could not refrain himself before all them that stood by him; and he cried, Cause every man to go out from me. And there stood no man with him, while Joseph made himself known unto his brethren.

2 And he wept aloud: and the Egyptians and the house of Pharaoh heard.

3 And Joseph said unto his brethren, I am Joseph; doth my father yet live? And his brethren could not answer him; for they were troubled at his presence.

4 And Joseph said unto his brethren, Come near to me, I pray you. And they came near. And he said, I am Joseph your brother, whom ye sold into Egypt.

5 Now therefore be not grieved, nor angry with yourselves, that ye sold me hither: for God did send me before you to preserve life.

6 For these two years hath the famine been in the land: and yet there are five years, in the which there shall neither be earing nor harvest.

7 And God sent me before you to preserve you a posterity in the earth, and to save your lives by a great deliverance.

8 So now it was not you that sent me hither, but God: and he hath made me a father to Pharaoh, and lord of all his house, and a ruler throughout all the land of Egypt.

9 Haste ye, and go up to my father, and say unto him, Thus saith thy son Joseph, God hath made me lord of all Egypt: come down unto me, tarry not:

10 And thou shalt dwell in the land of Goshen, and thou shalt be near unto me, thou, and thy children, and thy children's children, and thy flocks, and thy herds, and all that thou hast:

11 And there will I nourish thee; for yet there are five years of famine; lest thou, and thy household, and all that thou hast, come to poverty.

12 And, behold, your eyes see, and the eyes of my brother Benjamin, that it is my mouth that speaketh unto you.

Genesis 45:1-12—NRSV

THEN JOSEPH could no longer control himself before all those who stood by him, and he cried out, "Send everyone away from me." So no one stayed with him when Joseph made himself known to his brothers.

2 And he wept so loudly that the Egyptians heard it, and the household of Pharaoh heard it.

3 Joseph said to his brothers, "I am Joseph. Is my father still alive?" But his brothers could not answer him, so dismayed were they at his presence.

4 Then Joseph said to his brothers, "Come closer to me." And they came closer. He said, "I am your brother, Joseph, whom you sold into Egypt.

5 And now do not be distressed, or angry with yourselves, because you sold me here; for God sent me before you to preserve life.

6 For the famine has been in the land these two years; and there are five more years in which there will be neither plowing nor harvest.

7 God sent me before you to preserve for you a remnant on earth, and to keep alive for you many survivors.

8 So it was not you who sent me here, but God; he has made me a father to Pharaoh, and lord of all his house and ruler over all the land of Egypt.

9 Hurry and go up to my father and say to him, 'Thus says your son Joseph, God has made me lord of all Egypt; come down to me, do not delay.

10 You shall settle in the land of Goshen, and you shall be near me, you and your children and your children's children, as well as your flocks, your herds, and all that you have.

11 I will provide for you there—since there are five more years of famine to come--so that you and your household, and all that you have, will not come to poverty.'

12 And now your eyes and the eyes of my brother Benjamin see that it is my own mouth that speaks to you.

UNIFYING LESSON PRINCIPLE

Often, in retrospect, even the worst situation may have positive significance. How do we explain the good that comes out of such terrible circumstances? Joseph told his brothers that God had sent him to Egypt to preserve a remnant of the family of promise.

TOPICAL OUTLINE OF THE LESSON

I. Introduction
A. Understanding Your Purpose
B. Biblical Background

II. Exposition and Application of the Scripture
A. Release of Identity and the Shock (Genesis 45:1-3)
B. Hands of Fellowship and God's Providence (Genesis 45:4-8)
C. The Command and Promises Reinforced (Genesis 45:9-12)

III. Concluding Reflections

LESSON OBJECTIVES

At the completion of this lesson, the students will know that:

1. Everyone has a purpose in life to fulfill;
2. The way our purpose will be fulfilled is not through our own strength, but through the mercies of God; and,
3. Remaining calm under complex and terrible situations allows God to complete His plan for our lives.

POINTS TO BE EMPHASIZED

ADULT/YOUTH

Adult Topic: **Negative Actions, Positive Results**
Youth Topic: **Gotcha!**
Adult Key Verse: **Genesis 45:7**
Youth Key Verse: **Genesis 45:5**
Print Passage: **Genesis 45:1-12**

—Joseph revealed his true identity to his brothers.
—Joseph was able to interpret the events in his life as being part of God's larger plan to preserve life.
—Joseph explained that God worked good out of the events that his brothers meant for evil.
—Jacob's family was not the only clan Joseph saved from extinction. People from many places came to Egypt to buy grain (Genesis 41:57).
—The theme of the suffering servant runs throughout this portion of Scripture.
—Joseph was a type of Christ in that those closest to him betrayed him and God used the experience to bring about their redemption.

CHILDREN

Children Topic: **From Stranger to Family**
Key Verses: **Genesis 45:4-5**
Print Passage: **Genesis 45:1-12**

—His brothers displayed both pride and guilt in their relationship with Joseph.
—Joseph extended acceptance and forgiveness to his brothers and wanted them near him.
—Joseph saw God's plan at work throughout his journey from slavery to a position of power.
—Joseph saw himself as God's agent in preserving a remnant of the family of promise.

I. INTRODUCTION

A. Understanding Your Purpose

Today's lesson brings us to the climax of the story about Joseph and his brothers. After nearly twenty years, Joseph and his brothers were reconciled. During the years that he lived in Egypt, Joseph made a new life for himself. He married an Egyptian woman named Asenath, the daughter of Potiphera, priest of On. They were blessed with two sons, Manasseh, meaning "God has made me forget all my trouble," and Ephraim, meaning "God has made me fruitful in the land of my suffering" (Genesis 41:50-52, NIV). Joseph had no idea that he would one day see his brothers, let alone his father and beloved brother Benjamin. Many times when we look at the circumstances we face, it can be very difficult to see anything positive. How does good come out of a major accident? Well, it may lead to improving overall safety standards. Joseph's purpose for being in Egypt was greater than the hatred and jealousy of his brothers. It was all part of the divine plan of God to save not just Israel, but Egypt and all of the other nations and peoples impacted by the great famine.

B. Biblical Background

During the years of Egypt's bountiful harvests, Joseph collected massive amounts of grain for storage (Genesis 41:47-49). The famine came just as Joseph had predicted, and it engulfed not only Egypt but the whole earth (Genesis 41:56-57). People from all over came to Egypt to buy food. Among those looking for food were the sons of Jacob (Genesis 42:1-5). One of Joseph's responsibilities was to supervise the sale of grain to Egyptians and to foreigners (Genesis 42:6). When Jacob's sons appeared before Joseph, he immediately recognized them, but they had no idea who he was (Genesis 42:7-8). The brothers were able to buy food and return home to Canaan, but Simeon was held as a hostage by Joseph in Egypt (Genesis 42:9-28). Upon their return, they told their father, Jacob, that they had to take Benjamin to Egypt in order to redeem Simeon and convince Joseph of their honesty. Jacob was heartbroken and did not want to send Benjamin, having already lost (as he thought) two sons (Genesis 42:29-38).

The famine grew more severe with each passing month. Jacob told his sons to return to Egypt to buy more food (Genesis 43:1-2). Judah made a vow to his father that he would be surety for Benjamin and would take personal responsibility for his safe return (Genesis 43:9). Jacob reluctantly went along with the request. He advised the brothers to take double the money they needed and to return the money that Joseph had secretly given back to them (Genesis 43:11-15).

When Joseph saw Benjamin for the first time in years, he could not contain himself (Genesis 43:30). He had a great meal prepared for his brothers, filled their sacks with food, and sent them on their way (Genesis 44:1-14). But Joseph had his servants place a silver cup in Benjamin's sack. He ordered his servants to allow his brothers to leave and then pursue and overtake them. They were to search the sacks of each one. They did as they were told and brought the brothers back to Joseph's house (Genesis 44:14).

This was the perfect setup. Joseph accused his brothers of repaying his generosity with evil. He told them that Benjamin would become his slave for this grievous infraction (Genesis 44:17). Judah stepped forward and told Joseph in an impassioned way that Benjamin was the son of his father's old age and that to lose him would be the end of his father's life (Genesis 44:22). Judah had vowed that he would not return without Benjamin, but would offer himself in his place. He pleaded with Joseph to allow him to remain and permit Benjamin to return with his brothers, because Benjamin was Jacob's life, and without him he would die.

II. EXPOSITION AND APPLICATION OF THE SCRIPTURE

A. Release of Identity and the Shock
(Genesis 45:1-3)

THEN JOSEPH could not refrain himself before all them that stood by him; and he cried, Cause every man to go out from me. And there stood no man with him, while Joseph made himself known unto his brethren. And he wept aloud: and the Egyptians and the house of Pharaoh heard. And Joseph said unto his brethren, I am Joseph; doth my father yet live? And his brethren could not answer him; for they were troubled at his presence.

The moment of truth had finally arrived. Joseph would be able to shed the pain, disappointment, and anguish over not being with his family for more than twenty years. Judah's statement regarding his love and concern for his father pushed Joseph to the breaking point. He could not contain his emotions. His eyes must have welled up with tears as he tried to control his feelings. What would people think if the second most powerful man in Egypt were to begin crying like a frightened child? He ordered everyone out of the room, except his brothers. At long last he would be able to settle the family feud and friction that had gone on for so long. He was convinced that his brothers had had a change of heart and attitude toward him and his father. This was going to be a private family moment that he would not share with anyone but his brothers. Not even his wife and sons were privileged to share in the occasion.

The brothers must have been baffled because they were still in the dark. They had no idea what was about to happen. Without warning, Joseph began to weep so loudly that people outside of the room could hear him. The news even reached the palace of the Pharaoh that Joseph was weeping loudly in his home. Joseph, pushing back the tears, revealed himself to his brothers. "I am Joseph! Is my father still alive?" The rush of words revealed Joseph's unwavering love for his father. This text proves that even strong men are vulnerable to deep emotions. Strong men can cry and show that they care and have feelings as well. Some men today believe that it is a sign of weakness to show true emotion.

For the brothers, shock must have quickly given way to fear and dread. What would Joseph do to them now? When the revelation of Joseph's identity came, the brothers must have thought that he would surely take out his revenge against them. They thought that Joseph would kill them or enslave them. This was not a good situation. Is it possible that guilt resurfaced in their minds and they began to relive that day they sold Joseph into slavery?

Guilt is a powerful emotion. When we have committed sin, the guilt we carry never dies. Joseph's brothers were troubled by Joseph's presence and no doubt wondered what could possibly happen next.

We are reminded in the Scriptures that we reap what we sow (Galatians 6:7-9). This means that if we sow kindness and goodness, we will reap exactly kindness and goodness in return. There may be people we know who are wondering why their lives are filled with so much disappointment and pain. It may be that they have sown to the wind, and they are now reaping the whirlwind.

B. Hands of Fellowship and God's Providence (Genesis 45:4-8)

And Joseph said unto his brethren, Come near to me, I pray you. And they came near. And he said, I am Joseph your brother, whom ye sold into Egypt. Now therefore be not grieved, nor angry with yourselves, that ye sold me hither: for God did send me before you to preserve life. For these two years hath the famine been in the land: and yet there are five years, in the which there shall neither be earing nor harvest. And God sent me before you to preserve you a posterity in the earth, and to save your lives by a great deliverance. So now it was not you that sent me hither, but God: and he hath made me a father to Pharaoh, and lord of all his house, and a ruler throughout all the land of Egypt.

With his brothers still reeling from the revelation of his identity and their mouths ajar, Joseph invited his brothers to come closer and look at him. "Look at me; I am Joseph whom you sold into Egypt" (verse 4). This was a real bombshell that had just been dropped on the brothers. As far as they knew until that moment, Joseph was either dead or laboring in some Egyptian labor camp. He could not possibly be the second most important man in Egypt. But beneath the royal regalia and the shaved face typical of Egyptian royalty,

there stood Joseph, open to reuniting with his brothers and father.

We have here a very telling lesson in self-understanding. Joseph was neither caught up in his title nor his position. We must constantly view ourselves in the same light in which God sees us. We are sinners saved by grace, and that gives no one any bragging rights (Ephesians 2:8-10).

In these verses, we see the bigness of the heart of Joseph. We see what made him God's choice to go into Egypt. He had a good heart, which he had already shown by his generosity extended toward his brothers. He cautioned them not to be distressed by what they had done. Nor were they to be angry with themselves. At that moment, a lot of emotions were swirling: guilt, shame, and fear, probably all working at the same time. Joseph put their fears to rest. Essentially, he said, "Do not be upset with yourselves because you sold me into slavery" (verse 5). He let them know that God sent him to Egypt because He had a greater purpose for Joseph's being there. God had sent him there to save their lives. Joseph saw his purpose in Egypt as one connected to something larger than himself.

He reminded his brothers that the famine was quite severe and it was only in its second year. There were still five years to go in which nothing was going to happen in the fields. It might have been possible that, along with the absence of rain, the east wind coming out of the desert would dry up the land, and disaster would follow. Additionally, the source of the Nile River may have experienced drought as well. Therefore, the entire region of East and North Africa would have been affected. There would not be any planting or harvesting for the next five years (verse 6).

Joseph repeated his previous statement that God had sent him to Egypt to save the family and others from the famine (verse 7). God sent him ahead of them. He had to come in order to be in position to do what God wanted. In retrospect, God had perfected a great salvation through Joseph's presence in Egypt. Joseph told his brothers that God had made him like a father to the Pharaoh. Exactly what did he mean by that statement? It did not mean that Joseph was the Pharaoh's father. Nor did it have any reference to divinity. More than likely, it referred to Joseph as a man of wisdom and understanding who was able to give wise counsel and guidance to the king. This fits quite well with the role that Joseph played in Egypt, going back to the time when he first interpreted the Pharaoh's dreams. Whatever he would counsel, the king would be open to hearing. His brothers had no need to fear anything or anyone in all of Egypt.

God had done three things for him in his stay in Egypt. First, Joseph had been elevated to a position of great responsibility. Second, he had become a man of influence because he had the king's attention. Third, he had access to resources and people whom he could use for his purposes, if the occasion should arise. God had allowed Joseph to reach a point where he was over the household of the Pharaoh. More importantly, he was "a ruler throughout all the land of Egypt" (verse 8).

All believers must begin to see themselves as servants of God in whatever position they find themselves. There are many believers who have risen to high positions of leadership in government, education, and business. These positions must be viewed as opportunities to serve the greater good of the kingdom of God. In these high levels of responsibility, we can help others to find faith in the Lord Jesus Christ. God allows us to walk in favor so that we can be in positions to effect positive change in the world and in organizations that can influence what happens in the world.

C. The Command and Promises Reinforced (Genesis 45:9-12)

Haste ye, and go up to my father, and say unto him, Thus saith thy son Joseph, God hath made me lord of all Egypt: come down unto me, tarry not: And thou shalt dwell in the land of Goshen, and thou shalt be near unto me, thou, and thy children, and thy children's children, and thy flocks, and thy herds, and all that thou hast: And there will I nourish thee; for yet there are five years of famine; lest thou, and thy household, and all that thou hast, come to poverty. And, behold, your eyes see, and the eyes of my brother Benjamin, that it is my mouth that speaketh unto you.

Joseph told his brothers to go back hastily to Canaan. The word *haste* is used in a commanding tone. Joseph wanted them to tell his father that he was alive and that God had made him lord over all of Egypt: "Come down unto me" (verse 9). Joseph continued to give God all of the credit for what had happened in his life. He took no glory for himself, neither for his ascendancy to power or for his ability to interpret dreams. Joseph told his brothers that they would live in Goshen, a fertile plain located in northeast Egypt. It was there that the Israelites grew and flourished until the time of the Exodus. Evidently, Joseph did not live too far from that area. He wanted his entire extended family to be near him. They were to bring all they had, including their livestock. Living near Joseph would put him in a position to provide for their security and needs.

Verse 11 says, "...there will I nourish thee...." God had placed Joseph in a position of authority and made him forget his pain. This is the reason why he perpetuated his experience by naming his two sons *Manasseh* and *Ephraim* (see their meanings in the introduction section). Joseph made a solemn promise to his brothers that he was going to nourish them in Goshen. They would have no need of anything. The famine had already been very severe, and there were still five years to go. If they did not come down to Egypt, there was no way that they could survive. They would fall into poverty and die. Joseph reassured them of protection.

III. CONCLUDING REFLECTIONS

The story of Joseph's reconciliation with his brothers provides very powerful lessons on the need to cultivate a spirit and heart of forgiveness. All of us have either been the recipients of harsh, callous treatment or we have been responsible for giving it out to others. Joseph shows us how to live without being overcome by bitterness and resentment toward people who have willfully mistreated us. God has given to all believers the ministry of reconciliation (2 Corinthians 5:18). We are challenged each day to heal hurts and not cause them.

Joseph also shows us that we will never lose by seeking the welfare of others, even those who have sought nothing but evil for us. This is far easier to say than to do. The natural person wants to retaliate, and usually hopes nothing good will happen in the lives of his or her antagonists. In the life of Joseph, we see the sovereign power of God, who is able to reverse the evil that people have done to us by allowing us to heap coals of fire upon their heads through the good we do to them (Romans 12:14-21).

PRAYER

Heavenly Father, teach us to love You not just in words, but in deeds. May we be living reflections of Your grace and mercy. Root out of our hearts any presence of anger, bitterness, and malice so that we may be the living manifestations of Jesus Christ on the earth. In His name, we pray. Amen.

WORD POWER

Save (Hebrew: *chaqah- khaw-yah´*)—this means "to live," "to be alive." God used Joseph to accomplish his purpose in life. Since the beginning of his life, the hand of the Lord had been upon him, and Joseph knew this quite well. When the time came to fulfill his purpose, which was to save lives, Joseph knew it and carried it out.

HOME DAILY BIBLE READINGS
(November 12-18, 2007)

God Preserved a Remnant

MONDAY, November 12: "Restoration of God's Favor" (Psalm 85)

TUESDAY, November 13: "Food in Egypt" (Genesis 42:1-20)

WEDNESDAY, November 14: "Jacob's Difficult Decision" (Genesis 43:1-15)

THURSDAY, November 15: "Dining Together" (Genesis 43:16-34)

FRIDAY, November 16: "Joseph Tests His Brothers" (Genesis 44:1-13)

SATURDAY, November 17: "Judah's Plea" (Genesis 44:14-34)

SUNDAY, November 18: "Brothers Reconciled" (Genesis 45:1-15)

LESSON 13   November 25, 2007

JACOB BLESSED HIS FAMILY

DEVOTIONAL READING: **Psalm 145:1-13a**
PRINT PASSAGE: **Genesis 48:11-19**

BACKGROUND SCRIPTURE: **Genesis 48:8-21**
KEY VERSE: **Genesis 48:11**

Genesis 48:11-19—KJV

11 And Israel said unto Joseph, I had not thought to see thy face: and, lo, God hath shown me also thy seed.

12 And Joseph brought them out from between his knees, and he bowed himself with his face to the earth.

13 And Joseph took them both, Ephraim in his right hand toward Israel's left hand, and Manasseh in his left hand toward Israel's right hand, and brought them near unto him.

14 And Israel stretched out his right hand, and laid it upon Ephraim's head, who was the younger, and his left hand upon Manasseh's head, guiding his hands wittingly; for Manasseh was the firstborn.

15 And he blessed Joseph, and said, God, before whom my fathers Abraham and Isaac did walk, the God which fed me all my life long unto this day,

16 The Angel which redeemed me from all evil, bless the lads; and let my name be named on them, and the name of my fathers Abraham and Isaac; and let them grow into a multitude in the midst of the earth.

17 And when Joseph saw that his father laid his right hand upon the head of Ephraim, it displeased him: and he held up his father's hand, to remove it from Ephraim's head unto Manasseh's head.

18 And Joseph said unto his father, Not so, my father: for this is the firstborn; put thy right hand upon his head.

19 And his father refused, and said, I know it, my son, I know it: he also shall become a people, and he also shall be great: but truly his younger brother shall be greater than he, and his seed shall become a multitude of nations.

Genesis 48:11-19—NRSV

11 Israel said to Joseph, "I did not expect to see your face; and here God has let me see your children also."

12 Then Joseph removed them from his father's knees, and he bowed himself with his face to the earth.

13 Joseph took them both, Ephraim in his right hand toward Israel's left, and Manasseh in his left hand toward Israel's right, and brought them near him.

14 But Israel stretched out his right hand and laid it on the head of Ephraim, who was the younger, and his left hand on the head of Manasseh, crossing his hands, for Manasseh was the firstborn.

15 He blessed Joseph, and said, "The God before whom my ancestors Abraham and Isaac walked, the God who has been my shepherd all my life to this day,

16 the angel who has redeemed me from all harm, bless the boys; and in them let my name be perpetuated, and the name of my ancestors Abraham and Isaac; and let them grow into a multitude on the earth."

17 When Joseph saw that his father laid his right hand on the head of Ephraim, it displeased him; so he took his father's hand, to remove it from Ephraim's head to Manasseh's head.

18 Joseph said to his father, "Not so, my father! Since this one is the firstborn, put your right hand on his head."

19 But his father refused, and said, "I know, my son, I know; he also shall become a people, and he also shall be great. Nevertheless his younger brother shall be greater than he, and his offspring shall become a multitude of nations."

UNIFYING LESSON PRINCIPLE

One generation dies and another is born. What legacies do older generations want to leave for younger ones? Jacob moved to Egypt and lived out his last days; he blessed his grandsons and assured that they would continue to grow into a multitude, just as God had promised Abraham and Sarah.

TOPICAL OUTLINE OF THE LESSON

I. Introduction
   A. Importance of a Legacy
   B. Biblical Background

II. Exposition and Application of the Scripture
   A. Israel's Joy
      (Genesis 48:11)
   B. Israel Bestowed Blessings
      (Genesis 48:12-16)
   C. Israel Overruled Joseph's Objection
      (Genesis 48:17-19)

III. Concluding Reflections

LESSON OBJECTIVES

Upon completion of this lesson, the students will know that:

1. Leaving godly legacies for coming generations should be a driving force in the way we carry out our Christian responsibilities;
2. Each of us must be conscious of those who are looking at us as Christian role models; and,
3. Our lives are open books.

POINTS TO BE EMPHASIZED

ADULT/YOUTH

Adult Topic: **Leaving a Legacy**
Youth Topic: **Blessed**
Adult Key Verse: **Genesis 48:11**
Youth Key Verse: **Genesis 48:16**
Print Passage: **Genesis 48:11-19**

—How does this story of blessing relate to an earlier story of blessing in Genesis 27:1-45?
—Why would Jacob bless Ephraim, the younger son? How does this pattern echo previous events in Genesis?
—Jacob's blessing continues the line of descendants promised to Abraham and Sarah.
—Jacob needed to put his legal affairs in order and he did so by pronouncing blessings on his sons and grandsons.
—Placing one's right hand on another during the blessing ceremony signified the giving of the chief blessing.
—Jacob crossed his hands to give his blessing; thus, the younger grandson received favor over the firstborn.
—By bequeathing Joseph's share of blessing on Ephraim and Manasseh, the tribal allotments increased to thirteen. Eliminating the territorial share belonging to Levi reduced the total number of tribes to twelve.

CHILDREN

Children Topic: **Together Again**
Key Verse: **Genesis 47:11**
Print Passage: **Genesis 46:1-6, 28-30; 47:7, 11-12**

—God reassured Jacob that the move to Egypt was the right move at that time.
—Obeying God's call, Jacob took his family and his possessions to Egypt.
—Joseph presented himself to his father, Jacob.
—Pharaoh granted "the best part of the land" to Joseph's family.
—Joseph took seriously his calling to "preserve . . . a remnant" of God's chosen family.

I. INTRODUCTION

A. Importance of a Legacy

In our study of the patriarchs, we have been privileged to witness the beginning of a strong foundation of faith in God. Beginning with Abraham and Sarah, the patriarchs came to know God in the most intimate and personal of ways. They passed this knowledge of God and their personal experiences with Him along to the next generation. Abraham knew from personal experience that God would always provide (see Genesis 22:1-14). In today's lesson, we come to the passing of the torch of faith from one generation to the other. Jacob passed along to Joseph's sons the legacy of his faith in God. Christians today are the beneficiaries of that legacy.

B. Biblical Background

Today's lesson brings us to the end of our study of the Hebrew patriarchs. We have followed Abraham from the time of his initial call to the birth of Isaac, who was his son of promise (see Genesis 11:27-25:9). In Isaac, we met a man who was gentle and meek, but who became a man of deep faith in God (see Genesis 25:19-27; 46). His two sons, Esau and Jacob, competed for the right to be blessed by their father, but God had chosen Jacob to be the standard bearer of the promise first made to Abraham. We followed the saga of Jacob and the years of faithfulness to his father-in-law, Laban, as he served for the right to marry Rachel. Jacob was the most blessed of all of the patriarchs when it came to children. His two wives (Leah and Rachael) and two concubines (Bilhah and Zilpah) gave birth to eleven sons and one daughter (see Genesis 30:3, 9; 34:1; 35:23-27). Jacob was blessed to accumulate great wealth, flocks, herds, and servants.

II. EXPOSITION AND APPLICATION OF THE SCRIPTURE

A. Israel's Joy
(Genesis 48:11)

And Israel said unto Joseph, I had not thought to see thy face: and, lo, God hath shewed me also thy seed.

For the first time, we see one of the patriarchs meeting his son's sons. There is no mention of Abraham ever having met the two sons of Isaac. Therefore, Jacob counted himself among the most blessed men on all of the earth. Why? He had been given the opportunity to see Joseph, his long-lost and most beloved son, again. This happened after nearly twenty years of uncertainty about Joseph's fate. Jacob did not know whether Joseph was dead or alive. He had no idea about what could have possibly happened to him, other than what his sons had told him (see Genesis 37:32-35). The last time he saw Joseph was when he sent him to see about his brothers (Genesis 37:12-14). Jacob remarked that he had never expected to see Joseph's face again, but God had been gracious and kind, allowing him to see Joseph's children as well. Jacob attributed his great blessing to the favor of God. It was not chance that had brought him to that point—it was God.

The expression, "…I had not thought to see thy face" (verse 11), means that Jacob thought Joseph had died, according to the report of Joseph's brothers. Israel (Jacob) had believed his sons. There are many people who are not blessed to see future generations of their offspring. We must never take for granted that we will live long enough to see future generations of our own offspring. The knowing of one's offspring is a blessing that comes from God, and it is one that should be greeted with deep gratitude. It is critical that grandparents pass along to their grandchildren their legacy of godliness and faith.

Israel attributed the longevity of his life to the providence of God. God had promised "…I will also surely bring thee up again: and Joseph shall put his hand upon thine eyes" (Genesis 46:4). The lesson here is that God is faithful to His promise. Every child of God can count on the faithfulness of God.

B. Israel Bestowed Blessings
(Genesis 48:12-16)

And Joseph brought them out from between his knees, and he bowed himself with his face to the earth. And Joseph took them both, Ephraim in his right hand toward Israel's left hand, and Manasseh in his left hand toward Israel's right hand, and brought them near unto him. And Israel stretched out his right hand, and laid it upon Ephraim's head, who was the younger, and his left hand upon Manasseh's head, guiding his hands wittingly; for Manasseh was the firstborn. And he blessed Joseph, and said, God, before whom my fathers Abraham and Isaac did walk, the God which fed me all my life long unto this day, The Angel which redeemed me from all evil, bless the lads; and let my name be named on them, and the name of my fathers Abraham and Isaac; and let them grow into a multitude in the midst of the earth.

Joseph's two sons had been standing with their father, quite possibly in front of him. This accounts for the Bible's reference to "between his knees" (verse 12). As the second most important and powerful ruler in Egypt, Joseph was used to people bowing before him. In an act of deep humility and respect, he bowed before his father. When he was younger, Joseph dreamed of the day when his brothers and parents would bow before him. Jacob had chastised his son when he told him that he saw his entire family bowing before him. In this scene, the tables were reversed and Joseph was the one bowing.

The lesson is one of respect for parents, which is the first commandment with promise (see Exodus 20:12; Ephesians 6:1-3). There is also the implied lesson that we should respect those in authority (see Romans 13:1-3). Many youth grow up not learning to respect adults and especially those in authority. Hence, jails and prisons are full of young men and women who never learned this lesson that comes with a promise. Church leaders should encourage parents and grandparents to take seriously the need to provide spiritual and moral training for their children. Joseph honored his father and showed it.

He brought his two sons before Israel to be blessed by him. He brought Manasseh, the firstborn, in a position where the right hand of Jacob could be easily placed upon his head and the left hand on Ephraim (verse 13). This would ensure that the older son would be touched with the right hand of Jacob and the younger with Jacob's left hand.

Jacob first blessed Joseph and told him how God had been with him. He made three statements about the God he served and worshiped. First, He was the God who was served and worshiped by his fathers, Abraham and Isaac. He was the One before whom they both walked. He was the God who revealed Himself to them and gave them the covenant of promise. Second, He was the God who had fed him and taken care of him all of the days of his life. Jacob acknowledged the protection and provision of God. Third, He was the God who had redeemed Jacob from all evil (verses 15-16).

Israel passed along to Joseph and his sons a legacy of faithfulness to God that was rooted in the past experience of his fathers. It was not a faith based upon hearsay or the witness of someone else; it was one grounded in his own personal experience with God. Here is a lesson for every parent and grandparent to model. We must continue to pass along from one generation to the next our personal experience of God's love and grace. Many parents never take the time to share with their children their personal witness and testimony about how God has kept them throughout their days. The God of Israel is a personal God and He relates to us in a personal way if we arc open to Him.

Children of this generation are growing up as the most prosperous and blessed of any generation of African Americans. They are also growing up among the most violent youth in our history. They have lived in the midst of global terror attacks, war, famine, and ethnic conflict on a massive scale. Our children and grandchildren are growing up at a time when many of the battles for social and economic justice have been fought and won. The youth today are the first generation of African Americans who do not know the struggle against massive inequality and racial injustice. The baby boomers and the builders generation (those born in the 1920s and 30s) must not fail to teach this generation and tell them the story of our sojourn in this country. This may be the first generation that does not know the story of our struggle in America. We can extend the life and times of past generations by retelling their stories of trial and triumph. Black History Month is a few months away; churches should organize lecture series to help the youth see the hand of God in the lives of African-Americans.

It was important to Israel that his grandsons know his story and what God had brought him through. Jacob wanted his grandsons to bear his name and the names of Abraham and Isaac that would keep his name alive for future generations. They would both grow into a multitude of nations, just as God had promised.

C. Israel Overruled Joseph's Objection (Genesis 48:17-19)

And when Joseph saw that his father laid his right hand upon the head of Ephraim, it displeased him: and he held up his father's hand, to remove it from Ephraim's head unto Manasseh's head. And Joseph said unto his father, Not so, my father: for this is the firstborn; put thy right hand upon his head. And his father refused, and said, I know it, my son, I know it: he also shall become a people, and he also shall be great: but truly his younger brother shall be greater than he, and his seed shall become a multitude of nations.

When Joseph saw what his father was doing, he tried to steer the older son, Manasseh, to the right hand of Jacob. Joseph thought for sure that his father had made a grave mistake. He may have reasoned that his father was making this mistake as a result of poor eyesight or feebleness. Joseph reminded his father that Manasseh was the firstborn and that he should receive the blessing reserved for the firstborn. Jacob rebuffed his son and told him that he was fully aware of what he was doing. He told Joseph that both sons would become great.

But it was the younger son who would become greater than the older brother and would become the most populous nation between the two of them. True to what Israel predicted, the tribe of Manasseh was so large that when Joshua partitioned the tribes, Manasseh occupied both the East and West parts of the river Jordan (see the map of twelve tribes in Canaan at the back of your Bible).

Joseph intended to steer the blessing of God in the direction that he felt it should go and where he wanted it to go. He had no idea that God was planning something entirely different from what he thought. This teaches the lesson that we can never determine who God will or will not bless. He chooses whomever He wishes to bless and use for His purposes.

III. CONCLUDING REFLECTIONS

Every year, millions of Americans die; some are very famous and will leave a lasting mark upon the fabric of the nation's culture. Others are people we have never heard of, but their influence and presence will live for generations to come. These are people who have dedicated their lives to the service of the Lord Jesus Christ and who seek to make a difference every day. Every believer is called by God to make a difference in the world.

We must all be concerned about the legacies we will leave when we are called from time to eternity. Jacob left a legacy of faith and trust in God that he passed along to his children's children.

PRAYER

Almighty God, creator of the heavens and the earth, we pray that You will teach us to number our days so that we may apply our hearts to wisdom and understanding. Grant us the patience to serve You and the faith to trust You. In Jesus' name, we pray. Amen.

WORD POWER

Legacy—this word does not appear in the Bible. We have no Hebrew or Greek word for it. However, today's lesson rotates around it. The Webster Collegiate Dictionary defines it as "something transmitted." It is incumbent upon Christians to transmit their faith in God to their children, as we have seen in the lives of the patriarchs. Christians should be able to say to their children, "the God I serve" will do this or that.

HOME DAILY BIBLE READINGS
(November 19-25, 2007)
Jacob Blessed His Family
MONDAY, November 19: "Bring Your Father" (Genesis 45:16-20)

TUESDAY, November 20: "God's Reassurance" (Genesis 46:1-4)

WEDNESDAY, November 21: "The Reunion" (Genesis 46:28-34)

THURSDAY, November 22: "A Blessing" (Genesis 47:7-12)

FRIDAY, November 23: "Joseph's Promise" (Genesis 47:27-31)

SATURDAY, November 24: "A Grandfather's Blessing" (Genesis 48:8-21)

SUNDAY, November 25: "The Greatness and Goodness of God" (Psalm 145:1-13a)

God's Call to the Christian Community

GENERAL INTRODUCTION

The study for this quarter surveys the theme of God's call. The concept of "call" relates to God's self-disclosure in seeking us as participants in the world's redemption. God retains the prerogative to call those whom He will to specific tasks related to the ultimate goal of humanity's redemption. The sessions this quarter look at various passages in the gospel of Luke as they deal directly or indirectly with the way that God calls the community of faith to live out the purpose for which it was created.

Unit I, *God's Call at Christmas and Beyond,* consisting of five sessions, explores how God's call was received and acted upon by Elisabeth and Zacharias, Mary the mother of Jesus, and Jesus. The topic of Lesson 1, "Surprising Opportunities," underscores the fact that some people are aware that God is at work and might use miracles to fulfill His purposes. His message came to Zacharias in the temple concerning the call that would be on their lives and the life of their child. Lesson 2's topic, on "Significance and Purpose," reminds us of God's initiative of grace in calling whomever He wills for special tasks. Lesson 3 concerns Zacharias' song of praise, which focused not on personal blessings, but on the work of God. This would be seen specifically in his son John and in the Savior, whom John would proclaim. In Lesson 4, the topic "Reasons to Rejoice" focuses on Luke's account of Jesus' birth; we see that God's concern for those who are poor or oppressed is demonstrated in both the birth of Jesus and in the announcement to the shepherds. Lesson 5 presents the topic, "Hearing and Telling Good News." As Simeon declared by the Holy Spirit that Jesus was the means of salvation for all people, Jew and Gentile, the church should proclaim the Gospel of Jesus Christ to all people and races.

Unit II, *The Awareness of God's Instruction,* consists of four sessions and has as its focus the inspiration that comes to us through God's call on us. Because we have been called to a partnership with God, we can find inspiration to learn, love, pray, and trust. The topic of Lesson 6, "Questions and Answers," shows us that faith grows by active participation in discussion with other believers. Lesson 7 raises the following question, "What does Jesus teach us about loving our enemies?" In Lesson 8, Jesus teaches that we have a loving heavenly parent to whom we can persistently bring our needs and the desires of our hearts. In Lesson Nine's topic, "Combating Anxiety and Worry," Jesus says that anxiety about possessions reflects a lack of trust in God, a lack of interest in the kingdom, and a lack of generosity toward those in need.

Unit III, *God Summons Us to Respond,* consists of four sessions and considers our cooperation with God by responding to the call to labor in extending the community of faith. It also calls us to repent when we have failed or fallen short, to serve God with humility, and to be dedicated disciples. Lesson 10 presents the topic "Response Requires Work" and points out that to follow God's summons or call is to become involved in the work God gives us to do. Lesson 11 seeks to answer the following question: "How do we change our behavior so that we are better people?" The answer is found in Jesus' call for people to repent and to allow God to transform their lives. Lesson 12, based on the topic "The Necessity of Humility," spotlights Jesus' teaching in which He urges Christians to be proactive in befriending and welcoming those rejected by others. The final session, Lesson 13, focuses on Jesus' challenge to the crowd to leave everything behind and become His disciples. Discipleship requires looking ahead, counting the cost, and following through on commitments.

Madonna and Child

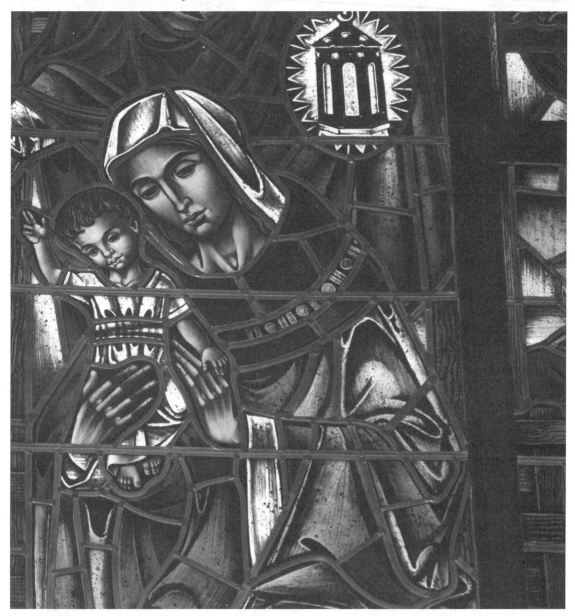

    The Madonna and Child is often the name of a work of art which shows the Virgin Mary and the Child Jesus. The image of the Madonna and Child, such as the one in this stained-glass representation, is one of the central icons of Christianity. After some initial resistance and controversy, the formula "Mother of God" *(Theotokos)* was adopted officially by the Christian Church at the Council of Ephesus, 431.

    The earliest known representation of the Madonna and Child may be the wall painting in the Catacomb of Priscilla, Rome, in which the seated Madonna suckles the Child, who turns His head to gaze at the spectator.

LESSON 1

December 2, 2007

CALLED TO BELIEVE

DEVOTIONAL READING: **Psalm 66:1-4, 16-20**
PRINT PASSAGE: **Luke 1:8-23**

BACKGROUND SCRIPTURE: **Luke 1:5-25**
KEY VERSE: **Luke 1:20**

Luke 1:8-23—KJV

8 And it came to pass, that while he executed the priest's office before God in the order of his course,
9 According to the custom of the priest's office, his lot was to burn incense when he went into the temple of the Lord.
10 And the whole multitude of the people were praying without at the time of incense.
11 And there appeared unto him an angel of the Lord standing on the right side of the altar of incense.
12 And when Zacharias saw him, he was troubled, and fear fell upon him.
13 But the angel said unto him, Fear not, Zacharias: for thy prayer is heard; and thy wife Elisabeth shall bear thee a son, and thou shalt call his name John.
14 And thou shalt have joy and gladness; and many shall rejoice at his birth.
15 For he shall be great in the sight of the Lord, and shall drink neither wine nor strong drink; and he shall be filled with the Holy Ghost, even from his mother's womb.
16 And many of the children of Israel shall he turn to the Lord their God.
17 And he shall go before him in the spirit and power of Elias, to turn the hearts of the fathers to the children, and the disobedient to the wisdom of the just; to make ready a people prepared for the Lord.
18 And Zacharias said unto the angel, Whereby shall I know this? for I am an old man, and my wife well stricken in years.
19 And the angel answering said unto him, I am Gabriel, that stand in the presence of God; and am sent to speak unto thee, and to shew thee these glad tidings.
20 And, behold, thou shalt be dumb, and not able to speak, until the day that these things shall be performed, because thou believest not my words, which shall be fulfilled in their season.
21 And the people waited for Zacharias, and marvelled that he tarried so long in the temple.

Luke 1:8-23—NRSV

8 Once when he was serving as priest before God and his section was on duty,
9 he was chosen by lot, according to the custom of the priesthood, to enter the sanctuary of the Lord and offer incense.
10 Now at the time of the incense offering, the whole assembly of the people was praying outside.
11 Then there appeared to him an angel of the Lord, standing at the right side of the altar of incense.
12 When Zechariah saw him, he was terrified; and fear overwhelmed him.
13 But the angel said to him, "Do not be afraid, Zechariah, for your prayer has been heard. Your wife Elizabeth will bear you a son, and you will name him John.
14 You will have joy and gladness, and many will rejoice at his birth,
15 for he will be great in the sight of the Lord. He must never drink wine or strong drink; even before his birth he will be filled with the Holy Spirit.
16 He will turn many of the people of Israel to the Lord their God.
17 With the spirit and power of Elijah he will go before him, to turn the hearts of parents to their children, and the disobedient to the wisdom of the righteous, to make ready a people prepared for the Lord."
18 Zechariah said to the angel, "How will I know that this is so? For I am an old man, and my wife is getting on in years."
19 The angel replied, "I am Gabriel. I stand in the presence of God, and I have been sent to speak to you and to bring you this good news.
20 But now, because you did not believe my words, which will be fulfilled in their time, you will become mute, unable to speak, until the day these things occur."
21 Meanwhile the people were waiting for Zechariah, and wondered at his delay in the sanctuary.

People find it hard to believe that the miraculous could happen to them. What evidence do we have that miracles can happen in our lives? God promised Elisabeth and Zecharias a miracle, and God fulfilled that promise.

22 And when he came out, he could not speak unto them: and they perceived that he had seen a vision in the temple: for he beckoned unto them, and remained speechless.

23 And it came to pass, that, as soon as the days of his ministration were accomplished, he departed to his own house.

22 When he did come out, he could not speak to them, and they realized that he had seen a vision in the sanctuary. He kept motioning to them and remained unable to speak.

23 When his time of service was ended, he went to his home.

TOPICAL OUTLINE OF THE LESSON

I. **Introduction**
   A. A Miracle in the Lives of Zacharias and Elisabeth
   B. Biblical Background

II. **Exposition and Application of the Scripture**
   A. An Angelic Appearance (Luke 1:8-12)
   B. A Divine Promise (Luke 1:13-17)
   C. A Faithless Priest (Luke 1:18-23)

III. **Concluding Reflections**

LESSON OBJECTIVES

Upon completion of this lesson, the students will know that:

1. Miracles still happen in our day;
2. Engaging in the work of the Lord wholeheartedly has its rewards;
3. God does not have a cutoff line for His ministers; and,
4. If God promised anything, He will deliver it.

POINTS TO BE EMPHASIZED

ADULT/YOUTH

Adult Topic: **Surprising Opportunities**
Youth Topic: **Called to Believe**
Adult Key Verse: **Luke 1:20**
Youth Key Verse: **Luke 1:19**
Print Passage: **Luke 1:8-23**

—What did it mean to serve as a priest in the order of Abijah and to offer incense in temple worship?
—John is a Semitic name meaning "God is gracious."
—Zacharias had doubts about the angel's prediction of a miraculous birth.
—Zacharias' service in the temple was a once-in-a-lifetime opportunity.
—Zacharias' unbelief was in response to a promised miracle, while Elisabeth's rejoicing was in response to a promise fulfilled.

CHILDREN

Children Topic: **Believing in Miracles**
Key Verse: **Luke 1:13**
Print Passage: **Luke 1:8-23**

—Although he was a priest ministering before God, Zacharias was unprepared for an angel's visitation.
—Zacharias found it difficult to see past the human realities of his and Elisabeth's ages.
—Zecharias' question asked for proof, a sign that the promise would be fulfilled.
—Elisabeth accepted her pregnancy as a personal gift from God.

I. INTRODUCTION

A. A Miracle in the Lives of Zacharias and Elisabeth

Today's lesson introduces us to Elisabeth and Zacharias, the parents of John the Baptist. They were a faithful and godly family of Aaronic descent, who had long desired to have children but had none. They had both grown old, and Elisabeth was well past her childbearing years. In the process of time, an angel of the Lord appeared to Zacharias and announced that God would give him and Elisabeth a son. The birth of John would be the answer to their prayers and the fulfillment of God's promise to give them a son. In this lesson, we meet faith and doubt in John's father, Zacharias. The birth of John fits into the miraculous genre as that of the immaculate conception of Jesus given the ages of his parents and the circumstances under which they lived.

B. Biblical Background

The birth of John the Baptist occurred during the days that Herod was the king of Judea. Living in the hill country, in a small village just outside of Jerusalem, was a priest named Zacharias who lived with his wife, Elisabeth (Luke 1:39, 65). Zacharias was among the thousands of priests who lived at that time. Zacharias was a member of the eighth course of Abijah, which was established during the reign of King David (1 Chronicles 24:10). During the time that David was king (940-910 B.C.), a rotating order of service was established so as to give every priest an opportunity to serve at the temple at least once in his lifetime. There were twenty-four courses or rotations, with each course serving for a period of one to two weeks. Each priest was blessed to just have one day to serve or perform some temple function in his lifetime.

Zacharias and Elisabeth are described as righteous before God. They walked or lived in accordance with the Law, keeping the commandments and ordinances of the Lord, and were blameless according to the Law (Deuteronomy 6:1-3; Philippians 3:6-9). This godly couple lived a life with which God was well-pleased. Yet with all of their righteousness, they were still missing the one thing that every Jewish woman wanted in order to feel fulfilled and blessed by God: a son.

Elisabeth was barren, but God appeared through an angel and gave Zacharias and Elisabeth good news about the future. This same angel later appeared to Mary to give good news about the birth of our Lord, Jesus Christ. The news was received by Zacharias while he was serving in the temple.

II. EXPOSITION AND APPLICATION OF THE SCRIPTURE

A. An Angelic Appearance (Luke 1:8-12)

And it came to pass, that while he executed the priest's office before God in the order of his course, According to the custom of the priest's office, his lot was to burn incense when he went into the temple of the Lord. And

the whole multitude of the people were praying without at the time of incense. And there appeared unto him an angel of the Lord standing on the right side of the altar of incense. And when Zacharias saw him, he was troubled, and fear fell upon him.

As stated previously, Zacharias was among the thousands of priests who made up the course of Abijah. Once a year, their course was selected to serve for a period of one to two weeks in Jerusalem at the temple. They would perform all of the Levitical functions and services associated with the daily temple services and sacrifices: cleaning the temple area, preparing the shewbread, lighting the candles, preparing the various sacrifices, and so forth. One of those functions was the burning of incense on the Golden Altar of Incense twice a day (see Exodus 30:7-8). The Golden Altar of Incense was among the original items of furniture built for use in the tabernacle (see Exodus 25-40). It was the last item standing between the Holy Place and Holy of Holies. Each day, the priest would light the incense twice a day creating a sweet aroma in the temple precincts (verse 9). Therefore, to be selected to burn the incense on any day was a high and holy privilege. Zacharias was executing his duties according to the customs that went back to the time of the tabernacle worship in the wilderness when events happened that would change his life forever.

Incense burning took place during the third hour of prayer at 9:00 a.m. and the ninth hour of prayer at 3:00 p.m. According to Psalm 55:17, there were three designated times for prayer: 9:00 a.m. (third hour), 12:00 p.m. (sixth hour), and 3:00 p.m. (ninth hour). Usually during the hours of prayer there were large gatherings of people in the two primary courtyards, the Court of Men and the Court of Women and Gentiles (see Acts 3:1-11). While Zacharias was inside the Holy Place, the people were outside waiting for the lighting of the incense so that they could fall down in adoration and worship of God.

While he was performing his duties, there appeared out of nowhere an angel of the Lord standing at the right side of the altar. Zacharias was completely stunned by the sight and was deeply troubled. His first thought must have been that here was someone who was not authorized to be in this place, let alone at the altar of incense. Trouble was followed by fear. Fear is one of the most common reactions to the appearance of heavenly beings (see Exodus 15:16; Judges 6:23; 2 Samuel 6:9). God dispatched angels to give special messages for notable occasions.

There are important lessons to be learned from the examples of Zacharias and Elizabeth. First, we are never too old to be used by God. Abraham was close to eighty when God called him. Second, this also points out that we should never assume that our age eliminates us from the performance of service for the Lord. Zacharias was at the temple serving in the capacity to which he had been appointed. When we engage ourselves in the service of the Lord, He takes care of our personal problems. Zacharias was a typical example. He was in the temple preparing the place for worship when the angel of the Lord appeared to him.

B. A Divine Promise
(Luke 1:13-17)

But the angel said unto him, Fear not, Zacharias: for thy prayer is heard; and thy wife Elisabeth shall bear thee a son, and thou shalt call his name John. And thou shalt have joy and gladness; and many shall rejoice at his birth. For he shall be great in the sight of the Lord, and shall drink neither wine nor strong drink; and he shall be filled

with the Holy Ghost, even from his mother's womb. And many of the children of Israel shall he turn to the Lord their God. And he shall go before him in the spirit and power of Elias, to turn the hearts of the fathers to the children, and the disobedient to the wisdom of the just; to make ready a people prepared for the Lord.

Zacharias' fear was evident because he was caught completely off guard by the angelic appearance and announcement. Fear was a natural reaction whenever human beings encountered the Lord or one of His messengers (Genesis 15:1; 21:17; Joshua 8:1; Judges 6:10; Luke 2:10; 5:10; 8:50; 12:7, 32; 18:4). The angel of the Lord told him not to fear, for he had not come to bring harm or bad news, but good news. The angel told Zacharias that God had heard and answered his prayer. We are not sure what Zacharias' prayer had been, and there has been much speculation among biblical scholars regarding this matter. The best possibilities have been as follows: 1) He was praying for a son. (2) He may have been praying for the Messiah to come, because Israel was under the rule of Rome. (3) He may have been praying for the salvation of his people, many of whom had taken on the culture and ways of Rome. We don't know, but we do know that God heard and answered his prayer (see Genesis 25:21; 1 Samuel 1:20-23; Psalm 118:21; Acts 10:31). There is the possibility that His prayer may have been a combination of all three. God does hear and answer the prayers of the righteous (see 2 Kings 20:1-7; Psalm 34:17).

The announcement was specific to him and Elisabeth. She was going to give birth to a son, and Zacharias was to name him John. The magnitude of the moment was captured in the name that was to be given to the child: John. God had already picked a name for him, which was an indication that this was a special child with a special calling upon his life (see 1 Kings 13:2).

John's birth was going to produce joy and gladness for his parents. Not only would they be filled with joy, but John's life and ministry would bring joy to thousands. We know that the preaching ministry of John ignited a flame of revival throughout Judea. His aged parents would experience joy on an unprecedented scale, which is what "gladness" means. *Gladness* is a fuller manifestation of joy—it is exceeding joy. What other reaction would be appropriate for two people who had demonstrated through their lives an unwavering faith and confidence in God?

John was coming with a distinct calling and purpose already established for his life. His greatness and standing in Jewish society would not come from people, but from God. He would be great in the sight of God. The greatest title that God bestows upon any human being is that of *servant* (see Joshua 1:1-2). The Bible reminds us that God is the One who makes us great. This is greatness that is lasting (see Genesis 12:2; Joshua 3:7; 1 Chronicles 17:8; 29:12). Yet people of faith have often sought greatness apart from the simple life of servanthood. One of the problems that Jesus had with His disciples was the quest for greatness (see Mark 10:35-45). Like Samson, John was not to drink any alcoholic drinks. John would be filled with the Holy Spirit from his mother's womb. God's anointing and calling was already upon his life. John's ministry would turn many of the children of Israel from the world and back to God (verse 16; also Luke 3:2-3, 7-14).

John's ministry would be unlike anything that Israel had seen in hundreds of years. He would have the fire and passion of Elijah. His ministry is described in Luke 1:17, using three distinctive phrases. The first says, "go before Him in the spirit and power of Elias." This is a clear reference to the messianic prophecy concerning the forerunner that would precede the coming of the Messiah (see Malachi 3:1). The second descriptive statement, "to turn the hearts of the fathers to the children, and the disobedient to the wisdom of the just," is a clear prophetic utterance bestowed upon John. The preaching of John would prepare families for the new age of the Messiah, when reconciliation and healing would take place (see Malachi 4:6). The third descriptive statement reads, "to make ready a people prepared for the Lord." Lord refers to God the Father, not to Jesus. John's primary mission was to prepare (Greek: *hetoimazo*—to equip internally or make ready) a people for service in the kingdom of God.

John clearly provides a model for ministry in the twenty-first-century African-American church. Pentecost was the dawn of the church age in which the Holy Spirit filled believers with the Spirit and power of God. The church is able to do exceedingly great things in the name of God. However, she must operate in the fullness of that authority. There is a clear mandate throughout the Scriptures to take time to teach and train children. Many parents are so disconnected from the lives of their children that reconciliation and healing needs to take place. Fathers must not leave their responsibilities of rearing and teaching their children the ways of God upon the shoulders of their children's mothers. Pastors and church leaders were and are challenged to take seriously the requirement to equip the saints for the work of the ministry (see Ephesians 4:11-16).

C. A Faithless Priest
(Luke 1:18-23)

And Zacharias said unto the angel, Whereby shall I know this? for I am an old man, and my wife well stricken in years. And the angel answering said unto him, I am Gabriel, that stand in the presence of God; and am sent to speak unto thee, and to shew thee these glad tidings. And, behold, thou shalt be dumb, and not able to speak, until the day that these things shall be performed, because thou believest not my words, which shall be fulfilled in their season. And the people waited for Zacharias, and marvelled that he tarried so long in the temple. And when he came out, he could not speak unto them: and they perceived that he had seen a vision in the temple: for he beckoned unto them, and remained speechless. And it came to pass, that, as soon as the days of his ministration were accomplished, he departed to his own house.

Zacharias' first response was one of doubt. He wanted to know how he would know that everything he had just been told was true. All that Zacharias saw were the ages of himself and his wife (verse 18). The angel told him that he was Gabriel, one of the archangels, who stood in the very presence of the Lord. He wanted Zacharias to know that his giving the news of the birth of Zacharias' son was as good as God Himself telling him (verse 19). Gabriel had been sent to speak specifically to Zacharias, giving him the good news. As a sign of the truthfulness of Gabriel's word, Zacharias would not be able to speak at all until the day that John was born (verse 20).

While Zacharias was inside the temple, the people were anxiously waiting for him, because it was taking longer than usual to light the incense (verse 21). When he finally did emerge from the Holy Place, his voice was gone. He could not tell the people what had happened to him, but something about his facial expressions or gestures gave the indication that he had been in the presence of a heavenly being. We are not sure how much longer Zacharias stayed in Jerusalem, but when his time was up, he departed to his house in the hill country of Judea. His experience of the presence of God had left him speechless. How would he explain what had happened when he returned home to Elisabeth? Shortly after his return, Elisabeth conceived, just as Gabriel had promised.

III. CONCLUDING REFLECTIONS

This first Sunday in Advent reminds us that God is more willing to use us than we may think. Just when we may have given up on new possibilities for ministry and mission, God opens fresh opportunities for service, as He did with Zacharias and Elisabeth. All of us have an opportunity to be used by God to do great works in His name. Yet few of us have the opportunity to engage in work that changes the very landscape of life for millions of people. Although we may never be used at that level, it is important to always make ourselves available without wavering and doubting. Our doubts, however, will never disqualify us from service to God. Zacharias and Elisabeth were two humble people laboring in obscurity as faithful servants of the Lord God. He saw their service and honored them with one of the greatest opportunities to be afforded any human being.

PRAYER

Heavenly Father, may we see every new day as an opportunity for a fresh start in Your kingdom. Forgive us of any doubts that we may have. Cleanse our thoughts and give us renewed determination to live for You every day of our lives. In Jesus' name, we pray. Amen.

WORD POWER

Dumb (Greek: *sioopoon*)—there are voluntary and involuntary dumbness. In this case, Zacharias experienced involuntary dumbness. Zacharias did not act in faith when the angel told him about the birth of his son. As a result, he could hear words, but he was not able to speak until John's birth. There are different consequences for lack of faith.

HOME DAILY BIBLE READINGS
(November 26—December 2, 2007)
Called to Believe

MONDAY, November 26: "Sing God's Praises" (Psalm 66:1–4)

TUESDAY, November 27: "Righteous before God" (Luke 1:5–7)

WEDNESDAY, November 28: "Incense Offering Interrupted" (Luke 1:8–13)

THURSDAY, November 29: "A Ministry Foretold" (Luke 1:14–17)

FRIDAY, November 30: "Zacharias Sees a Vision" (Luke 1:18–23)

SATURDAY, December 1: "Elisabeth Conceives" (Luke 1:24–25)

SUNDAY, December 2: "God Listened to My Prayer" (Psalm 66:16–20)

LESSON 2   December 9, 2007

CALLED TO BE A VESSEL

DEVOTIONAL READING: **Psalm 40:1-5**
PRINT PASSAGE: **Luke 1:26-38**

BACKGROUND SCRIPTURE: **Luke 1:26-38**
KEY VERSE: **Luke 1:38**

Luke 1:26-38—KJV

26 And in the sixth month the angel Gabriel was sent from God unto a city of Galilee, named Nazareth,

27 To a virgin espoused to a man whose name was Joseph, of the house of David; and the virgin's name was Mary.

28 And the angel came in unto her, and said, Hail, thou that art highly favoured, the Lord is with thee: blessed art thou among women.

29 And when she saw him, she was troubled at his saying, and cast in her mind what manner of salutation this should be.

30 And the angel said unto her, Fear not, Mary: for thou hast found favour with God.

31 And, behold, thou shalt conceive in thy womb, and bring forth a son, and shalt call his name JESUS.

32 He shall be great, and shall be called the Son of the Highest: and the Lord God shall give unto him the throne of his father David:

33 And he shall reign over the house of Jacob for ever; and of his kingdom there shall be no end.

34 Then said Mary unto the angel, How shall this be, seeing I know not a man?

35 And the angel answered and said unto her, The Holy Ghost shall come upon thee, and the power of the Highest shall overshadow thee: therefore also that holy thing which shall be born of thee shall be called the Son of God.

36 And, behold, thy cousin Elisabeth, she hath also conceived a son in her old age: and this is the sixth month with her, who was called barren.

37 For with God nothing shall be impossible.

38 And Mary said, Behold the handmaid of the Lord; be it unto me according to thy word. And the angel departed from her.

Luke 1:26-38—NRSV

26 In the sixth month the angel Gabriel was sent by God to a town in Galilee called Nazareth,

27 to a virgin engaged to a man whose name was Joseph, of the house of David. The virgin's name was Mary.

28 And he came to her and said, "Greetings, favored one! The Lord is with you."

29 But she was much perplexed by his words and pondered what sort of greeting this might be.

30 The angel said to her, "Do not be afraid, Mary, for you have found favor with God.

31 And now, you will conceive in your womb and bear a son, and you will name him Jesus.

32 He will be great, and will be called the Son of the Most High, and the Lord God will give to him the throne of his ancestor David.

33 He will reign over the house of Jacob forever, and of his kingdom there will be no end."

34 Mary said to the angel, "How can this be, since I am a virgin?"

35 The angel said to her, "The Holy Spirit will come upon you, and the power of the Most High will overshadow you; therefore the child to be born will be holy; he will be called Son of God.

36 And now, your relative Elizabeth in her old age has also conceived a son; and this is the sixth month for her who was said to be barren.

37 For nothing will be impossible with God."

38 Then Mary said, "Here am I, the servant of the Lord; let it be with me according to your word." Then the angel departed from her.

We want to know that we are significant to someone and that our lives count for something. How does God address these needs by calling us to serve? Mary is an example of how God can call us to significance and purpose.

TOPICAL OUTLINE OF THE LESSON

I. Introduction
A. Position of Women
B. Biblical Background

II. Exposition and Application of the Scripture
A. The Messenger Sent (Luke 1:26-29)
B. The Message Delivered (Luke 1:30-33)
C. The Method Explained (Luke 1:34-38)

III. Concluding Reflections

LESSON OBJECTIVES

Upon completion of this lesson, the students will know that:
1. All children of God are significant to God, and there is a mission to be carried out in each child's life;
2. God can use anybody to carry out His plans, irrespective of age; and,
3. Small tasks in the house of God, when done with a sense of calling, honor God.

POINTS TO BE EMPHASIZED

ADULT/YOUTH
Adult Topic: Significance and Purpose
Youth Topic: Called to Be a Servant
Adult Key Verse: Luke 1:38
Youth Key Verse: Luke 1:28
Print Passage: Luke 1:26-38
—The Virgin Birth asserts that Jesus Christ was truly human as well as truly God.
—*Jesus* is the Greek equivalent of the Semitic name *Joshua,* which means "the Lord is salvation."
—The angel's words to Mary recall the prophecies of 2 Samuel 7:13-16 and Isaiah 9:6-7.
—Mary responded positively to being chosen as God's faithful servant.
—The text is a reminder of God's initiative of grace.
—What does it mean in biblical culture to be favored by God?
—Women in biblical culture were seen as inferior, yet God chose a woman to be a favored servant.

CHILDREN
Children Topic: Being God's Servant
Key Verse: Luke 1:38
Print Passage: Luke 1:26-38
—Note the differences and similarities between Zecharias' angel visitation and Mary's.
—The angel's first words affirmed Mary's value to God.
—This is the first time we encounter Mary's "pondering" of spiritual things; Mary's faith was a thoughtful faith.
—Mary questioned how this conception might take place, and yet her question was not counted as unbelief.
—Although Mary asked for no sign of the promise, the angel told her that Elisabeth had conceived in her old age.

I. INTRODUCTION

A. Position of Women

In the ancient world, women were regarded as subservient to men. This defined role of submission and second-class citizenship extended thousands of years back to the time of Abraham, when women were kept out of sight of other men and visitors to the home (Genesis 18:9). In this culture, the women did most of the work, which is reflected in the poem of the virtuous woman of Proverbs 31:10-31. While the poem is beautiful in its description, it really paints a graphic picture of the tireless work that faced women in the ancient world.

Jesus elevated the place and role of women in ministry, as did the apostle Paul, who was often supported by women and had them as part of his missionary teams (Acts 18:2, 18, 26; Romans 16:1; 1 Corinthians 16:19). Even in our contemporary world, God still chooses people that the world may have little, if any, confidence in to be vessels to be used by God. Mary's life took on eternal significance when God chose her to bear the Savior of the world.

B. Biblical Background

There are two accounts of the birth of Jesus Christ in the New Testament. The first is found in the gospel of Matthew (Matthew 1:18-25), and the second is found in the gospel of Luke (Luke 2:1-7). Together they give us a very good picture of the details surrounding the birth of the Promised Jewish Messiah. In Christian tradition, this event has come to be known as "The Annunciation." Luke's account of the birth of Jesus begins with the visit of the angel Gabriel to Mary, a young teenage girl living in the small village of Nazareth. Six months after Elisabeth had conceived in her old age, God sent Gabriel to Nazareth to inform Mary that she was going to have a baby and that this baby would be the Son of God. The Promised Messiah and heir to the throne of David would finally come forth. In this account, we are not told anything about Mary's family or their reaction to the news that she was pregnant and not married. Clearly, given the nature of that culture, it must have been an extremely heavy burden for Mary and her parents to bear.

Nazareth was located in the hill country of lower Galilee. For Christians, this is one of the holiest places on the earth, ranking second only to Bethlehem and Jerusalem. Today, the largest active Christian church in all of Israel is located in Nazareth and sits on top of the site believed to have been the home of Mary and Joseph.

II. EXPOSITION AND APPLICATION OF THE SCRIPTURE

A. The Messenger Sent
(Luke 1:26-29)

And in the sixth month the angel Gabriel was sent from God unto a city of Galilee, named Nazareth, To a virgin espoused to a man whose name was Joseph, of the house of David; and the virgin's name was Mary. And the angel came in unto her, and said, Hail, thou that art highly favoured, the Lord is with thee: blessed art thou among

women. And when she saw him, she was troubled at his saying, and cast in her mind what manner of salutation this should be.

Six months after visiting Elisabeth and Zacharias, Gabriel was sent to Nazareth, a small town in Galilee, to the home of a young virgin named Mary. Mary's family lived about eighty miles north of her cousin Elisabeth. Nazareth was not on a main road; it was a village that a person specifically had to be traveling to—not a village that a person would go through on the way to somewhere else.

We are told that Mary was engaged to be married to a young man named Joseph whose family were descendants of the same tribe as David (Matthew 1:18). Jewish marriages occurred in two stages. The first stage of engagement involved a formal agreement between the fathers that a wedding was to take place, and a settlement was made on the bride price. Deuteronomy 22:13-30 discusses the legal requirements of ancient Hebrew marriages. From the moment of the engagement, the couple was considered to be legally married. A year later, the groom would come to the home of the bride, and would take the bride to formally live with him (Matthew 25:1-13). Jewish women married at very early ages, usually in their early-to-mid teens.

Gabriel came to where Mary was located. There is a story told in Nazareth today that Mary received the news of the annunciation while she was drawing water from the local well. Gabriel's appearance no doubt startled Mary as he delivered God's message. There were three parts to the message: First, Gabriel told Mary that she was highly favored of the Lord. This literally means "to be graced by God." Mary had received God's abundant grace in ways she could not fully comprehend at that moment. This had come about due to God's own prerogative and providence, not because of anything she had done.

Second, Gabriel told her that the Lord was with her. This was a clear promise of protection. That God would be with one was one of the clearest evidences in the Old Testament of God's favor (Judges 6:15-17). Whatever Mary was about to face, it would not harm or overcome her. God would be her stronghold and sure foundation (Joshua 1:3-5; Psalm 27:1ff). Third, Mary was told that of all of the women on the earth she was the most blessed among them. "Thou that art highly favoured" (Luke 1:28) means that Mary received special grace, which was very uncommon. In the first century B.C., the messianic expectation was so very high that all women longed for the privilege to be the birth mother of the Messiah.

Mary did not seek or yearn for this privilege, yet God honored her. Mary's reaction was one of deep dread and fear. What was she to make of the announcement and the salutation? How could she understand what was happening? Remember, she had no idea that this was going to happen to her.

The appearance of Gabriel to Mary speaks to us about God's willingness to relate to human beings on a personal level. Although God is transcendent, He is near to each of us. These verses describe a God who relates to even those that the world seeks to marginalize. Women were not considered socially important in that day, yet God came to Mary in the presence of His angel and included her in His grand design of human redemption. God could have chosen a queen—someone who would have given high visibility to the birth, but Jesus came to the world in the womb of a lowly virgin from an out-of-the-way place in Galilee.

B. The Message Delivered
(Luke 1:30-33)

And the angel said unto her, Fear not, Mary: for thou hast found favour with God. And, behold, thou shalt conceive in thy womb, and bring forth a son, and shalt call his name Jesus. He shall be great, and shall be called the Son of the Highest: and the Lord God shall give unto him the throne of his father David: And he shall reign over the house of Jacob for ever; and of his kingdom there shall be no end.

Was Mary afraid? Yes—for several reasons. She was speaking face-to-face with what she must have thought was a strange man. This was something that was just not done in that culture. When she realized that Gabriel was an angel of the Lord, she was still afraid. After all, a woman speaking face-to-face with an angel was also highly unusual in ancient Hebrew history. Mary was told to "Fear not, Mary..." (verse 30). Who was this strange man who called her by name? Gabriel announced a second time that she had found favor with God (2 Samuel 15:25; Psalms 5:12; 30:7). At issue here was not Mary's particular piety; rather, the emphasis was on God's sovereignty.

There were several things that Gabriel told Mary that must have shaken her to the very foundations of her young life. This announcement would put her and her family in grave jeopardy, because to have a child outside of marriage in ancient Jewish culture was the ultimate form of personal disgrace. There were clearly defined penalties according to the Mosaic Law (see Deuteronomy 22:14ff). Typically, childlessness meant shame and pregnancy removed this disgrace, but the opposite was true for unmarried women. What in this period was more disgraceful than a pregnancy in one who, it was thought, ought to preserve her virginity until marriage? In the eyes of the community, Mary had violated the Law of God. But Mary experienced the miracle of conception without sexual intercourse. Mary was told that she would conceive in her womb (Isaiah 7:14). She would give birth to a Son and His name was to be Jesus, which means "the Lord is salvation." Who was this child who would be born of Mary? What would His life be like? First, there was the declaration of greatness. He would be great from the moment of His conception. God was and is the One who makes us great (Deuteronomy 8:18; 1 Chronicles 29:12-14; Psalm 75:6-7). Jesus would be the Son of the Highest, and God would give to Him the very throne of David. This referred to the Davidic Covenant in 2 Samuel 7:12-14, where God promised to make David's descendants into an everlasting kingdom and to establish his throne forever (Psalms 2:7; 89:27-29).

Here we have one of the greatest and most noble Christological pictures of Jesus Christ found anywhere in the New Testament. *Christological* means that which pertains to the person and work of Jesus Christ. It is a particularly powerful statement, because Gabriel announced that in Jesus, God would fulfill all of the promises made to Abraham and David regarding the establishment of a perpetual throne and kingdom. Through the seed of Abraham, every family on the earth would be blessed. But, these words went a step further than what first appeared and pointed to the inauguration of a new kingdom and covenant that would be fulfilled through the greatness of Jesus' sacrifice on the cross. Although this is not explicitly stated, it was at least implied. Let us take into account the angel of the Lord's message to Joseph that Mary's child's name would be Jesus, because He would save His people from their sins (Matthew 1:21).

One question that the text raises for us is this: How do we gain this kind of favor with God? How do we become the kind of people that God chooses to use in ways that defy even our feeble imaginations? There was nothing Mary did, nor was there some service she rendered, that earned her the right to be chosen to bear God's Son. God graciously chose her and still chooses whom He will, even today. All of us have been chosen by God for a special purpose. It may be that because we are looking for the dramatic, the simple assignments go undone, and hence our calling to greatness is lost. Greatness is not to be found in how many people know our names nor by the loftiness of our achievements, but it is found in the willingness to be a humble servant of the Lord. The greatest title that God can give to anyone is that of *servant* (see Joshua 1:1). We are reminded in the narrative that God is the One who exalts and raises us up. God can make one great, even though others may be committed to one's destruction.

C. The Method Explained
(Luke 1:34-38)

Then said Mary unto the angel, How shall this be, seeing I know not a man? And the angel answered and said unto her, The Holy Ghost shall come upon thee, and the power of the Highest shall overshadow thee: therefore also that holy thing which shall be born of thee shall be called the Son of God. And, behold, thy cousin Elisabeth, she hath also conceived a son in her old age: and this is the sixth month with her, who was called barren. For with God nothing shall be impossible. And Mary said, Behold the handmaid of the Lord; be it unto me according to thy word. And the angel departed from her.

Mary accepted the news from the angel, but she wanted to know how something of this nature was going to be possible. She had never

even been with a man in private, let alone had sexual relations with one. How could this be? In Zacharias' experience, he wanted a sign from God specifying how he would know if what Gabriel had told him was true. Mary sought no such sign; her response was clearly faith in motion. Doubt was not present—just the need to know more about what was going to happen. This was a model of faith, even though Mary did not fully understand.

Gabriel answered Mary's question by telling her that the power of the Holy Spirit would come upon her and overshadow her. Here we face one of the greatest mysteries of God. How did Mary conceive or become pregnant by the Holy Spirit? For certain, it was not through some form of divine intercourse. Rather, it was the power of God miraculously embedding in her the seed of His own personhood, taking up residence as an embryo to be carried to full term. And it would be in the fullness of time that Jesus would come forth (see Galatians 4:4). Any further explanations regarding the Virgin Birth become more than our feeble minds can explain or understand. What was in her womb was holy and was the very Son of God.

The miracle of Mary's pregnancy was highlighted against the backdrop of her cousin Elisabeth's pregnancy. Elisabeth was an older woman who was well past child-bearing age. Her barrenness had been turned into joy. Elisabeth was six months pregnant at the time of the annunciation to Mary. God can do anything, and nothing was or is too hard for Him (Genesis 18:14; Jeremiah 32:27). Mary presented herself to God to be used in His service. Mary's words are among the most submissive, yet strong words of commitment found in the Scriptures: "Behold the handmaid of the Lord; be it unto to me according to thy word" (verse 38). With that statement, Mary submitted herself to fulfilling God's plan for her life. Gabriel departed and returned to the presence of the Lord.

III. CONCLUDING REFLECTIONS

This lesson brings to a close the second week in the season of Advent. In this lesson, we see an image of God who refused to remain cut off from the brokenness and sin of the human condition. Rather than come into the world with pomp and majesty, He chose the most humble of ways and the least likely candidate to fulfill His plan. Here, we have the foundation of the Incarnation and the centerpiece of the Christian church's faith in the redemptive plan of God. Jesus Christ came into the world through the Virgin Birth. "The Word became flesh and lived among us..." (John 1:14). Our task is to make Him live continuously through us by submitting to the leadership and will of the Father.

PRAYER

Heavenly Father, thank You for the demonstration of faithfulness and trust that we saw in Mary. May we, like her, be willing to submit ourselves to You for the greater works promised by Your Son, Jesus Christ. Forgive us for not trusting You and serving You with our whole hearts. In the name of Jesus Christ, we pray. Amen.

WORD POWER

Impossible *(adunate)*—this means that it is impossible for any word from God to be either without power or void of power. The angel brought the Good News to Mary and told her that the word from God would not be void of power. All of us can count on God, for He has spoken peace, and no power can reverse His Word.

HOME DAILY BIBLE READINGS
(December 3-9, 2007)

Called to Be a Vessel

MONDAY, December 3: "God's Wondrous Deeds" (Psalm 40:1–5)

TUESDAY, December 4: "An Unexpected Visitor" (Luke 1:26–29)

WEDNESDAY, December 5: "Mary's Son's Future" (Luke 1:30–33)

THURSDAY, December 6: "The Miraculous Conception" (Luke 1:34–35)

FRIDAY, December 7: "Nothing Is Impossible!" (Luke 1:36–38)

SATURDAY, December 8: "Elisabeth Blesses Mary" (Luke 1:39–45)

SUNDAY, December 9: "Mary Sings to the Lord" (Luke 1:46–56)

LESSON 3   December 16, 2007

CALLED TO PROCLAIM

DEVOTIONAL READING: **Malachi 3:1-4**   BACKGROUND SCRIPTURE: **Luke 1:57-80**
PRINT PASSAGE: **Luke 1:67-80**   KEY VERSE: **Luke 1:64**

Luke 1:67-80—KJV

67 And his father Zacharias was filled with the Holy Ghost, and prophesied, saying,
68 Blessed be the Lord God of Israel; for he hath visited and redeemed his people,
69 And hath raised up an horn of salvation for us in the house of his servant David;
70 As he spake by the mouth of his holy prophets, which have been since the world began:
71 That we should be saved from our enemies, and from the hand of all that hate us;
72 To perform the mercy promised to our fathers, and to remember his holy covenant;
73 The oath which he sware to our father Abraham,
74 That he would grant unto us, that we being delivered out of the hand of our enemies might serve him without fear,
75 In holiness and righteousness before him, all the days of our life.
76 And thou, child, shalt be called the prophet of the Highest: for thou shalt go before the face of the Lord to prepare his ways;
77 To give knowledge of salvation unto his people by the remission of their sins,
78 Through the tender mercy of our God; whereby the dayspring from on high hath visited us,
79 To give light to them that sit in darkness and in the shadow of death, to guide our feet into the way of peace.
80 And the child grew, and waxed strong in spirit, and was in the deserts till the day of his shewing unto Israel.

Luke 1:67-80—NRSV

67 Then his father Zechariah was filled with the Holy Spirit and spoke this prophecy:
68 "Blessed be the Lord God of Israel, for he has looked favorably on his people and redeemed them.
69 He has raised up a mighty savior for us in the house of his servant David,
70 as he spoke through the mouth of his holy prophets from of old,
71 that we would be saved from our enemies and from the hand of all who hate us.
72 Thus he has shown the mercy promised to our ancestors, and has remembered his holy covenant,
73 the oath that he swore to our ancestor Abraham, to grant us
74 that we, being rescued from the hands of our enemies, might serve him without fear,
75 in holiness and righteousness before him all our days.
76 And you, child, will be called the prophet of the Most High; for you will go before the Lord to prepare his ways,
77 to give knowledge of salvation to his people by the forgiveness of their sins.
78 By the tender mercy of our God, the dawn from on high will break upon us,
79 to give light to those who sit in darkness and in the shadow of death, to guide our feet into the way of peace."
80 The child grew and became strong in spirit, and he was in the wilderness until the day he appeared publicly to Israel.

BIBLE FACT

Luke, a physician, also wrote the book of Acts. He was a close associate of the apostle Paul and the only Gentile New Testament author. This prophetic hymn of Zechariah is known as the "Benedictus," which comes from its opening word in the Latin translation.

UNIFYING LESSON PRINCIPLE

We often talk about experiences that change us. What differences do these transforming events make in how we live? At John's birth, Zacharias proclaimed the vision of God's future for his son, John, who would prepare people for the coming of the Messiah.

TOPICAL OUTLINE OF THE LESSON

I. Introduction
   A. Zacharias and the Birth of John
   B. Biblical Background

II. Exposition and Application of the Scripture
   A. Horn of Salvation (Luke 1:67-70)
   B. Holy Covenant (Luke 1:71-75)
   C. Hallowed Mission (Luke 1:76-80)

III. Concluding Reflections

LESSON OBJECTIVES

Upon completion of this lesson, the students will know that:

1. God has ways by which He transforms our lives to fulfill our calling if we are responsive to His will;
2. Parents are endowed with the responsibility of helping their children to grow in the admonition and fear of the Lord; and,
3. Unaccomplished missions stem from misguided lives.

POINTS TO BE EMPHASIZED
ADULT/YOUTH

Adult Topic: Life-Changing Events
Youth Topic: Called to Spread the Word
Adult Key Verse: Luke 1:64
Youth Key Verse: Luke 1:76
Print Passage: Luke 1:67-80

—God is praised for the fulfillment of the people's hopes.
—John the Baptist's role as a preacher of repentance is predicted.
—Some scholars suggest that the gospel writer has Luke 3:1-6 in mind as the "day he [John] appeared publicly" (verse 80).
—Immediately after his response of faithfulness, Zacharias' voice returned.
—Zacharias, once unable to speak because of his doubt, was enabled by the Holy Spirit to speak of things no one could know by human insight.

CHILDREN

Children Topic: Preparing for God's Messenger
Key Verse: Luke 1:76
Print Passage: Luke 1:57-67, 76-77, 80

—The circumstances of John's birth had already begun to turn people's attention to something great that God was doing.
—The neighbors and relatives assumed that tradition would hold in the naming of the baby.
—Elisabeth was the first to shatter the preconceived ideas of "business as usual" by stating emphatically that the baby was to be called John.
—The first thing Zacharias did when he regained his voice was to praise God, proclaim what the Lord was going to do, and tell what John's role would be.

I. INTRODUCTION

A. Zacharias and the Birth of John

Again, we are reminded of the theme of Advent, which is preparation for the celebration of the coming of the Messiah. After John was born, Zacharias announced to all who were present at his naming ceremony that his son had been born for a divine purpose. You may be one of those Christians still trying to understand what your purpose in life is supposed to be. Zacharias' prophecy will help us see that the ultimate aim of God is the salvation of the world. The birth of John changed life forever in ancient Judea. His preaching sparked the beginning of a major revival in Israel. May this season of the year spark a time of revival and spiritual renewal in your life and church. Our purpose is the same as that of John: to make ready a people prepared for the Lord Jesus Christ.

B. Biblical Background

Elisabeth had no complications with her pregnancy. After the departure of Mary back to Nazareth, she continued to wait for the day of her delivery. When she reached the ninth month and the appointed day, she gave birth to a son, just as the angel Gabriel had promised. The aged woman who had been barren, and broken in spirit because of it, did the improbable—she gave birth. The birth of this son was met with great rejoicing by Elisabeth's neighbors, cousins, and extended family.

In that culture, the family and friends would gather for a naming ritual, which included the act of circumcision of all Jewish males on the eighth day (see Genesis 17:10-12; Leviticus 12:3; Philippians 3:5). In the Old Testament, the normal time to name a child appears to have been at birth (Genesis 4:1; 25:25-26; 29:32-35). The family wanted to call the baby Zacharias after his father, but Elisabeth said that his name was John. The family and neighbors wanted to know where she got that name, because no one in her family had that name. They appealed to Zacharias and wanted to know what he wanted to call the child. He asked for a writing tablet and wrote that his name would be John. The family and friends marveled, and instantly the tongue of Zacharias was loosed and he was filled with the Holy Spirit. He began to prophesy regarding the role that John would play in God's redemptive plan.

II. EXPOSITION AND APPLICATION OF THE SCRIPTURE

A. Horn of Salvation
(Luke 1:67-70)

And his father Zacharias was filled with the Holy Ghost, and prophesied, saying, Blessed be the Lord God of Israel; for he hath visited and redeemed his people, And hath raised up an horn of salvation for us in the house of his servant David; As he spake by the mouth of his holy prophets, which have been since the world began.

When Zacharias' speech was restored, the Holy Spirit filled his mouth with words of prophecy. At that very moment, the power of the Holy Spirit overshadowed Zacharias and he spoke God's Word (Acts 4:8, 31; 9:17; 13:9). What does it mean to prophesy? It literally means to speak for God, to serve as the mouthpiece of the Creator.

Zacharias began by pronouncing a blessing upon the God of Israel. The Greek word for blessed is *eugolgetos*–eulogy. It literally means to speak well of someone or to offer words of praise and celebration. In the New Testament, this word is used only in reference to God (Ephesians 1:3; 1 Peter 1:3). Why is God to be praised? God is to be praised because of what He does for His people. God is to be praised because He has visited His people. God came to ransom them from the power and presence of sin. Zacharias knew that in the coming of John, God was about to raise up a prophet the likes of which had not been in Israel in hundreds of years. God had not just come, but He had come for a purpose.

The prophetic words of Zacharias were filled with messianic overtones. God had raised up a horn of salvation. *Horn* means "strength" and "courage." In the ancient world and even now, it was and is believed that the strength and courage of animals reside in their horns. Hence, the coming of God in human flesh was and is described as the "horn of salvation." God had raised up someone who was filled with power, courage, and strength to bring salvation to His people (Matthew 1:21).

Jesus Christ became the means by which the redemptive plan of God was brought to completion (see John 1:14; 1 Corinthians 5:18-19). The coming of Jesus Christ into the world was the final piece in the redemptive plan of God to overthrow the powers of spiritual wickedness and darkness (John 1:4-5). Jesus

Christ became sin for the sins of every human being from the beginning of time (Romans 8:3; 1 Corinthians 5:21). In Him, the very righteousness of God was revealed. Zacharias was aware that God was sending a Messiah, because Mary had visited with them and in those three months of sharing together, he must have learned of the intention of God to bring to pass every prophetic word regarding the salvation of His people.

The coming of Jesus Christ was in fulfillment of the promises made to David that God would raise up a King after him whose throne would be established forever (see 2 Samuel 7:12-14). Within Israel there developed the belief in a coming King-Messiah who would be a son of David. The prophet Nathan announced to David that God had heard the desires of his heart to build a temple in His honor. However, David would not be permitted to do it, but his heir would build the temple and would occupy the throne of Jerusalem forever (see 2 Samuel 7:1-17); (verses 12-16 are known as the Davidic Covenant). After the time of David, all of the prophets interpreted the covenant between God and David in messianic overtones (Isaiah 11:1,10; Jeremiah 5:2-5; 23:5; 33:15,17, 22; Zechariah 12:8). David was the ideal king. He had been chosen by God to lead His people over his other brothers. He was not the oldest, tallest, nor what some would consider the brightest, but he was God's choice, and that made all the difference in the world.

Finally, the Messiah was the One spoken about by the holy prophets. These were men who had been set apart and were dedicated to the preaching of the Word of God. Their proclamations had been going on since the world began. At long last, the head of the Serpent (the devil) would be bruised by the One whom God was sending (Genesis 3:15).

God's people must see that the purpose of the Messiah's coming was to save the world from its sins. As we move toward the celebration of the birth of Christ, it is critical to keep in mind that in Jesus Christ, God did for us what we cannot do for ourselves. He has saved us and qualified us for heaven. There is nothing that we can do to effect our own salvation (see Ephesians 2:8-10). Just as Abraham was saved by faith, so are we.

B. Holy Covenant
(Luke 1:71-75)

That we should be saved from our enemies, and from the hand of all that hate us; To perform the mercy promised to our fathers, and to remember his holy covenant; The oath which he sware to our father Abraham, That he would grant unto us, that we being delivered out of the hand of our enemies might serve him without fear, In holiness and righteousness before him, all the days of our life.

At the time of Zacharias' prophesy, Rome dominated Israel. Israel had not enjoyed true independence since 63 B.C. when the Romans under Julius Caesar conquered Syria and took Judea as one of its prizes. There were real expectations that the Messiah would conquer their enemies and restore the kingdom of Israel to the golden age of Davidic rule and prosperity. Israel was surrounded by historical enemies who wanted to see them destroyed. But God had preserved them as a remnant because of the promise made to Abraham and David. However, there was a deeper meaning to the work of the Messiah as Savior. He would save the world from its arch-enemy who was and is Satan. The Messiah's coming would fulfill the promises made to the patriarchs. He would stand as witness that the covenant relationship between God and Abraham had been honored. God had made a covenant with Abraham that

He would bless him and his descendants. The covenant between God and Israel became the basis upon which the promises stood. Israel was called upon to obey and keep the commandments of God and the word of the covenant; thereby they would become a special people to God (Exodus 19:1-7; Deuteronomy 6:1-8). Through Abraham and his seed, all of the families of the earth would be blessed (Genesis 12:1-5; 15:1-7; 17:1-8). This blessing came in the person of Jesus Christ. Abraham became the father of all of the faithful because of his unfailing trust in God and His promises. It was Abraham's faith that made him righteous in the eyes of God (Romans 4:1-25; Galatians 3:17; Hebrews 11:8).

The Messiah came to deliver Israel out of the hands of her enemies. The purpose for this deliverance is stated in the words to "serve him without fear." The word *serve* (Greek: *latreuo)* is instructive because it literally means to render some sort of religious service or to worship. God's people would be empowered through the Messiah to serve God without intimidation and fear. The service would be performed in holiness and righteousness. Holiness (Greek: *hosiotes),* in this instance, refers to personal piety or full consecration. Piety has to do with an individual's lifestyle. Deliverance and salvation from sin are for the purpose of living a pious lifestyle. Believers are called to live above and beyond the world. The Messiah empowers us to live just this way (see Ephesians 4:24; 1 Thessalonians 4:1; 2 Thessalonians 2:13; 2 Timothy 1:9). Righteousness is the result of our new lives in Christ. The power of God to save is revealed in the preaching of the gospel of salvation which came through Jesus Christ (see Romans 1:16-17).

Boldness, courage, commitment, piety, and determination are all words that should describe the believers of this generation. We stand at a point in time when we have seen all that God has done. Therefore, our worship and service should never be halfhearted or lethargic. Personal piety and the road to spiritual formation are not areas of deep concern in many congregations today. Hence, we are rearing a generation of believers rooted in the need to achieve personal satisfaction through personal gain. Zacharias reminds us that the Messiah's coming was for God's purpose of salvation.

C. Hallowed Mission
(Luke 1:76-80)

And thou, child, shalt be called the prophet of the Highest: for thou shalt go before the face of the Lord to prepare his ways; To give knowledge of salvation unto his people by the remission of their sins, Through the tender mercy of our God; whereby the dayspring from on high hath visited us, To give light to them that sit in darkness and in the shadow of death, to guide our feet into the way of peace. And the child grew, and waxed strong in spirit, and was in the deserts till the day of his shewing unto Israel.

Zacharias returned to speaking about John's mission. John would be the prophet of the Highest. He was born for one purpose only and that was to prepare the way of the Messiah (Isaiah 40:1; Malachi 3:1). He would be a voice crying in the wilderness, preparing the way of the Lord (Luke 3:3-6). John's mission was specific. He was not a miracle worker, nor was he called to raise up a new community of believers. Simply put, he was called to prepare, through preaching, the way for the coming of Jesus Christ.

John's preaching would be about salvation. He would give the people knowledge about the coming Messiah. His preaching was directed to all of the people of God. For all of them needed salvation (Romans 10:1-17). The word *remission* means "to release" or "to set free." John's preaching would highlight God's commitment to freeing His people from sin, which would reach its fullness in the sacrificial death of Jesus (1 Corinthians 15:1-4; Ephesians 1:7).

Zacharias stated that the salvation that John would preach about would come through the tender mercy of God. God's compassion and love surpasses human understanding. He loves us in spite of our tendencies to rebel and disobey. One of the attributes of the nature of God is His mercy (Psalms 103:1-9; 107:1-2).

The use of the word *dayspring* is a reference to the coming of the Messiah (see Numbers 24:17; Malachi 4:2). The Greek word *anatole* (dayspring) literally means "that which springs up." This Greek word was also used to translate the Hebrew word for "branch," or "sprout," which was a concept with messianic overtones (see Isaiah 11:1-10; Malachi 4:2). For instance, the prophet Malachi foretold of one like a Sun of Righteousness who would come with healing in his wings. Within this context, the word clearly was a reference to Jesus Christ as the Light of the World (see John 8:12; 9:5). Why is there a need for the light of the Messiah? Human beings are sitting in darkness and face the grim prospect of death. In Jesus Christ, God brought both life and light. The world needs the message of the Gospel. There are people who have never heard the Gospel of Jesus Christ. There may be people in our congregations who have made a commitment to come to a local church but have never come to salvation in Jesus Christ. This Christmas season might be the perfect time to introduce them to the Dayspring of eternal life.

The passage closes with a postscript about the life and ministry of John. He grew physically and spiritually. He went and lived in the Judean desert or wilderness until the day when he began preaching the repentance and remission of sins.

III. CONCLUDING REFLECTIONS

Today we take another step closer to the celebration of Christmas. This lesson has reminded us that the primary purpose for which Christ came into the world was to save human beings from their sins. Take the time this holiday season to remind someone you care about that Jesus Christ has made it possible for us to walk in the light of life.

PRAYER

Heavenly Father, in whose hands are the deep places of the earth, thank You for loving insignificant people like us and for forgiving us. We are thankful for Your tender mercies, which are new every day. May we remember that Jesus Christ is the reason that we celebrate this season of the year. In His name, we pray. Amen.

WORD POWER

Immediately (Greek: *parachrema*)—this means "instantly," "forthwith." This word occurs nineteen times in the New Testament and seventeen times in the gospel of Luke. Thirteen of the times the word is mentioned in the gospel of Luke are in connection with the miracle of healing. The healing of Zacharias was instantaneous. He could speak normally. This was the reason why the people marveled when Zacharias spoke after nine months.

HOME DAILY BIBLE READINGS
(December 10-16, 2007)
Called to Proclaim
MONDAY, December 10: "A Messenger Is Coming" (Malachi 3:1–4)
TUESDAY, December 11: "Elisabeth Births a Son" (Luke 1:57–61)
WEDNESDAY, December 12: "His Name Is John" (Luke 1:62–66)
THURSDAY, December 13: "God Sends a Powerful Savior" (Luke 1:67–75)
FRIDAY, December 14: "Preparing the Way" (Luke 1:76–80)
SATURDAY, December 15: "Warnings to the Crowds" (Luke 3:7–14)
SUNDAY, December 16: "A Powerful One Is Coming" (Luke 3:15–20)

LESSON 4 December 23, 2007

CALLED TO REJOICE

DEVOTIONAL READING: **Psalm 96:1-6**
PRINT PASSAGE: **Luke 2:1-14**

BACKGROUND SCRIPTURE: **Luke 2:1-20**
KEY VERSE: **Luke 2:11**

Luke 2:1-14—KJV

AND IT came to pass in those days, that there went out a decree from Caesar Augustus, that all the world should be taxed.

2 (And this taxing was first made when Cyrenius was governor of Syria.)

3 And all went to be taxed, every one into his own city.

4 And Joseph also went up from Galilee, out of the city of Nazareth, into Judaea, unto the city of David, which is called Bethlehem; (because he was of the house and lineage of David:)

5 To be taxed with Mary his espoused wife, being great with child.

6 And so it was, that, while they were there, the days were accomplished that she should be delivered.

7 And she brought forth her firstborn son, and wrapped him in swaddling clothes, and laid him in a manger; because there was no room for them in the inn.

8 And there were in the same country shepherds abiding in the field, keeping watch over their flock by night.

9 And, lo, the angel of the Lord came upon them, and the glory of the Lord shone round about them: and they were sore afraid.

10 And the angel said unto them, Fear not: for, behold, I bring you good tidings of great joy, which shall be to all people.

11 For unto you is born this day in the city of David a Saviour, which is Christ the Lord.

12 And this shall be a sign unto you; Ye shall find the babe wrapped in swaddling clothes, lying in a manger.

13 And suddenly there was with the angel a multitude of the heavenly host praising God, and saying,

14 Glory to God in the highest, and on earth peace, good will toward men.

Luke 2:1-14—NRSV

IN THOSE days a decree went out from Emperor Augustus that all the world should be registered.

2 This was the first registration and was taken while Quirinius was governor of Syria.

3 All went to their own towns to be registered.

4 Joseph also went from the town of Nazareth in Galilee to Judea, to the city of David called Bethlehem, because he was descended from the house and family of David.

5 He went to be registered with Mary, to whom he was engaged and who was expecting a child.

6 While they were there, the time came for her to deliver her child.

7 And she gave birth to her firstborn son and wrapped him in bands of cloth, and laid him in a manger, because there was no place for them in the inn.

8 In that region there were shepherds living in the fields, keeping watch over their flock by night.

9 Then an angel of the Lord stood before them, and the glory of the Lord shone around them, and they were terrified.

10 But the angel said to them, "Do not be afraid; for see—I am bringing you good news of great joy for all the people:

11 to you is born this day in the city of David a Savior, who is the Messiah, the Lord.

12 This will be a sign for you: you will find a child wrapped in bands of cloth and lying in a manger."

13 And suddenly there was with the angel a multitude of the heavenly host, praising God and saying,

14 "Glory to God in the highest heaven, and on earth peace among those whom he favors!"

UNIFYING LESSON PRINCIPLE

Everyone looks for reasons to rejoice. How can we rejoice in the midst of all that life brings? The shepherds, whose lives were hard and who were often disparaged, received the announcement of God's fulfilled promise of the Messiah and declared their joy to all.

TOPICAL OUTLINE OF THE LESSON

I. Introduction
   A. Christmas
   B. Biblical Background

II. Exposition and Application of the Scripture
   A. Preparation for the Birth (Luke 2:1-7)
   B. Declaration of the Birth (Luke 2:8-12)
   C. Exultation Because of the Birth of Christ (Luke 2:13-14)

III. Concluding Reflections

LESSON OBJECTIVES

Upon completion of this lesson, the students will know that:

1. God can use anybody to carry out His purpose;
2. No one is outside the scope of God's infinite love; and,
3. Messengers have come and gone, but the message is still the same—Jesus is Lord.

POINTS TO BE EMPHASIZED

ADULT/YOUTH

Adult Topic: **Reasons to Rejoice**
Youth Topic: **Called to Greet the Messiah**
Adult Key Verse: **Luke 2:11**
Youth Key Verse: **Luke 2:10**
Print Passage: **Luke 2:1-14**

—Why is the City of David so important to the story of Jesus' birth?
—Caesar Augustus ruled from 27 B.C. to A.D. 14.
—In Luke's account of Jesus' birth, God's concern for those who were poor or oppressed is demonstrated in both the birth of Jesus and in the announcement to the shepherds.
—The announcement of the angel communicates a particular Christology, a way to understand God's work in Jesus Christ as the Messiah, who would usher in the reign of God.
—The first announcement of Jesus' birth came to shepherds who were despised by the socially elite people of the day.

CHILDREN

Children Topic: **Rejoicing About the Good News**
Key Verse: **Luke 2:20**
Print Passage: **Luke 2:1-14**

—Luke presents the account of Jesus' birth in a matter-of-fact manner similar to a brief news report.
—With the entry of the shepherds and angels, Luke adds contrasting emotions.
—One angel wasn't enough for this divine announcement; it required a multitude of the heavenly host.
—Humble, lowly shepherds received a message and a concert fit for royalty.
—The shepherds did not keep their story a secret, nor contain their joy.

I. INTRODUCTION

A. Christmas

For Christians, Christmas is the celebration of the coming of our Savior and Lord in human form. Yet this time of the year means many different things to many different people. For some, the season is too sad and too depressing for them to remember that it is a season of joy.

The celebration of Christmas is not an occasion that we should take lightly, because it is deeply rooted in the fabric of our faith. The celebration of Christmas goes back nearly 1700 years to the mid-fourth century, when it was first declared to be a holy day by the Western church.

In the year of our Lord's birth, no one thought much of Mary or Joseph, two lowly, insignificant peasants from Nazareth. Who cared about another pregnant Jewish girl? Why would anyone want to give up his or her room at the inn for a young family with no clout? Mary and Joseph went to Bethlehem to register and pay their taxes, and, while they were there, the greatest of all miracles took place.

B. Biblical Background

The coming of Christ into the world was not by chance. His coming was under the strategic timing and providential will of God. His birth was not one day before or behind the appointed time. God decided the fulness of time for the coming of Christ (see Galatians 4:4). The world had fully been prepared for His coming. There were five factors that paved the way for the birth of Jesus Christ at that appointed time.

First, the Jewish religion had given the world monotheism, or the belief in one God; this was rooted in revelation and personal experience. The Jews had a deep sense of righteousness and holiness that was not found in any other religious system. Their prophets foretold of the coming One who would right the wrongs of sin and usher in a new kingdom of peace and prosperity (see Isaiah 11:6; 65:25).

Second, the people of the world were spiritually starved. The worship of idol gods, self, pleasure, and philosophical ethics had left many people empty, void of meaning, and barren.

Third, the world was at peace under Roman rule. The world was an open door for the spread of the Gospel—without any restraint. The *Pax Romana,* or the peace of Rome throughout the provinces, made it easier to spread good news.

Fourth, the world spoke Greek as a basic language. The Greek language was the *Lingua Franca* (common language) of that day. The conquest of Alexander the Great had given the world a common language and culture.

Fifth, the Roman road network allowed Christian missionaries to reach the farthest parts of the Roman Empire. It also brought commercial travelers to metropolitan centers, where Christian believers were concentrated.

II. EXPOSITION AND APPLICATION OF THE SCRIPTURE

A. Preparation for the Birth
(Luke 2:1-7)

AND IT came to pass in those days, that there went out a decree from Caesar Augustus, that all the world should be taxed. (And this taxing was first made when Cyrenius was governor of Syria.) And all went to be taxed, every one into his own city. And Joseph also went up from Galilee, out of the city of Nazareth, into Judaea, unto the city of David, which is called Bethlehem; (because he was of the house and lineage of David:) To be taxed with Mary his espoused wife, being great with child. And so it was, that, while they were there, the days were accomplished that she should be delivered. And she brought forth her firstborn son, and wrapped him in swaddling clothes, and laid him in a manger; because there was no room for them in the inn.

Luke stated that the birth of the Messiah came about at a decisive point in history. Caesar Augustus, ruler of the Roman Empire, had issued an official edict that required everyone in the kingdom to go to their ancestral homelands and register to be taxed. This registration first occurred when Cyrenius or Quirinius was governor of the Roman province of Syria. The kingdom of Judea was under this provincial Roman ruler. Herod was the Judean king who served at the pleasure of Caesar Augustus. The Romans would sometimes permit their subjects to live under their own rulers, and, hence, Herod's kingship.

Joseph and Mary left Nazareth, probably joining others on the road that led from Galilee to Judea. Luke reported that they went up from Galilee. There would have been large bands of pilgrims who would have been traveling back to their homelands. Travel to Bethlehem and Jerusalem always meant going up, because of their height of nearly 2,500 feet above sea level. Joseph was from Bethlehem, six miles south of Jerusalem (see 1 Samuel 16:1-4). Bethlehem was an old city with an ancient history. Rachel, the beloved wife of Jacob, died in Bethlehem and was buried there (Genesis 35:9). Naomi and Ruth returned to Bethlehem when their husbands died (Ruth 1:9). Bethlehem was the place that had been prophesied as the birthplace of the Messiah, and because it was Jesus' birthplace, it was and is the second most important city to Christians, after Jerusalem. The modern city of Bethlehem borders West Jerusalem.

Mary was in the final trimester of her pregnancy. She could deliver her baby at any time. Luke wrote in his account of the birth of Jesus Christ that when the days were accomplished that she should be delivered, Mary gave birth to her firstborn Son, wrapped Him in swaddling clothes, and laid Him in a manger because there was no room for them in the inn. "Swaddling" bands consisted of cloths tied together in bandage-like strips. After an infant was born, the umbilical cord was cut and tied, then the baby was washed, rubbed with salt, and wrapped with strips of cloth (Ezekiel 16:4). The manger was the eating trough of farm animals. It was not some comfortable rocker that is often depicted in paintings and on Christmas cards.

There are several reasons why there may not have been room for Joseph and Mary in the small inn at Bethlehem. First, there was a general census being taken and the inn was no doubt filled with Roman government workers and registrars. Second, the couple might have simply arrived too late to get a room. After all, Mary was pregnant and could not move as fast as Joseph. Third, it may be that Joseph and Mary were simply not affluent enough to demand and warrant a room or special consideration. They simply had to stay where the animals were kept.

B. Declaration of the Birth
(Luke 2:8-12)

And there were in the same country shepherds abiding in the field, keeping watch over their flock by night. And, lo, the angel of the Lord came upon them, and the glory of the Lord shone round about them: and they were sore afraid. And the angel said unto them, Fear not: for, behold, I bring you good tidings of great joy, which shall be to all people. For unto you is born this day in the city of David a Saviour, which is Christ the Lord. And this shall be a sign unto you; Ye shall find the babe wrapped in swaddling clothes, lying in a manger.

Just outside of Bethlehem is an area known as the "Shepherds' Fields." This site is believed to be the area where the angel of the Lord first appeared and gave the shepherds the Good News about the birth of Jesus Christ. In the evening, shepherds would secure their flocks in a sheepfold so that it was easier to keep watch over them. There were probably several shepherds gathered in this area because of its suitability for grazing. The job of a shepherd was not glamorous, and was often ranked as one of the most despised occupations in Israel. Shepherds were lowly people who were not highly regarded.

While they were watching the sheep, an angel of the Lord appeared out of nowhere. There was a brightness that lit up the night sky. This was a divine appearance. The shepherds were gripped by fear because they had never seen anything like this. We are not told the name of the angel who appeared to them, for that is not important. What is important is the message the angel gave them: "Fear not: for, behold, I bring you good tidings of great joy" (verse 10). The words *good tidings* mean "good news" or "gospel." The shepherds, being outsiders, had no idea what this good news was. They were not among the religious elite, exposed to the teachings of the prophets and living with a great messianic hope and awareness. This news was not just for them, but was for all people everywhere.

God had come into the world in the form of a little baby. "Born this day" (verse 11), indicates that what they were hearing about was happening at that very moment. They were just outside of the ancient city of Bethlehem on the hills surrounding the city. Bethlehem was and is called the City of David because it was the place of his birth and early childhood.

What was the news? It was that a Savior had been born. Human beings were lost in sin, and God sent a Savior who would rescue the world from sin's grip. This Savior was Christ the Lord. The word *Christ* comes from the Hebrew root word *Messiah,* and it literally means "anointed one." The word *Christ* is really the title for the office of the Messiah. It was not, as it is commonly used today, a proper name for Jesus of Nazareth. Throughout the New Testament, Jesus is repeatedly referred to as "the Christ" (see Matthew 16:16; Mark 8:29; Luke 9:20; Acts 2:36; 17:3). While visiting Caesarea Philippi, Jesus asked His disciples a question: "But whom say ye that I am?" (Matthew 16:15). Peter responded by saying, "Thou art the Christ, the Son of the living God" (Matthew 16:16b). There was a belief that developed sometime during the Inter-testamental period that the coming of the Messiah would be preceded by either Elijah or one of the prophets. Some thought that it might be Jeremiah or one of the others. However, the One who was born was both Christ and Lord.

The angel told the shepherds how they would know this particular baby. They were given a sign. They would find the babe wrapped in swaddling clothes and lying in a manger. Bethlehem was not a very large city, and it would not be hard to find a newborn in the city, especially one who was lying in a manger. It certainly would be easy to identify the babe given the very clear description of what to look for. This was the second time that swaddling clothes and a manger were mentioned. This heightened the humility surrounding the birth of the Lord Jesus Christ.

God came into the world, but He did not reveal Himself first to the religious leaders. Neither did He present Himself to the Sadducees, the men who supervised the temple, nor to the Pharisees, the most pious among the people, nor to the Scribes. The most highly educated among them knew that Jesus had been born. They had studied the prophets and knew all of the details and traditions surrounding the appearance of the Messiah, yet when He was born, none of them were there. The lowly and despised shepherds were the first to receive the news. How ironic that in the city of David, shepherds would be the first to see and worship the Savior of the world. This Good News was for everyone, including the shepherds. Please note the three titles of the Babe: *Savior, Christ,* and *Lord.* These three titles together summarize the saving work of Jesus and His sovereign position. The word *Christ* means "Anointed." This title refers to the royal messianic position. The word *Lord* was the title for "ruler" and the one who had dominion over everything.

In many traditional nativity scenes, there are shepherds with sheep along with three royally dressed wise men or magi, camels and donkeys and other farm animals. The reality is that none of the wise men is mentioned in the text, and it is highly unlikely that any of these men were present in this stable after Christ was born.

What is the message of Christmas for this generation? It is that the Gospel is for everyone. The world still needs to hear this eternal word—that God was in Christ, reconciling the world unto Himself. In Him, the world has been brought near by the blood of Christ. The challenge is to look beyond the fluff of the holidays and see the Savior of sinners.

C. Exultation Because of the Birth of Christ (Luke 2:13-14)

And suddenly there was with the angel a multitude of the heavenly host praising God, and saying, Glory to God in the highest, and on earth peace, good will toward men.

While the angel was speaking, there appeared a multitude of angels praising God for the birth of the Messiah. They were angels who had never sinned and required no Savior. In Jesus Christ, heaven and earth would now be reconciled, and the breach brought on by the rebellion of Adam and Eve would be healed. Their praise came in a threefold declaration of praise. First was the call to give God the highest glory. *Glory* means brightness or to shine. God's mercy, grace, and love all shone in the birth of Jesus Christ. Second, the birth of Jesus brought peace to the earth. The world would no longer be at odds or enmity with God (see Romans 5:6-8). Rome gave the world peace through its military, but it could not give peace to troubled hearts and disturbed minds. God in Christ has given the world peace. Third, many New Testament scholars believe that the words "good will toward men" (verse 14) would have been better represented by the words "men in whom He takes pleasure." The world experienced the peace of God because it was God's good pleasure to give humankind His peace. Christmas reminds us that God is to be praised because of what He has given to the world in Jesus Christ—peace, life, and hope.

III. CONCLUDING REFLECTIONS

This lesson reminds us that God often uses people who are the least likely to be selected. Mary and Joseph were virtual nobodies in Israel. No one had ever heard of them, but God chose them to be the means by which a new kingdom of grace would be brought to pass. In them, God showed the world that He could and does choose based upon His own criteria. Likewise, the fact that the shepherds received the Good News first points to the fact of God's willingness to use people who are social rejects and exalt them to the status of first earthly witnesses of the incarnation of the Son of God.

PRAYER

Heavenly Father, thank You for including the least of the earth in the divine plan of human redemption. Your grace and mercy know no limits. Thank You for sending Jesus Christ into the world in the fullness of time so that we might know true joy and salvation. In Jesus' name, we pray. Amen.

WORD POWER

Savior (Greek: *soter*)—this means one who provides salvation or relief from physical and spiritual oppression. In ancient Greek, the term referred to gods and individual personalities whose significant actions brought some type of relief. Mary rejoiced in God her Savior, the One who, through His mighty power, would protect and deliver Israel. This Savior brought light into the world and saved us from eternal hell.

HOME DAILY BIBLE READINGS
(December 17-23, 2007)

Called to Rejoice

MONDAY, December 17: "Sing a New Song" (Psalm 96:1–6)
TUESDAY, December 18: "Joseph and Mary" (Matthew 1:18b–21)
WEDNESDAY, December 19: "Traveling to Bethlehem" (Luke 2:1–5)
THURSDAY, December 20: "Jesus, Firstborn Son" (Luke 2:6–7)
FRIDAY, December 21: "Angels Proclaim the News" (Luke 2:8–14)
SATURDAY, December 22: "Shepherds Visit the King" (Luke 2:15–20)
SUNDAY, December 23: "Judging with God's Truth" (Psalm 96:7–13)

CALLED TO WITNESS

DEVOTIONAL READING: **Isaiah 49:5-6**
PRINT PASSAGE: **Luke 2:22-35**

BACKGROUND SCRIPTURE: **Luke 2:22-38**
KEY VERSE: **Luke 2:34**

Luke 2:22-35—KJV

22 And when the days of her purification according to the law of Moses were accomplished, they brought him to Jerusalem, to present him to the Lord;
23 (As it is written in the law of the Lord, Every male that openeth the womb shall be called holy to the Lord;)
24 And to offer a sacrifice according to that which is said in the law of the Lord, A pair of turtledoves, or two young pigeons.
25 And, behold, there was a man in Jerusalem, whose name was Simeon; and the same man was just and devout, waiting for the consolation of Israel: and the Holy Ghost was upon him.
26 And it was revealed unto him by the Holy Ghost, that he should not see death, before he had seen the Lord's Christ.
27 And he came by the Spirit into the temple: and when the parents brought in the child Jesus, to do for him after the custom of the law,
28 Then took he him up in his arms, and blessed God, and said,
29 Lord, now lettest thou thy servant depart in peace, according to thy word:
30 For mine eyes have seen thy salvation,
31 Which thou hast prepared before the face of all people;
32 A light to lighten the Gentiles, and the glory of thy people Israel.
33 And Joseph and his mother marvelled at those things which were spoken of him.
34 And Simeon blessed them, and said unto Mary his mother, Behold, this child is set for the fall and rising again of many in Israel; and for a sign which shall be spoken against;
35 (Yea, a sword shall pierce through thy own soul also,) that the thoughts of many hearts may be revealed.

Luke 2:22-35—NRSV

22 When the time came for their purification according to the law of Moses, they brought him up to Jerusalem to present him to the Lord
23 (as it is written in the law of the Lord, "Every firstborn male shall be designated as holy to the Lord"),
24 and they offered a sacrifice according to what is stated in the law of the Lord, "a pair of turtledoves or two young pigeons."
25 Now there was a man in Jerusalem whose name was Simeon; this man was righteous and devout, looking forward to the consolation of Israel, and the Holy Spirit rested on him.
26 It had been revealed to him by the Holy Spirit that he would not see death before he had seen the Lord's Messiah.
27 Guided by the Spirit, Simeon came into the temple; and when the parents brought in the child Jesus, to do for him what was customary under the law,
28 Simeon took him in his arms and praised God, saying,
29 "Master, now you are dismissing your servant in peace, according to your word;
30 for my eyes have seen your salvation,
31 which you have prepared in the presence of all peoples,
32 a light for revelation to the Gentiles and for glory to your people Israel."
33 And the child's father and mother were amazed at what was being said about him.
34 Then Simeon blessed them and said to his mother Mary, "This child is destined for the falling and the rising of many in Israel, and to be a sign that will be opposed
35 so that the inner thoughts of many will be revealed—and a sword will pierce your own soul too."

TOPICAL OUTLINE OF THE LESSON

I. Introduction
   A. Called to Be Witnesses
   B. Biblical Background

II. Exposition and Application of the Scripture
   A. Presentation in the Temple (Luke 2:22-24)
   B. Proclamation in the Temple (Luke 2:25-32)
   C. Revelation in the Temple (Luke 2:33-35)

III. Concluding Reflections

LESSON OBJECTIVES

Upon completion of this lesson, the students will know that:

1. Jesus was formally dedicated in the temple;
2. Jesus was and is a sign to be spoken against, but He is the Savior of the world; and,
3. It is incumbent upon every Christian to bear witness to Jesus Christ.

POINTS TO BE EMPHASIZED
ADULT/YOUTH

Adult Topic: Hearing and Telling Good News
Youth Topic: Called to Be Faithful
Adult Key Verse: Luke 2:34
Youth Key Verses: Luke 2:29-30
Print Passage: Luke 2:22-35

—By their participation in rites of purification, Joseph and Mary demonstrated that they were devout Jews.
—Jewish mothers were considered "unclean" for seven days after the birth of their children.
—Simeon was in the right place at the right time and gave Joseph and Mary their first insight regarding their Son Jesus as the Messiah.
—The Holy Spirit led Simeon to the temple in order that he could see the consolation of Israel and share the joy this brought.
—Anna responded by telling others in the temple the miraculous Good News about Jesus. Both Simeon and Anna were among those who anticipated the coming of the Messiah.

CHILDREN

Children Topic: Praising God for Promises Kept
Key Verse: Luke 2:28
Print Passage: Luke 2:22-35

—Mary and Joseph went to the temple to fulfill their obedience to the Law of Moses, not to show off the baby.
—Simeon recognized Jesus as God's promised Messiah, one who would bring salvation to all people, and he praised God.
—What started as a customary act of obedience became a time of further revelation and amazement for Mary and Joseph.

I. INTRODUCTION

A. Called to Be Witnesses

All Christians should agree that we are called to be witnesses of the love and grace of God. However, many Christians find it extremely difficult to talk to the unsaved or tell about God's gift of salvation through Jesus Christ. In this lesson, we will learn that we have been empowered with the Holy Spirit to share the Good News of God's amazing grace and love that was manifested through Jesus Christ. We are called to expand and enlarge the kingdom of God.

In Mark chapter 5, Jesus healed a man who had been demon-possessed. The healed man wanted to go with Jesus on His missionary travels. In verse 19, Jesus said, "Go home to thy friends, and tell them how great things the Lord hath done for thee, and hath had compassion on thee." And he went away and began to publish in Decapolis how great things Jesus had done for him: and all men did marvel (Mark 5:19-20).

What is the point of the story? God did something for you one day. He made you a new creature in Jesus Christ, and that is a story worth telling (see 1 Corinthians 5:17). The psalmist stated that God brought him up out of a horrible pit and planted his feet on a solid rock. Your story of faith begins with what God has done in your life and how Jesus Christ makes the difference for you. You have a personal account of how God saved you one day. You have a testimony of how He cleansed your life, took you from the very bottom of skid row and put you back on the right road. Tell your story and it will draw people to Jesus. The power is in the Word. Your testimony is the vehicle.

B. Biblical Background

The lesson today focuses on the formal dedication and naming of Jesus when He was an infant. According to the custom and covenant between God and Israel, each male child was to be formally circumcised on the eighth day (see Genesis 17:11-12; Luke 2:21). Joseph now had a family living in Bethlehem, so it was highly likely that Mary and Joseph remained in their home rather than return to Nazareth so soon after the birth of Jesus. The seventy-five-mile journey would have been too much for the young mother and newborn. Mary and Joseph remained in Bethlehem for several months before departing for Egypt and eventually coming back to Nazareth (see Matthew 2:11, 13, 19-23).

In this lesson, we see another man whom God had filled with the Holy Spirit, who was strategically placed to bear witness to the arrival of the Messiah in the world. Everyone who had been associated with the coming of the Messiah and witness of the forerunner, John, had been persons filled with the Holy Spirit. When Jesus was born, thousands of years had passed and the hope and consolation of Israel had been delayed. Simeon, like many devout Jews, wanted to see with his own eyes the gift of God (see Isaiah 40:1-11). His hymn of praise has become known in Christian tradition as the *Nunc Dimittis,* taken from the first two words of the Latin text: *"Nunc Dimittis servum trium Domine ...,"* or "Lord, now lettest thou thy servant depart in peace..." (Luke 2:29).

II. EXPOSITION AND APPLICATION OF THE SCRIPTURE

A. Presentation in the Temple (Luke 2:22-24)

And when the days of her purification according to the law of Moses were accomplished, they bought him to Jerusalem, to present him to the Lord; (As it is written in the law of the Lord, Every male that openeth the womb shall be called holy to the Lord;) And to offer a sacrifice according to that which is said in the law of the Lord, A pair of turtledoves, or two young pigeons.

Eight days after He was born, Jesus was circumcised, just as all Jewish males were. This act placed Jesus within the covenant community of Israel. The first question that we must address is: Why would the Son of God need to be circumcised? As a Son of Abraham and descendant of David, Jesus had to submit to the Law in order to be considered an orthodox Jew. If he had not been circumcised, He could never have made the claim that He had come not to destroy the Law but to fulfill the Law. Further, Jesus would not have been able to fulfill all righteousness as He told John at His baptism (see Matthew 3:13-15; 5:17). J. C. Ryle noted that, "Circumcision was absolutely necessary before our Lord could be heard as a teacher in Israel." Every teacher of the Law had to meet the requirements of the Law in order to enter any synagogue. Jesus was born under the Law; therefore, He had to meet all of the demands of the Law (see Galatians 4:4).

At the appointed time, Mary and Joseph took Jesus to Jerusalem to the temple to perform the required rituals of purification. Luke incorporated three separate ritual ceremonies in verses 22-23. First, there was the ritual of purification associated with childbirth, as noted in Leviticus 12:1-8. Second, there was the ritual of the presentation of the firstborn to the Lord (see Exodus 13:2, 12, 15, 34:19). Third, just as Hannah brought Samuel to the tabernacle at Shiloh, so each firstborn child was brought before the Lord to be dedicated to Him (see 1 Samuel 1-2). According to the Law, nothing and no unclean person could enter the holy sanctuary; for to do so would defile the holy place. Childbirth was not considered unclean, nor was it considered immoral. What was considered unclean in ancient Hebrew culture were the discharges associated with childbirth. Hence, a period of purification was specified by God to render the person holy again and ritually clean. Mary and Joseph appeared at the temple in Jerusalem with the appropriate sin offering and sacrifices to the Lord.

God, by His nature, is holy; holiness is a foundational attribute of God (see Leviticus 19:2; 20:7, 26 Isaiah 6:3; 30:15; 40:25). Nothing unclean or unholy could come before the Lord God without first being sanctified. Before Aaron and his sons could serve in the tabernacle, they had to wash themselves of any uncleanness (see Exodus 30:17-21; 40:12). The laws of purity extended into every aspect of ancient Hebrew life (see Leviticus 11:25-28; 14:1-10; 15:1-27; 16:1-10).

During my first trip to Israel, I did not pay much attention to the ritual baths, because it seemed a rather odd thing to me that someone would wash himself or herself before entering the temple or a synagogue. Would it not be just as important to pray and seek forgiveness before going into the temple or synagogue? However, I have come to understand the importance of ritual cleansing in the ancient world. One of the ways I have come to understand the importance of ritual purity is by observing the number of ritual baths that were placed at the entrance to the temple in Jerusalem and at other holy sites throughout Israel. Cleanliness was critical to ancient people. One dare not come into the presence of a holy God with unclean hands or hearts.

As previously mentioned, no one who was unclean could enter into the presence of a holy God. In the Qumran community, which was located near the Dead Sea roughly twenty miles from Jerusalem, there are several ruins of ritual baths that were used in the ceremonies of ritual cleansing. We take this very lightly today and do not give much thought or do much teaching on holiness and moral living. Yet, we are reminded in the New Testament that God is holy, and we are called to live holy lives (see 1 Thessalonians 2:10-12; 4:3; 5:23; 1 Peter 1:14-15).

Holiness has a two-dimensional meaning. On the one hand, we are holy because we have been set aside for the purpose of the Lord Jesus Christ. What is that purpose? It is to preach and carry the Gospel to the ends of the earth. Christians are called to present themselves as living sacrifices, which are holy and acceptable to God (see Romans 12:1). The other dimension has to do with right living or moral living. Our standards of morality are very much shrouded in the freedom of this post-modern age, which in many cases, defines right and wrong by its own standards. Christians are reminded in this lesson that there are still standards of holiness that God has established that form the basis for our relationship with Him.

B. Proclamation in the Temple (Luke 2:25-32)

And, behold, there was a man in Jerusalem, whose name was Simeon; and the same man was just and devout, waiting for the consolation of Israel: and the Holy Ghost was upon him. And it was revealed unto him by the Holy Ghost, that he should not see death, before he had seen the Lord's Christ. And he came by the Spirit into the temple: and when the parents brought in the child Jesus, to do for him after the custom of the law, Then took he him up in his arms, and blessed God, and said, Lord, now lettest thou thy servant depart in peace, according to thy word: For mine eyes have seen thy salvation, Which thou hast prepared before the face of all people; A light to lighten the Gentiles, and the glory of thy people Israel.

We are now introduced to a pious man who had been awaiting the coming of the Messiah. There are no biographical details given about the life of Simeon. Indeed, for Luke such details were not as important as who Simeon was and his witness concerning the Christ child. He was righteous according to the dictates of the Law. He was an aged man with a distinguished piety and reputation. Simeon is described as a man living with great hope and expectation. He was looking for the consolation of the Lord. We are not told how long he had been living with the hope and expectation of the coming Messiah. However, among the aged people of his day, Simeon saw the "Consolation" of Israel.

The Lord revealed to Simeon that he would not die until he had seen the Messiah with his own two eyes. How this revelation came to him we do not know. The Lord reveals to His servants, in timely ways, what He wishes to reveal; it is not our duty to probe into the mysteries of God. Simeon was directed by the Holy Spirit to go to the temple. He had no idea why he was being directed there. We do not know the time of day nor the day of the week when he went to the temple. It may have been the first hour of prayer at 9:00 a.m. When Mary and Joseph appeared in the temple precincts with Jesus, Simeon knew right away that this was the Christ. People had looked for a family with a royal entourage to be Christ's family. Instead, there were two parents of humble origins who had come to merely fulfill the obligations of the Law. They sought no special attention. How Simeon came to address them, we do not know. But the Spirit of God let him know that this was the Christ! He took the Child in his arms and blessed the name of the Lord.

When Simeon saw Jesus and had held Him in his arms, he was ready to die. His days and dreams had been fulfilled. He had seen the Messiah and held Him in his arms. God had kept His promise to Simeon, and he recognized it and thanked God for the blessing. Death had lost the power to claim him in fear. Simeon saw with his own eyes the salvation of the Lord, which God had prepared for all people. Jesus came as light, not just to descendants of Abraham and David, but for the whole human race. He came as light to the Gentiles and glory for the Israelites.

Christians are witnesses of the light of life in Jesus Christ. Jesus has taught us that we are the light of the world. We are that city which is sitting on a hill that cannot be hidden. We are witnesses of the matchless grace of God. In Jesus Christ, God became a living human being to redeem us from the curse of the Law. When Simeon saw Jesus, he saw the fulfillment of every promise made to the patriarchs and the validation of every prophetic message preached about the coming day of the Lord's glory.

C. Revelation in the Temple
(Luke 2:33-35)

And Joseph and his mother marvelled at those things which were spoken of him. And Simeon blessed them, and said unto Mary his mother, Behold, this child is set for the fall and rising again of many in Israel; and for a sign which shall be spoken against; (Yea, a sword shall pierce through thy own soul also,) that the thoughts of many hearts may be revealed.

Mary and Joseph had a lot to digest in the weeks and months leading up to the birth of Jesus and the miraculous things that happened afterward. They had seen and spoken with angels, and had been visited by strange shepherds who had received the news of the Child's birth from angels. They heard the witness of devout men and women who had declared and confirmed every prophetic word of God about Jesus the Messiah. Simeon's words, no doubt, were further confirmation of all that had gone on before. His words caused them to marvel at how God was working.

Simeon gave the baby back to Mary and blessed them. We are not sure whether he blessed Joseph and Mary or Mary and Jesus or all three. He did speak directly to Mary that Jesus would become a stumbling block for many in Israel. "Behold, this child…" (verse 34) tells us that Jesus was a special Child. There were other children who were brought to the temple to undergo the ritual of dedication; but Jesus was unique, and this was the reason Simeon used a demonstrative pronoun to call attention to His uniqueness. Many had fallen and many are still falling, for they refused and still refuse to see Jesus as the Son of God. Isaiah prophesied a long time ago that He would be "a stone of stumbling and for a rock of offence" (Isaiah 8:14). Jesus' life and ministry of preaching and teaching would be a thorn in the side of those who ultimately rejected Him. Just as there were those who would turn away, there were many who received Jesus, and these became sons and daughters of God. They were lifted to a new status as joint-heirs with Christ. He would become the stone whom the builders would reject. The words of Isaiah would ring true in the life of the Savior of men and women, "He is despised and rejected of men..." (Isaiah 53:3).

In the words of Simeon, Mary heard what amounted to the first prediction of the anguish she would suffer as a mother. Thirty-three years later, just outside the city walls of Jerusalem, at a place called Golgotha, her heart would be pierced by the sword of hatred and rejection as she watched her firstborn Son die in humiliation and shame. Maybe then all that she had pondered in her heart would resurface as a revelation of who Jesus Christ was and is today.

III. CONCLUDING REFLECTIONS

One of the major teaching points that can be lost in this lesson is the need to understand the radical demands for holy living. In many of our churches, people would rather talk about a lot of other things than the need to be pious and devout. Piety is really about our relationship to God and the world. Many may think of piety as a lost virtue that is not to be pursued. But we are reminded again and again that God has not changed. What He demanded then, He demands now. "Be ye holy, for I am holy" (1 Peter 1:16).

PRAYER

Heavenly Father, we bless You that we can have hope in Your Word. Just as You fulfilled Your promise to Simeon, You have done the same for us. We thank You for the precious gift of eternal life through our Lord Jesus Christ. May we live lives that make us to be worthy of our being called sons and daughters of God. In the name of Jesus, we pray. Amen.

WORD POWER

Is Set (Greek: *keima`*)—this means to be by divine intent set, put forward to see, appointed, held up conspicuously. Simeon said "this Child" probably holding Jesus up, "is set" (verse 34). Jesus was, is, and will be a sign that people will speak against. There were Bible scholars in Jesus' day who were enemies of the Cross, just as there are enemies today. Their attitudes should serve as reminders of the prophecy of Simeon.

HOME DAILY BIBLE READINGS
(December 24-30, 2007)

Called to Witness

LESSON 6   January 6, 2008

INSPIRED TO INQUIRE

DEVOTIONAL READING: **Psalm 148:7-14**   BACKGROUND SCRIPTURE: **Luke 2:41-52**
PRINT PASSAGE: **Luke 2:41-52**   KEY VERSE: **Luke 2:49**

Luke 2:41-52—KJV

41 Now his parents went to Jerusalem every year at the feast of the passover.

42 And when he was twelve years old, they went up to Jerusalem after the custom of the feast.

43 And when they had fulfilled the days, as they returned, the child Jesus tarried behind in Jerusalem; and Joseph and his mother knew not of it.

44 But they, supposing him to have been in the company, went a day's journey; and they sought him among their kinsfolk and acquaintance.

45 And when they found him not, they turned back again to Jerusalem, seeking him.

46 And it came to pass, that after three days they found him in the temple, sitting in the midst of the doctors, both hearing them, and asking them questions.

47 And all that heard him were astonished at his understanding and answers.

48 And when they saw him, they were amazed: and his mother said unto him, Son, why hast thou thus dealt with us? behold, thy father and I have sought thee sorrowing.

49 And he said unto them, How is it that ye sought me? wist ye not that I must be about my Father's business?

50 And they understood not the saying which he spake unto them.

51 And he went down with them, and came to Nazareth, and was subject unto them: but his mother kept all these sayings in her heart.

52 And Jesus increased in wisdom and stature, and in favour with God and man.

Luke 2:41-52—NRSV

41 Now every year his parents went to Jerusalem for the festival of the Passover.

42 And when he was twelve years old, they went up as usual for the festival.

43 When the festival was ended and they started to return, the boy Jesus stayed behind in Jerusalem, but his parents did not know it.

44 Assuming that he was in the group of travelers, they went a day's journey. Then they started to look for him among their relatives and friends.

45 When they did not find him, they returned to Jerusalem to search for him.

46 After three days they found him in the temple, sitting among the teachers, listening to them and asking them questions.

47 And all who heard him were amazed at his understanding and his answers.

48 When his parents saw him they were astonished; and his mother said to him, "Child, why have you treated us like this? Look, your father and I have been searching for you in great anxiety."

49 He said to them, "Why were you searching for me? Did you not know that I must be in my Father's house?"

50 But they did not understand what he said to them.

51 Then he went down with them and came to Nazareth, and was obedient to them. His mother treasured all these things in her heart.

52 And Jesus increased in wisdom and in years, and in divine and human favor.

BIBLE FACT

Above are the first recorded words of Jesus. Joseph and Mary were amazed at His words and apparently forgot the prophecies about their young son. How often do we forget His promises? No more of Jesus' words were recorded until His baptism by John the Baptist.

UNIFYING LESSON PRINCIPLE

We have questions for which we seek answers. How does inquiry within the community of faith lead to maturity? Entering into dialogue in the temple, Jesus grew in faith and wisdom.

TOPICAL OUTLINE OF THE LESSON

I. Introduction
A. Teaching Ministry
B. Biblical Background

II. Exposition and Application of the Scripture
A. Staying in Jerusalem (Luke 2:41-44)
B. Learning in Jerusalem (Luke 2:45-48)
C. The Priority of Jesus (Luke 2:49-50)
D. Growing in Nazareth (Luke 2:51-52)

III. Concluding Reflections

LESSON OBJECTIVES

Upon completion of this lesson, the students will know that:

1. Jesus took the ministry of teaching, preaching, and healing seriously;
2. We, His followers, should emulate Him in bringing others to His kingdom; and,
3. Parents have important roles to play in the spiritual growth of their children.

POINTS TO BE EMPHASIZED

ADULT/YOUTH

Adult Topic: Questions and Answers
Youth Topic: Inspired to Inquire!
Adult Key Verse: Luke 2:49
Youth Key Verse: Luke 2:47
Print Passage: Luke 2:41-52

— Israelite men were supposed to attend festivals (Exodus 23:14-17 and Deuteronomy 16:16).

—The Feast of Passover and of Unleavened Bread lasted seven days.

—Jesus caused His parents understandable concern when He was missing from among their travel companions.

—Jesus had remained in Jerusalem in meaningful interaction with the teachers in the temple who were amazed at His depth of insight.

—Consider the implications of this passage as the only biblical text that refers to Jesus' childhood.

—Luke establishes in verses 41-52 that Jesus was a true Israelite, brought up from birth in the moral and ritual life of Judaism.

—Jesus' reference to "my Father's house" indicates His special relationship with God.

CHILDREN

Children Topic: Inspired to Ask Questions
Key Verse: Luke 2:46
Print Passage: Luke 2:41-52

—Jesus taught us to seek more knowledge of God.

—Jesus understood the importance of listening to and learning from others.

—Jesus taught us that it is important not only to listen but also to understand what we hear.

—Jesus wanted to be close to His Father, and that is why He went to God's house.

I. INTRODUCTION

A. Teaching Ministry

The teaching ministry is an essential and vital part of the church's ministry. Many believers take for granted their privilege to learn and grow in the Christian faith. The ministry of Jesus was a three-pronged approach of preaching, teaching, and healing. We read a lot about the teaching ministry of Jesus in the Gospels. Through the example of His own ministry, Jesus showed us that teaching must be at the top of every church's agenda. Finally, it must be the centerpiece for every believer's plan to grow in grace and in the knowledge of the Lord Jesus Christ.

B. Biblical Background

This is the only canonical gospel record we have of Jesus' early childhood. This record from Luke clearly shows Jesus in the earliest stages of transition from childhood to young manhood. In that culture, boys usually began to take their places with the men at the age of thirteen.

It was customary for people to travel in large caravans with the women and children leading the way. During the trip, families and friends would keep watch over each other's children. Mary may have thought that Jesus was with Joseph and he may have thought that Jesus was with Mary.

Sometime during that first day, they discovered that Jesus was missing. When they realized that Jesus was not with the caravan, Mary and Joseph hastily returned to Jerusalem to search for Him. Three days after the ordeal began on the road to Nazareth, they found Jesus sitting in the midst of the teachers, listening to them and asking them questions.

When they found the young lad, Mary gently rebuked Him, telling Him how He had caused them some serious anxiety and stress. Jesus replied, saying, "How is it that ye sought me? Wist ye not that I must be about my Father's business?" (Luke 2:49).

II. EXPOSITION AND APPLICATION OF THE SCRIPTURE

A. Staying in Jerusalem
(Luke 2:41-44)

Now his parents went to Jerusalem every year at the feast of the passover. And when he was twelve years old, they went up to Jerusalem after the custom of the feast. And when they had fulfilled the days, as they returned, the child Jesus tarried behind in Jerusalem; and Joseph and his mother knew not of it. But they, supposing him to have been in the company, went a day's journey; and they sought him among their kinsfolk and acquaintance.

Jesus grew up in a home of very pious and devout Jews. We have no record of Jesus attending the other two main festivals (Pentecost and the Feast of Tabernacles) as a boy. However, Passover was and is the preeminent Jewish religious festival. It was celebrated every year and continues to be celebrated even today in commemoration of God's great act of the deliverance of Israel from slavery in Egypt. Passover was also significant in ancient Hebrew religious tradition because it was the beginning of the Jewish year (see Exodus 12:2). The name *Passover* comes from a Hebrew word, *Pesach*, which means "to step over" or "to overstep." The origin of the festival is found in Exodus 12.

It is significant that the first feast we read about that the Messiah attended was the annual Passover celebration. This act looked back to the sacrifice of blood and forward to another sacrifice that would be made in the same city twenty-one years later at Calvary. At that sacrifice, Jesus would be the Passover Lamb.

Verse 43 states that when the days were fulfilled (the seven days that the festival lasted), the family began its return trip to Nazareth. This was a long journey by foot and would take several days of hard travel in addition to the climate change of going from Jerusalem to Jericho. The roads were narrow, dusty, and often filled with limestone rocks and stones which are still very prevalent in Israel. There were numerous caves, from which roaming bands of marauders could easily attack travelers. It was a dangerous trip. The first part of the journey would be downhill, 2,500 feet to the plains of Jericho, and then north through the Jordan Valley until they arrived at the Jezreel Valley and turned east toward Nazareth. Once near Nazareth, the party would face an uphill climb of over 1,000 feet above sea level. There was a central route through the hill country, but it ran through Samaria, and it was unlikely that an orthodox Jewish family would take that route.

Jesus remained in Jerusalem. We are not told what made Him do this, but it comes out later in the passage when we see Him in the temple, conversing with the doctors and lawyers of the Jewish religion. His parents thought that Jesus was somewhere in the crowd and never thought to consider that He might not be in the crowd until the caravan stopped that night and He could not be found. They had traveled a day's journey, which would probably put the caravan at or near the plains of Jericho.

B. Learning in Jerusalem (Luke 2:45-48)

And when they found him not, they turned back again to Jerusalem, seeking him. And it came to pass, that after three days they found him in the temple, sitting in the midst of the doctors, both hearing them, and asking them questions. And all that heard him were astonished at his understanding and answers. And when they saw him, they were amazed: and his mother said unto him, Son, why hast thou thus dealt with us? behold, thy father and I have sought thee sorrowing.

When Joseph and Mary discovered that Jesus was not present, they had to turn around and go back up the road that ran to Jerusalem. The three days is a reference to the total time it took to find Jesus, and does not refer to their searching Jerusalem for three days. On the first day, they headed toward Galilee; on the second day they returned to Jerusalem; and on the third day they found Him. After three days, they found Jesus in the temple sitting among the doctors, listening to them and asking questions. Jesus was patient enough to listen to them. Note that *hearing* is mentioned first, indicating that He was in the temple as a learner; and it was as such that He questioned the doctors. People were astonished at His demeanor and maturity. Who was this young lad of twelve who felt comfortable talking with the leading scholars of the Law?

Mary spoke first and told Jesus how anxious she and Joseph had been that they had not found Him. No doubt they were quite tired from their search. They had missed Him with the group, and there was grave concern regarding His welfare. They were happy to find Him, but He had caused them a great deal of stress.

There is much to be learned from Jesus' life at this early age. Here we see the Master of teachers sitting and listening to the great minds of His day. How can one grow in grace and in the knowledge of the Lord Jesus Christ unless he or she listens to the teaching of the Word of God? Jesus did not need to have any man teach Him, but He listened and spoke with the scholars as an example for us, that we might see the importance of listening and being taught.

C. The Priority of Jesus
(Luke 2:49-50)

And he said unto them, How is it that ye sought me? wist ye not that I must be about my Father's business? And they understood not the saying which he spake unto them.

Jesus appeared surprised that Mary and Joseph would inquire as to where He had been. It would appear that they would understand that He was exactly where He was supposed to be, in His Father's house. Here, at the age of twelve, Jesus clearly set the stage for what would be His life's calling—the Father's business. He had come to give His life as a ransom and to seek and to save the lost. We can be certain that there were more words spoken than these in verse 49, but we have no record of them. Jesus distanced Himself from Joseph, who was not His true Father, because God was His real Father. He was the object of the worship of that house. The Father's business had to do with the deeper realities of life, which were all bound up in the rites and rituals of the temple religion. His business was not that of a carpenter but as a Savior of lost humanity. Even at His age, priority had to be given to what was most important and central to who He was.

Jesus' words teach us about the urgency of the kingdom's work. We see this in His questions: Jesus asked why they were seeking Him. Did they not know that He must be about

His Father's business? (see verse 49). There was a real sense of urgency in Jesus' words. His Father's business was the driving force behind His actions. The zeal to carry out the work of His Father could not wait a day longer.

I wonder sometimes if Christians today sense any urgency at all in what they do and how they serve God. Is it possible that we have become so relaxed with Christianity that we have lost sight of the seriousness of the human condition? The words of Jesus teach us that time is too precious to waste doing things that do not add to the kingdom of God. Many of God's people spend enormous amounts of their time engaged in activities that make no difference in the world. Those activities may not even add to the value of their church's ministry. When you consider your own life and ministry, can you make the same claim as Jesus—that you are about your Father's business?

Joseph and Mary were unable to comprehend the statement made by Jesus. They did not know that Jesus was the Savior of the world.

D. Growing in Nazareth
(Luke 2:51-52)

And he went down with them, and came to Nazareth, and was subject unto them: but his mother kept all these sayings in her heart. And Jesus increased in wisdom and stature, and in favour with God and man.

How is it that they did not understand the words of Jesus or His actions? During the period of His greatest miracles and works, even His disciples were not sure who Jesus was. At the annunciation and birth of Jesus, not everyone saw the same things. Only the shepherds saw the angels in the heavens singing and glorifying God. Jesus left Jerusalem and went home to Nazareth with His parents and was subject to them. Jesus did not disrespect them nor treat them as less than His parents. The Law required that children honor and obey their parents. Children should learn from the humility and obedience of Christ; He was industrious and not ashamed to work in the carpenter's shed. Mary kept all of these things, the things that had happened in the young life of Jesus, in her heart. Jesus grew and increased in wisdom and age. He lived with the grace of God upon Him as He gained favor with both God and man.

III. CONCLUDING REFLECTIONS

How seriously do you take the need for the study of the Bible? Is church work ever a valid substitute for the active engagement of the mind with the Word of God? I have watched with fascination how men and women in churches become so absorbed with working in their respective congregations that they never take the time to examine whether or not they are growing spiritually. Working for God is never a reason for dismissing our need to grow in wisdom, knowledge, and spiritual understanding. For adults, youth, and children, obedience to the Word of God is a duty we must perform. Jesus set an example for all of us. Though He was the Son of God, He was also the "Son of Mary." He worked with His earthly father, Joseph, as a carpenter. Jesus teaches us that it is no dishonor to be a carpenter, dishwasher, garbage collector, or CEO. Jesus, through His actions, conferred honor on virtuous industry.

PRAYER

Heavenly Father, we beseech You for wisdom and understanding to serve You in ways that advance Your kingdom. Give us a clearer vision of what our priorities in ministry must be. May we walk in the knowledge that to serve You is to first love and obey Your Word. Give us a hunger and thirst for the things that You love. Forgive us of our sins. In the name of Jesus, we pray. Amen.

WORD POWER

Not Understand (Greek: *ou suniemi*)—the first word, ou, means "not" or "absolutely no." The second word, suniemi, means "understand." Put together, the phrase means "to not comprehend, not understand, not perceive, or to not have insight." In verse 50, Joseph and Mary did not seem to have the slightest perception of the true identity of Jesus Christ. The same is true of many Christians today; they are yet to grasp the true identity of Jesus Christ.

HOME DAILY BIBLE READINGS
(December 31, 2007—January 6, 2008)
Inspired to Inquire

MONDAY, December 31: "A Horn for God's People" (Psalm 148:7–14)
TUESDAY, January 1: "The Passover Feast Instituted" (Numbers 9:1–5)
WEDNESDAY, January 2: "First Passover Observed" (Exodus 12:11–14)
THURSDAY, January 3: "The Annual Pilgrimage" (Luke 2:41–45)
FRIDAY, January 4: "About the Father's Business" (Luke 2:46–50)
SATURDAY, January 5: "Growing Up in Nazareth" (Luke 2:51–52)
SUNDAY, January 6: "Praise the Lord!" (Psalm 148:1–6)

LESSON 7   January 13, 2008

INSPIRED TO LOVE

DEVOTIONAL READING: **Psalm 37:1-11**
PRINT PASSAGE: **Luke 6:27-36**

BACKGROUND SCRIPTURE: **Luke 6:27-36**
KEY VERSE: **Luke 6:35**

Luke 6:27-36—KJV

27 But I say unto you which hear, Love your enemies, do good to them which hate you,
28 Bless them that curse you, and pray for them which despitefully use you.
29 And unto him that smiteth thee on the one cheek offer also the other; and him that taketh away thy cloak forbid not to take thy coat also.
30 Give to every man that asketh of thee; and of him that taketh away thy goods ask them not again.
31 And as ye would that men should do to you, do ye also to them likewise.
32 For if ye love them which love you, what thank have ye? for sinners also love those that love them.
33 And if ye do good to them which do good to you, what thank have ye? for sinners also do even the same.
34 And if ye lend to them of whom ye hope to receive, what thank have ye? for sinners also lend to sinners, to receive as much again.
35 But love ye your enemies, and do good, and lend, hoping for nothing again; and your reward shall be great, and ye shall be the children of the Highest: for he is kind unto the unthankful and to the evil.
36 Be ye therefore merciful, as your Father also is merciful.

Luke 6:27-36—NRSV

27 "But I say to you that listen, Love your enemies, do good to those who hate you,
28 bless those who curse you, pray for those who abuse you.
29 If anyone strikes you on the cheek, offer the other also; and from anyone who takes away your coat do not withhold even your shirt.
30 Give to everyone who begs from you; and if anyone takes away your goods, do not ask for them again.
31 Do to others as you would have them do to you.
32 "If you love those who love you, what credit is that to you? For even sinners love those who love them.
33 If you do good to those who do good to you, what credit is that to you? For even sinners do the same.
34 If you lend to those from whom you hope to receive, what credit is that to you? Even sinners lend to sinners, to receive as much again.
35 But love your enemies, do good, and lend, expecting nothing in return. Your reward will be great, and you will be children of the Most High; for he is kind to the ungrateful and the wicked.
36 Be merciful, just as your Father is merciful.

BIBLE FACT

We who are truly born again are obliged to love. People who are difficult to love are just the people whom Jesus directs us to extend this grace. We must not expect them to reciprocate us accordingly. Only then will our reward be great in heaven.

UNIFYING LESSON PRINCIPLE

Every person needs to learn how to express love to others. What does Jesus teach us about loving our enemies? Jesus taught His disciples to love their enemies, do good to those who hated them, and do to others as they would have others do to them.

TOPICAL OUTLINE OF THE LESSON

I. **Introduction**
   A. Sermon on the Mount
   B. Biblical Background

II. **Exposition and Application of the Scripture**
   A. Preparation of the Disciples (Luke 6:27)
   B. Particulars of the Instruction (Luke 6:28-30)
   C. Parameters of the Golden Rule (Luke 6:31)
   D. Principles to Govern Conduct (Luke 6:32-36)

III. **Concluding Reflections**

LESSON OBJECTIVES

Upon completion of this lesson, the students will know that:

1. Love is a prerequisite to an authentic Christian life;
2. Jesus is the supreme example of how to act in love toward others; and,
3. Love is reciprocal.

POINTS TO BE EMPHASIZED

ADULT/YOUTH

Adult Topic: **Responding to Opposition**
Youth Topic: **Inspired to Love**
Adult Key Verse: **Luke 6:35**
Youth Key Verse: **Luke 6:27**
Print Passage: **Luke 6:27-36**

—Loving your enemies is a divine prescription for combating attitudes of hate and mistreatment.
—In ancient times, a cloak was the outer garment and a coat was the undergarment or tunic.
—The phrase "expect nothing in return" probably meant prohibition of the collection of interest on loans.
—Loving our enemies is a reflection of God's generosity and love for us.
—By telling listeners to "love your enemies," Jesus was challenging them to relate to one another beyond what the Law required.
—This text holds up the ideals of love, forgiveness, and generosity.
—Love seeks mercy more than justice.

CHILDREN

Children Topic: **Showing Love to Others**
Key Verses: **Luke 6:27-28**
Print Passage: **Luke 6:27-36**

—Jesus teaches us about love for others.
—Jesus shows us how to be kind to others, no matter what they may do to us.
—We must be willing to pray for our friends and our enemies.
—When we love and expect nothing in return, we are living God's Word.

I. INTRODUCTION

A. Sermon on the Mount

Today's lesson comes from Jesus' Sermon on the Plains (Luke 6:17-49). There is a parallel passage in Matthew 5:1—7:29 where these same teachings take place on the side of a mountain. Jesus practiced what He preached, and He sought to instill these same traits in His first followers (John 13:13-17). It is much easier to talk about loving our enemies and those who hate us than it is to unconditionally practice this principle. However, this is the challenge of this lesson. The Sermon on the Plains is a practical lesson about the ethics of life in the kingdom of God. Christians are people who have embraced the call to enter the kingdom of God and live by its standards. Kingdom life is evidenced by honesty and integrity in our speech and actions. If we say that we are going to do something, we must make every effort to try and get it done. If you join a ministry, you vow to support that ministry by your actions, and you do all you can to help it succeed. Our words validate our characters.

Kingdom living is not vengeful or spiteful (Romans 12:13-14, 20-21). Kingdom people are unconditionally committed to the ethics of love. We love each other and our enemies. Pray for the people who persecute you. By doing this, you show that you are sons and daughters of God. Our love for others must go beyond the norm and beyond our circle of friends and associates. We are to love and treat each other with respect and dignity. Love is the real evidence of a changed life. In John 13:34-35, Jesus prescribed a new standard of identity for those who call themselves His disciples. "A new commandment I give unto you, That ye love one another; as I have loved you, that ye also love one another. By this shall all men know that ye are my disciples, if ye have love one to another."

B. Biblical Background

In the previous lessons, we studied the birth narratives of John the Baptist and Jesus. We examined the first public appearance of Jesus at the Jerusalem temple. Between the ages of twelve and thirty we hear absolutely nothing about Jesus' growth into full manhood. Jesus began His public ministry at the age of thirty (Luke 3:23). According to the Gospels, He was baptized by John in a place known as Bethany beyond the Jordan out near the Judean wilderness (John 1:28). After fasting forty days and being tempted by the devil, Jesus returned to Galilee and conducted a teaching ministry, probably in the area of Lower Galilee, which would be near Nazareth (Luke 4:14,16). During those early days, Jesus had some success and developed a reputation as being a Spirit-filled teacher with authority (Luke 4:15, 37).

When did Jesus formally begin His preaching ministry? It was after John had been put into prison (Matthew 4:12). His ministry was concentrated in and around the fishing town of Capernaum in the region of Galilee, which is located about seventy-five miles north of Jerusalem. Why did Jesus concentrate His efforts in Galilee? There are several reasons. First, the Galileans were much more open to hearing and accepting new ideas and teachings. Second, the people were less politically connected and motivated, unlike the religious elitists in Jerusalem and Judea. Third, it was near His home of Nazareth, and it was a major population center.

Jesus gathered around Himself a small group of men who were mostly peasants, fishermen, and tax collectors. These men formed His first inner circle of friends and disciples (Luke 5:10, 27; 6:12-16). In this lesson, we see how Jesus conducted His first major teaching session with His disciples and the multitudes of people who were starting to gather around Him. He taught them lessons about relationships and how to live in the kingdom of God.

II. EXPOSITION AND APPLICATION OF THE SCRIPTURE

A. Preparation of the Disciples
(Luke 6:27)

But I say unto you which hear, Love your enemies, do good to them which hate you.

Jesus taught that love is the supreme manifestation of obedience to God (Mark 12:28-31). Loving God means loving everyone whom God created, including one's enemies. Jesus exhorted those who were present that day to "hear," which meant not only to listen to the instruction but to take the instruction and apply it to their lives. What were they listening to? They were listening to words that were radically different from any teaching that they had ever heard.

In the Mosaic Law, there were stipulations that related to how justice and love were to be lived out among the Hebrew people. One such law was the command to love one's neighbor (Leviticus 19:18). Jews of that day felt that a neighbor was someone who was of similar background and ethnicity. Jesus redefined who one's neighbor was and said that even people who were different from the accepted norm were to be loved (Luke 10:25-36). This exhortation to love extended to even those who hated one and were opposed to everything one stood for.

The exhortation to love one's enemies was followed by an equally demanding call to do the same with the people who hated God's people. Jesus said it was not enough to love—love must be followed by actions. Then and now, this means that we seek our enemies' best interests in spite of how they have treated us. Paul taught that Christians were to do good to all people and especially those who were of the household of faith (Galatians 6:10).

B. Particulars of the Instruction
(Luke 6:28-30)

Bless them that curse you, and pray for them which despitefully use you. And unto him that smiteth thee on the one cheek offer also the other; and him that taketh away thy cloke forbid not to take thy coat also. Give to every man that asketh of thee; and of him that taketh away thy goods ask them not again.

In these verses, Jesus offered four practical suggestions for Christians to demonstrate love for their enemies: First, the people were to bless the ones who cursed them. This was the command to wish them well in every endeavor, and not to ask God to punish them. Second was the exhortation to pray for the people who disrespected and reviled one publicly, without regard for one's feelings. All of those who have sought to live at a nobler spiritual plateau have known the sting of public rebuke. Third was the command not to retaliate against people, even when they inflicted the worst indignity on one, that of slapping one in the face. Jesus said to turn the other cheek. In the ancient world, much as it is today, to be slapped in public was the worst form of humiliation. Finally, Jesus said to give freely and without restrictions. If people had their cloaks taken, they were to give their coats as well. When poorer people took what they needed to live and survive, those who had more should not ask for their belongings back. The idea of these exhortations was to remain open and vulnerable to these insults again.

Jesus said that when you consider everything that people have done to undermine and destroy your life, your reaction must still be driven by the ethics of unconditional love (1 Corinthians 13:4-5). One of the challenges of these teachings across the years has been how to understand such radical demands. In a sense, these teachings are framed in the form of hyperbolical teachings, which means that they represent exaggerated speech that is intended to convey a serious message. Did Jesus literally mean what He said? Of course, He meant what He said. These teachings are intended to serve as models to followers of the Lord for how not to respond to those who are opposed to the kingdom, who mistreat and abuse you, and who without warrant take advantage of your generosity and commitment to follow Jesus. Jesus lived by what He taught, and these words are still the supreme model for us today.

C. Parameters of the Golden Rule
(Luke 6:31)

And as ye would that men should do to you, do ye also to them likewise.

Verse 31 has come to be known as the "Golden Rule." No one is exactly sure when this description of the verse entered the language of the church; it may have been in the sixteenth, seventeenth, or eighteenth century. What is clear is what Jesus said about the law of reciprocity. This simply means to treat others in the same manner that you wish to be treated. This command is stated in the positive in Leviticus 19:18, NRSV: "You shall not take vengeance…but you shall love your neighbor as yourself…." Jesus identified this as one of only two commandments that, if kept, would fulfill all the Law (Matthew 22:37-40).

Each of us wants to be loved, admired, respected, obeyed, and appreciated; therefore, we should sow the seeds of the aforementioned heart attitudes. We will surely reap what we sow. The Law of sowing and reaping can be applied to these heart attitudes: 1) You reap what you sow; 2) You reap at a different season; and, 3) You reap more than you sow. As long as the earth lasts, no human being can alter this law (see Galatians 6:7). There are similar types of teachings found in the ancient Jewish rabbinical writings which say: "What you hate do to no one," and "Judge a fellow guest's needs by your own." The application of these words in the lives of believers would eliminate much of the infighting and conflict that goes on in many congregations today.

D. Principles to Govern Conduct
(Luke 6:32-36)

For if ye love them which love you, what thank have ye? for sinners also love those that love them. And if ye do good to them which do good to you, what thank have ye? for sinners also do even the same. And if ye lend to them of whom ye hope to receive, what thank have ye? for sinners also lend to sinners, to receive as much again. But love ye your enemies, and do good, and lend, hoping for nothing again; and your reward shall be great, and ye shall be the children of the Highest: for he is kind unto the unthankful and to the evil. Be ye therefore merciful, as your Father also is merciful.

What are principles? They are rules or teachings that are generally true in every culture and generation. Jesus gave some strong principles for His disciples to live by. He continued to press into the hearts of His disciples that a radically different nature of the ethics of love was to characterize their lives. It had to be so different that there was nothing else that could compare to it. What makes you different if you love the people who love you? Many people do not have difficulty relating to people with whom they feel a deep sense of kinship. We find it easier to work with them than we do with those with whom we disagree. Society has been polarized into three groups of people: the upper class, middle class, and lower class. People within each social stratum gravitate to each other. Churches are segregated among colors. In mainline denominations in America, churches that some foreigners attend are referred to as "language churches." Jesus taught us to look beyond our perceived superiority and love people as He loved and still loves them (see verses 32 and 34).

How different are you if you do good to the people who do good to you? It takes a great deal of love and obedience to seek the welfare and goodwill of those who would like to see you falter and fail. During the Babylonian exile, God sent word by the prophet Jeremiah to His people that they were to seek the welfare of the city in which they had been exiled (see Jeremiah 29:7). In seeking the goodwill of their enemies, they would find peace.

Jesus said that if you lend to people who are going to pay you back, what will make your life stand out? All of these statements summon believers to examine how they think about their own relationship with the Lord Jesus Christ and whether or not they are models of the life of Christ. Again, the call to discipleship and kingdom living is clearly a call to live at a higher level of spirituality. Why would anyone think of you as being a superior saint when your life looks, basically, like everyone else's lives? Jesus challenged the people to live differently, think differently, and most of all, act differently.

The exhortation reached its zenith in the call to be children of the Highest, which is a clear reference to God. We often hear the excuse, "I am not perfect. Therefore, I cannot do these things." However, the command is to be like the Father, who is merciful and kind to even the lowest and worst sinner. God is no respecter of persons because He is kind to the just and to the unjust. How do we become like God? We find favor with God by loving our enemies, doing good to them, and lending while not expecting to get anything back. God is the God of all of creation; therefore, His love and kindness extend even to those who do not call upon His name or who may even hate His name. By manifesting the nature of God, Jesus promised that the believer's reward would be great. He did not specify what this reward would be, and no effort should be made to speculate. Our minds are not capable of fully comprehending the depth of all that God has prepared for those who love Him and have lived in obedience to His Word (see 1 Corinthians 2:9-16). Moses was faithful to God in everything He was asked to do and God called him His servant (Joshua 1:1-4). The rewards of believers are the favor and blessings of God that come because they have sought to live lives of faithful obedience to Him (see Deuteronomy 6:3; 28:1-14). Obedience to God is the highest virtue of faithfulness. Just as God is merciful and faithful in the extension of His mercy, so are His children to do and be the same (Psalm 107).

III. CONCLUDING REFLECTIONS

The Christian ethic of loving one's enemies was a centerpiece of the nonviolent theology of Dr. Martin Luther King, Jr. His belief in the dignity of all men and women was the clarion call to live out the creeds of their professions of faith. Love is stronger than hatred, and peace is a nobler alternative to violence and war. Christians must not only pray for peace in the world; they must be at the center of bringing peace to every place they go.

This lesson should provoke serious reflection upon what it means to be a Christian. Is there evidence in your life that you have been with Jesus? When the apostles Peter and John stood before the Sanhedrin Council, we are told that the Jewish religious leaders took notice that they had been with Jesus (see Acts 4:13). Is there evidence in your life that you have been born again? Is there evidence in your life that you are committed to developing a Christlike character? Is there evidence in your life that you are growing in grace each day? When you look at yourself, do you see any evidence or signs of a deep abiding relationship with God through our Lord Jesus Christ?

Our lives will bear the fruit of righteousness. Are you living a kingdom life in your home, marriage, with your children, and on your job? It is not enough to talk in a pious manner if we fail to exhibit true Christian behavior.

PRAYER

Heavenly Father, teach us to love as You love. May we be more willing to live out our creeds, manifest the virtues of obedience to Your Word, and have patience toward one another. Thank You for sending the Lord Jesus Christ to show us a more excellent way. Forgive us our sins. In the name of Jesus Christ, we pray. Amen.

WORD POWER

Love (Greek: *agapao*)—there are different words for "love" in the Bible; but the one that is used here is agapao. The word implies high esteem or high regard for its object. Agape is the love of God toward His Son—Jesus Christ, and toward the human race (see John 3:16). Phileo, on the other hand, is an instinctive, affectionate attachment based on judgment and calculation.

HOME DAILY BIBLE READINGS
(January 7-13, 2008)

Inspired to Love

MONDAY, January 7: "Trust in the Lord" (Psalm 37:1–11)
TUESDAY, January 8: "Love Your Neighbor" (Leviticus 19:17–18)
WEDNESDAY, January 9: "Love Your Enemies" (Luke 6:27–28)
THURSDAY, January 10: "Absorb Injustice" (Luke 6:29–30)
FRIDAY, January 11: "Set the Standard" (Luke 6:31)
SATURDAY, January 12: "Expect Nothing in Return" (Luke 6:34–36)
SUNDAY, January 13: "Posterity for the Peaceable" (Psalm 37:35–40)

LESSON 8   January 20, 2008

INSPIRED TO PRAY

DEVOTIONAL READING: **Psalm 28:6-9**   BACKGROUND SCRIPTURE: **Luke 11:5-13**
PRINT PASSAGE: **Luke 11:5-13**   KEY VERSE: **Luke 11:9**

Luke 11:5-13—KJV

5 And he said unto them, Which of you shall have a friend, and shall go unto him at midnight, and say unto him, Friend, lend me three loaves;
6 For a friend of mine in his journey is come to me, and I have nothing to set before him?
7 And he from within shall answer and say, Trouble me not: the door is now shut, and my children are with me in bed; I cannot rise and give thee.
8 I say unto you, Though he will not rise and give him, because he is his friend, yet because of his importunity he will rise and give him as many as he needeth.
9 And I say unto you, Ask, and it shall be given you; seek, and ye shall find; knock, and it shall be opened unto you.
10 For every one that asketh receiveth; and he that seeketh findeth; and to him that knocketh it shall be opened.
11 If a son shall ask bread of any of you that is a father, will he give him a stone? or if he ask a fish, will he for a fish give him a serpent?
12 Or if he shall ask an egg, will he offer him a scorpion?
13 If ye then, being evil, know how to give good gifts unto your children: how much more shall your heavenly Father give the Holy Spirit to them that ask him?

Luke 11:5-13—NRSV

5 And he said to them, "Suppose one of you has a friend, and you go to him at midnight and say to him, 'Friend, lend me three loaves of bread;
6 for a friend of mine has arrived, and I have nothing to set before him.'
7 And he answers from within, 'Do not bother me; the door has already been locked, and my children are with me in bed; I cannot get up and give you anything.'
8 I tell you, even though he will not get up and give him anything because he is his friend, at least because of his persistence he will get up and give him whatever he needs.
9 "So I say to you, Ask, and it will be given you; search, and you will find; knock, and the door will be opened for you.
10 For everyone who asks receives, and everyone who searches finds, and for everyone who knocks, the door will be opened.
11 Is there anyone among you who, if your child asks for a fish, will give a snake instead of a fish?
12 Or if the child asks for an egg, will give a scorpion?
13 If you then, who are evil, know how to give good gifts to your children, how much more will the heavenly Father give the Holy Spirit to those who ask him!"

BIBLE FACT

Prayer is no laggard work; it is engaging the soul and heart in the presence of God. Prayer cannot be sporadic, but rather must be conscientious and persistent. This persistence overcomes our doubt and insensitivity. Both adults and youth should learn how to pray.

UNIFYING LESSON PRINCIPLE

We long for a relationship with someone who cares enough to listen to and respond to our needs. To whom can we go? Jesus taught that we have a loving heavenly Parent to whom we can persistently bring our needs and the desires of our hearts.

TOPICAL OUTLINE OF THE LESSON

I. Introduction
   A. Prayer
   B. Biblical Background

II. Exposition and Application of the Scripture
   A. The Friend Who Visited at Midnight
   (Luke 11:5-7)
   B. The Lesson of Persistence in Prayer
   (Luke 11:8-10)
   C. The Reasonableness of Prayer
   (Luke 11:11-13)

III. Concluding Reflections

LESSON OBJECTIVES

Upon completion of this lesson, the students will know that:
1. God answers prayer;
2. Prayer requires discipline and commitment;
3. We all have equal access to the throne of grace; and,
4. Prayer solidifies our relationship with God and establishes our trust in Him.

POINTS TO BE EMPHASIZED

ADULT/YOUTH
Adult Topic: **Finding a Listening Ear**
Youth Topic: **Inspired to Pray!**
Adult/Youth Key Verse: **Luke 11:9**
Print Passage: **Luke 11:5-13**

—Being persistent achieves its purpose in human relationships and can achieve an even greater purpose when we are persistent with God.

—Jesus appears to applaud the persistent efforts of the friend as our example of not giving up in prayer.

—If loving parents will do anything to provide for their children, how much more can we expect from God—who loves us?

—In the parable, Jesus mentions that the friend asks for bread in order to help fulfill the requirements of hospitality. The request for bread is in order to feed another.

—Even an annoyed friend will give bread to a neighbor. God willingly gives the Holy Spirit to those who ask.

—Jesus' comparison moves from friends to parents in order to help the listeners develop a deeper understanding of God's desire to give us what we need.

—Jesus teaches that the focus of prayer should be the desire for the Holy Spirit.

CHILDREN
Children Topic: **God Hears and Answers Prayer**
Key Verse: **Luke 11:9**
Print Passage: **Luke 11:5-13**

—Jesus encourages us to pray to God.

—Jesus teaches that God listens to our prayers.

—Jesus teaches that God loves us and cares for us.

—Jesus teaches us that sometimes we have to wait for answers to our prayers.

I. INTRODUCTION

A. Prayer

Today's lesson is about prayer and the need to be persistent in petitioning God the Father. The Scriptures teach that God does hear and answer prayer (Psalm 34:6; Isaiah 65:24). The Bible is full of the prayers of the saints who have faced dangerous and life-threatening situations (2 Kings 19:14-19; 20:1-6). Through their prayers, they found strength and help in their darkest moments. Christians in the first century prayed often for guidance, boldness, and direction in the work of missions (Acts 1:14; 2:42; 4:31; 6:4; 13:1-3). One important prerequisite to prayer is helplessness. When we are helpless, we are ready to pray. But as long as there are other plans to solve problems at hand, then there will be the belief that prayer is not needed. Only the one who is helpless is ready to pray (Matthew 9:12). Luke tells us that when Jesus was praying, the sweat that was coming out from Him was like blood (Luke 22:44).

In the Gospels, one of the most poignant pictures we have of Jesus is His consistent and intimate prayer life (John 17). Jesus shared with His disciples the need to continue in prayer even when it looked as though things would never change. It is clear from the Gospels that Jesus practiced the privilege of prayer (see Luke 6:12f). In the teachings of Jesus, prayer was the outpouring of the human heart in adoration to God. Through prayer, one would be thrust into the throne room of heaven, where he or she could "obtain mercy, and find grace to help in time of need" (Hebrews 4:16).

Many deeply spiritual saints have written about the importance of prayer. Richard Foster wrote, "Prayer catapults us onto the frontier of the spiritual life." Harry Emerson Fosdick wrote, "Prayer is the soul of religion...Failure in prayer is the loss of religion itself in its inward and dynamic aspect of fellowship with the eternal." Prayer is our opportunity to encounter our heavenly Father on the plane of our deepest need. Prayer is the one moment that we have to experience the invisible God in our visible world. Prayer is warfare. The moment you are about to pray, the enemy begins to play on your mind. The telephone may ring off the hook, the children may be calling for attention, and so forth. When such things happen, stay on your knees.

B. Biblical Background

The parable of the friend who knocked at midnight is found only in the gospel of Luke. It follows Jesus' instructions on how to pray (Luke 11:1-4). Jesus was at the halfway point in His ministry (Luke 9:51). According to Luke's account of His ministry, more of His time would be devoted to teaching the disciples and preparing them for their missions to the world (Luke 10:1-16; 24:46-47). During this time, there were occasions when Jesus would slip away from His disciples to have time alone to meditate and pray. The weight of Calvary was starting to close in on His heart and spirit.

During one of my trips to Israel, I was able to view a small cave that overlooks the Sea of Galilee. It is nestled in the hillside away from the main road that ran from Capernaum to Gennesaret and Magdala. Tradition has it that Jesus would go to this place and pray, and this may be where He was when one of His disciples observed Him in prayer and wanted to be taught to pray. What followed was a second lesson on the Lord's Prayer. The first lesson occurred during the Sermon on the Mount, where Jesus gave a series of lessons on life in the kingdom of God (Matthew 6:9-13). There is a question we must answer in regard to this prayer and its place in the Gospel. Is this a different prayer from the one found in Matthew? No, it is not a different prayer. It is the same prayer taught at a different time under different circumstances. There are some minor variations between the two prayers, because the circumstances under which they were taught were different. There were also two compilers: Matthew and Luke. It is quite possible that Jesus taught the same lessons again and again, varying them according to the context. When teaching a lesson or sharing principles for living, the content of what He said quite possibly varied from place to place. When Paul retold the account of his conversion on the road to Damascus, in each instance he emphasized different aspects of his testimony (Acts 9:1-9; 22:6-21; 26:12-18). It was and is natural for a teacher to change the emphasis of a lesson as the context changes.

II. EXPOSITION AND APPLICATION OF THE SCRIPTURE

A. The Friend Who Visited at Midnight (Luke 11:5-7)

And he said unto them, Which of you shall have a friend, and shall go unto him at midnight, and say unto him, Friend, lend me three loaves; For a friend of mine in his journey is come to me, and I have nothing to set before him? And he from within shall answer and say, Trouble me not: the door is now shut, and my children are with me in bed; I cannot rise and give thee.

This parable was one that Jesus' disciples readily related to and understood. Many of them had just returned from preaching the Gospel throughout Galilee and they had been dependent upon others for their food and lodging (Luke 9:1-6; 10:1-17). In order to teach a lesson about the necessity of persistence in prayer, Jesus told a parable about a man who had a friend show up at his home at midnight. It would not be unusual for this to happen, given that in the ancient world people would often travel during the hours of darkness to escape the oppressive heat. Traveling during the hours of darkness meant that people would arrive at their destinations late in the evening. Mary and Joseph reached Bethlehem at night, and there was no room for them in the inn (Luke 2:9). Remember, there were no real hotels or travelers' inns in those days where one could simply go and rent a room for the night. Often inns were the residences of local people who would open their doors for strangers to reside with them. This kind of cordial hospitality still exists today in the Middle East and Africa.

Meals were prepared daily, and usually there was nothing left over for the next day. When the friend showed up unexpectedly, the man whose house he visited went into a panic because he had to provide for his guest. He hurriedly got dressed and went to another friend's home to see if he would lend him some loaves of bread. If there was going to be anything left that would keep overnight, it would be bread. He pleaded with another friend to help him out. From within the small home, he heard the reply: Go away. This friend was already in bed and could not get out of bed without disturbing the entire family.

Homes in Galilee were made out of balsam, a stone that is common in that part of Israel. They were one-room residences that had flat roofs and the ground as the floor. The family would sleep together on mats that could be rolled up and easily stored in the morning. Therefore, to wake up, look for a light, and make one's way to the door and down the street would cause quite a commotion. We would assume that it was asking a lot of a friend to show up at midnight and expect to be housed and fed. However, in that culture it was no more than a friend was expected to do.

Being a friend is one level of relationship and it is possible for a friend to say no to a request. Abraham was a friend of God, but Abraham did not receive an immediate answer to his request.

B. The Lesson of Persistence in Prayer (Luke 11:8-10)

I say unto you, Though he will not rise and give him, because he is his friend, yet because of his importunity he will rise and give him as many as he needeth. And I say unto you, Ask, and it shall be given you; seek, and ye shall find; knock, and it shall be opened unto you. For every one that asketh receiveth; and he that seeketh findeth; and to him that knocketh it shall be opened.

Jesus said that although the man refused initially to get out of bed and give the loaves of bread to his friend, because the man was persistent, his friend was finally persuaded to give in to the request. He would not just give him the loaves, but would give him all that he needed to meet the needs of the moment. In that culture, it was unthinkable for a man not to give what was needed by a neighbor. The honor of the one being asked was at stake, and to refuse the friend's request, even though it was midnight, would be to bring shame upon the one being asked. Abraham was persistent until God gave him his heart's desire. Verse 8 says, "…I say to you, though he will not rise and give, yet because of His persistence…." The word *persistence* in the original is "shameless boldness." Here, Jesus taught that the disciple was to be bold when the person requested things from God. In verses 5-7, the man went to his friend boldly in the night. Boldness in requesting things from God is a proof of intimacy with Him, and it is an assurance that God is alive and answers prayer.

The point of the parable was quite clear to those who first heard it. Jesus stated that God would certainly hear and answer our prayers. We can have total confidence that He will hear us, even in our "midnights" (Psalm 121; Acts 16:25-26). We may pray confidently, therefore, not because we trust in our own persistence, but because we know that in the time of need, God is even more trustworthy than a neighbor. How often have you prayed for days, weeks, months, and even years? Just when it looked as though God had turned a closed ear to your need, in His own time and way He answered your prayer (Isaiah 55:8-11).

The words of verses 9-10 are among the most familiar of Jesus' sayings, and there is an exact parallel in Matthew 7:7-8. Jesus taught that the key to answered prayer begins with asking. The petitioner must be willing to seek and to do everything humanly possible to receive from God what he or she is asking for in prayer. Seeking does not imply that you start out looking and then, when it does not look like you will have success, quit. Rather, the word implies a continuous process of looking faithfully and diligently until you succeed. Knocking can imply a kind of banging on the door to be heard. Jesus said that everyone who did these three things would get an answer to his or her petitions. If you ask, you will receive; seek, and you will find; knock, and the door will eventually be opened.

What are the lessons for us today about prayer? First, there is clearly the example of praying. In our fast-paced world of high tech communications and constant going and coming, many believers simply do not see the necessity of cultivating consistent quiet time in prayer. Persistence in prayer is also about developing a persistent commitment to the cultivation of the inner life, which begins with prayer and meditation on the Word of God. Second, seeking reminds us of the necessity of staying with our petitions until they are answered. Moreover, we are reminded that believers must do everything necessary to see that their prayers are answered. Why pray about youth gangs if there is never an action plan to become involved with ministering to them? Why pray about congregational unity when we make no effort to create and foster peace? Why pray for more missionaries to go to the foreign fields when we never recruit or support missions? Third, this implies the necessity to speak the need until you are heard. Congregations can make a huge difference in their communities when they become advocates for justice and equality. Knocking implies speaking loudly enough to be heard.

C. The Reasonableness of Prayer
(Luke 11:11-13)

If a son shall ask bread of any of you that is a father, will he give him a stone? or if he ask a fish, will he for a fish give him a serpent? Or if he shall ask an egg, will he offer him a scorpion? If ye then, being evil, know how to give good gifts unto your children: how much more shall your heavenly Father give the Holy Spirit to them that ask him?

Jesus asked a series of three rhetorical questions that had a positive response implied within the question. The love of a father will ensure that he gives his best to his son or daughter. If a son were to ask for bread from his father, would the father give anything less than that? No, he would give his son what he asked for. If a son asked for a fish, would he give him a serpent? No, he would give him a fish. Or if he asked for an egg, would he give him a scorpion? The answer is no! If evil men knew then how to give good gifts to their children, it stood to reason that the heavenly Father would give not just good gifts, but He would give the Holy Spirit, who is the best gift of all to those who ask. Here, the teaching diverges from what Jesus said in the gospel of Matthew. At this point, Jesus was also teaching a lesson about the need for those who followed Him to have the power and presence of the Holy Spirit living and dwelling within them. Persistent prayer had and has its reward. Not only will God give good gifts to those who ask; He will also give the Holy Spirit as a plus. Having the Holy Spirit as a gift from the Father is the crown of all gifts.

Jesus pointed to the gracious nature of a loving and merciful heavenly Father who heard and answered the prayers of His children. We learn a valuable lesson about parenting and giving. We cannot assume that all parents are willing to give their children good gifts. Jesus shows that God should be our model for giving. God gives good gifts to those who love and obey Him, and the greatest of all of those gifts is the gift of eternal life.

III. CONCLUDING REFLECTIONS

The lack of cultivation of a life of prayer is probably the biggest failure of the postmodern Christian church. Many churches gather each week for an hour on Wednesdays or some other day of the week to have "Prayer Meeting." These services are often attended by a small percentage of the congregation. When one examines the prayer life of the first-century Christian church, it becomes obvious that there is a wide chasm of difference between their prayer lives and ours. While we cannot generalize across the board and say that churches do not practice prayer, we can say that the churches do not practice consistent prevailing prayer for power, boldness, deliverance, and holiness. Many congregations will come together to pray in a time of internal crisis or when they propose to build a new building and they want God's blessings and favor. But there is a real need for congregations to gather in solemn assemblies and seek the face of God in sincere prayer and repentance.

PRAYER

Heavenly Father, creator and sustainer of all life, we bless You that everything we need is found in You. We are confident of this one thing—that in You we live, move, and have our being. Grant to your servants the grace to persist in prayer for the lost people of the world. Forgive us of our sins. In the name of Jesus Christ, we pray. Amen.

WORD POWER

Importunity *(anaideia)*—this means impudence, shamelessness, and unyielding perseverance. This word also carries the idea of boldness without shame. Some Bible teachers have taught that when one asks for something repeatedly, it is a sign of faithlessness. Jesus here teaches that persistence in prayer will be rewarded beyond what one requests.

HOME DAILY BIBLE READINGS
(January 14-20, 2008)

Inspired to Pray

MONDAY, January 14: "Answered Prayer" (Psalm 28:6–9)
TUESDAY, January 15: "Teach Us to Pray" (Luke 11:1–4)
WEDNESDAY, January 16: "A Friend's Request" (Luke 11:5–8)
THURSDAY, January 17: "Ask and Receive" (Luke 11:9–12)
FRIDAY, January 18: "Persistent in Prayer" (Luke 18:1–17)
SATURDAY, January 19: "God's Gift of the Holy Spirit" (Luke 11:13; Acts 2:1–4)
SUNDAY, January 20: "Praise the Lord!" (Psalm 138:1–3)

LESSON 9   January 27, 2008

INSPIRED TO TRUST

DEVOTIONAL READING: **Psalm 31:1-5**   BACKGROUND SCRIPTURE: **Luke 12:22-34**
PRINT PASSAGE: **Luke 12:22-34**   KEY VERSE: **Luke 12:22**

Luke 12:22-34—KJV

22 And he said unto his disciples, Therefore I say unto you, Take no thought for your life, what ye shall eat; neither for the body, what ye shall put on.

23 The life is more than meat, and the body is more than raiment.

24 Consider the ravens: for they neither sow nor reap; which neither have storehouse nor barn; and God feedeth them: how much more are ye better than the fowls?

25 And which of you with taking thought can add to his stature one cubit?

26 If ye then be not able to do that thing which is least, why take ye thought for the rest?

27 Consider the lilies how they grow: they toil not, they spin not; and yet I say unto you, that Solomon in all his glory was not arrayed like one of these.

28 If then God so clothe the grass, which is to day in the field, and to morrow is cast into the oven; how much more will he clothe you, O ye of little faith?

29 And seek not ye what ye shall eat, or what ye shall drink, neither be ye of doubtful mind.

30 For all these things do the nations of the world seek after: and your Father knoweth that ye have need of these things.

31 But rather seek ye the kingdom of God; and all these things shall be added unto you.

32 Fear not, little flock; for it is your Father's good pleasure to give you the kingdom.

33 Sell that ye have, and give alms; provide yourselves bags which wax not old, a treasure in the heavens that faileth not, where no thief approacheth, neither moth corrupteth.

34 For where your treasure is, there will your heart be also.

Luke 12:22-34—NRSV

22 He said to his disciples, "Therefore I tell you, do not worry about your life, what you will eat, or about your body, what you will wear.

23 For life is more than food, and the body more than clothing.

24 Consider the ravens: they neither sow nor reap, they have neither storehouse nor barn, and yet God feeds them. Of how much more value are you than the birds!

25 And can any of you by worrying add a single hour to your span of life?

26 If then you are not able to do so small a thing as that, why do you worry about the rest?

27 Consider the lilies, how they grow: they neither toil nor spin; yet I tell you, even Solomon in all his glory was not clothed like one of these.

28 But if God so clothes the grass of the field, which is alive today and tomorrow is thrown into the oven, how much more will he clothe you—you of little faith!

29 And do not keep striving for what you are to eat and what you are to drink, and do not keep worrying.

30 For it is the nations of the world that strive after all these things, and your Father knows that you need them.

31 Instead, strive for his kingdom, and these things will be given to you as well.

32 "Do not be afraid, little flock, for it is your Father's good pleasure to give you the kingdom.

33 Sell your possessions, and give alms. Make purses for yourselves that do not wear out, an unfailing treasure in heaven, where no thief comes near and no moth destroys.

34 For where your treasure is, there your heart will be also.

UNIFYING LESSON PRINCIPLE

We all face pressure and may experience anxiety. What can we do to combat anxiety and worry? Jesus says that when we trust in God, we have no need to worry.

TOPICAL OUTLINE OF THE LESSON

I. Introduction
A. Anxiety
B. Biblical Background

II. Exposition and Application of the Scripture
A. The Cause of Anxiety and Worry (Luke 12:22)
B. The Case Against Anxiety and Worry (Luke 12:23-30)
C. The Cure for Anxiety and Worry (Luke 12:31-34)

III. Concluding Reflections

LESSON OBJECTIVES

Upon the completion of this lesson, the students will know:

1. What anxiety is and how it can creep upon us unawares;
2. That anxiety is part of the human experience and it has no boundaries; and,
3. That Jesus recognized the damage anxiety can do in our lives and He offers a solution for it.

POINTS TO BE EMPHASIZED

ADULT/YOUTH
Adult Topic: Combating Anxiety and Worry
Youth Topic: Inspired to Trust
Adult Key Verse: Luke 12:22
Youth Key Verse: Luke 12:34
Print Passage: Luke 12:22-34

—To add a "cubit" to one's life would be to add about seventeen to twenty inches to one's body length, thereby supporting the absurdity of thinking that worry serves a useful purpose.

—To worry about material wants is to worry about things that interfere with our deeper spiritual needs.

— Jesus calls His followers to seek Him, trust in Him, and not be ensnared in the trap of worldly pursuits.

—Trusting God in the good times and the bad times is a recurring theme of the Scriptures. The Psalms, for example, are a good companion to any study about trusting God because they give us a human view of the experience of trust.

—Wood was scarce in Palestine, and dried grasses and wildflowers were used to feed the oven fires.

—Early Christians would interpret "little flock" as a reference to the church.

CHILDREN
Children Topic: Trusting God
Key Verse: Luke 12:34
Print Passage: Luke 12:22-34

—Jesus teaches us not to worry but to believe in Him.

—Jesus teaches us to look at all we have and be thankful.

—God will provide for our needs.

—We have to believe that God knows what we need.

I. INTRODUCTION

A. Anxiety

Anxiety is the most prevalent cause of emotional and mental distress. Anxiety is a state of uneasiness and apprehension brought on when we are preoccupied with future uncertainties. Anxiety is inner anguish over a matter that may or may not happen. The treatment and development of drugs and therapies for anxiety and its attendant illnesses is a $250 billion global business. Westerners are covering up their fears and inner pain in a sea of prescription and non-prescription pills.

Everyone struggles with anxiety at some point. We have all worried about circumstances in our lives or in the lives of people we care about. We may have worried over things that have no direct bearing on our lives. Some people attend weekly worship services while their minds are racing 100 miles per minute, thinking about all of the problems, issues, concerns, and drama that envelops their lives. Jesus cared about people and their problems. Our Lord revealed His sensitivity to the problems and concerns that the people of His day felt. In this lesson, we will learn that God does care about us and that we can cast all our cares upon Him because He cares for each one of us (1 Peter 5:7).

B. Biblical Background

Today's lesson is part of a discussion about material possessions that began with Luke 12:13. Jesus had just finished encouraging His disciples to be strong in the face of opposition when someone in the crowd asked Him to settle a family dispute over an inheritance. The man called Jesus "Master," which was a title of respect. He recognized that Jesus was a highly regarded teacher in Galilee. In the Law of Moses, there were specific rules and guidelines for how inheritances were to be handled (Numbers 27:1-11; Deuteronomy 21:15-17). The man approached Jesus because traditionally these types of disputes were questions of the law, and it was up to the rabbis to offer the proper interpretation of the laws regarding inheritances (see Luke 9:51—24:53). We do not know about either of the persons involved in the dispute. We have no knowledge as to whether the petitioner was the younger or the older person in the dispute. Nor do we have any information about the nature of the inheritance. Anything we say regarding that would be mere speculation. We do know that Jesus took that occasion as an opportunity to teach a practical lesson about material possessions, and the need for His disciples to release themselves from anxiety over their accumulation of possessions.

II. EXPOSITION AND APPLICATION OF THE SCRIPTURE

A. The Cause of Anxiety and Worry (Luke 12:22)

And he said unto his disciples, Therefore I say unto you, Take no thought for your life, what ye shall eat; neither for the body, what ye shall put on.

The word *therefore* connected what Jesus

had just finished saying to what was about to follow. He had just finished talking about the folly of putting too much stock and confidence in earthly possessions. Why spend your time amassing great wealth only to leave it here for someone else to enjoy when life could be better spent serving God? Jesus said, "Take no thought..." (verse 22). The grammatical structure reveals an ongoing issue, and as such, Jesus commanded them to stop worrying about how they were going to live and survive. What was the cause of their anxiety and worry? They had been with Jesus for nearly two or three years, and there appeared to be no plan to meet personal needs other than to pray and evangelize (see Luke 11:3). Jesus had already told them that foxes had holes and birds had nests, but the Son of Man had no place to lay His head (Luke 9:58).

Jesus told His disciples that worrying about their needs for food and clothing was not going to help them at all. It may be that the disciples were so concerned with how they were going to survive that they were losing sight of the mission. Remember, these were not extremely poor men who followed Jesus. They were independent small business owners, and each made a pretty good living fishing or collecting taxes. They were not used to missing their pay (Mark 10:28-30).

B. The Case Against Anxiety and Worry (Luke 12:23-30)

The life is more than meat, and the body is more than raiment. Consider the ravens: for they neither sow nor reap; which neither have storehouse nor barn; and God feedeth them: how much more are ye better than the fowls? And which of you with taking thought can add to his stature one cubit? If ye then be not able to do that thing which is least, why take ye thought for the rest? Consider the lilies how they grow: they toil not, they spin not; and yet I say unto you, that Solomon in all his glory was not arrayed like one of these. If then God so clothe the grass, which is to day in the field, and to morrow is cast into the oven; how much more will he clothe you, O ye of little faith? And seek not ye what ye shall eat, or what ye shall drink, neither be ye of doubtful mind. For all these things do the nations of the world seek after: and your Father knoweth that ye have need of these things.

Jesus gave three reasons why worrying was not necessary. These are found in verses 23-25. He followed that up with some practical lessons from nature about ravens and lilies in verses 27-28. He concluded by reminding His disciples that by worrying they were acting like the nations of the world. Let's look at the three reasons that Jesus cited for why worrying was not a good idea.

First, life is about more than food and clothing. The disciples may have been spending time worrying about things that were of no concern to them. They had already been with Jesus for a while, and their daily needs had been met. Life was about more than the next meal or what they would put on. Mission and ministry were the primary things for them to be concerned with. It may be that Jesus reminded them of who they were and what they had been called to do. They were God's very elect, chosen and anointed, and as such, God would take care of them. He would supply their every need according to the vast riches of His storehouse. The apostle Paul learned the blessedness of trusting God to provide and shared that spiritual gem with both the church at Philippi and with all Christians (Philippians 4:6, 19).

In verse 24, the ravens provided the second lesson for not worrying. The ravens had to eat, and yet they did not plant fields of grain; nor did they have vast storehouses. Here Jesus argued from the lesser to the greater; if God fed the ravens, how much were they better than the fowls? Ravens were regarded as unclean birds in the ancient world, and they were among the birds that the ancient Israelites were forbidden to eat (Leviticus 11:15; Deuteronomy 14:14). The point that Jesus made was that if God took care of unclean creatures, why would the disciples worry about their own survival? The passing comment that, unlike human beings, the birds had neither storehouses nor barns subtly reminds the reader that the rich fool's barns offered him no security at all (verse 23).

The third reason not to worry is found in verse 25 where Jesus talked about the futility of worrying. What did worrying produce? Could it add to the disciples' lives? Could it add to their height? The obvious answer was no—it could do neither of these things. Who even today can add one day or one minute to the time that will be spent on this earth? But we can certainly reduce our days through ceaseless worry. Job thought of the pointlessness of spending time worrying about what God had already determined to be the boundaries of one's lifespan (Job 14:6). Yet people spend billions of dollars a year trying to lengthen their days.

The conclusion to the whole matter can be seen in verse 26 where Jesus pointed out that if you cannot do even the little things, why worry about the rest? Jesus looked out across the expanse of the Galilean hillside and said, in essence, to look at all of the lilies; none of the lilies worked to survive. Not even Solomon in all of his glory could compare to the least of these. The flowers did not work. They had neither fishing boat nor nets, and yet God provided for them. The flowers of the fields did not have barns with which to store nutrients, and were totally dependent upon God for rain and sunshine, yet they bloomed year after year.

Jesus no doubt spoke these words in the spring of the year, sometime in early March-April when the fields were coming out with plants and flowers. In Israel in the spring of the year, one could observe a vast variety of flowers. Jesus could have been speaking about any of a number of different types of flowers that bloomed at that time of year.

God takes care of the very least of the earth's plant life: grass. Grass is here one day but gone the next; how much more would God clothe His children? Grass has a very short time to grow in Israel. The fields dry up very quickly when the spring rains cease, and the heat produced by the cloudless days of summer dries up the earth.

Jesus called into question the faith and confidence that His disciples had in God. "Ye of little faith" (verse 28). The statement implied that the disciples had trouble trusting God. Further still, the words "little faith" denoted a short memory when it came to recalling the things that God had already done in their very midst (Matthew 8:26; 14:31; 16:5-8).

In verses 29-30, Jesus challenged His disciples to stop looking for what they were going to eat or wear. He wanted them to remove all of the doubts they had about their needs being met. Worrying about the material things of life ranked them with the other nations of the world. Jesus said the nations of the world spent a lot of their time seeking worldly things. It was not to be this way among the disciples. Jesus reminded them that their Father knew that they needed these things and He would make sure that they had them (Luke 11:9-13).

C. The Cure for Anxiety and Worry (Luke 12:31-34)

But rather seek ye the kingdom of God; and all these things

shall be added unto you. Fear not, little flock; for it is your Father's good pleasure to give you the kingdom. Sell that ye have, and give alms; provide yourselves bags which wax not old, a treasure in the heavens that faileth not, where no thief approacheth, neither moth corrupteth. For where your treasure is, there will your heart be also.

Jesus said to His disciples that rather than spend their time worrying about how they would survive, "But rather seek ye the kingdom of God; and all these things shall be added unto you" (verse 31). Don't be anxious about life; establish your primary purpose for living, which is the expansion and promotion of the great purpose of God. His purpose is that the world might be saved and know the true and living God and that all might come to the knowledge of salvation in Him. Jesus will not have us spend time being anxious about how we are going to make ends meet; rather, we are to trust God for our provisions. Don't be anxious; seek first His kingdom, and all the things you need will be provided.

The words of Jesus are shaped into a present command and a future promise. The word *seek* expresses the present command and means to look diligently. It means to crave and yearn for a thing so much that it literally consumes your life. In the Greek language, seek is in the present imperative tense, which means we are to make it a matter of grave urgency, immediately. The future promise states that because we have made the Lord's purpose our primary goal and principal priority, He will provide for all of our future needs as they arise. David wrote in Psalm 37:3-5, "Trust in the Lord, and do good; so shalt thou dwell in the land, and verily thou shalt be fed. Delight thyself also in the Lord; and he shall give thee the desires of thine heart. Commit thy way unto the Lord; trust also in him; and he shall bring it to pass."

We are to seek the kingdom of God. The kingdom of God is not in a spatial, geographical, fixed location. It has no borders and boundaries like the United States. Rather, it is wherever God is King and Jesus Christ is Lord. God's kingdom is not defined and built upon a foundation of bricks, marble, and fine stones. It is not built upon the foundation of earthly power. Rather, it is wherever God is acknowledged as creator and sustainer of all life. The kingdom is where God is obeyed and trusted as King of kings. Because we have made God's purpose our main goal, we need not worry or be anxious about what we will eat, drink, or wear. He knows and will provide.

Seeking the kingdom of God will bring success. It would be God's good pleasure to give the disciples the kingdom. Jesus turned the tables from seeking earthly treasures to seeking the incorruptible treasures of heaven. They were bidden to sell their possessions and give alms or charitable gifts to the poor. The presence of thieves indicated that riches and possessions could and can very quickly be taken away. Moths could and can destroy the finest wardrobes and ruin the most expensive garments.

Verse 34 is proverbial and really speaks about one's commitment and loyalty to the things of God. Jesus pointed out that wherever a person pins his or her greatest hopes and expends the greatest amount of energy is where that person's treasures lie (see verse 34). The references to the heart and to treasure are figurative for "priorities" and "that which is valued." What we value most will be the things that we invest in. There is a clear call to the church of this generation to reassess its priorities and commitments to a kingdom agenda. Where have congregations invested the bulk of their resources? What have they done to build and fortify the kingdom of God against failure?

III. CONCLUDING REFLECTIONS

Believers who spend time worrying about how they are going to make it through life reveal their lack of faith in God. Worrying is pointless and produces nothing productive for the kingdom of God. Believers should spend their time doing the things that increase their faith in the living God. God gives us gifts so that we can make investments in the lives of the poor and helpless of the world. Commitment to Jesus Christ means detachment from the things of this world. God is calling for the post-modern church to divest itself of its own interests for the greater interests of our heavenly Father. What is the remedy for worry? The answer is to trust God and do good.

PRAYER

Heavenly Father, may we rejoice that You have given to us the good things of the earth to meet all of our basic needs. Thank You for the examples in nature that constantly remind us of Your providential care and compassion. Forgive us for not trusting You completely. In the name of Jesus Christ, we pray. Amen.

WORD POWER

Anxious (Greek: *merimnao'*)—this means to be troubled with care, distracted by future concerns, saddled by divided loyalty. This word anxious is preceded by another word (do not), which means "don't be," or "stop." Jesus here told His disciples to stop an action that was already in progress. He cautioned them not to be distracted or have divided opinions regarding the ability of the Father (God) to provide for their earthly and eternal needs.

HOME DAILY BIBLE READINGS
(January 21-27, 2008)

Inspired to Trust

MONDAY, January 21: "Trust God" (Psalm 31:1–5)
TUESDAY, January 22: "Valuable to God" (Luke 12:22–24)
WEDNESDAY, January 23: "Worry Won't Help!" (Luke 12:25–26)
THURSDAY, January 24: "Clothed by God" (Luke 12:27–28)
FRIDAY, January 25: "God Knows Your Needs" (Luke 12:29–31)
SATURDAY, January 26: "Receive the Kingdom" (Luke 12:32–34)
SUNDAY, January 27: "Trust God, Not Princes" (Psalm 146:1–7)

LESSON 10   February 3, 2008

SUMMONED TO LABOR

DEVOTIONAL READING: **Psalm 78:1-4**
PRINT PASSAGE: **Luke 10:1-12, 17-20**

BACKGROUND SCRIPTURE: **Luke 10:1-12, 17-20**
KEY VERSE: **Luke 10:2**

Luke 10:1-12, 17-20—KJV

AFTER THESE things the Lord appointed other seventy also, and sent them two and two before his face into every city and place, whither he himself would come.

2 Therefore said he unto them, The harvest truly is great, but the labourers are few: pray ye therefore the Lord of the harvest, that he would send forth labourers into his harvest.

3 Go your ways: behold, I send you forth as lambs among wolves.

4 Carry neither purse, nor scrip, nor shoes: and salute no man by the way.

5 And into whatsoever house ye enter, first say, Peace be to this house.

6 And if the son of peace be there, your peace shall rest upon it: if not, it shall turn to you again.

7 And in the same house remain, eating and drinking such things as they give: for the labourer is worthy of his hire. Go not from house to house.

8 And into whatsoever city ye enter, and they receive you, eat such things as are set before you:

9 And heal the sick that are therein, and say unto them, The kingdom of God is come nigh unto you.

10 But into whatsoever city ye enter, and they receive you not, go your ways out into the streets of the same, and say,

11 Even the very dust of your city, which cleaveth on us, we do wipe off against you: notwithstanding be ye sure of this, that the kingdom of God is come nigh unto you.

12 But I say unto you, that it shall be more tolerable in that day for Sodom, than for that city.

…..

17 And the seventy returned again with joy, saying, Lord, even the devils are subject unto us through thy name.

18 And he said unto them, I beheld Satan as lightning fall from heaven.

Luke 10:1-12, 17-20—NRSV

AFTER THIS the Lord appointed seventy others and sent them on ahead of him in pairs to every town and place where he himself intended to go.

2 He said to them, "The harvest is plentiful, but the laborers are few; therefore ask the Lord of the harvest to send out laborers into his harvest.

3 Go on your way. See, I am sending you out like lambs into the midst of wolves.

4 Carry no purse, no bag, no sandals; and greet no one on the road.

5 Whatever house you enter, first say, 'Peace to this house!'

6 And if anyone is there who shares in peace, your peace will rest on that person; but if not, it will return to you.

7 Remain in the same house, eating and drinking whatever they provide, for the laborer deserves to be paid. Do not move about from house to house.

8 Whenever you enter a town and its people welcome you, eat what is set before you;

9 cure the sick who are there, and say to them, 'The kingdom of God has come near to you.'

10 But whenever you enter a town and they do not welcome you, go out into its streets and say,

11 'Even the dust of your town that clings to our feet, we wipe off in protest against you. Yet know this: the kingdom of God has come near.'

12 I tell you, on that day it will be more tolerable for Sodom than for that town.

…..

17 The seventy returned with joy, saying, "Lord, in your name even the demons submit to us!"

18 He said to them, "I watched Satan fall from heaven like a flash of lightning.

UNIFYING LESSON PRINCIPLE

We are often summoned to struggle for purposes greater than ourselves. How do we respond to the summons? When Jesus appointed seventy disciples to prepare His way, they obeyed despite the probability of hardship and rejection.

19 Behold, I give unto you power to tread on serpents and scorpions, and over all the power of the enemy: and nothing shall by any means hurt you.
20 Notwithstanding in this rejoice not, that the spirits are subject unto you; but rather rejoice, because your names are written in heaven.

19 See, I have given you authority to tread on snakes and scorpions, and over all the power of the enemy; and nothing will hurt you.
20 Nevertheless, do not rejoice at this, that the spirits submit to you, but rejoice that your names are written in heaven."

TOPICAL OUTLINE OF THE LESSON

I. **Introduction**
   A. Fulfilling the Great Commission
   B. Biblical Background

II. **Exposition and Application of the Scripture**
   A. The Preparation for the Mission (Luke 10:1-4)
   B. The Plan of the Mission (Luke 10:5-12)
   C. The Proofs of the Mission's Success (Luke 10:17-20)

III. **Concluding Reflections**

LESSON OBJECTIVES:

Upon completion of this lesson, the students will know that:

1. There should be no unemployed Christians in God's vineyard;
2. Many are called, but few are chosen;
3. Each Christian is equipped with a gift to profit others in the vineyard; and,
4. Prayer raises up laborers for the kingdom work.

POINTS TO BE EMPHASIZED

ADULT/YOUTH

Adult Topic: **Response Requires Work**
Youth Topic: **Summoned to Labor**
Adult/Youth Key Verse: **Luke 10:2**
Print Passage: **Luke 10:1-12, 17-20**

—Jesus appointed and sent disciples to prepare the way for His future visits and to prepare people for the kingdom of God.
—Jesus let the seventy know the difficulties and dangers of discipleship (verse 3), but He assured them that His presence, power, and strength would be with them.
—The reasoning behind sending out people in pairs is found in Deuteronomy 17:6 and 19:15; two witnesses were required in order to establish a fact in any court of Jewish law.
—In New Testament times, travelers were dependent on the hospitality of others.

CHILDREN

Children Topic: **Working for God**
Key Verse: **Luke 10:2**
Print Passage: **Luke 10:1-12**

—The Lord sent seventy disciples to different places, and they obeyed.
—Jesus told them they were going to have a difficult time.
—If Jesus sends us to do something, He will be with us.
—Jesus wants us to tell others about Him and to be His messengers.

I. INTRODUCTION

A. Fulfilling the Great Commission

No man or woman has the right to call himself or herself a Christian if he or she denies, disobeys, and neglects the Great Commission and the charge to spread the Gospel to the ends of the earth (Matthew 28:19-20; Acts 1:8). No congregation can call itself a Christian church that does not see the mission of the church and the spread of the teachings of our Savior as the primary reason for its existence. This post-modern generation and the previous two generations of African-American Christians have not been as aggressive in the arena of foreign and home missions as the generations of the eighteenth and nineteenth centuries.

We have more work to do in the area of foreign missions. At the end of the nineteenth century, African-American Christians were at the forefront of the evangelization of Africa. For more than one hundred years, beginning with Lott Carey and his departure to Liberia, West Africa in 1815, Black Christians sent missionaries to Africa, built churches, and supported them. Much of the leadership for the evangelization of Africa came from North Carolina and Virginia. Dr. Sandy Martin, a National Baptist Deacon who teaches at the University of Georgia, writes in his book, *Black Baptists and African Missions,* "Virginia Baptists considered Africa second only to their own state as an object of missionary concern, though undoubtedly blacks in other parts of the South were unchurched and in need of material and educational assistance." The popular belief among both white and Black Baptists was that blacks were more suited for missionary work in Africa. Between 1895 and 1920, there arose a generation of African-American Christians who had a strong, determined sense of purpose to evangelize Africa. They did their best, but a sense of apathy arose among African-American Christians who came after them. The zeal for missions has gone down; we are now preoccupied with modern edifices at the expense of supporting mission work. We must regain our vision of a global Christian movement. In this lesson, we are reminded of the primary reason that Jesus called and gathered a group of followers around Him.

B. Biblical Background

The account of the sending out of the seventy disciples is unique to the gospel of Luke. Each of the gospel writers recorded a time when Jesus commissioned the twelve disciples and sent them out to preach, heal, and cast out demons. They all report the instructions that Jesus gave to the disciples before sending them forth (Matthew 10:1-42; Mark 6:7-13; Luke 9:1-6). This mission occurred after the sending of the Twelve in Luke 9:1-6 and their subsequent return from a successful mission of preaching and healing (Luke 9:10). Between the first mission of the twelve and the sending of the seventy, a great deal happened in the life of Jesus and in the lives of the disciples (Luke 9:10-62). Among the most significant occurrences were the opportunities for Jesus to enlist more men and women into service for the kingdom of God. There were people who continued to express interest, some of whom accepted the invitation and joined the band of Jesus' most intimate followers. Then there were others for whom the demands of committed discipleship were too much to bear (Luke 9:57-62). It was from this new, larger group of disciples that Jesus drew the seventy.

Why would Jesus enlist more people to serve as roaming missionaries? The answer has to do with the growth of the work. There developed the recognition that the mission in Galilee and the Decapolis required more than just the Twelve. Jesus included others who looked forward in time to the birth and growth of the Christian church, which started on the Day of Pentecost. This larger mission in Galilee and the Decapolis involved both opportunity and challenge. This was an opportunity to be partners with God in the expansion of the kingdom. It was a challenge in that there was nothing glamorous about the work of missions.

II. EXPOSITION AND APPLICATION OF THE SCRIPTURE

A. The Preparation for the Mission
(Luke 10:1-4)

AFTER THESE things the Lord appointed other seventy also, and sent them two and two before his face into every city and place, whither he himself would come. Therefore said he unto them, The harvest truly is great, but the labourers are few: pray ye therefore the Lord of the harvest, that he would send forth labourers into his harvest. Go your ways: behold, I send you forth as lambs among wolves. Carry neither purse, nor scrip, nor shoes: and salute no man by the way.

"After these things" looks back to the lessons about commitment to being disciples. Evidently, there were people who heard and accepted the call to share in the work of the kingdom of God. We do not know how large the crowd was from which Jesus selected this group of seventy, nor do we have any other biographical information about who they were. At that point, it was not important. Jesus organized them into teams of two and sent them out in various directions to the places where He was planning to go and preach. Why send them out in teams of two people? This was because in those days, in order for a matter to be validated, it required at least two witnesses (Deuteronomy 17:6; 19:15; 1 Timothy 5:19). In the wisdom writings of Ecclesiastes, the notion of teamwork is spelled out where two are always better than one (Ecclesiastes 4:9-10). Organizing the disciples into teams of two would enable them to support each other.

The first thing Jesus did was to define the magnitude of the work by pointing out that the harvest was truly great. Here, our Lord revealed His ability to teach, using the everyday language of the people. Jesus saw the harvest of lost souls rotting in the fields because of a lack of workers.

It would have been easy for Jesus to have become discouraged and overwhelmed by the magnitude of the challenge. But He enlisted His disciples to pray for workers. The reason was plain—"the harvest is plentiful" (verse 2, NIV). The problem was and is not having enough workers—"the workers are few" (verse 2, NIV). There was more work than there were workers to accomplish the tasks. Prayer was the key to achieving the results that would be needed. Prayer was and is one of the best and most powerful ways to help Christ's cause in the world. Jesus did not call for more training; He called upon the disciples to pray first before going out. The One who owns the harvest can provide the means to reap His fields. God is Lord of the harvest. There is urgency in the task. Pray that He will send forth workers.

Jesus never pulled any punches with His disciples about what to expect in their work. They would go forth as lambs facing hungry wolves. The wolf was described as an animal that was extremely ferocious and terrifying. Wolves were viewed as savage creatures (Acts 20:29); they devoured (Genesis 49:27), tore to pieces (Ezekiel 22:27), and they especially preyed upon helpless sheep (Matthew 10:16; John 10:12). In ancient Israel, wolves were feared because they were animals of the night who would kill their prey and feast upon it all night long (Habakkuk 1:8; Zephaniah 3:3). The seventy missionaries understood in no uncertain terms what they were facing. But, as sheep in the Lord's pasture, they did not need to serve in fear, because God would take care of them.

In verse 4, Jesus told the disciples not to carry any money or extra shoes. No doubt, they saw this as a very strange statement. Jesus wanted them to be totally dependent upon God for their provisions. They were not to spend time in lengthy greetings, which were common in that day. The urgency of the task demanded that they move with deliberate speed (2 Kings 4:29).

The lessons are very obvious. First, missions work must be given a high priority by the Christian church. This was the second time that Jesus sent out a group to preach repentance and to heal. Second, missions work must be thoroughly organized and filled with people who understand the nature of the assignment and are prepared to accept the risks. Third, missionaries must be sent forth. Saul and Barnabas did not go on their own, but were sent by the church at Antioch after much prayer and fasting for guidance (Acts 13:1-3). A lot of what is termed "missions work" in many churches is no more

than monthly meetings that discuss the need for more involvement; but these groups never get much beyond the talking stage. Discipleship means less talk and more action.

There are points to ponder here: 1) the harvest is plentiful; 2) prayer is an essential part of a successful evangelism; 3) "...Go...I send you" (verse 3). Jesus backed up His disciples with a command; 4) They must travel light; and, 5) they must greet no one. This means the disciples must remain focused and not engage in fraternal greetings.

B. The Plan of the Mission (Luke 10:5-12)

And into whatsoever house ye enter, first say, Peace be to this house. And if the son of peace be there, your peace shall rest upon it: if not, it shall turn to you again. And in the same house remain, eating and drinking such things as they give: for the labourer is worthy of his hire. Go not from house to house. And into whatsoever city ye enter, and they receive you, eat such things as are set before you: And heal the sick that are therein, and say unto them, The kingdom of God is come nigh unto you. But into whatsoever city ye enter, and they receive you not, go your ways out into the streets of the same, and say, Even the very dust of your city, which cleaveth on us, we do wipe off against you: notwithstanding be ye sure of this, that the kingdom of God is come nigh unto you. But I say unto you, that it shall be more tolerable in that day for Sodom, than for that city.

The instructions for the mission were clear, and it was evident that these disciples were going to be gone for several days. When they entered a town and found a place to reside, they were to pronounce peace upon that house (verse 5). If the owner or tenant of the house was a person of peace, then their peace was to remain, but if not, they were to retract their blessings and move on (verse 6). Kingdom workers must realize that power and authority existed in Jesus' directly commissioned messengers, since they conveyed the message of God's peace. Whatever food their hosts put before them was to be graciously received (verse 7). It must be noted that the spiritual benefit the worker brought with the kingdom message was worthy of support.

During a 2004 mission trip to a small town in Nigeria called Tombia, we were invited to have Sunday dinner with one of our hosts. There were members of the team who were very reluctant to eat any of the food set before them, because they felt that the sanitation standards in that country were different from what they are in America. Such an attitude is uncalled for by missionaries who take the Word of Christ to heart.

The mission consisted of preaching the Good News of the kingdom of God and healing the sick. The mission was a model of the itinerant ministry of Jesus as He traveled throughout Galilee (Matthew 4:23-25). As the disciples healed and preached, they were to let people know that the kingdom of God had come near to them. If they were not received, they were to go out into the streets and shake the dust off of their shoes as a sign of disapproval. Their peace would return to them. This was a very serious act in the ancient world and signaled God's scorn upon a city.

Jesus said that those who heard the Gospel and saw the miracles of healing yet still refused to believe, would receive a harsh punishment. It would be more tolerable for Sodom and Gomorrah in the Day of Judgment than for those nations who heard but rejected the Gospel. Why? The people of Jesus' day had a firsthand account of the incarnation of God's Son into the world. They saw His many and mighty demonstrations of power. They heard the profound yet simple teachings of divine truth. They

were witnesses of the most powerful ministry in Israel's history, but they turned away.

How harsh the judgment of the great western nations of the world in the last day will be! The world's leaders have a chance to even the playing field and make life better for the people they have exploited and used for economic gain; yet they keep oppressing these helpless people through the IMF (International Monetary Fund) and by other clandestine means.

C. The Proofs of the Mission's Success (Luke 10:17-20)

And the seventy returned again with joy, saying, Lord, even the devils are subject unto us through thy name. And he said unto them, I beheld Satan as lightning fall from heaven. Behold, I give unto you power to tread on serpents and scorpions, and over all the power of the enemy: and nothing shall by any means hurt you. Notwithstanding in this rejoice not, that the spirits are subject unto you; but rather rejoice, because your names are written in heaven.

We are not told how long the seventy disciples were gone. When they returned, they did so with joy, and reported to Jesus that things went better than they had expected. Even the demons were subject to them through the name of Jesus. They discovered that there was power in the name of Jesus. In the latter days of His earthly ministry, Jesus would teach His disciples the importance of His name (John 14:13-14, 26; 15:16; 16:23-26). In the preaching and healing of the early church, the name of Jesus would be synonymous with power (Acts 2:38; 3:6, 16; 4:17; 5:28; 9:15; 10:48).

Jesus encouraged the disciples by stating that Satan fell from heaven like lightning and by pointing out that the fact that the demons were subject to the disciples was further evidence of his defeat. The disciples had been given power over serpents and scorpions. Therefore, when they went forth in the future they were not to go in fear, but in the power of the Holy Spirit and with the knowledge that God would keep them.

What was to be the cause of their outpouring of joy? It was not that they had defeated the demonic powers, but that their names had been written in heaven (verse 20). In other words, the disciples were personally known by God, and their eternal presence before Him was certain.

III. CONCLUDING REFLECTIONS

Each year I lead a team of short-term missionaries on two trips to the West African nation of Nigeria. In the summer, our association travels to East Africa. In all of these travels, the words of Jesus about the dangers associated with missionary work ring loud and clear. There is nothing glamorous about the work of missions, but this work is what the Lord Jesus Christ commissioned us to do. Think of it this way—if you were the last Christian on the face of the earth, you would still be required to carry out the Great Commission with the assurance that God would give the increase in your labors.

PRAYER

Heavenly Father, almighty and everlasting God, we are grateful that You are the God who does not dwell in temples made with hands. Stir within each of us the passion to do Your will and to serve You with boldness. We will continuously seek Your kingdom and all of its righteousness. Forgive us of the times and days when we have failed to serve You faithfully. In the name of Jesus Christ, we pray. Amen.

WORD POWER

Laborer (Greek: *ergates)*—this means toiler, laborer, or worker, especially an agricultural laborer. The root word for laborer in Greek carries the idea of pain, struggle, and uneasiness. Work in an agricultural environment is hard work. Jesus used the word laborer (ergates) to drive home the importance of the laborers' work and what it entailed (and still does entail). Their labor was and is full of agony, anguish, and struggle.

HOME DAILY BIBLE READINGS
(January 28—February 3, 2008)
Summoned to Labor
> **MONDAY, January 28:** "Instruct the Believers" (Psalm 78:1–4)
> **TUESDAY, January 29:** "The Twelve on a Mission" (Luke 9:1–10)
> **WEDNESDAY, January 30:** "The Seventy Go in Pairs" (Luke 10:1–3)
> **THURSDAY, January 31:** "Travel Lightly in Peace" (Luke 10:4–7)
> **FRIDAY, February 1:** "Proclaim God's Kingdom" (Luke 10:8–12)
> **SATURDAY, February 2:** "They Returned with Joy" (Luke 10:17–20)
> **SUNDAY, February 3:** "See God's Work" (Psalm 66:1–7)

LESSON 11   February 10, 2008

SUMMONED TO REPENT

DEVOTIONAL READING: **Psalm 63:1-6**   BACKGROUND SCRIPTURE: **Luke 13:1-9**
PRINT PASSAGE: **Luke 13:1-9**   KEY VERSE: **Luke 13:3**

Luke 13:1-9—KJV

THERE WERE present at that season some that told him of the Galilaeans, whose blood Pilate had mingled with their sacrifices.

2 And Jesus answering said unto them, Suppose ye that these Galilaeans were sinners above all the Galilaeans, because they suffered such things?

3 I tell you, Nay: but, except ye repent, ye shall all likewise perish.

4 Or those eighteen, upon whom the tower in Siloam fell, and slew them, think ye that they were sinners above all men that dwelt in Jerusalem?

5 I tell you, Nay: but, except ye repent, ye shall all likewise perish.

6 He spake also this parable; A certain man had a fig tree planted in his vineyard; and he came and sought fruit thereon, and found none.

7 Then said he unto the dresser of his vineyard, Behold, these three years I come seeking fruit on this fig tree, and find none: cut it down; why cumbereth it the ground?

8 And he answering said unto him, Lord, let it alone this year also, till I shall dig about it, and dung it:

9 And if it bear fruit, well: and if not, then after that thou shalt cut it down.

Luke 13:1-9—NRSV

AT THAT very time there were some present who told him about the Galileans whose blood Pilate had mingled with their sacrifices.

2 He asked them, "Do you think that because these Galileans suffered in this way they were worse sinners than all other Galileans?

3 No, I tell you; but unless you repent, you will all perish as they did.

4 Or those eighteen who were killed when the tower of Siloam fell on them—do you think that they were worse offenders than all the others living in Jerusalem?

5 No, I tell you; but unless you repent, you will all perish just as they did."

6 Then he told this parable: "A man had a fig tree planted in his vineyard; and he came looking for fruit on it and found none.

7 So he said to the gardener, 'See here! For three years I have come looking for fruit on this fig tree, and still I find none. Cut it down! Why should it be wasting the soil?'

8 He replied, 'Sir, let it alone for one more year, until I dig around it and put manure on it.

9 If it bears fruit next year, well and good; but if not, you can cut it down.'"

BIBLE FACT

Pilate was a ruthless Roman governor who hated the Galileans because of their disdain for Rome. To quell an insurrection, he massacred some Galileans in the temple. Jesus used this tragedy to teach the importance of God's patience and quick repentance.

UNIFYING LESSON PRINCIPLE

As we look at our lives, we see things about ourselves that we would like to change. How do we change our behavior so that we are better people? Jesus called people to repent and to allow God to transform their lives.

TOPICAL OUTLINE OF THE LESSON

I. **Introduction**
   A. Repentance
   B. Biblical Background

II. **Exposition and Application of the Scripture**
   A. The Deaths of the Innocents (Luke 13:1)
   B. The Necessity of Personal Repentance (Luke 13:2-5)
   C. The Purpose of Personal Repentance (Luke 13:6-9)

III. **Concluding Reflections**

LESSON OBJECTIVES

Upon completion of this lesson, the students will know that:
1. God wants us to turn our lives around for our own sakes;
2. Repentance and forsaking of sin are the initial steps in Christendom;
3. Refusal to repent of sins is a direct ticket to hell; and,
4. A repentant life can have a positive influence on government bureaucracy.

POINTS TO BE EMPHASIZED
ADULT/YOUTH

Adult Topic: Turning Our Lives Around
Youth Topic: Summoned to Turn Around
Adult/Youth Key Verse: Luke 13:3
Print Passage: Luke 13:1-9

—Jesus taught that we are accountable for our priorities and for how we deal with others.

—When our lives, our hearts, our thoughts, and our actions lead us away from God, we are turning from true life.

—In order to live in the relationship with God that God intended, we must turn our lives around, reject sin, and accept God.

—Part of the message of the barren fig tree is that God is patient, always giving us the chance to change, but also firm and resolute in making sure we realize the consequences of living unfruitful lives.

—The call and our positive response to repentance allow us to overcome the power of sin.

—Jesus rejected the first-century Jewish view that disasters were retribution for individual sins.

—Fig trees take three years to reach maturity. If a tree does not produce fruit by that time, it may not produce at all. The tree in Jesus' parable was given a second chance.

CHILDREN

Children Topic: Given Another Chance
Key Verse: Luke 13:6
Print Passage: Luke 13:6-9

—Rather than cutting it down, Jesus gave the fig tree another chance to grow.

—People who follow Christ know that He gives all of us many chances.

—Jesus keeps providing for our needs so that we can live better lives.

—To become good disciples, we need to become more Christlike.

I. INTRODUCTION

A. Repentance

Today's lesson teaches us that repentance is necessary in order to bring about real, lasting change in our lives. Many people want to change their behaviors and attitudes, but are not sure how to do it. Jesus taught that real change begins with repentance. He preached a simple yet uncompromising message, "The time is fulfilled, and the kingdom of God is at hand: repent ye, and believe the gospel" (Mark 1:15). Jesus preached that anyone expecting to enter the kingdom of God must make a complete change in his or her life. Deep inner change begins with repentance. The word *repent* comes from the Greek word *metanoeo,* and it literally means "to change one's mind for the better, to amend; to abhor one's past sins." Repentance means that a person looks at his or her faults, failures, and shortcomings and becomes sorry to the point of being sick and tired of them. Feeling godly sorrow for one's sins is one definition that is often cited for repentance. True repentance takes that sorrow one step further to the absolute resolve to turn completely away from sin. One can be sorry for a sin and go right back to doing what he or she hates. We can be extremely remorseful for our actions and still not turn from the very thing that we hate (see Romans 7:13-25). The apostle James wrote that hearers and not doers of God's Word have looked into a mirror and forgotten what they saw (see James 1:23-24). We have not repented if we keep living carnal and worldly lives and nothing in our lives has changed.

The new birth means that our lives change completely. God changes us permanently, inside and out. Repentance means that we have denounced our sins. We hate what we see in our lives, and we desire real change. Repentance means that we have disowned our sins, and we have denounced and disconnected ourselves from the things that separated us from God. Without true and sincere repentance, there is no conversion and salvation. There are times when the people of God must enter a great period of repentance and return to Him (2 Chronicles 7:12-14). When Jesus came preaching the kingdom of God, His Word was accompanied by the declaration that God's people must repent and believe the message of the Gospel.

B. Biblical Background

This story is the conclusion of a long series of lessons that began in Luke 12:1. There, Jesus was responding to some comments that were raised about God's justice. In this unit, Jesus made reference to the tower of Siloam that fell and killed eighteen people in Jerusalem. The reference to the tower of Siloam spoke to a common Jewish belief in the first century that anyone who suffered a tragic ending must have been a sinner receiving justly deserved divine punishment. Jesus rejected this teaching as inconsistent with the very nature of God.

Jesus used the parable of a barren fig tree. This parable is about a tree that had been given ample opportunity to produce healthy fruit but had remained unfruitful after three years. Jesus used that moment to remind the people in that crowd that unless they too repented, they would face a fate far worse than physical death.

Jesus told a parable to instill a deeper lesson about repentance. Parables were a common form of instruction used by Jesus, which He used frequently during His three-year ministry. Essentially, a parable is a short story that contains moral, ethical, or spiritual truths. All of the short stories He told were based on the everyday lives of the people who first heard them, including the parable in this lesson. This parable is found only in Luke, as is the parable of the "Rich Fool" that was part of Jesus' discourse (Luke12:13-21).

II. EXPOSITION AND APPLICATION OF THE SCRIPTURE

A. The Deaths of the Innocents
(Luke 13:1)

THERE WERE present at that season some that told him of the Galilaeans, whose blood Pilate had mingled with their sacrifices.

At this present location, some people came to Jesus and told Him about how Pilate massacred some Galilean worshipers while they were performing their annual sacrifice at the temple precincts. Pilate was the Roman governor of Judea from A.D. 26-36. He was ruthless and showed little regard for Jewish religious traditions and practices. A great deal of what we have learned about the religious, economic, social, and political climate during the time of Jesus has come from the writings of Flavius Josephus, who was a Jewish historian. He recorded several incidents that revealed the corrupt and antagonistic nature of Pilate toward the Jews.

Josephus recorded that the Galileans were the most subversive people in the land. The Galileans were not under the jurisdiction of Pilate, but of Herod. Herod and Pilate did not like each other. While the Galileans were sacrificing at Jerusalem, Pilate came suddenly upon them and killed them. The blood of the slain worshipers and the blood of the animals filled the whole place. Why did they inform Jesus about this incident? It might have been due to their desire to get Him to say something about Pilate, so that they could bring Jesus into a confrontation with Pilate. However, based on Jesus' answer, it would appear that the people had concluded that the Galileans deserved punishment for their ruthlessness. This event is only recorded by Luke, and there is no other record of it in any of the Gospels or other non-biblical writings. Jesus led them into a deeper understanding of the urgency of repentance.

B. The Necessity of Personal Repentance
(Luke 13:2-5)

And Jesus answering said unto them, Suppose ye that these Galilaeans were sinners above all the Galilaeans, because they suffered such things? I tell you, Nay: but, except ye repent, ye shall all likewise perish. Or those eighteen, upon whom the tower in Siloam fell, and slew them, think ye that they were sinners above all men that dwelt in Jerusalem? I tell you, Nay: but, except ye repent, ye shall all likewise perish.

Jesus went right to the heart of the question. Did the people in His audience believe that the Galileans whom Pilate killed were greater sinners than any other Galileans (verse 2)? These Galileans suffered a horrific and senseless fate for no apparent reason other than Pilate's anger. People die daily at the hands of others for no apparent reason. Are they sinners who get what they deserve? Jesus attacked the popular belief of that day that if something tragic happened in a person's life, he or she must have committed some grievous sin (John 9:1-3). Eliphaz, a dear friend of Job, accused Job of having committed some obvious sin. Why else would he be experiencing such dire events as the trials that he suffered (Job 4:7)? Jesus stated that unless they too repented, they could experience the same fate. What did Jesus mean? The likely interpretation of His words revolves around the uncertainty and the frailty of life. The occurrence of a tragic incident has nothing to do with whether or not people are heinous sinners. In the aftermath of hurricane Katrina's destruction, some religious leaders made baseless assertions that God brought massive destruction upon New Orleans as retribution for the city's corruption. Such pronouncements reveal a lack of understanding about the nature of the human pilgrimage.

Jesus debunked the belief that a person who suffered deserved punishment by asserting that there was a far worse fate that could come upon a man or woman who did not repent of his or her sins. This fate resulted, and still does result, in eternal damnation and separation from God. The failure to respond to the call of God leaves one susceptible to far more tragic eternal consequences. Repentance and confession of one's sins are the first prerequisites for being saved (Acts 3:19). All of us are sinners who have turned away from God (Psalm 119:176; Isaiah 53:6; Romans 3:23). As sinners, all of us deserve our just due, but God's gracious mercy has spared us (Romans 6:23; Ephesians 2:4-5, 8-10).

Jesus cited a second incident of seemingly senseless death in which the tower of Siloam fell and tragically killed eighteen people in Jerusalem (verse 4). Siloam was a pool of water located in the southern end of the Old City that was used as a source of water and for ritual bathing (John 9:7, 11). The wall or a tower collapsed, killing people who simply may have been at the pool engaging in ritual bathing at the wrong time. Were they considered sinners who received punishment for sin in their lives? Jesus replied, *No!* These people were no worse than anyone else. The tumbling of the tower down onto the people in or near the pool was an unfortunate and untimely accident. Life is full of these sorts of occurrences. Often in our efforts to find a logical explanation for some tragedy, we will say, "God allowed this fatal car accident to kill this family of four for His own purposes." Again, such thinking presumes that God stages tragic accidents for some larger divine purpose that people can find only through seeing Him as the cause of it. God would never do this sort of thing as a means to reveal His will.

For the third time, Jesus repeated the call to repent. The repetition of the word *repent* clearly highlighted the importance of the subject. Unless we repent, we will likewise face a similar eternal fate.

C. The Purpose of Personal Repentance (Luke 13:6-9)

He spake also this parable; A certain man had a fig tree planted in his vineyard; and he came and sought fruit thereon, and found none. Then said he unto the dresser of his vineyard, Behold, these three years I come seeking fruit on this fig tree, and find none: cut it down; why cumbereth it the ground? And he answering said unto him, Lord, let it alone this year also, till I shall dig about it, and dung it: And if it bear fruit, well: and if not, then after that thou shalt cut it down.

Jesus continued His teaching session by telling a parable about a man who had an unfruitful fig tree in his vineyard. This was a story that would be relatively easy for the people of that day to pick up and understand. Figs were an important staple in the Hebrew diet along with wheat, barley, honey, milk, dates, olives, pomegranates, and fish. Figs were among the three samples of fruit brought back by the twelve spies (Number 13:23). They were a ready source of energy and nourishment (2 Samuel 30:11-12). Near the Mount of Olives there is the small village of Bethphage, which means "house of unripe figs." The name probably comes from the numerous fig trees that grow in that location. It was in Bethphage where Jesus began His triumphal entry into Jerusalem and where He cursed the unfruitful fig tree (see Matthew 21:17-23; Luke 19:29-44). Fig trees required tenderness and cultivation in order to produce a bountiful harvest (see Proverbs 27:13). When properly cultivated, they can grow to heights of fifteen to forty feet.

The owner of the vineyard came looking for fruit, and he found nothing. For three years, the tree had grown, taking up space and consuming the nutrients of the soil. Three years was the minimal amount of time that fig trees were to be left alone and allowed to produce (see Leviticus 19:23). At the end of three years, a fig tree should bear fruit. In this case, the tree had produced nothing and the owner decided that it must be cut down. His hired worker prevailed upon the owner to give the tree one more chance. He would take a personal interest in the tree and work to see if it would produce fruit. He was going to dig around it and fertilize it. The worker told the owner that if at the next harvest the tree did not produce, then it could be cut down.

The most obvious question concerns the meaning of the parable. Through this parable, Jesus continued to teach about the necessity of personal repentance. The tree was given time to produce a fruitful harvest, but it had failed. The interpretation has been obvious to believers for centuries. The tree represented Israel, which had been given ample opportunities to turn from wicked and sinful ways. The owner of the vineyard was God the Father, who sent His Son Jesus into the world to redeem the world from sin. The worker in the vineyard was Jesus, who asked the Father to give Israel one more opportunity to produce the fruits of righteousness. If at that point there was no change and no fruitfulness in the Israelites' lives, then they could be destroyed. As a people, they had been given every advantage and opportunity to serve the true and living God.

The parable teaches valuable lessons at three levels. At the first level is God the Father, who is merciful and just. He is the God of second chances, who is patient with us in spite of our unwillingness to produce the fruits of righteousness and justice. We see an image of a God who gives His people every advantage and the resources necessary to succeed on His behalf. The people, however, misuse and even abuse that position of favor.

Second, we see Jesus, who intercedes on behalf of the people of God. He serves as our Advocate with the Father, making intercession on our behalf. In this parable, we see an image of Jesus, who willingly worked then and now among us and through us to produce ripe fruit. The death of Jesus on the cross was and is the greatest symbol of God's active grace and love.

Finally, we see an image of the people of God, who have been given ample opportunities and resources to reach out and bring the lost into the kingdom of God's righteousness. However, they often fail to respond. There is a time in the life cycle of every congregation when God uses the congregation in miraculous and powerful ways to affect real change and spiritual growth in the lives of the unrepentant and spiritually dead. As the tree in the parable was given three years, so are congregations given time to produce the fruits of righteousness. The picture is painfully clear—the church of the Lord Jesus Christ is called to be fruitful (see Matthew 13:8; Mark 4:1-8; John 15:1-8; Romans 7:4; Galatians 5:22-23). This lesson is equally applicable to the lives of individual believers, who are just as accountable for being fruitful in their service to God.

III. CONCLUDING REFLECTIONS

The tsunami of December 2004 claimed the lives of hundreds of thousands of people in Southeast Asia. Many of those countries are Muslim, Hindu, Buddhist, or belong to other traditional religions unique to that part of the world. Did the magnitude of the tragedy signal that God wreaked havoc and punishment upon them because of their religion? Some people would say *Yes!* Jesus would say *No!* Life is full of uncertainty, and calamitous things can happen without notice to any one of us. What is critical is that we must always live in a state of repentant expectancy.

PRAYER

Heavenly Father, teach us to trust You in every way. May we be more willing to examine our lives and then seek Your forgiveness. We thank You for the love and grace You have shown us in the sending of Jesus Christ to die for our sins. We repent of every word, action, and attitude that does not reflect Your character. In the name of Jesus Christ, we pray. Amen.

WORD POWER

Perish (Greek: *apollumai*)—this means to devote or give over to eternal damnation, or to be delivered up to eternal misery. Jesus used this word (perish) to drive home the reality of eternal hell. Jesus does not confine anybody to hell, but if anybody refuses to accept Jesus and repent of sin, that person is a candidate for hell. In order to qualify for eternal life, repentance of sins is the prerequisite.

HOME DAILY BIBLE READINGS
(February 4-10, 2008)
Summoned to Repent

MONDAY, February 4: "My Soul Is Satisfied" (Psalm 63:1–6)
TUESDAY, February 5: "Turn from Your Ways" (Luke 3:7–14)
WEDNESDAY, February 6: "Jesus Calls for Repentance" (Mark 1:14–15)
THURSDAY, February 7: "Repent or Perish" (Luke 13:1–5)
FRIDAY, February 8: "Bear Fruit of Repentance" (Luke 13:6–9)
SATURDAY, February 9: "Paul Calls for Repentance" (Acts 26:19–23)
SUNDAY, February 10: "Choose God's Way" (Psalm 1:1–6)

LESSON 12   February 17, 2008

SUMMONED TO BE HUMBLE

DEVOTIONAL READING: **Psalm 25:1-10**
PRINT PASSAGE: **Luke 14:1, 7-14**

BACKGROUND SCRIPTURE: **Luke 14:1, 7-14**
KEY VERSE: **Luke 14:11**

Luke 14:1, 7-14—KJV

AND IT came to pass, as he went into the house of one of the chief Pharisees to eat bread on the sabbath day, that they watched him.

.....

7 And he put forth a parable to those which were bidden, when he marked how they chose out the chief rooms; saying unto them,

8 When thou art bidden of any man to a wedding, sit not down in the highest room; lest a more honourable man than thou be bidden of him;

9 And he that bade thee and him come and say to thee, Give this man place; and thou begin with shame to take the lowest room.

10 But when thou art bidden, go and sit down in the lowest room; that when he that bade thee cometh, he may say unto thee, Friend, go up higher: then shalt thou have worship in the presence of them that sit at meat with thee.

11 For whosoever exalteth himself shall be abased; and he that humbleth himself shall be exalted.

12 Then said he also to him that bade him, When thou makest a dinner or a supper, call not thy friends, nor thy brethren, neither thy kinsmen, nor thy rich neighbours; lest they also bid thee again, and a recompence be made thee.

13 But when thou makest a feast, call the poor, the maimed, the lame, the blind:

14 And thou shalt be blessed; for they cannot recompense thee: for thou shalt be recompensed at the resurrection of the just.

Luke 14:1, 7-14—NRSV

ON ONE occasion when Jesus was going to the house of a leader of the Pharisees to eat a meal on the sabbath, they were watching him closely.

.....

7 When he noticed how the guests chose the places of honor, he told them a parable.

8 "When you are invited by someone to a wedding banquet, do not sit down at the place of honor, in case someone more distinguished than you has been invited by your host;

9 and the host who invited both of you may come and say to you, 'Give this person your place,' and then in disgrace you would start to take the lowest place.

10 But when you are invited, go and sit down at the lowest place, so that when your host comes, he may say to you, 'Friend, move up higher'; then you will be honored in the presence of all who sit at the table with you.

11 For all who exalt themselves will be humbled, and those who humble themselves will be exalted."

12 He said also to the one who had invited him, "When you give a luncheon or a dinner, do not invite your friends or your brothers or your relatives or rich neighbors, in case they may invite you in return, and you would be repaid.

13 But when you give a banquet, invite the poor, the crippled, the lame, and the blind.

14 And you will be blessed, because they cannot repay you, for you will be repaid at the resurrection of the righteous."

BIBLE FACT

Jesus used parables to teach spiritual truth, principles, and lessons. In the text, Jesus taught about humility and showing hospitality to all. Today, many "sow seed" for earthly returns instead of heavenly ones. We must not forget Jesus' teaching on humility.

UNIFYING LESSON PRINCIPLE

Our society values and rewards people who put themselves first. What is a better way to live? Jesus told a parable about humility at a meal where people had been clamoring for the best seats.

TOPICAL OUTLINE OF THE LESSON

I. Introduction
A. What Is Biblical Humility?
B. Biblical Background

II. Exposition and Application of the Scripture
A. The Pharisee: False Piety (Luke 14:1)
B. The Guest: False Popularity (Luke 14:7-11)
C. The Host: False Hospitality (14:12-14)

III. Concluding Reflections

LESSON OBJECTIVES

Upon completion of this lesson, the students will know that:

1. Humility is one of the basic tenets of Christian living;
2. If we are humble, God knows how to elevate us to unexpected positions;
3. The propensity to elevate ourselves is always with us; and,
4. True humility comes through an encounter with Jesus Christ.

POINTS TO BE EMPHASIZED

ADULT/YOUTH

Adult Topic: The Necessity of Humility
Youth Topic: Summoned to Be Humble
Adult/Youth Key Verse: Luke 14:11
Print Passage: Luke 14:1, 7-14

—Watching guests as they selected places of honor at a meal led Jesus to tell a parable about humility.

—Jesus reminded hearers that it is better to select a place of lesser honor and to be invited by the host to "move up" than to be asked to "move down" when someone of higher status arrives.

—Jesus had an additional message for the host, telling him that when giving a luncheon or dinner, he should invite the poor, the lame, and the blind—those unable to reciprocate—rather than family, friends, and rich neighbors who would invite him in return.

—Hosting a feast on the Sabbath did not breach Sabbath laws. The food was prepared on the previous day.

—The wedding banquet parable parallels Proverbs 19:17 and 25:6-7.

—In rabbinical literature, banquets often symbolize the kingdom of God.

CHILDREN

Children Topic: Putting Others First
Key Verse: Luke 14:11
Print Passage: Luke 14:1, 7-14

—Jesus taught that we should do things for others.

—God will bless us when we put others before ourselves.

—Jesus wants us to accept others as they are.

—Jesus wants us to live as He has taught us.

I. INTRODUCTION

A. What Is Biblical Humility?

Today's lesson contains some of the teachings of Jesus about humility and pride. Humility requires us to remember that God is the one who exalts us. It is one of the greatest virtues of the Christian faith, yet one of the least practiced. The exact opposite of humility is pride, which is tantamount to self-worshiping and self-praising. Jesus taught His disciples that pride is to be vigorously resisted because of what it does to the human spirit. Humility in the spiritual sense is an inward grace of the soul that allows one to think of oneself no more highly than he or she ought to think (Ephesians 4:1-2).

Jesus Christ is the supreme example of humility (Matthew 11:29; Mark 10:45). Biblical humility is not stupidity as some may think; rather, it is following the example of Jesus Christ.

B. Biblical Background

Jesus told the parable about chief seats during the latter days of His earthly ministry. According to Luke's account, as Jesus made His way to Jerusalem He went throughout all of the villages and towns preaching, teaching, and healing (Luke 13:22). The events of this lesson took place during those travels. The setting for the telling of the parable comes at the end of a Sabbath teaching session at a local synagogue (Luke 13:10). Jesus was invited to the home of one of the chief Pharisees for bread and further discussion, which was customary in that day. This particular invitation became another occasion for His opponents to watch Him for the purpose of finding fault with Him.

Jesus often found Himself at odds with the Jewish religious leaders over the Sabbath. In Matthew 12:1-7, Jesus was confronted by a group of Pharisees who raised objections over His disciples picking the heads of grain to eat. They accused the disciples of breaking the Sabbath law which forbade work on the Sabbath (Matthew 12:1-2). Jesus responded by citing an example from the life of David—about how David went into the house of God and ate the showbread, which could be eaten by no one except the priests (1 Samuel 21:1-6; Matthew 12:4). Jesus also made reference to the work of the priests and Levites, who were exempt from the Sabbath rules regarding the prohibition against working on the Sabbath (Matthew 12:5). He infuriated His opponents over His declaration that He was greater than the Sabbath (Matthew 12:7-8).

There were constant confrontations with the religious leaders over the observance of the Sabbath. Was it lawful to heal on the Sabbath (Matthew 12:9-13)? Was it lawful to save one's animals on the Sabbath (Luke 14:1-5)? Was it lawful to do justice or what was morally right on the Sabbath, even if it meant breaking the Sabbath rule (Mark 3:1-6)? In Luke 14:7-14, Jesus taught the wisdom of humility.

II. EXPOSITION AND APPLICATION OF THE SCRIPTURE

A. The Pharisee: False Piety
(Luke 14:1)

AND IT came to pass, as he went into the house of one of the chief Pharisees to eat bread on the sabbath day, that they watched him.

Jesus was invited to the home of a leading Pharisee for a Sabbath meal. We do not know whether this man was the ruler of the synagogue or just one of the primary leaders. It was not uncommon for visiting rabbis to be invited to break bread with the leader of the local synagogue. This meal was prepared the day before because to cook food on the Sabbath would be a violation of the Law.

The Pharisees were among the most vocal opponents of Jesus for a variety of reasons. They were a group of men numbering about 6,000 who devoted much of their lives to the study and keeping of the Law of Moses and the oral traditions of the elders. Much of their opposition toward Jesus stemmed from differences between their interpretation of the Law and that of Jesus.

Jesus considered the Pharisees to be self-righteous (Matthew 5:20). He indicated that they were often concerned about how they appeared publicly. They wanted to be regarded as very religious and pious men (see Luke 18:9-14). Jesus considered the Pharisees to be puffed up with pride—so much so that He called them hypocrites (Matthew 23; Luke 12:1). Jesus was in continuous conflict with the Pharisees throughout much of His ministry.

However, we must remember that not all of the Pharisees were hostile toward Jesus. Some of the Pharisees had high regard for Jesus and would even invite Him for meals (Luke 7:36-50; 14:1). Some were attracted to and even believed in Jesus (John 3:1-21; 7:45-53; 9:13-16) and went so far as to protect early Christians (Acts 5:34-39; 23:6-9). Nicodemus was so impressed by Jesus that he came to see Him by night (John 3:1ff). Paul asserted that he was a Pharisee before his conversion (Philippians 3:5). Whatever the Pharisees thought of Jesus, they nonetheless respected His ability to gather large crowds of people around Him to hear the Gospel.

B. The Guest: False Popularity
(Luke 14:7-11)

And he put forth a parable to those which were bidden, when he marked how they chose out the chief rooms; saying unto them, When thou art bidden of any man to a wedding, sit not down in the highest room; lest a more honourable man than thou be bidden of him; And he that bade thee and him come and say to thee, Give this man place; and thou begin with shame to take the lowest room. But when thou art bidden, go and sit down in the lowest room; that when he that bade thee cometh, he may say unto thee, Friend, go up higher: then shalt thou have worship in the presence of them that sit at meat with thee. For whosoever exalteth himself shall be abased; and he that humbleth himself shall be exalted.

Jesus was very observant of human nature. As the guests arrived for the dinner that had been prepared in His honor, He noticed how they all sought to get the best seats (verse 7). What Jesus observed was a practice common among the Pharisees and people of high social standing—seeking the places of honor at social gatherings. It was not the only time that He said something about the desire to get the best seats at a feast (Matthew 23:6; Luke 11:43). Jesus was not afraid to confront the Pharisees about their behavior, because it profoundly impacted their relationships with other people.

Wedding feasts, banquets, and other social gatherings were very important events during Jesus' day. In addition to being the host, it was always important to be invited to a gathering that featured the social elite of the community. At those gatherings, where one sat and who sat with one were important (Luke 5:29-30). Seats of prominence were quite important. Weddings and funerals were opportunities for the socially elite to advertise their imagined merit and distinction. Jesus took this occasion to teach His host and the guests a lesson in humility.

Customarily, the most important guests arrived later than the other guests. Jesus said that if one arrived before all of the guests had arrived, that person should not seek out the best seat. Jesus quoted from Proverbs 25:6-7, which offers counsel against seeking the chief seats at the king's banquet. What was the reason for this recommended self-abasement? One could be attending a dinner, and someone who was more honorable or important than himself or herself could arrive later. One would then be forced to take the lowest seat in the house. This act would be one of great humiliation and shame. The picture that Jesus painted is of one who went to a presidential banquet and took a seat at the head table next to the presiding officer. This would be the equivalent of the seat of the speaker for the occasion. When the speaker arrived, the person would then be asked to move to the lowest seat on the floor. The embarrassment of such a situation would be heightened when one was asked to get up in the midst of the program and go to the last seat in the room.

Rather than take a higher-level seat, Jesus said to take the last seat on the floor and wait to be invited to join those who occupied the seats at the head table. By waiting to be invited up to the higher level of seats, one would gain honor and glory in the sight of all those who were present. Jesus was not suggesting that the key to gaining personal recognition at a banquet was to feign humiliation, all the while waiting to be recognized in front of the other guests. The point that Jesus made was that it was always better to be invited to come up higher rather than to be asked to take a step down, especially to the lowest level possible.

This lesson became very clear to me during a 2006 mission trip to Port Harcourt, Nigeria. My team and I were invited to have dinner at the home of a prominent and wealthy citizen. At the dinner table, the seats were assigned according to the social status and standing of the guests. Since the dinner had been prepared in honor of our team members I was invited to sit next to the host and his wife. All of the other team members were invited to be seated in the order of their position on the team. No one was invited to sit at the head table who was not a member of the mission team, although some may have been prominent Nigerian citizens. It was simply the protocol of the culture of Nigeria that the special guests should have the primary seats of honor.

Verse 11 is one of the most familiar sayings of Jesus. This is the theme of social reversal, which is a common theme in Luke and the rest of the New Testament. This verse has what has been referred to as *eschatological* meaning. It points to a future time when all of the injustices and wrongs perpetrated against the least of the earth will be atoned for. Those who have been last will be made first and vice versa (see Matthew 18:4; 23:12; Luke 1:52-53; 6:21; 10:15; 18:14; Romans 12:14; Philippians 2:5-11; 1 Timothy 6:17; James 4:6, 1; 1 Peter 5:5).

C. The Host: False Hospitality
(Luke 14:12-14)

Then said he also to him that bade him, When thou makest a dinner or a supper, call not thy friends, nor thy brethren, neither thy kinsmen, nor thy rich neighbours; lest they also bid thee again, and a recompence be made thee. But when thou makest a feast, call the poor, the maimed, the lame, the blind: And thou shalt be blessed; for they cannot recompense thee: for thou shalt be recompensed at the resurrection of the just.

Jesus told the elite people that if they wanted to do something that would have real value, they should do something to help the poor, maimed, lame, and blind. What benefit would it be to you if you invited your friends, brothers, relatives, and rich neighbors to a feast? These are people who can reciprocate. When they have a feast, they can invite you, thereby paying you back for your invitation. This was and is a challenge: to move beyond one's circle of friends and associates to touch the lives of the least of the earth.

Jesus identified with the poor, because God the Father was and is concerned about the poor. The Old Testament is replete with divine demands for justice and equity. In Deuteronomy 15:7-15, we discern the attitude of God toward the poor. What do we see here? We see that we must be compassionate toward the poor and hungry. Deuteronomy 15:7 states, "If there be among you a poor man of one of thy brethren within any of thy gates in thy land which the Lord thy God giveth thee, thou shalt not harden thine heart, nor shut thine hand from thy poor brother." The people of Israel were forbidden to turn their backs and look in the other direction when poverty afflicted one of their own, especially when they were the recipients of grace and blessings from God.

In His final discourse in Matthew 25:31-46, Jesus made it clear to His followers that they must be concerned about the plight of the least of the earth. This was such a high priority that Jesus connected entry into the kingdom of God with an active concern for suffering humanity. Jesus identified six areas of Christian social concern: the hungry, the thirsty, strangers (homeless), the naked, the sick, and those in prisons. These represented and still represent people on the lowest rung of the socio-economic ladder. They are the people without political clout, influence, and those who have little or no hope of upward mobility. Jesus directed His entire preaching, teaching, and healing ministry toward reaching the least of the earth. He sought to reach all men and women, but it was the poor who gladly received His Word.

Service must always be rendered without an eye toward personal recognition in the here and now. There will come a day when God will repay those who have faithfully served His interests and people. In verse 14, Jesus closed the discourse by pointing out that in the final day at the Resurrection, those who had been and were considerate of the poor and helpless would be blessed (Psalm 41:1-4). God will repay those who were kind in the end, for He was and is not unjust to forget one's work and labor of love shown to the saints (Hebrews 6:10).

III. CONCLUDING REFLECTIONS

Jesus never pulled any punches about the expectations of God the Father. There are two lessons that stand out in this passage. The first has to do with humility. God expects us to walk in humility, recognizing that He is the creator and sustainer of all life. Therefore, no man or woman is in a position to think more of himself or herself than they should. Humility keeps us grounded through true self-assessment. As we reflect upon who we are, we are always reminded that we are servants of God, called to serve His purpose, and His purpose only, in the world. Our goal must never be to build personal kingdoms for ourselves.

The second lesson is the importance of embracing those who are considered to be the least of the earth. I have a member who founded an executive search company that seeks out minority candidates to serve on corporate and nonprofit boards of directors. One of the projects he leads for the United Way is called Project Inclusion. Through this effort, his firm seeks to include people who have traditionally been left out of the boardrooms of major corporations and nonprofits. God wants us to think of ways that we can be more inclusive of those that we can serve who may never be able to pay us back.

PRAYER

Heavenly Father, we thank You for saving us from sin. May we be constantly aware of our own pride and arrogance that may get in the way of Your love manifesting itself through us. Grant Your servants the wisdom and discernment to know the difference between pride and self-confidence. Thank You for lifting us to new levels of service in Your kingdom. In the name of Jesus, we pray. Amen.

WORD POWER

Shall be humbled (Greek: *tapeinotheesetai*)—this means to depress, to humiliate, or to bring low. The phrase "shall be humbled" is one word in Greek. Jesus is saying that the reward of pride lies in the future. Any form of pride, whether open or clandestine, is noted by God. The proud in heart will be humbled or brought low.

HOME DAILY BIBLE READINGS
(February 11-17, 2008)
Summoned to Be Humble

MONDAY, February 11: "Prayer of Humility" (Psalm 25:1–10)
TUESDAY, February 12: "Jesus Heals on the Sabbath" (Luke 14:1–6)
WEDNESDAY, February 13: "Disgraced at a Banquet" (Luke 14:7–9)
THURSDAY, February 14: "Exalted Though Humble" (Luke 14:10–11)
FRIDAY, February 15: "The Guest List" (Luke 14:12–14)
SATURDAY, February 16: "A Life of Humility" (Ephesians 3:1–10)
SUNDAY, February 17: "Tending the Flock with Humility" (1 Peter 5:1–5)

UNIT III: God Summons Us to Respond!   CHILDREN'S UNIT: God Summons Us to Respond!   WINTER QUARTER

LESSON 13   February 24, 2008

SUMMONED TO BE A DISCIPLE

DEVOTIONAL READING: **Psalm 139:1-6**
PRINT PASSAGE: **Luke 14:25-33**

BACKGROUND SCRIPTURE: **Luke 14:25-33**
KEY VERSE: **Luke 14:27**

Luke 14:25-33—KJV

25 And there went great multitudes with him: and he turned, and said unto them,
26 If any man come to me, and hate not his father, and mother, and wife, and children, and brethren, and sisters, yea, and his own life also, he cannot be my disciple.
27 And whosoever doth not bear his cross, and come after me, cannot be my disciple.
28 For which of you, intending to build a tower, sitteth not down first, and counteth the cost, whether he have sufficient to finish it?
29 Lest haply, after he hath laid the foundation, and is not able to finish it, all that behold it begin to mock him,
30 Saying, This man began to build, and was not able to finish.
31 Or what king, going to make war against another king, sitteth not down first, and consulteth whether he be able with ten thousand to meet him that cometh against him with twenty thousand?
32 Or else, while the other is yet a great way off, he sendeth an ambassage, and desireth conditions of peace.
33 So likewise, whosoever he be of you that forsaketh not all that he hath, he cannot be my disciple.

Luke 14:25-33—NRSV

25 Now large crowds were traveling with him; and he turned and said to them,
26 "Whoever comes to me and does not hate father and mother, wife and children, brothers and sisters, yes, and even life itself, cannot be my disciple.
27 Whoever does not carry the cross and follow me cannot be my disciple.
28 For which of you, intending to build a tower, does not first sit down and estimate the cost, to see whether he has enough to complete it?
29 Otherwise, when he has laid a foundation and is not able to finish, all who see it will begin to ridicule him,
30 saying, 'This fellow began to build and was not able to finish.'
31 Or what king, going out to wage war against another king, will not sit down first and consider whether he is able with ten thousand to oppose the one who comes against him with twenty thousand?
32 If he cannot, then, while the other is still far away, he sends a delegation and asks for the terms of peace.
33 So therefore, none of you can become my disciple if you do not give up all your possessions.

BIBLE FACT

A disciple accepts the views of the teacher and is in total agreement in practicing all of the master's orders. John's disciples strictly followed his lifestyle; the Pharisees' disciples carried out their instructions. Jesus' true disciples emulate Him in public and in private.

UNIFYING LESSON PRINCIPLE

People look for a cause or a purpose that they can passionately support. What is worth giving up everything for? Jesus challenged the crowd to leave everything behind and become His disciples.

TOPICAL OUTLINE OF THE LESSON

I. Introduction
   A. Discipleship
   B. Biblical Background

II. Exposition and Application of the Scripture
   A. The Call to Bear the Cross (Luke 14:25-27)
   B. The Necessity of Counting the Cost (Luke 14:28-32)
   C. The Summons to Give up Our Possessions (Luke 14:33)

III. Concluding Reflections

LESSON OBJECTIVES

Upon completion of this lesson, the students will know that:
1. Being a disciple of Jesus Christ will cost you something;
2. Following Christ as a disciple brings an eternal reward; and,
3. When you carry your cross to follow Christ, there can be no looking back.

POINTS TO BE EMPHASIZED

ADULT/YOUTH

Adult Topic: Becoming Passionate Supporters
Youth Topic: Summoned to Be a Disciple
Adult/Youth Key Verse: Luke 14:27
Print Passage: Luke 14:25-33

—God gives us the freedom to choose whom we will follow, but we are accountable for the choices we make.
—Following Jesus requires something of us. Salvation is free, but discipleship is costly.
—Counting the cost of following Jesus Christ is strategic to being His disciple.
—The phrase "give up" (verse 33) is probably better translated "renounce."
—The word "hate" in verse 26 uses an idiom that would have been understood differently in Jesus' time than it is today.
—A martyr carrying a cross (verse 27) on the way to the crucifixion site was a familiar sight to Jesus' hearers.
—Jesus' words about building a tower (verse 28) were spoken in an age of unfinished structures. Herod was a reckless builder who believed that one's glory came from towers, palaces, and the like.

CHILDREN

Children Topic: Becoming a Follower
Key Verse: Luke 14:33
Print Passage: Luke 14:25-33

—Jesus wants us to understand what it means to be disciples.
—Jesus wants us to be willing to follow Him.
—Jesus is looking for a commitment from us.
—Jesus wants us to give up everything that keeps us from being close to Him.

I. INTRODUCTION

A. Discipleship

In today's lesson, we will learn some very important lessons about discipleship and the high personal cost of following Jesus Christ. What did it cost people in first-century Galilee to become disciples of Jesus of Nazareth? Do the words of Jesus about discipleship mean the same things today? The answer is a resounding *Yes!* Discipleship today requires the same deep commitment and passion as it did in the first century. There *is* nothing in the Word of God that has been watered down to fit the tastes of this post-modern age. Jesus called men and women to embrace the ideals and teachings of the kingdom of God without reservation. He challenged His first followers to become so committed that they would be considered radical and fanatical. Why? First, Jesus never called men and women to follow a set of religious traditions, teachers, organizations, or philosophies. Rather, Jesus called men and women to follow Him. This was a far different type of commitment than that which existed in the world in which He preached and lived.

Second, Jesus called men and women to a lifestyle that was considered to be nothing less than extreme (Luke 9:57-62). Third, Jesus came preaching and teaching a doctrine that was viewed as strange, extreme, and far to the left of the neo-conservative Jewish thinking and practices of His day (Luke 4:32, 36; 20:2-8). Jesus broke through the pious and hypocritical theology of His contemporaries. He brought God's promise of love in place of the traditions of the elders with their demands for strict adherence to the Law of Moses. Fourth, Jesus promised a new outpouring and endowment of the Holy Spirit, which would replace the emptiness of the Jewish traditions. Those who lived during the era of Jesus' ministry could not have been surprised when His ministry ended with a violent crucifixion at Golgotha. The Jewish authorities thought that Calvary would be the end of the movement begun in Galilee, but Jesus had gathered a band of disciples who would continue the work.

B. Biblical Background

This passage marks a turning point in the teaching ministry of Jesus. In the previous lesson, which began with Luke 14:1, 7-14, Jesus had been involved in discussions with the Pharisees and other religious leaders over how to understand and define the concept of the kingdom of God (Luke 13:18, 20; 14:15). When Jesus left the home of the chief Pharisee, He turned His attention and teaching back to the crowds of people who were following Him. Many of them expected Jesus to lead an insurrection against the Roman authorities and establish a reincarnated Davidic kingdom of peace and prosperity (2 Samuel 7:12-14; Isaiah 11:1-16; 65:9-25). Instead of peace, prosperity, and power to the people, Jesus offered a cross and separation from family and possessions.

Jesus made it clear that those who followed Him must give their undivided loyalty to Him. There was no middle ground whereby one could ease into this new relationship and slowly adjust to the new demands of discipleship. It was all or nothing from the very start. He made it clear that without accepting these demands, no one could be His disciple. There must be total agreement with Him. Jesus gave two examples of the necessity of weighing carefully what He was asking people to do. The first was the parable about a man who intended to build a tower, but ran out of money and left the tower unfinished (Luke 14:28-30). The second parable was about a king going to war unprepared because he did not sit and first evaluate the situation to see if he had enough men and equipment to win the battle (Luke 14:31). Jesus made it clear in no uncertain terms that unless one was willing to meet His requirements, one could not be His disciple.

II. EXPOSITION AND APPLICATION OF THE SCRIPTURE

A. The Call to Bear the Cross
(Luke 14:25-27)

And there went great multitudes with him: and he turned, and said unto them, If any man come to me, and hate not his father, and mother, and wife, and children, and brethren, and sisters, yea, and his own life also, he cannot be my disciple. And whosoever doth not bear his cross, and come after me, cannot be my disciple.

When Jesus left the home of the chief Pharisee, there were people waiting outside for Him. He turned and began to teach them about the demands and the cost of following Him (verse 25). Many leaders measure their success and effectiveness by the numbers of people who adore them and heap accolades of praise upon them. Jesus was never impressed with the crowds of people who surrounded Him. His entire ministry attracted large crowds of people who joined themselves to Him for a variety of reasons (Matthew 5:1; 8:1, 18; 9:8, 33; 15:30; 19:2; Luke 5:15). On one occasion, He spoke about the demands of following Him; because of the hardships involved, many of His would-be disciples went away and did not follow Him anymore (John 6:60-66).

Jesus offered three measurements for what it would it take to be His disciples. The first is found in verse 26, the second is in verse 27, and the third is found in verse 33. In verse 26, Jesus gave an open invitation to anyone who wanted to follow Him to do so. However, before making the decision, a person must be prepared to make an unconditional commitment to Him. Jesus demanded loyalty and devotion so deep that it would appear as though everyone else was hated, including father, mother, wife, children, sisters, and brothers. Did Jesus literally mean that one must hate his or her family before one can become His disciple? No! Jesus meant that anyone who wanted to follow Him must place no earthly relationship above one's relationship with Him. Everything that we hold dear must be subordinate to Jesus Christ. If a person was not willing to make Jesus Christ first in every way, even first above their family ties, it would be impossible to be His disciple.

This radical redefinition of "hatred" extended not just to family and friends, but to one's very own life. This demand is heightened further in verse 27 with the call to take up a cross. Jesus made a positive demand using a negative statement—"whosoever doth not bear his cross cannot... be my disciple." Jesus raised a question with the crowd. What price were they willing to pay for the privilege of being disciples of Jesus? Discipleship came and still comes with a cross. The cross was not a strange sight to first-century people, for they often saw men carrying crosses to prominent places to face capital punishment. The idea of a cross to Jews was repugnant. After all, death on a cross was not a Jewish form of punishment, but a Roman form of punishment. Jews would stone a person to death (Acts 7:58). The Romans would crucify men; and this was usually done at very prominent locations so that many people could see and learn lessons in submission. The cross meant certain death. When a man took up that crossbeam to carry it, he knew that he was on the way to his own death. The point of the cross is submission to Jesus Christ. One must be prepared to die for the cause of Jesus Christ.

B. The Necessity of Counting the Cost (Luke 14:28-32)

For which of you, intending to build a tower, sitteth not down first, and counteth the cost, whether he have sufficient to finish it? Lest haply, after he hath laid the foundation, and is not able to finish it, all that behold it begin to mock him, Saying, This man began to build, and was not able to finish. Or what king, going to make war against another king, sitteth not down first, and consulteth whether he be able with ten thousand to meet him that cometh against him with twenty thousand? Or else, while the other is yet a great way off, he sendeth an ambassage, and desireth conditions of peace.

In this first illustration, Jesus used an example that was very common and familiar to the people of Israel. Towers were common sights around Israel. They were used primarily as places to station lookouts who could sound the alarm in case of attacks on the city (2 Kings 17:9; 2 Chronicles 20:24; Nehemiah 3:26). Towers were also used to station guards to protect vineyards and fields (Isaiah 5:2). In the Psalms, a tower is used as a metaphor for the watchful protection of God (Psalms 18:2; 61:3) and as a metaphor for the work of the prophets (Jeremiah 6:7).

As previously stated, anyone considering following Jesus must first consider the enormous cost. Jesus made this point crystal clear with two illustrations of what can happen when one fails to count the cost. Jesus began the first illustration of the unfinished tower with a rhetorical question. "For which of you, intending to build a tower, sitteth not down first, and counteth the cost, whether he hath sufficient to finish it" (verse 28). The use of the word "intending" carries the force of the illustration. The hypothetical builder started with the determination and resolve to complete the work, but failed to consider every possible contingency. He really meant to build the tower. But, after laying the foundation, he discovered that he did not have enough money to complete the project. The laying of a foundation indicated that a rather sizeable structure had already been constructed. The builder had big intentions, but he lacked the financial resources to fulfill his vision. Consequently, because he could not finish the tower, people in the community would come by and look at the unfinished structure and mock the owner. *Mocking* denotes ridicule and making fun of someone. The unfinished building would stand as a testimony to the lack of foresight and careful financial planning on the part of the owner.

I have had the opportunity to travel to Turkey, which was the Roman province of Asia Minor during the first century. Throughout Turkey, there are thousands of unfinished buildings and houses. The reason has to do with how building construction was and is financed. People would begin with whatever resources they had, and when they finally got enough money, they would finish the project. Bank financing was and is rarely used or available for the average homeowner.

The second illustration about counting the cost is about a king who decided to go to war against an enemy that had a force twice the size of his own (verse 31). One of the laws of combat states that one never engages an enemy without the capacity to exert overwhelming firepower along with a larger number of combat soldiers. On going to war, the king was about to commit military suicide. Before making the decision to go to war, he should have gotten a clear assessment from his subordinates about the advisability of going into combat, and only then should he have decided if going to war made sense. Once he realized that he was out-numbered two to one, he would have done the most prudent thing available—pursue terms of peace. He would do this well in advance of the two opposing armies meeting each other.

In these two illustrations, Jesus taught a very important lesson about discipleship. In the first illustration, the lesson points to the need of considering the consequences of starting something that we cannot finish. How many people declare themselves for Jesus on Sunday morning, but lack the resolve to see their con-version through? They may return to work on Monday and announce their commitment to Christ, only to have their resolve dry up under the searing rays of trials and trouble. When a person is unable to continue in the Christian faith because of trials, he or she becomes a mockery and a joke to people around him or her. In the second illustration, the king would be forced to retreat because he had met a greater force. The greatest harm done to the cause of Jesus Christ in the world today comes from

people who refuse to reckon the high cost of what it means to follow Him.

C. The Summons to Give up Our Possessions (Luke 14:33)

So likewise, whosoever he be of you that forsaketh not all that he hath, he cannot be my disciple.

This is the third of three statements Jesus made about discipleship. It was and is even more demanding and brings home the point that discipleship involves renouncing every-thing that the world holds dear. At the center of worldliness is materialism. Materialism is the desire to acquire wealth, land, clothes, and anything else of a material nature. The quest for possessions leaves people morally and spiritually bankrupt (1 Timothy 6:6-9; 1 John 2:15-17). Jesus said if one is going to be one of His disciples, then there must be a complete detachment from the things of the world (Mark 10:17-31). Materialism splits our loyalty and causes us to focus more on what we have rather than on what God has called us to be (Luke 12:13-21). A disciple must make Jesus the first object of his or her loyalty and affection (Mat-thew 6:24; Luke 12:31).

One of the great theological tragedies of the postmodern Christian church has been the over-emphasis on material possessions as being a sign of God's favor. That belief and teaching stresses that if one is experiencing an unusual bounty of material prosperity, it is due to God's favor and, therefore, one is among the most blessed. Rarely stressed is the biblical demand about forsaking all for the cause of Jesus Christ. An appropriate question for generations of Christians might be: "Am I really Christian, given my lifestyle, commitment, and obedience to Jesus Christ?"

III. CONCLUDING REFLECTIONS

These words that Jesus said are among the most difficult statements of the Master regarding the cost of discipleship. Committed discipleship means that we shift the center of our lives away from ourselves to God and His purposes. We must move out of the center and let Him become the center of our lives. In Colossians 1:18, Paul says that in all things, Jesus must have the preeminence; this means that He must be first in our lives. In Romans 6:16ff, Paul wrote about believers becoming the servants of righteousness by serving the cause of God in Christ. In Colossians 3:1-3, Paul wrote, "If ye then be risen with Christ, seek those things which are above, where Christ sitteth on the right hand of God. Set your affection on things above, not on things on the earth. For ye are dead, and your life is hid with Christ in God."

We are called to renounce all self-dependence, self-interest, and self-pursuits that are contrary to the will and way of God. This form of thinking is not the contemporary way of thinking for most Christians. We live in a day and time when the emphasis is more on "me" and what "I" want than at any other time in our history. Gone is the sense of collective mission, community personality, and the highest good for the least of the earth. A Christian is called to be counter-culture. Everything we do and everything we are about must be seasoned and saturated by what God's will is.

PRAYER

Heavenly Father, teach us how to love You with our whole being. May we learn the lessons of sacrifice and service which characterized Your Son, Jesus Christ. Teach us, then, to number our days, that we may apply wisdom to our hearts. Forgive us of our sins. In the name of Jesus Christ, we pray. Amen.

WORD POWER

Cross (Greek: *stauros*)—this is the well-known instrument of a most cruel and ignominious punishment. It was borrowed by the Romans and the Greeks from the Phoenicians. The guiltiest criminals, the basest slaves, and insurrectionists ended up on the cross. To bear one's cross is to consider the pain and the shame as nothing compared to the joy of following Christ.

HOME DAILY BIBLE READINGS
(February 18-24, 2008)

Summoned to Be a Disciple

MONDAY, February 18: "You Know Me" (Psalm 139:1–6)
TUESDAY, February 19: "Conditions of Discipleship" (Luke 14:25–27)
WEDNESDAY, February 20: "First, Count the Cost" (Luke 14:28–33)
THURSDAY, February 21: "The Rich Ruler's Response" (Luke 18:18–25)
FRIDAY, February 22: "Rewards of Discipleship" (Luke 18:28–30)
SATURDAY, February 23: "First Disciples Called" (Luke 5:1–11)
SUNDAY, February 24: "Saul Called to Be a Disciple" (Acts 9:1–6, 11–16)

MONARCHY

God, the People, and the Covenant

GENERAL INTRODUCTION

The study for this quarter surveys the theme of covenant. This quarter focuses on the covenant of God with the people of Israel. God's faithfulness to the covenant is shown throughout the monarchy, the exile, and the restoration of the people to Jerusalem. Through the years, the people wavered between unfaithfulness and faithlessness to the covenant. Various prophets and kings led the way in restoring their covenant relationship with God.

Unit I, *Signs of God's Covenant,* consists of five sessions and begins with the topic "A Symbol of God's Presence" in Lesson 1. It focuses on the ark of the covenant, the symbol of God's presence with the people of Israel, which David brought into Jerusalem. Lesson 2 deals with how God made a lasting covenant with David through the prophet Nathan. In Lesson 3, we see how Solomon was charged to build a more permanent place for the ark to rest. In Lesson 4, the question raised is: "Whose Promises Can You Trust?" The answer is given as follows: God is faithful in keeping promises, as Solomon recognized and declared to the Israelites, and as Jesus' resurrection demonstrated. Lesson 5 presents the topic, "Mending a Broken Relationship," and points out that the healing of broken relationships must begin with listening and then must follow with an affirmation to restore and maintain our relationship with God.

Unit II, *The Covenant in Exile,* consists of four sessions. Lesson 6 focuses on Daniel and his three friends as they begin life in the foreign land of Babylon. Even in Babylon, these four men kept their covenant with God and found that God was faithful to them. Lesson 7 reviews the story of Shadrach, Meschach, and Abednego and the fiery furnace. We see God's faithfulness in this familiar story. Lesson 8 seeks to answer the question, "What does it matter if you compromise your convictions?" The topic of lesson 9, "Intercession in Crisis," focuses on Daniel's prayer that links the people's current situation with their unfaithfulness to the covenant.

Unit III, *Restoration and Covenant Renewal,* consists of four sessions and focuses on a time when exiled Israelites were allowed to return home to Judah and Jerusalem. The topic of lesson 10 is "First Things First!" and highlights Haggai's main concern about the reconstruction of the temple in Jerusalem. Lesson 11 seeks to answer the following question: "How do we discern a worthy vision and recognize a visionary leader?" God gave Nehemiah a vision of rebuilding the walls and the leadership ability to seek the king's favor and motivate people to work. In Lesson 12, we see how Nehemiah and the Israelites found God's help to counteract the plots against them and continued the work on the wall—finishing in record time. The topic of Lesson 13, "Restored and Renewed," focuses on Ezra's challenge to the returned Israelite exiles to reestablish their covenant relationship with God and with one another.

The Ishtar Gate

THE ISHTAR GATE, one of the eight gates of the inner city of Babylon, was built during the reign of Nebuchadnezzar II (604-562 B.C.E.). Only the foundations of the original ancient gate were found, going down some forty-five feet. The gateway pictured here was reconstructed in the Pergamon Museum in Berlin from the glazed bricks found at the excavation site. While its original height was different in size, the reconstructed gate is forty-seven feet tall.

One of eight fortified gates of the inner city of Babylon, it served as the main entrance into the city. The original gate was built about 575 B.C.E. The gate remains one of the most impressive monuments rediscovered in the ancient Near East.

Ishtar Gate was dedicated to the goddess Ishtar by King Nebuchadnezzar II, who orchestrated elaborate building projects in Babylon (ca. 604-562 B.C.E.). His goal was to beautify his capitol city. Nebuchadnezzar restored the temple of Marduk, the chief god, and also built himself a magnificent palace with the famous Hanging Gardens, reported by the Greek historian Herodotus to have been one of the wonders of the world.

The Bible records that it was Nebuchadnezzar who destroyed Jerusalem, brought the kingdom of Judah to an end, and carried off the Jews into exile. The Ishtar Gate was the starting point for the processions. The Babylonians would assemble in front of it and march through the triumphal arch and proceed along the Sacred Way to the seven-story Ziggurat, which was crowned near the temple of Marduk.

LESSON 1   March 2, 2008

THE ARK COMES TO JERUSALEM

DEVOTIONAL READING: **Psalm 150**
PRINT PASSAGE: **1 Chronicles 15:1-3,
14-16, 25-28**

BACKGROUND SCRIPTURE: **1 Chronicles 15:1-28**
KEY VERSE: **1 Chronicles 15:3**

1 Chronicles 15:1-3, 14-16, 25-28—KJV

AND DAVID made him houses in the city of David, and prepared a place for the ark of God, and pitched for it a tent.

2 Then David said, None ought to carry the ark of God but the Levites: for them hath the LORD chosen to carry the ark of God, and to minister unto him for ever.

3 And David gathered all Israel together to Jerusalem, to bring up the ark of the LORD unto his place, which he had prepared for it.

…..

14 So the priests and the Levites sanctified themselves to bring up the ark of the LORD God of Israel.

15 And the children of the Levites bare the ark of God upon their shoulders with the staves thereon, as Moses commanded according to the word of the LORD

16 And David spake to the chief of the Levites to appoint their brethren to be the singers with instruments of musick, psalteries and harps and cymbals, sounding, by lifting up the voice with joy.

…..

25 So David, and the elders of Israel, and the captains over thousands, went to bring up the ark of the covenant of the LORD out of the house of Obed-edom with joy.

26 And it came to pass, when God helped the Levites that bare the ark of the covenant of the LORD, that they offered seven bullocks and seven rams.

27 And David was clothed with a robe of fine linen, and all the Levites that bare the ark, and the singers, and Chenaniah the master of the song with the singers: David also had upon him an ephod of linen.

28 Thus all Israel brought up the ark of the covenant of the LORD with shouting, and with sound of the cornet, and with trumpets, and with cymbals, making a noise with psalteries and harps.

1 Chronicles 15:1-3, 14-16, 25-28—NRSV

DAVID BUILT houses for himself in the city of David, and he prepared a place for the ark of God and pitched a tent for it.

2 Then David commanded that no one but the Levites were to carry the ark of God, for the LORD had chosen them to carry the ark of the LORD and to minister to him forever.

3 David assembled all Israel in Jerusalem to bring up the ark of the Lord to its place, which he had prepared for it.

…..

14 So the priests and the Levites sanctified themselves to bring up the ark of the LORD, the God of Israel.

15 And the Levites carried the ark of God on their shoulders with the poles, as Moses had commanded according to the word of the LORD.

16 David also commanded the chiefs of the Levites to appoint their kindred as the singers to play on musical instruments, on harps and lyres and cymbals, to raise loud sounds of joy.

…..

25 So David and the elders of Israel, and the commanders of the thousands, went to bring up the ark of the covenant of the Lord from the house of Obed-edom with rejoicing.

26 And because God helped the Levites who were carrying the ark of the covenant of the LORD, they sacrificed seven bulls and seven rams.

27 David was clothed with a robe of fine linen, as also were all the Levites who were carrying the ark, and the singers, and Chenaniah the leader of the music of the singers; and David wore a linen ephod.

28 So all Israel brought up the ark of the covenant of the LORD with shouting, to the sound of the horn, trumpets, and cymbals, and made loud music on harps and lyres.

Families, groups, and nations all have symbols of their belonging to one another and their history together. What symbols really matter in our lives? David brought the ark of God, a symbol of the covenant, back to the people of Israel and reminded them of their covenantal relationship with God.

TOPICAL OUTLINE OF THE LESSON

I. Introduction
A. The Ark of the Covenant
B. Biblical Background

II. Exposition and Application of the Scripture
A. The Ark Is Relocated
   (1 Chronicles 15:1-3)
B. The Role of the Priests and the Levites
   (1 Chronicles 15:14-16)
C. The Joyful Procession
   (1 Chronicles 15:25-28)

III. Concluding Reflections

LESSON OBJECTIVES

Upon completion of this lesson, the students will understand that:

1. The ark of the covenant symbolized God's presence;

2. God attaches importance to the symbols of His presence;

3. The sanctuary symbolizes God's presence; and,

4. God does not reside in houses of stone.

POINTS TO BE EMPHASIZED

ADULT/YOUTH
Adult Topic: **A Symbol of God's Presence**
Youth Topic: **God Is with Us!**
Adult/Youth Key Verse: **1 Chronicles 15:3**
Print Passage: **1 Chronicles 15:1-3, 14-16, 25-28**
—So sacred was the ark that only Levites were designated to carry it and then only with poles so that no one would touch the ark.
—Who were the Levites, and why did God choose them to carry the ark?
—In the ark was the tablet of the Ten Commandments, the Covenant of God given to Moses on Mt. Sinai.
—The ark of the covenant illustrates the importance of worship as a central event.
—The ark of the covenant symbolizes God's presence with His people.
—First Chronicles 15 describes the ceremony and celebration with which David had the ark delivered to Jerusalem to be housed in a temporary tent.

CHILDREN
Children Topic: **King David Leads Worship**
Key Verse: **1 Chronicles 15:28a**
Print Passage: **1 Chronicles 15:1-3, 14-16, 25-28**
—King David led the nation of Israel in worshiping God.
—King David prepared a special place for the ark of God and organized Israel for its processional return to Jerusalem.
—King David followed God's instructions in completing the task of returning the ark of the covenant.
—The people worshiped as the ark was brought back into the city.

I. INTRODUCTION

A. The Ark of the Covenant

Inasmuch as God is spirit and spirits are invisible, it is sometimes difficult for people to relate to Him as someone who is real. In the absence of a physical God who can be seen and touched, people throughout history have come up with all kinds of outlandish ideas and graven images as representations of God, eventually replacing the homage due Him with homage to their chosen idol.

In an effort to meet the people's needs and yet guard them against falling into idolatry, God chose the ark as a symbolic representation of His presence among the people. This lesson focuses upon that ark and the great care attached to it as a symbolic representation of God's covenant to provide, protect, and empower His people. It is also designed to help us know that our God does not dwell in some faraway, unreachable place; He is here in our midst, within our grasp.

As we study this lesson, we should pay attention to symbols in our local churches. We must bear in mind that symbols, in actuality, point to something beyond themselves. Do we realize the role those symbols play in worship and faith understanding? Do we revere them as some denominations do? As Baptists, religious symbols are merely that, but we know that they point us ultimately to God.

B. Biblical Background

The word *ark* means a "box" or "chest" that was designed to hold the stone tablets of "the covenant of the Lord" (1 Kings 8:21); thus the term "ark of the covenant" refers both to the container and the purpose for which it was made. Because of its close association with God, it is sometimes referred to as "the ark of God" (1 Samuel 3:3); and in the book of Psalms, it is called "the ark of his might" (Psalm 78:61, NIV). The title, "ark of the covenant" is the most significant name given to it, because it contained the "tablets of stone" upon which God had written the Decalogue. It also contained a two-quart jar of manna (Exodus 16:13-21).

As the symbol of God's guidance and protection when Israel advanced through the wilderness, it was the ark that went before the tribes three days in advance "to seek out a resting place for them" (Numbers 10:33, NRSV). It also preceded them at other times, as the symbol of God's might—whether it was a means for scattering or conquering their enemies, or parting the waters of Jordan as the Israelites entered Canaan (Joshua 3:3).

II. EXPOSITION AND APPLICATION OF THE SCRIPTURE

A. The Ark Is Relocated
(1 Chronicles 15:1-3)

AND DAVID made him houses in the city of David, and prepared a place for the ark of God, and pitched for it a tent. Then David said, None ought to carry the ark of God but the Levites: for them hath the Lord chosen to carry the ark of God, and to minister unto him for ever. And David gathered all Israel together to Jerusalem, to bring up the ark of the Lord unto his place, which he had prepared for it.

Through the liberality of the king of Tyre (1 Chronicles 14:1), David was able to erect not only a palace for himself, but also a suitable residence for his entire family. Meanwhile, the ark was put under a tent in foreign territory. David was not pleased that the ark, which was a symbol of God's presence, was not situated in a place befitting it. David understood the importance of the ark of the Lord. Prior to this time, the ark of the Lord had been in the house of Abinadab of Gibeah. There was great rejoicing when this sacred object was being moved; however, when the oxen that were bearing the ark shook, Uzza touched the sacred object out of curiosity, even though there was a stipulation that only the Levites were permitted to touch the ark. Right there on the spot, Uzza died mysteriously. David was displeased with the Lord and ordered the ark to be taken to the house of Obed-edom. While the ark was there for a period of three months, the Lord blessed the house of Obed-edom, a Philistine, and all his household. David heard about it (see 2 Samuel 6:4-12). Because of this news, David, perhaps out of jealousy, made plans for the relocation of the ark of the Lord to the city of David.

We must take note of some principles here; first, anyone who dares to take good care of God's property will surely receive unannounced and unspecified blessings. Second, God is no respecter of persons. Rather, God is looking for those who truly fear Him from the heart. Third, God wants us to obey simple instructions. No matter how unappealing an instruction is, we must carry it out. Uzza is a case in point. It was a common understanding that only the Levites were to touch the ark of the Lord.

David made sure this time around that only the Levites would carry or touch the ark of the Lord. In Numbers, chapters 4:1-4, 15 and 7:9, God gave specific instructions regarding the carrying and servicing of the ark of the Lord. This is the reason why David insisted that, "None-ought to carry the ark but the Levite." David issued this instruction because he had learned from his past mistake when Uzza was struck in the presence of all the people. We should learn a simple lesson here: the work of the Lord should be carried out with a sense of divine mandate. David did not construct a tent for the ark of the Lord; instead, we are told that he prepared a place for it. The word *prepared* shows that this place meant more than just a tent.

Finally, David gathered all Israel together. He did this to raise the consciousness of his people to the reality of God's presence among them. It was also done so that many of the younger generations of the Israelites who had witnessed the long-continued disorders of the kingdom might have the opportunity to know something about the ark. Human beings are prone to forgetting important matters in their lives. David realized the importance of calling all the people together so that they could remember that the Lord was still in their midst.

B. The Role of the Priests and the Levites (1 Chronicles 15:14-16)

So the priests and the Levites sanctified themselves to bring up the ark of the Lord God of Israel. And the children of the Levites bare the ark of God upon their shoulders with the staves thereon, as Moses commanded according to the word of the Lord. And David spake to the chief of the Levites to appoint their brethren to be the singers with instruments of musick, psalteries and harps and cymbals, sounding, by lifting up the voice with joy.

The priests and the Levites consecrated themselves in order to bring up the ark of the

Lord, the God of Israel. The word *consecrate* as used here means "a constant cleansing of the Levites." The ark was a tangible representation of God; therefore, the handlers of it had to constantly purify themselves. God called the Levites and priests to be the custodians of this sacred object, but to do this, they had to remain holy. They could not come close to or touch corpses. The Levites and the priests had different roles. In the Mosaic commandments, the Levites were not allowed to sacrifice. Their duties included slaughtering of the animals, praising, and caring for the temple courts (see Ezekiel 44:6-16). They were the priests' assistants in maintaining a smooth administration in the temple. They were associated with the priestly functions, but they were not allowed at the altar and the innermost sanctuary. Admittance to the Levite corps was through descent from Levi (see Exodus 6:17-25; Numbers 3:14-39).

This special sanctification, which was required on all grave and important occasions, consisted in observing strict abstinence as well as cleanliness in both person and dress (see Genesis 35:2; Exodus 19:10, 15). The priests were keenly aware of the importance of these rules and knew that to neglect them could cause serious consequences (2 Chronicles 30:3).

The Levites carried the ark of God with poles on their shoulders, as Moses had commanded in accordance with the Word of the Lord. We should take note here that everything should be done decently and in order in our service to the Lord. It is to the glory and honor of God that we carry out our own sacred duties with the utmost sense of respect. When was the last time your church's pastor or leader called attention to the sacredness of church equipment? Some years ago, one church observed the Lord's Supper, and when the service was over, the cups, the bread, and the trays were left in the sanctuary. We should treat all the sacred objects in the sanctuary with reverence. It is true that we are under grace, but sacred objects are reminders of God's presence among us.

We believe, as the writer of Hebrews says, that "Jesus is the same yesterday, and today, and forever" (Hebrews 13:8). This reminds us that God has not lowered His standards when it comes to the objects of worship. Our modernity should be tempered with humility in the presence of God. The priests and the Levites sanctified themselves because of the sacredness of their calling and duty. When it comes to who we are in Christ at present, Peter says, "But ye are a chosen generation, a royal priesthood, an holy nation…" (1 Peter 2:9). This is what scholars call "propositional truth"—a truth that can be believed. If we believe the Word of God as recorded by Peter, then it stands to reason that we Christians today are priests as well. Carriers of the ark of God were to maintain proper balance and distance to prevent themselves from touching it. In our contemporary worship setting, we must take care to handle the affairs of God with respect and to carry out assigned duties with care. Carrying an object on the shoulders symbolized a burden bearer. In fact, the Levites were the burden bearers of the Israelites.

David ordered the chief of the Levites to appoint the singers with instruments. The transporting of the ark was to be more than just moving it from one place to another. Rather, it was to be an elaborate religious celebration with pomp and pageantry befitting such a holy activity. Thus, David instructed the Levites to choose individuals who were known to be the most proficient musicians and singers among them and to appoint them for the solemn procession.

The performers were arranged in three choirs, or bands, and the names of the principal leaders were given (1 Chronicles 15:17-18, 21), with the instruments respectively used by each.

David truly knew how to serve God. One may wonder why David made this elaborate preparation for the conveying of God's ark. Looking back at his life, David remembered God choosing him over King Saul. David went through the Valley of the Shadow of Death, and God brought him out. Absalom conspired against David; the Lord caused David to escape the evil plot. David sinned against God when he committed a heinous offense against Uriah. He confessed his sins, and the Lord pardoned him. David remembered many other things God helped him to accomplish, and David could not do less than honor God. This was one of the reasons for the elaborateness of this occasion.

C. The Joyful Procession
(1 Chronicles 15:25-28)

So David, and the elders of Israel, and the captains over thousands, went to bring up the ark of the covenant of the Lord out of the house of Obed-edom with joy. And it came to pass, when God helped the Levites that bare the ark of the covenant of the Lord, that they offered seven bullocks and seven rams. And David was clothed with a robe of fine linen, and all the Levites that bare the ark, and the singers, and Chenaniah the master of the song with the singers: David also had upon him an ephod of linen. Thus all Israel brought up the ark of the covenant of the Lord with shouting, and with sound of the cornet, and with trumpets, and with cymbals, making a noise with psalteries and harps.

Finally, David and the elders of Israel and the commanders of units of a thousand went with rejoicing to bring the ark of the covenant of the Lord from the house of Obed-Edom. This was intended to communicate that this joyful activity was to be participated in by all people, irrespective of rank or status. According to verse 26, God helped the Levites who carried the ark of the covenant of the Lord. Seven bulls and seven rams were sacrificed. The Levites, remembering the fate that fell upon Uzza, were careful when they took up the ark. So the phrase, "God helped them" should be understood to mean that He encouraged them, silenced their fears, and strengthened their faith.

In the sacrificial system, the type of animal required was suitable to the rank of the beneficiary. Bulls and rams were offered as sacrifices for the high priest, as well as for the entire congregation. The number *seven* is used frequently in biblical numerology to indicate rest or completion. Taken together, this sacrifice of seven bulls and rams may be understood to refer to both the importance and the completion of this activity. The activity of transporting the ark from place to place was now complete and in its final resting place, the city of Jerusalem.

David was clothed in a robe of fine linen. Also dressed in fine linen were all the Levites who were carrying the ark, the singers, and Kenaniah, the worship leader. Fine linen was a symbol of purity, so it was particularly fitting that the participants were clothed in fine linen garments.

The recounting of this activity concludes with great expressions of rejoicing. The sacred music was played, David danced, the singers sang, and the common people shouted. This shows us that times of corporate worship are times of rejoicing. It also shows us that it is no disparagement to the greatest of human beings to show themselves zealous in acts of devotion to God.

III. CONCLUDING REFLECTIONS

Our spiritual heritage of worship is recorded in this account of the people of Israel. Our forebears in African-American plantation mission churches were also characterized first by their spiritual reverence for God. Second, they were characterized by their adoration of and gratitude to the God of our salvation, which was expressed in high, enthusiastic singing, accompanied by joyful shouts and dancing.

However, as we enjoy more and more socioeconomic success, it seems we are in danger of losing our spiritual heritage. This danger is twofold: the first danger lies in our growing lack of respect and adoration for the things of God. We show less and less respect to our spiritual leaders and to the house of God and, therefore, to God Himself. Second, we are in danger of losing the spiritual heritage of adoration and praise. This can be seen either in our unwillingness to freely praise or in our all-too-willing decision to substitute the worship of God for a sensuous and secularized focus on personal enjoyment.

As a people of the New Testament church age, living between David's time of the ark of the covenant and the fulfillment of the New Jerusalem of John's vision, how grateful we should be that the contents of the ark—"the tablets of stone"—have been written upon our hearts and the manna yet falls from heaven!

PRAYER

Gracious God, we praise You for being a covenant-keeping God. Thank You for including us in Your plan of salvation. Our inclusion is not because of works of righteousness on our part, but by Your love and grace. Enable us to be faithful to Your covenant, in order that we will be Your true ambassadors. In Christ's name, we pray. Amen.

WORD POWER

Kuwn [koon] *(prepared)*—the Hebrew word for *prepared* found in our Key Verse indicates that the place David constructed for the ark of the Lord was a real house. The Hebrew word kuwn helps us to know that it was firmly established and completed. It was a house with a foundation. The ark was situated in a final resting place.

HOME DAILY BIBLE READINGS
(February 25—March 2, 2008)

The Ark Comes to Jerusalem

MONDAY, February 25: "Praise the Lord!" (Psalm 150)

TUESDAY, February 26: "The Ark of God" (1 Chronicles 15:1-3, 11-15)

WEDNESDAY, February 27: "Music, Joy, and Celebration" (1 Chronicles 15:16-24)

THURSDAY, February 28: "Bringing the Ark of the Covenant" (1 Chronicles 15:25-29)

FRIDAY, February 29: "Before the Ark" (1 Chronicles 16:1-6)

SATURDAY, March 1: "A Psalm of Thanksgiving" (1 Chronicles 16:7-36)

SUNDAY, March 2: "Worship Before the Ark" (1 Chronicles 16:37-43)

GOD'S COVENANT WITH DAVID

DEVOTIONAL READING: **Psalm 78:67-72**

PRINT PASSAGE: **1 Chronicles 17:1, 3-4, 6-15**

BACKGROUND SCRIPTURE: **1 Chronicles 17:1-27**

KEY VERSES: **1 Chronicles 17:7c-8**

1 Chronicles 17:1, 3-4, 6-15—KJV

NOW IT came to pass, as David sat in his house, that David said to Nathan the prophet, Lo, I dwell in an house of cedars, but the ark of the covenant of the LORD remaineth under curtains.

.....

3 And it came to pass the same night, that the word of God came to Nathan, saying,

4 Go and tell David my servant, Thus saith the LORD, Thou shalt not build me an house to dwell in.

.....

6 Wheresoever I have walked with all Israel, spake I a word to any of the judges of Israel, whom I commanded to feed my people, saying, Why have ye not built me an house of cedars?

7 Now therefore thus shalt thou say unto my servant David, Thus saith the LORD of hosts, I took thee from the sheepcote, even from following the sheep, that thou shouldest be ruler over my people Israel:

8 And I have been with thee whithersoever thou hast walked, and have cut off all thine enemies from before thee, and have made thee a name like the name of the great men that are in the earth.

9 Also I will ordain a place for my people Israel, and will plant them, and they shall dwell in their place, and shall be moved no more; neither shall the children of wickedness waste them any more, as at the beginning,

10 And since the time that I commanded judges to be over my people Israel. Moreover I will subdue all thine enemies. Furthermore I tell thee that the LORD will build thee an house.

11 And it shall come to pass, when thy days be expired that thou must go to be with thy fathers, that I will raise up thy seed after thee, which shall be of thy sons; and I will establish his kingdom.

12 He shall build me an house, and I will stablish his throne for ever.

1 Chronicles 17:1, 3-4, 6-15—NRSV

NOW WHEN David settled in his house, David said to the prophet Nathan, "I am living in a house of cedar, but the ark of the covenant of the LORD is under a tent."

.....

3 But that same night the word of the LORD came to Nathan, saying:

4 Go and tell my servant David: Thus says the LORD: You shall not build me a house to live in.

.....

6 Wherever I have moved about among all Israel, did I ever speak a word with any of the judges of Israel, whom I commanded to shepherd my people, saying, Why have you not built me a house of cedar?

7 Now therefore thus you shall say to my servant David: Thus says the LORD of hosts: I took you from the pasture, from following the sheep, to be ruler over my people Israel;

8 and I have been with you wherever you went, and have cut off all your enemies before you; and I will make for you a name, like the name of the great ones of the earth.

9 I will appoint a place for my people Israel, and will plant them, so that they may live in their own place, and be disturbed no more; and evildoers shall wear them down no more, as they did formerly,

10 from the time that I appointed judges over my people Israel; and I will subdue all your enemies. Moreover I declare to you that the LORD will build you a house.

11 When your days are fulfilled to go to be with your ancestors, I will raise up your offspring after you, one of your own sons, and I will establish his kingdom.

12 He shall build a house for me, and I will establish his throne forever.

13 I will be his father, and he shall be my son: and I will not take my mercy away from him, as I took it from him that was before thee:

14 But I will settle him in mine house and in my kingdom for ever: and his throne shall be established for evermore.

15 According to all these words, and according to all this vision, so did Nathan speak unto David.

13 I will be a father to him, and he shall be a son to me. I will not take my steadfast love from him, as I took it from him who was before you,

14 but I will confirm him in my house and in my kingdom forever, and his throne shall be established forever.

15 In accordance with all these words and all this vision, Nathan spoke to David.

TOPICAL OUTLINE OF THE LESSON

I. **Introduction**
   A. The General Concept of a Covenant
   B. Biblical Background

II. **Exposition and Application of the Scripture**
   A. David Desires to Build a House for God (1 Chronicles 17:1)
   B. God Forbids David to Build the Temple (1 Chronicles 17:3-4)
   C. God Reminds David of His Abiding Presence (1 Chronicles 17:6-10)
   D. God's Promises to David and His Response (1 Chronicles 17:11-15)

III. **Concluding Reflections**

LESSON OBJECTIVES

Upon completion of this lesson, the students will understand:

1. The biblical concept of a covenant and the requirements of the parties involved;

2. God's faithfulness to His covenant from generation to generation; and,

3. How the Davidic covenant applies to the church today.

POINTS TO BE EMPHASIZED

ADULT/YOUTH

Adult Topic: **Covenanting**

Youth Topic: **God's Special Promise**

Adult Key Verses: **1 Chronicles 17:7c-8**

Youth Key Verse: **1 Chronicles 17:12**

Print Passage: **1 Chronicles 17:1, 3-4, 6-15**

—David, the sovereign king of Israel, demonstrated his respect for God and for God's covenant.

—The Messiah is the fulfillment of God's promise to David.

—God declared, through Nathan, His promise and plan for the kingdom by means of David and his offspring.

—God's covenant with David extends to all subsequent generations through Jesus Christ.

CHILDREN

Children Topic: **David Accepts God's Covenant**

Key Verse: **1 Chronicles 17:26**

Print Passage: 1 Chronicles 17:1, 3-4, 6-15

—God used the prophet Nathan to give a special message.

—David desired to build a place to house the ark of the covenant, but it was not God's desire for David to build it.

—God initiated the covenant and David accepted it.

I. INTRODUCTION

A. The General Concept of a Covenant

The Hebrew word *berith* means to "cut," "fetter," or "bind." The word *fetter* carries the idea of "a chain or shackles to bind the feet, or something that confines or restricts." In essence, a covenant is like a fetter that restricts the parties to remain faithful to the letter of the covenant.

In the Bible, God made covenants with Adam, Abraham, Noah, David, Solomon, and others. A covenant constituted a divine announcement of God's holy will to extend the benefits of His unmerited grace to human beings who were willing by faith to receive it, and who, by entering into a personal commitment to God, bound themselves to Him by ties of absolute obligation.

B. Biblical Background

David was the eighth and youngest son of Jesse, a citizen of Bethlehem. His early occupation was that of tending his father's flock. The prophet Samuel paid an unexpected visit to Bethlehem, having been guided there by divine direction (1 Samuel 16:1-13). There he offered up sacrifice and called the elders of Israel and Jesse's family to the sacrificial meal. Jesse's sons appeared before Samuel, a judge of Israel, but Samuel failed to discover the one chosen by God to succeed Saul, the sitting king of Israel who had forsaken God. David was summoned, and Samuel immediately recognized him as the chosen of God to succeed Saul. Then Samuel poured the anointing oil on David's head.

II. EXPOSITION AND APPLICATION OF THE SCRIPTURE

A. David Desires to Build a House for God
(1 Chronicles 17:1)

NOW IT came to pass, as David sat in his house, that David said to Nathan the prophet, Lo, I dwell in an house of cedars, but the ark of the covenant of the Lord remaineth under curtains.

Here we find David at rest, as "The Lord had given him rest round about" (2 Samuel 7:1), particularly with the Philistines and all those that were enemies to his settlement on the throne. As he was sitting in his house, meditating over the kindness that God had lavished upon him, his thoughts turned to the fact that, though he was sitting in a luxurious house made of cedar, the ark of God stood in a mere tent.

"A house of cedar" indicates the wealth of David, because cedar paneling was too expensive to be used in ordinary homes owned by average people. Considering the hand of God in his life, moving him from a field to a palace,

David made up his mind to do something for the ark of the Lord. He decided that the ark ought to also have a fine resting place, and he communicated this thought to the prophet Nathan. This is the first time in this book that a prophet's name appears.

David shared his thoughts with Nathan, knowing him to be a prophet of the Lord on whom he could rely for godly counsel.

B. God Forbids David to Build the Temple (1 Chronicles 17:3-4)

And it came to pass the same night, that the word of God came to Nathan, saying, Go and tell David my servant, Thus saith the Lord, Thou shalt not build me an house to dwell in.

David's ruthless warfare had disqualified him from building a temple for the Lord (1 Chronicles 22:8; 28:3; 2 Samuel 8:2). Although Nathan's initial response was one of encouragement (1 Chronicles 17:2), as he felt that it was an honorable undertaking, God had other plans. Nathan's approval was not in accordance with God's plan. We are told by the prophet Isaiah that God's ways are not like our ways (Isaiah 55:8).

The lesson here is obvious. The leaders of God's people should remain open to new possibilities and fresh encounters from the Lord. They should not be dogmatic in their ideas, no matter how good something looks. Nathan received a different instruction from the Lord. He humbled himself by retracting his premature approval of David's plan.

We must also take note. First, we should see that although we may have good intentions about what should be done in the service of God, it is wise to seek godly counsel. Second, we need to see that even though God superseded the human counsel of Nathan, He nevertheless communicated His plans for David through His chosen prophet, Nathan.

C. God Reminds David of His Abiding Presence (1 Chronicles 17:6-10)

Wheresoever I have walked with all Israel, spake I a word to any of the judges of Israel, whom I commanded to feed my people, saying, Why have ye not built me an house of cedars? Now therefore thus shalt thou say unto my servant David, Thus saith the Lord of hosts, I took thee from the sheepcote, even from following the sheep, that thou shouldest be ruler over my people Israel: And I have been with thee whithersoever thou hast walked, and have cut off all thine enemies from before thee, and have made thee a name like the name of the great men that are in the earth. Also I will ordain a place for my people Israel, and will plant them, and they shall dwell in their place, and shall be moved no more; neither shall the children of wickedness waste them any more, as at the beginning, And since the time that I commanded judges to be over my people Israel. Moreover I will subdue all thine enemies. Furthermore I tell thee that the Lord will build thee an house.

Through the prophet Nathan, God reminded David that throughout the time of the Judges, whom He appointed, He had never had a house built for Him. The literal rendering is, "I was walking in a tent and in a dwelling." The evident intention, as we may see from 1 Chronicles 17:6, is that God was a traveling God. God did not regard outward pomp in His service; His presence was as surely with His people when the ark was in a tent as when it was in the temple. What an encouragement this should be for those servants of the Lord who labor in small buildings or mere storefronts. God is as available to the storefront preacher as He is to the mega-church pastor.

The name "Lord of hosts" (verse 7) is one used to describe all the forces that operate at God's command throughout the world. It is an old title for God, who, in the role of divine warrior, was the leader of the armies of Israel. He was believed to be enthroned upon the cherubim on the ark of the covenant. As a warrior-king of Israel, David would have been familiar with that name and its significance.

We should note what God says in verse 10, "…Furthermore I tell thee that the LORD will build thee an house." The word *house* here means "a dynasty." God saw the intent of David and rewarded him with a greater blessing. God had given David success and victory over his enemies, protecting him when pursued, and prospering him in the process. He had cut off David's enemies that stood in the way of his advancement and settlement. He had crowned him not only with power and dominion in Israel, but also with honor and reputation among the surrounding nations. He had given David a great name, one which was to be both feared and respected.

D. God's Promises to David and His Response
(1 Chronicles 17:11-15)

And it shall come to pass, when thy days be expired that thou must go to be with thy fathers, that I will raise up thy seed after thee, which shall be of thy sons; and I will establish his kingdom. He shall build me an house, and I will stablish his throne for ever. I will be his father, and he shall be my son: and I will not take my mercy away from him, as I took it from him that was before thee: But I will settle him in mine house and in my kingdom for ever: and his throne shall be established for evermore. According to all these words, and according to all this vision, so did Nathan speak unto David.

The promises began. David had purposed to build God a house, and in response, God promised to build him a house. The house which God promised David was more than a mere dwelling; God's house would be a dynasty. If we sincerely purpose to do good things in the service of God, but providence prevents our doing them, we will not lose our reward. This is what the songwriter meant who wrote, "You can't beat God giving!"

God had promised to make David a name (verse 9). Here, God promised to make him a house, which would bear up that name. This was the language of Nathan himself, who was specially directed to assure David of personal blessings and prosperity, and of a continuous line of royal descendants.

The fulfillment of these promises began with Solomon, his immediate successor, and extended to the royal line of Judah. The statement, "when thy days be fulfilled, and thou must go to be with thy fathers" (verse 11), was a promise that David himself would come to his grave in peace; and then "I will raise up thy seed." This favor was so much the greater because it was more than God had done for Moses or Joshua or any of the judges whom He had called to feed His people. This establishing of the kingdom refers first to Solomon, but ultimately to Jesus Christ, who would sit on David's throne.

What great satisfaction David must have received while he lived, to have the absolute assurance of a divine promise that his family would flourish even after he was no longer alive! Indeed, next to the happiness of our souls and the church of God, we should desire the happiness of our progeny, that those who come from us may be praising God on earth when we are praising Him in heaven. However, it is important to remember that David possessed some qualities which made him worthy of receiving these magnificent promises.

First, David had a tender heart. When he sinned, he repented with all his heart and asked God to create in him a clean heart (Psalm 51:10). David was not a vindictive man. There were occasions when he had the opportunity to kill Saul, but he refused to do so. Also, he collected all the materials necessary to build God's house. God rewarded his intention. God's declaration, "I will establish his throne for ever" (1 Chronicles 17:12) carries us forward to the ultimate successor to the throne of David, Jesus Christ (Luke 1:32-33), who is often called the Son of David.

It is the Son of David to whom these promises pointed and in whom they had their full accomplishment. He was of the "seed of David" (Acts 13:23). To him, God "gave the throne of his father David" (Luke 1:32), all power both in heaven and earth, and authority to execute judgment. The Lord promised that He would establish His house, His throne, and His kingdom forever. We see in verse 14 another incredible conclusion: "for ever." This word *forever* finds its fulfillment in no person other than Christ and in no place other than His kingdom. David's house and kingdom have long since come to an end; only the Messiah's kingdom is everlasting, and of the increase of His government and peace, there will be no end (Isaiah 9:7).

With the words, "I will not take my mercy away from him," Nathan returns to David's more immediate successors (see the context in the parallel passage in 2 Samuel 7:14-15), who would not be overthrown as was "him that was before thee," namely Saul. As David's spiritual seed and joint heirs, we can rejoice in this promise. God has promised us that, "His mercy endureth for ever" (Psalms 106:1; 107:1).

Another incredible promise is found in verse 14, where God says, "I will settle him in mine house and in my kingdom for ever." God asserted His right of supreme sovereignty in Israel. David and Solomon, as with their successors, were rulers whom God, in His providence, permitted authority over Israel. God also determined that David's throne would be established forevermore. The descendents of David inherited the throne in a long succession, though not continuously. These verses are a good example of an Old Testament prophecy in which some elements find fulfillment in the immediate future, while others will be realized only in the more distant future.

We naturally expect the prophet to revert to David before concluding, after having spoken of the building of Solomon's temple (1 Chronicles 17:12). The promise that his house would be blessed proved to be compensation for the denial of his request to build the temple; hence, this assurance is appropriately repeated at the conclusion of the prophet's address.

The prophet Nathan showed himself to be a true prophet of the Lord in that he faithfully delivered to David all that the Lord had said to him. What a word of instruction that ought to be to those of us today who are called to speak His Word; that we too should emulate great servants of the Lord, like Nathan and the apostle Paul, in giving the whole counsel of God (Acts 20:20-21).

The scene ends with David sitting in the tent sanctuary he had erected for the ark, reflecting in amazement at his own journey from his humble beginnings of following sheep to becoming the leader of Israel. He then offers God a prayer of appreciation. What an encouragement to God's people today whose beginnings are mere and meager, to know that God can transform them into something more and greater!

III. CONCLUDING REFLECTIONS

There are elements in the experience of David which seem foreign and perhaps even repugnant to Christians. Yet he "served the purpose of God in his own generation" (Acts

13:36, NRSV). His accomplishments were many and varied—man of action, poet, tender lover, generous foe, stern dispenser of justice, loyal friend—he was all that human beings find wholesome and admirable. All of this was by the will of God, who made him and shaped him for his destiny.

God in His sovereign wisdom chooses and uses each of us for particular reasons and for particular seasons. The house that we labor to build may or may not come into fruition during our lifetimes; but whether it does or not is not necessarily an indication of our success or failure. The measure of our success is not in our fame or our fortune but in our faithfulness.

David, for all of his success, fame, and fortune, was not allowed to build the temple. Yet, which of us can call him a failure? It was and is David and not Saul whom the Jews look back on with pride and affection as the founder of their kingdom.

In assessing our ministries, we must remember that one person plants and another waters, but it is God who gives the increase (1 Corinthians 3:5-10). It is neither the one who plants nor the one who waters to whom the credit should be given for the harvest. If God allows us the privilege of harvesting—to God be the glory! If, on the other hand, we are given the privilege of merely planting or watering, still to God be the glory!

The seed of David, Jesus Christ, tells us to seek first the kingdom of God and its righteousness and the rest will be added unto us. David put God first in all he did. He made mistakes, but God overlooked them because of the way he sought repentance. David saw the ark of the Lord outside and planned to build a house for it. God saw his good intention and rewarded him excessively.

PRAYER

Most righteous and everlasting God, our heavenly Father, how we praise You for Your Word that continues to be a lamp unto our feet and a light unto our paths. Help us to be content with Your plans for the future. In the name of Your Son, our Savior, Jesus the Christ, we pray. Amen.

WORD POWER

Throne (Hebrew: *Kisse*)—this word can refer to any kind of seat or chair. In this context, it refers to a seat of honor. It also refers to an exalted royal position of authority. Part of the covenant that God made with David was that a seed from David would sit in an exalted position of authority. This was a reference to Jesus Christ.

HOME DAILY BIBLE READINGS
(March 3-9, 2008)
God's Covenant with David

MONDAY, March 3: "God Chose David" (Psalm 78:67-72)
TUESDAY, March 4: "No House for God" (1 Chronicles 17:1-6)
WEDNESDAY, March 5: "God's House for David" (1 Chronicles 17:7-10)
THURSDAY, March 6: "A House of Ancestors" (1 Chronicles 17:11-15)
FRIDAY, March 7: "Great Deeds of God" (1 Chronicles 17:16-19)
SATURDAY, March 8: "A House of Israel" (1 Chronicles 17:20-22)
SUNDAY, March 9: "The House of David" (1 Chronicles 17:23-27)

LESSON 3

March 16, 2008

GOD CALLS SOLOMON TO BUILD
THE TEMPLE

[handwritten: aday-]

[handwritten: 1 King 3 - 3, 28   2 Sam 5:14   2 Sam 5:4   1 King 4, 37   Solomon ZERubbel Helced.]

DEVOTIONAL READING: **Psalm 132**
PRINT PASSAGE: **1 Chronicles 28:5-10, 20-21**

BACKGROUND SCRIPTURE: **1 Chronicles 28:1-28**
KEY VERSE: **1 Chronicles 28:10**

1 Chronicles 28:5-10, 20-21—KJV

5 And of all my sons, (for the LORD hath given me many sons,) he hath chosen Solomon my son to sit upon the throne of the kingdom of the LORD over Israel.

6 And he said unto me, Solomon thy son, he shall build my house and my courts: for I have chosen him to be my son, and I will be his father.

7 Moreover I will establish his kingdom for ever, if he be constant to do my commandments and my judgments, as at this day.

8 Now therefore in the sight of all Israel the congregation of the LORD, and in the audience of our God, keep and seek for all the commandments of the LORD your God: that ye may possess this good land, and leave it for an inheritance for your children after you for ever.

9 And thou, Solomon my son, know thou the God of thy father, and serve him with a perfect heart and with a willing mind: for the LORD searcheth all hearts, and understandeth all the imaginations of the thoughts: if thou seek him, he will be found of thee; but if thou forsake him, he will cast thee off for ever.

10 Take heed now; for the LORD hath chosen thee to build an house for the sanctuary: be strong, and do it.

.....

20 And David said to Solomon his son, Be strong and of good courage, and do it: fear not, nor be dismayed: for the LORD God, even my God, will be with thee; he will not fail thee, nor forsake thee, until thou hast finished all the work for the service of the house of the LORD.

21 And, behold, the courses of the priests and the Levites, even they shall be with thee for all the service of the house of God: and there shall be with thee for all manner of workmanship every willing skilful man, for any manner of service: also the princes and all the people will be wholly at thy commandment.

1 Chronicles 28:5-10, 20-21—NRSV

5 And of all my sons, for the LORD has given me many, he has chosen my son Solomon to sit upon the throne of the kingdom of the LORD over Israel.

6 He said to me, 'It is your son Solomon who shall build my house and my courts, for I have chosen him to be a son to me, and I will be a father to him.

7 I will establish his kingdom forever if he continues resolute in keeping my commandments and my ordinances, as he is today.'

8 Now therefore in the sight of all Israel, the assembly of the LORD, and in the hearing of our God, observe and search out all the commandments of the LORD your God; that you may possess this good land, and leave it for an inheritance to your children after you forever.

9 "And you, my son Solomon, know the God of your father, and serve him with single mind and willing heart; for the LORD searches every mind, and understands every plan and thought. If you seek him, he will be found by you; but if you forsake him, he will abandon you forever.

10 Take heed now, for the LORD has chosen you to build a house as the sanctuary; be strong, and act."

.....

20 David said further to his son Solomon, "Be strong and of good courage, and act. Do not be afraid or dismayed; for the LORD God, my God, is with you. He will not fail you or forsake you, until all the work for the service of the house of the LORD is finished.

21 Here are the divisions of the priests and the Levites for all the service of the house of God; and with you in all the work will be every volunteer who has skill for any kind of service; also the officers and all the people will be wholly at your command."

UNIFYING LESSON PRINCIPLE

People long to know that the tasks they do have meaning. How can we know that our tasks are meaningful? David affirmed that God had chosen Solomon for the specific task of building a sanctuary for the worship of God.

TOPICAL OUTLINE OF THE LESSON

I. Introduction
A. The Choice of God
B. Biblical Background

II. Exposition and Application of the Scripture
A. God Chose Solomon (1 Chronicles 28:5-7)
B. Exhortation to the Nation (1 Chronicles 28:8-10)
C. Father-to-Son Exhortation (1 Chronicles 28:20-21)

III. Concluding Reflections

LESSON OBJECTIVES

Upon completion of this lesson, the students will have a clearer understanding of the following:

1. God uses different people at different times for different tasks, just as He used David for one task and Solomon for another;
2. Being chosen for specific tasks involves recognizing one's gifts as well as one's limitations; and,
3. Teamwork is an important element in achieving God's eternal purposes.

POINTS TO BE EMPHASIZED
ADULT/YOUTH

Adult Topic: Chosen for a Specific Task
Youth Topic: Called for a Purpose
Adult Key Verse: 1 Chronicles 28:10
Youth Key Verse: 1 Chronicles 28:6
Print Passage: 1 Chronicles 28:5-10, 20-21

—Through David, God declared that Solomon was chosen to build the temple and to reign as king.
—God affirmed the covenant by declaring God's promise to and expectations for Solomon and the nation.
—David recognized that God called him to perform certain tasks, but the task of rebuilding the temple was reserved for his son.
—David's testimony to Solomon was based on his experience with God.
—God reaffirmed His covenant in declaring His promise and expectation to Solomon and Israel.

CHILDREN

Children Topic: Solomon Is Given a Task
Key Verse: 1 Chronicles 28:10
Print Passage: 1 Chronicles 28:1-3, 5-10

—God selected David's son, Solomon, to build the temple.
—David instructed Solomon to obey God's commands and remain focused on God's call upon his life.
—David passed his plans for the temple on to Solomon and encouraged Solomon to follow through.
—David reminded Solomon that God would be with him through the process if he were obedient.

I. INTRODUCTION

A. The Choice of God

While lying on his deathbed, David summoned all the leaders of Israel: the officers of the tribes, the captains of the various divisions, the stewards, and all of his sons, including Solomon. He made an impressive declaration of his recognition of the government of God in both his own appointment to kingship and also that of his son. He reviewed the history of his own attempts to build the temple—attempts that did not come to fruition because he had shed abundant blood (1 Chronicles 22:8-10). Solomon was God's choice to carry out the desire of David's heart. In giving this command and these instructions, the deepest stratum of David's character and make-up is revealed, and we see what gained him the reputation as being "a man after God's own heart." Foremost in these verses are David's convictions and principles, upon which came his charge to his successor son, a charge that would serve to govern him in the future.

David's charge was twofold: "Know God" and "Serve God." This was followed by a promise and a warning equally clear and forceful, "If thou seek him, he will be found of thee; but if thou forsake him, he will cast thee off for ever" (1 Chronicles 28:9).

B. Biblical Background

Historically, when all the biblical references are collated, it is found that there is mention of both a tabernacle and a tent. In the first reference, the Tent of Meeting is pitched outside the camp (Exodus 33:7). Here, Moses and others were to commune with God and to inquire of Him. This tent was guarded by Joshua, an Ephraimite, but not by Levites. Its function was to provide the meeting place for God and Moses (Numbers 12:4; Deuteronomy 31:15).

The tabernacle was erected at Sinai in the second year after the Exodus, two weeks before Passover (Exodus 40:2, 17). When the congregation journeyed, the entire tabernacle was disassembled and carried in covered wagons (Numbers 3-4). Before Israel departed from Sinai, the tabernacle had been erected for fifty days (Numbers 10:11-12). The journey of Israel took them from Horeb in Arabia to Kadesh-Barnea in the Negev of Judah. Of the forty years spent marching to Canaan, almost thirty-eight were spent at Kadesh. The tabernacle remained there through those years except for one year spent going south to the Red Sea.

After the crossing of the Jordan River, a place was found for the sacred tent near Jericho at Gilgal (Joshua 4:19; 5; 10). This site was temporary, and in time the tabernacle was moved to Shiloh in Ephraim, a central location convenient for the men to attend the three annual pilgrimage feasts (Joshua 18:1; 19:51). When war erupted with the Philistines in Samuel's time, the people decided to bring the ark of the covenant from Shiloh (1 Samuel 4:1ff). The outcome was tragic: the Philistines captured the ark and sent Israel into retreat.

The next reference to the tabernacle is at Nob with Ahimelech as high priest (1 Samuel 21:1ff). After Saul had all the priests of Nob, slain, except Abiathar, the ark was removed to Gibeon (1 Chronicles 16:39; 21:29). After David captured Jebus and built himself a palace, he prepared a place for the ark of God and a tent in Zion. David pitched a tent for the ark, which he had brought to Jerusalem.

With David's removal of the ark to Jerusalem, there remained a tabernacle with its altar at Gibeon and another with the ark in Jerusalem, both soon to be replaced with the temple. Of all the materials of the tabernacle, only the ark remained the same in the temple. The last references to the tabernacle in the history of Israel, then, concern the time when it was transported, along with its sacred vessels, to Jerusalem, where, from all indications, the tabernacle and vessels were kept as sacred relics in the temple. Thus, the tabernacle disappeared from history.

II. EXPOSITION AND APPLICATION OF THE SCRIPTURE

A. God Chose Solomon
(1 Chronicles 28:5-7)

And of all my sons, (for the Lord hath given me many sons,) he hath chosen Solomon my son to sit upon the throne of the kingdom of the Lord over Israel. And he said unto me, Solomon thy son, he shall build my house and my courts: for I have chosen him to be my son, and I will be his father. Moreover I will establish his kingdom for ever, if he be constant to do my commandments and my judgments, as at this day.

In this section, David is indirectly praising God because He has blessed him with many sons, and from among his sons, the Lord chose Solomon as successor to the throne of Israel. In essence, what David is saying here is, "It was not my ambition, my valor, nor my merit that led to my enthronement as king." A careful examination of 1 Chronicles 17:11 reveals that rule over God's people was not limited to David, but it also included his descendants.

An emphatic statement was made in 1 Chronicles 28:6 (NRSV): "It is your son Solomon who shall build my house and my courts...." Solomon was chosen above all his brethren because he was quiet and beloved of God.

God adopted Solomon as His own child with an emphatic statement, "...for I have chosen him to be my son, and I will be his father" (1 Chronicles 28:6). The first clause is cast in a perfect tense, meaning that the choice of God was deliberate and the reason for choosing Solomon was only known to Him.

The second clause, "I will be his father," also points out the deliberate act of God. God, whose ways were and are past understanding by the finite human mind, chose Solomon to build the temple and would honor Solomon as His son in the same way that He had honored David. Being God's child carried many blessings. We note that throughout the reign of Solomon, there was no war.

God chose and chooses whom He will. For instance, David was the youngest son of Jesse, yet God chose to make him king. Solomon was one of the youngest sons of David, yet God chose him to sit upon the throne and to build the temple.

In verse 7, we arrive at another "I will" statement by God. "I will establish his kingdom for ever." As in the other clauses, this too is in the perfect tense. What God had done was complete from A to Z. We may ask what David and Solomon did to deserve this royal treatment from God. What did they do to earn a favor of this magnitude? We know that this prophecy of an everlasting kingdom will find its ultimate fulfillment in the kingdom of the Messiah (Isaiah 9:7; Luke 1:33). However, as to Solomon, this promise of the establishment of his kingdom was conditional: if Solomon remained true to the Lord, his kingdom would endure (1 Chronicles 22:10; 28:6-7).

But Solomon failed to keep to the law of God. During the reformation of Nehemiah, he made reference to the failure of Solomon: "Did not Solomon king of Israel sin by these things?" (Nehemiah 13:26). Solomon's desire for pagan women caused him to sin.

B. Exhortation to the Nation
(1 Chronicles 28:8-10)

Now therefore in the sight of all Israel the congregation of the Lord, and in the audience of our God, keep and seek for all the commandments of the Lord your God: that ye may possess this good land, and leave it for an inheritance for your children after you for ever. And thou, Solomon my son, know thou the God of thy father, and serve him with a perfect heart and with a willing mind: for the Lord searcheth all hearts, and understandeth all the imaginations of the thoughts: if thou seek him, he will be found of thee; but if thou forsake him, he will cast thee off for ever. Take heed now; for the Lord hath chosen thee to build an house for the sanctuary: be strong, and do it.

David concluded his instructions with a strong exhortation to the people. The exhortation was spoken in an open arena and had two components.

First, David wished to drive home the importance of his warnings. None of the Israelites would be able to say, "I was not there. I did not hear him." He charged them to adhere steadfastly to God and to their duty. The Lord was their God; therefore, His commandments must be their rules. To "seek out" the commandments meant they must make a conscious effort to keep them and seek them. Obviously, those who did not know God's commandments would not keep them. Therefore, the children of Israel needed to be inquisitive concerning their duty; they must search the Scriptures, take advice, seek the Law at the mouth of those whose lips were to keep this knowledge, and pray to God to teach and direct them.

Second, David gave them this charge publicly to let them realize that God was their witness, and the congregation was assembled so that they would have both good counsel and fair warning. If they failed to take heed, it would be their own fault, and both God and man would be witnesses against them (see 1 Timothy 5:21; 2 Timothy 4:1-2).

David accentuated this charge by telling the people that obedience to the charge was the way to be happy, to have the peaceable possession of the land themselves, and to preserve it for their children.

C. Father-to-Son Exhortation
(1 Chronicles 28:20-21)

And David said to Solomon his son, Be strong and of good courage, and do it: fear not, nor be dismayed: for the Lord God, even my God, will be with thee; he will not fail thee, nor forsake thee, until thou hast finished all the work for the service of the house of the Lord. And, behold, the courses of the priests and the Levites, even they shall be with thee for all the service of the house of God: and there shall be with thee for all manner of workmanship every willing skilful man, for any manner of service: also the princes and all the people will be wholly at thy commandment.

"As for you, my son Solomon…" (1 Chronicles 28:9, NIV). The king then turned his attention to Solomon, addressing him personally. He impressed upon him the importance of sincerity and practical piety. David told his son, "Know the God of your father" (1 Chronicles 28:9, NRSV). David, as a father, exhorted his son to follow hard after God. He did not mean with head knowledge, for Solomon possessed that already. Rather, he meant a serious encounter with God, which could only be known by loving and serving Him.

Solomon was charged to look upon God as the God of his father, David. He was born in God's house and, therefore, was bound in duty to belong to God. David commanded Solomon to "… serve Him with a loyal heart and with a willing mind" (1 Chronicles 28:9, NKJV). ("Heart" and "mind" refer to our true personalities. We cannot serve God rightly if we do not know Him; and it is in vain that we know Him, if we do not serve Him with our minds and hearts.)

David here wanted Solomon to recognize that God looked not only at his outward deeds, but also at his heart. David emphasized one important thing—if Solomon failed to adhere to his father's instructions, the Lord would reject him.

These instructions given to Solomon ought to be great inducements to us. First, as parents, we must bequeath to our children a lasting, godly legacy. We also must remember that the secrets of our souls are open before God. We must be sincere, because if we deal deceitfully, God sees it and judges us likewise. We also must be mindful of our thoughts, and engage them in God's service, because He fully understands all our imaginations, both good and bad. Second, we ought to recognize that we will be either happy or miserable here, and forever, depending upon whether we do or do not serve God. If we seek Him diligently, we will find Him.

David encouraged Solomon to recognize that he had been chosen by God for the work and that he should give himself wholeheartedly to the task with the assurance that God was with him. His final words included first a caution: "Take heed." David wanted his son to be wary of any and every thing that led to evil. Second, David admonished, "Be strong, and do it" (1 Chronicles 28:10). Solomon had to recognize that the completion of the task would require strength, courage, and determination.

When we engage in the work of the Lord, there will be temptations—from within and from without. There will be times when we will not feel like going on; the human frailties of weariness, boredom, and discouragement will set in. Likewise, from without, we will encounter circumstances and situations, individuals and incidents, that will attempt to sap our energy and redirect our thinking. But we must resolve to be strong, to be determined, and to complete the task. Just as God encouraged Joshua when he became the leader of the Israelites, David said to Solomon, "Be strong and of good courage, and do it; fear not, nor be dismayed" (1 Chronicles 28:20).

As a caring parent who reminded his son for good measure, David repeated his exhortation to Solomon, "Be strong and be of good courage, and do it." He then added to the exhortation two thoughts which anticipated the types of danger that Solomon would face. The first is "fear," the term generally used to imply anxiety and loss of courage about something or someone who stands in the way. He added another phrase, "nor be dismayed." The meaning of both words is essentially the same; but "dismayed" carries the idea of dreading something that lies ahead. David told Solomon not to allow anything seen or unseen to deter him from the task "…for the LORD God, even my God, will be with thee; he will not fail thee, nor forsake thee, until thou hast finished all the work for the service of the house of the LORD" (1 Chronicles 28:20).

III. CONCLUDING REFLECTIONS

The concept of David's throne existing forever finds its fulfillment in the Lord Jesus Christ. Solomon, recognizing this, sought for God's assurance as soon as he was made king. He desired that God would fulfill His whole promise to David, that there would never fail to be an heir to the throne (1 Kings 8:25-26). God clearly honored this promise throughout all the history of Judah.

Nevertheless, the promise of God to bless the throne of David was not unconditional. For David's throne to be blessed, the successors had to walk uprightly, as David had done (1 Kings 9:6-7). When Solomon failed to walk purely before God as David had done, God took His favor away from him. Yet, for David's sake, God remembered His covenant with Solomon.

Though torn asunder, the throne of David remained a reality, and God upheld His promise that "David may always have a lamp before me in Jerusalem" (1 Kings 11:36, NRSV). This promise became a constant reminder of hope to God's people thereafter (2 Kings 8:19; 2 Chronicles 21:7). To this day, the concept of the throne of David is alive in the hearts of the Jewish people who still await the birth of David's son, the Messiah. For Christians, of course, this promise is already fulfilled in Jesus Christ, who is David's seed forever.

PRAYER

Dear God, our heavenly Father, we praise You for stooping down to include sinful people like us in Your program. Strengthen and guide us now as we endeavor to walk worthy of the privilege which You have bestowed upon us. In Jesus' name, we pray. Amen.

WORD POWER

Take Heed (Hebrew: *ra-ah*)—the phrase "take heed" is one word in Hebrew, as opposed to the two words we use in the English translation. It is in the imperative mood, meaning that it is a command that David issued to Solomon. David realized the importance of obeying God in all matters; therefore, Solomon would have to be vigilant.

HOME DAILY BIBLE READINGS
(March 10-16, 2008)

God Calls Solomon to Build the Temple
MONDAY, March 10: "God's Promise to David" (Psalm 132:1-12)
TUESDAY, March 11: "God Chose Solomon" (1 Chronicles 28:1-5)
WEDNESDAY, March 12: "David Advises Solomon" (1 Chronicles 28:6-8)
THURSDAY, March 13: "With Single Mind and Willing Heart" (1 Chronicles 28:9-10)
FRIDAY, March 14: "David's Plan for the Temple" (1 Chronicles 28:11-19)
SATURDAY, March 15: "God Is with You" (1 Chronicles 28:20-21)
SUNDAY, March 16: "For God's Chosen" (Psalm 132:13-18)

FULFILLMENT OF GOD'S PROMISE

DEVOTIONAL READING: **Psalm 135:1-5**
PRINT PASSAGE: **2 Chronicles 6:12-17; Luke 24:44-49**

BACKGROUND SCRIPTURE: **2 Chronicles 6; Luke 24**
KEY VERSE: **2 Chronicles 6:10**

2 Chronicles 6:12-17; Luke 24:44-49—KJV

12 And he stood before the altar of the LORD in the presence of all the congregation of Israel, and spread forth his hands:

13 For Solomon had made a brasen scaffold, of five cubits long, and five cubits broad, and three cubits high, and had set it in the midst of the court: and upon it he stood, and kneeled down upon his knees before all the congregation of Israel, and spread forth his hands toward heaven,

14 And said, O LORD God of Israel, there is no God like thee in the heaven, nor in the earth; which keepest covenant, and shewest mercy unto thy servants, that walk before thee with all their hearts:

15 Thou which hast kept with thy servant David my father that which thou hast promised him; and spakest with thy mouth, and hast fulfilled it with thine hand, as it is this day.

16 Now therefore, O LORD God of Israel, keep with thy servant David my father that which thou hast promised him, saying, There shall not fail thee a man in my sight to sit upon the throne of Israel; yet so that thy children take heed to their way to walk in my law, as thou hast walked before me.

17 Now then, O LORD God of Israel, let thy word be verified, which thou hast spoken unto thy servant David.

.....

44 And he said unto them, These are the words which I spake unto you, while I was yet with you, that all things must be fulfilled, which were written in the law of Moses, and in the prophets, and in the psalms, concerning me.

45 Then opened he their understanding, that they might understand the scriptures,

46 And said unto them, Thus it is written, and thus it behoved Christ to suffer, and to rise from the dead the third day:

2 Chronicles 6:12-17; Luke 24:44-49—NRSV

12 Then Solomon stood before the altar of the LORD in the presence of the whole assembly of Israel, and spread out his hands.

13 Solomon had made a bronze platform five cubits long, five cubits wide, and three cubits high, and had set it in the court; and he stood on it. Then he knelt on his knees in the presence of the whole assembly of Israel, and spread out his hands toward heaven.

14 He said, "O LORD, God of Israel, there is no God like you, in heaven or on earth, keeping covenant in steadfast love with your servants who walk before you with all their heart—

15 you who have kept for your servant, my father David, what you promised to him. Indeed, you promised with your mouth and this day have fulfilled with your hand.

16 Therefore, O LORD, God of Israel, keep for your servant, my father David, that which you promised him, saying, 'There shall never fail you a successor before me to sit on the throne of Israel, if only your children keep to their way, to walk in my law as you have walked before me.'

17 Therefore, O LORD, God of Israel, let your word be confirmed, which you promised to your servant David.

.....

44 Then he said to them, "These are my words that I spoke to you while I was still with you—that everything written about me in the law of Moses, the prophets, and the psalms must be fulfilled."

45 Then he opened their minds to understand the scriptures,

46 and he said to them, "Thus it is written, that the Messiah is to suffer and to rise from the dead on the third day,

47 And that repentance and remission of sins should be preached in his name among all nations, beginning at Jerusalem.
48 And ye are witnesses of these things.
49 And, behold, I send the promise of my Father upon you: but tarry ye in the city of Jerusalem, until ye be endued with power from on high.

47 and that repentance and forgiveness of sins is to be proclaimed in his name to all nations, beginning from Jerusalem.
48 You are witnesses of these things.
49 And see, I am sending upon you what my Father promised; so stay here in the city until you have been clothed with power from on high."

TOPICAL OUTLINE OF THE LESSON

I. Introduction
A. God Fulfills His Promise
B. Biblical Background

II. Exposition and Application of the Scripture
A. Solomon's Prayer of Dedication (2 Chronicles 6:12-15)
B. Prayer for the Continuation of David's Dynasty (2 Chronicles 6:16-17)
C. Jesus' Resurrection Is the Fulfillment of Prophecy (Luke 24:44-46)
D. Jesus Gives the Great Commission (Luke 24:47-49)

III. Concluding Reflections

LESSON OBJECTIVES

Upon completion of this lesson, the students will know that:
1. God keeps His promises;
2. Sometimes God's promises are not fulfilled in our lifetimes; and,
3. The promises made to David were partially fulfilled in Solomon and ultimately fulfilled in Jesus Christ.

POINTS TO BE EMPHASIZED

ADULT/YOUTH
Adult Topic: **Whose Promises Can You Trust?**
Youth Topic: **God Keeps Promises**
Adult Key Verse: **2 Chronicles 6:10**
Youth Key Verse: **Luke 24:44**
Print Passage: **2 Chronicles 6:12-17; Luke 24:44-49**

—In dedicating the temple, Solomon praised God for fulfilling the promise God had made to David.

—Jesus declared that His resurrection fulfilled the promise made through the Law, the prophets, and the Psalms.

—Both Solomon and Jesus called for faithfulness as a response to God's promises.

—Solomon's prayer recognized that God fulfills promises but also that Israel was responsible to continue to be faithful to God.

CHILDREN
Children Topic: **Jesus Is Alive**
Key Verse: **Luke 24:5**
Print Passage: **Luke 24:1-12**

—God's promise was fulfilled when God raised Jesus from the dead.

—Several women visited the tomb and found it empty.

—God sent messengers to tell the women that God had fulfilled the promise.

—God's methods of fulfillment of promises may incorporate the miraculous and unexpected.

I. INTRODUCTION

A. God Fulfills His Promise

It should be remembered from our previous lesson that after David had conquered the Promised Land, he began the work of settling down permanently in the land. He first built a palace for himself and his family. He then erected a tent for the ark of the covenant. He began making plans and collecting the materials for the construction of the temple, the "house of God" in which the ark would be placed. But God did not permit David to build the temple; rather, his son, Solomon, would be given that privilege.

This lesson centers on the dedication of the temple, on which construction was now complete, and upon Solomon's prayer of thanksgiving to God for having kept His promise to David regarding the erection of the temple.

This lesson also discusses how Jesus appeared to His disciples, as He had promised them He would. His appearance prompted mixed emotions among them. The Lord opened up the Scriptures and explained to them that His resurrection was a fulfillment of what had been prophesied to David. That promise was that there would come One who would be the everlasting Son of David, who would sit on his throne.

B. Biblical Background

Some of the earliest structures built by human hands were shrines where people could worship their gods. The Tower of Babel was the first structure mentioned in the Bible which implies the existence of a temple (Genesis 11:4). It was intended as a place to worship God, and it symbolized the self-confidence of human beings attempting to climb up to heaven.

In Mesopotamia, each city had a temple dedicated to its patron deity. The god was looked upon as the owner of the land, and if that land was not blessed by that deity, it would be unproductive, resulting in poor revenues for his or her temple. The local king or ruler acted as steward for the god.

After Israel had grown into nationhood, a central temple became a necessity, since it would be a gathering point for all the people, a symbol of their unity in the worship of their God. This need was supplied by the tabernacle during the trek through the wilderness, and by recognized shrines during the period of the judges (for example, Shechem, Joshua 8:30ff; 24: lff; Shiloh, 1 Samuel 1:3). The lack of a shrine for Yahweh was ever in the mind of David and provided the impetus for his desire to build the temple.

Luke 24:44-49 should be linked to the promises made by the Lord to David concerning the continuation of his dynasty. It should be pointed out again that Jesus was referred to as the "Son of David" who would sit on David's throne. As such, it demonstrates the unity of the two Testaments; and it also serves as proof that God's promises extend over and beyond the limitations of time.

II. EXPOSITION AND APPLICATION OF THE SCRIPTURE

A. Solomon's Prayer of Dedication
(2 Chronicles 6:12-15)

And he stood before the altar of the Lord in the presence of all the congregation of Israel, and spread forth his hands: For Solomon had made a brasen scaffold, of five cubits long, and five cubits broad, and three cubits high, and had set it in the midst of the court: and upon it he stood, and kneeled down upon his knees before all the congregation of Israel, and spread forth his hands toward heaven, And said, O Lord God of Israel, there is no God like thee in the heaven, nor in the earth; which keepest covenant, and shewest mercy unto thy servants, that walk before thee with all their hearts: Thou which hast kept with thy servant David my father that which thou hast promised him; and spakest with thy mouth, and hast fulfilled it with thine hand, as it is this day.

The word *altar* literally means "high," and referred to any raised structure with a flat top, on which offerings to a deity were sacrificed. The altar, therefore, in all ancient religious practices, took shape from the idea of a raised table of stone or turf on which an offering of blood, and later burned flesh or harvest of agriculture, was set before the deity. The altar was a feature of universal worship adopted by worship in the Old Testament and developed as an object of ritual and sanctity. It was the centerpiece of every sanctuary and the place of sacrifice. Thus, the term "the altar of the Lord" referred to the raised structure on which sacrifices were made to God.

We are told that, "And he stood before the altar of the Lord…and kneeled down upon his knees before all the congregation of Israel" (2 Chronicles 6:12-13). In the first position, he pronounced blessings upon the people; in the second, he offered a prayer to God. In so doing, Solomon performed the duties of both prophet and priest. The prophet pronounced God's blessings upon the people while the priest offered the sacrifices of the people to God.

For this dedication, Solomon constructed a special platform which bore resemblance in structure to those lavers in the temple—a sort of round and elevated pulpit. (The description is found in verse 13.)

After ascending the brazen scaffold, he assumed those two attitudes in succession and with different objects in view. Note that Solomon stood while he addressed and blessed the multitude (2 Chronicles 6:3-11). Afterward, he kneeled and stretched his hands toward heaven in reverent form to acknowledge the faithfulness of God.

There was no seat in this pulpit; the king either stood or kneeled all the time. In so doing, the king publicly acknowledged that he, too, was no more than God's servant, administering a kingdom that was not his own. This should be noted by many preachers today who behave as if they are either exempt from or above the worship required of all of God's people, remaining in the office or study until the preaching hour. In so doing, they act more like entertainers than worshipers.

In verse 14, Solomon declared the doctrinal truth that the God of Israel was incomparably perfect. He could not describe Him, but this they knew: there was none like God in heaven or on earth. All the creatures had their fellow-creatures, but the Creator had and has no equal. He was and is infinitely above all and over all. He kept His covenant and showed mercy to all people. These are synonymous expressions; that is, they are two ways of saying the same thing. God is, and will be, true to every word that He has spoken. Everyone who serves Him in sincerity will certainly find Him both faithful and kind.

In verse 15, Solomon praised the Lord for His faithfulness, that He kept the promises He made to Solomon's father long ago by fulfilling them in Solomon's lifetime, and in the presence of the whole earth. Solomon's form of expression here is known as an "anthropomorphism" (a term derived from the Greek, *anthropos*, man, and *morphem*, form) which describes God as having human form with human characteristics. For example, to say that God "walks," is to assign human characteristics to God, who is Spirit. The biblical writers used this concept to aid us in our limited capacity to understand the attributes of God, which defy human description. Simply put, whatever God promises with His mouth, He brings to fruition by the work of His hands.

B. Prayer for the Continuation of David's Dynasty (2 Chronicles 6:16-17)

Now therefore, O Lord God of Israel, keep with thy servant David my father that which thou hast promised him, saying, There shall not fail thee a man in my sight to sit upon the throne of Israel; yet so that thy children take heed to their way to walk in my law, as thou hast walked before me. Now then, O Lord God of Israel, let thy word be verified, which thou hast spoken unto thy servant David.

"Now Lord God of Israel, keep for your servant David my father the promises you made to him…" (verse 16, NIV). Solomon's prayer looked to the future. He had acknowledged in the previous verses that God had kept His promise up to the present time by allowing him to sit on the throne and to build the temple. He now looked to the future and prayed that God would continue to honor His Word by ensuring that the throne of David would continue throughout all generations.

C. Jesus' Resurrection Is the Fulfillment of Prophecy (Luke 24:44-46)

And he said unto them, These are the words which I spake unto you, while I was yet with you, that all things must be fulfilled, which were written in the law of Moses, and in the prophets, and in the psalms, concerning me. Then opened he their understanding, that they might understand the scriptures, And said unto them, Thus it is written, and thus it behoved Christ to suffer, and to rise from the dead the third day.

When the Lord appeared to His disciples after His resurrection, they were filled with joy, yet they were confused (Luke 24:38). Their confusion was accompanied by a sense of unbelief as to how He could be present with them when they had witnessed His crucifixion. So, the Lord first convinced them that it was indeed Him, and not a spirit or ghost, by urging them to take a look at His feet and hands, which still bore the marks of His crucifixion. He then went a bit further by taking a piece of meat and eating it in their presence. Then He began to talk with them.

Jesus reminded them of the words He had spoken to them prior to the Crucifixion. "Now you will understand what seemed so dark to you when I told you about the Son of man being put to death and rising again (Matthew 16:21; 17:22; Mark 8:31; Luke 9:22; 18:31-34) that all things must be fulfilled which were written in the law of Moses, and in the prophets, and in the psalms, concerning me."

Jesus wanted the disciples to see how everything that He had said to them and everything that had been written about Him all fit together. The three divisions of the Old Testament during Jesus' time are mentioned here, as each of them featured words concerning Christ: (1) the Law of Moses, the Pentateuch (or the five books written by Moses); (2) the prophets, containing not only the books that are purely prophetical, but also the historical books; and (3) the Psalms, containing the other writings, which they called the *Hagiographa,* or sacred writings. In other words, He showed them, from three different parts of the Old Testament, that everything that had happened to Him was part of God's plan.

In verse 45, we are told that, "Then opened he their understanding, that they might understand the scriptures." He explained to them the necessity for His suffering and death and how the cross related to the promise of the kingdom (see 1 Peter 1:10-12).

D. Jesus Gives the Great Commission (Luke 24:47-49)

And that repentance and remission of sins should be preached in his name among all nations, beginning at Jerusalem. And ye are witnesses of these things. And, behold, I send the promise of my Father upon you: but tarry ye in the city of Jerusalem, until ye be endued with power from on high.

Because of His death and resurrection, the message of repentance and forgiveness of sins should be preached in Jesus' name to all nations, beginning at Jerusalem, for they were witnesses to His death and His resurrection. This became the outline for Luke in his second book (Acts).

In verse 48, Jesus told them, "And ye are witnesses of these things." But privilege always brings responsibility; they were to be witnesses to all that He had said and done (see also Acts 1:8). A witness is someone who sincerely tells what he or she has seen and heard (Acts 4:20). The word *witness* is used in one way or another twenty-nine times in the book of Acts. As Christians, we are not judges or prosecuting attorneys sent to condemn the world; rather, we are witnesses who point to Jesus Christ and tell sinners how to be saved.

Jesus renews the promises of the Father regarding the coming Holy Spirit in verse 49, "And, behold, I send the promise of my Father upon you...." How could a group of common people ever hope to fulfill that kind of a commission?

God promised to provide them with power (Luke 24:49; Acts 1:8), and He did. On the Day of Pentecost, the Holy Spirit came upon the church and empowered them to preach the Word (Acts 2). After Pentecost, the Spirit continued to fill them with great power (see Acts 4:33).

Witnessing is not something that we do for the Lord; it is something that He does through us, if we are filled with the Holy Spirit. There is a great difference between a "sales talk" and a Spirit-empowered witness. People do not come to Christ at the end of an argument. It must be remembered that Simon Peter came to Jesus because Andrew went after him with a testimony (John 1:41). We go forth in the authority of His name, and in the power of His Spirit, heralding His Gospel of grace.

III. CONCLUDING REFLECTIONS

Christ's apostles could never have planted His Gospel and set up His kingdom in the world as they did if they had not been imbued with power. The Lord told them to wait in Jerusalem for the promise of the Father. That promise was that they would receive power from the Holy Spirit.

That promise of power is much discussed today and is the point of much confusion. The confusion is most often referred to as the "anointing," and it is caused by those who do not distinguish the ministry of the Spirit in the Old Testament from His ministry in the New Testament.

In the Old Testament, selected people of God who preceded Jesus, like David and Saul, experienced the ministry of the Holy Spirit by His "anointing." This anointing was a temporary empowerment, such that these individuals could accomplish unusual and extraordinary feats. However, in this church age, we are more blessed than they were in two ways. First, the ministry of the Holy Spirit is not restricted to a few chosen individuals; rather, He ministers to all of the elect. Second, Jesus' ministry is not a temporary anointing, but a permanent indwelling. That means all believers have Him as a permanent resident inside our hearts. So, contrary to the false teachings of some today, we have no need to "tarry" or wait for Him. Each of us has been anointed to go forth under His power.

PRAYER

Most gracious, eternal God our Father, we do praise and thank You for Your everlasting promises, which You have fulfilled in our lives through Your Son and Your Holy Spirit. Help us to be obedient to Your commands to go out and tell others about Your saving grace. In Jesus' name, we pray. Amen.

WORD POWER

Performed (Hebrew: *quwm-koom*)—this word could also mean "fulfilled" or "accomplished." The Lord caused everything to work in favor of Solomon. In this context, the word is cast in the imperfect tense, which means the original intention of David to build a house for the ark originated with God.

HOME DAILY BIBLE READINGS
(March 17-23, 2008)

Fulfillment of God's Promise

MONDAY, March 17: "Praise for God's Goodness" (Psalm 135:1-5)

TUESDAY, March 18: "Dedication of the Temple" (2 Chronicles 6:1-11)

WEDNESDAY, March 19: "Solomon's Prayer" (2 Chronicles 6:12-17)

THURSDAY, March 20: "Pray Toward This Place" (2 Chronicles 6:18-31)

FRIDAY, March 21: "Repent and Pray" (2 Chronicles 6:36–39)

SATURDAY, March 22: "God's Promise Remembered" (2 Chronicles 6:40-42)

SUNDAY, March 23: "God's Promise Fulfilled" (Luke 24:44-49)

JOSIAH RENEWS THE COVENANT

DEVOTIONAL READING: **Psalm 119:25-40**

PRINT PASSAGE: **2 Chronicles 34:15, 18-19, 25-27, 29, 31-33**

BACKGROUND SCRIPTURE: **2 Chronicles 34**

KEY VERSE: **2 Chronicles 34:31**

2 Chronicles 34:15, 18-19, 25-27, 29, 31-33—KJV

15 And Hilkiah answered and said to Shaphan the scribe, I have found the book of the law in the house of the LORD. And Hilkiah delivered the book to Shaphan.

.....

18 Then Shaphan the scribe told the king, saying, Hilkiah the priest hath given me a book. And Shaphan read it before the king.
19 And it came to pass, when the king had heard the words of the law, that he rent his clothes.

.....

25 Because they have forsaken me, and have burned incense unto other gods, that they might provoke me to anger with all the works of their hands; therefore my wrath shall be poured out upon this place, and shall not be quenched.
26 And as for the king of Judah, who sent you to inquire of the LORD, so shall ye say unto him, Thus saith the LORD God of Israel concerning the words which thou hast heard;
27 Because thine heart was tender, and thou didst humble thyself before God, when thou heardest his words against this place, and against the inhabitants thereof, and humbledst thyself before me, and didst rend thy clothes, and weep before me; I have even heard thee also, saith the LORD.

.....

29 Then the king sent and gathered together all the elders of Judah and Jerusalem.

.....

31 And the king stood in his place, and made a covenant before the LORD, to walk after the LORD, and to keep his commandments, and his testimonies, and his statutes, with all his heart, and with all his soul, to perform the words of the covenant which are written in this book.

2 Chronicles 34:15, 18-19, 25-27, 29, 31-33—NRSV

15 Hilkiah said to the secretary Shaphan, "I have found the book of the law in the house of the LORD"; and Hilkiah gave the book to Shaphan.

.....

18 The secretary Shaphan informed the king, "The priest Hilkiah has given me a book." Shaphan then read it aloud to the king.
19 When the king heard the words of the law he tore his clothes.

.....

25 Because they have forsaken me and have made offerings to other gods, so that they have provoked me to anger with all the works of their hands, my wrath will be poured out on this place and will not be quenched.
26 But as to the king of Judah, who sent you to inquire of the LORD, thus shall you say to him: Thus says the LORD, the God of Israel: Regarding the words that you have heard,
27 because your heart was penitent and you humbled yourself before God when you heard his words against this place and its inhabitants, and you have humbled yourself before me, and have torn your clothes and wept before me, I also have heard you, says the LORD.

.....

29 Then the king sent word and gathered together all the elders of Judah and Jerusalem.

.....

31 The king stood in his place and made a covenant before the LORD, to follow the Lord, keeping his commandments, his decrees, and his statutes, with all his heart and all his soul, to perform the words of the covenant that were written in this book.

32 And he caused all that were present in Jerusalem and Benjamin to stand to it. And the inhabitants of Jerusalem did according to the covenant of God, the God of their fathers.
33 And Josiah took away all the abominations out of all the countries that pertained to the children of Israel, and made all that were present in Israel to serve, even to serve the LORD their God. And all his days they departed not from following the LORD, the God of their fathers.

32 Then he made all who were present in Jerusalem and in Benjamin pledge themselves to it. And the inhabitants of Jerusalem acted according to the covenant of God, the God of their ancestors.
33 Josiah took away all the abominations from all the territory that belonged to the people of Israel, and made all who were in Israel worship the LORD their God. All his days they did not turn away from following the LORD the God of their ancestors.

TOPICAL OUTLINE OF THE LESSON

I. **Introduction**
   A. Josiah Inherits a Decayed Throne
   B. Biblical Background

II. **Exposition and Application of the Scripture**
   A. Discovery and Reading of the Law Book (2 Chronicles 34:15, 18-19)
   B. God's Anger Is Kindled and Josiah Repents (2 Chronicles 34:25-27)
   C. Assembly of Elders and Covenant Renewal (2 Chronicles 34:29, 31-33)

III. **Concluding Reflections**

LESSON OBJECTIVES

Upon completion of this lesson, the students will know that:

1. Issues that contributed to broken relationships of the past can help in restoring relationships in the present;

2. Ignorance of Scripture leads to a broken relationship with God; and,
3. One person's commitment to godliness can impact an entire community.

POINTS TO BE EMPHASIZED

ADULT/YOUTH

Adult Topic: **Mending a Broken Relationship**
Youth Topic: **Mending a Broken Relationship**
Adult/Youth Key Verse: **2 Chronicles 34:31**
Print Passage: **2 Chronicles 34:15, 18-19, 25-27, 29, 31-33**

—Josiah inherited the throne from a king who was unfaithful to the covenant.
—With the discovery of the Book of the Law and during the process of initiating reform, Josiah realized that the depth of the Israelites' spiritual depravity was greater than he imagined.
—Josiah's actions and mandates to his people demonstrated a call to faithfulness to God.

CHILDREN

Children Topic: **Josiah Obeys the Law**
Key Verse: **2 Chronicles 34:31a**
Print Passage: **2 Chronicles 34:14, 19, 21-23, 27, 29-31**

—In Josiah's time, the Book of the Law was found.
—Josiah was grieved when he heard the Law, for he realized

that the people were not obeying it.
—Josiah did not look for excuses for Israel's wrong-doings but instead sought to restore the covenant relationship with God.

I. INTRODUCTION

A. Josiah Inherits a Decayed Throne

The phrase, "But he did evil in the sight of the Lord," is used repeatedly to describe those kings in Israel and Judah who walked contrary to the commandments of God and thus severed the relationship between God and His people. That phrase is applied to both of Josiah's predecessors: Manasseh and his son, Amon. Manasseh, the son of Hezekiah, seemed determined to restore every form of abomination that his godly father, who ruled before him, had destroyed. As a result, the strong hand of God was stretched out against him, and with the Assyrians as their scourge, the king was carried away in irons, broken and defeated. Manasseh was followed in succession by his son, Amon, who followed in his father's footsteps, doing evil in the sight of the Lord. Amon was so utterly corrupt that his own servants conspired against him and killed him.

Then Josiah inherited a throne that for two reigns had behaved unfaithfully to the covenant and thus instigated a broken relationship with God. In the process of restoring and cleansing the temple, a remarkable thing occurred. The Book of the Law was discovered, and it was brought to King Josiah by the priest.

B. Biblical Background

Josiah was only eight years old when he started to reign over Judah. Much like his great-grandfather, Hezekiah, Josiah loved the Lord and began to demonstrate this actively by the time he was sixteen. The kings of Judah were considered minors until they had completed their thirteenth birthdays; three years after Josiah had reached that age he began his reform measures. In the twelfth year of his reign, at the age of twenty, Josiah began to take a lively interest in purging his kingdom from all the monuments of idolatry that had been erected during his father's brief reign.

Josiah went so far as to scatter the smashed idols and other paraphernalia over the graves of their worshipers and to burn the bones of the pagan priests on their very altars. And this purge was not limited to Judah. In Israel, particularly Naphtali to the north, the work of purging idolatry went on.

It was in Josiah's eighteenth reigning year, at the age of twenty-six, that he commissioned Shaphan, Maaseiah, and Joah to repair and refurbish the temple. These men took money that had been collected for that purpose from all over Israel and Judah gave it to Hilkiah, the high priest, to enable him to hire workmen and to purchase materials for the task ordered by the king. The supervisors were Levites, two from the Merari branch and two from the Kohath branch. Those four were skillful musicians, a statement that probably attested to their artistry and sensitivity in all things pertaining to the temple and worship.

II. EXPOSITION AND APPLICATION OF THE SCRIPTURE

A. Discovery and Reading of the Law Book (2 Chronicles 34:15, 18-19)

And Hilkiah answered and said to Shaphan the scribe, I have found the book of the law in the house of the LORD. And Hilkiah delivered the book to Shaphan. ... Then Shaphan the scribe told the king, saying, Hilkiah the priest hath given me a book. And Shaphan read it before the king. And it came to pass, when the king had heard the words of the law, that he rent his clothes.

Strange as it may seem, the books of Moses apparently had all been destroyed, except for this one copy preserved in the temple. How or when this happened is a mystery, but it most likely occurred during the near-total eradication of the worship of Yahweh in the days of Manasseh and Amon (2 Chronicles 33). The found book probably was the official scroll of the Pentateuch, usually kept by the side of the ark (Deuteronomy 31:25-26), but misplaced during the previous administrations when the ark had been moved about (2 Chronicles 35:3).

Who was Hilkiah? He was a priest and an overseer during the reign of Hezekiah. His experience had helped Josiah to reign successfully. He was the one who discovered the Book of the Law and gave it to Shaphan the scribe. In his statement to Shaphan, he said, "I have found the book." It was as if he had been looking for the Book of the Law that had guided Hezekiah during his reign. How important to us is the Bible? Shaphan wasted no time in reporting the discovery of the Book of the Law to King Josiah.

When Josiah heard what was in the Book, he realized how far his subjects had deviated from the Law of God. Upon hearing the news, the king tore his robes, an ancient expression of grief. The king then issued a command to Hilkiah and the others that the entire text be studied and that the mind of the Lord in relation to it be ascertained. He was concerned that his ancestors had incurred God's anger by not obeying His Word. Josiah's personal display of grief and dismay is an indictment of us today. We pray for revival; we bring in eminent preachers; yet nothing happens because our hearts are not as tender as Josiah's heart.

Josiah's actions here are commendable to everyone today. Whenever we read or hear the Word of God, it ought to affect our hearts to the extent that we recognize the state of our relationship with God. Who among us, when confronted with the reality of God's Word, will not find ourselves lacking? This should cause each of us to be possessed with a holy fear of the wrath of God. It ought to cause us to rend, not our garments, but our hearts.

B. God's Anger Is Kindled and Josiah Repents (2 Chronicles 34:25-27)

Because they have forsaken me, and have burned incense unto other gods, that they might provoke me to anger with all the works of their hands; therefore my wrath shall be poured out upon this place, and shall not be quenched. And as for the king of Judah, who sent you to inquire of the LORD, so shall ye say unto him, Thus saith the LORD God of Israel concerning the words which thou hast heard; Because thine heart was tender, and thou didst humble thyself before God, when thou heardest his words against this place, and against the inhabitants thereof, and humbledst thyself before me, and didst rend thy clothes, and weep before me; I have even heard thee also, saith the LORD.

There were two issues at stake in this section of the text. First, God said, "They have forsaken me..." (2 Chronicles 34:25). Forsaking God is a violation of the first commandment, which states, "Thou shalt have no other gods before me" (Exodus 20:3). They had traded their souls for other gods. As a result, they showed no belief in God, and maligned the purpose for which God had raised them up—to be a lighthouse to the world.

Second, they burned incense. They were commanded in Exodus 30:1, 9, 34, and several other passages to construct an altar upon which they would burn incense. Incense-burning was closely connected to the holiest place. Only Aaron and his descendants were allowed to burn incense. In the New Testament, some priests were chosen by lot to burn incense morning and evening (see Luke 1:9). King Uzziah burnt incense, and he paid dearly for it when leprosy broke out on his forehead (see 2 Chronicles 26:16-21). When the people chose to burn incense on their own, they had, by that act, abolished the priesthood. They had committed a truly grievous offense.

Realizing the magnitude of their offense, Josiah sent Hilkiah and his colleagues to the prophetess, Huldah, who resided in a suburb of Jerusalem (2 Chronicles 34:20-24). This should be an eye opener to all of us that God can use anyone to carry out His divine purpose. The prophetess sent a message to Josiah, which we find in verse 27, "Because thine heart was tender, and thou didst humble thyself before God, when thou heardest his words against this place, and against the inhabitants thereof, and humblest thyself before me, and didst rend thy clothes, and weep before me; I have even heard thee also, saith the LORD."

In this passage, there are notable clues that lend insight into why Josiah received favor from the Lord. First, his heart was tender. When David, his ancestor, sinned, he asked the Lord to purge him and create in him a clean heart (Psalm 51:10). Josiah's heart was soft and the Lord recognized it. Josiah also humbled himself; he tore his clothes and wept. Those outward signs were indicative of inward change. God recognized the inward attitude of Josiah; he would be spared because of his wholehearted devotion to the Lord. The Israelites' impending doom would be postponed until after Josiah's death.

The Lord God stands ever ready to restore those of a broken spirit and a penitent heart. Society looks at those who shed tears over how far they have strayed from the Lord as weak people. God knows our hearts, and when we truly realize how far we have fallen short of God's expectation, we can run to God humbly. As a nation, the rulers are not exempt from re-tracing their steps, particularly when they know that they have led their people astray. Church leaders are also called upon to follow Josiah's example when they realize that their following is not in compliance with God's purpose.

C. Assembly of Elders and Covenant Renewal (2 Chronicles 34:29, 31-33)

Then the king sent and gathered together all the elders of Judah and Jerusalem. ...And the king stood in his place, and made a covenant before the LORD, to walk after the LORD and to keep his commandments, and his testimonies, and his statutes, with all his heart, and with all his soul, to perform the words of the covenant which are written in this book. And he caused all that were present in Jerusalem and Benjamin to stand to it. And the inhabitants of Jerusalem did according to the covenant of God, the God of their fathers. And Josiah took away all the abominations out of all the countries that pertained to the children of Israel, and made all that were present in Israel to serve, even to serve the LORD their God. And all his days they departed not from following the Lord the God of their fathers.

Josiah demonstrated a true spirit of repentance. He did not humble himself alone; he involved the whole nation. He called all the people together—great and small, young and old, rich and poor—along with all the elders. The responsibility for their broken relationship with God was a concern for all and sundry—thus, everyone would have to be involved in the act of repentance and renewal.

It is not often that we hear a report of an entire congregation truly humbling itself before almighty God, searching for a new direction in life. The only time we hear news is when a pastor or church leader falls from his or her position of authority as a result of moral failure. Isn't it time for leaders to call for holy assembly, whereby members and leaders alike truly seek the face of the Lord?

In verse 31, we are told, "And the king stood in his place, and made a covenant before the LORD, to walk after the LORD, and to keep his commandments, and his testimonies, and his statues, with all his heart, and with all his soul, to perform the words of the covenant which are written in this book." Josiah was a king who feared the Lord.

To stress the importance of the occasion, though there were priests and Levites present, the king himself read the book to the people (verse 30). Having read from the book—the articles of agreement between God and Israel—the king, as representative of the people, stood and affirmed his intent to renew the covenant and to keep God's commandments with all of his heart and soul, according to all that was written in the book.

The spirit of godly leadership requires responsibility. Thus, even though the leader himself may not have committed the breach, he is nevertheless held responsible for the actions of those under his care. Josiah acknowledged this fact by first repenting and renewing his vows of fidelity.

Josiah led by example. The king mandated all the people to stand and do as he had done (verse 32)—that is, to vow to strive with all of their hearts to abide by the covenant agreement written in the Book. This was required of everyone in the region under Josiah's domain. Sin and its consequences had connections. This was why the king involved all their neighbors. The king made sure that he destroyed all the idols to avoid the temptation of falling back into the same sin again.

The result of King Josiah's reformation is stated in verse 33: "And all his days they departed not from following the LORD, the God of their fathers." Thus, for the entirety of his reign, the king kept Israel from returning to her former state of idolatry. He did this in spite of the fact that many of the Israelites wanted nothing but to have him out of the way. Then, they would have their high places and their idolatrous images again. Josiah was sincere in what he did, but the majority of the people was opposed to it and still hankered after their idols.

Thus, the sad footnote to this narrative is that the reformation, though well designed and well executed by the king, had little or no effect upon the people. It was with reluctance that they parted with their idols; in their hearts, they were still joined to them, and wished for them again. This God saw, and from that time forward—when one might have thought the foundations had been laid for perpetual security and peace—the decree went forth for their destruction.

III. CONCLUDING REFLECTIONS

This narrative, unfortunately, does not end on a good note, for what follows is proof that the people responded to God's commands with their deeds but not with their hearts. The prophet Jeremiah, a contemporary of Josiah who agreed with the reform, wrote, "And yet for all this her treacherous sister Judah hath not turned unto me with her whole heart, but feignedly, saith the LORD. And the LORD said unto me, The backsliding Israel hath justified herself more than treacherous Judah" (Jeremiah 3:10-11). Within four to five years of Josiah's death, the Israelites had gone on to provoke God to anger with their rebellion and disobedience (Jeremiah 25:3-7). Their actions brought ruin upon them, which the prophet Jeremiah was to bear lying on his right side for forty days, representing the number of years of Israel's sin.

Josiah was Judah's last good king, and in some respects, her greatest. It was his reformation of 621 B.C. that did more than all else to restore Israel's commitment to God's Book. And it was loyalty to this same written Word that provided the glimmer of hope for Judaism during the Exile (see Daniel 9:2), during its precarious restoration (Ezra 7:10; Malachi 4:6), and down through the centuries until the coming of Christ (Matthew 5:17-18).

As our title suggests, mending a broken relationship requires that we do all that is within our power to bequeath a lasting, godly heritage for the coming generation.

PRAYER

Dear God, our heavenly Father, we praise and thank You for being a God who stands ever ready to restore our broken relationships—with You and with one another. Help us now, we pray, to keep the commandments of Your Word ever before us, that we might walk therein and continue in our wonderful relationship with You and others. In Jesus' name, we pray. Amen.

WORD POWER

The Book of the Law of the Lord—what is it? Many of the reforms of Josiah reflect many of the themes in Deuteronomy. Therefore, the Book of the Law technically includes the first five books of the Bible known as the *Pentateuch*. This book survived religious suppression during Manasseh's and Amon's evil reigns.

HOME DAILY BIBLE READINGS
(March 24- 30, 2008)

Josiah Renews the Covenant

MONDAY, March 24: "Revive Me" (Psalm 119:25-32)
TUESDAY, March 25: "Josiah Seeks God's Way" (2 Chronicles 34:1-7)
WEDNESDAY, March 26: "A Big Discovery" (2 Chronicles 34:8-18)
THURSDAY, March 27: "Josiah Repents" (2 Chronicles 34:19-21)
FRIDAY, March 28: "God Hears Josiah" (2 Chronicles 34:22-28)
SATURDAY, March 29: "The Covenant Renewed" (2 Chronicles 34:29-33)
SUNDAY, March 30: "Teach Me" (Psalm 119:33-40)

DANIEL KEEPS COVENANT IN A FOREIGN LAND

DEVOTIONAL READING: **Psalm 141:1-4**

PRINT PASSAGE: **Daniel 1:8-20**

BACKGROUND SCRIPTURE: **Daniel 1**

KEY VERSE: **Daniel 1:8**

Daniel 1:8-20—KJV

8 But Daniel purposed in his heart that he would not defile himself with the portion of the king's meat, nor with the wine which he drank: therefore he requested of the prince of the eunuchs that he might not defile himself.

9 Now God had brought Daniel into favour and tender love with the prince of the eunuchs.

10 And the prince of the eunuchs said unto Daniel, I fear my lord the king, who hath appointed your meat and your drink: for why should he see your faces worse liking than the children which are of your sort? then shall ye make me endanger my head to the king.

11 Then said Daniel to Melzar, whom the prince of the eunuchs had set over Daniel, Hananiah, Mishael, and Azariah,

12 Prove thy servants, I beseech thee, ten days; and let them give us pulse to eat, and water to drink.

13 Then let our countenances be looked upon before thee, and the countenance of the children that eat of the portion of the king's meat: and as thou seest, deal with thy servants.

14 So he consented to them in this matter, and proved them ten days.

15 And at the end of ten days their countenances appeared fairer and fatter in flesh than all the children which did eat the portion of the king's meat.

16 Thus Melzar took away the portion of their meat, and the wine that they should drink; and gave them pulse.

17 As for these four children, God gave them knowledge and skill in all learning and wisdom: and Daniel had understanding in all visions and dreams.

18 Now at the end of the days that the king had said he should bring them in, then the prince of the eunuchs brought them in before Nebuchadnezzar.

Daniel 1:8-20—NRSV

8 But Daniel resolved that he would not defile himself with the royal rations of food and wine; so he asked the palace master to allow him not to defile himself.

9 Now God allowed Daniel to receive favor and compassion from the palace master.

10 The palace master said to Daniel, "I am afraid of my lord the king; he has appointed your food and your drink. If he should see you in poorer condition than the other young men of your own age, you would endanger my head with the king."

11 Then Daniel asked the guard whom the palace master had appointed over Daniel, Hananiah, Mishael, and Azariah:

12 "Please test your servants for ten days. Let us be given vegetables to eat and water to drink.

13 You can then compare our appearance with the appearance of the young men who eat the royal rations, and deal with your servants according to what you observe."

14 So he agreed to this proposal and tested them for ten days.

15 At the end of ten days it was observed that they appeared better and fatter than all the young men who had been eating the royal rations.

16 So the guard continued to withdraw their royal rations and the wine they were to drink, and gave them vegetables.

17 To these four young men God gave knowledge and skill in every aspect of literature and wisdom; Daniel also had insight into all visions and dreams.

18 At the end of the time that the king had set for them to be brought in, the palace master brought them into the presence of Nebuchadnezzar,

19 And the king communed with them; and among them all was found none like Daniel, Hananiah, Mishael, and Azariah: therefore stood they before the king.
20 And in all matters of wisdom and understanding, that the king enquired of them, he found them ten times better than all the magicians and astrologers that were in all his realm.

19 and the king spoke with them. And among them all, no one was found to compare with Daniel, Hananiah, Mishael, and Azariah; therefore they were stationed in the king's court.
20 In every matter of wisdom and understanding concerning which the king inquired of them, he found them ten times better than all the magicians and enchanters in his whole kingdom.

TOPICAL OUTLINE OF THE LESSON
I. Introduction
A. Daniel and His Friends Uphold Their Convictions
B. Biblical Background

II. Exposition and Application of the Scripture
A. Daniel and His Friends Make Their Convictions Known (Daniel 1:8-13)
B. The Guard Has Respect for Their Convictions (Daniel 1:14-16)
C. Favored for Their Convictions (Daniel 1:17-20)

III. Concluding Reflections

LESSON OBJECTIVES
Upon completion of this lesson, the students will know that:
1. Believers will be challenged to hold on to their convictions;
2. Those around you become allies when you decide to hold on to your Christian convictions; and,
3. Holding on to convictions can sometimes lead to unexpected rewards.

POINTS TO BE EMPHASIZED
ADULT/YOUTH
Adult Topic: **Holding to Your Convictions!**
Youth Topic: **Go Along to Get Along?**
Adult/Youth Key Verse: **Daniel 1:8**
Print Passage: **Daniel 1:8-20**
—There is timeliness to the book of Daniel that offers strength and inspiration to Christians who struggle to remain faithful in a hostile environment.
—Daniel and his companions resolved not to eat the food prepared for them by the royal cooks, but they worked out a scenario whereby they would not jeopardize their positions as officials of the king.
—The young men placed their trust and loyalty in God, and God took care of them.
—The story of Daniel and his three friends is a narrative on the Diaspora of the Babylonian exile.
—Daniel appears as the epitome of a wise man, completely faithful to God and Jewish tradition.

CHILDREN
Children Topic: **Daniel Makes a Choice**
Key Verses: **Daniel 1:8, 9**
Print Passage: **Daniel 1:3-4, 6-17**
—God rewards those who faithfully follow His laws.
—Daniel and his friends faced making a choice about whether to follow God's laws or the king's instructions.
—God gave Daniel favor with the palace master.
—Daniel resolved to follow God despite the consequences.

I. INTRODUCTION

A. Daniel and His Friends Uphold Their Convictions

God's people had refused to repent and obey Him, so by the hand of the Babylonians, they were driven into exile. The conquerors took many of the Hebrew youth to Babylon for training in the king's court. As such, Daniel and his three friends, Hananiah, Mishael, and Azariah, were among the chosen. The king's plan was to brainwash these young men so that they would eventually adopt the ways and mindset of the Babylonians. During their training period, they were supposed to learn the wisdom and the language of their captors. They were also to eat the king's diet, which, of course, was contrary to the dietary laws of God's chosen people. Likely, the food had also been offered to the idols of the land, and for the Hebrew youths to eat it would be blasphemous.

The king's plan to transform these four teenagers and the others was a three-year arrangement that began with changing their names. *Daniel* ("God is my judge") was changed to "Belteshazzar" ("Bel protect his life"). *Bel* was the name of a Babylonian god. *Hananiah* ("Jehovah is gracious") became *Shadrach* ("the command of the moon god"). *Mishael* ("Who is like God?") became *Meshach* ("who is like Aku"—one of the heathen gods), and *Azariah* ("Jehovah is my helper") became *Abednego* ("the servant of Nego"— another heathen god).

B. Biblical Background

The food that was offered to Daniel and his three friends violated two aspects of Jewish dietary laws. The first law concerned eating food that was considered "unclean"; the second referred to the prohibition against eating foods that had been offered to idols. As to the first, the distinction between clean and unclean foods was an ancient tradition that antedated Mosaic Law (see Leviticus 11). Whether a creature was "clean" or "unclean" had nothing to do with the quality of the beast; it all depended on what God said about the animal. When He gave these laws, no doubt the Lord had the health of His people in mind (Exodus 15:26; Deuteronomy 7:15), but the main purpose of the dietary code was to remind the Israelites that they belonged to God and were obligated to keep themselves separated from everything that would defile them "…be holy; for I am holy…" (Leviticus 11:44).

The second prohibition was that the Jews were to abstain from food that had been offered to idols. This law was connected to the first commandment, which prohibited idolatry (Exodus 20:3, 5). It was the practice of the pagans to ask their gods to bless their food before they ate it, in much the same way that we ask God to bless the food we eat prior to consuming it. Thus, to eat food blessed or offered to idols was, in effect, to recognize and worship that god. Therefore, Daniel and his friends' decision not to eat the food from the king's table was their way of displaying, in an ungodly environment, their convictions and devotion to God.

II. EXPOSITION AND APPLICATION OF THE SCRIPTURE

A. Daniel and His Friends Make Their Convictions Known (Daniel 1:8-13)

But Daniel purposed in his heart that he would not defile himself with the portion of the king's meat, nor with the wine which he drank: therefore he requested of the prince of the eunuchs that he might not defile himself. Now God had brought Daniel into favour and tender love with the prince of the eunuchs. And the prince of the eunuchs said unto Daniel, I fear my lord the king, who hath appointed your meat and your drink: for why should he see your faces worse liking than the children which are of your sort? then shall ye make me endanger my head to the king. Then said Daniel to Melzar, whom the prince of the eunuchs had set over Daniel, Hananiah, Mishael, and Azariah, Prove thy servants, I beseech thee, ten days; and let them give us pulse to eat, and water to drink. Then let our countenances be looked upon before thee, and the countenance of the children that eat of the portion of the king's meat: and as thou seest, deal with thy servants.

Daniel's determination not to defile himself had nothing to do with any harmful elements in the food and drink of the Babylonians. Nebuchadnezzar had made abundant provisions for the captives. Theirs was a life of luxury, not deprivation, for they were given a portion of food and wine daily from the king's own table. Rather, the food and drink were used in a figurative sense to represent a conscience defiled by sin; thus, it refers here to moral defilement.

This food did not conform to the requirements of Mosaic Law. First, the fact that it was prepared by Gentiles rendered it unclean. Also, without a doubt, many things forbidden by the Law were served on the king's table, so to partake of such food would defile the Jewish youth. Further, this royal food likely had been sacrificed and offered to pagan gods before it was served to the king. To partake of such food would be contrary to Exodus 34:15, where the Jews were forbidden to eat flesh sacrificed to pagan gods.

The word *purposed* in Hebrew is *suwm*. Grammatically, it is in the imperfect tense; therefore, it was a one-time decision or act, but one that affected a lifetime. In this context, Daniel and his three friends had come to a decision to hold to their convictions as Jews by refusing to eat what was offered. These Hebrew boys maintained their convictions in a foreign land. The Babylonians could change the young men's homes, textbooks, menu, and names, but they could not change their hearts.

Daniel and his friends purposed in their hearts that they would obey God's Word. They refused to conform to the world. Of course, they could have made excuses and "gone along to get along" with the crowd. They might have justified their behavior and said, "Everybody's doing it, so why not?" or "We had better obey the king!" or "We'll obey on the outside but keep our faith privately." But they did not compromise their faith in any fashion. They dared to believe God's Word and trust God for victory. It is one thing to have a private conviction, but it is an entirely different thing to stand by it at a difficult time.

Daniel, on behalf of his friends, spoke to the chief official and requested that they be allowed to abstain from eating what was being offered. Notice here that their approach was not to stage a protest or go on a hunger strike, but rather to simply make a request. Sometimes, we assume that our actions must be radical when, in fact, a little diplomacy might produce better results.

In verse 9, we are told that "God allowed Daniel to receive favor and compassion from the palace master." This is meant to communicate that it was not Daniel's looks, wit, or wisdom that brought him into favor; God had done this. Far too often, we as believers are apt to take credit for what God has done, or is doing; therefore, we become guilty of stealing the glory that belongs to Him.

Interesting also is Daniel's approach to the situation. He could have led an open rebellion to make his protest known. Instead, he chose to gain the permission of the chief eunuch to do what was right in the eyes of the Lord. The fact that he was willing to even broach the subject must have been impressive to the eunuch.

The term *eunuch* referred "to men who had been emasculated." The practice of emasculation was widespread throughout the Near East, and such men served as close attendants to the royal harem. The chief official expressed his reluctance to grant Daniel's request because he had been given the responsibility for overseeing the young captives' physical and mental development to ensure that they would become prepared for the roles the king had in mind for them. He feared that Daniel and his friends' lack of food would make them appear to be underweight in comparison to the other young captives. This would cause trouble for him with the king.

In the light of this, Daniel essentially said, "Please test your servants for ten days, and let them give us vegetables to eat and water to drink. (The Hebrew word for *vegetables*, meaning "sown things," may also include grains.) Daniel and his friends requested organic foods. As a matter of fact, it is believed that many of the diseases that afflict us today can be traced back to inorganic food that we consume every day. In our attempt to mass produce and preserve foods today, we are using all kinds of chemicals, which, when introduced into the body, can compromise our immune systems. Since the Mosaic Law designated no vegetables as unclean, Daniel could eat any vegetable put before him without defiling himself. After ten days, there was no marked deterioration that would jeopardize the life of anyone in authority. Daniel requested that after the ten days were over, the palace master should examine him and his friends and see who looked robust and fresh (see verse 13).

B. The Guard Has Respect for Their Convictions (Daniel 1:14-16)

So he consented to them in this matter, and proved them ten days. And at the end of ten days their countenances appeared fairer and fatter in flesh than all the children which did eat the portion of the king's meat. Thus Melzar took away the portion of their meat, and the wine that they should drink; and gave them pulse.

Even though the guard was afraid to change the king's orders lest anything happen to the youth and to himself, he considered Daniel's proposal to be safe. So he agreed to the test. Daniel and his friends showed the truth of the old phrase that is good to keep in mind: "You can catch more flies with honey than you can with vinegar!" At the conclusion of the ten days, the four young men who had lived on vegetables appeared healthier than those who had dined on the king's rich food. Since the four looked better and not worse than the others, as Ashpenaz had imagined (verse 10), he did not object to the diet Daniel had requested for himself and his friends. So they were allowed to continue on a diet of vegetables.

This should not be taken to mean that the vegetarian diet was superior to the carnivorous diet; rather, it should be ascribed to the special blessing of God. This shows that God blesses those who obey His commands and prospers those who trust Him. This incident would have been a great lesson for the nation of Israel. God demanded obedience to the Law, and their punishment came because of their disobedience. But when He imposes discipline, God protects and sustains those who obey Him and trust Him for their sustenance.

In this section, we see the mighty hand of God at work. In verse 15, the phrase "fairer and fatter" indicates that Daniel and his friends were healthier than those who consumed the king's delicacies.

The lesson here is obvious: any person that stands by his or her convictions honors God; and God, in turn, honors the person.

We should learn from these Hebrew boys that God will honor us if we are able to withstand the temptation to compromise our convictions.

C. Favored for Their Convictions
(Daniel 1:17-20)

As for these four children, God gave them knowledge and skill in all learning and wisdom: and Daniel had understanding in all visions and dreams. Now at the end of the days that the king had said he should bring them in, then the prince of the eunuchs brought them in before Nebuchadnezzar. And the king communed with them; and among them all was found none like Daniel, Hananiah, Mishael, and Azariah: therefore stood they before the king. And in all matters of wisdom and understanding, that the king enquired of them, he found them ten times better than all the magicians and astrologers that were in all his realm.

The Bible says, "A good man obtaineth favour of the Lord..." (Proverbs 12:2). Daniel and his friends knew who God was, and they were not ashamed of Him while in exile. God was not ashamed of them either. These youth, who were being prepared by Nebuchadnezzar for positions of responsibility in the royal court, were indirectly being prepared by God for a greater role in His royal kingdom.

To serve His purposes, God gave these young men "knowledge and skill in every aspect of literature and wisdom" (verse 17, NRSV). Knowledge has to do with reasoning skills and thought processes. Because God had so endowed them, these young men were able to think clearly and logically. Wisdom and skill go hand-in-hand. Daniel and his friends were given insight and discernment, along with the ability to apply these things to their specific situations and circumstances as needed.

God gave Daniel all of these gifts and then some. In addition to knowledge and skill, God endowed Daniel with both dreams and visions. Though the knowledge of others in Babylon may have equaled Daniel's in those subjects, he was superior to them all in one area—he had the God-given ability to understand divinely planted visions and dreams. This fact serves as a foreword to the following narrative, which tells of the prominence of Daniel as an agent of God's revelation. All abilities and endowments, whether natural or acquired, are from God and are to be used for Him.

The final test of Daniel's and the other boys' convictions was demonstrated when the king summoned the boys to appear before him. A personal interview by the king himself revealed an amazing outcome, and among them was found none like Daniel, Hananiah, Mishael, and Azariah; therefore, they stood before the king (verse 19).

In our focal text, the entire group, including many besides our special four, had participated in the three years of training. All of them were presented to Nebuchadnezzar. The king, via personal examination, fixed upon the very individuals whom Providence had distinguished with peculiar gifts, which rendered them superior to the others. The Bible affirms, "And in all matters of wisdom and understanding, that the king enquired of them, he found them ten times better than all the magicians and astrologers that were in all his realm" (Daniel 1:20).

By the king's own admission, Daniel and his friends surpassed the knowledge of the royal advisers, magicians, and astrologers in his entire realm. In fact, these young men were ten times better! "Ten times" is an idiom meaning that they possessed superior knowledge. In the modern-day academic environment, we say that they obtained *summa cum laude,* an institution's highest honor to a college graduate.

III. CONCLUDING REFLECTIONS

As believers seeking to hold to our convictions, we will be faced with various tests and temptations. It is wise, therefore, to keep in mind two things: first, it must be remembered that God, as a loving Father, is deeply concerned with the spiritual maturity of His children. Therefore, He tests each and every one of them (James 1:3; 1 Peter 1:7; Hebrews 12:5-7). Second, the temptations we face are always multiple in their sources; they originate in the lusts of our flesh and are ignited by the world and Satan (Genesis 3:1-7; James 1:13-15).

This narrative of Daniel and his friends demonstrates both tests and temptations. The natural bodily desire for food in this narrative was ignited into temptation by the foods and delicacies from the king's table. The test permitted by God was to see whether or not Daniel and his friends would abandon their convictions. They withstood the temptation and gained the victory in the testing of their faith.

PRAYER

Dear God, our heavenly Father, we thank You for the testimony of Daniel and his three friends. We pray, therefore, that when temptations arise in our lives, we will be strengthened to respond in faith by holding to our convictions. In Jesus' name, we pray. Amen.

WORD POWER

Purpose (Hebrew: *suwm* "seem")—**this word is cast in the imperfect tense; therefore, it has the idea of an action taken in the past, yet one that continues in the present without breaking, as long as life lasts. It is a decided purpose. Daniel purposed in his heart not to defile himself, and he would not yield.**

HOME DAILY BIBLE READINGS
(March 31—April 6, 2008)

Daniel Keeps Covenant in a Foreign Land

MONDAY, March 31: "A Prayer for God's Support" (Psalm 141:1-4)

TUESDAY, April 1: "God's House Besieged" (Daniel 1:1-2)

WEDNESDAY, April 2: "The King's Plan" (Daniel 1:3-7)

THURSDAY, April 3: "Daniel's Resolution" (Daniel 1:8-10)

FRIDAY, April 4: "The Ten-Day Test" (Daniel 1:11-14)

SATURDAY, April 5: "Four Fine Young Men" (Daniel 1:15-17)

SUNDAY, April 6: "Tested and True" (Daniel 1:18-21)

LESSON 7   April 13, 2008

THREE REFUSE TO BREAK COVENANT

DEVOTIONAL READING: **Psalm 121**
PRINT PASSAGE: **Daniel 3:10-13, 16-18, 21, 24**

BACKGROUND SCRIPTURE: **Daniel 3**
KEY VERSES: **Daniel 3:17-18**

Daniel 3:10-13, 16-18, 21, 24— KJV

10 Thou, O king, hast made a decree, that every man that shall hear the sound of the cornet, flute, harp, sackbut, psaltery, and dulcimer, and all kinds of musick, shall fall down and worship the golden image:
11 And whoso falleth not down and worshippeth, that he should be cast into the midst of a burning fiery furnace.
12 There are certain Jews whom thou hast set over the affairs of the province of Babylon, Shadrach, Meshach, and Abed-nego; these men, O king, have not regarded thee: they serve not thy gods, nor worship the golden image which thou hast set up.
13 Then Nebuchadnezzar in his rage and fury commanded to bring Shadrach, Meshach, and Abednego. Then they brought these men before the king.

.....

16 Shadrach, Meshach, and Abed-nego, answered and said to the king, O Nebuchadnezzar, we are not careful to answer thee in this matter.
17 If it be so, our God whom we serve is able to deliver us from the burning fiery furnace, and he will deliver us out of thine hand, O king.
18 But if not, be it known unto thee, O king, that we will not serve thy gods, nor worship the golden image which thou hast set up.

......

21 Then these men were bound in their coats, their hosen, and their hats, and their other garments, and were cast into the midst of the burning fiery furnace.

.....

24 Then Nebuchadnezzar the king was astonied, and rose up in haste, and spake, and said unto his counsellors, Did not we cast three men bound into the midst of the fire? They answered and said unto the king, True, O king.

Daniel 3:10-13, 16-18, 21, 24—NRSV

10 You, O king, have made a decree, that everyone who hears the sound of the horn, pipe, lyre, trigon, harp, drum, and entire musical ensemble, shall fall down and worship the golden statue,
11 and whoever does not fall down and worship shall be thrown into a furnace of blazing fire.
12 There are certain Jews whom you have appointed over the affairs of the province of Babylon: Shadrach, Meshach, and Abednego. These pay no heed to you, O King. They do not serve your gods and they do not worship the golden statue that you have set up."
13 Then Nebuchadnezzar in furious rage commanded that Shadrach, Meshach, and Abednego be brought in; so they brought those men before the king.

.....

16 Shadrach, Meshach, and Abednego answered the king, "O Nebuchadnezzar, we have no need to present a defense to you in this matter.
17 If our God whom we serve is able to deliver us from the furnace of blazing fire and out of your hand, O king, let him deliver us.
18 But if not, be it known to you, O king, that we will not serve your gods and we will not worship the golden statue that you have set up."

.....

21 So the men were bound, still wearing their tunics, their trousers, their hats, and their other garments, and they were thrown into the furnace of blazing fire.

.....

24 Then King Nebuchadnezzar was astonished and rose up quickly. He said to his counselors, "Was it not three men that we threw bound into the fire?" They answered the king, "True, O king."

Many people are willing to take risks when they hold firm convictions. What is worth dying for? Three Hebrews held captive in King Nebuchadnezzar's court risked their lives by refusing to bow down and worship anything but the Lord God.

TOPICAL OUTLINE OF THE LESSON

I. Introduction
A. The King Erects a Golden Image
B. Biblical Background

II. Exposition and Application of the Scripture
A. The Evil Plot (Daniel 3:10-13)
B. Faith in Action (Daniel 3:16-18)
C. Saved in Fiery Trial (Daniel 3:21, 24)

III. Concluding Reflections

LESSON OBJECTIVES

Upon completion of this lesson, the students will know that:

1. Idolatry is a common phenomenon among Christians;
2. Standing firm in faith may thrust believers into conflict with human rules and regulations; and,
3. God protects and delivers those who hold to their faith in Him.

POINTS TO BE EMPHASIZED

ADULT/YOUTH

Adult Topic: **Holding on to Your Faith**
Youth Topic: **Standing Up to False Gods**
Adult/Youth Key Verses: **Daniel 3:17-18**
Print Passage: **Daniel 3:10-13, 16-18, 21, 24**

—Nebuchadnezzar erected a statue and demanded that everyone worship it.
—The choice faced by Shadrach, Meshach, and Abednego was a choice between life and death.
—As young faithful Jews, Shadrach, Meshach, and Abednego could only serve one God (reference the first and second commandments).
—The faithful disobedience of Shadrach, Meshach, and Abednego was complicated by their positions in the king's court.
—The fourth person in the fiery furnace is believed by some to have been Christ, the Son of God.

CHILDREN

Children Topic: **Three Friends Take a Stand**
Key Verse: **Daniel 3:28a**
Print Passage: **Daniel 3:8-9, 12-13, 16-18, 21, 24-26**

—Shadrach's, Meshach's, and Abednego's faith remained strong in the face of extremely difficult circumstances.
—The three friends remained resolute in their stance even though they were not assured of God's deliverance from the fire.
—God is omnipresent and can be trusted to be present with the faithful even in seemingly impossible situations.
—An unbelieving king was brought to an acknowledgment of God's power.
—God's omnipotence was demonstrated through God's ability to make the impossible possible in the lives of the young men.
—God uses those who are seemingly weak to confound the world.

I. INTRODUCTION

A. The King Erects a Golden Image

The image erected by the king was humongous. The dimensions of the image would be fitting for an obelisk; it was ninety feet high (about the height of a present-day eight-story building) and only nine feet wide. It must have been overlaid with gold. Without a doubt, the use of gold in this image was inspired by Daniel's interpretation of the king's dream (Daniel 2:36, 38).

When the king erected this image is not known. It had to follow the events recorded in chapter 2, because Daniel's three companions were in the positions of authority (3:12) to which they had been appointed (2:49). The Septuagint adds in 3:1 that this event occurred in Nebuchadnezzar's nineteenth year (587 B.C.), one year before the fall of Jerusalem (cf. 2 Kings 25:8). However, a consideration of Daniel 3 seems to indicate that the events recorded there took place nearer the beginning of Nebuchadnezzar's long reign.

The events associated with the king's erecting the image suggest that he wanted to unify his empire and consolidate his authority as ruler. The image was to become the unifying center of Nebuchadnezzar's kingdom. Therefore, anyone who refused to bow in recognition of his reign would be cast into the fiery furnace.

B. Biblical Background

Nebuchadnezzar, which means "Nebo, protect the crown!" or the "frontiers," was the son and successor of Nabopolassar, who delivered Babylon from its dependence on Assyria and laid Nineveh in ruins. He was the greatest and most powerful of all the Babylonian kings.

Nebuchadnezzar subdued the whole of Palestine and took Jerusalem, carrying a great multitude of the Jews away captive. This was where the experience of Daniel and his friends started (Daniel 1:1, 2; Jeremiah 27:19, 40:1).

Daniel was a teenager when he was taken captive to Babylon around 605 B.C. Because of his commitment to God, he did not violate the life of righteousness which distinguished him among his peers. In addition to being a young man of righteousness and integrity, Daniel possessed prophetic abilities and unusual knowledge to interpret dreams and visions.

II. EXPOSITION AND APPLICATION OF THE SCRIPTURE

A. The Evil Plot
(Daniel 3:10-13)

Thou, O king, hast made a decree, that every man that shall hear the sound of the cornet, flute, harp, sackbut, psaltery, and dulcimer, and all kinds of musick, shall fall down and worship the golden image: And whoso falleth not down and worshippeth, that he should be cast into the midst of a burning fiery furnace. There are certain Jews whom thou hast set over the affairs of the province of Babylon, Shadrach, Meshach, and Abed-nego; these men, O king, have not regarded thee: they serve not thy gods, nor worship the golden image which thou hast set up. Then Nebuchadnezzar in his rage and fury commanded to bring Shadrach, Meshach, and Abed-nego. Then they brought these men before the king.

Prior to this passage, the king had elevated Daniel to a position of prominence in his kingdom. In time, the king had a dream that no one among his counselors was able to interpret. God favored Daniel and he gave the king an accurate interpretation of the dream. As a result, the king advanced Daniel to a higher position. However, his promotion caused jealousy among the king's counselors.

To further complicate matters, the king, in his arrogance, created an image and decreed that everyone in his domain bow to it when particular music emanated from the king's palace. At the sound of the music, all who heard it were to bow down and worship. After the decree was made, a group of Chaldeans (verse 8) approached the king and reminded him of his decree, underscoring what it meant to those who disobeyed it.

Their real concern was not disobedience to the king. They went to the king and reported Daniel's friends in order to undermine them in their positions of authority. They quoted the decree of the king in order to lend weight to their accusation.

They also reminded him of the penalty, which by the law was to be inflicted upon offenders. They were to be cast into a fiery furnace. Shadrach, Meshach, and Abednego were reported to the king as refusing to bow down and worship (Daniel 3:12) the king's monument. They made sure that the identity and state of origin of the violators was made plain to the king.

Those who were jealous and envious of Daniel and his friends saw their refusal to worship the golden image as an opportunity to have them stripped of their authority. They reminded the king of the stature to which the three accused had been elevated.

The group suggested that the three young Hebrews had committed a malicious crime, filled with contempt for the king and his authority: "… these men, O king, have not regarded thee: they serve not thy gods, nor worship the golden image which thou hast set up" (Daniel 3:12).

Upon hearing this allegation, Nebuchadnezzar lost control. How could anyone dare to go against the king's order? Such a deed was unthinkable, especially from a group of foreigners. Unable to cool his temper, the king summoned Shadrach, Meshach, and Abednego to be brought before him.

The king's reactions were extreme; however, we must not be quick to judge him. If you find yourself angered when people do not follow your directions, you need to ask these questions: "Why am I reacting this way? Is the Holy Spirit in control, or is Satan in control? Is my ego getting the better of me?"

B. Faith in Action
(Daniel 3:16-18)

Shadrach, Meshach, and Abed-nego, answered and said to the king, O Nebuchadnezzar, we are not careful to answer thee in this matter. If it be so, our God whom we serve is able to deliver us from the burning fiery furnace, and he will deliver us out of thine hand, O king. But if not, be it known unto thee, O king, that we will not serve thy gods, nor worship the golden image which thou hast set up.

The three Hebrew boys were found guilty of disobeying the king's order. In verses 14-15, the king had asked them whether or not their disobedience was deliberate; if not, he was willing to give them an opportunity to demonstrate their obedience. Perhaps the king was trying to give them a way out of the situation. However, the three young men answered with the phrase, "We are not careful to answer thee" (verse 16).

This phrase begs for our attention as it could be interpreted, "It is not necessary for us to argue with you, Your Highness. You, the king, have made your decree and we, the Hebrew boys, have vowed not to bow down to any graven image. Therefore, we are not going to enter into any argument with you."

This is faith in action—faith that will not succumb in the face of the threat of death. The boys needed no time for further deliberation, even though this was a matter of life and death. One would think they might have considered the matter for awhile before they gave their response. We know that, in the natural world, life is indeed desirable, and death is dreadful. But the second commandment, "Thou shalt have no other gods before me" (Exodus 20:3) was clear, and no room was left to question what was right.

Shadrach, Meshach, and Abednego were resolved to die in their integrity rather than live in iniquity. Hesitation, or bargaining with sin, is fatal; unhesitating decision is the only safety, where the path of duty is clear (Matthew 10:19, 28). *Faith* is an action word, and each of us will come to a point in life when we will have to demonstrate the faith we profess.

These Hebrew boys demonstrated uncommon courage in the face of a despot who had the power to cast them into the fire—into death. Theirs was a strong reply from unexpectedly brave people. Shadrach, Meshach, and Abednego recognized God's sovereignty and power.

"But if not…" was another daring statement in this section. The final choice was in the hands of the Lord. These faithful Hebrew boys knew that God could deliver them, but they were also aware that their God might choose not to save them. Their God demanded unequivocal obedience and had forbidden them to worship any other gods.

One who obeys God completely is not presuming divine protection and deliverance. Obeying God was more important than life to these three, so if God chose not to deliver them, they would still obey Him.

C. Saved in Fiery Trial (Daniel 3:21, 24)

Then these men were bound in their coats, their hosen, and their hats, and their other garments, and were cast into the midst of the burning fiery furnace. … Then Nebuchadnezzar the king was astonied, and rose up in haste, and spake, and said unto his counsellors, Did not we cast three men bound into the midst of the fire? They answered and said unto the king, True, O king.

In the custom of the Babylonians, criminals were stripped prior to execution, but in this case the Hebrew boys were bound with their coats. This action suggests that the king was especially enraged; therefore, the servants performed their duty in a hateful manner. Additionally, the king had ordered the flames seven times hotter than was customary for such a punishment.

Once in the furnace, to the astonishment of the king, there was another man in the fire. The king asked, "Did not we cast three men bound into the midst of the fire?" (Daniel 3:24). Nebuchadnezzar was watching the proceedings intently from a safe distance. As he peered into the furnace, probably through the lower opening, what he saw amazed him. The men who had been tied up in their coats were walking around in the furnace, unbound. And, instead of three men in the furnace, he saw four, and the fourth was like a son of the gods.

In verse 24, the words *three* and *bound* are very important. Without a doubt, the king had ordered three men cast into the fire, but now there were four. Also, the three were now unbound and walking around unburned and unharmed by the flames. This fourth man is believed to be the pre-incarnate Christ, or an angel who came to shield the boys from the intensity of the fire. Though Nebuchadnezzar did not know of the Son of God, he did recognize that the fourth person was a supernatural being.

III. CONCLUDING REFLECTIONS

There is much to reflect on in this lesson: First, we should note the immediacy of the Hebrews' decision. Those who would avoid sin must not parley with temptation. That is to say, when we have purposed to stand, then we should not pause, hesitate, and ponder.

Second, we should weigh the potential harm that we may face for our decision to stand. These young men faced death, yet they did not bargain.

Third, we should notice that it was not their courage but their confidence that sustained them. It was their confidence in God that enabled them to look with so much contempt upon death. They trusted in the living God, and by faith they saw God at work.

Fourth, their confidence was complete; that is, it was not simply limited to God's delivering them from the furnace, but extended to His *ability* to deliver them out of the furnace. As faithful servants of God, we must recognize that He is able to control and overrule all the powers that are armed against us, even the forces of nature, like fire and water.

PRAYER

Gracious, eternal, and ever-faithful God, our Father, how we praise You as the God who enters with us into the fiery furnaces of life. May we face the difficulties and trying circumstances of life with the complete confidence that our God is able. In Your Son, Jesus, we pray. Amen.

WORD POWER

Serve (Aramaic: *palach*)—this word appears two times in the Key Verse; however, the second time the word is used, it is prefixed with a negative ("not" Aramaic: *la*). Combined with the word not, it denotes a strong feeling toward something, or a strong objection to compromise. No matter what the king planned to do, the Hebrews would not *(la)* change their minds.

HOME DAILY BIBLE READINGS
(April 7-13, 2008)
Three Refuse to Break Covenant

MONDAY, April 7: "God's Protection Forevermore" (Psalm 121:1-4)
TUESDAY, April 8: "King Nebuchadnezzar's Golden Statue" (Daniel 3:1-7)
WEDNESDAY, April 9: "The Refusal to Worship the Statue" (Daniel 3:8-15)
THURSDAY, April 10: "Brought before the King" (Daniel 3:16-23)
FRIDAY, April 11: "Not a Hint of Fire" (Daniel 3:24-27)
SATURDAY, April 12: "A New Decree" (Daniel 3:28-30)
SUNDAY, April 13: "God Will Keep You" (Psalm 121:5-8)

DANIEL'S LIFE-AND-DEATH TEST

DEVOTIONAL READING: **Psalm 119:57-64**   BACKGROUND SCRIPTURE: **Daniel 6**
PRINT PASSAGE: **Daniel 6:4-7, 10, 16,**   KEY VERSE: **Daniel 6:10**
19, 21, 25-26

Daniel 6:4-7, 10, 16, 19, 21, 25-26—KJV

4 Then the presidents and princes sought to find occasion against Daniel concerning the kingdom; but they could find none occasion nor fault; forasmuch as he was faithful, neither was there any error or fault found in him.
5 Then said these men, We shall not find any occasion against this Daniel, except we find it against him concerning the law of his God.
6 Then these presidents and princes assembled together to the king, and said thus unto him, King Darius, live for ever.
7 All the presidents of the kingdom, the governors, and the princes, the counsellors, and the captains, have consulted together to establish a royal statute, and to make a firm decree, that whosoever shall ask a petition of any God or man for thirty days, save of thee, O king, he shall be cast into the den of lions.

.....

10 Now when Daniel knew that the writing was signed, he went into his house; and his windows being open in his chamber toward Jerusalem, he kneeled upon his knees three times a day, and prayed, and gave thanks before his God, as he did aforetime.

.....

16 Then the king commanded, and they brought Daniel, and cast him into the den of lions. Now the king spake and said unto Daniel, Thy God whom thou servest continually, he will deliver thee.

.....

19 Then the king arose very early in the morning, and went in haste unto the den of lions.

.....

21 Then said Daniel unto the king, O king, live for ever.

.....

Daniel 6:4-7, 10, 16, 19, 21, 25-26—NRSV

4 So the presidents and the satraps tried to find grounds for complaint against Daniel in connection with the kingdom. But they could find no grounds for complaint or any corruption, because he was faithful, and no negligence or corruption could be found in him.
5 The men said, "We shall not find any ground for complaint against this Daniel unless we find it in connection with the law of his God."
6 So the presidents and satraps conspired and came to the king and said to him, "O King Darius, live forever!
7 All the presidents of the kingdom, the prefects and the satraps, the counselors and the governors are agreed that the king should establish an ordinance and enforce an interdict, that whoever prays to anyone, divine or human, for thirty days, except to you, O king, shall be thrown into a den of lions.

.....

10 Although Daniel knew that the document had been signed, he continued to go to his house, which had windows in its upper room open toward Jerusalem, and to get down on his knees three times a day to pray to his God and praise him, just as he had done previously.

.....

16 Then the king gave the command, and Daniel was brought and thrown into the den of lions. The king said to Daniel, "May your God, whom you faithfully serve, deliver you!"

.....

19 Then, at break of day, the king got up and hurried to the den of lions.

.....

21 Daniel then said to the king, "O king, live forever!

.....

25 Then king Darius wrote unto all people, nations, and languages, that dwell in all the earth; Peace be multiplied unto you.
26 I make a decree, That in every dominion of my kingdom men tremble and fear before the God of Daniel: for he is the living God, and stedfast for ever.

25 Then King Darius wrote to all peoples and nations of every language throughout the whole world: "May you have abundant prosperity!
26 I make a decree, that in all my royal dominion people should tremble and fear before the God of Daniel: For he is the living God, enduring forever.

TOPICAL OUTLINE OF THE LESSON

I. Introduction

A. Daniel's Prominence Produced Jealousy and Envy
B. Biblical Background

II. Exposition and Application of the Scripture

A. The Plot Against Daniel (Daniel 6:4-7)
B. Prayers to God (Daniel 6:10)
C. The Lions' Den and the God of Daniel (Daniel 6:16, 19, 21)
D. Everlasting God of Daniel (Daniel 6:25-26)

III. Concluding Reflections

LESSON OBJECTIVES

Upon completion of this lesson, the students will know that:

1. Those who are faithful to God will be tempted to compromise;
2. Honoring God can sometimes brings believers into conflict with societal laws; and,
3. God is magnified among believers who refuse to compromise.

POINTS TO BE EMPHASIZED

ADULT/YOUTH

Adult Topic: **Faith Without Compromise!**
Youth Topic: **Defiance!**
Adult Key Verse: **Daniel 6:10**
Youth Key Verse: **Daniel 6:16**
Print Passage: **Daniel 6:4-7, 10, 16, 19, 21, 25-26**

—Daniel had a position of status that aroused jealousy on the part of others and led to conspiracy against him.
—Daniel maintained his priorities and prayer life even though doing this could have led to his death.
—Daniel's daring faith was a witness to God's power and trustworthiness, and His power and trustworthiness were confirmed in God's protection of Daniel.
—Daniel's uncompromising stand resulted in the king's acknowledgement of God's sovereignty.

CHILDREN

Children Topic: **Daniel Faces the Lions**
Key Verse: **Daniel 6:22a**
Print Passage: **Daniel 6:4-7, 10, 16, 19, 21, 25-26**

—Faithful believers were and are sometimes persecuted for their faith.
—Daniel continued his practice of prayer in defiance of civil authority.
—Daniel's faith in God helped him stand firm even in the face of death.
—God stood with Daniel in the lions' den and saved his life.
—Daniel, who lived out his faith, influenced the king to proclaim the power of God.

I. INTRODUCTION

A. Daniel's Prominence Produced Jealousy and Envy

When Darius conquered Babylon and received the crown, he remodeled the government, dividing his empire into 120 districts. He appointed princes over each of them. These men were assigned to administer justice, preserve the public peace, and levy the king's revenue. Over these princes he appointed three presidents who were to manage the public accounts, receive appeals from the princes, and handle complaints against them in cases of mismanagement. This was done to ensure that Darius would not sustain loss, either politically or economically. Of these three presidents, Daniel was appointed chief, effectively making him the prime minister of state.

Daniel was a native of a foreign kingdom, and a ruined one, and because of that he was despised as a stranger and a captive. But Darius, it seems, was very quick-sighted in judging human capacities and was soon aware that Daniel possessed something extraordinary. Therefore, Darius appointed him second-in-command, directly under himself. Daniel's meteoric ascendancy aroused the anger and jealousy of the other two presidents who, being native-born, likely thought that such honor should have been bestowed upon one of them.

B. Biblical Background

Daniel, which means "God is my judge" or "judge of God," is one of the four great prophets, though he is not mentioned as such in the Old Testament. He descended from one of the noble families of Judah (Daniel 1:3-6), and probably was born in Jerusalem about 623 B.C., during the reign of Josiah.

At the first deportation of the Jews by Nebuchadnezzar, Daniel and three other youths were carried off to Babylon, along with some of the vessels of the temple. While in exile, Daniel entered into the service of the king of Babylon, and in accordance with the custom of the age, received the Chaldean name *Belteshazzar* ("Bel" meant "protect the king").

A pivotal moment in Daniel's life was when he aptly interpreted King Nebuchadnezzar's dream. He was rewarded with a purple robe and elevation to the rank of third ruler. The incident also sealed his reputation as a great interpreter.

Because of this reputation, Daniel was summoned to interpret the handwriting that appeared on the wall during a party hosted by Belshazzar, a successor to the Chaldean throne. "In that night was Belshazzar the king of the Chaldeans slain" (Daniel 5:30).

Daniel prospered as a foreigner in a foreign land, yet he remained faithful to God. The Lord spared Daniel's life to see his people restored to their homeland. In his old age, Daniel had a series of visions regarding redemption through Jesus Christ.

II. EXPOSITION AND APPLICATION OF THE SCRIPTURE

A. The Plot Against Daniel
(Daniel 6:4-7)

Then the presidents and princes sought to find occasion against Daniel concerning the kingdom; but they could find none occasion nor fault; forasmuch as he was faithful, neither was there any error or fault found in him. Then said these men, We shall not find any occasion against this Daniel, except we find it against him concerning the law of his God. Then these presidents and princes assembled together to the king, and said thus unto him, King Darius, live for ever. All the presidents of the kingdom, the governors, and the princes, the counsellors, and the captains, have consulted together to establish a royal statute, and to make a firm decree, that whosoever shall ask a petition of any God or man for thirty days, save of thee, O king, he shall be cast into the den of lions.

The other officials envied Daniel and sought a way to get rid of him. His ruin and disgrace would not be enough to satisfy their vengeful hearts; they wanted him dead. Their task was complicated by the fact that there was nothing character-wise that his detractors could use to accuse him. Daniel was a man of impeccable character. In the book of the prophecies of Ezekiel, Daniel was mentioned as a man having a pattern of righteousness (Ezekiel 14:14, 20).

In those days, there were no surveillance cameras, but the government employed a secret service-type agency to constantly check on Daniel. The main duty of their covert agents was to observe Daniel in the management of his duties. They sought something on which to ground an accusation against him concerning the kingdom—some instance of neglect or partiality, some hasty word spoken, some disgruntled worker, or some necessary business overlooked. They searched meticulously, but they could find nothing against him. Daniel always acted honestly, and now even more so, because in his divine wisdom he was aware of their treachery.

When their efforts proved fruitless, these men devised another means by which to accuse Daniel. The only way they could get him was through his devotion to his God. They said among themselves: "...we shall not find any occasion against this Daniel, except we find it against him concerning the law of his God" (Daniel 6:5). It is an excellent thing, and does much for the glory of God, when believers' lifestyles are such that their most watchful, spiteful enemies can find no blame in them, except in matters of their God.

In order to carry out their plot, Daniel's enemies had to go through the king. They persuaded the king to issue a decree prohibiting prayers to any god other than himself (see Daniel 6:7-9). They initiated a meeting with the king. Then these presidents and princes assembled together with the king, and said thus to him, "King Darius, live forever...." The literal translation of the phrase "assembled together" (verse 6) is "assembled hastily and tumultuously." It was a hastily-called meeting, in an attempt to force the king into this plot, not allowing him time to think it over or to consult with Daniel.

In approaching the king, the princes and presidents gave the impression that all those in authority had collectively come to this decision. Yet we may be sure that Daniel, the chief of the three presidents, did not agree to it. So absolute was the king's authority in the East that he was regarded not merely as the ruler, but as the owner of the people. A weak despot like Darius could easily be persuaded that such a decree would test the loyalty of the just-conquered Chaldeans and tame their proud spirits—giving added assurance to his personal safety. The princes proposed a thirty-day period of testing. During that time, if anyone was found praying to any god other than the king, they would be cast into the den of lions.

B. Prayers to God
(Daniel 6:10)

Now when Daniel knew that the writing was signed, he went into his house; and his windows being open in his chamber toward Jerusalem, he kneeled upon his knees three times a day, and prayed, and gave thanks before his God, as he did aforetime.

Daniel's daily routine involved praying to his God three times a day. Thus, upon hearing of the king's decree, he decided to continue his regular practice of prayer. So as usual, "…he went into his house…his windows being open in his chamber toward Jerusalem…" (Daniel 6:10). Jerusalem was the place where God had chosen to put his name. When the temple was dedicated, Solomon prayed that should his people find themselves captive in another land one day, they could still pray to God, looking back toward the land that He had given them and the city where He had built His house. Then He would hear their cry and maintain their cause (1 Kings 8:48-49). Evidently, it was this promise that Daniel had in mind in his daily devotions and prayer. He did this three times every day, according to the example of David, "Evening, morning, and at noon, will I pray…" (Psalm 55:17).

It is a good discipline to have regular intervals devoted to prayer, just as we have our regular dining hour. It helps us to remember that if our souls require regular spiritual refreshment, prayer matters in the lives of believers. When Daniel found out that the decree had been signed to pray to Darius, he went home and prayed to God. Daniel opposed earthly authority in a way that shames us as Christians today. It was his custom to pray constantly. He did not pray only when a situation was dire; rather, he prayed because it was his way of life.

C. The Lions' Den and the God of Daniel
(Daniel 6:16, 19, 21)

Then the king commanded, and they brought Daniel, and cast him into the den of lions. Now the king spake and said unto Daniel, Thy God whom thou servest continually, he will deliver thee. . . . Then the king arose very early in the morning, and went in haste unto the den of lions. …Then said Daniel unto the king, O king, live for ever.

It is indeed noteworthy that in carrying out his edict by throwing Daniel into the den of lions, the king still viewed Daniel as a man of integrity. He acknowledged that Daniel's actions were not in defiance of him, but rather out of obedience to his God. He even went so far as to try to give Daniel encouragement: "Thy God whom thou servest continually, he will deliver thee" (Daniel 6:16). In Daniel's example, we see the positive impact that a person who holds onto her or his faith can have upon others. Even though the king was bound by his own decree to cast Daniel into the den of lions, he was so impressed with the God of Daniel (through previous encounters) that he also had confidence in Daniel's deliverance.

Daniel shows us here the extent to which one may have to go in order to hold on to one's faith. He shows us that faithfulness also requires courage. It involves courage to remain faithful in the face of a humanly impossible predicament. The penalty for being faithful was the most horrific of deaths—to be thrown into the midst of a den of hungry lions. Despite this, we see here that those who throw away their souls to save their lives only serve to make a bad bargain for themselves.

The king spent a restless night, and at dawn he hurried to the lions' den. Darius hoped against hope that Daniel might have been rescued by the God whom he served (Daniel 6:16). What a contrast between Darius in his palace and Daniel in the lions' den! Darius had no peace in the palace, yet Daniel was perfectly at peace with himself and the Lord amid the lions.

Darius called out to Daniel, who responded, "O king, live for ever" (Daniel 6:21). Daniel was alive, safe, well, and unhurt in the lions' den.

Daniel embodies for us a valuable lesson, later reiterated by our Lord, about how we ought to respond to those who persecute us for righteousness' sake (Matthew 5:10). Daniel shows us here the extent to which one may have to go in order to hold on to faith in God. Adverse circumstances in life are an opportunity for God to demonstrate His awesome power, if we have faith in Him.

D. Everlasting God of Daniel (Daniel 6:25-26)

Then king Darius wrote unto all people, nations, and languages, that dwell in all the earth; Peace be multiplied unto you. I make a decree, That in every dominion of my kingdom men tremble and fear before the God of Daniel: for he is the living God, and stedfast for ever.

The one who by his own decree was revered for a month as a god (Daniel 6:7), now made a proclamation that all subjects of his nation, all the peoples, nations, and persons of every language (cf. Daniel 3:4, 7; 4:1-2; 5:19; 7:14) must fear and revere Daniel's God. This was an amazing turnaround on Darius's part! The reason for this, Darius wrote, was that Daniel's God was the living God (cf. Daniel 6:26), whereas the gods of the Medes and Persians were dead idols. Our God is eternal, His kingdom is indestructible (cf. Daniel 7:14), and He intervenes and delivers those who trust Him. He works by miraculous power to perform His will, including the miraculous delivery of Daniel. Such a God is to be truly revered and worshiped. In spite of the opposition of the satraps and administrators, Daniel was honored and lived a good long life, encompassing the reigns of Darius and Cyrus.

One of the cardinal beliefs of Christian doctrine is the immutability of God (an unchanging God). We are still serving the God of Daniel. What He did for Daniel, He can do for us if we let Him take the glory. The Persian despot finally acknowledged the God of Daniel as the only true God. We now see the reason why God allowed Daniel to go through the lions' den. It was through this ordeal that God received the glory among unbelievers.

III. CONCLUDING REFLECTIONS

Daniel's prayer is instructive in providing us with seven vital elements of prayer that all of us ought to observe.

1. *A place of prayer.* Daniel prayed in his house, sometimes alone and sometimes, we may presume, with his family about him. Every believer's house ought to be a house of prayer. God must have an altar, and on it we must offer spiritual sacrifices of prayer and praise.

2. *Thanksgiving.* In every prayer, Daniel gave thanks to God. When we pray to God for the mercies we want, we must praise Him for those we have received.

3. *Faith.* Daniel believed the Word; he trusted that God would hear and answer His prayers with favor. We ought to pray in faith and not with doubt (James 1:6).

4. *Obedience.* Daniel prayed because he had been commanded to pray. We likewise have been commanded and ought to respond by "praying always" (Ephesians 6:18).

5. *Worship.* Solomon prescribed that prayers should be made "toward the city" (Jerusalem) (1 Chronicles 11:4-8). Daniel could not worship literally in the Holy City, but his posture showed that he wished to do so.

6. *Humility.* Daniel knelt down on his knees; the posture of a beggar. We are as beggars before the One who is able to provide for our needs.

7. *Regularity.* Daniel prayed three times a day, every day. Prayer must be a regular part of our daily routines.

PRAYER

Most merciful and gracious God our Father, we are grateful to know that the God of Daniel is our God. We find strength in reading how You shut the mouths of the lions in the den with Daniel. May we be so encouraged as to live our lives in such a manner as did Daniel. In Jesus' name, we pray. Amen.

WORD POWER

Prayer (Aramaic: *tselá*)—this word means to kneel down in a position of humility. Such posture demonstrates deep devotion. It also shows the place prayer takes in one's life. Daniel did not just kneel on this occasion because of the immensity of the problem; rather, it was his custom to do so.

HOME DAILY BIBLE READINGS
(April 14-20, 2008)
Daniel's Life-and-Death Test
MONDAY, April 14: "Prayer and Commitment" (Psalm 119:57-64)
TUESDAY, April 15: "An Honest Leader" (Daniel 6:1-4)
WEDNESDAY, April 16: "A Dishonest Plot" (Daniel 6:5-9)
THURSDAY, April 17: "The King's Distress" (Daniel 6:10-14)
FRIDAY, April 18: "The Charge Stands" (Daniel 6:15-18)
SATURDAY, April 19: "Daniel Trusted in God" (Daniel 6:19-23)
SUNDAY, April 20: "The Living God" (Daniel 6:24-28)

LESSON 9   April 27, 2008

DANIEL'S PRAYER FOR THE PEOPLE

DEVOTIONAL READING: **Psalm 130**
PRINT PASSAGE: **Daniel 9:1-7, 17-19**

BACKGROUND SCRIPTURE: **Daniel 9**
KEY VERSE: **Daniel 9:17**

Daniel 9:1-7, 17-19—KJV

IN THE first year of Darius the son of Ahasuerus, of the seed of the Medes, which was made king over the realm of the Chaldeans;

2 In the first year of his reign I Daniel understood by books the number of the years, whereof the word of the LORD came to Jeremiah the prophet, that he would accomplish seventy years in the desolations of Jerusalem.

3 And I set my face unto the LORD God, to seek by prayer and supplications, with fasting, and sackcloth, and ashes:

4 And I prayed unto the LORD my God, and made my confession, and said, O Lord, the great and dreadful God, keeping the covenant and mercy to them that love him, and to them that keep his commandments;

5 We have sinned, and have committed iniquity, and have done wickedly, and have rebelled, even by departing from thy precepts and from thy judgments:

6 Neither have we hearkened unto thy servants the prophets, which spake in thy name to our kings, our princes, and our fathers, and to all the people of the land.

7 O Lord, righteousness belongeth unto thee, but unto us confusion of faces, as at this day; to the men of Judah, and to the inhabitants of Jerusalem, and unto all Israel, that are near, and that are far off, through all the countries whither thou hast driven them, because of their trespass that they have trespassed against thee.

…..

17 Now therefore, O our God, hear the prayer of thy servant, and his supplications, and cause thy face to shine upon thy sanctuary that is desolate, for the Lord's sake.

18 O my God, incline thine ear, and hear; open thine eyes, and behold our desolations, and the city which is called by thy name: for we do not present our supplications before thee for our righteousnesses, but for thy great mercies.

Daniel 9:1-7, 17-19—NRSV

IN THE first year of Darius son of Ahasuerus, by birth a Mede, who became king over the realm of the Chaldeans—

2 in the first year of his reign, I, Daniel, perceived in the books the number of years that, according to the word of the LORD to the prophet Jeremiah, must be fulfilled for the devastation of Jerusalem, namely, seventy years.

3 Then I turned to the Lord God, to seek an answer by prayer and supplication with fasting and sackcloth and ashes.

4 I prayed to the LORD my God and made confession, saying, "Ah, Lord, great and awesome God, keeping covenant and steadfast love with those who love you and keep your commandments,

5 we have sinned and done wrong, acted wickedly and rebelled, turning aside from your commandments and ordinances.

6 We have not listened to your servants the prophets, who spoke in your name to our kings, our princes, and our ancestors, and to all the people of the land.

7 "Righteousness is on your side, O Lord, but open shame, as at this day, falls on us, the people of Judah, the inhabitants of Jerusalem, and all Israel, those who are near and those who are far away, in all the lands to which you have driven them, because of the treachery that they have committed against you."

…..

17 Now therefore, O our God, listen to the prayer of your servant and to his supplication, and for your own sake, Lord, let your face shine upon your desolated sanctuary.

18 Incline your ear, O my God, and hear. Open your eyes and look at our desolation and the city that bears your name. We do not present our supplication before you on the ground of our righteousness, but on the ground of your great mercies.

Some people willingly offer prayers of confession and intercession. What drives them to approach God? Daniel was so overcome by grief over the devastation of Jerusalem and the exile of his people that he made intercession and confession on their behalf for their sin against God.

19 O Lord, hear; O Lord, forgive; O Lord, hearken and do; defer not, for thine own sake, O my God: for thy city and thy people are called by thy name.

19 O Lord, hear; O Lord, forgive; O Lord, listen and act and do not delay! For your own sake, O my God, because your city and your people bear your name!"

TOPICAL OUTLINE OF THE LESSON

I. Introduction
A. Historical Preamble
B. Biblical Background

II. Exposition and Application of the Scripture
A. Scripture Reading and Meditation (Daniel 9:1-2)
B. Intercessory Prayer (Daniel 9:3-7)
C. Plea for Deliverance (Daniel 9:17-19)

III. Concluding Reflections

LESSON OBJECTIVES

Upon completion of this lesson, the students will know:

1. Intercessory prayer is praying for others;
2. Intercessory prayer is significant in the life of the believer; and,
3. Everyone, individually and corporately, stands in need of intercessory prayer.

POINTS TO BE EMPHASIZED

ADULT/YOUTH

Adult Topic: **Intercession in Crisis**
Youth Topic: **Confess!**
Adult Key Verse: **Daniel 9:17**
Youth Key Verses: **Daniel 9:4-5**
Print Passage: **Daniel 9:1-7, 17-19**

—Daniel offers a prayer that links the people's current situation with their unfaithfulness to the covenant.
—Daniel's prayer reflects a sense of urgency.
—Daniel's prayer is offered through both word and action.
—The prayers of God's people in the Old Testament often recounted the things God had done for them.

CHILDREN

Children Topic: **Daniel Asks God for Help**
Key Verse: **Daniel 9:19**
Print Passage: **Daniel 9:1-7, 17-19**

—God's covenantal love for believers is steadfast.
—In spite of the covenant, the people of Israel continued to rebel against God.
—Daniel sensed his duty to intercede on behalf of God's people.
—God does not hold God's people faultless who repeatedly rebel against His Word and who show little or no evidence of repentance.
—God will listen to our fervent prayers even if these prayers are offered during a time of divine chastisement.

INTRODUCTION

A. Historical Preamble

Sometime after the deportation of Jerusalem in 597 B.C., Jeremiah sent a letter to the exiles in Babylon to tell them how to behave in their new land. He first addressed those who felt they had no hope. The exiles had lost everything but their lives and what few possessions they could carry with them to Babylon. They had lost their freedom and were now captives. No matter how they looked at it, the situation seemed hopeless.

Jeremiah then addressed those with false hopes. The false prophets had convinced certain people that their stay in Babylon would be brief, perhaps only two years. Jeremiah told them that they would be there for seventy years. Therefore, it was important that the exiles move forward and live their lives by establishing homes, planting gardens, and having families so that there would be people available to return to Judea when the time of captivity ended.

Third, Jeremiah addressed the faithful remnant whose hope remained true. He reminded them that true hope was based on the revealed Word of God, not on the dream messages of self-appointed prophets. Therefore, there was no need to be discouraged. It was this letter that Daniel read, prompting the actions covered in this lesson (Jeremiah 29:10-11).

B. Biblical Background

The book of Daniel is prominent in the division of the Jewish Bible called the *Hagiographa* (sacred writings). However, the book of Daniel, as we have it in our Bible, consists of two distinct parts. The first part, consisting of the first six chapters, is chiefly historical; the second part, consisting of the remaining six chapters, is chiefly prophetical.

The historical part of the book deals with the period of the captivity. The book of Daniel reveals the history of Israel's captivity. This is the only book of the Bible that furnishes any series of events for that dark and dismal period in Israel's history. It was a period when the Israelites hung their harps on the trees that grew by the Euphrates. For more details on their lethargic minds, read Psalm 137.

Daniel's narrative may be said to intervene between Kings and Chronicles on the one hand, and Ezra on the other, to fill out the sketch that the author of Chronicles gives in a single verse in his last chapter: "And them that had escaped from the sword carried he [i.e., Nebuchadnezzar] away to Babylon; where they were servants to him and his sons until the reign of the kingdom of Persia" (2 Chronicles 36:20).

II. EXPOSITION AND APPLICATION OF THE SCRIPTURE

A. Scripture Reading and Meditation
(Daniel 9:1-2)

IN THE first year of Darius the son of Ahasuerus, of the seed of the Medes, which was made king over the realm of the Chaldeans; In the first year of his reign I Daniel understood by books the number of the years, whereof the word of the Lord came to Jeremiah the prophet, that he would accomplish seventy years in the desolations of Jerusalem.

This section of the book of Daniel falls into the prophetic part. Daniel began by saying, "In the first year of Darius..." (verse 1). Darius was appointed by Cyrus as administrator of Babylon. The date of this chapter is, therefore, 537 B.C., one year before Cyrus permitted the Jews to return from exile, and sixty-nine years after Daniel had been carried to Babylon. These dates help every reader of the book of Daniel to know that the events described in his book are historical facts.

Daniel had been a diligent student of the book of Jeremiah. The book that is referred to contains Jeremiah's prophecies. Apart from the prophecies of Jeremiah, there were a series of letters written to the exiles (see Jeremiah 25:11-12; 29:10). Daniel paid particular attention to one clause, "...the number of the years...."

At this point, Daniel was advanced in age. While reading Jeremiah 25:1-14, the Lord caused him to see that his people would be in Babylon for seventy years. Daniel realized that the seventy years of captivity were about to come to an end. Today, God is still able to speak in dreams and visions to people, but His primary way of speaking is through His Word.

B. Intercessory Prayer
(Daniel 9:3-7)

And I set my face unto the Lord God, to seek by prayer and supplications, with fasting, and sackcloth, and ashes: And I prayed unto the Lord my God, and made my confession, and said, O Lord, the great and dreadful God, keeping the covenant and mercy to them that love him, and to them that keep his commandments; We have sinned, and have committed iniquity, and have done wickedly, and have rebelled, even by departing from thy precepts and from thy judgments: Neither have we hearkened unto thy servants the prophets, which spake in thy name to our kings, our princes, and our fathers, and to all the people of the land. O Lord, righteousness belongeth unto thee, but unto us confusion of faces, as at this day; to the men of Judah, and to the inhabitants of Jerusalem, and unto all Israel, that are near, and that are far off, through all the countries whither thou hast driven them, because of their trespass that they have trespassed against thee.

"And I set my face unto the Lord God, to seek by prayer..." (Daniel 9:3). Daniel knew what to do when he discovered that the captivity was coming to an end. He prayed three times a day. We must realize that God's promises are to be plucked by serious prayer. God's promises are the ground on which we should, like Daniel, rest our hope. The verses we have here are a penitential prayer. In token of his deep humiliation before God for his own sins, the sins of his people, and his own sense of unworthiness, he prayed, fasted, and put on sackcloth.

Daniel prayed and made his confession to the Lord. Why did Daniel pray when God had already determined the time of release of His people? Do we need to pray when we know that God has revealed His will? Daniel prayed so that the release would materialize. He prayed so that the people would not fall back into sin, thereby prolonging their release. Daniel prayed because the suffering of his people must come to an end. When we pray, we must make confession, not only for the sins of which we are guilty (commonly called "confession"), but we also must make confession of our faith in God and dependence upon Him, our sorrow for sin, and our resolution against it.

Part of Daniel's prayer reads, "...O Lord, the great and dreadful God, keeping the covenant and mercy to them that love him, and to them that keep his commandments" (verse 4). In prayer, we should look both at God's greatness and His goodness, and His majesty and mercy in conjunction. If He is a God to be feared for His justice, He is one to be trusted for mercy. In this prayer, Daniel made mention of those who received answers to their prayers. These are the ones who love God and keep His commandments. Daniel helps us to understand that one may profess to love God through words, but not demonstrate that love through actions. True love for God entails fidelity to His commandments.

There are two elements of penitent prayer: first is admission of guilt and the willingness to forsake our sin completely. "We have sinned..." (verse 5).

The second element involves naming the sin. "We ...have committed iniquity..." (verse 5). This means we have sinned in every way. "We ...have done wickedly" means that "we have arrogantly gone away from Your path." "We have rebelled..." (verse 5). They had literally sinned with hard hearts and stiff necks. Daniel asserted that his people had departed from God's known precepts and from His judgments. They had violated the express laws God had given them via Moses and, second, had refused to be governed by them.

Israel's rebellion had caused them to harden their hearts toward the prophets God sent to them. "Neither have we hearkened unto thy servants the prophets, which spake in thy name to our kings, our princes, and our fathers, and to all the people of the land" (verse 6). Israel was like many people today who either ignore or mock God's messengers, failing to recognize the authority of the One for whom they speak. Thus, in rejecting the messenger, they end up rejecting the One who sent the message. Whenever God's people refuse to be warmed by the words of His messengers, He turns up the heat of adversity.

Daniel acknowledged the righteousness of God in dealing with those who had broken His laws. He did not accuse God of dealing with His people unjustly, but, rather, confessed that God was indeed just; and it was because of His holiness that He had allowed his people to be taken captive. Daniel affirmed the result of their sin—"confusion of faces." This was another way of saying "we are ashamed—shamed by our guilt and by our betrayal of trust." Their present calamity clearly demonstrated their guilt to the men of Judah, and to the inhabitants of Jerusalem and all Israel; for they had been all alike in their guilt before God. This shame belonged to all Israel and Judah. The result of sin and rebellion resulted in God's hand-delivering the Israelites to their enemies. They had no one else to blame. They alone had caused the problems that came upon them.

Whenever the people of God behave in such blatant and obstinate ways, we put the veracity of His Word to the test, to the extent that if God does not execute judgment upon us, it disproves the reliability of His Word. Does God chastise us today? Yes! The problem with us today is that we tend to cover up our pain, rather than repent before Him.

C. Plea for Deliverance
(Daniel 9:17-19)

Now therefore, O our God, hear the prayer of thy servant, and his supplications, and cause thy face to shine upon

thy sanctuary that is desolate, for the Lord's sake. O my God, incline thine ear, and hear; open thine eyes, and behold our desolations, and the city which is called by thy name: for we do not present our supplications before thee for our righteousnesses, but for thy great mercies. O Lord, hear; O Lord, forgive; O Lord, hearken and do; defer not, for thine own sake, O my God: for thy city and thy people are called by thy name.

"Now therefore, O our God, hear the prayer of thy servant, and his supplications, and cause thy face to shine…" (verse 17). When Daniel finished cataloging the various sins of the nation, he began this section with the word *now*. In effect, Daniel remembered the importance of confession. He remembered what Solomon said in 2 Chronicles 7:14: "If my people, who are called by my name, shall humble themselves and pray…."

Daniel was specific in putting God into remembrance of what God had promised for a different occasion. Isaiah 43:26 says, "Put me in remembrance…." In "reminding" God, he was not trying to wake God from sleep; rather, God wanted us to remind Him of His words. It was to help God's people to be conscious of Him being their all in all. Daniel wanted God to lift up the light of His countenance upon the people so that He would forgive their sins and thereby hasten their deliverance. Daniel prayed that God would hear his prayer and return them to Jerusalem, so that they could rebuild the temple that had been in ruins for a long time.

Daniel's was a prayer of agony. "O my God, incline thine ear, and hear; … for we do not present our supplications before thee for our righteousnesses, but for thy great mercies" (verse 18). Daniel appealed to God on the basis of His honor rather than on the basis of the needs of the people. He asked that God would take heed and listen to his prayer and that He would look down upon the state of His people, and upon His holy city that was in ruins, and respond in favor.

Daniel cried, "O Lord, hear; O Lord, forgive; O Lord, hearken and do…" (verse 19). These short repetitions, characteristic of Hebrew writings, show the intense fervor of Daniel's pleadings as he prayed that God would not only hear and forgive, but also act quickly toward the deliverance of His people. Daniel implied that the seventy years were all but complete. "…defer not, for thine own sake, O my God" (Daniel 9:19). Daniel was asking God not for the sake of the people, but for the sake of His holy name. His appeal was to the mercy of God and to the ancient demonstrations of His favor to Israel and to the concern of His own glory in their interests.

Daniel's prayer demonstrates to us that God gives us the privilege not only to pray, but also to plead; this is not to move Him, as He knows what He will do, but to move ourselves, to excite our fervency, and to encourage our faith. But notice, also, that the basis for our pleadings is never our works of righteousness, as we have none; rather, it is based upon His righteousness and His mercy. When He extends His mercy and forgiveness to us in our lowliness, He demonstrates the exceeding abundance of His greatness.

III. CONCLUDING REFLECTIONS

Like all Old Testament prophets, Daniel had a great impact on his own era. In Daniel, we see God acting in grace in the lives of pagan individuals, to bring them into knowledge of Him. The apparent conversion of Nebuchadnezzar is among the most striking of all Old Testament events, particularly when contrasted with Pharaoh's response some thousand years earlier.

At the same time, Daniel must have had several very vital influences on the captive Israelites. His early example of commitment to God (Daniel 1) was an encouraging testimony to the fact that believers can remain true to their faith in a pagan culture and still find acceptance and even advancement. Rather than withdrawing from his world, Daniel influenced the course of history. Daniel's righteousness, described by Ezekiel as being legendary in his own day, stood to the exiles as a beacon, pointing them toward the way to live for God, no matter where they were.

One final influence on his own people and the present world comes from the prophetic sections of the book of Daniel (chapters 7-12).

Daniel ministered effectively to his generation, and today we are still influenced by his prophetic utterances. Each of us is writing history in the annals of life. We are born to serve God and leave a legacy to those who come after us, so that they will want to know and serve our God.

PRAYER

Most gracious and faithful God, our heavenly Father, we join Daniel in bowing down before Your presence, acknowledging You as the one living and true God. Help us, we pray, to dutifully exercise the priestly privilege of praying for others, as others have surely prayed for us. In Jesus' name, we pray. Amen.

WORD POWER

Confession (Hebrew: *yada;* Greek: *homologeo*)—both Hebrew and Greek carry the same idea. The word is an admission of sin, or acknowledgment of one's sin. It also means saying the same thing. Whatever God declares as sin, let us agree with God. Some call sin alternative behavior; but that is not in agreement with God's Word. We cannot give sin any other name.

HOME DAILY BIBLE READINGS
(April 21-27, 2008)

Daniel's Prayer for the People
- MONDAY, April 21: "The Assurance of Redemption" (Psalm 130)
- TUESDAY, April 22: "Preparing to Pray" (Daniel 9:1-3)
- WEDNESDAY, April 23: "A Righteous God" (Daniel 9:4-10)
- THURSDAY, April 24: "God's Response to Sin" (Daniel 9:11-14)
- FRIDAY, April 25: "Hear, O God" (Daniel 9:15-19)
- SATURDAY, April 26: "A Word Gone Out" (Daniel 9:20-23)
- SUNDAY, April 27: "God's Strong Covenant" (Daniel 9:24-27)

LESSON 10   May 4, 2008

THE TEMPLE REBUILT

DEVOTIONAL READING: **Psalm 84:1-4**
PRINT PASSAGE: **Haggai 1:1-4, 7-10, 12-15**

BACKGROUND SCRIPTURE: **Haggai 1, Ezra 5**
KEY VERSE: **Haggai 1:8**

Haggai 1:1-4, 7-10, 12-15—KJV

IN THE second year of Darius the king, in the sixth month, in the first day of the month, came the word of the LORD by Haggai the prophet unto Zerubbabel the son of Shealtiel, governor of Judah, and to Joshua the son of Josedech, the high priest, saying,

2 Thus speaketh the LORD of hosts, saying, This people say, The time is not come, the time that the LORD's house should be built.

3 Then came the word of the LORD by Haggai the prophet, saying,

4 Is it time for you, O ye, to dwell in your cieled houses, and this house lie waste?

. . . . .

7 Thus saith the LORD of hosts; Consider your ways.

8 Go up to the mountain, and bring wood, and build the house; and I will take pleasure in it, and I will be glorified, saith the LORD.

9 Ye looked for much, and, lo, it came to little; and when ye brought it home, I did blow upon it. Why? saith the LORD of hosts. Because of mine house that is waste, and ye run every man unto his own house.

10 Therefore the heaven over you is stayed from dew, and the earth is stayed from her fruit.

. . . . .

12 Then Zerubbabel the son of Shealtiel, and Joshua the son of Josedech, the high priest, with all the remnant of the people, obeyed the voice of the LORD their God, and the words of Haggai the prophet, as the LORD their God had sent him, and the people did fear before the LORD.

13 Then spake Haggai the LORD's messenger in the LORD's message unto the people, saying, I am with you, saith the LORD.

14 And the LORD stirred up the spirit of Zerubbabel the son of Shealtiel, governor of Judah, and the spirit of Joshua the son of Josedech, the high priest, and the spirit of all the remnant of the people; and they came and did work in the house of the LORD of hosts, their God,

15 In the four and twentieth day of the sixth month, in the second year of Darius the king.

Haggai 1:1-4, 7-10, 12-15—NRSV

IN THE second year of King Darius, in the sixth month, on the first day of the month, the word of the LORD came by the prophet Haggai to Zerubbabel son of Shealtiel, governor of Judah, and to Joshua son of Jehozadak, the high priest:

2 Thus says the LORD of hosts: These people say the time has not yet come to rebuild the Lord's house.

3 Then the word of the LORD came by the prophet Haggai, saying:

4 Is it a time for you yourselves to live in your paneled houses, while this house lies in ruins?

. . . . .

7 Thus says the LORD of hosts: Consider how you have fared.

8 Go up to the hills and bring wood and build the house, so that I may take pleasure in it and be honored, says the LORD.

9 You have looked for much, and, lo, it came to little; and when you brought it home, I blew it away. Why? says the LORD of hosts. Because my house lies in ruins, while all of you hurry off to your own houses.

10 Therefore the heavens above you have withheld the dew, and the earth has withheld its produce.

. . . . .

12 Then Zerubbabel son of Shealtiel, and Joshua son of Jehozadak, the high priest, with all the remnant of the people, obeyed the voice of the LORD their God, and the words of the prophet Haggai, as the LORD their God had sent him; and the people feared the LORD.

13 Then Haggai, the messenger of the LORD, spoke to the people with the LORD's message, saying, I am with you, says the LORD.

14 And the LORD stirred up the spirit of Zerubbabel son of Shealtiel, governor of Judah, and the spirit of Joshua son of Jehozadak, the high priest, and the spirit of all the remnant of the people; and they came and worked on the house of the LORD of hosts, their God,

15 on the twenty-fourth day of the month, in the sixth month.

TOPICAL OUTLINE OF THE LESSON

I. Introduction
A. The Exiles' Misplaced Priority
B. Biblical Background

II. Exposition and Application of the Scripture
A. Haggai and the Word of the Lord (Haggai 1:1-4)
B. The Command to Rebuild (Haggai 1:7-10)
C. The People's Obedience (Haggai 1:12-15)

III. Concluding Reflections

LESSON OBJECTIVES

Upon completion of this lesson, the students will know:

1. How one's priorities reveal one's true beliefs;
2. How misplaced priorities lead to a loss of spiritual well-being; and,
3. How placing God first leads to personal blessings in all areas of our lives.

POINTS TO BE EMPHASIZED

ADULT/YOUTH
Adult Topic: **First Things First!**
Youth Topic: **Rebuild!**
Adult Key Verse: **Haggai 1:8**
Youth Key Verse: **Haggai 1:4**
Print Passage: **Haggai 1:1-4, 7-10, 12-15**

—Haggai delivered his prophetic message calling upon the leadership and the people to rebuild the temple.
—Rebuilding the temple was a powerful, symbolic act that revealed the priorities of the people.
—The Israelites returned from Babylonian captivity with great anticipation and enthusiasm for rebuilding, yet the obstacles they faced discouraged them.
—The people experienced difficulties as a direct result of their disobedience to God.
—After Cyrus, ruler of the Persian Empire, conquered Babylon, he issued a decree that allowed exiles to return to their homelands.

CHILDREN
Children Topic: **The People Go to Work**
Key Verse: **Haggai 1:14**
Print Passage: **Haggai 1:1-4, 7-10, 12-13**

—The Jews, upon returning to Jerusalem, were summoned to rebuild the temple to honor God.
—The returning exiles gave higher priority to their personal needs and desires than to their duty to rebuild God's house.
—In order for God's vision for God's people to be successful, Zerubbabel and the people worked together.
—As the people obeyed God, God promised to be with them.

I. INTRODUCTION

A. The Exiles' Misplaced Priority

Daniel sought the face of the Lord for an end to the misery of those exiled. His prayers were answered, but as soon as they got back to their home country, the Israelites focused on their personal well-being rather than on what they had committed to do for the Lord. They returned to Judah in 538 B.C., some sixteen years before Haggai first spoke out.

They had come with the specific intention of rebuilding the ruined temple of their God. The people had quickly laid the foundation of the temple, but then enthusiasm had flagged. Their efforts shifted to preparing houses to live in and to clearing fields so crops might grow. For over a decade, work on the temple had been abandoned, and the funds they had brought with them for the building program were spent in a futile effort to make the little community self-sufficient.

In essence, the people of Judah had forgotten that it was the call of every believer to put God first. God's blessing follows full commitment, and that blessing cannot be found apart from it. Haggai's message, then, was a call to recommitment. It was an explanation of dashed hopes, for through Haggai, the Lord now explained what had been happening.

B. Biblical Background

When some of the exiles returned from Babylon, their priority was building the temple. The purpose of Haggai's ministry was to awaken the lazy people and encourage them to finish God's temple.

It was easy to get the work started after they first arrived in the Holy Land, because everyone was dedicated and enthusiastic. They rebuilt the altar and started the sacrifices again, and in 535 B.C., the foundation was laid for the new temple. But after months of trial and opposition, the work lagged and finally stopped. The children of God were determined to worship God, but there was considerable opposition to the work on the temple. It was not until 520 B.C. that the people took up the work again; and in 515 B.C. the temple was finally completed. It was the work of four godly men that finally brought the task to completion—Zerubbabel, the governor; Joshua, the high priest; and Haggai and Zechariah, the prophets (see Ezra 5:1 and 6:14).

In this book, we have four sermons from Haggai, and each of them has a specific date. In each message, Haggai points out a particular sin that will keep Israel, and us, from accomplishing God's will and finishing His work.

II. EXPOSITION AND APPLICATION OF THE SCRIPTURE

A. Haggai and the Word of the Lord
(Haggai 1:1-4)

IN THE second year of Darius the king, in the sixth month, in the first day of the month, came the word of the Lord by Haggai the prophet unto Zerubbabel the son of Shealtiel, governor of Judah, and to Joshua the son of Josedech, the high priest, saying, Thus speaketh the Lord of hosts, saying, This people say, The time is not come, the time that the Lord's house should be built. Then came the word of the Lord by Haggai the prophet, saying, Is it time for you, O ye, to dwell in your cieled houses, and this house lie waste?

Haggai began his message with specific dates "…in the sixth month, on the first day of the month" (verse 1). In terms of specificity, Haggai gave us historical fact which corresponds with secular history.

The Jews, having no king of their own, dated events among them by the reign of the world kings to whom they were subject. *Darius* was a common name for Persian kings, as was *Pharaoh* for kings of Egypt, and *Caesar* for kings of Rome.

Sixteen years had passed since the laying of the foundation for the temple, and the whole enterprise had come to a standstill. In the midst of this came the Word of the Lord through the prophet Haggai. He used God's name, *Jehovah,* which implies covenant title, and His unchangeableness. Using this name among the Jews would remind them of who God was. Haggai was attempting to emphasize that God was the One who was speaking.

Haggai was stirred up to speak to the governor as the civil leader, and to Jehozadak as the spiritual leader. He did this to establish them as his associates in giving God's commands. In essence, the priest, prophet, and ruler would jointly testify in God's name. *Zerubbabel* means

"one born in Babylon." He was the heir apparent to the throne of David, being the grandson of King Jehoiachin (1 Chronicles 3:17-19; cf. Matthew 1:12), where Jehoiachin is called *Jeconiah.*

Verse 2 begins with a declaration from the Most High through the prophet Haggai. It is a high honor to be a spokesperson for the Most High God. "Thus speaketh the Lord of hosts," is a prophetic response common in the Old Testament. Such a phrase was intended to get the attention of the people. It was to say that this message was from the Lord of hosts (literally, "the Lord *[Yahweh]* of armies").

Haggai used another title, "the LORD Almighty," fourteen times. Haggai wanted the Jews to understand the gravity of their misplaced priority. The phrase "this people" was used to remind them that they were formally God's people but because they had put God's work aside, they were now referred to as "this people." Haggai did not say, "my" people, since these people had neglected the service of God.

What exactly did they think? Inwardly they said, "…the time is not come, the time that the LORD's house should be built" (verse 2). They believed that the proper time for rebuilding the temple had not come.

The Lord did not take kindly to their idleness in building His temple. They had no excuse for having abandoned this important project. They had become selfish, and their priorities were misplaced. God displayed His love by sending a serious warning to them. Then came the Word of the Lord by Haggai the prophet (Haggai 1:2, 4), saying, "The time is not come, the time that the Lord's house should be built…Is it time for you, O ye, to dwell in your cieled houses, and this house lie waste?"

We must note here that the Lord did not rebuke them for building their paneled houses. He rebuked them for putting the Lord's work on hold to do so. Their enthusiasm for the Lord's house settled down and took a back seat to personal comfort as they became prosperous. They forgot the source of their blessing. Anyone who forgets the source of his or her blessing runs the risk of losing it.

B. The Command to Rebuild
(Haggai 1:7-10)

Thus saith the Lord of hosts; Consider your ways. Go up to the mountain, and bring wood, and build the house; and I will take pleasure in it, and I will be glorified, saith the Lord. Ye looked for much, and, lo, it came to little; and when ye brought it home, I did blow upon it. Why? saith the Lord of hosts. Because of mine house that is waste, and ye run every man unto his own house. Therefore the heaven over you is stayed from dew, and the earth is stayed from her fruit.

As stressed earlier, the prophet Haggai was very specific. He used verbs quite accurately, such as we see in this section. "Thus saith the LORD of hosts; Consider your ways. Go up to the mountain…" (verses 7-8). There are two important verbs that arrest our attention, the first one being *consider*. In this context, the word *consider* is a command. The prophet, as a spokesman for God, commanded them to *consider*. It was an order, and they were expected to carry it out.

They were also to "go up to the mountain." The word *go* is also a command. They were to stand up and go to a specific place where the right wood for building was located. Haggai specifies this as being the first necessary action, but not to the exclusion of obtaining other materials. Stones were also needed. Either the old walls were not standing, or the new walls were only partly built.

When the people obeyed the commands and carried out God's Word to precision, God said, "I will take pleasure in it, and I will be glorified" (verse 8). In neglecting the temple, which was the mirror of God's presence, they had dishonored God. In completing the building project, they would glorify God.

Verse 9 should resonate with all believers who are serving God at their own convenience. It is the Lord's pleasure for His children to have peace all around; however, we serve God haphazardly and we expect Him to say *amen* to us. This is the crux of this verse. "Ye looked for much," (verse 9) means that, literally, they looked to see great dividends, but their reward was small. The word *look* is cast in the Hebrew infinitive, which means "continued looking." They had hoped to be blessed and accumulate much even though they were neglecting the temple. Verse 8 reminds us that the greater the Israelites' greediness, the more bitter their disappointment would be.

"…and lo, it came to little, and when ye brought it home, I did blow upon it" (verse 9). This was the reason why Haggai commanded them to consider and take stock and see how their gains were made for the wind. The Lord caused their situation to be stressful. They worked hard, but there was no blessing from the Lord. The irony is that even the little crop that they brought into their barns quickly dissipated.

With His mere breath, God caused even the little gain they did receive to scatter and perish like blighted corn. God's unfinished house was the reason for the problems of the people. Their priority was their own houses, but theirs was a misplaced priority.

Heaven ought to open for children of God, but according to their deeds, "…the heaven over you is stayed from dew and the earth is stayed from her fruit" (verse 10). In essence, heaven or the sky is personified (given human qualities or characteristics). The statement implies that even inanimate nature obeyed Jehovah's will and would withhold its goods from the people (see Jeremiah 2:12-13).

C. The People's Obedience
(Haggai 1:12-15)

Then Zerubbabel the son of Shealtiel, and Joshua the son of Josedech, the high priest, with all the remnant of the people, obeyed the voice of the Lord their God, and the words of Haggai the prophet, as the Lord their God had sent him, and the people did fear before the Lord. Then spake Haggai the Lord's messenger in the Lord's message unto the people, saying, I am with you, saith the Lord And the Lord stirred up the spirit of Zerubbabel the son of Shealtiel, governor of Judah, and the spirit of Joshua the son of Josedech, the high priest, and the spirit of all the remnant of the people; and they came and did work in the house of the Lord of hosts, their God, In the four and twentieth day of the sixth month, in the second year of Darius the king.

It was the prophet Samuel who made a classic statement after Saul failed to fully carry out the order to destroy the Amalakites. He said, "To obey is better than sacrifice…" (1 Samuel 15:22). Unlike Saul, the people obeyed the word of the prophet. Obedience has always been the pillar of true relationship with God.

There are three types of obedience:

1. *Partial obedience.* This type of obedience is obeying only part of the instruction that has been given.

2. *Postponed obedience.* This type could also be termed as delayed obedience. In this case, the instruction is well received, but it may be pushed back to be done at a convenient time. Such was the obedience of Governor Felix (see Acts 24:25).

3. *Full obedience.* This is the kind of obedience which carries out instructions to the letter. According to this section, the remnant of the people, that is, all those who had returned from the exile, obeyed the voice of the Lord.

All the people carried out the instruction by going to the mountains to get the wood. We read, "…and the people did fear before the LORD" (Haggai 1:7-9). Verse fourteen captures the essence of their obedience: "And the LORD stirred up the spirit of Zerubbabel the son of Sheatiel, governor of Judah, and the spirit of Joshua the son of Josedech, the high priest, and the spirit of all the remnant of the people; and they came and did work…."

They collected the wood and stones and other materials (compare with Haggai 1:8) for the work. They did not actually build or lay the secondary foundations of the temple; for this was not done until three months afterwards. It was done on the twenty-fourth day of the ninth month (Haggai 2:18). God gave them enthusiasm and perseverance in the good work, although they were slothful in their own endeavors.

God is honored and people are blessed when we obey Him. In his preciseness, Haggai said, "On the four and twentieth day of the sixth month, in the second year of Darius the king…" (verse 15). This was when the people heard the word, thought about it, and started to work in full obedience.

III. CONCLUDING REFLECTIONS

There are some parallels to be drawn here between the experience of God's people of old and His people today. Any efforts on the part of God's people to build His house would encounter various forms of opposition. When the Jews encountered opposition from those on the outside, they readily abandoned the temple effort and turned their efforts to building their own houses. Shortly thereafter, by divine intervention, the opposition was made to cease. However, rather than returning to the work of building God's house, they continued in the work not only of building, but also of adorning of their own houses.

We witness the same things happening today in the church. Whenever God's people set out to build a house for God, there is always opposition from the outside—purchasing land, getting bank loans, obtaining building permits, meeting or changing zoning requirements, and so forth. It is a common scene to see sites with signs proclaiming "the future home" of various churches, but to see no progress for years. Sometimes there may even be large holes where the foundation was laid, but the walls never go up.

God is appealing to us: "Consider your ways…Ye looked for much, and lo, it came to little; and when ye brought it home, I did blow upon it…" (Haggai 1:7, 9). The Jews were finally moved by the Word of the Lord, and God favored them. As soon as they obeyed, God promised His presence.

PRAYER

Gracious, merciful, eternal God, our Father, we praise You for dwelling among us and granting us the privilege of drawing nigh to Thee. Help us to so honor Your presence by putting You first in all that we say and do. In Christ's name, we pray. Amen.

WORD POWER

Obey (Hebrew: *shama*)—this word means to hear, to listen with the intention of carrying out the instruction or command. There is delayed obedience; there is postponed obedience, of which Governor Felix was a typical example; and finally there is full obedience. In the context of this lesson, the remnant of the people fully obeyed the Lord.

HOME DAILY BIBLE READINGS

(April 28—May 4, 2008)

The Temple Rebuilt

MONDAY, April 28: "In God's House" (Psalm 84:1-4)

TUESDAY, April 29: "Time to Rebuild the Temple" (Haggai 1:1-11)

WEDNESDAY, April 30: "The Work Begins" (Haggai 1:12-15)

THURSDAY, May 1: "Rebuilding the Foundation" (Ezra 3:8-13)

FRIDAY, May 2: "Help Rejected" (Ezra 4:1-4)

SATURDAY, May 3: "The Rebuilding Questioned" (Ezra 5:1-5)

SUNDAY, May 4: "The Decree of King Cyrus" (Ezra 5:6-17)

LESSON 11   May 11, 2008

REBUILDING THE WALL

DEVOTIONAL READING: **Psalms 137:1-7; 138:1-5**
PRINT PASSAGE: **Nehemiah 2:1-8, 11, 17-18**

BACKGROUND SCRIPTURE: **Nehemiah 1:1–2:20**
KEY VERSE: **Nehemiah 2:18**

Nehemiah 2:1-8, 11, 17-18—KJV

AND IT came to pass in the month Nisan, in the twentieth year of Artaxerxes the king, that wine was before him: and I took up the wine, and gave it unto the king. Now I had not been beforetime sad in his presence.

2 Wherefore the king said unto me, Why is thy countenance sad, seeing thou art not sick? this is nothing else but sorrow of heart. Then I was very sore afraid,

3 And said unto the king, Let the king live for ever: why should not my countenance be sad, when the city, the place of my fathers' sepulchres, lieth waste, and the gates thereof are consumed with fire?

4 Then the king said unto me, For what dost thou make request? So I prayed to the God of heaven.

5 And I said unto the king, If it please the king, and if thy servant have found favour in thy sight, that thou wouldest send me unto Judah, unto the city of my fathers' sepulchres, that I may build it.

6 And the king said unto me, (the queen also sitting by him,) For how long shall thy journey be? and when wilt thou return? So it pleased the king to send me; and I set him a time.

7 Moreover I said unto the king, If it please the king, let letters be given me to the governors beyond the river, that they may convey me over till I come into Judah;

8 And a letter unto Asaph the keeper of the king's forest, that he may give me timber to make beams for the gates of the palace which appertained to the house, and for the wall of the city, and for the house that I shall enter into. And the king granted me, according to the good hand of my God upon me.

…..

11 So I came to Jerusalem, and was there three days.

…..

Nehemiah 2:1-8, 11, 17-18—NRSV

IN THE month of Nisan, in the twentieth year of King Artaxerxes, when wine was served him, I carried the wine and gave it to the king. Now, I had never been sad in his presence before.

2 So the king said to me, "Why is your face sad, since you are not sick? This can only be sadness of the heart." Then I was very much afraid.

3 I said to the king, "May the king live forever! Why should my face not be sad, when the city, the place of my ancestors' graves, lies waste, and its gates have been destroyed by fire?"

4 Then the king said to me, "What do you request?" So I prayed to the God of heaven.

5 Then I said to the king, "If it pleases the king, and if your servant has found favor with you, I ask that you send me to Judah, to the city of my ancestors' graves, so that I may rebuild it."

6 The king said to me (the queen also was sitting beside him), "How long will you be gone, and when will you return?" So it pleased the king to send me, and I set him a date.

7 Then I said to the king, "If it pleases the king, let letters be given me to the governors of the province Beyond the River, that they may grant me passage until I arrive in Judah;

8 and a letter to Asaph, the keeper of the king's forest, directing him to give me timber to make beams for the gates of the temple fortress, and for the wall of the city, and for the house that I shall occupy." And the king granted me what I asked, for the gracious hand of my God was upon me.

…..

11 So I came to Jerusalem and was there for three days.

…..

When a person of vision is in charge of a task, people will join in the work with a passion. How do we discern a worthy vision and recognize a visionary leader? God gave Nehemiah a vision of rebuilding the walls of Jerusalem and the leadership ability to seek the king's favor and motivate people to work.

17 Then said I unto them, Ye see the distress that we are in, how Jerusalem lieth waste, and the gates thereof are burned with fire: come, and let us build up the wall of Jerusalem, that we be no more a reproach.

18 Then I told them of the hand of my God which was good upon me; as also the king's words that he had spoken unto me. And they said, Let us rise up and build. So they strengthened their hands for this good work.

17 Then I said to them, "You see the trouble we are in, how Jerusalem lies in ruins with its gates burned. Come, let us rebuild the wall of Jerusalem, so that we may no longer suffer disgrace."

18 I told them that the hand of my God had been gracious upon me, and also the words that the king had spoken to me. Then they said, "Let us start building!" So they committed themselves to the common good.

TOPICAL OUTLINE OF THE LESSON

I. **Introduction**
   A. Nehemiah Receives Bad News
   B. Biblical Background

II. **Exposition and Application of the Scripture**
   A. Nehemiah's Prayer Answered (Nehemiah 2:1-6)
   B. Nehemiah Makes a Request (Nehemiah 2:7-8)
   C. Nehemiah Views the Wall (Nehemiah 2:11)
   D. Invitation to Rebuild the Walls (Nehemiah 2:17-18)

III. **Concluding Reflections**

LESSON OBJECTIVES

Upon completion of this lesson, the students will know that:

1. Godly leaders rely upon God for direction and guidance;
2. Humility, patience, and wisdom are hallmarks of a godly leader;

3. Having a good reputation among those outside of the faith is an invaluable asset for the Kingdom; and,
4. God functions at different levels to achieve His divine purposes.

POINTS TO BE EMPHASIZED

ADULT/YOUTH

Adult Topic: **Following a Visionary Leader!**

Youth Topic: **Rebuild!**

Adult Key Verse: **Nehemiah 2:18**

Youth Key Verse: **Nehemiah 2:17**

Print Passage: **Nehemiah 2:1-8, 11, 17-18**

—Nehemiah was so concerned about the state of ruin of Jerusalem that he left a palace job to return to Jerusalem with the risky mission of rebuilding the wall.

—Nehemiah was willing to use his influence to help his people and not just himself.

—By rebuilding, God's people were publicly demonstrating their faithfulness to God.

CHILDREN

Children Topic: **Nehemiah Sees a Need**

Key Verse: **Nehemiah 2:8b**

Print Passage: **Nehemiah 2:1-8, 11, 17-18**

—Nehemiah was called by God to provide the leadership necessary for rebuilding the temple wall.

—Nehemiah approached rebuilding the wall with divine inspiration, dedication and preparation.

INTRODUCTION

A. Nehemiah Receives Bad News

God moves in mysterious ways in order to carry out His purposes. God, in His foreknowledge of all things, placed Nehemiah in the palace of the king of Persia. While serving at the Persian winter palace in Susa, in the month of Kislev (which is in November and December), Nehemiah received a report from his brother and several other men who had recently come from Judah. They told him of the desolate and disgraceful state of the holy city. They told him that the walls of the city were broken down and that the gates had been burned, leaving the city defenseless against enemy attacks, among other things.

They informed him of how the people had begun rebuilding the walls (Ezra 4:12) but were stopped by Artaxerxes, who was pressured by the Samaritans. On receiving this dismal report, Nehemiah sat down and wept (cf. Ezra 10:1). He resolved to pray and fast for a number of days and seek guidance from God as to what he should do. His praying was continual, "day and night" (Nehemiah 1:6). While Nehemiah was praying, his burden, Jerusalem, became greater and his vision of what needed to be done became clearer.

B. Biblical Background

Nehemiah was the son of Hachaliah (Nehemiah 1:1) and probably part of the tribe of Judah. He was one of the "Jews of the dispersion," and a cupbearer at the palace of Shushan. The position was one of great responsibility and trust. The officer's chief responsibility was to guard the king's person. Whether or not the cupbearer was also a eunuch is debatable. In the LXX (Septuagint) version of the Bible, Nehemiah is described as a "eunuch" instead of a "cupbearer." Whether he was a eunuch or not is unknown; but what is certain is that his position allowed him intimate contact with the king and queen.

The piety of his heart, his deeply religious spirit, and his constant sense of communion with and absolute dependence upon God, were strikingly exhibited throughout his dealings. These virtues can be seen, first, in the long prayer recorded in Nehemiah 1:5-11, and, second, and most remarkably, in what have been called his "interjectional prayers." These were short but moving addresses to almighty God which occur frequently in his writings. Therein is revealed the instinctive outpouring of a heart deeply moved, but ever resting itself upon God. Nehemiah looked to God alone for aid in trouble, for the frustration of evil designs, and for final reward and acceptance.

Nehemiah demonstrated the true spirit of a compatriot. He heard that the situation in Jerusalem had deteriorated—in particular that the wall around the city had collapsed. In essence, Jerusalem had no protection against vandals. Nehemiah did more than lament; he took action. He used his position before the king to ask for a leave of absence to go back to his homeland and work for the Lord.

II. EXPOSITION AND APPLICATION OF THE SCRIPTURE

A. Nehemiah's Prayer Answered
(Nehemiah 2:1-6)

AND it came to pass in the month Nisan, in the twentieth year of Artaxerxes the king, that wine was before him: and I took up the wine, and gave it unto the king. Now I had not been beforetime sad in his presence. Wherefore the king said unto me, Why is thy countenance sad, seeing thou art not sick? this is nothing else but sorrow of heart. Then I was very sore afraid, And said unto the king, Let the king live for ever: why should not my countenance be sad, when the city, the place of my fathers' sepulchres, lieth waste, and the gates thereof are consumed with fire? Then the king said unto me, For what dost thou make request? So I prayed to the God of heaven. And I said unto the king, If it please the king, and if thy servant have found favour in thy sight, that thou wouldest send me unto Judah, unto the city of my fathers' sepulchres, that I may build it. And the king said unto me, (the queen also sitting by him,) For how long shall thy journey be? and when wilt thou return? So it pleased the king to send me; and I set him a time.

In this section, Nehemiah tells us the exact month when he made the move to approach the king. "Nisan" corresponds to our March-April. Nehemiah knew the time to present his case. It was done when the king's "wine was before him: and I took up the wine and gave it unto the king." The cupbearers were very careful to follow every detail in carrying out their duties. So, as was customary, the wine was brought in and placed before the king. Nehemiah then washed the cup in the king's presence, and poured a little of the wine in his left hand and drank it in the king's presence. This was done to ensure that the wine was safe for the king to drink.

Satan always has a way to bring fear; he is the author of confusion. Nehemiah said, "Then I was very sore afraid" (verse 2). Servants were not permitted to look sad or express any negative emotions while in the king's presence, for this might suggest dissatisfaction with the king (Esther 4:2). To do so might jeopardize Nehemiah's position, or even his life.

The king recognized the face of his chief cupbearer and asked, "... Why is thy countenance sad, seeing thou art not sick? this is nothing else but sorrow of heart" (Nehemiah 2:2). The king was unaccustomed to seeing his cupbearer looking sad; he was struck by the dejection on Nehemiah's face. Prior to this occasion, Nehemiah had not been in the king's presence with a sad countenance.

We see the hand of God moving in the affairs of history behind the scenes. The king could have asked that Nehemiah be removed immediately; instead, God used Nehemiah's condition to work behind the scenes.

Nehemiah knew that his request was a bold one. As already stated, a few years earlier this same king had stopped the rebuilding of Jerusalem; now, Nehemiah was going to ask that the order be reversed. The cupbearer was, in fact, risking his life.

Without reflection upon any person, and with all the respect, deference, and good-will imaginable toward the king, his master, Nehemiah said, customarily, "Let the king live for ever: why should not my countenance be sad, when the city, the place of my fathers' sepulchres, lieth waste…?" (verse 3).

Nehemiah called Jerusalem "the place of his fathers' sepulchres"—the place where his ancestors were buried. All nations, even those that had no expectation of the resurrection of the dead, had looked upon the sepulchers of their ancestors as sacred, to some degree, and not to be violated. It was, perhaps, with this idea in mind that he responded, justifying himself in his grief. As mortals, there is a time to be sad and to show grief. He assigned the ruins of Jerusalem as the true cause of his grief.

A word of instruction is in order here: Whenever the house of God is in a state of disrepair or desolation, it ought to be a matter of grief and sadness to all that have a concern for God's honor—all who are living members of Christ's mystical body.

B. Nehemiah Makes a Request (Nehemiah 2:7-8)

Moreover I said unto the king, If it please the king, let letters be given me to the governors beyond the river, that they may convey me over till I come into Judah; And a letter unto Asaph the keeper of the king's forest, that he may give me timber to make beams for the gates of the palace which appertained to the house, and for the wall of the city, and for the house that I shall enter into. And the king granted me, according to the good hand of my God upon me.

"Then the king said unto me, For what dost thou make request?" (verse 4). Artaxerxes's heart responded to Nehemiah's statements. So he asked Nehemiah what he could do as king to remedy the situation. With Judea being a Persian province, the cupbearer may have reasoned that perhaps the king would now be sensitive to Jerusalem's condition. "So I prayed to the God of heaven" (verse 4). Between the king's question (verse 4) and Nehemiah's answer (verse 5), the cupbearer breathed a brief prayer. This short prayer, whatever its unvoiced words were, built on his praying for four months. It is good to pray on all occasions.

Nehemiah is a good example of how believers should relate to unsaved officials as they seek to do the work of God. Nehemiah respected the king and sought to work within the lines of authority that existed in the empire. He didn't

say, "I have a commission from the Lord to go to Jerusalem, and I'm going whether you like it or not!" When it comes to matters of conscience, we must always obey God rather than human beings (Acts 5:29). But even in our dealings with human authority, we must show respect (see Romans 13 and 1 Peter 2:13-25). Daniel and his friends took the same approach as did Nehemiah, and God honored them as well (Daniel 1).

As the Persian monarchs did not permit their wives to be present at their state festivals, this must have been a private occasion. Nehemiah 2:6 states that the king asked, "For how long shall thy journey be? And when wilt thou return?" This question indicated that the king would give his permission. Nehemiah responded immediately with a specific time frame, again indicating forethought on his part. Originally, this may have been a short time that was later extended; for he remained in Jerusalem twelve years (5:14) and then returned to the king for several years (13:6).

Nehemiah then asked for the biggest favor yet. Knowing he would face opposition from his enemies, he requested letters of permission from the king to allow him to pass through the various provinces in the Trans-Euphrates, the large area west of the Euphrates River. Artaxerxes's permission to rebuild the city of Jerusalem was the decree Daniel had prophesied ninety-five years earlier in 539 B.C., the decree "to restore and build Jerusalem" (Daniel 9:25), which was to begin after the seventy weeks of prophetic years of Daniel (Daniel 9:24-27).

Again, we see here the hand of the almighty God at work in the life of a visionary leader. The king granted the request of Nehemiah. Nehemiah did not claim the glory; rather, he said, "according to the good hand of my God upon me" (Nehemiah 2:8). Though Nehemiah had worked diligently to prepare himself for the time when he would have opportunity to share his burden with the king, and though he demonstrated unusual wisdom in responding to the king's questions, he knew that ultimately his success depended on God's help.

C. Nehemiah Views the Wall
(Nehemiah 2:11)

So I came to Jerusalem, and was there three days.

"So I came to Jerusalem, and was there three days..." (verse 11). Nehemiah knew there was no way he could share with the people in Jerusalem what God led him to accomplish without first doing some research and planning. After taking time (three days), presumably to think, pray, and get acquainted with some people there, he then made a careful survey of the walls to analyze the situation. He did so at night, apparently to avoid letting others know his plans before they were firmly fixed in his mind.

During these night hours, he gained perspective and, as outlined in chapter 3, developed an effective plan to accomplish the task he had come to Jerusalem to perform. What looked like an impossible situation became possible for Nehemiah. A leader should be wise to pray and plan for any project before its execution. When there is clear direction from the Lord, even though opposition may come, one can rest assured that God is still the same.

D. Invitation to Rebuild the Walls
(Nehemiah 2:17-18)

Then said I unto them, Ye see the distress that we are in, how Jerusalem lieth waste, and the gates thereof are burned with fire: come, and let us build up the wall of Jerusalem, that we be no more a reproach. Then I told them of the hand of my God which was good upon me; as also the king's words that he had spoken unto me. And they said, Let us rise up and build. So they strengthened their hands for this good work.

"Then said I unto them, Ye see the distress that we are in, how Jerusalem lieth waste, and the gates thereof are burned with fire... (verse 17). Nehemiah refrained from assigning blame for the situation, and he included himself in the general plight. "Come, and let us build up the wall of Jerusalem, that we be no more a reproach" (verse 17). After Nehemiah had completed his secret survey and was satisfied that he had developed a workable plan, the time had come to reveal to the Jews why he was in Jerusalem. First, he challenged them to notice their deplorable circumstances, which had brought them trouble and disgrace (cf. Nehemiah 1:3). Then he challenged them to rebuild the walls of Jerusalem (Nehemiah 2:18). A visionary leader must learn how to get others to do what they otherwise would not be inclined to do.

"Then I told them of the hand of my God which was good upon me; as also the king's words that he had spoken unto me" (Nehemiah 2:18). Nehemiah followed his exhortation to them with a personal testimony as to how God's gracious hand (cf. 2:8) had granted him favor before King Artaxerxes. What a climax this must have been to his speech! None in Israel could deny the direct providence of God in reversing Artaxerxes's decree in Ezra 4:23.

When Nehemiah gave his challenge, the effect was immediate and wholehearted. The people's negative feelings became positive. Despair turned to hope. And they said, "Let us rise up and build..." (verse 18). So they strengthened their hands for this good work. The wall was finished fifty-two days later (Nehemiah 6:15).

III. CONCLUDING REFLECTIONS

Let us bear in mind that the word *visionary* is not found in the Bible; however, the concept is certainly there time and time again. A visionary leader, then, may be defined as "one whose vision is divinely empowered to discern things extra-physical." A visionary is one who receives messages that are spiritual in nature, invisible to the natural eye.

In the church age, a visionary leader is one to whom God has communicated through His Spirit, His will, and His way. The visionary, then, is one empowered to see what is not discernible to others. A visionary leader has the welfare of people in mind. A visionary leader is prayerful. A visionary leader refuses to quit when opposition mounts. Nehemiah faced serious opposition from the people he was protecting, but he refused to abandon the project at hand.

We have the responsibility of not only recognizing, but also of following God's visionary leaders. We must do so, aware of the fact that failure to follow God's leaders is, in effect, refusing to follow God Himself. On the contrary, when believers follow ungodly leadership, they participate in their sin and place themselves under the judgment that is coming to all false prophets.

PRAYER

Most wise and gracious God, our heavenly Father, thank You for continually providing us with godly, visionary leaders like Nehemiah. Help us to recognize those leaders whom You have placed among us today, and give us the humility to accept, follow, and support their leadership. In Jesus' name, we pray. Amen.

WORD POWER

Strengthened (Hebrew: *chazak* [khaw-zak])—this means to prevail, to be courageous, or to be resolute. The word is in *piel stem*, which expresses intense or intentional action. Therefore, all the people worked with Nehemiah intensely until the work was done. It is in the imperfect tense, which means that there was no break in their work until the walls came together.

HOME DAILY BIBLE READINGS
(May 5-11, 2008)

Rebuilding the Wall

MONDAY, May 5: "A Lament for Jerusalem" (Psalm 137:1-7)
TUESDAY, May 6: "Weeping and Fasting" (Nehemiah 1:1-4)
WEDNESDAY, May 7: "Nehemiah's Confession" (Nehemiah 1:5-11)
THURSDAY, May 8: "Permission to Return" (Nehemiah 2:1-10)
FRIDAY, May 9: "A Secret Inspection" (Nehemiah 2:11-16)
SATURDAY, May 10: "Determination to Rebuild" (Nehemiah 2:17-20)
SUNDAY, May 11: "Giving Thanks to God" (Psalm 138:1-5)

LESSON 12   May 18, 2008

UP AGAINST THE WALL

DEVOTIONAL READING: **Psalm 70**
PRINT PASSAGE: **Nehemiah 4:1-3, 7-9, 13-15; 6:15**

BACKGROUND SCRIPTURE: **Nehemiah 4–6**
KEY VERSE: **Nehemiah 4:6**

Nehemiah 4:1-3, 7-9, 13-15; 6:15—KJV

BUT IT came to pass, that when Sanballat heard that we builded the wall, he was wroth, and took great indignation, and mocked the Jews.
2 And he spake before his brethren and the army of Samaria, and said, What do these feeble Jews? will they fortify themselves? will they sacrifice? will they make an end in a day? will they revive the stones out of the heaps of the rubbish which are burned?
3 Now Tobiah the Ammonite was by him, and he said, Even that which they build, if a fox go up, he shall even break down their stone wall.

…..

7 But it came to pass, that when Sanballat, and Tobiah, and the Arabians, and the Ammonites, and the Ashdodites, heard that the walls of Jerusalem were made up, and that the breaches began to be stopped, then they were very wroth,
8 And conspired all of them together to come and to fight against Jerusalem, and to hinder it.
9 Nevertheless we made our prayer unto our God, and set a watch against them day and night, because of them.

…..

13 Therefore set I in the lower places behind the wall, and on the higher places, I even set the people after their families with their swords, their spears, and their bows.
14 And I looked, and rose up, and said unto the nobles, and to the rulers, and to the rest of the people, Be not ye afraid of them: remember the Lord, which is great and terrible, and fight for your brethren, your sons, and your daughters, your wives, and your houses.
15 And it came to pass, when our enemies heard that it was known unto us, and God had brought their counsel to nought, that we returned all of us to the wall, every one unto his work.

…..

15 So the wall was finished in the twenty and fifth day of the month Elul, in fifty and two days.

Nehemiah 4:1-3, 7-9, 13-15; 6:15—NRSV

NOW WHEN Sanballat heard that we were building the wall, he was angry and greatly enraged, and he mocked the Jews.
2 He said in the presence of his associates and of the army of Samaria, "What are these feeble Jews doing? Will they restore things? Will they sacrifice? Will they finish it in a day? Will they revive the stones out of the heaps of rubbish—and burned ones at that?"
3 Tobiah the Ammonite was beside him, and he said, "That stone wall they are building—any fox going up on it would break it down!"

…..

7 But when Sanballat and Tobiah and the Arabs and the Ammonites and the Ashdodites heard that the repairing of the walls of Jerusalem was going forward and the gaps were beginning to be closed, they were very angry,
8 and all plotted together to come and fight against Jerusalem and to cause confusion in it.
9 So we prayed to our God, and set a guard as a protection against them day and night.

…..

13 So in the lowest parts of the space behind the wall, in open places, I stationed the people according to their families, with their swords, their spears, and their bows.
14 After I looked these things over, I stood up and said to the nobles and the officials and the rest of the people, "Do not be afraid of them. Remember the LORD, who is great and awesome, and fight for your kin, your sons, your daughters, your wives, and your homes."
15 When our enemies heard that their plot was known to us, and that God had frustrated it, we all returned to the wall, each to his work.

…..

15 So the wall was finished on the twenty-fifth day of the month Elul, in fifty-two days.

UNIFYING LESSON PRINCIPLE

With every worthy cause come detractors—those who will ridicule or work against the cause. How can we carry on? Nehemiah and the Israelites found God's help to counteract the plots against them, and they continued the work on the wall, finishing it in record time.

TOPICAL OUTLINE OF THE LESSON

I. Introduction
A. The Enemies Scoff at Nehemiah's Plan
B. Biblical Background

II. Exposition and Application of the Scripture
A. Sanballat Mocks the Work (Nehemiah 4:1-3)
B. Sanballat's Conspiracy (Nehemiah 4:7-9)
C. Surveillances Set (Nehemiah 4:13-15)
D. Mission Accomplished! (Nehemiah 6:15)

III. Concluding Reflections

LESSON OBJECTIVES

Upon completion of this lesson, the students will know that:

1. The accomplishment of God-given tasks often involves challenges;
2. God provides inner and spiritual resources to accomplish His tasks; and,
3. Remaining steadfast in the face of detractors and relying on God for strength are the marks of a Christlike spirit.

POINTS TO BE EMPHASIZED

ADULT/YOUTH
Adult Topic: **Finishing the Task!**
Youth Topic: **Keep on Building**
Adult Key Verse: **Nehemiah 4:6**
Youth Key Verse: **Nehemiah 4:14**
Print Passage: **Nehemiah 4:1-3, 7-9, 13-15; 6:15**

—Nehemiah demonstrated uncommon honesty and integrity throughout the rebuilding process.
—Nehemiah's rebuilding project was a demonstration of faith and practical action in harmony.
—Although the narrative was written in the first person, the focus of the text was on what God achieved within the community.
—Internal and external threats to the building project and measures taken by Nehemiah to counter them illustrate the reality of human conflict and God's power to overcome it.
—Nehemiah responded to threats with prayers and by calling upon the community to rally.
—Sanballat's plots did not surprise or discourage Nehemiah.

CHILDREN
Children Topic: **The People Complete the Work**
Key Verse: **Nehemiah 4:6**
Print Passage: **Nehemiah 4:1-3, 7-9, 13-15; 6:15**

—Nehemiah had enemies who tried to sabotage the rebuilding of the wall.
—When others plotted against them, Nehemiah and the workers prayed and set up a guard.
—When our vision for action is motivated by our desire to implement God's plan, God will provide everything we need to be successful.
—Nehemiah believed that God could be trusted to give hope, power, and strength to those who were faithful.

I. INTRODUCTION

A. The Enemies Scoff at Nehemiah's Plan

Sanballat served as governor of Samaria in the latter half of the fifth century B.C. It was under his leadership that the Samaritan faction showed its bitter animosity toward the Jews, upon discovering the systematic design of refortifying Jerusalem. Their opposition was confined at first to scoffs and insults. The governors circulated all sorts of disparaging reflections that were intended to increase the feelings of hatred and contempt for the Jews among their party and acquaintances.

The insults referred to the weakness of the Jews with respect to their wealth and numbers; the absurdity of their purpose in trying to reconstruct the walls and celebrate the Feast of Dedication all in one day; the idea of raising the walls on their old foundations; and the use of the charred and moldering debris of the ruins as the materials to restore the buildings. Last, they were deemed to be foolish if they hoped that any wall they could raise would be strong enough to serve as a fortress of defense. Sanballat even went so far as to accuse Nehemiah of planning a rebellion against Persian rule, repeatedly summoning him to account for his actions (Nehemiah 6:1-7).

B. Biblical Background

After the death of David, Solomon built the temple for the Lord on Mount Moriah. He also greatly strengthened and adorned the city, and it became the great center of all the civil and religious affairs of the nation (Deuteronomy 12:5, 14; 14:23; 16:11-16; Psalm 122). After the disruption of the kingdom upon the accession of Rehoboam (the son of Solomon) to the throne, Jerusalem became the capital of Judah, the kingdom of the two tribes. Subsequently, the city was taken and retaken by the Egyptians, the Assyrians, and by the kings of Israel (2 Kings 14:13, 14; 2 Chronicles 12:9; 26:9). Finally, for the abounding iniquities of the nation, Jerusalem was taken and utterly destroyed by Nebuchadnezzar, and the Jews were taken to exile.

The books of Ezra and Nehemiah contain the history of the rebuilding of the city and the temple, and the restoration of the kingdom of the Jews, consisting of a portion of all the tribes. Within these pages falls the story of Nehemiah's unwavering dedication to the task God assigned to him. The restored kingdom lasted for two centuries under the dominion of Persia, until 331 B.C., and thereafter for about a century and a half under the rulers of the Greek empire in Asia, until 167 B.C.

For a century, the Jews maintained their independence under native rulers, the Asmonean princes. At the close of this period they fell under the rule of Herod and of members of his family, but they were practically under Rome until the time of the destruction of Jerusalem in A.D. 70.

II. EXPOSITION AND APPLICATION OF THE SCRIPTURE

A. Sanballat Mocks the Work
(Nehemiah 4:1-3)

BUT IT came to pass, that when Sanballat heard that we builded the wall, he was wroth, and took great indignation, and mocked the Jews. And he spake before his brethren and the army of Samaria, and said, What do these feeble Jews? will they fortify themselves? will they sacrifice? will they make an end in a day? will they revive the stones out of the heaps of the rubbish which are burned? Now Tobiah the Ammonite was by him, and he said, Even that which they build, if a fox go up, he shall even break down their stone wall.

The words *wroth* (furious) and *indignant*, when used together, mean "burning with rage." Sanballat was displeased when he heard that Nehemiah had returned to Jerusalem to help the Jews. His displeasure turned to intense anger, and he started to mock the Jews. He accused them of rebelling against King Artaxerxes (Nehemiah 2:19), and by a series of questions, he began to ridicule them.

Sanballat used his authority as governor of Samaria to attack the Jews with a verbal assault. Verse 2 reveals that Sanballat summoned his family members and the army of Samaria to attempt to weaken the Jews through open mockery. He quipped, "What do these feeble Jews?" (Nehemiah 4:2). The verb from which the adjective *feeble* was derived is used to describe a woman who was no longer able to bear children, or of the inhabitants of a defeated land (see Hosea 4:3).

In verse 2, Sanballat asked a series of questions in hopes of discouraging the Jews. "Will they fortify themselves?" The governor wondered how a remnant of feeble Jews could hope to build a wall strong enough to protect the city from an army. "Will they sacrifice?" That is, could they possibly complete the walls so that they could then give sacrifices of thanksgiving? This implies, "It will take more than prayer and worship to rebuild the city!" This question was blasphemy against Jehovah, for Sanballat was denying that God would help His people.

"Will they make an end in a day?" This reference to "a day" suggests that the Jews did not know the difficulty of the task and would soon call it quits. Verse 2 continues: "Will they revive the stones out of the heaps of rubbish which are burned?" And how, Sanballat asked, could they use burned, weakened bricks from the heaps of debris? The stones were taken out of the rubbish heaps and probably were so old and damaged that they would never last when set into the wall. In spite of what Sanballat said, there was still plenty of good material for the builders to use. One of the strongest materials was human will. The enemies were not able to bend the will of the Jewish people.

Tobiah joined in the mockery. He was one of the visiting dignitaries at the Samaritan army inspection standing nearby, and he joined Sanballat in the ridicule. His ridicule focused upon the finished product. Tobiah was even crueler in his joking when he said, "Even that which they build, if a fox go up, he shall even break down their stone wall" (verse 3). He was implying that even if they were able to build a wall, it would be so weak that a fox, weighing only a few pounds, would break it down.

Of course, much that Sanballat and Tobiah said was true from a human point of view; for the Jewish remnant was weak and poor, and the work was too great for them. But they had great faith in a great God—and that is what made the difference.

B. Sanballat's Conspiracy
(Nehemiah 4:7-9)

But it came to pass, that when Sanballat, and Tobiah, and the Arabians, and the Ammonites, and the Ashdodites, heard that the walls of Jerusalem were made up, and that the breaches began to be stopped, then they were very wroth, And conspired all of them together to come and to fight against Jerusalem, and to hinder it. Nevertheless we made our prayer unto our God, and set a watch against them day and night, because of them.

"But it came to pass, that when Sanballat, and Tobiah, and the Arabians, and the Ammonites, and the Ashodites, heard that the walls of Jerusalem were made up, and that the breaches began to be stopped, then they were very wroth" (verse 7). The Jewish workers' rapid progress naturally increased the threat to their enemies, who became very angry. They then decided to take more overt and corporate action.

The enemies of progress then increased from two to four. The city was now completely surrounded by enemies! To the north were Sanballat and the Samaritans; to the east, Tobiah and the Ammonites; to the south, Geshem and the Arabs; and to the west, the Ashdodites. Ashdod was perhaps the most important city in Philistia at that time, and the Philistines did not want to see a strong community in Jerusalem.

As the enemy saw the work progressing, they became angrier. A common enemy and a common cause brought four different groups together to stop the work on the walls of Jerusalem.

In Nehemiah 2:8, the detractors conspired to fight against Jerusalem. They never ran out of strategies for killing the progress of the Jews' work. As the detractors saw the work progressing, it became obvious that it would take more than ridicule to stop the Jewish people's improvement project. So, the enemies came together and planned a secret attack.

Nehemiah realized the danger ahead and that the enemy had increased; and he put the power of prayer to work. Nehemiah and the Jews prayed and watched the moves of the enemy. The corporate strategy of Judah's enemies was met by a corporate response. The people prayed to God for help. Nehemiah suspected that his enemies would launch an attack, so he set a watch against them day and night. The workers held both tools and weapons (Nehemiah 4:17) and were prepared to fight when the signal was given.

C. Surveillances Set
(Nehemiah 4:13-15)

Therefore set I in the lower places behind the wall, and on the higher places, I even set the people after their families with their swords, their spears, and their bows. And I looked, and rose up, and said unto the nobles, and to the rulers, and to the rest of the people, Be not ye afraid of them: remember the Lord, which is great and terrible, and fight for your brethren, your sons, and your daughters, your wives, and your houses. And it came to pass, when our enemies heard that it was known unto us, and God had brought their counsel to nought, that we returned all of us to the wall, every one unto his work.

Nehemiah wanted to make sure that there were no openings for the enemy to sneak into Jerusalem. He did not take chances. "Therefore set I in the lower places behind the wall, and on the higher places, I even set the people after their families with their swords, their spears, and their bows" (verse 13). There was no Jewish army, and Nehemiah did not anticipate these problems, so he enlisted every family to fight for their protection and future. This must have been a difficult decision for Nehemiah. To place whole families together—including women and children—put tremendous pressure on fathers, particularly.

In case of outright attack, they would have no choice but to stay and fight for and with their family members. But Nehemiah knew that it was the only decision he could make if they were to survive and succeed in rebuilding the walls. So, he armed entire families, knowing that they would stand together and encourage one another. The Jews not only repaired the walls near their own houses (Nehemiah 3:28-32), but they stood with their families to protect their homes and their city.

Nehemiah encouraged the officials and the people to fight courageously and confidently, knowing that the enemies were set to destroy them. Obviously, fear gripped the people. So Nehemiah gathered them together and spoke words of encouragement to them, charging them to face the situation courageously and to fight to save their families, remembering the great and awesome Lord who was on their side.

He reminded them that they were involved in a great work. After all, they were serving a great God and doing a great work rebuilding the walls of a great city. He also reminded them that they were not working alone, even though they could not see all of their fellow workers on the wall. God was with all of them and would come to their defense.

If we fear the Lord, we need not fear the enemy. Nehemiah's heart was captivated by the "great and terrible" God of Israel, and he knew that God was strong enough to meet the challenge. When we face a situation that creates fear in our hearts, we must remind ourselves of the greatness of God.

When the enemy learned that Jerusalem was armed and ready, they backed off (Nehemiah 4:15). God had frustrated their plot. "The LORD bringeth the counsel of the heathen to nought; he maketh the devices of the people of none effect. The counsel of the LORD standeth for ever, the thoughts of his heart to all generations" (Psalm 33:10-11). It is good to remind ourselves that the will of God comes from His heart, and that we need not be afraid.

D. Mission Accomplished! (Nehemiah 6:15)

So the wall was finished in the twenty and fifth day of the month Elul, in fifty and two days.

"So the wall was finished in the twenty and fifth day of the month Elul, in fifty and two days" (verse 15). Whatever has a beginning has an end. The wall was completed with God's help on the twenty-fifth day of Elul, which was about September 20th. The project began in the last few days of July and continued through August and into September.

The previous November-December (Kislev) was when Nehemiah had first heard about the problem (Nehemiah 1:1-3), and in March-April (Nisan), he presented his plan to the king (Nehemiah 2:5). The trip to Jerusalem took two or three months (April or May to June or July)—as long as or longer than the building program itself.

The enemies of God's work abound, but we must realize that any project started with the approval of God will be completed. God will gather both seen and unseen forces to carry out His plans.

III. CONCLUDING REFLECTIONS

When we engage in Kingdom work, we must be aware that we are in spiritual warfare. The Christian's battle is not against flesh and blood, but against Satan and his demonic forces that use flesh and blood to oppose the

Lord's work. Nevertheless, we have a Captain for whom we fight, a banner under which we fight, and certain rules of war by which we are to govern ourselves. Therefore, we must apply ourselves to the work that God has commissioned us to do as Christian soldiers.

If we hope to win the war and finish the work, we must use the spiritual equipment God has provided (Ephesians 6:10-18; 2 Corinthians 10:1-6). If we focus on the *visible* enemy alone and forget the *invisible* enemy, we are sure to start trusting our own resources—and this will lead to defeat.

We have seen, throughout all the lessons in this series, the importance the prophets' attachment to prayer, irrespective of the challenges they faced—whether it was a king like Nebuchadnezzar, jealous peers in the court, roaring lions in the den, or ridiculing adversaries. The prophets always faced their adversities in faith and with the spiritual weapon of prayer.

As we continue in our Christian pilgrimage, we must not lose focus on Christ the King. Therefore, let us heed the instructions of the apostle Paul and "Put on the whole armor of God" (Ephesians 6:11, NRSV).

PRAYER

Dear God, our heavenly Father, we praise You today as One whose presence cannot be contained within walls; yet as One who has come to dwell within our hearts. May we be empowered to remember always that our bodies are Your temples—may You be pleased to dwell therein. In Christ's name, we pray. Amen.

WORD POWER

Mind (Hebrew: *leb*)—we tend to think of the human mind as the place where thinking takes place, as opposed to the heart, where feelings are created. However, in the Old Testament, no separate words for *heart* and *mind* existed—heart and mind were the same thing. A person's mind is reflective of that person's entire inner self. The people of Nehemiah's time employed their entire selves to work for the Lord.

HOME DAILY BIBLE READINGS
(May 12-18, 2008)

Up Against the Wall

    MONDAY, May 12: "A Cry for Help" (Psalm 70)
    TUESDAY, May 13: "Mocking Enemies" (Nehemiah 4:1-6)
    WEDNESDAY, May 14: "A Plot to Confuse the Builders" (Nehemiah 4:7-11)
    THURSDAY, May 15: "The Plot Is Foiled" (Nehemiah 4:12-15)
    FRIDAY, May 16: "Always at the Ready" (Nehemiah 4:16-23)
    SATURDAY, May 17: "Attempts to Stop the Building" (Nehemiah 6:1-14)
    SUNDAY, May 18: "The Wall Is Finished" (Nehemiah 6:15-19)

LESSON 13   May 25, 2008

CALL TO RENEW THE COVENANT

DEVOTIONAL READING: **Psalms 19:7-14; 27:11-14**   BACKGROUND SCRIPTURE: **Nehemiah 8**
PRINT PASSAGE: **Nehemiah 8:1-3, 5-6,**   KEY VERSE: **Nehemiah 8:3**
13-14, 17-18

Nehemiah 8:1-3, 5-6, 13-14, 17-18—KJV

AND ALL the people gathered themselves together as one man into the street that was before the water gate; and they spake unto Ezra the scribe to bring the book of the law of Moses, which the LORD had commanded to Israel.

2 And Ezra the priest brought the law before the congregation both of men and women, and all that could hear with understanding, upon the first day of the seventh month.

3 And he read therein before the street that was before the water gate from the morning until midday, before the men and the women, and those that could understand; and the ears of all the people were attentive unto the book of the law.

.....

5 And Ezra opened the book in the sight of all the people; (for he was above all the people;) and when he opened it, all the people stood up:

6 And Ezra blessed the LORD, the great God. And all the people answered, Amen, Amen, with lifting up their hands: and they bowed their heads, and worshipped the LORD with their faces to the ground.

.....

13 And on the second day were gathered together the chief of the fathers of all the people, the priests, and the Levites, unto Ezra the scribe, even to understand the words of the law.

14 And they found written in the law which the LORD had commanded by Moses, that the children of Israel should dwell in booths in the feast of the seventh month.

.....

17 And all the congregation of them that were come again out of the captivity made booths, and sat under the booths: for since the days of Jeshua the son of Nun unto that day had not the children of Israel done so. And there was very great gladness.

Nehemiah 8:1-3, 5-6, 13-14, 17-18—NRSV

ALL THE people gathered together into the square before the Water Gate. They told the scribe Ezra to bring the book of the law of Moses, which the LORD had given to Israel.

2 Accordingly, the priest Ezra brought the law before the assembly, both men and women and all who could hear with understanding. This was on the first day of the seventh month.

3 He read from it facing the square before the Water Gate from early morning until midday, in the presence of the men and the women and those who could understand; and the ears of all the people were attentive to the book of the law.

.....

5 And Ezra opened the book in the sight of all the people, for he was standing above all the people; and when he opened it, all the people stood up.

6 Then Ezra blessed the LORD, the great God, and all the people answered, "Amen, Amen," lifting up their hands. Then they bowed their heads and worshiped the LORD with their faces to the ground.

.....

13 On the second day the heads of ancestral houses of all the people, with the priests and the Levites, came together to the scribe Ezra in order to study the words of the law.

14 And they found it written in the law, which the LORD had commanded by Moses, that the people of Israel should live in booths during the festival of the seventh month,

.....

17 And all the assembly of those who had returned from the captivity made booths and lived in them; for from the days of Jeshua son of Nun to that day the people of Israel had not done so. And there was very great rejoicing.

UNIFYING LESSON PRINCIPLE

The rebuilding of life requires reestablishing right relationships. What relationships are important to reestablish? Ezra challenged the returned Israelite exiles to reestablish their covenantal relationship with God and with one another.

18 Also day by day, from the first day unto the last day, he read in the book of the law of God. And they kept the feast seven days; and on the eighth day was a solemn assembly, according unto the manner.

18 And day by day, from the first day to the last day, he read from the book of the law of God. They kept the festival seven days; and on the eighth day there was a solemn assembly, according to the ordinance.

TOPICAL OUTLINE OF THE LESSON

I. Introduction
   A. People Need Restoration
   B. Biblical Background

II. Exposition and Application of the Scripture
   A. Request and Reading of the Book of the Law (Nehemiah 8:1-3)
   B. Reading and Worshiping of the Lord (Nehemiah 8:5-6)
   C. Readiness of the Leaders (Nehemiah 8:13-14)
   D. Reading and Obedience (Nehemiah 8:17-18)

III. Concluding Reflections

LESSON OBJECTIVES

Upon completion of this lesson, the students will know:

1. What it means to be restored and renewed in relationships;
2. What it means to be renewed and restored in their relationship with God; and,
3. The importance of renewal services held in local churches.

POINTS TO BE EMPHASIZED

ADULT/YOUTH

Adult Topic: **Restored and Renewed**
Youth Topic: **Rebuilding the Relationship**
Adult Key Verse: **Nehemiah 8:3**
Youth Key Verses: **Nehemiah 8:2-3**
Print Passage: **Nehemiah 8:1-3, 5-6, 13-14, 17-18**

—The people gathered to have Ezra read from the book of the law of Moses.
—On the first day when Ezra opened the book, the people stood; they responded with "amens" when Ezra blessed the Lord.
—God's Word is the baseline for faithful, obedient living.
—Recommitment to the law was a crucial element in the restoration of the covenant community.

CHILDREN

Children Topic: **Ezra Reads the Law**
Key Verse: **Nehemiah 8:10b**
Print Passage: **Nehemiah 8:1-3, 5-6, 13-14, 17-18**

—Ezra led the people in corporate worship, which strengthened their faith and renewed their sense of duty to God.
—God's purpose became clear through the reading of the Scriptures and through prayer.
—After Ezra read from the Book of the Law, the people offered sacrifices to God.

I. INTRODUCTION

A. People Need Restoration

While in Babylon, Ezra gained the favor of King Artaxerxes, who granted him permission to return to Jerusalem (this was the second return, circa 457 B.C.). However, this time only approximately 1,754 of the exiles chose to make the journey, compared with the nearly 50,000 who had returned with Zerubbabel seventy-nine years earlier.

Much can happen within the timeframe of two generations. The temple was complete and in use, but something was still missing—a right attitude toward almighty God. The people still lacked understanding. They were not wholeheartedly obedient to God.

God set His hand to begin restoration of the spiritual temple, a remnant of Judah. He used Ezra to do this. Ezra was a man of sterling character and strong conviction. His example can be encouraging to any who desire to be faithful to God. He was "a scribe skilled in the law of Moses" (Ezra 7:6, NRSV) and "even a scribe of the words of the commandments of the LORD, and of His statutes to Israel" (Ezra 7:11).

In a testimony to his convictions, we read that "Ezra had prepared his heart to seek the law of the LORD, and to do it, and to teach in Israel statues and judgments" (Ezra 7:10).

B. Biblical Background

The Feast of Booths, or Ingathering, fell on the fifteenth day of the seventh month, five days after the Day of Atonement, and encompassed seven days (Exodus 23:16-17; 34:22). The first and eighth days were designated days of rest—a requirement from the Lord. "That your generations may know that I made the children of Israel dwell in booths when I brought them out of the land of Egypt…" (Leviticus 23:33-43).

However, a generation had come up that knew nothing about the Feast of Booths. While they were in exile, some younger generations were out of touch with the past. They failed to observe the feast, probably because their parents were disillusioned when they were in exile.

The returned exiles observed this feast under the rule of Darius (Ezra 3:4) and in the time of Ezra, at which time Ezra read the law and led the people in penitence. The celebration is said to have been different from anything done since the days of Joshua (Nehemiah 8:13-18).

Zechariah 14:16-19 envisions all nations coming up to Jerusalem year by year to keep the Feast of Tabernacles. During the rebuilding of the wall in Jerusalem, the Book of the Law was discovered. The people were eager to know their history of worship, and God provided leaders like Ezra and Nehemiah to help them learn. As Ezra read God's Law, the people discovered that they had not been observing the feast. From that point on, it was reinstated.

The punishment for those who neglected to come to the Feast was that no rain would fall upon them; but in the case of Egypt, the inundation of the Nile would fail. The Jews continued to observe the Feast, even during the days of Jesus (see John 7:2, 8ff).

II. EXPOSITION AND APPLICATION OF THE SCRIPTURE

A. Request and Reading of the Book of the Law
(Nehemiah 8:1-3)

AND ALL the people gathered themselves together as one man into the street that was before the water gate; and they spake unto Ezra the scribe to bring the book of the law of Moses, which the Lord had commanded to Israel. And Ezra the priest brought the law before the congregation both of men and women, and all that could hear with understanding, upon the first day of the seventh month. And he read therein before the street that was before the water gate from the morning until midday, before the men and the women, and those that could understand; and the ears of all the people were attentive unto the book of the law.

"And all the people gathered themselves together as one man…" (verse 1). The phrase, "All the people," indicates that people came from all over, from various countries and villages, for this special occasion. The occasion was the celebration of the feast of the seventh month (Nehemiah 7:73). The beginning of every month was ushered in as a sacred festival, but the commencement of the seventh month was kept with distinguished honor as "the Feast of Trumpets," which lasted for at least two days.

Before a mighty revival could take place among them, the people needed to realize that their oneness was crucial. The Jews had lost touch with the reality of their existence, and as such they all came to hear from the Book of the Lord. They all gathered at the street that was before the water gate on the south wall. This was the first time Ezra was mentioned in the book of Nehemiah.

Because the people were longing to reconnect with God, they invited Ezra to bring the Book of the Law. This book had been in the hands of Ezra for at least twelve years. Word must have been circulating among the people regarding the nature and existence of the book, but the occasion had come to bring it out. A public reading of Scripture was required by the Law to be done every seventh year; but during the long period of their captivity, this worthy practice, along with many others, had fallen into neglect.

That there was a strong and general desire among the returned exiles in Jerusalem to hear the Word of God read to them indicates their great longing to recommit themselves to the Lord. The book that had been in private hands among the learned men was made public to everyone. In order to reconnect to God, a deep longing for knowledge of His Word was and is imperative.

Ezra was more than ready to read this book in public, because the people's hearts were ready to receive the Word of the Lord. Any preacher of the Word is happy when members of the church make a request like this.

The reading was extensive; it lasted six hours, with Ezra's reading of the Law, alternating with a thorough exposition of what was read by the Levites. The gathering included men and women and all those that could understand. Because they were the ones who requested the reading of the Law, they were attentive. The word *understanding* and its derivatives are mentioned six times in this chapter (verses 2, 3, 7, 8, 12, and 13). Only those persons old enough to understand the Scriptures were permitted to be in the assembly.

B. Reading and Worshiping of the Lord
(Nehemiah 8:5-6)

And Ezra opened the book in the sight of all the people;

(for he was above all the people;) and when he opened it, all the people stood up: And Ezra blessed the Lord, the great God. And all the people answered, Amen, Amen, with lifting up their hands: and they bowed their heads, and worshipped the Lord with their faces to the ground.

"And Ezra opened the book in the sight of all the people; (for he was above all the people;) and when he opened it, all the people stood up" (verse 5). Ezra stood in a conspicuous place on this occasion. He lifted the scroll and unrolled it to the passage he would read. The people who were seated in the square honored the Word of God by standing up. They knew they would be hearing the very Word of God. The people remained standing while the Law was read and explained (verse 7).

Ezra started reading and teaching early in the morning and continued through midday (verse 3), which means the congregation stood and listened for five or six hours. This continued for an entire week. What a stark contrast with and a terrible indictment on those today who are wearied after a two-hour service! We will not be able to attain the spiritual level of the people of God if we continue our traditional three-point preaching style.

Seeing the response of the people, Ezra blessed the Lord, the great God. In most churches today, there is a blessing *after* the reading of the Scripture, but there is certainly nothing wrong with praising the Lord for His Word *before* we read and hear it. The response of the people to Ezra was spontaneous. "And all the people answered, Amen, Amen, with lifting up their hands: and they bowed their heads, and worshipped the LORD with their faces to the ground" (verse 6). The people affirmed the words by saying "Amen, Amen," which means "So be it!" It was a united congregation that honored the Scriptures and was willing to

devote half of its day to hearing God's Word read and taught.

Our churches today have a desperate need to show more respect for the Word of God during their worship services. We are not excited in the house of the Lord. The preacher or the worship leader often has to prod congregants by asking, "May I have an amen?" We should not have to be asked to say "amen" if we are truly worshiping God.

Every church has a liturgy, either a good one or a bad one. We should wonder how the Holy Spirit feels when Bibles are put on the church floor or used as portable filing cabinets for miscellaneous papers or even left behind in church where they are stacked up in a corner to collect dust. We defend the Bible as the Word of God, but we don't always treat it like the Word of God.

C. Readiness of the Leaders (Nehemiah 8:13-14)

And on the second day were gathered together the chief of the fathers of all the people, the priests, and the Levites, unto Ezra the scribe, even to understand the words of the law. And they found written in the law which the Lord had commanded by Moses, that the children of Israel should dwell in booths in the feast of the seventh month.

The detailed study of the Law of God caused many of the leaders to come to Ezra the next day for further instruction, especially concerning proper observance of the Feast of Tabernacles. The hearts of the leaders were moved. Many leaders today have gone to religious meetings and other convention gatherings series and returned home as spiritually dry as winter leaves.

In their reading, the people discovered that they were to observe the Feast of Tabernacles from the fifteenth to the twenty-second day of the seventh month. The purpose of this feast was to look back and remember the nation's forty years of wandering in the wilderness. The feast was a time for looking around at the harvest blessings from the hand of God, and it was an occasion for looking ahead to the glorious kingdom God promised His people Israel (Zechariah 14:4, 9, 16-20). It was a week-long festival of joyful praise and thanksgiving, focusing on the goodness of the Lord.

D. Reading and Obedience
(Nehemiah 8:17-18)

And all the congregation of them that were come again out of the captivity made booths, and sat under the booths: for since the days of Jeshua the son of Nun unto that day had not the children of Israel done so. And there was very great gladness. Also day by day, from the first day unto the last day, he read in the book of the law of God. And they kept the feast seven days; and on the eighth day was a solemn assembly, according unto the manner.

"And all the congregation of them that were come again out of the captivity made booths, and sat under the booths: for since the days of Jeshua the son of Nun unto that day had not the children of Israel done so. And there was very great gladness" (verse 17).

It is one thing to desire the Word of the Lord, but it is another to obey what is required. It was not the fact of the celebration of the Feast of Booths that was so special; it was the way that the people celebrated; everybody participated enthusiastically and in the spirit of obedience. Because every family made a booth, some of the people had to move from the houses into the streets and squares of the city. Apparently, in previous years, not all the Jews had made booths and lived in them for the week of the feast. They had given only token acknowledgment of the feast. Furthermore, the joyful attitude of the people was beyond anything the nation had ever seen. It was truly a week of joyful celebration that brought glory to the Lord.

The next day, the leaders met with Ezra and proclaimed a day of celebration throughout the land. The Day of Atonement was celebrated on the tenth day of the month, and the Feast of Tabernacles was celebrated from the fifteenth day to the twenty-second day. This meant that the leaders had just a few days available for getting the word out to the Jews in the surrounding villages that everybody was going to celebrate the Feast of Tabernacles. It is not enough to hear the Word of God; we must obey what it tells us to do (James 1:22-25). The people not only had joy in hearing the Word; they also had "great gladness" in their obedience to it.

This was the last and great day of the feast (see Numbers 29:35). In later times, other ceremonies, which increased the rejoicing, were added (John 7:37). Ezra continued the "Bible conference" during the entire week of the feast, day by day reading and explaining the Word of God. The combination of joyful fellowship, feasting, and hearing the Word must have strengthened the people greatly.

After this week, the people returned to their regular daily schedules. It is quite amazing how the Jews on this occasion brought back God to their consciousness. The Feast of Booths, which had been long neglected, was reinstated. The youth were blessed to have a strong heritage. The elders in different communities were happy because their young ones were brought back into the fold of God. The question for us is this: How do we ensure that we are truly reconnected with God both today and in future generations?

III. CONCLUDING REFLECTIONS

The Bible uses two different terms to describe two different activities, which, given our current practices, the church would do well to reflect upon. Those two terms and events are *revival* and *renewal.*

The biblical use of the term *revival*, in both the Hebrew and the Greek languages, literally means "to come back to life from the dead" (see 1 Kings 17:22). Evangelism is good news; revival is new life. Evangelism is working for God; revival is God working in a sovereign way on our behalf. Therefore, to speak of "holding a revival" is a misnomer. No human being can kindle the interest, quicken the conscience of a people, or generate that intensity of spiritual hunger that signifies revival.

The term *renewal* is used in the title of this lesson. It has its roots in the Old Testament (Psalms 5; 10; 103:5; Isaiah 40:31; 41:1) The New Testament words are *anakainizo* and *ananeoo.* In Romans 12:2, this renewal (*anakainosis)* is applied to one's mental faculties and indicates the reinvigorating effect of Christian committal on conduct. It happened in Nehemiah's day, and it can happen again in our day.

PRAYER

Dear God, our heavenly Father, we thank You for the gift of Your Holy Spirit that You have given to us to convict us of our sins and to guide us back to You. We are grateful for Your Word that promises us that if we confess our sins, repent and turn from our wicked ways, You stand ready to forgive and restore us. Renew in us a clean spirit that we might serve Thee in all Thy ways. In Jesus' name, we pray. Amen.

WORD POWER

Understand (Hebrew: *biyn-bene*)—this word appears three times in the text studied today. It means "to hear and be able to discern," or "to perceive subjectively." The people who came to hear the words from the Book of the Law had discerning spirits. They were able to subjectively know the very Word of God. As a result, their obedience was spontaneous.

HOME DAILY BIBLE READINGS

(May 19-25, 2008)

Call to Renew the Covenant

MONDAY, May 19: "Take Courage" (Psalm 27:11-14)

TUESDAY, May 20: "The Festival of Booths" (Leviticus 23:33-43)

WEDNESDAY, May 21: "Do Not Appear Empty-handed" (Deuteronomy 16:13-17)

THURSDAY, May 22: "Hear the Word" (Nehemiah 8:1-6)

FRIDAY, May 23: "Teach the Word" (Nehemiah 8:7-12)

SATURDAY, May 24: "Study the Word" (Nehemiah 8:13-18)

SUNDAY, May 25: "Delight in God's Law" (Psalm 19:7-14)

Images of Christ

GENERAL INTRODUCTION

In this quarter of study, all three units display the images of Christ as found in the letter to the Hebrews, the four gospels, and the letter of James. The themes of "Creation," "Call," and "Covenant" find their apex in Christ. In fact, Christ is the foundation of *creation,* the means of the *call,* and the center of the *covenant* relationship.

Unit I, *Images of Christ in Hebrews,* consists of five sessions that explore five images. Lesson 1 affirms the fact that God spoke to us through His beloved Son, Jesus Christ. In Lesson 2, we learn that God chose Jesus to be the perfect and permanent intercessor for humanity. In Lesson 3, titled "Guilt Removed," we learn that Jesus shed His blood for the redemption of humanity. The power of the blood of Christ covers and protects believers in Christ. Lesson 4 raises the question: "What makes a leader credible?" The answer is seen in Jesus' actions and godly discipline, which demonstrated that He is a leader who can be trusted. Lesson 5, on "Finding Stability and Permanence Today," details how God gave us eternal life through Jesus so that humans would have a firm foundation for living in relationship to God and others.

Unit II, *Images of Christ in the Gospels,* features four lessons that consider Christ as teacher, as healer, as servant, and as the Messiah. Lesson 6, on "Teaching that Transforms," features Jesus demonstrating the authority of His teaching by dominating and controlling the demons.

In Lesson 7, we learn that faith in the power of Jesus Christ will lead to wholeness, though not necessarily a physical cure. Lesson 8, on the topic "To Be a Servant," shows us how Jesus Christ demonstrated what it means to be a humble servant. In Lesson 9, "Getting to Know a Person," we see how Peter's confession of Jesus was a milestone in his understanding of Jesus as the Messiah.

Unit III, *Images of Christ in Us,* consists of five sessions that locate five images of Christ in the letter of James. These images illustrate how Christians are to model Christ in their lives by being doers of the Word, impartial disciples, wise speakers, people of godly behavior, and people of a prayerful community. In Lesson 10, James tells us that as God's people we must not only hear the Word of God, but also respond to it with transforming action. Those who hear the Word of God are empowered to carry it out. In Lesson 11, on the topic "Honoring All People," James teaches that Christians should make no distinctions in their treatment of people based on people's material wealth. Lesson 12 is titled "Thoughtful Speech." In this lesson, James exhorts people to discipline their tongues by accepting the wisdom and peace that come from above. In Lesson 13 on "Living Responsibly," James says that people must submit themselves to God who frees them from behaving in ungodly ways. Living by God's wisdom results in a wholesome lifestyle.

In the final session, titled "Powerful and Effective Living," James teaches that our lifestyle is to be shaped by an attitude of prayer. Prayer is talking to God and waiting to hear what God speaks to us.

Images
of Christ

JESUS AS GOD'S SON

DEVOTIONAL READING: **Proverbs 8:22-31**   BACKGROUND SCRIPTURE: **Hebrews 1**
PRINT PASSAGE: **Hebrews 1:1-4, 8-12**   KEY VERSE: **Hebrews 1:3**

Hebrews 1:1-4, 8-12—KJV

GOD, WHO at sundry times and in divers manners spake in time past unto the fathers by the prophets,
2 Hath in these last days spoken unto us by his Son, whom he hath appointed heir of all things, by whom also he made the worlds;
3 Who being the brightness of his glory, and the express image of his person, and upholding all things by the word of his power, when he had by himself purged our sins, sat down on the right hand of the Majesty on high;
4 Being made so much better than the angels, as he hath by inheritance obtained a more excellent name than they.

.....

8 But unto the Son he saith, Thy throne, O God, is for ever and ever: a sceptre of righteousness is the sceptre of thy kingdom.
9 Thou hast loved righteousness, and hated iniquity; therefore God, even thy God, hath anointed thee with the oil of gladness above thy fellows.
10 And, Thou, Lord, in the beginning hast laid the foundation of the earth; and the heavens are the works of thine hands:
11 They shall perish; but thou remainest; and they all shall wax old as doth a garment;
12 And as a vesture shalt thou fold them up, and they shall be changed: but thou art the same, and thy years shall not fail.

Hebrews 1:1-4, 8-12—NRSV

LONG AGO God spoke to our ancestors in many and various ways by the prophets,
2 but in these last days he has spoken to us by a Son, whom he appointed heir of all things, through whom he also created the worlds.
3 He is the reflection of God's glory and the exact imprint of God's very being, and he sustains all things by his powerful word. When he had made purification for sins, he sat down at the right hand of the Majesty on high,
4 having become as much superior to angels as the name he has inherited is more excellent than theirs.

.....

8 But of the Son he says, "Your throne, O God, is forever and ever, and the righteous scepter is the scepter of your kingdom.
9 You have loved righteousness and hated wickedness; therefore God, your God, has anointed you with the oil of gladness beyond your companions."
10 And, "In the beginning, Lord, you founded the earth, and the heavens are the work of your hands;
11 they will perish, but you remain; they will all wear out like clothing;
12 like a cloak you will roll them up, and like clothing they will be changed. But you are the same, and your years will never end."

BIBLE FACT

In the ancient biblical world, a scepter was a staff borne by a ruler as the badge of his royal authority (Ezekiel 19:11, 14). King Ahasuerus used his scepter to usher Esther to his presence (Esther 4:11; 5:2). Jesus Christ has the scepter of righteousness—a rod of straightforwardness. He will judge with righteousness because He proceeded from righteousness.

UNIFYING LESSON PRINCIPLE

People search for authoritative and credible voices to answer life's questions. Who can speak to us about the deeper meanings of life? God spoke to us through His beloved Son, Jesus Christ.

TOPICAL OUTLINE OF THE LESSON

I. **Introduction**
   A. Jesus: The Supreme Revelation of God
   B. Biblical Background

II. **Exposition and Application of the Scripture**
   A. Diverse Revelation (Hebrews 1:1)
   B. Supreme Revelation (Hebrews 1:2a)
   C. Credentials of the Son (Hebrews 1:2b-4)
   D. Jesus Christ Is Superior to All (Hebrews 1:8-12)

III. **Concluding Reflections**

LESSON OBJECTIVES

Upon completion of this lesson, the students are expected to understand that:

1. Jesus is God's Son;
2. Jesus is superior to all other agents whom God has used as a revelation of Himself; and,
3. The life of the believer in Christ is far superior to life without Him.

POINTS TO BE EMPHASIZED

ADULT/YOUTH

Adult Topic: **Finding Deeper Meaning in Life**
Youth Topic: **Here Comes the Son!**
Adult Key Verse: **Hebrews 1:3**
Youth Key Verse: **Hebrews 1:2**
Print Passage: **Hebrews 1:1-4, 8-12**

—God spoke to the Jewish people through the prophets, but now God speaks directly through Jesus, the Son.
—Jesus is the reflection of God's glory and imprint of God's being, and He sustains the universe with God's Word.
—After Jesus died on the cross for the sins of the world, He ascended into heaven where He sits on the seat of power next to the Father and where He is far superior even to the angels.
—Hebrews clearly states that Jesus is the Son of God.
—The writer of Hebrews is concerned about the superiority of Jesus over all other agents whom God has used throughout history as a revelation of God's Way.
—The writer makes a strong argument for both the divine and human images of Christ.
—Only Jesus is seen as reflecting the image of God and displaying God's power in His actions.

CHILDREN

Children Topic: **God's Son, Jesus**
Key Verse: **Matthew 3:17**
Print Passage: **Matthew 3:13-17**

—John prepared for Jesus to come.
—John called for the people to change their sinful ways.
—When Jesus asked John to baptize Him, John thought that Jesus should baptize him instead.
—Jesus stated that the reason He wanted to be baptized was in order for righteousness to be fulfilled.
—At the moment of Jesus' baptism, the Holy Spirit descended like a dove.
—God identified Jesus as His Son.

I. INTRODUCTION

A. Jesus: The Supreme Revelation of God

The purpose of the letter of Hebrews is twofold—to inform and to exhort the Jewish converts to hold to their belief in Jesus. The writer proceeds first with the argument that Christianity is superior to Judaism. In presenting his case, the writer uses the word *consider* repeatedly throughout the epistle in reference to Jesus. The readers are led to "consider Him" in His priesthood and sacrifice. This consideration is to include the difference between Christ and the angels, Moses, Aaron, Melchisedec, and the entire Levitical system. This consideration, the writer argues, will lead one logically to the conclusion that Jesus is superior in both His person and His works.

Properly informed regarding the supremacy of Jesus, the second idea of the epistle is found in the word *exhortation (paraklesis),* with its companion verb, "I exhort" (Hebrews 13:22). The writer is asking his recipients to pursue a course of conduct. The persecution, trials, and difficulties of these Jewish Christians would be made easier if they would not only "consider him" (Hebrews 12:3), but also bear with Him—for Christ, our example, endured all sorts of contradictions (Hebrews 13:22, ASV). We too should take this epistle as a personal one because the issues in this epistle are relevant to the contemporary Christian experience.

B. Biblical Background

The epistle to the Hebrews is a rich part of the New Testament canon. It exalts the person and work of the Lord Jesus Christ. But despite its unquestioned value, little is known about its authorship. Many names have been conjectured for the authorship of Hebrews, but the question remains unsolved. The tradition of Pauline authorship is very old and has never been decisively disproved.

In modern times, it has generally been asserted that the style and internal characteristics of Hebrews rule out Paul as the author. But arguments built on such considerations are notoriously subjective and have also been used to prove highly unsound propositions. Still it must be admitted that when Hebrews is read in the Greek and compared with the known letters of Paul, the overall impression is that here one meets a spiritual mind clearly attuned to Paul—but it is, in subtle ways, quite different.

In some respects, Barnabas fits the requirements for authorship of this epistle. Since he was a Levite (Acts 4:36), an interest in the Levitical system such as the author of Hebrews displayed would be natural for him. However, authorship by Barnabas cannot be proven any more than authorship by Paul can be disproved. But it has more to commend it than the other alternative suggestions.

In the final analysis, however, neither the question of the exact authorship nor the exact destination of the epistle is of great consequence to us. Regardless of who wrote it or to whom it was first sent, the Christian church has rightly regarded it through the ages as a message from God.

There are other scholars who say that the best we can say about the authorship of Hebrews is that "God knows the author." Bible scholars are not even sure of the exact date of this epistle, but none dispute that it is one of the richest epistles.

II. EXPOSITION AND APPLICATION OF THE SCRIPTURE

A. Diverse Revelation
(Hebrews 1:1)

GOD, WHO at sundry times and in divers manners spake in time past unto the fathers by the prophets.

The author begins without mentioning his name. The reason is that the message he was about to give was more important than any apostolic greeting. This epistle could be referred to as a general epistle because of its content. The author says that at various times God made Himself known in many portions *(polumeros)*. This Greek word has two parts: *polu and meros,* meaning "many portions." This is where the English word *metropolis* is derived.

The author is saying that God, the Creator of heaven and earth, revealed Himself progressively, or in piecemeal, rather than all at once. He revealed one portion to one prophet and another portion to another. He used different means—subjective and objective experiences, audible voices, the *Urim* and *Thummim* (revelation and truth), dreams, and visions. He revealed Himself in many ways in order that His message would not be overwhelming to His creatures. He spoke audibly to Abraham, in a burning bush to Moses, and in a vision to Isaiah.

The Old Testament revelations were fragmentary in substance and manifold in form; the very multitude of prophets shows that they prophesied only in part. Every generation, from Adam until the arrival of Jesus Christ, had one form of revelation of God or another. There is no excuse for any human being to not know God (see Romans 1:18-20).

B. Supreme Revelation
(Hebrews 1:2a)

Hath in these last days spoken unto us by his Son.

"In these last days…" is also translated, "At the last part of these days." The rabbis divided the whole of time into two ages: "this age" or "world" or "the age to come" (Hebrews 2:5; 6:5). The days of the Messiah mark the transition period or "last part of these days," the close of the existing dispensation and the beginning of the final dispensation, of which Christ's second coming will be the crowning event. Even though God still speaks in various ways today, the supreme revelation is in the Lord Jesus Christ, His Son. God has spoken to us in these last days through His Son, Jesus.

As believers today, we must guard against individuals who claim to be speaking "new revelations" from God. God has spoken to us supremely in His Word that became flesh (John 1:14). The Lord Jesus Christ is the latest Word from heaven. The Bible encourages us to test all spirits, as there are many using pseudo psychology to entrap their victims. Many preachers today falsely claim to have a word from the Lord; we must not become their prey.

Nabal, the husband of Abigail, took time to verify the authenticity of the servants who came from David asking for food. Nabal responded, "Who is David? and who is the son of Jesse? there be many servants now a days that break away every man from his master" (1 Samuel 25:10). If anyone comes to us in the name of the Lord, we too must take time to do some checking.

C. Credentials of the Son
(Hebrews 1:2b-4)

Whom he hath appointed heir of all things, by whom also he made the worlds; Who being the brightness of his glory, and the express image of his person, and upholding all things by the word of his power, when he had by himself purged our sins, sat down on the right hand of the Majesty on high; Being made so much better than the angels, as he hath by inheritance obtained a more excellent name than they.

In this section, the author sets forth the Son's super-credentials, based on two facts. First, the Son was an appointed heir of all things. How was He an appointed heir of all things? He was "heir of all things" by right of creation, and especially by right of redemption. Jesus will inherit everything because He is the eternal Son of God (see Isaiah 9:67; Micah 5:2).

His inheritance is complete dominion. There is no competitor with Him. He is the sole owner of everything on earth, under the earth, and in heaven. The promise to Abraham that he should be heir of the world had its fulfillment in Christ (Romans 4:13; Galatians 3:16; 4:7). The second fact is that "Through whom also He made the worlds." The Greek word for worlds can also mean "ages." Thus, *worlds* indicate all things and persons belonging to them: the universe, including all space and ages of time, and all material and spiritual existences. The Son is the Lord of all history. The Father appointed His Son heir of all things before Creation.

Another important aspect of the Son is that He is the reflection and exact image of God Himself (Hebrews 1:3). In John 14:9, Jesus told Phillip, "...He who has seen Me has seen the Father..." Jesus is the brightness of God's glory. He possesses the very character of God. The words *express image* in Greek is *charakteer,* where we get our word for *character* in English. Whatever the character that Jesus displayed while He was on earth is the very character of God. Just as the sun is seen by its brightness, so is the Father seen by the brightness of the Son. As one writer put it, "It is Light from Light." The sun is never seen without shining, nor is the Father seen without the Son. God's revelation in the Son has a definitive quality which previous revelation lacked. The One who is both Creator and Heir is also a perfect reflection of the God who has spoken in the Son.

In the second part of verse 3 we read, "Jesus sustains all things by his powerful word." This statement points to the omnipotence of Jesus. Through His omnipotence, coupled with His love, He purged our sins once and for all. The purging was done by His own blood and not that of bulls and goats. This purging of our sins means He has purified us and claimed us for the Father.

After purging our sins, Jesus then sat down at the right hand of God. He did not sit there in judgment; rather, He has become our advocate. This sitting of the Son at God's right hand was by the act of the Father (Ephesians 1:20; Hebrews 8:1). It was never used of His pre-existing state as co-equal with the Father, but always of His exalted state as Son of man, after His sufferings, and as Mediator for human beings in the presence of God (Romans 8:34).

It was also a return to His divine glory (John 6:62; 17:5).

This exalted position, which was accomplished by the Father, showed that Jesus was superior to the angels (Hebrews 1:3). Paul showed that His humbled form was neither an objection to His divine Messiahship, nor a diminishing of His Sonship. As the Law was given by the ministration of angels and Moses, it was inferior to the Gospel given by the divine Son—who is as God (Hebrews 1:4-14) and has been made, as the exalted Son of Man (Hebrews 2:5-18), much better than the angels. The manifestations of God by various means and at different times in the Old Testament did not bring humanity and God into personal union, as did the manifestation of God incarnate.

Jesus is the Son of God in a manner far exalted above that in which angels are called "sons of God" (see Job 1:6; 38:7). The full meaning of "the Son of God" is inexpressible through human speech. All of our descriptions and appellations are but fragments of its glory. Paul says, "For we know in part and we prophesy in part" (1 Corinthians 13:9). John the revelator also said Christ had "a name written that no man knew but He Himself" (Revelation 19:12).

D. Jesus Christ Is Superior to All
(Hebrews 1:8-12)

But unto the Son he saith, Thy throne, O God, is for ever and ever: a sceptre of righteousness is the sceptre of thy kingdom. Thou hast loved righteousness, and hated iniquity; therefore God, even thy God, hath anointed thee with the oil of gladness above thy fellows. And, Thou, Lord, in the beginning hast laid the foundation of the earth; and the heavens are the works of thine hands: They shall perish; but thou remainest; and they all shall wax old as doth a garment; And as a vesture shalt thou fold them up, and they shall be changed: but thou art the same, and thy years shall not fail.

The word *but* is an adversative conjunction which sets contrast to what has been said before. Here Jesus is addressed as God and His throne is forever. The text says: "Thy throne, O God, is for ever and ever; a scepter of righteousness is the scepter of thy kingdom...." There are two characteristics of the kingdom of Christ: (1) everlasting duration and (2) righteousness (Psalms 45:2; 89:14). A scepter is a rod of authority used by kings. However, in the case of Christ, He carried the scepter of righteousness. The quotation found in verses 8-9 is taken from Psalm 45:6-7, which describes the final triumph of God's messianic King. Jesus Christ is accorded the rank of full deity. He possesses an eternal kingdom. His manifested love of righteousness and hatred of iniquity made Him to be anointed by the Father above all other hosts of heaven.

The reference to "partakers" is a significant theme for the writer. The same word *metochoi* ("partakers or sharers") is used to describe Christians in Hebrews 3:1, 14 (it is also used in Hebrews 12:8). Since the King has attained His joy and dominion through a life of steadfast righteousness, He has been anointed above His fellows—the angels—who are partakers, though His inferiors, in the glories, holiness, and joys of heaven.

Verses 10 and 12 are directly taken from Psalm 102. These two verses indicate that Jesus the Lord was the one who would appear in the future to Israel and other nations (see Psalm 102:12-16).

We must also take note that Jesus Christ is being described here in His pre-incarnate existence. Jesus Christ formed the foundation of the earth, according to verse 10, and the heavens are His handiwork. The earth and all created beings will perish—except Jesus Christ, who will endure forever. Verse 12b is making allusion to the end of this age; the section says, "...as a vesture shalt thou fold them up, and they shall be changed" (Hebrews 1:12). Paul made allusion to what will happen at the coming of Jesus Christ. He said, "In a moment, in the twinkling of an eye…this mortal shall have put on immortality" (see 1 Corinthians 15:52-54). The Son will not experience metamorphosis (or any changes).

Jesus Christ is the champion of our salvation. The writer of this epistle is encouraging all believers to know that Christ is superior to other created beings. Others will suffer change in various ways. Scientists know that this world is suffering from climatic change known as global warming. The earth is getting warmer because of all kinds of pollution. We human beings know that we are not getting younger; by the end of this class today, we will be older than when we came in.

Whatever language the scientists are using, Christians should remember that only Christ remains unchanged.

III. CONCLUDING REFLECTIONS

The writer of the book of Hebrews uses three words repeatedly that are, therefore, worth reflecting upon as we conclude this lesson: *better, perfect,* and *eternal.*

When you combine these three important words, you discover that Jesus Christ and the life He gives is *better* because these blessings are *eternal* and they give us a *perfect* standing before God. The religious system under the Mosaic Law was imperfect because it could not accomplish a once-and-for-all redemption that was eternal. Only Jesus Christ, the Son of the living God, could accomplish this with His blood.

PRAYER

Dear God, our heavenly Father, we thank and praise You for Your Son. Help us to understand and become more appreciative of whom He is to You, and what He means to us, so that we may grow into His likeness in Your sight. Amen.

WORD POWER

Brightness (Greek: *apaugasma* [apoo-gasmar])—This means reflected brightness, effulgence. Jesus is God in essence. He reflects the glory of God. Jesus Himself said, "He that hath seen me hath seen the Father" (John 14:9). He is the true image of God. He perfectly reflects the majesty of God.

HOME DAILY BIBLE READINGS

(May 26—June 1, 2008)

Christ as God's Son

MONDAY, May 26: "From the Beginning" (Proverbs 8:22-31)
TUESDAY, May 27: "Appointed Heir" (Hebrews 1:1-5)
WEDNESDAY, May 28: "In the Beginning" (John 1:1-5)
THURSDAY, May 29: "The Firstborn" (Hebrews 1:6-9)
FRIDAY, May 30: "The Work of God's Hands" (Hebrews 1:10-12)
SATURDAY, May 31: "Full of Grace and Truth" (John 1:14-18)
SUNDAY, June 1: "Heir of All Things" (Hebrews 1:13-14)

LESSON 2   June 8, 2008

CHRIST AS INTERCESSOR

DEVOTIONAL READING: **Jeremiah 31:31-34**   BACKGROUND SCRIPTURE: **Hebrews 7**
PRINT PASSAGE: **Hebrews 7:20-28**   KEY VERSE: **Hebrews 7:25**

Hebrews 7:20-28—KJV

20 And inasmuch as not without an oath he was made priest:

21 (For those priests were made without an oath; but this with an oath by him that said unto him, The Lord sware and will not repent, Thou art a priest for ever after the order of Melchisedec:)

22 By so much was Jesus made a surety of a better testament.

23 And they truly were many priests, because they were not suffered to continue by reason of death:

24 But this man, because he continueth ever, hath an unchangeable priesthood.

25 Wherefore he is able also to save them to the uttermost that come unto God by him, seeing he ever liveth to make intercession for them.

26 For such an high priest became us, who is holy, harmless, undefiled, separate from sinners, and made higher than the heavens;

27 Who needeth not daily, as those high priests, to offer up sacrifice, first for his own sins, and then for the people's: for this he did once, when he offered up himself.

28 For the law maketh men high priests which have infirmity; but the word of the oath, which was since the law, maketh the Son, who is consecrated for evermore.

Hebrews 7:20-28—NRSV

20 This was confirmed with an oath; for others who became priests took their office without an oath,

21 but this one became a priest with an oath, because of the one who said to him, "The Lord has sworn and will not change his mind, 'You are a priest forever'"—

22 accordingly Jesus has also become the guarantee of a better covenant.

23 Furthermore, the former priests were many in number, because they were prevented by death from continuing in office;

24 but he holds his priesthood permanently, because he continues forever.

25 Consequently he is able for all time to save those who approach God through him, since he always lives to make intercession for them.

26 For it was fitting that we should have such a high priest, holy, blameless, undefiled, separated from sinners, and exalted above the heavens.

27 Unlike the other high priests, he has no need to offer sacrifices day after day, first for his own sins, and then for those of the people; this he did once for all when he offered himself.

28 For the law appoints as high priests those who are subject to weakness, but the word of the oath, which came later than the law, appoints a Son who has been made perfect forever.

BIBLE FACT

Priests have come and gone, religious leaders have emerged and faded into history. They were human beings subject unto death. Some of them still have large followings, some of whom are dying for their deceased leaders. But our Eternal Intercessor died, was resurrected, and appeared to many people. He is now interceding for us in the presence of our heavenly Father.

UNIFYING LESSON PRINCIPLE

Sometimes we need someone to speak up for us—to take our side. Who speaks on our behalf? God chose Jesus to be the perfect and permanent intercessor for humanity.

TOPICAL OUTLINE OF THE LESSON

I. Introduction
A. The Priesthood
B. Biblical Background

II. Exposition and Application of the Scripture
A. Christ Was Made Priest by an Oath (Hebrews 7:20-22)
B. The Unchangeable Priest (7:23-25)
C. Qualities of Christ as the High Priest (7:26-28)

III. Concluding Reflections

LESSON OBJECTIVES

Upon completion of this lesson, the students will understand:

1. The status and role of a priest as intercessor;
2. How the priesthoods of Melchisedec and Christ are superior to the priesthood of the Levitical system; and,
3. What the priesthood of Christ means to us today.

POINTS TO BE EMPHASIZED

ADULT/YOUTH

Adult Topic: **Who Can Speak for Us?**
Youth Topic: **We Have a Friend in High Places**
Adult/Youth Key Verse: **Hebrews 7:25**
Print Passage: **Hebrews 7:20-28**

—Jesus was without sin—the perfect High Priest who was able to offer the perfect sacrifice. He did it once for all persons for all time.
—Access to God is through Jesus Christ, who makes it possible for us to talk with God.
—Hebrews uses passages from the Old Testament to demonstrate that Jesus is the Messiah and that the new covenant has superseded the old.
—Genesis 14:17-20 is used to support the author's argument about Jesus as High Priest.
—The mysterious priesthood of Melchisedec is seen as a model for Jesus' role rather than that of the Levitical priesthood.
—Jesus was not a priest, according to the Law, because He was of the tribe of Judah and not of Levi.
—The priesthoods of Melchisedec and Christ are both considered to be of the same status and are superior to the Levitical priesthoods.
—The eternal character of the priesthoods of Jesus and Melchisedec is used as one reason for their superior status over the Levitical priesthood.

CHILDREN

Children Topic: **Jesus Prays for Us**
Key Verse: **John 17:11**
Print Passage: **John 17:6-11, 20-21a**

—Jesus prayed for God's chosen people.
—Jesus tells God that He has fulfilled His mission.
—Jesus asks for protection for the people when He returns to God.
—Jesus includes all people in His prayer.

I. INTRODUCTION

A. The Priesthood

The term *priest* (Hebrew: *kohen;* Greek: *hierus;* and Latin: *sacerdos),* always denotes "one who offers sacrifices." In the beginning, every man was his own priest and presented his own sacrifices before God (Job 5:1). Afterward, that office passed on to the head of the family, as in the cases of Noah (Genesis 8:20) and the three patriarchs—Abraham (12:7; 13:4), Isaac (26:25), and Jacob (31:54).

The term *priest* first occurs in Genesis 14:18 and was applied to Melchisedec. Under the Levitical arrangements, the office of the priesthood was limited to the tribe of Levi, and then to only one family of that tribe—the family of Aaron. Certain laws respecting the qualifications of priests are given in Leviticus 21:16-23. Additionally, there are ordinances also regarding the priests' dress (Exodus 28:40-43) and the manner of their consecration to the office (29:1-37).

The priests represented the people before God and offered the various sacrifices prescribed in the Law. The whole priestly system of the Jews was a shadow of the body of Christ. The priests all foreshadowed the one great Priest who offered one sacrifice for sins "once for all" (Hebrews 10:10, 12). There is now no human priesthood, since the word *priest* now applies to all believers (1 Peter 2:9; Revelation 1:6). All true believers are now "kings and priests unto God" (Revelation 1:6). As priests, they have free access into the holiest of all, and they offer up the sacrifices of praise and thanksgiving and the sacrifices of grateful service from day to day.

B. Biblical Background

Who was Melchisedec? Mentioned only twice in the Old Testament, what we know of Melchisedec is recorded in Genesis 14:18-20, with a subsequent mention in Psalm 110:4. The general significance of his history is set forth in detail in the verses preceding our lesson (Hebrews 7:1-19). In Hebrews, the writer points out the superiority of his priesthood to that of Aaron in several respects: (1) Abraham paid him tithes; (2) he blessed Abraham; (3) he is the type of priest who lives forever; (4) Levi, yet unborn, paid him tithes in the person of Abraham; (5) the permanence of his priesthood in Christ implied the abrogation of the Levitical system; (6) he was made priest not without an oath; and (7) his priesthood can neither be transmitted nor interrupted by death.

Melchisedec's mysterious personage has given rise to a great deal of modern speculation. It is an old tradition among the Jews that he was Shem, the son of Noah, who may have survived to this time, also an angel, the Holy Spirit, Christ, and others. These speculations are not based on historical fact and cannot be theologically sustained. Melchisedec was a real, historical king-priest who served as a type of Jesus Christ.

II. EXPOSITION AND APPLICATION OF THE SCRIPTURE

A. Christ Was Made Priest by an Oath (Hebrews 7:20-22)

And inasmuch as not without an oath he was made priest: (For those priests were made without an oath; but this with an oath by him that said unto him, The Lord sware and will not repent, Thou art a priest for ever after the order of Melchisedec:) By so much was Jesus made a surety of a better testament.

What is an oath? It is a solemn statement to validate a promise. To underscore the importance of an oath, even Jesus Christ was not made priest without an oath. Why did God have to confirm the priesthood of Jesus with an oath? He did it to show the certainty and unchangeableness of the thing promised or sworn. Historically, God swore to Abraham that in his seed all the nations of the earth would be blessed (Genesis 22:16-18). Christ's consecration showed that His ministry was and is endless and cannot be terminated by death.

No priest in the order of Aaron was ever ordained and established on the basis of God's personal oath. The oath of God gave a solemn weight to Christ's priesthood, which was made after the order of Melchisedec (Hebrews 7:21).

This is better understood by the Greek translation: "For they indeed, the existing legal priests without the solemn promise, on oath are made priests." The writer then repeated the divine oath of Psalm 110:4, which by its very solemnity argued for the superiority of the new Priest who was majestically inducted into His role.

Verse 22 says "By so much was Jesus made a surety of a better testament." This is the first occurrence of a very important word in Hebrews—*testament*. This word, which is usually translated "covenant," is used twenty-one times in this epistle, and it is the equivalent of "last will and testament." The word "surety" means "one who guarantees that the terms of an agreement will be carried out." Perhaps the nearest equivalent we have to this today is a bondsman who posts bail for someone under indictment to guarantee that the indicted person will appear in court and stand trial. The presence of this oath gives to the priesthood of our Lord a greater degree of permanence and assurance.

As the mediator between God and humankind (1 Timothy 2:5), Jesus Christ is God's great surety. Our risen and ever-living Savior guarantees that the terms of God's covenant will be fulfilled completely. God will not abandon His people; He has saved us and He has guaranteed that He will keep us.

Why is the priesthood of Jesus better than the Levitical priesthood? There are basically two reasons: 1) God promised blessings to the Jewish nation if they kept the Mosaic laws; God promises forgiveness of sin and eternal life to all who trust and obey Him; 2) the Levitical priests were fallible men; death prevented them from continuing in office, but Jesus shed His own blood to take away the sins of the whole world, and death has no dominion over Him. On the contrary, the Levitical priests were not required by the law to shed their personal blood. They were to offer the blood of selected animals.

B. The Unchangeable Priest (Hebrews 7:23-25)

And they truly were many priests, because they were not suffered to continue by reason of death: But this man, because he continueth ever, hath an unchangeable priesthood. Wherefore he is able also to save them to the

uttermost that come unto God by him, seeing he ever liveth to make intercession for them.

Pastors come and they go; deacons are ordained and they pass on; church boards come and they go; rulers come and they go. Right now, the wheels are in motion to elect another American president, as the current one is finishing his term of office. Through all of these changes, Jesus Christ remains the same.

In the Levitical system there were many priests, and the high priest's office was always changing hands. When one high priest died, another assumed his position. Josephus, a Jewish historian, estimated that there were some 83 different high priests between the time of Aaron and the fall of the temple in A.D. 70. The priesthood of Jesus continues forever because He does not die (7:24). "He continues forever" means that Jesus has an unchangeable priesthood.

The fact that the *unchanging* Christ continues as High Priest means, logically, that there is an "unchangeable priesthood." The Greek word translated *unchangeable* carries the idea of "valid and unalterable." This same word is used at the end of legal contracts. Our Lord's priesthood in heaven is "valid and unalterable." It is does not pass from one to another.

Because of the permanent nature of His priesthood, we can have confidence in the midst of this unstable and changing world. Jesus' ministry of intercession for salvation is eternal (7:25). He is able to save to the uttermost. Unfortunately, this verse is often misquoted as "He is able to save *from* the uttermost" instead of "*to* the uttermost." To be sure, Christ can save any sinner from any condition; but that is not the import of the verse. The emphasis is on the fact that He saves completely, forever, all who put their faith in Him.

Because He is our High Priest forever, He can save forever. The Hebrews readers were to hold fast to their professions of faith. They should continue reckoning themselves among those who came to God through Jesus, knowing that He could see them through every trial and difficulty. He lived and lives to intercede for them. In saying this, the author reverted to a truth he had already enunciated (Hebrews 4:14-16), inviting the readers to avail themselves boldly of the mercy and grace accessible to them through Jesus' priesthood. As they did so, they would find that their Captain and High Priest was able to finish what He started.

There was but the one sin offering on earth that was "once for all." But the intercession for us in the heavens continues, leading us to the conclusion that we can never be separated from the love of God in Christ.

C. Qualities of Christ as the High Priest (Hebrews 7:26-28)

For such an high priest became us, who is holy, harmless, undefiled, separate from sinners, and made higher than the heavens; Who needeth not daily, as those high priests, to offer up sacrifice, first for his own sins, and then for the people's: for this he did once, when he offered up himself. For the law maketh men high priests which have infirmity; but the word of the oath, which was since the law, maketh the Son, who is consecrated for evermore.

The phrase "for such a High Priest became us" means that Jesus as the High Priest was in every respect qualified to be the champion of our eternal salvation. There are four qualities specified in the text:

A) Holy *(hosios)*—this means that Jesus Christ is holy, pious, and perfectly fit to carry out the demands of God. The writer of Hebrews declares, "Follow peace with all men, and holiness, without which no man shall see the Lord" (Hebrews 12:14). In order to satisfy the demands of God, the High Priest of our salvation must be holy.

B) Harmless *(akakos)*—this means free from all kinds of evil. Jesus Christ harmed no one. He came to uplift the ones who were oppressed by the powerful. Women were raised from being second-class citizens to being co-heirs with Him (see Galatians 3:28).

C) Undefiled *(amiantos)*—this means that there is no form of bodily imperfection, but more importantly there should be no character flaw.

D) Separate from sinners *(kechoorismenos)*—just as the Levitical high-priest was separated from the people in the sanctuary and became higher than the sinful community, Jesus as God was higher and entirely devoted to the service of God.

Being perfect, Jesus was able to exercise a perfect ministry for His people. The Old Testament priests were "set apart" for their ministry, so in that sense they were "holy." But they were not always holy in character. They were sinners like the people to whom they ministered. The characteristics ascribed here to Jesus—holy, harmless, blameless, and undefiled—could be claimed by no Jewish priest.

When He was ministering on earth, our Lord was a friend of publicans and sinners (Matthew 9:10; 11:19), but His contact with them did not defile His character or His conduct. There was contact without contamination. He was not *isolated,* but He was separated.

Today, He is "separate from sinners" because of His position, which is higher than the heavens; but He is not separated from the people to whom He ministers. He is always available to us at His throne of grace. The Levitical priests died like the people they served, but Jesus died a criminal's death.

Jesus did and does not need to offer sacrifices daily. His offering of Himself was and is sufficient for all times (Hebrews 7:27). His one act of self-offering was definitive and sufficient.

We must not imagine that God the Father is angry with us so that God the Son must constantly appeal to Him not to judge us. The Father and the Son are in total agreement in the plan of salvation (Hebrews 13:20-21). We should not imagine our Lord Jesus is in heaven repeatedly "offering His blood" as a sacrifice for our sins. The work of salvation was completed on the cross.

Before He died on the cross, Jesus said, "It is finished *[tetelestai]*" (John 19:30). This was a cry of accomplishment, meaning, "I have executed the great designs of the almighty God. I have satisfied the demands of His justice. I have completed all that was written in the prophets."

The door to the Holy of Holies now swings open for us. Through this cry, heaven's gate is open to all believing souls. There is no need of an earthly intermediary as there was in the Old Testament.

Intercession involves our Lord's representation of His people at the throne of God. Through Christ, believers are able to draw near to God in prayer and offer spiritual sacrifices to Him (Hebrews 4:14–16; 1 Peter 2:5). It has been well said that Christ's life in heaven is His prayer for us. It is what He *is* that determines what He *does.* The Son was made a priest after the Law and is therefore perfected forever (Hebrews 7:28). In contrast with the Levitical priests, the Son is a perfected High Priest.

In verse 28, there are two important facts which set Jesus apart from the Levitical priests. First, the Levitical priests were chosen by human institution, but Christ was chosen by an oath of God. Second, they were weak, fallible, and subject to death; but Christ is strong and infallible. Jesus Christ endures forever. Accordingly, believers can go to Him at all times, fully confident of His capacity to serve their every need.

III. CONCLUDING REFLECTIONS

Let us close this lesson by reflecting for a moment upon the significance of the change in the priesthood, for you and me, in the church today. The former was weak and unprofitable and made nothing perfect; the latter brought in a better hope, by which we draw near to God. The Levitical priesthood brought nothing to perfection; it could not justify us. It could not sanctify persons from inward pollution; it could not cleanse the consciences of the worshipers from dead works.

The priesthood of Christ carries in it, and brings along with it, a better hope. It shows us the true foundation of all the hope we have toward God for pardon and salvation. It clearly discovers the great objects of our hope, and so it tends to work in us a more strong and lively hope of acceptance with God.

PRAYER

Dear God our Father, thank You for the privilege we have been given to come before Your presence on behalf of others. We ask that You would forgive and bless the members of our families, our friends, and those in our fellowship. In Jesus' name, we pray. Amen.

WORD POWER

Made like (Greek: *aphomoioo* [afo-moio])—this literally means "to make a facsimile, or to produce an exact carbon copy of an object." In our text, the writer of Hebrews was showing the similarities between Jesus Christ and Melchisedec. This prince of Salem was a copy of Jesus.

HOME DAILY BIBLE READINGS
(June 2-8, 2008)

Christ as Intercessor
> MONDAY, June 2: "Preparing for a New Covenant" (Jeremiah 31:31-34)
> TUESDAY, June 3: "The Old Order of Priests" (Hebrews 7:1-3)
> WEDNESDAY, June 4: "King Melchisedec" (Genesis 14:17-20)
> THURSDAY, June 5: "Introduction of a New Order" (Hebrews 7:4-17)
> FRIDAY, June 6: "The Permanent Priesthood" (Hebrews 7:18-24)
> SATURDAY, June 7: "Interceding for All Who Approach God" (Hebrews 7:25-26)
> SUNDAY, June 8: "Perfect Forever" (Hebrews 7:27-28)

LESSON 3   **June 15, 2008**

CHRIST AS REDEEMER

JACKSON BECKY

DEVOTIONAL READING: **John 4:21-26**
PRINT PASSAGE: **Hebrews 9:11-18; 10:12-14, 17-18**

BACKGROUND SCRIPTURE: **Hebrews 9:11–10:18**
KEY VERSE: **Hebrews 9:12**

Hebrews 9:11-18; 10:12-14, 17-18—KJV

11 But Christ being come an high priest of good things to come, by a greater and more perfect tabernacle, not made with hands, that is to say, not of this building;

12 Neither by the blood of goats and calves, but by his own blood he entered in once into the holy place, having obtained eternal redemption for us.

13 For if the blood of bulls and of goats, and the ashes of an heifer sprinkling the unclean, sanctifieth to the purifying of the flesh:

14 How much more shall the blood of Christ, who through the eternal Spirit offered himself without spot to God, purge your conscience from dead works to serve the living God?

15 And for this cause he is the mediator of the new testament, that by means of death, for the redemption of the transgressions that were under the first testament, they which are called might receive the promise of eternal inheritance.

16 For where a testament is, there must also of necessity be the death of the testator.

17 For a testament is of force after men are dead: otherwise it is of no strength at all while the testator liveth.

18 Whereupon neither the first testament was dedicated without blood.

.....

12 But this man, after he had offered one sacrifice for sins for ever, sat down on the right hand of God;

13 From henceforth expecting till his enemies be made his footstool.

14 For by one offering he hath perfected for ever them that are sanctified.

.....

17 And their sins and iniquities will I remember no more.

18 Now where remission of these is, there is no more offering for sin.

Hebrews 9:11-18; 10:12-14, 17-18—NRSV

11 But when Christ came as a high priest of the good things that have come, then through the greater and perfect tent (not made with hands, that is, not of this creation),

12 he entered once for all into the Holy Place, not with the blood of goats and calves, but with his own blood, thus obtaining eternal redemption.

13 For if the blood of goats and bulls, with the sprinkling of the ashes of a heifer, sanctifies those who have been defiled so that their flesh is purified,

14 how much more will the blood of Christ, who through the eternal Spirit offered himself without blemish to God, purify our conscience from dead works to worship the living God!

15 For this reason he is the mediator of a new covenant, so that those who are called may receive the promised eternal inheritance, because a death has occurred that redeems them from the transgressions under the first covenant.

16 Where a will is involved, the death of the one who made it must be established.

17 For a will takes effect only at death, since it is not in force as long as the one who made it is alive.

18 Hence not even the first covenant was inaugurated without blood.

.....

12 But when Christ had offered for all time a single sacrifice for sins, "he sat down at the right hand of God,"

13 and since then has been waiting "until his enemies would be made a footstool for his feet."

14 For by a single offering he has perfected for all time those who are sanctified.

.....

17 he also adds, "I will remember their sins and their lawless deeds no more."

18 Where there is forgiveness of these, there is no longer any offering for sin.

UNIFYING LESSON PRINCIPLE

People feel a need to be absolved of their wrongdoing. Who can take away our guilt? In Mark, we see Jesus offering forgiveness, and in Hebrews, we read that Jesus shed His blood for the redemption of humanity.

TOPICAL OUTLINE OF THE LESSON

I. Introduction
   A. Guilt: The Biblical Concept
   B. Biblical Background

II. Exposition and Application of the Scripture
   A. The Heavenly Sanctuary (Hebrews 9:11-18)
   B. One-Time Sacrifice Perfects Us (Hebrews 10:12-14)
   C. Cessation of Sin Offering (Hebrews 10:17-18)

III. Concluding Reflections

LESSON OBJECTIVES

At the conclusion of this lesson, the students are expected to understand:

1. What guilt is and the problem that guilt presents to healthy living;
2. How the sacrificial system of the Old Testament was designed to deal with the problem of guilt; and,
3. The role that the death and blood sacrifice of Christ plays in absolving sin and guilt.

POINTS TO BE EMPHASIZED

ADULT/YOUTH

Adult Topic: Guilt Removed
Youth Topic: Jesus to the Rescue
Adult/Youth Key Verse: Hebrews 9:12
Print Passage: Hebrews 9:11-18; 10:12-14, 17-18

—In the role of High Priest, Jesus sacrificed Himself once and for all for the sins of the world.
—Jesus redeemed us by paying the price for our sins with His blood so that we might serve God.
—The writer presents Jesus as the fulfillment and completion of the Jewish system of sacrifice.
—In today's world that minimizes sin, Jesus' great and costly sacrifice says sin is serious.
—This passage explores differences between the old covenant and the new covenant regarding sacrifice for sins, and it asserts the superiority of the new to the old.
—Christ functions as both Priest and sacrificial offering here.
—Jesus' offering of Himself as the perfect and pure human sacrifice is said to take away the very consciousness of sin (Hebrews 10:1-3).

CHILDREN

Children Topic: Jesus Forgives
Key Verse: Mark 2:5
Print Passage: Mark 2:1-12

—A paralyzed man's friends brought him to Jesus in an unusual way.
—Jesus forgave the paralyzed man's sins.
—Jesus was sensitive to the thoughts and motives of others.
—The teachers of the Law questioned Jesus' motives in their hearts.
—Jesus responded to the teachers' unvoiced questions.
—Jesus not only forgave the paralyzed man's sins but also gave him the ability to walk.

I. INTRODUCTION

A. Guilt: The Biblical Concept

For the biblical writers, guilt was not understood primarily as an inward feeling of remorse or a bad conscience. Rather, it was seen as involving a situation that had arisen because of sin committed against God or one's neighbor. Thus, in the Bible, guilt appears to have two primary presuppositions for its existence. First, human beings were and are responsible and accountable for their actions, thoughts, and attitudes. Second, these actions, thoughts, and attitudes constitute a state of guilt when relationships between human beings and God or other human beings have been broken because of sin.

The principal ingredient in the biblical concept of guilt appears to be the dimension of responsibility. Human beings are accountable for what they do and for the consequences of what they do. This accountability lies at the center of the biblical understanding of guilt. So great was this sense of responsibility that people could be guilty without even being aware of it (Leviticus 5:17-19). When a person sinned, guilt was the natural consequence. Often, guilt was depicted in the Old Testament as a burden or weight that could crush a person (Psalm 38:4, 6), or as a cancer that could destroy a person from within (Psalm 32:3-4).

B. Biblical Background

Because of the understanding that all people were guilty before God and each other, there developed in Israel a sacrificial system to "purify" the people involved by their paying a penalty for the wrong done. This ritual was not designed simply to relieve the conscience of the guilty party, but rather to make restitution—to lay aside the burden of guilt and restore the broken relationship caused by the guilt. In the New Testament, Paul made frequent use of this idea (Romans 5:6-11; 2 Corinthians 5:16-21; Colossians 1:19-20).

Because of the biblical understanding of the importance of the community (i.e., the people of God), guilt could be both collective and individual. What one person did could cause guilt to come upon an entire group of people (cf., especially the story of Achan, Joshua 7). The basis for this view was the Hebrew belief in corporate solidarity—the significance of the people being viewed as a whole and not just as an aggregate of individuals. Individuals could sin, however, and bring guilt and the consequences of sin upon themselves.

Guilt brought with it serious consequences, such as separation from God and one's neighbor, with specific penalties for sins committed. The New Testament writers used a particular word with regard to guilt *(genochos)*, which usually means "deserving of punishment" (Matthew 26:66; 1 Corinthians 11:27; James 2:10). According to Paul, all human beings were guilty before God (Romans 1:18-3:20). In both the Old Testament and New Testament, it is only because of God's grace that guilt can be set aside through God's forgiveness.

II. EXPOSITION AND APPLICATION OF THE SCRIPTURE

A. The Heavenly Sanctuary
(Hebrews 9:11-18)

But Christ being come an high priest of good things to come, by a greater and more perfect tabernacle, not made with hands, that is to say, not of this building; Neither by the blood of goats and calves, but by his own blood he entered in once into the holy place, having obtained eternal redemption for us. For if the blood of bulls and of goats, and the ashes of an heifer sprinkling the unclean, sanctifieth to the purifying of the flesh: How much more shall the blood of Christ, who through the eternal Spirit offered himself without spot to God, purge your conscience from dead works to serve the living God? And for this cause he is the mediator of the new testament, that by means of death, for the redemption of the transgressions that were under the first testament, they which are called might receive the promise of eternal inheritance. For where a testament is, there must also of necessity be the death of the testator. For a testament is of force after men are dead: otherwise it is of no strength at all while the testator liveth. Whereupon neither the first testament was dedicated without blood.

In this section, the tabernacle here refers to the body of Jesus, and thus it is greater and more perfect than any earthly building made with human hands.

The writer wanted his readers, and us, to focus attention on the things of heaven and not on the things of earth and, in so doing, to recognize the supremacy of the heavenly over the earthly. So he contrasted the earthly tabernacle, in which the Levitical priests ministered, with the heavenly tabernacle in which Christ ministered and ministers.

The sacrificial offering of the blood of Jesus is greater than that of goats and calves because it obtained eternal redemption (9:12). The heavenly sanctuary is better than the earthly one because Jesus shed His own blood in order to make entry possible to all.

The earthly sanctuary could only be entered through the shed blood of a bullock and a goat on the Day of Atonement (Leviticus 16:6, 15). The sacrificial system in the Old Testament was taxing on both the high priest and the people.

In addition to the goat offered for the people, the blood of which was sprinkled before the mercy seat, the high priest brought forth a second goat—namely, the scapegoat. Over it he confessed the people's sins, putting them on the head of the goat, which was sent as the sin-bearer into the wilderness out of sight, implying that the atonement effected by the goat sin offering resulted in the transfer of the people's sins onto the goat, and their consequent removal from sight. However, Jesus, by His own blood rather than by animal blood, entered into the holy place once and for all and obtained eternal redemption. Thus, the value of His sacrifice was and is immeasurably greater than the animal offerings of the Levitical system (Hebrews 7:27; 10:10).

Under the former system of atonement, an animal's blood was carried by the high priest into the Holy of Holies, but Jesus Christ presented Himself in the presence of God as the final and complete sacrifice for all sin. Of course, the animal sacrifices were repeated, while Jesus Christ offered Himself only once. Finally, no animal sacrifices ever purchased "eternal redemption." Their blood could only "cover" sin until the time when Christ's blood would "take away sin" (John 1:29). Through Christ we have "eternal redemption." It is not conditioned upon our merit or good works; it is secured once and for all by the finished work of Jesus Christ.

In verse 13 the author argues, "For if the blood of bulls and the ashes of a heifer sprinkling the unclean, sanctifieth to the purifying of the flesh…." This means that if the blood of mere brutes could purify, how much more shall inward purification and complete and eternal salvation be wrought by the blood of Christ, in whom was the fullness of the Godhead? Through the blood of Christ, we are restored to peace and living in communion with God in the heavenly holy place.

The blood of Christ was and is better because it purified and continues to purify both the flesh and the conscience (9:14). The eternal Spirit is the Holy Spirit, which means all three Persons of the Trinity are involved in the cleansing. The animals offered had no spirit or will to consent in the act of sacrifice; they were offered according to the Law. But Jesus, from eternity, with His divine and everlasting Spirit, concurred with the Father's will of redemption. The voluntary nature of the offering gives it special efficacy. Christ was able to offer the perfect sacrifice pleasing to the Father.

Christ was and is the Mediator of the New Testament (9:15). The New Testament provides two gifts to a believer: redemption and inheritance. Jesus ratified these two gifts by means of His death. At the moment that His death took place, the necessary effect was that the called would receive the fulfillment of the promise to Abraham (see Galatians 3:13-14).

Before the inheritance of the New Testament could come in, there had to be deliverance from the penalties incurred by the transgressions. The atoning sacrifices under the first testament reached only as far as removing outward, ceremonial defilement. But in order to obtain the inheritance, which was and is a reality, there had to be a real propitiation, since

God could not enter into covenantal relationship with us as long as our past sins were not atoned for (Romans 3:24-25).

The blessings under the Old Testament depended upon the obedience of God's people. If they obeyed God, He blessed them; if they disobeyed, He withheld His blessings. Not only were the blessings temporary, but also they were primarily temporal. Israel's Canaan inheritance involved material blessings. Our eternal inheritance is primarily spiritual in nature (Ephesians 1:3). Note that the emphasis is on eternality (Hebrews 9:12, 15). A believer in Jesus Christ can have confidence because all that he or she has in Christ is eternal.

In legal terminology, the death of the testator is required for the testament to take effect (9:16-17). *Testament* is the word translated "covenant" (verse 15). It means "a legal will"— for where a testament (will) is, there must of necessity be the death of the testator. Before the provisions of a will can take effect, the one who made it must die. Therefore, it was necessary for Jesus Christ to die so that the terms of the New Testament could be enforced.

Even the Old Testament was established on the basis of blood. This was taken from Exodus 24:3-8, the account of Moses and the people of Israel ratifying the Old Testament. The Book of the Law was sprinkled with blood, along with the people and the tabernacle and its furnishings.

Not only was blood used at the beginning of the ministry of the Old Testament, but it also was used in the regular administration of the tabernacle service. Under the Old Testament, people and objects were purified by blood, water, or fire (Numbers 31:21-24). This was, of course, ceremonial purification; it meant that the persons and objects were acceptable to God after purification. The purification did not alter the nature of the person or object. God's principle was and is that blood must be shed before sin can be forgiven (Leviticus 17:11).

B. One-Time Sacrifice Perfects Us
(Hebrews 10:12-14)

But this man, after he had offered one sacrifice for sins for ever, sat down on the right hand of God; From henceforth expecting till his enemies be made his footstool. For by one offering he hath perfected for ever them that are sanctified.

"But this man, after he had offered one sacrifice for sins for ever, sat down on the right hand of God" (verse 12). Again, the writer contrasts the Old Testament high priest with Jesus Christ, our Great High Priest. The fact that Jesus sat down after He ascended to the Father is proof that His work was completed (Hebrews 1:3, 13; 8:1). The ministry of the priests in the tabernacle and temple was never done and never different. They offered the same sacrifices day after day. This repetition was proof that their sacrifices did not take away sin. What tens of thousands of animal sacrifices could not accomplish, Jesus accomplished with one sacrifice—forever.

The phrase "sat down" refers us again to Psalm 110:1: "Sit thou at my right hand, until I make thine enemies thy footstool." Christ was and is in the place of exaltation and victory. When He returns, He will overcome every enemy and establish His righteous kingdom. Christ is now awaiting the execution of His Father's will, that all His foes should be subjected to Him. The Son waits until the Father sends Him to triumph over all His enemies (Hebrews 10:13). He is now sitting at the right hand of God (Hebrews 10:12). His present sitting on the unseen throne is a prerequisite to His coming to subdue His enemies openly.

He will then come forth to a visibly manifested kingdom and will conquer His foes.

Those who have trusted Him need not fear, for they have been "perfected forever." Believers are "complete in Him" (Colossians 2:10). We have a perfect standing before God because of the finished work of Jesus Christ. The sanctification (consecration to God) of the elect believers (1 Peter 1:2) is perfect in Christ once for all; however, the development of that sanctification is progressive.

C. Cessation of Sin Offering
(Hebrews 10:17-18)

And their sins and iniquities will I remember no more. Now where remission of these is, there is no more offering for sin.

"And their sins and their iniquities will I remember no more" (Hebrews 8:12). To remember sin no more does not mean to forget, but to not hold sin against us any longer. Paul declares that, "There is therefore now no condemnation to them which are in Christ Jesus…" (Romans 8:1).

How do we know personally that we have this perfect standing before God? We know because of the witness of the Holy Spirit which indwells us as believers. The witness of the Spirit is based on the work of the Son and is given through the words of Scripture. The writer (Hebrews 10:16-17) quoted Jeremiah 31:33-34, part of a passage he also had quoted in Hebrews 8:7-12. The Old Testament worshiper could not claim to have "no more conscience of sins" (Hebrews 10:2). But the New Testament believer can joyfully proclaim that personal sins and iniquities are remembered no more. There is "no more offering for sin" (Hebrews 10:18) and no more remembrance of sin.

"Now where remission of these is, there is

no more offering for sin" (verse 18). If the New Testament (Hebrews 8:6-13) involves forgiveness of sin and sin being remembered no more (Hebrews 8:12; 10:17), then there is no longer a need to atone for sin. Reverting to his basic text on the benefits of the New Testament (cf. 8:8-12), the author quoted a portion of Hebrews 10:16; he also quoted Jeremiah 31:33 .

III. CONCLUDING REFLECTIONS

Forgiveness is the legal act of God whereby He removes the charges that were held against the sinner because proper satisfaction or atonement for those sins has been made. There are several Greek words used to describe forgiveness. One is *charizomai*, which is related to the word "grace" and means "to forgive out of grace." It is used regarding the cancellation of a debt (Colossians 2:13). The context emphasizes that our debts were nailed to the cross, with Christ's atonement freely forgiving the sins that were charged against us.

The most common word for "forgiveness" is *aphiemi*, which means "to let go of, release, or send away." The noun form is used in Ephesians 1:7, where it is stressed that the believer's sins have been forgiven or sent away because of the riches of God's grace, as revealed in the death of Christ. Forgiveness forever solves the problem of all sins in the believer's life—past, present, and future (Colossians 2:13). This is distinct from the daily cleansing from sin that is necessary to maintain fellowship with God (1 John 1:9).

PRAYER

Most holy and righteous God our heavenly Father, thank You for giving us the gift of Your Son as a cleansing sacrifice for our sins. Help us, we pray, to walk worthy of His atoning blood. In His name, we pray. Amen.

WORD POWER

Covenant *(diatheke* [dia-thake])—this word could mean "agreement" or a "will or testament." The author uses *diatheke* throughout this section, employing two different meanings and tying them together. The death of Christ put into immediate operation the blessings of the New Testament, and this frees us from the bondage and penalties of the Old Testament.

HOME DAILY BIBLE READINGS
(June 9-15, 2008)
Christ as Redeemer
> MONDAY, June 9: "I Am He" (John 4:21-26)
> TUESDAY, June 10: "Mediator of a New Covenant" (Hebrews 9:11-15)
> WEDNESDAY, June 11: "On Our Behalf" (Hebrews 9:16-24)
> THURSDAY, June 12: "Once for All Time" (Hebrews 9:25-28)
> FRIDAY, June 13: "A One-Time Sacrifice" (Hebrews 10:1-10)
> SATURDAY, June 14: "For Our Sanctification" (Hebrews 10:11-14)
> SUNDAY, June 15: "Forgiveness Forever" (Hebrews 10:15-18)

CHRIST AS LEADER *PHILIPPEN 5:2 ISAIAH*

DEVOTIONAL READING: **Proverbs 3:5-12**   BACKGROUND SCRIPTURE: **Hebrews 12:1-13**
PRINT PASSAGE: **Hebrews 12:1-13**   KEY VERSE: **Hebrews 12:1**

Hebrews 12:1-13—KJV

WHEREFORE SEEING we also are compassed about with so great a cloud of witnesses, let us lay aside every weight, and the sin which doth so easily beset us, and let us run with patience the race that is set before us,

2 Looking unto Jesus the author and finisher of our faith; who for the joy that was set before him endured the cross, despising the shame, and is set down at the right hand of the throne of God.

3 For consider him that endured such contradiction of sinners against himself, lest ye be wearied and faint in your minds.

4 Ye have not yet resisted unto blood, striving against sin.

5 And ye have forgotten the exhortation which speaketh unto you as unto children, My son, despise not thou the chastening of the Lord, nor faint when thou art rebuked of him:

6 For whom the Lord loveth he chasteneth, and scourgeth every son whom he receiveth.

7 If ye endure chastening, God dealeth with you as with sons; for what son is he whom the father chasteneth not?

8 But if ye be without chastisement, whereof all are partakers, then are ye bastards, and not sons.

9 Furthermore we have had fathers of our flesh which corrected us, and we gave them reverence: shall we not much rather be in subjection unto the Father of spirits, and live?

10 For they verily for a few days chastened us after their own pleasure; but he for our profit, that we might be partakers of his holiness.

11 Now no chastening for the present seemeth to be joyous, but grievous: nevertheless afterward it yieldeth the peaceable fruit of righteousness unto them which are exercised thereby.

12 Wherefore lift up the hands which hang down, and the feeble knees;

13 And make straight paths for your feet, lest that which is lame be turned out of the way; but let it rather be healed.

Hebrews 12:1-13—NRSV

THEREFORE, SINCE we are surrounded by so great a cloud of witnesses, let us also lay aside every weight and the sin that clings so closely, and let us run with perseverance the race that is set before us,

2 looking to Jesus the pioneer and perfecter of our faith, who for the sake of the joy that was set before him endured the cross, disregarding its shame, and has taken his seat at the right hand of the throne of God.

3 Consider him who endured such hostility against himself from sinners, so that you may not grow weary or lose heart.

4 In your struggle against sin you have not yet resisted to the point of shedding your blood.

5 And you have forgotten the exhortation that addresses you as children—"My child, do not regard lightly the discipline of the Lord, or lose heart when you are punished by him;

6 for the Lord disciplines those whom he loves, and chastises every child whom he accepts."

7 Endure trials for the sake of discipline. God is treating you as children; for what child is there whom a parent does not discipline?

8 If you do not have that discipline in which all children share, then you are illegitimate and not his children.

9 Moreover, we had human parents to discipline us, and we respected them. Should we not be even more willing to be subject to the Father of spirits and live?

10 For they disciplined us for a short time as seemed best to them, but he disciplines us for our good, in order that we may share his holiness.

11 Now, discipline always seems painful rather than pleasant at the time, but later it yields the peaceful fruit of righteousness to those who have been trained by it.

12 Therefore lift your drooping hands and strengthen your weak knees,

13 and make straight paths for your feet, so that what is lame may not be put out of joint, but rather be healed.

UNIFYING LESSON PRINCIPLE

People want to follow leaders who will give them direction. What makes a leader credible? By His action and godly discipline, Jesus demonstrates that He is a leader who can be trusted.

TOPICAL OUTLINE OF THE LESSON

I. **Introduction**
   A. Suffering
   B. Biblical Background

II. **Exposition and Application of the Scripture**
   A. Encouragement for the Race of Faith (Hebrews 12:1-2)
   B. Endurance Under Discipline (Hebrews 12:3-11)
   C. Tune Up Your Spiritual Vitality (Hebrews 12:12-13)

III. **Concluding Reflections**

LESSON OBJECTIVES

Upon completion of this lesson, the students are expected to have a greater understanding of:

1. How suffering is one of the means by which faith is perfected;
2. Jesus as the perfect model for suffering;
3. Suffering as a necessary requirement to produce holiness; and,
4. How suffering serves to produce trustworthy leaders.

POINTS TO BE EMPHASIZED

ADULT/YOUTH

Adult Topic: **Trustworthy Leadership**
Youth Topic: **Supreme Commander**
Adult Key Verse: **Hebrews 12:1**
Youth Key Verse: **Hebrews 12:10**
Print Passage: **Hebrews 12:1-13**

—Hebrews uses a sports metaphor of the marathon race to describe the Christian life, complete with Christ as pacesetter and past faith heroes as cheering fans.

—Jesus is the Author (originator) and Perfecter (one who completes) of our faith. He is its Alpha and Omega—its beginning and its end.

—Jesus set the example by enduring the pain and shame of the Cross to achieve the joy and victory of eternal life with God the Father. Follow His example.

—Christians learn discipline through the endurance of trials.

—Jesus is presented as the perfect leader who was tempted but did not give in.

—Suffering is seen as discipline that purifies and strengthens.

—The discipline of suffering is seen as being a necessary refinement in order for humans to be blessed with God's holiness.

CHILDREN

Children Topic: **Follow the Leader**
Key Verse: **Luke 5:11**
Print Passage: **Luke 5:1-11**

—Jesus used every opportunity to teach.

—Jesus told Simon how to make a bountiful catch.

—Jesus made "catching fish" a model for "catching people."

—Jesus invited Simon and his companions to follow Him.

—The first four disciples were commissioned as "fishers of people."

I. INTRODUCTION

A. Suffering

Pain, or distress, is one of the most persistent of all human problems. Even those who experience relatively minor suffering in their own lives are constantly confronted with the suffering of others in their own families, among acquaintances, or even in distant lands.

Suffering can take on many forms—physical pain, frustrated hopes, depression, isolation, loneliness, grief, anxiety, spiritual crisis, and more. Such unpleasantness comes to Christians and non-Christians alike. Certainly, people in biblical times struggled with the presence of suffering in their lives. They must have sought ways to understand it and cope with it to include their belief in God's power and God's goodness (1 Peter 1:10-12).

B. Biblical Background

In the Bible, suffering was regarded as an intrusion into this created world. Creation was made good (Genesis 1:31). When sin entered, suffering also entered in the form of conflict, pain, corruption, drudgery, and death (Genesis 3:15-19). In the new heaven and new earth, suffering will have been abolished (Isaiah 65:17; Revelation 21:4 ff).

The work of Christ was to deliver humankind from suffering, corruption, sin, and death (Romans 8:21; 1 Corinthians 15:26). Though Satan is regarded as having power to make human beings suffer (Job 1:12; 2:6), they suffer only at the hand of God, and it is God who controls and sends suffering (Isaiah 45:7; Amos 3:6; Acts 2:23).

In bearing their witness to the sufferings of the coming Messiah, the Old Testament writers were taught how God can give a new meaning to suffering. Their own experience of serving God in His redemptive purposes in Israel taught them that the love of God must involve sharing in the affliction and shame of those He was seeking to redeem (Isaiah 63:9; Jeremiah 9:1-2; 20:7-10). Therefore, His true servant, who will perfectly fulfill His redeeming will, will be a suffering servant (Isaiah 53).

Such suffering will not arise simply as a result of faithfulness to God in pursuing a vocation; indeed, it will constitute the very vocation a person must fulfill. A new vicarious meaning and purpose can now be seen in such unique suffering, wherein one can suffer in the place of—and as the inclusive representative of—all.

II. EXPOSITION AND APPLICATION OF THE SCRIPTURE

A. Encouragement for the Race of Faith (Hebrews 12:1-2)

WHEREFORE SEEING we also are compassed about with so great a cloud of witnesses, let us lay aside every weight, and the sin which doth so easily beset us, and let us run with patience the race that is set before us, Looking unto Jesus the author and finisher of our faith; who for the joy that was set before him endured the cross, despising the shame, and is set down at the right hand of the throne of God.

"Since we are surrounded by so great a cloud of witnesses…" (verse 1). The great cloud represents heroes of the faith. It is not suggested here that these men and women are now in heaven watching us as we run the race, like people seated in a stadium. The word *witness* does not mean "spectator." Our English word *martyr* comes directly from the Greek word translated "witness." Therefore, the people are not witnessing what we are doing; rather, they are now examples of those who have trod where we are treading, and we can be encouraged that God will see us through.

In the light of this fact, the writer encourages us to lay aside those things that hinder us and run with endurance the race set before us (verse 1). No athlete would actually participate in a competition wearing weights because they would slow him or her down. The modern analogy to this would be a baseball player who swings a bat with a heavy metal collar on it before he steps to the plate. Too much weight will drain an athlete's endurance.

What are the "weights" that we should remove in order to win the race? They are anything and everything that hinders our progress. They may even be "good" things in the eyes of others. But a winning athlete does not choose between the good and the bad; but rather, between the better and the best.

We should also get rid of "the sin that so easily entangles" *(euperiston:* "ambushes or encircles or anything that thwarts a race"). While he does not name any specific sin, the writer was probably referring to the sin of unbelief. It was unbelief that kept Israel out of the Promised Land, and it is unbelief that hinders us from entering into our spiritual inheritance in Christ. The phrase *by faith* (or *through faith*) is used twenty-one times in Hebrews 11, indicating that it is faith in Christ that enables us to endure.

The writer encourages us to focus our eyes on Jesus. He is the supreme model for how we ought to face our trials. He is the author (the originator), the pioneer, finisher, and perfecter of our faith. Jesus, our supreme example, fixed His eyes on eternal glory that was and is the joy set before Him. Today's believer is to face his or her trials by keeping his or her eyes on the joy that person will share with Jesus at the end.

Our Lord endured far more than did any of the heroes of faith named in Hebrews 11; therefore, He is a perfect example for us to follow. He endured the pain and shame of the cross and even temporary rejection by the Father. On the cross, He suffered for all the sins of the world. Yet, He endured and finished the work the Father gave Him to do (John 17:4).

What enabled our Lord to endure the cross? Please keep in mind that during His ministry on earth, our Lord did not use His divine powers for His personal needs. Satan tempted Him to do this (Matthew 4:1-4), but Jesus refused. It was our Lord's faith that enabled Him to endure. He kept the eye of faith on "the joy that was set before Him." From Psalm 16:8-10, He knew that He would come out of the tomb. Jesus knew that He would be exalted in heaven in glory. So "the joy that was set before Him" would include Jesus' completing the Father's will, His resurrection and exaltation, and His joy in presenting believers to the Father in glory (Jude 24).

After enduring the cross and scorning its shame, Jesus assumed that triumphant position at the right hand of the throne of God which pictures His and the believers' final victory (Hebrews 10:12-14).

B. Endurance Under Discipline (Hebrews 12:3-11)

For consider him that endured such contradiction of sinners against himself, lest ye be wearied and faint in your minds. Ye have not yet resisted unto blood, striving against sin. And ye have forgotten the exhortation which speaketh unto you as unto children, My son, despise not thou the chastening of the Lord, nor faint when thou art rebuked of him: For whom the Lord loveth he chasteneth, and scourgeth every son whom he receiveth. If ye endure chastening, God dealeth with you as with sons; for what son is he whom the father chasteneth not? But if ye be without chastisement, whereof all are partakers, then are ye bastards, and not sons. Furthermore we have had fathers of our flesh which corrected us, and we gave them reverence: shall we not much rather be in subjection unto the Father of spirits, and live? For they verily for a few days chastened us after their own pleasure; but he for our profit, that we might be partakers of his holiness. Now no chastening for the present seemeth to be joyous, but grievous: nevertheless afterward it yieldeth the peaceable fruit of righteousness unto them which are exercised thereby.

Throughout this epistle, the writer emphasized the importance of the future hope. His readers were prone to look back and want to go back, but he encouraged them to follow Christ's example and look ahead by faith. The heroes of faith named in the previous chapter lived for the future, and this enabled them to endure. Though the readers of Hebrews had suffered persecution, they had not yet "resisted unto blood" (Hebrews 12:4). None of them was yet a martyr. But in Jesus' battle against sin, He shed His own blood. By "sin," the author probably primarily meant the sinful ones who opposed them, but doubtless also had their own sin in mind as well which they had to resist in order to maintain a steadfast Christian profession.

"And you have forgotten the exhortation that addresses you as children…" (Hebrews 12:5, NRSV). This quotation is an exhortation because they were ready to give up. The key words in this quotation are "son," "children," and "sons." These words are used six times in Hebrews 12:5-8. A parent who would repeatedly chasten an infant child would be considered a monster. God deals with us as adult children because we have been adopted and given an adult standing in His family (Romans 8:14-18; Galatians 4:1-7).

The next key word in this section is *chastening (paideia).* It is a Greek word that means "child training, instruction, and disciplinary correction." A Greek boy was expected to "work out" in the gymnasium until he reached maturity. It was a part of his preparation for adult life. The writer viewed the trials of the Christian life as spiritual discipline that could help a believer mature. Instead of trying to escape the difficulties of life, we should be "exercised" by them so that we may grow (12:11). All of God's children are subject to His discipline. In the phrase "every son," the writer uses again the Greek word *metochoi* (companions, sharers) to indicate that each and every one of God's children are companions who share in this experience of discipline.

In speaking of those who are not disciplined and are thus illegitimate (Greek: *nothoi*—this means a child born outside of lawful wedlock), the author probably was thinking of Christians whose disloyalty to the faith resulted in their loss of inheritance (for example, "reward") which was acquired by the many sons and daughters. In the Roman world, an "illegitimate child" had no inheritance rights. Therefore, what such Christians endured was severe judgment.

On the other hand, believers who undergo God's discipline are being prepared by this educational process. If you endure chastening, you demonstrate your acceptance of God as your Father.

Each of us was raised by one or both parents or a guardian. If the parental figure was faithful, then we were subject to be disciplined. If a child is left alone, without discipline, that child will grow up to become a selfish tyrant. The point the writer made (Hebrews 12:7-8) is that a father chastens only his own sons, and this is proof that they are his children. We may feel like spanking the neighbors' children (and our neighbors may feel like spanking ours), but we cannot do it. God's chastening is proof that we are indeed His children.

No chastening is pleasant at the time it is administered—neither to the parent nor to the child—but its benefits are profitable. Undoubtedly, few children believe it when their parents say, "This hurts me more that it hurts you," but it is true just the same. The Father does not enjoy having to discipline His children, but the benefits afterward make the chastening an evidence of His love.

What are some of the benefits? For one thing, there is "the peaceable fruit of righteousness." Instead of continuing to sin, the child strives to do what is right. There is also peace instead of war; the rebellion has ceased, and the child is in loving fellowship with the Father. Chastening also encourages a child to grow in spiritual matters—reading the Word of God, prayer, meditation, and witnessing. All of this leads to a new joy.

When we are suffering, it is easy to think that God does not love us. So the writer gave three proofs that chastening comes from the Father's heart of love. Chastening is evidence of the Father's love. Satan wants us to believe that the difficulties of life are proof that God does *not* love us, but just the opposite is true. Sometimes God's chastening is seen in His *rebukes* from His Word or by way of circumstances.

At other times, He shows His love by punishing us with some actual suffering. The word *paideia* also carries the idea of chastening by the infliction of evils and calamities. Whatever the experience, we can be sure that His chastening hand is controlled by His loving heart. The Father does not want us to be pampered babies; He wants us to become mature adult sons and daughters who can be trusted with the responsibilities of life.

C. Tune Up Your Spiritual Vitality (Hebrews 12:12-13)

Wherefore lift up the hands which hang down, and the feeble knees; And make straight paths for your feet, lest that which is lame be turned out of the way; but let it rather be healed.

Of course, the important thing is how God's child responds to chastening. He/she can despise it or faint under it (Hebrews 12:5), both of which are wrong. A child of God can also rebel and turn away from God, which may indicate that his or her encounter with Christ is initially faulty. A legitimate child should show reverence to the Father by submitting to His will (Hebrews 12:9) and using the experience as spiritual exercise (Hebrews 12:11; 1 Timothy 4:7-8). Hebrews 12:12-13 sounds like a coach's orders to the team: "Lift up your hands! Strengthen those knees!" The author quotes Isaiah 35:3; in essence, he advises his readers to renew their strength so that they can endure the race of faith.

In contemporary speech, the author is saying, "Get those lazy feet on the track!" (Proverbs 4:26). "Tune up your spiritual vitality and stop idling!" When a car is not performing well, we take it to the auto mechanic for a tune-up. Similarly, Christians must remember that the race is still on and there is no room for slackness. Keep pushing on until the final whistle is blown.

III. CONCLUDING REFLECTIONS

Suffering can have new meaning for those who are members of the body of Christ. They can share in the sufferings of Christ and regard themselves as pledged to a career or vocation of suffering (1 Peter 4:1-2)— since the members of the body must be conformed to the Head in this respect (Romans 8:29; Philippians 3:10), as well as in respect of His glory. Whatever form the suffering of a Christian takes, it can be regarded as a cross which may be taken up in following the way of Christ. Such suffering is the inevitable way to resurrection and glory. It is by tribulation that persons enter the kingdom of God (John 16:21; Acts 14:22).

The coming of the new age is preceded by birth pangs on earth, in which the church has its decisive share (Matthew 24:21-22; Revelation 12:1-2, 13-17). Since the sufferings of Christ are sufficient in themselves to set us free, it is entirely by grace, and not in any way by necessity, that the sufferings in which His people participate with Him can be regarded as filling what is lacking in His affliction (Colossians 1:24) and as giving fellowship in His vicarious and redemptive suffering.

PRAYER

Dear God, our heavenly Father, we thank You today for Your Son, Jesus, who through His suffering provided us the model for how we ought to face our times of suffering. Help us to remember that He was victorious over His suffering, and because of His victory, we too shall be victorious. In His name, we pray. Amen.

WORD POWER

Lay aside *(apothitemi)*—this word is made up of two words: *apo* (away from), and *thitemi* (to put something down). The word (when it is put together) forms a compound word. Finally, it means "to lay apart horizontally," "to let die," or "to cast something aside without touching it." The writer is saying to put sin down horizontally and let it die.

HOME DAILY BIBLE READINGS
(June 16-22, 2008)

Christ as Leader

MONDAY, June 16: "Seek God's Leadership and Discipline" (Proverbs 3:5-12)
TUESDAY, June 17: "Endure the Race" (Hebrews 12:1-3)
WEDNESDAY, June 18: "Endure Trials and Discipline" (Hebrews 12:4-7)
THURSDAY, June 19: "Necessity of Discipline" (Hebrews 12:8-11)
FRIDAY, June 20: "Be Strong and Be Healed" (Hebrews 12:12-13)
SATURDAY, June 21: "Be Humble like Christ" (Philippians 2:1-4)
SUNDAY, June 22: "Follow Christ's Example" (Philippians 2:5-11)

THE ETERNAL CHRIST

DEVOTIONAL READING: **Psalm 118:5-9**   BACKGROUND SCRIPTURE: **Hebrews 13:1-16**
PRINT PASSAGE: **Hebrews 13:1-16**   KEY VERSE: **Hebrews 13:8**

Hebrews 13:1-16—KJV

LET BROTHERLY love continue.

2 Be not forgetful to entertain strangers: for thereby some have entertained angels unawares.

3 Remember them that are in bonds, as bound with them; and them which suffer adversity, as being yourselves also in the body.

4 Marriage is honourable in all, and the bed undefiled: but whoremongers and adulterers God will judge.

5 Let your conversation be without covetousness; and be content with such things as ye have: for he hath said, I will never leave thee, nor forsake thee.

6 So that we may boldly say, The Lord is my helper, and I will not fear what man shall do unto me.

7 Remember them which have the rule over you, who have spoken unto you the word of God: whose faith follow, considering the end of their conversation.

8 Jesus Christ the same yesterday, and to day, and for ever.

9 Be not carried about with divers and strange doctrines. For it is a good thing that the heart be established with grace; not with meats, which have not profited them that have been occupied therein.

10 We have an altar, whereof they have no right to eat which serve the tabernacle.

11 For the bodies of those beasts, whose blood is brought into the sanctuary by the high priest for sin, are burned without the camp.

12 Wherefore Jesus also, that he might sanctify the people with his own blood, suffered without the gate.

13 Let us go forth therefore unto him without the camp, bearing his reproach.

14 For here have we no continuing city, but we seek one to come.

15 By him therefore let us offer the sacrifice of praise to God continually, that is, the fruit of our lips giving thanks to his name.

16 But to do good and to communicate forget not: for with such sacrifices God is well pleased.

Hebrews 13:1-16—NRSV

LET MUTUAL love continue.

2 Do not neglect to show hospitality to strangers, for by doing that some have entertained angels without knowing it.

3 Remember those who are in prison, as though you were in prison with them; those who are being tortured, as though you yourselves were being tortured.

4 Let marriage be held in honor by all, and let the marriage bed be kept undefiled; for God will judge fornicators and adulterers.

5 Keep your lives free from the love of money, and be content with what you have; for he has said, "I will never leave you or forsake you."

6 So we can say with confidence, "The Lord is my helper; I will not be afraid. What can anyone do to me?"

7 Remember your leaders, those who spoke the word of God to you; consider the outcome of their way of life, and imitate their faith.

8 Jesus Christ is the same yesterday and today and forever.

9 Do not be carried away by all kinds of strange teachings; for it is well for the heart to be strengthened by grace, not by regulations about food, which have not benefited those who observe them.

10 We have an altar from which those who officiate in the tent have no right to eat.

11 For the bodies of those animals whose blood is brought into the sanctuary by the high priest as a sacrifice for sin are burned outside the camp.

12 Therefore Jesus also suffered outside the city gate in order to sanctify the people by his own blood.

13 Let us then go to him outside the camp and bear the abuse he endured.

14 For here we have no lasting city, but we are looking for the city that is to come.

15 Through him, then, let us continually offer a sacrifice of praise to God, that is, the fruit of lips that confess his name.

16 Do not neglect to do good and to share what you have, for such sacrifices are pleasing to God.

UNIFYING LESSON PRINCIPLE

In a world of rapid change, people seek stability and permanence. Where can we find such grounding? God gave Jesus eternal life so that humans would have a firm foundation for living in relationship to God and others.

TOPICAL OUTLINE OF THE LESSON

I. Introduction
A. Stability and Permanence
B. Biblical Background

II. Exposition and Application of the Scripture
A. Exhortation for Love Rooted in Kinship (Hebrews 13:1-3)
B. Exhortation for Marital Fidelity (Hebrews 13:4)
C. Exhortation for Contentment (Hebrews 13:5-6)
D. Exhortation for Religious Direction (Hebrews 13:7-16)

III. Concluding Reflections

LESSON OBJECTIVES

Upon completion of this lesson, the students are expected to have a greater understanding of:

1. The concept of eternity and the eternality of Christ;
2. The unchangeableness of the love of God in Christ Jesus; and
3. The role that love plays in providing stability and permanence.

POINTS TO BE EMPHASIZED

ADULT/YOUTH

Adult Topic: **Finding Stability and Permanence Today**
Youth Topic: **Someone You Can Count On**
Adult/Youth Key Verse: **Hebrews 13:8**
Print Passage: **Hebrews 13:1-16**

—Hebrews closes with practical advice for living the Christian life based on mutual love.
—Hebrews advises hearers to follow those who led them to Christianity and not to be led astray by strange teachings, for "Jesus Christ is the same yesterday and today and forever" (13:8).
—The writer concludes that since Jesus is always the same, and we can trust Him to not go back on His Word, then we should live like Him.
—First Corinthians 13 is good background for this passage.
—First John 4:7-21 expounds on the practice of love for one another as Christians.
—Love is a characteristic of God portrayed throughout the Old Testament and New Testament.
—Hebrews has as its major focus the themes of perfection and completion; to conclude with these admonitions to love one another fits well with the notion of love perfecting one's faith.

CHILDREN

Children Topic: **Jesus Is Forever**
Key Verse: **Hebrews 13:8**
Print Passage: **Luke 24:36-49**

—After His resurrection, Jesus appeared to His disciples.
—Jesus revealed His identity by allowing His disciples to touch Him.
—Jesus reminded the disciples that He had fulfilled the Law and the prophecy.
—Jesus assured the disciples that they would receive power from God.
—Jesus promised His disciples the power to witness.

I. INTRODUCTION

A. Stability and Permanence

The world as a whole is in a state of flux. Changes occur rapidly. Many countries around the world are unstable. Many rulers have become tyrants. In Africa, the Sudanese government is committing a horrific offense by killing its own people. In the Darfur region, children are roaming the desert seeking a place of refuge. In North Korea, the people are tools in the hands of a totalitarian government. The United Nations has no power to bring stability to the world. There is no peace in the Middle East. The super powers of the world cannot bring peace and stability. As a matter of fact, they are contributing more to the instability of the world.

In the midst of these uncertainties, the question we need to ask is, "Where can we find peace and stability?" In the Bible, we find hope. Jesus said, "…in me ye might have peace. In the world ye shall have tribulation…" (John 16:33). Jesus Christ is humanity's only source of hope. Peace and eternal life are found in Him only. Jesus is the same yesterday, today, and tomorrow.

B. Biblical Background

The first twelve chapters of Hebrews form a closely-knit argument for the superiority of Christ. Chapter 13, however, is somewhat of a departure from the argument and something of an appendix dealing with a number of practical points. The Christians to whom the epistle was written were being challenged to wake up from their spiritual slumber. They had become weak, and their Christian love was waning. In light of this, the author expounded upon the fact that Christians were and are to be concerned for the needs of others. Those for whom Christ died could not and cannot live for themselves only.

Christianity is faith in action, and that means to love in a concrete way. The believer, therefore, is commanded by God to "…love thy neighbor as thyself" (Mark 12:31). Every normal person has a sense of personal dignity and self-worth; therefore, every normal person is filled with a sense of self-love. This self-love is the basis of love for one's neighbor. We are to love our neighbors with the same degree of zeal and consistency with which we love ourselves. And since there is no practical limit to the claims of self-love, there is no practical limit to our duties toward our neighbors.

When we as believers express love for others, we fulfill the idea of "Christ-likeness," for the life of Christ is the standard by which Christians measure virtue in themselves and others. When we demonstrate Christian love in our various communities, unbelievers will want to know about our God, whose light illuminates our hearts.

II. EXPOSITION AND APPLICATION OF THE SCRIPTURE

A. Exhortation for Love Rooted in Kinship (Hebrews 13:1-3)

LET BROTHERLY love continue. Be not forgetful to entertain strangers: for thereby some have entertained angels unawares. Remember them that are in bonds, as bound with them; and them which suffer adversity, as being yourselves also in the body.

The concept of love to which the believer is exhorted is expressed in the Bible by the employment of two different words. The first word is *agapao*, which speaks of God's love (John 3:16). *Agapao*, or agape, is the love produced in the heart of the yielded believer by the Holy Spirit (Romans 5:5) and the love defined by Paul in 1 Corinthians 13. That is not the kind of love addressed by the writer of Hebrews in this passage. Rather, it is *phileo*, which speaks of a love rooted in a sense of kinship—human affection and fondness.

In the ancient world, hotels as we know them today were non-existent; inns, such as they were, came few and far between. Therefore, hospitality to strangers was a virtue that was much esteemed. Moreover, in so doing, "some have entertained angels unawares" (Hebrews 13:2).

Compassion is an essential part of Christian living. In verse 3, the believers were exhorted to remember those who suffered because of their faith in Christ. Believers today are likewise commanded to be mindful of those who are imprisoned, whether they are believers or not. One of the richest fields for evangelism is the prison community.

B. Exhortation for Marital Fidelity (Hebrews 13:4)

Marriage is honourable in all, and the bed undefiled: but whoremongers and adulterers God will judge.

The writer compares that which is sexually moral with that which is immoral. Sex among married couples is honorable, while sex outside of the marriage bond is immoral, and those who practice such will suffer the condemnation of God. Believers are exhorted to honor marriage. The word "honor" is *timios*, which means "held as of great price, esteemed, especially dear." When marriage is honored, it follows that the marital bed will be honored and kept from defilement.

The statement here, like the rest of the passage, goes beyond mere advice; it is a commandment. Believers are commanded to honor both their marriages and the marriages of others, seeking always to maintain purity. Marriage is an institution of God and, as such, must be highly esteemed.

C. Exhortation for Contentment (Hebrews 13:5-6)

Let your conversation be without covetousness; and be content with such things as ye have: for he hath said, I will never leave thee, nor forsake thee. So that we may boldly say, The Lord is my helper, and I will not fear what man shall do unto me.

In our world today, the word *conversation* is limited in meaning to refer to conversing between two or more persons. However, in A.D. 1611, when the *Authorized (King James) Version* of the Bible was translated, it retained the original Greek meaning: "manner of life, behavior." The term "covetous," which essentially means to be greedy and to lust for what belongs to another, refers to one who pursues selfish aims—whether sexual, financial, political, or otherwise—without regard for the rights of others. So the writer cautions Christians against the love of money.

Being content means "to be satisfied, or to have enough." At the time of this writing, there was a popular sect known as the Stoics, whose favorite doctrine was one of "self-sufficiency" that humankind should be sufficient to themselves for all things, and able by the power of their own will to handle whatever the circumstances of life brought before them. What was said to them extends also to us. God will neither withdraw His *presence* ("never leave thee") nor His *help* ("nor forsake thee") (verse 5).

This affirmation shows great faith: "The Lord is my helper, and I will not fear what man shall do unto me" (verse 6). This idea comes from Psalm 118:6. It is a messianic psalm and is fulfilled in Jesus Christ, so we may claim this promise for ourselves. This reiterates the point that whatever a person attempts to do against us will not succeed because the Lord is our Helper and our Protector, and therefore we have no need to fear.

D. Exhortation for Religious Direction (Hebrews 13:7-16)

Remember them which have the rule over you, who have spoken unto you the word of God: whose faith follow, considering the end of their conversation. Jesus Christ the same yesterday, and to day, and for ever. Be not carried about with divers and strange doctrines. For it is a good thing that the heart be established with grace; not with meats, which have not profited them that have been occupied therein. We have an altar, whereof they have no right to eat which serve the tabernacle. For the bodies of those beasts, whose blood is brought into the sanctuary by the high priest for sin, are burned without the camp. Wherefore Jesus also, that he might sanctify the people with his own blood, suffered without the gate. Let us go forth therefore unto him without the camp, bearing his reproach. For here have we no continuing city, but we seek one to come. By him therefore let us offer the sacrifice of praise to God continually, that is, the fruit of our lips giving thanks to his name. But to do good and to communicate forget not: for with such sacrifices God is well pleased.

Believers are here exhorted to remember both the examples and the teachings of those leaders who have gone on and to honor them by imitation. In essence, the godly lives of former leaders provide a pattern for us to follow. They, too, suffered persecution, but yet they persevered by their dependence upon the promises of the Word of God.

"Jesus Christ is the same yesterday, and to-day, and for ever" (verse 8). He (is) the same, and (shall be the same) unto the ages (that is, unto all ages)." Verse 8 emphasizes the unchangeable nature and the permanence of Jesus as Messiah. We should recognize that the same God who helped our leaders yesterday (in, out, and through slavery) has not changed, either in His Person or in His power.

The writer reinforces his appeal (verse 14) to go to Jesus by reminding Christians that they have no stake in any earthly city, Jewish or otherwise. All earthly cities are transient and temporary. But Christians are looking for a city that is yet to come. Those Jews who clung to the earthly sanctuary were representatives of all who clung to this earth. The earthly Jerusalem proved to be no "abiding city," having been destroyed shortly after this epistle was written, and with it fell the Jewish civil and religious organization.

Verse 15 begins with an emphatic phrase, "By him…," that is, through Jesus and not the Jewish priests, people offered acceptable sacrifices to God. This spiritual sacrifice was to be offered continually. In systems like Judaism, sacrifices were offered at set times; but for Christians, praise was and is to go up all the time. The believer-priests of the New Testament, as well as those today, were and are to offer sacrifices of praise, rather than animal sacrifices.

The writer—having already made the point that Christians are relieved of the burdensome requirements of animal sacrifices and exhorted them to offer spiritual sacrifices instead—cautioned them against becoming speakers only. They did have tangible sacrifices to offer and he provided them with two examples: *To do good* is a general way of expressing it; however, "sharing" *(koinonia,* fellowship) is more specific. Today, it signifies sharing with others such things as we have: money, goods, and, of course, those intangibles that make up "fellowship."

are both equally impossible. The perfection of God renders Him devoid of all change, not only in His Being, but also in His purposes and promises. By virtue of this, He is exalted above all that is and all that is becoming, and is free from all growth or decay.

Nevertheless, divine immutability should not be understood as implying immobility, as if there was no movement in God. The Bible does indeed teach us that God is always in action. He enters into relationships with human beings, but there is no change in His being, His attributes, His purpose, His motives of action, or His promises.

III. CONCLUDING REFLECTIONS

It is important to understand and maintain the immutability or unchangeable nature of God against false doctrines that claim that God is subject to change. In God, being absolute perfection, improvement and deterioration

PRAYER

Dear God, our heavenly Father, we praise and thank You for Your unchangeable goodness and mercy. Thank You for continuing to offer us Your forgiveness for our sins. We thank You for the gift of Your Son, our eternal Savior. In Jesus' name, we pray. Amen.

WORD POWER

Immutable *(ametathetos* [ame-ta-the-tos])—this is the root word for "mutate" or "change." This word is found in Hebrews 6:18. The word begins with "a," which in Greek turns the word to an opposite. A good example is *theist,* which means "the one who believes in God"; however, *atheist* means "unbeliever in God." The word *immutable* means "God remains unchanged and faithful to His Word and His promises."

HOME DAILY BIBLE READINGS
(June 23-29, 2008)
The Eternal Christ

LESSON 6   July 6, 2008

CHRIST AS TEACHER

1 peter 5 - 8
ELIA - 8 - 19
SAME - 7
Jude 9 '9

DEVOTIONAL READING: **Isaiah 11:1-3**
PRINT PASSAGE: **Luke 4:31-37; 20:1-8**

DEVI 8 - 10-12
GAI - 10-21

BACKGROUND SCRIPTURE: **Luke 4:31-37; 20:1-8**
KEY VERSE: **Luke 4:32**

Luke 4:31-37; 20:1-8—KJV

31 And came down to Capernaum, a city of Galilee, and taught them on the sabbath days.

32 And they were astonished at his doctrine: for his word was with power.

33 And in the synagogue there was a man, which had a spirit of an unclean devil, and cried out with a loud voice,

34 Saying, Let us alone; what have we to do with thee, thou Jesus of Nazareth? art thou come to destroy us? I know thee who thou art; the Holy One of God.

35 And Jesus rebuked him, saying, Hold thy peace, and come out of him. And when the devil had thrown him in the midst, he came out of him, and hurt him not.

36 And they were all amazed, and spake among themselves, saying, What a word is this! for with authority and power he commandeth the unclean spirits, and they come out.

37 And the fame of him went out into every place of the country round about.

…..

AND IT came to pass, that on one of those days, as he taught the people in the temple, and preached the gospel, the chief priests and the scribes came upon him with the elders,

2 And spake unto him, saying, Tell us, by what authority doest thou these things? or who is he that gave thee this authority?

3 And he answered and said unto them, I will also ask you one thing; and answer me:

4 The baptism of John, was it from heaven, or of men?

5 And they reasoned with themselves, saying, If we shall say, From heaven; he will say, Why then believed ye him not?

6 But and if we say, Of men; all the people will stone us: for they be persuaded that John was a prophet.

7 And they answered, that they could not tell whence it was.

Luke 4:31-37; 20:1-8—NRSV

31 He went down to Capernaum, a city in Galilee, and was teaching them on the sabbath.

32 They were astounded at his teaching, because he spoke with authority.

33 In the synagogue there was a man who had the spirit of an unclean demon, and he cried out with a loud voice,

34 "Let us alone! What have you to do with us, Jesus of Nazareth? Have you come to destroy us? I know who you are, the Holy One of God."

35 But Jesus rebuked him, saying, "Be silent, and come out of him!" When the demon had thrown him down before them, he came out of him without having done him any harm.

36 They were all amazed and kept saying to one another, "What kind of utterance is this? For with authority and power he commands the unclean spirits, and out they come!"

37 And a report about him began to reach every place in the region.

…..

ONE DAY, as he was teaching the people in the temple and telling the good news, the chief priests and the scribes came with the elders

2 and said to him, "Tell us, by what authority are you doing these things? Who is it who gave you this authority?"

3 He answered them, "I will also ask you a question, and you tell me:

4 Did the baptism of John come from heaven, or was it of human origin?"

5 They discussed it with one another, saying, "If we say, 'From heaven,' he will say, 'Why did you not believe him?'

6 But if we say, 'Of human origin,' all the people will stone us; for they are convinced that John was a prophet."

7 So they answered that they did not know where it came from.

8 And Jesus said unto them, Neither tell I you by what authority I do these things.

8 Then Jesus said to them, "Neither will I tell you by what authority I am doing these things."

TOPICAL OUTLINE OF THE LESSON

I. Introduction
   A. Teach, Teacher, Teaching
   B. Biblical Background

II. **Exposition and Application of the Scripture**
   A. Jesus Taught with Authority (Luke 4:31-32)
   B. The Demon-possessed Man Recognized Jesus (Luke 4:33-34)
   C. Jesus Expelled the Demons (Luke 4:35-37)
   D. Jesus' Authority Is Questioned (Luke 20:1-8)

III. **Concluding Reflections**

LESSON OBJECTIVES

Upon completion of this lesson, the students will know that:
1. Teaching is more than just giving out information;
2. Those who teach the Bible will encounter satanic opposition;
3. Teachers of the Scriptures are endowed with power to transform lives; and,
4. The teachings of the Scriptures are superior to other teachings.

POINTS TO BE EMPHASIZED
ADULT/YOUTH
Adult Topic: **Teaching that Transforms**
Youth Topic: **Christ Tells It like It Is!**
Adult/Youth Key Verse: **Luke 4:32**
Print Passage: **Luke 4:31-37; 20:1-8**
—Jesus was teaching in Capernaum on the Sabbath, and He astounded people because He taught with authority.
—Jesus' authority was questioned by everyone except the demons.
—Capernaum was the headquarters of Jesus' ministry.
—Jesus taught at the synagogue in Capernaum (Matthew 7:28-29; Mark 1:21-28).
—Jesus demonstrated the authority of His teaching by dominating and controlling demons.
—A dread of demons is reflected throughout the Gospels; people in biblical times seemed to feel a sense of helplessness in the presence of demons.
—The religious leaders of the day recognized Jesus' teaching authority and tried to challenge it at every opportunity.

CHILDREN
Children Topic: **Jesus Taught with Power**
Key Verse: **Luke 4:32**
Print Passage: **Luke 4:31-37; 6:17-22**
—Jesus taught with great authority and power.
—Jesus ordered the evil spirit to depart from the man.
—Jesus had healing in His voice as well as in His hands.
—Jesus blessed the poor, the hungry, the sorrowful, and the hated.
—Jesus possessed extraordinary power to teach and heal.

I. INTRODUCTION

A. Teach, Teacher, Teaching

We can better present this lesson on "Christ as Teacher" if we have some understanding of the role of teachers in the Bible. Therefore, let's begin with a brief survey of the most frequently used words that describe teaching or the role of the teacher. The Old Testament word *badal*, "to separate" or "to divide," refers to the ability to distinguish the necessary from the unimportant. In that vein, a teacher solved difficult problems, both spiritual and otherwise. The teacher was endowed with the ability to put issues in correct perspective (Psalm 119:34; Daniel 8:16).

The word *zahar*, "to shine," is used when Moses enlightened the people about the principles sent by God (Exodus 18:20). The teacher illuminated for the student. The teacher made and makes what is obscure come to the light so that the student can have a deeper understanding of the subject matter.

In the New Testament, some of the important words are as follows: *didasko*, ("to teach")—which conveys both lecturing and imparting knowledge; emphasis is on the instructor and implies fitness for the task (see Matthew 28:19; Ephesians 4:11); *diermeneuo* ("to interpret")—which is used to refer to the task of explaining; the teacher explained the lesson to the students—(Luke 24:27; 1 Corinthians 14:5); this is where we derive the word *hermeneutics*, which is the "method of interpretation"; *paratithemi* ("to place beside")—which refers to the ability to adapt the lesson to the existing situation. This technique was employed by the Lord Jesus in parables.

These words are clear evidence of the responsibilities of the teacher. The teacher could and can fulfill this responsibility only by understanding the basis of true teaching, a basis which can come only from the Word of God. The teaching ministry of the Lord Jesus Christ was an excellent example of this, earning Him the title *Rabbi* or "Master Teacher" (John 3:2).

B. Biblical Background

This lesson chronicles the behavior of a man with "an unclean spirit" (Luke 4:33) or demon. It is helpful, therefore, to see what the Bible teaches about such a phenomenon.

The New Testament writers always thought of devils or demons as spiritual beings that were hostile to both God and human beings. The "prince" of these maligned beings was accorded the name *Beelzebub*, so that demons generally were regarded as his agents in human society.

In the gospels, the outburst of demonic opposition to the work of God in Christ is most evident, and the evangelists depict Christ in continual conflict with evil forces. To expel demons was no easy matter, as the disciples discovered in Matthew 17:19 and Mark 9:28. The fact that Christ was able to expel the evil spirit with apparent ease led His enemies to link Him perversely with demonic forces instead of recognizing His divine origin (see Luke 11:15; John 7:20).

II. EXPOSITION AND APPLICATION OF THE SCRIPTURE

A. Jesus Taught with Authority
(Luke 4:31-32)

And came down to Capernaum, a city of Galilee, and taught them on the sabbath days. And they were astonished at his doctrine: for his word was with power.

Jesus went from Nazareth down to the city of Capernaum, because the lakeside city was on a lower level. Capernaum became the center of Christ's activities and was His headquarters during His Galilean ministry. It was in this vicinity that He called his first disciples (John 1:35-42). Jesus arrived there on the Sabbath and, as was His custom, He went into the synagogue and began to teach. He delivered several messages in this synagogue including His address on "The Bread of Life" (John 6:24-65). His teachings there differed from that of the other rabbis, for most of them quoted other more prominent rabbis to give authority to their words.

Jesus taught with the authority of one greater than His predecessors. His authoritative tone astonished those in attendance. The word *astonish* denoted "surprise." They wondered where and how He attained such knowledge. He was too young to have been to any rabbinical school. His parents were too poor to give Him the formal education of their day. All these factors combined contributed to their sense of wonderment.

B. The Demon-possessed Man Recognized Jesus
(Luke 4:33-34)

And in the synagogue there was a man, which had a spirit of an unclean devil, and cried out with a loud voice, Saying, Let us alone; what have we to do with thee, thou Jesus of Nazareth? art thou come to destroy us? I know thee who thou art; the Holy One of God.

There was a man present in the audience who had become possessed by a demon, and the demon caused the man to cry out loudly, "What have you to do with us, Jesus of Nazareth? Have you come to destroy us? I "know" who you are, the Holy One of God." The word "know" *(oida)* indicates a thorough knowledge of something. For example, it is one thing to know what an apple is as it hangs on a tree, but it is another experience to pluck the apple and eat it.

The demon recognized Jesus as one having authority over him. The original Greek reads "Aha! What …Jesus? I know who you are, the Holy One of God." This is usually taken as a question, but it may be a statement. The demon recognized the opposition between Jesus and all of his kind. His employment of the title "Holy One of God" is an unusual title (only used here, Mark 1:24, and in John 6:69). It stresses the thought of consecration to God's service, and for that reason the demon knew there was no chance for him to continue to torment his victim.

We should see this as an example of what James had in mind when he wrote "the devils also believe, and tremble" (James 2:19). The demons knew who Jesus was and this knowledge caused them to shudder at the sight of Him. However, their knowledge of Him was not accompanied by saving faith and acceptance of Him as Savior. Light and darkness did not and do not associate. Jesus represented light, and the demon represented darkness.

Indeed, in our day-to-day living we will encounter individuals who, like the demons, have knowledge of Jesus but lack the faith to believe and accept Him as Savior. There is a crucial difference between knowledge and faith. Saving faith is not mere intellectual acceptance of a theological proposition. It goes much deeper, involving the heart and the whole inner being, expressing itself outwardly in a change in our lives.

Head knowledge about Jesus without heart knowledge of Him is satanic. The demon in the possessed man recognized the power inherent in Jesus Christ. We should ask ourselves as individuals: "Do I know Jesus Christ? Do I recognize His presence through the Holy Spirit? Do I avail myself of Him?" Jesus said, "I am the good shepherd, and know my sheep and am known of mine" (John 10:14). Do you hear His voice? Are you able to distinguish His voice from other competing voices around you?

C. Jesus Expelled the Demons (Luke 4:35-37)

And Jesus rebuked him, saying, Hold thy peace, and come out of him. And when the devil had thrown him in the midst, he came out of him, and hurt him not. And they were all amazed, and spake among themselves, saying, What a word is this! for with authority and power he commandeth the unclean spirits, and they come out. And the fame of him went out into every place of the country round about.

Jesus rebuked the demon. There are two words used in the New Testament for "rebuke." The one used here, *epitimao,* means "to rebuke another, the rebuke failing to bring the offender to acknowledge personal sin." The other word, *elegcho,* results in conviction of sin and sometimes a confession of sin on the offender's part. The former was used by Luke to describe Satan, the fallen angels, and the demons who were incorrigible. They refused to be convicted of their sins, and they would not acknowledge them or repent. Jesus commanded them to "hold thy peace" (verse 35), meaning, literally, "to close the mouth with a muzzle; to muzzle," and, metaphorically, "to stop the mouth, to make speechless, reduce to silence."

Jesus forbade them to utter a single word.

He used the same word used to refer to muzzling an ox (Deuteronomy 25:4; 1 Corinthians 9:9). It is used in the Lord's muzzling the Sadducees (Matthew 22:34) and stilling the storm (Mark 4:39). It is roughly equivalent to our "Shut up!" Grammatically speaking, it is a sharp command to be obeyed at once. The same holds true of the command, "Come out!" At Jesus' command, the demon protested by throwing the man down, but it came out without doing him any further harm.

The people had witnessed some fraudulent exorcisms before, but they were always accompanied by a great demonstration of chanting and casting spells. Jesus' exorcism was done with only a spoken phrase, and it amazed them. The word used for "amazed" suggests that they were struck with astonishment to the point of panic and fright. They questioned among themselves, inquiring of one another about the authority and power of this man Jesus. This questioning among themselves continued long after their departure, causing the fame of Jesus to spread throughout the country.

Jesus, at this point, helped His audience to know that truly the kingdom of Satan could not stand against the kingdom of God. The two were and are diametrically opposed. The demon who had taken residence in the life of the man was expelled by the Lord Jesus Christ. This phenomenon contributed to their amazement, for no rabbi had ever cast out demons. By casting out the demon, Jesus established His authority over evil forces.

Jesus said in Matthew 12:28, "...If I cast out devils by the Spirit of God, then the kingdom of God is come..." By expelling the demon from the man, Jesus publicly announced the presence of the Father's kingdom, which supersedes the kingdom of Satan.

The people of God should believe that their presence in this world represents God. One thing that Satan will do is try to make Christians believe that they have no power and that their prayers have no effect. But we are not ignorant of his devices (2 Corinthians 2:11). The authority we have is in Christ and we must constantly keep our position in Him in our hearts so that Satan will not steal it away from us.

D. Jesus' Authority Is Questioned (Luke 20:1-8)

AND IT came to pass, that on one of those days, as he taught the people in the temple, and preached the gospel, the chief priests and the scribes came upon him with the elders, And spake unto him, saying, Tell us, by what authority doest thou these things? or who is he that gave thee this authority? And he answered and said unto them, I will also ask you one thing; and answer me: The baptism of John, was it from heaven, or of men? And they reasoned with themselves, saying, If we shall say, From heaven; he will say, Why then believed ye him not? But and if we say, Of men; all the people will stone us: for they be persuaded that John was a prophet. And they answered, that they could not tell whence it was. And Jesus said unto them, Neither tell I you by what authority I do these things.

On a particular day when Jesus was teaching, the religious leaders all gathered together. This group consisted of the chief priests (the present ruling high priest, those who had formerly held this high office, and other high dignitaries from whose ranks the high priest was usually chosen), the scribes (the men of letters, those who studied and taught God's law, and the experts in the Jewish religion), and the elders (the heads of tribes). This group of individuals made up the Sanhedrin, the Jewish Supreme Court, which served as the official representative of the Jewish people.

They confronted Jesus, telling Him to let them know by what authority He was doing the healings and miracles. In other words, they were saying, "Show us your credentials." It was an attempt to embarrass Him. If He admitted that He had no credentials, the people likely would lose respect for Him. On the other hand, if He considered Himself to be authorized to say these things, He would be claiming for Himself authority that belonged to God alone. In doing so, He would be guilty of blasphemy. It should be remembered that it was of the charge of blasphemy that the religious leaders were constantly accusing Jesus, and ultimately this was the "crime" for which they crucified Him.

Jesus recognized their plot to trap Him, so He confounded them by asking them this question: "The baptism of John, was it from heaven, or of men?" (verse 4). In so doing, He drove them into a corner. If they had answered that the baptism of John had a heavenly source, then He would have asked them, "Why then believed ye him not?" (verse 5). On the other hand, if they claimed that the baptism of John was of human origin, the crowds of pilgrims who had come from Galilee might have stoned them, for they believed that John was a prophet. Trying to avoid entanglement in their own trap, they answered that they did not know the source. Upon hearing their answer, the Lord said, "Neither tell I you by what authority I do these things" (verse 8).

Today, there are people who have yet to grasp the truth about the power of Jesus. Inwardly, they question whether Jesus' power is still present. When they see the intervention of God in healing an individual, they raise the question of authenticity. They have forgotten that all power belongs to Jesus, and His power is present when and where His people gather.

III. CONCLUDING REFLECTIONS

Jesus' last words spoken during His earthly ministry, best known from Matthew 28:19-20, have become known as the Great Commission. This suggests that the greatest command of the church is to make disciples by "teaching them…" (verse 20). As such, teaching was and is not an option; rather, it was and is central to the church's mission in the world.

We should note, however, that the teaching referred to in verse 20 is not simply the communication of information, but has a goal of transformation. That idea, expressed by the apostle Paul in Romans 12:1-2, employs the same word used by the Lord when He was on the Mount of Transfiguration. It was a word that denoted a physical change in His appearance brought about by an inward change that revealed His deity. Christian teaching is to bring change from the inside. Christian teaching is to bring new life and readiness for eternity. Christian teaching should aim to empower learners to become enablers. Christian teaching should produce stable lives. Christians should teach to produce believers who will not be swayed by various and false doctrines that are being preached.

PRAYER

Dear God, our heavenly Father, how grateful we are for the privilege of studying Your Word. Thank You for the godly teachers You have placed in our midst, and for the teaching ministry of Your Holy Spirit. Help us now to be diligent in our study of Your Word. In the name of Your Son Jesus, we pray. Amen.

WORD POWER

Authority *(eksousia* [ek-sou-sia])—this word describes power of choice, or freedom to do as one pleases. It is an endowed power which is at one's disposal, and one can bring it out (ek) to subdue any other power. This is the power that Jesus used on the man in today's text. The demon recognized the awesome power in Christ, and he pleaded to not be expelled.

HOME DAILY BIBLE READINGS
(June 30—July 6, 2008)

Christ as Teacher
MONDAY, June 30: "Spirit-anointed Teacher" (Isaiah 11:1-3)
TUESDAY, July 1: "Filled with God's Spirit" (Luke 4:14-15)
WEDNESDAY, July 2: "With Authority" (Luke 4:31-37)
THURSDAY, July 3: "Blessed Are You" (Luke 6:17-23)
FRIDAY, July 4: "Woes and Blessings" (Luke 6:24-31)
SATURDAY, July 5: "Love Your Enemies" (Luke 6:32-36)
SUNDAY, July 6: "Authority Questioned" (Luke 20:1-8)

LESSON 7   July 13, 2008

CHRIST AS HEALER

DEVOTIONAL READING: **Isaiah 61:1-4**
PRINT PASSAGE: **Mark 1:29-45**

BACKGROUND SCRIPTURE: **Mark 1:29-45**
KEY VERSE: **Mark 1:34**

Mark 1:29-45—KJV

29 And forthwith, when they were come out of the synagogue, they entered into the house of Simon and Andrew, with James and John.

30 But Simon's wife's mother lay sick of a fever, and anon they tell him of her.

31 And he came and took her by the hand, and lifted her up; and immediately the fever left her, and she ministered unto them.

32 And at even, when the sun did set, they brought unto him all that were diseased, and them that were possessed with devils.

33 And all the city was gathered together at the door.

34 And he healed many that were sick of divers diseases, and cast out many devils; and suffered not the devils to speak, because they knew him.

35 And in the morning, rising up a great while before day, he went out, and departed into a solitary place, and there prayed.

36 And Simon and they that were with him followed after him.

37 And when they had found him, they said unto him, All men seek for thee.

38 And he said unto them, Let us go into the next towns, that I may preach there also: for therefore came I forth.

39 And he preached in their synagogues throughout all Galilee, and cast out devils.

40 And there came a leper to him, beseeching him, and kneeling down to him, and saying unto him, If thou wilt, thou canst make me clean.

41 And Jesus, moved with compassion, put forth his hand, and touched him, and saith unto him, I will; be thou clean.

42 And as soon as he had spoken, immediately the leprosy departed from him, and he was cleansed.

Mark 1:29-45—NRSV

29 As soon as they left the synagogue, they entered the house of Simon and Andrew, with James and John.

30 Now Simon's mother-in-law was in bed with a fever, and they told him about her at once.

31 He came and took her by the hand and lifted her up. Then the fever left her, and she began to serve them.

32 That evening, at sundown, they brought to him all who were sick or possessed with demons.

33 And the whole city was gathered around the door.

34 And he cured many who were sick with various diseases, and cast out many demons; and he would not permit the demons to speak, because they knew him.

35 In the morning, while it was still very dark, he got up and went out to a deserted place, and there he prayed.

36 And Simon and his companions hunted for him.

37 When they found him, they said to him, "Everyone is searching for you."

38 He answered, "Let us go on to the neighboring towns, so that I may proclaim the message there also; for that is what I came out to do."

39 And he went throughout Galilee, proclaiming the message in their synagogues and casting out demons.

40 A leper came to him begging him, and kneeling he said to him, "If you choose, you can make me clean."

41 Moved with pity, Jesus stretched out his hand and touched him, and said to him, "I do choose. Be made clean!"

42 Immediately the leprosy left him, and he was made clean.

43 And he straitly charged him, and forthwith sent him away;

44 And saith unto him, See thou say nothing to any man: but go thy way, shew thyself to the priest, and offer for thy cleansing those things which Moses commanded, for a testimony unto them.

45 But he went out, and began to publish it much, and to blaze abroad the matter, insomuch that Jesus could no more openly enter into the city, but was without in desert places: and they came to him from every quarter.

43 After sternly warning him he sent him away at once,

44 saying to him, "See that you say nothing to anyone; but go, show yourself to the priest, and offer for your cleansing what Moses commanded, as a testimony to them."

45 But he went out and began to proclaim it freely, and to spread the word, so that Jesus could no longer go into a town openly, but stayed out in the country; and people came to him from every quarter.

TOPICAL OUTLINE OF THE LESSON

I. **Introduction**
   A. Healing in the Bible
   B. Biblical Background

II. **Exposition and Application of the Scripture**
   A. Jesus Healed Peter's Mother-in-Law (Mark 1:29-31)
   B. Jesus Healed Many with Various Diseases (Mark 1:32-34)
   C. Jesus Preached and Cast Out Demons (Mark 1:35-39)
   D. Jesus' Cleansing of a Leper and the Impact It Had (Mark 1:40-45)

III. **Concluding Reflections**

LESSON OBJECTIVES

Upon completion of this lesson, the students will know:

1. The extent and importance of the healing ministry of Jesus Christ;
2. The relationship of spiritual healing to physical healing; and,
3. That the reason why some are healed and some are not is best known to God.

POINTS TO BE EMPHASIZED

ADULT/YOUTH

Adult Topic: **Finding Healing and Wholeness**

Youth Topic: **The Doctor Is In!**

Adult/Youth Key Verse: **Mark 1:34**

Print Passage: **Mark 1:29-45**

—Jesus healed the mother-in-law of Simon Peter on the Sabbath in Capernaum. He also healed many after sundown when the Sabbath was over.

—By touching him, Jesus healed the leper who expressed his faith. Jesus told him to go to the priests so that he could be cleansed.

—Jesus struggled with being seen only as a healer and not as a teacher of the Good News.

CHILDREN

Children Topic: **Jesus Healed**

Key Verse: **Mark 1:34**

Print Passage: **Mark 1:29-34, 40-45**

—Many sought Jesus for healing when they heard about His healing of other people.

—Jesus' touch healed Simon Peter's mother-in-law.

—Jesus healed many with various diseases.

—Jesus gave the healed leper instructions that the leper did not follow because he joyously told others about his healing.

I. INTRODUCTION

A. Healing in the Bible

In the Scriptures, healing is restoration to a state of health by physical means or by a miracle (the methods are not necessarily mutually exclusive). Healing by means of medicines and surgical tools was supported by the Scriptures. Local application of ointments and bandaging of wounds was certainly standard treatment in Old Testament times. The use of a plaster made of a cake of figs to be laid upon Hezekiah's boil was recognized as appropriate treatment and was advocated by God's prophet (Isaiah 38:21).

Using medicine to heal wounds or diseases is not prohibited in the Bible. However, some interpret James 5:14 (concerning the anointing with oil) as not merely referring to a religious rite, but as an injunction to accompany the prayer of faith with the application of whatever oil or balm seemed to be required in the particular instance of illness. Such applications were extensively used in Bible times and may be regarded as similar to the present-day use of certain applications, such as oil of wintergreen for rheumatic symptoms.

Modern medicines in the form of tablets, ointments, and liquids all came from different plants. Knowing that God created these plants and has given us the knowledge to make use of them is a blessing.

B. Biblical Background

There are at least three kinds of healing in the New Testament: physical healing, spiritual healing, and thorough healing. The three main words used to describe them are *therapeuo,* which is used ten times in reference to our Lord's miracles; *iaomai,* which carries the idea of restoration; and *diasozo,* which means "to preserve through danger, or to bring safely through" (see Luke 7:3).

In most cases of our Lord's healings, there was an implicit demand for faith to be exercised by the sufferer (Matthew 9:29; Mark 10:52), although there are exceptions (for example, John 5:1-9). It is interesting to note that on two occasions (Mark 8:23; John 9:6), Christ used saliva to anoint a person's eyes for healing. It is believed that He did so partly to strengthen their faith, but partly to teach that divine healing may go hand in hand with the use of recognized medical remedies.

II. EXPOSITON AND APPLICATION OF THE SCRIPTURE

A. Jesus Healed Peter's Mother-in-Law
(Mark 1:29-31)

And forthwith, when they were come out of the synagogue, they entered into the house of Simon and Andrew, with James and John. But Simon's wife's mother lay sick of a fever, and anon they tell him of her. And he came and took her by the hand, and lifted her up; and immediately the fever left her, and she ministered unto them.

We discover in this section that Peter was married, and that his mother-in-law lived with him and his wife. Jesus made His home with Peter while He was in Capernaum. Upon entering the house, they discovered that Peter's mother-in-law was ill. The phrase "lay sick" is in the imperfect tense, speaking of continuous action; she had been in that condition for a while. The word *fever* in the noun form is the Greek word for "fire" *(pur)*. Thus, she had been lying in the house for a long time, burning with fever.

Jesus, the Great Physician, came and stood over her. He took her by the hand and lifted her up. She was healed instantly with no recovery time needed, as indicated by the reading "…immediately the fever left her, and she ministered unto them" (verse 31). Moreover, the verb form for *served,* or *ministered,* is in the imperfect tense, which indicates that she served them continuously, which would include preparing the meal, without relapsing to her feverish condition.

It is worth noting here that, unlike that of some modern-day faith healers, the healing here was immediate and complete. However, there was no recording of the woman's faith, or even of her saying any words of positive confession.

B. Jesus Healed Many with Various Diseases
(Mark 1:32-34)

And at even, when the sun did set, they brought unto him all that were diseased, and them that were possessed with devils. And all the city was gathered together at the door. And he healed many that were sick of divers diseases, and cast out many devils; and suffered not the devils to speak, because they knew him.

This incident recorded by Matthew indicates that "all" were healed (Matthew 8:16). The news of this incident spread and people came from around the country—some seeking healing, others deliverance from demons, and many others simply to see the Great Physician. The number of the people coming to Jesus was so great, Luke records, that the whole city was gathered together at the door. Some came to satisfy their curiosity, and they were not disappointed.

In verse 34, we are told that Jesus healed as many as went to Him. He healed them all of "various diseases" or all kinds of illnesses. This included those who had been diagnosed as incurable, or even terminal. In so doing, He also "cast out many devils and suffered not the devils to speak, because they knew Him." The tense indicates that the demons were continuously trying to be heard, but He did not permit them to speak.

As alluded to here and recorded elsewhere (James 2:19), the demons were well acquainted with Jesus, though their acquaintance is not to be accorded with faith. Jesus did not permit them to speak because they were considered destructive agents in the vineyard of God. No farmer would allow pests to take control of his farm products. The farmer would take pest control measures and get rid of the pests without mercy. Human beings are created in the image of God, and for demons to take over the image of God would be tantamount to saying that the demons had power over God. The demons were destroyers, and they had to be expelled without consideration.

C. Jesus Preached and Cast Out Demons (Mark 1:35-39)

And in the morning, rising up a great while before day, he went out, and departed into a solitary place, and there prayed. And Simon and they that were with him followed after him. And when they had found him, they said unto him, All men seek for thee. And he said unto them, Let us go into the next towns, that I may preach there also: for therefore came I forth. And he preached in their synagogues throughout all Galilee, and cast out devils.

Jesus arose early in the morning—an indication that it was the last watch of the night, from three to six a.m., a long while before daylight and in the early part of the watch while it was still a bit dark. He left Peter's house, departed the city to a solitary place—and prayed there.

It is instructive for us to observe here that the prayer life of Jesus involved rising early in the morning and departing for a place of solitude. It is consistent with His instructions to His disciples and to us to set aside a "prayer closet," a "secret place" we are to reserve for our times of prayer (Matthew 6:5-6).

The prayer life of Jesus was successful for three reasons: 1) It was planned. He got up very early in the morning to be alone with the Father before the hustle and bustle of the day began. 2) It was private. He went alone without asking the disciples to go with Him. 3) It was prolonged. Jesus did not usually pray short prayers.

The disciples, upon arising, discovered that the Lord was not in their midst and began searching for Him. Mark's use of the term "searched" is an indication that they "tracked Him down." Their search involved looking for Him in various places and finally finding Him outside the city in a solitary place. They said to Him, "All men seek for thee" (verse 37).

We are to observe here another important lesson from the Lord. Jesus knew that He had a busy day awaiting Him. He knew that the number of people coming to Him for healing was bound to increase, and this would be accompanied by increased demonic opposition. So, in preparation for the difficulties which lay ahead, He arose early in the morning to pray. This tells us that whenever we anticipate a difficult task, we should prepare for it by praying. Furthermore, the more difficult the task, the more time we should spend in prayer.

These verses (38-39) summarize much, if not most, of the earthly ministry of the Lord Jesus: "…for therefore came I forth." Through this proclamation, Jesus took seriously His mission to reach the next towns.

D. Jesus' Cleansing of a Leper and the Impact It Had (Mark 1:40-45)

And there came a leper to him, beseeching him, and kneeling down to him, and saying unto him, If thou wilt, thou canst make me clean. And Jesus, moved with compassion, put forth his hand, and touched him, and saith unto him, I will; be thou clean. And as soon as he had spoken, immediately the leprosy departed from him, and he was cleansed. And he straitly charged him, and forthwith sent him away; And saith unto him, See thou say nothing to any man: but go thy way, shew thyself to the priest, and offer for thy cleansing those things which Moses commanded, for a testimony unto them. But he went out, and began to publish it much, and to blaze abroad the matter, insomuch that Jesus could no more openly enter into the city, but was without in desert places: and they came to him from every quarter.

The phrase "And there came a leper to him…" (verse 40) is spoken in a manner that indicates this was no isolated incident; rather, it happened continuously. The leper beseeched, implored, and begged Him, saying, "If thou wilt…." There are two Greek words which may be translated "to be willing, to desire." One expresses a desire that comes from one's emotions and the other a desire that comes from one's reason. The first is used here.

The leper appealed to the tenderheartedness of the Messiah. "Thou canst make me clean." He employed the word *dunamai*, meaning "to have power" or "to be able." The leper did not doubt the ability of the Lord to heal. He had heard of what Jesus did in nearby Capernaum. What he doubted was the Lord's "will" or "desire."

This too ought to prove instructive for us. The leper did not doubt God's ability but, rather, His will, and he beseeched Him for His will. Ought not we to pray in like manner in times of illness or distress? Should we not also pray to God for His will to be done rather than giving Him instructions or orders?

At this point, the Lord Jesus was moved with compassion. He put out his hand and said, "I will; be thou clean" (verse 41). Be reminded here that Levitical law forbade a Jew to touch a leper, and as we know, our Lord lived under and obeyed the law. So how was He able to touch the leper?

The rule of Greek grammar that governs this construction is that the action of the present participle goes on simultaneously with the action of the leading verb. That is, Jesus was saying "I will," at the time he was touching the leper. But the thought "I will," the determination to follow out His desire to cleanse the leper, and the act of cleansing him all preceded the spoken words and the outstretched hand.

The Lord did not touch the leper in order to heal him, but to show him and the people around that he was cleansed of his leprosy. This gives us a wonderful truth. Leprosy was associated with sin, and when we (repentant sinners) come crying, "Unclean, unclean, Lord if You will, make me clean," the Lord Jesus is moved with compassion, stretches out His hand and touches us, saying, "I will. Be cleansed!" And, as in the case of the leper, He cleanses us before He touches us. In John 1:12, justification precedes regeneration in the divine economy.

Jesus charged the leper to keep quiet and not tell the source of his healing. Why did Jesus instruct him not to proclaim his healing? There are at least four cardinal reasons: 1) The report of Jesus healing the man may have prejudiced the priest who needed to pronounce him clean. 2) Jesus did not want people to see Him primarily as a miracle worker. 3) The man's testimony would provoke a quick reaction to Jesus from the religious leaders who were constantly watching Him. 4) Jesus may have wanted to ensure that the man would not be distracted from making his requisite visit to the priest.

The leper was required by Law to go to the priest and be declared clean (see Leviticus 14:1-32). It appears that, following his appearance before the priest, he simply could not keep the miracle to himself and went out and told others about the miracle that had happened. The news of this event caused so many people to come looking for Jesus that He had to take refuge in the wilderness; but even this did not keep people from pursuing Him.

Although he did not follow Jesus' instructions, it is difficult for us to criticize the leper for his disobedience. When God does something miraculous in our lives, we just can't keep it to ourselves!

III. CONCLUDING REFLECTIONS

Throughout the ages, miracles of healing have been claimed, not only by orthodox Christians, but also by followers of various cults. These claims are still being made today by both Christians and non-Christians alike. There are even some, such as the Christian Scientists, and certain "Word Ministries" that claim healing through the denial of the existence of disease. The latter alleges the ability to activate this healing power by "positive confession" (for example, "I do not receive this" or by "pleading of the blood of Jesus"). Some religious groups conduct "miracle healing" services wherein many individuals give testimony to healings that occurred after the doctors had given up.

In assessing these modern-day reports, we should be careful to take note that some of these cases are great exaggerations or outright fraudulence, being produced by unethical spokespersons for personal and financial gain. Nevertheless, we who believe in Him know that He is able to do what no other power can do. The God of the Old Testament and the New Testament is the same. If He healed then, He can heal today as well.

PRAYER

Almighty God, our heavenly Father, we thank You for spiritual and physical healing. We praise and thank You for our assurance that when our earthly tabernacles have dissolved, we have other buildings, eternal in the heavens. Help us, we pray, to submit our every desire for physical healing to Your will. In Your Son's name, we pray. Amen.

WORD POWER

Cast out *(ekballo* [ek-ba-llo])—means "to eject, expel, or banish a person from a society." In the Key Verse, the words *cast out* show that Jesus expelled the demons with the notion of violence. He considered them to be like little foxes destroying the vineyard. Demons could not be treated with ease. They were deadly foes, and that was why Jesus did not entertain any discussion with them.

HOME DAILY BIBLE READINGS
(July 7-13, 2008)
Christ as Healer
MONDAY, July 7, "Anointed by God" (Isaiah 61:1-4)
TUESDAY, July 8, "He Cured Many" (Mark 1:29-34)
WEDNESDAY, July 9, "To Neighboring Towns" (Mark 1:35-39)
THURSDAY, July 10, "The Word Spread" (Mark 1:40-45)
FRIDAY, July 11, "The Needs for Healing Grow" (Mark 2:1-2)
SATURDAY, July 12, "Healed by Faith" (Mark 2:3-5)
SUNDAY, July 13, "Astonished beyond Measure" (Mark 7:31-37)

LESSON 8   **July 20, 2008**

CHRIST AS SERVANT

DEVOTIONAL READING: **Isaiah 53:4-6**
PRINT PASSAGE: **John 13:1-8, 12-20**

BACKGROUND SCRIPTURE: **John 13:1-20**
KEY VERSE: **John 13:15**

John 13:1-8, 12-20—KJV

NOW BEFORE the feast of the passover, when Jesus knew that his hour was come that he should depart out of this world unto the Father, having loved his own which were in the world, he loved them unto the end.

2 And supper being ended, the devil having now put into the heart of Judas Iscariot, Simon's son, to betray him;

3 Jesus knowing that the Father had given all things into his hands, and that he was come from God, and went to God;

4 He riseth from supper, and laid aside his garments; and took a towel, and girded himself.

5 After that he poureth water into a bason, and began to wash the disciples' feet, and to wipe them with the towel wherewith he was girded.

6 Then cometh he to Simon Peter: and Peter saith unto him, Lord, dost thou wash my feet?

7 Jesus answered and said unto him, What I do thou knowest not now; but thou shalt know hereafter.

8 Peter saith unto him, Thou shalt never wash my feet. Jesus answered him, If I wash thee not, thou hast no part with me.

.....

12 So after he had washed their feet, and had taken his garments, and was set down again, he said unto them, Know ye what I have done to you?

13 Ye call me Master and Lord: and ye say well; for so I am.

14 If I then, your Lord and Master, have washed your feet; ye also ought to wash one another's feet.

15 For I have given you an example, that ye should do as I have done to you.

16 Verily, verily, I say unto you, The servant is not greater than his lord; neither he that is sent greater than he that sent him.

17 If ye know these things, happy are ye if ye do them.

John 13:1-8, 12-20—NRSV

NOW BEFORE the festival of the Passover, Jesus knew that his hour had come to depart from this world and go to the Father. Having loved his own who were in the world, he loved them to the end.

2 The devil had already put it into the heart of Judas son of Simon Iscariot to betray him. And during supper

3 Jesus, knowing that the Father had given all things into his hands, and that he had come from God and was going to God,

4 got up from the table, took off his outer robe, and tied a towel around himself.

5 Then he poured water into a basin and began to wash the disciples' feet and to wipe them with the towel that was tied around him.

6 He came to Simon Peter, who said to him, "Lord, are you going to wash my feet?"

7 Jesus answered, "You do not know now what I am doing, but later you will understand."

8 Peter said to him, "You will never wash my feet." Jesus answered, "Unless I wash you, you have no share with me."

.....

12 After he had washed their feet, had put on his robe, and had returned to the table, he said to them, "Do you know what I have done to you?

13 You call me Teacher and Lord--and you are right, for that is what I am.

14 So if I, your Lord and Teacher, have washed your feet, you also ought to wash one another's feet.

15 For I have set you an example, that you also should do as I have done to you.

16 Very truly, I tell you, servants are not greater than their master, nor are messengers greater than the one who sent them.

17 If you know these things, you are blessed if you do them.

UNIFYING LESSON PRINCIPLE

No one is too good to serve others. How are we to know whom and when to serve? Jesus Christ demonstrated what it means to be a humble servant.

18 I speak not of you all: I know whom I have chosen: but that the scripture may be fulfilled, He that eateth bread with me hath lifted up his heel against me.
19 Now I tell you before it come, that, when it is come to pass, ye may believe that I am he.
20 Verily, verily, I say unto you, He that receiveth whomsoever I send receiveth me; and he that receiveth me receiveth him that sent me.

18 I am not speaking of all of you; I know whom I have chosen. But it is to fulfill the scripture, 'The one who ate my bread has lifted his heel against me.'
19 I tell you this now, before it occurs, so that when it does occur, you may believe that I am he.
20 Very truly, I tell you, whoever receives one whom I send receives me; and whoever receives me receives him who sent me."

TOPICAL OUTLINE OF THE LESSON

I. **Introduction**
   A. The Biblical Practice of Foot Washing
   B. Biblical Background

II. **Exposition and Application of the Scripture**
   A. The Night of Passover Feast (John 13:1)
   B. Extreme Humility (John 13:2-8)
   C. A Model for Serving Others (John 13:12-17)
   D. Judas's Betrayal (John 13:18-20)

III. **Concluding Reflections**

LESSON OBJECTIVES

Upon completion of this lesson, the students are expected to:

1. Understand the practice of foot washing and the significance of Jesus' washing the disciples' feet;
2. Have a greater understanding of the biblical concept of servanthood; and,
3. Learn calmness in the presence of a betrayal.

POINTS TO BE EMPHASIZED

ADULT/YOUTH
Adult Topic: To Be a Servant
Youth Topic: Stooping Down to Lift Up
Adult Key Verse: John 13:15
Youth Key Verse: John 13:14
Print Passage: John 13:1-8, 12-20

—Jesus set an example for the disciples, telling them they were to wash one another's feet.
—Jesus defines what it means to be a disciple in terms of servanthood.
—The foot-washing incident by Jesus and its connection with the Eucharistic meal is unique to the gospel of John.
—John focuses on the divinity of Christ as the Son of God.
—John portrays Jesus as having insight into or knowledge of the inner makeup and thoughts of human beings.

CHILDREN
Children Topic: Jesus, a Serving Example
Key Verse: John 13:15
Print Passage: John 13:1-16

—Jesus gave His disciples an example of servanthood.
—Peter did not understand what Jesus was doing.
—When Jesus explained that being His follower required cleansing by Him, Peter welcomed Jesus' act of servanthood.
—A willingness to serve others is one way to glorify God.

.

I. INTRODUCTION

A. The Biblical Practice of Foot Washing

Though never a major rite in the Mosaic ritual, foot washing, the washing of hands and feet of the priests, did have a place (Exodus 30:17-21). This practice, like so many others in the Old Testament, may have had a sanitary function as well as a ritualistic one. In those days, guests were offered water and vessels for washing their feet (Genesis 18:4; 19:2). As a special act of affection and humility, a host might even wash the guest's feet (1 Samuel 25:41). In prominent households where there were slaves, this menial task was assigned to them.

Some interpreters see the act of Jesus' washing the disciples' feet and the subsequent practice of some sects to be more symbolic of ritualistic cleansing from sin, rather than an act of humility. They equate the washing as a cleansing from the defilement of present sin, with baptism symbolizing cleansing from all guilt—the one partial and temporary, the latter complete and permanent. A number of smaller denominations (for example, Primitive Baptists) even practice foot washing as an ordinance, citing 1 Timothy 5:10 as further affirmation of its elevated status within their ranks.

B. Biblical Background

The biblical concept of servanthood is expressed in several ways. Generally speaking, a servant is a person whose allegiance is bound to another. The most prevalent idea of servanthood in the Old Testament was that of a slave, who was regarded as property though possessing also certain rights (see Exodus 21:1-11; Leviticus 25:39-55). The concept of a servant, however, differs from that of a slave—in that the emphasis is upon service and obedience rather than obligation.

The New Testament writers differ from the Old Testament in distinguishing between servant and slave, often using the former to mean slave while the latter moves in the direction of child or son. New Testament writers assert the concept of being a slave to sin (John 8:34), but it is also used in a positive sense of being a slave to Christ or a slave to righteousness (Romans 6:16ff).

Paul himself indicates, however, that this language is a rather exceptional metaphor. When he and other writers refer to themselves as "servants of Jesus Christ," it is not the metaphor of slavery, but rather the Old Testament covenantal use of "servant," which implies controlled thinking. The decisive factor in the shift is Jesus, who reversed the customary patterns of authority (both pagan and Jewish) first by His teaching, and then by His own fulfillment of the servant role (Matthew 23:8-12; Mark 10:35-45).

II. EXPOSITION AND APPLICATION OF THE SCRIPTURE

A. The Night of the Passover Feast
(John 13:1)

NOW BEFORE the feast of the passover, when Jesus knew that his hour was come that he should depart out of this world unto the Father, having loved his own which were in the world, he loved them unto the end.

Passover was the first of three annual festivals, at which all men were required to appear in the sanctuary (Exodus 23:14-17). The noun *pesah* is derived from the verb *pasha* ("to pass over"), in the sense of "to spare," "to leap over," or "show mercy" (Exodus 23:15).

The historical Passover is related to the tenth plague on Egypt—the death of the firstborn of Egypt. In order to be protected from the angel of death, Israel was instructed to prepare a lamb for each household. Blood was to be applied to the lintel and doorpost (Exodus 12:7). The sign of the blood would secure the safety of each house so designated.

In this verse, it is worth noting that John's gospel account differs in many respects from that of the Synoptic Gospels (Matthew, Mark, and Luke). No mention is made of the preparation by Peter and John, the procedure during the meal, the discourse concerning the significance of the bread and cup, or of the contention for a position of favor that took place among the disciples at the supper.

The emphasis for John was upon the love that Jesus had for His disciples. The key statement is, "Jesus knew that his hour was come…, having loved his own which were in the world, he loved them unto the end" (John 13:1). The stress here is not on the new covenant, which is prominent in the Synoptic gospels, but on Jesus' personal love for His disciples. The meaning can be made clear by a paraphrase of this verse: "Jesus…because he loved his own that were in the world, made one final demonstration of that love."

The Greek word (love) used here is *agapao*, which translates "to be full of good will and exhibit the same." Another important phrase is "…He loved them unto the end." This means that when Jesus was only a few hours away from the cross, He did not allow His impending shameful death to cause Him to forget His own. Jesus was and is truly the same yesterday, today and forever.

B. Extreme Humility
(John 13:2-8)

And supper being ended, the devil having now put into the heart of Judas Iscariot, Simon's son, to betray him; Jesus knowing that the Father had given all things into his hands, and that he was come from God, and went to God; He riseth from supper, and laid aside his garments; and took a towel, and girded himself. After that he poureth water into a bason, and began to wash the disciples' feet, and to wipe them with the towel wherewith he was girded. Then cometh he to Simon Peter: and Peter saith unto him, Lord, dost thou wash my feet? Jesus answered and said unto him, What I do thou knowest not now; but thou shalt know hereafter. Peter saith unto him, Thou shalt never wash my feet. Jesus answered him, If I wash thee not, thou hast no part with me.

By the time that Jesus and His disciples were assembled in the upper room, He was aware that Judas had already yielded to the devil's suggestion that he betray the Master; nevertheless, Jesus allowed him to participate in the meal.

Jesus' awareness did not prevent Him from sharing in His last meal with the disciples. Before the meal started He rose and laid aside His garments, took a towel, and girded Himself. This action shocked the disciples, for they were aware that such attire was that of a slave preparing to serve.

The disciples, when they entered the room, had looked for someone to wash their feet, but since no one was present to do this, they simply ignored this unpleasant task and reclined for supper. The Lord, however, seeing the need, poured water into a basin and began to wash the disciples' feet, and then to wipe them with the towel with which he was girded. Notice here that a mark of a true servant is to take notice of a need and then take the initiative to fulfill the need without being asked.

When the Lord came to Peter to wash his feet, Peter protested, "Lord, dost thou wash my feet?" (verse 6). Peter resisted the Master's attempt because he regarded it as the work of a slave. In so doing, he failed to associate Jesus' act with His impending death. Furthermore, his refusal was a display of pride and false humility characteristic of unredeemed individuals who were so confident in their own ability to save themselves that they instinctively resisted the suggestion that they needed divine cleansing. They desired to do everything for themselves.

Peter would have preferred to wash Jesus' feet rather than allowing Jesus to wash his feet, protesting, *Thou shalt never wash my feet!* (verse 8). The "my" is very emphatic, and it perhaps has more significance than if Jesus had already washed the feet of the others. He said something like, "Whatever you may have done to the others, I will never let you wash my feet." Jesus then told Peter plainly that there could be nothing in common between them and that their friendship must be abandoned, unless Peter allowed Him to perform this act. At this point Peter had no choice but to submit (verse 9). In verse 10, there are two Greek words for washing: *Nipto* (washing of extremities—the hands and feet) and *Louo* (bathing). According to social norms of those times, once people had bathed their bodies they needed only to wash their hands and feet before eating meals. The lesson to Peter and us is this: that just those who have been bathed need only to wash their feet; likewise, believers who have been bathed by the Lord through His Word and the Spirit need only to wash themselves daily by confession of sin and meditating in the Word of God.

C. A Model for Serving Others
(John 13:12-17)

So after he had washed their feet, and had taken his garments, and was set down again, he said unto them, Know ye what I have done to you? Ye call me Master and Lord: and ye say well; for so I am. If I then, your Lord and Master, have washed your feet; ye also ought to wash one another's feet. For I have given you an example, that ye should do as I have done to you. Verily, verily, I say unto you, The servant is not greater than his lord; neither he that is sent greater than he that sent him. If ye know these things, happy are ye if ye do them.

When the Lord had finished washing the disciples' feet, had taken off the towel, and had put His garments back on, He sat down again and asked them. "Know ye what I have done to you?" (verse 12). He then proceeded to explain to them the significance of His action.

First, He reaffirmed His status among them: "You call me Master and Lord; and ye say well; for so I am." (verse 13). Then He said, "If I, then, your Lord and Master, have washed your feet; you also ought to wash one another's feet" (verse 14).

In contrast to the self-seeking of the disciples, Jesus took the place of humility. He set an example of service, not of strife; of self-abasement rather than self-exaltation. His washing of their feet was an accurate picture of what it means to "take on the form of a servant" (see Philippians 2:6-8).

Second, rather than spending their energies on self-exaltation, the disciples were to imitate Him and devote themselves to the cleansing of one another. They were to take on the attitudes and actions of bondservants.

Third, Jesus remained calm even though His death was a few hours away.

Indeed, that is the essence of this lesson, for the twelve disciples and for those of us today who would call ourselves disciples of Christ. We, too, must abandon the desire to be served and become servants; we also must stop seeking a title and pick up a towel, and remain calm in the face of opposition.

D. Judas's Betrayal
(John 13:18-20)

I speak not of you all: I know whom I have chosen: but that the scripture may be fulfilled, He that eateth bread with me hath lifted up his heel against me. Now I tell you before it come, that, when it is come to pass, ye may believe that I am he. Verily, verily, I say unto you, He that receiveth whomsoever I send receiveth me; and he that receiveth me receiveth him that sent me.

The treachery of Judas did not come as a surprise to Jesus. "I speak not of you all: I know whom I have chosen…" (verse 18). As the all-knowing God, Jesus knew and knows the thoughts of human beings. However, in the divine plan of salvation, it was inevitable that the Savior of the world would be betrayed by a human being.

Jesus implied His understanding of this divine decree when He said, "but that the scripture may be fulfilled; He that eateth bread with Me hath lifted up his heel against me" (verse 18). This prophecy had already been told in Psalm 41:9. Jesus was aware of the treachery of Judas and how it would show itself, but He kept this knowledge to Himself. In other words, the venomous act of Judas was part of the divine plan from the beginning. Therefore, any attempt to expose Judas would have been an act to derail the fulfillment of that which had already been prophesied, which Jesus would never have done.

Jesus went on to say, "Now I tell you before it come, that when it is come to pass, ye may believe that I am he" (verse 19). Herein, Jesus offered His foreknowledge of Judas's deed as proof of His messiahship. In other words, He was saying to them, "I am the Messiah, and as such, I have foreknowledge of all things. When Judas betrays Me, instead of you becoming angry or distraught, rejoice, because it will be further proof to you that I am He who was prophesied."

This Father-Son-disciples relationship is stated repeatedly in the Gospels (Matthew 10:40, 41; Mark 9:37; 12:6; Luke 4:18; 10:16). "He who receiveth whomsoever I send receiveth me; and he that receiveth me receiveth him that sent me" (verse 20). Those who carry out the mandates of Jesus are to be looked upon as His representatives. And because of His relationship to the Father, they, in turn, become the Father's representatives also. Therefore, when anyone receives, accepts, or aids His representatives, the person is, in essence, doing these things to the Father. Likewise, anyone who rejects or betrays one of God's representatives—as did Judas—has done the same to God Himself.

III. CONCLUDING REFLECTIONS

The term "servant" was frequently used in the Old Testament to refer to those who were obedient to God, and was therefore applied to Israel as she fulfilled her vocation. Certainly, other figures in the Old Testament were described as "servants of God," especially the prophets, the patriarchs, and other individuals, such as Moses and David (see Genesis 26:24; Exodus 14:31; Deuteronomy 34:5).

However, the preeminent "Servant of Jehovah" is none other than the Lord Jesus Christ Himself. Isaiah described the character of the servant as chosen by the Lord (42:1; 49:1) and endued with the Spirit (42:1). He was taught by the Lord (50:4), and found His strength in Him (49:2, 5). It was the Lord's will that He should suffer (53:10). He was weak, unimpressive, and scorned by men (42:3), and uncomplaining (50:6; 53:7).

Despite His innocence (53:9), He was subjected to constant suffering (50:6; 53:3), so as to be reduced to near despair (49:4). But His trust was in the Lord (49:4; 50:7-9); He obeyed Him (50:4-5) and persevered (50:7) until he was victorious (42:4; 50:8-9).

Of His mission, the prophet Isaiah said that His mission to Israel was to bring the rebellious nation back to God (49:5), but His work extended farther. He was a light to the nations, bringing judgment and salvation to the end of the earth (42:1, 3-4). This mission could be accomplished only through His suffering, wherein He took the place of the people of the Lord and bore the penalty that should be theirs (53:4-6, 8), interceding for them (53:12). His suffering ended in death (53:8, 9; 53:12) as a sin offering on their behalf (53:10), thus accomplishing their acquittal (53:11). His mission accomplished, He was exalted to glory and worldwide influence (52:13, 15; 53:12).

Jesus demonstrated the true spirit of servant-hood by giving His life. He demonstrated servant-hood in a most practical manner when He stooped to wash His disciples' feet. This willingness to serve must be emulated by all who claim to be His disciples.

PRAYER

Almighty God, we thank You and praise You for loving us so that You sent Your Son to be born, to live among us, and to die as a servant to us and all humanity. May we be granted the grace to imitate Him and to live as His servants through serving others. In Jesus' name, we pray. Amen.

WORD POWER

Example *(hupodeigma—hoop-od-deig-me)*— this is a compound word in Greek. The word is prefixed with a preposition *hupo* ("under"), and a verb *deigma* ("to show"). In essence, Jesus put down a practical example for His followers to emulate. It is an exhibit for emulation. In the presence of a betrayal (Judas), Jesus exhibited an uncommon spirit of servant-hood.

HOME DAILY BIBLE READINGS
(July 14-20, 2008)
Christ as Servant
MONDAY, July 14: "The Suffering Servant" (Isaiah 53:4-6)
TUESDAY, July 15: "To the End" (John 13:1-2a)
WEDNESDAY, July 16: "Unless I Wash You" (John 13:2b-11)
THURSDAY, July 17: "An Example" (John 13:12-17)
FRIDAY, July 18: "Whoever Receives Me" (John 13:18-20)
SATURDAY, July 19: "What Do You Want?" (Matthew 20:20-23)
SUNDAY, July 20: "Not to Be Served" (Matthew 20:24-28)

LESSON 9   July 27, 2008

CHRIST AS MESSIAH

DEVOTIONAL READING: **Isaiah 43:1-7**
PRINT PASSAGE: **Matthew 16:13-23**

BACKGROUND SCRIPTURE: **Matthew 16:13-23**
KEY VERSE: **Matthew 16:15**

Matthew 16:13-23—KJV

13 When Jesus came into the coasts of Caesarea Philippi, he asked his disciples, saying, Whom do men say that I the Son of man am?

14 And they said, Some say that thou art John the Baptist: some, Elias; and others, Jeremias, or one of the prophets.

15 He saith unto them, But whom say ye that I am?

16 And Simon Peter answered and said, Thou art the Christ, the Son of the living God.

17 And Jesus answered and said unto him, Blessed art thou, Simon Barjona: for flesh and blood hath not revealed it unto thee, but my Father which is in heaven.

18 And I say also unto thee, That thou art Peter, and upon this rock I will build my church; and the gates of hell shall not prevail against it.

19 And I will give unto thee the keys of the kingdom of heaven: and whatsoever thou shalt bind on earth shall be bound in heaven: and whatsoever thou shalt loose on earth shall be loosed in heaven.

20 Then charged he his disciples that they should tell no man that he was Jesus the Christ.

21 From that time forth began Jesus to shew unto his disciples, how that he must go unto Jerusalem, and suffer many things of the elders and chief priests and scribes, and be killed, and be raised again the third day.

22 Then Peter took him, and began to rebuke him, saying, Be it far from thee, Lord: this shall not be unto thee.

23 But he turned, and said unto Peter, Get thee behind me, Satan: thou art an offence unto me: for thou savourest not the things that be of God, but those that be of men.

Matthew 16:13-23—NRSV

13 Now when Jesus came into the district of Caesarea Philippi, he asked his disciples, "Who do people say that the Son of Man is?"

14 And they said, "Some say John the Baptist, but others Elijah, and still others Jeremiah or one of the prophets."

15 He said to them, "But who do you say that I am?"

16 Simon Peter answered, "You are the Messiah, the Son of the living God."

17 And Jesus answered him, "Blessed are you, Simon son of Jonah! For flesh and blood has not revealed this to you, but my Father in heaven.

18 And I tell you, you are Peter, and on this rock I will build my church, and the gates of Hades will not prevail against it.

19 I will give you the keys of the kingdom of heaven, and whatever you bind on earth will be bound in heaven, and whatever you loose on earth will be loosed in heaven."

20 Then he sternly ordered the disciples not to tell anyone that he was the Messiah.

21 From that time on, Jesus began to show his disciples that he must go to Jerusalem and undergo great suffering at the hands of the elders and chief priests and scribes, and be killed, and on the third day be raised.

22 And Peter took him aside and began to rebuke him, saying, "God forbid it, Lord! This must never happen to you."

23 But he turned and said to Peter, "Get behind me, Satan! You are a stumbling block to me; for you are setting your mind not on divine things but on human things."

BIBLE FACT

"Messiah" is from the Hebrew *Mashiach*, or "anointed one." Most Jews rejected Christ, thinking their Messiah would end Roman occupation. Today, Jewish Christians are called Messianic Jews.

UNIFYING LESSON PRINCIPLE

We come to know people not by what others say about them but by having a personal relationship with them. How well do we ever really know another person? Peter's confession of Jesus was a milestone in his understanding of Jesus as the Messiah.

TOPICAL OUTLINE OF THE LESSON

I. **Introduction**
    A. Jesus: The Son of Man
    B. Biblical Background

II. **Exposition and Application of the Scripture**
    A. Jesus' Inquiries about His Identity (Matthew 16:13-15)
    B. Simon Peter's Response (Matthew 16:16-20)
    C. Jesus Predicts His Death and Resurrection (Matthew 16:21-23)

III. **Concluding Reflections**

LESSON OBJECTIVES

Upon completion of this lesson, the students will:

1. Have an increased understanding of the personhood of Jesus;
2. Have an increased understanding of the role of Jesus as Messiah; and,
3. Recognize the importance of judging individuals based upon their deeds rather than upon hearsay.

POINTS TO BE EMPHASIZED

ADULT/YOUTH

Adult Topic: **Getting to Know a Person**
Youth Topic: **What's My Line?**
Adult Key Verse: **Matthew 16:15**
Youth Key Verse: **Matthew 16:16**
Print Passage: **Matthew 16:13-23**

—Jesus began for the first time to explain that He must go to Jerusalem where He would be killed and rise again, and when Peter tried to stop Him, Jesus said, "Get thee behind me, Satan."
—Even though Peter gives the great affirmation that Jesus is the Son of God, he is evidently confused about what this means.
—Jesus is beginning His journey to His death.
—Peter identifies Jesus in light of Malachi 3:1-4.
—Peter's confession is somewhat different in Mark 8:27-33 and Luke 9:18-22.
—Ephesians 2:20 expresses the view that all the apostles serve as the foundation of the church.
—There was no official church established until after the Day of Pentecost.
—Matthew's gospel is very much concerned with establishing Jesus' messiahship and with the authority of the church.

CHILDREN

Children Topic: **Jesus Is the Messiah**
Key Verse: **Matthew 16:16**
Print Passage: **Matthew 16:13-20**

—Jesus asked His disciples how people identified Him.
—Some of the disciples were unsure of who Jesus was.
—Peter identified Jesus as the Messiah through the inspiration of the Holy Spirit.
—Jesus did not yet want His identity revealed publicly.
—Jesus said He would build the church on the kind of faith Peter expressed.

I. INTRODUCTION

A. Jesus: The Son of Man

The incidents of this lesson occurred during the last few weeks of Jesus' earthly ministry. In recognition of the fact that His time on earth was drawing to a close, Jesus began to withdraw from public appearances to spend more intimate time with His disciples. In so doing, His teachings were directed toward preparing them for the dramatic events that lay ahead.

If they were to persevere through these difficult times, it was essential that the disciples understand who Jesus was. Of course, this teaching was simply a continuation of that which had been given earlier, but now could be imparted with greater emphasis, since they were away from the crowds.

In testing the disciples about their understanding of His identity, Jesus referred to Himself as "the Son of man." This self-designation deserves closer examination. To begin with, it is important to note that Jesus used this title more than any other to refer to Himself. The term is found in a number of Old Testament passages where the phrase means simply "man" (Psalm 8:5), and at times Jesus' use of it corresponds with this meaning (Matthew 8:20). But the majority of contexts indicate that in using this title Jesus was thinking of Daniel 7:13, where the Son of man was a heavenly figure, an individual, and at the same time the ideal representative of the people of God.

Though "Son of man" was used only by Jesus for Himself, what it signified is otherwise expressed, especially in Romans 5 and 1 Corinthians 15, where Christ is described as the "man from heaven" or the "second Adam." Both Adam and Christ had the representative relationship to the whole of humankind that was involved in the concept "Son of man." But Christ was and is regarded as one whose identification with all humankind was and is far deeper and more complete than that of Adam. In His redeeming action, salvation was and is provided for all people.

B. Biblical Background

The term "Messiah" is derived from a Hebrew verb meaning, "to anoint, smear with oil." As a title, it was sometimes used of non-Israelite figures like Cyrus (see Isaiah 45:1), sometimes in referring to the altar (see Exodus 29:36), and sometimes of the prophet (see 1 Kings 19:16); but, most frequently it referred to the king of Israel as in 1 Samuel 26:11 and Psalm 89:20.

The primary sense of the title is "king" as the anointed man of God, but it also suggests election—that is, the king was chosen, elected, and, therefore, honored. It was generally understood to refer to a political leader, and was so used by Israel, who in her early stages sought only a ruler, visible and powerful, who would reign there and then. However, the evidence of later Judaism points to a Messiah not only as king, but also as a future king—a ruler who would appear at the end of time. Such an appearance would fulfill prophecy.

This lesson focuses on the identification of Jesus as the long-awaited Messiah who had appeared proclaiming that the kingdom of God was at hand.

II. EXPOSITION AND APPLICATION OF THE SCRIPTURE

A. Jesus' Inquiries about His Identity (Matthew 16:13-15)

When Jesus came into the coasts of Caesarea Philippi, he asked his disciples, saying, Whom do men say that I the Son of man am? And they said, Some say that thou art John the Baptist: some, Elias; and others, Jeremias, or one of the prophets. He saith unto them, But whom say ye that I am?

The region of Caesarea Philippi was a distance of approximately 24 miles from "the other side" (16:5) where the Lord had fed the five thousand. It was a place enlarged and beautified by Philip the Tetrarch and was named in honor of Caesar Augustus. To distinguish Caesarea from its namesake, to which reference is made in this verse—the far more important seaport south of Mt. Carmel—and to indicate its founder, it was called Caesarea Philippi.

When the Lord and His disciples arrived there, and while alone from the crowds, He asked them, "Whom do men say that I the Son of man am?" (verse 13). The statement is cast in the imperfect tense, which by interpretation means, "He kept on asking them." It was not a one-time question. As indicated in the Introduction, this title "Son of man" was a self-designation, used exclusively by the Lord Himself, but a usage with which the disciples were familiar.

In asking this question, the Lord was trying to determine to what extent they had been influenced by the opinions of others about His identity. Followers of Christ must guard against being influenced by the world's opinion of Him. Virtually every known cult is founded upon a less-than-biblical identity of Jesus.

They answered that some people were of the opinion that He was John the Baptist brought back to life. There were others who thought that He was Elijah, or Jeremiah (John 16:14). It must be remembered here that John the Baptist had gone forth in the spirit and power of Elijah (Luke 1:17), and was therefore going to be called "Elijah" by no less than Jesus Himself, as the following chapter in Matthew indicates (Matthew 17:12). Yet, he was not literally Elijah, and it was the literal, personal forerunner Elijah whom many of the Jews expected and wrongly identified as Jesus, partly as a result of their misinterpretation of Malachi 4:5. These first two groups seem to have viewed Jesus as a forerunner of the Messiah.

Still others identified Jesus with Jeremiah, who, according to some legends, would return as a forerunner of the Messiah to reconstruct the tent, the ark, and the altar of incense. Finally, there were those who did not think that Jesus was the Messiah, but perhaps one of the other prophets who had risen again (Luke 9:19).

Jesus repeatedly queried His disciples regarding His identity. In the original texts, enormous stress is placed on "But you...." This personal pronoun, "you," second person plural, stands at the very heart of the question. It appears first as a word all by itself, and then is included again as an element in the verb (see verse 15, NIV).

In New Testament Greek, the word to be emphasized is positioned first in the sentence. The import of this grammatical construction is to emphasize the personal nature of the question. It was a question that each of the disciples must answer personally. The time of the prophesied dramatic events was drawing near, and He knew that they must now have no doubts about His true identity if they were going to be able to persevere as His disciples.

A person may be able to function in the church effectively without having knowledge of a great deal of things, but no one can be mistaken, or even halfhearted, about the identity of Jesus.

B. Simon Peter's Response (Matthew 16:16-20)

And Simon Peter answered and said, Thou art the Christ, the Son of the living God. And Jesus answered and said unto him, Blessed art thou, Simon Barjona: for flesh and blood hath not revealed it unto thee, but my Father which is in heaven. And I say also unto thee, That thou art Peter, and upon this rock I will build my church; and the gates of hell shall not prevail against it. And I will give unto thee the keys of the kingdom of heaven: and whatsoever thou shalt bind on earth shall be bound in heaven: and whatsoever thou shalt loose on earth shall be loosed in heaven. Then charged he his disciples that they should tell no man that he was Jesus the Christ.

It must be kept in mind that this question had been addressed to all of these men, not just to one of them. However, in the Gospels and in the book of Acts, Peter frequently represented the twelve disciples. Therefore, when Peter answered, it must be understood as being representative of all of them—with him acting as their spokesman.

Peter's response, "Thou art the Christ," was a declaration that Jesus was the long-awaited Anointed One, the one who, as Mediator, was set apart or ordained by the Father and anointed with the Holy Spirit, to be His people's chief prophet (Deuteronomy 18:15, 18; Isaiah 55:4), only High Priest (Psalm 110:4; Hebrews 6:20), and eternal King (Psalm 2:6; Zechariah 9:9).

When Peter added, "the Son of the living God," he meant that Jesus was the only begotten, unique in all humankind. His relationship was and is without beginning or end; He is, always has been, and will be forevermore, the Son of God.

In Jesus' response to Peter, He wanted to emphasize Peter's limitations as a human being. Therefore, He referred to him as "Simon Bar Jonah," that is, "Simon, son of Jonah," a human son of a human father. Jesus replied, "...for your flesh and blood hath not revealed it unto thee" (verse 17). In other words, this knowledge did not come as a result of Peter's human calculation or intuition. The insight needed to arrive at this conclusion came to him from "my Father who is in heaven" (verse 17).

Just as Peter received the knowledge of Jesus' identity from God, so we do today. The revelation of Jesus is given to all of us by the choice of the Father through the agency of the Holy Spirit. No human being apart from the enablement of God can come to the true knowledge of Jesus Christ. The preaching of the cross is "foolishness to them that perish" (1 Corinthians 1:18); but blessed, happy, and fortunate are those to whom such knowledge is revealed.

The interpretation of this passage (Matthew 16:18) varies widely; however, the bulk of the evidence suggests the following interpretation. Jesus did indeed promise Peter that He would build the church on him, but with the following qualifications: 1) This blessing was not on Peter as he was by nature; but, rather, on him considered as a product of grace. It was not on the weak, unstable man that Peter was by nature, when Christ found him; the blessing was to come to the mature, courageous, and enthusiastic witness Peter was to become, as illustrated by his confession. 2) It was not on Peter by himself, or on him as one possessing any special authority over the others; but, rather, it was on Peter as the representative of the twelve disciples—that is, it was upon Peter taking his stand with the eleven. 3) It was not on Peter as the foundation. In the primary or basic sense of the term, there was and is only one foundation; that was not Peter, but on Jesus Christ Himself, of course (1 Corinthians 3:11). This point is made clear by the next phrase, "I will build My church" (Matthew 16:18).

"The gates of Hades" should rightly be interpreted "the gates of hell." This figure referred to Satan and his legions as though they were coming out of hell's gates in order to attack and destroy the church (the bride of Christ). In other words, Satan and all his demonic forces arrayed together will not overpower the church.

The church to which Jesus referred is the universal church, the spiritual body of believers of Christ throughout the generations. Jesus is not here promising that individual churches, or even entire denominations, will not be overcome by Satan. To the contrary, local churches and entire denominations may become doctrinally impure and thus overpowered by the forces of the evil one. But the true church, the body of Christ, the church of the redeemed, His bride, will not be overcome by Satan.

Verse 19 refers to church authority—"binding" and "loosening"—which corresponds with what was permitted or not permitted. Peter and the apostles were given the authority to bind and to loose. Whatever they allowed and disallowed in the church would have divine authority.

According to John 20:22-23 (NRSV), "If you forgive the sin of any, they are forgiven...." The disciples were given authority to determine wrongdoing in the church.

The work of God demands authority over demonic forces, and the authority to cast them out is available to the servants of God with good conscience and integrity. This authority is not for self-aggrandizement; rather, it is to be used for the glory of God. When the leaders of the church exercise discipline, they do so in the name of heaven, or better, in the delegated authority of the Head of the church.

The disciples were commanded to tell no one that Jesus was the Messiah. The people would have interpreted the term "messiah" in the political sense (cf. John 6:15). This might have fanned the flames of enthusiasm about Him, as a potential deliverer from the Roman yoke. When an open announcement was finally made to the Jewish religious authorities, Jesus himself made it (Matthew 26:63-64).

C. Jesus Predicts His Death and Resurrection (Matthew 16:21-23)

From that time forth began Jesus to shew unto his disciples, how that he must go unto Jerusalem, and suffer many things of the elders and chief priests and scribes, and be killed, and be raised again the third day. Then Peter took him, and began to rebuke him, saying, Be it far from thee, Lord: this shall not be unto thee. But he turned, and said unto Peter, Get thee behind me, Satan: thou art an offence unto me: for thou savourest not the things that be of God, but those that be of men.

The expression "From that time..." marked a new direction in the ministry of Jesus. This expression occurs twice in the book of Matthew (4:17). In 4:17, it introduces the beginning of

Jesus' ministry, inaugurating the nearness of the kingdom of God. But in this section, it was announcing the cross and the rejection of the Messiah.

The elders, the chief priests, and the scribes were the group called the Sanhedrin (the religious council). The mention of Jerusalem indicates that the death sentence that would be passed on Jesus was official. Peter could not believe what Jesus was saying; hence, Peter called the Master aside to rebuke Him. Referring to Peter as Satan was a serious charge. Peter, at that point, was standing in the way of God's plan and was unwittingly speaking for Satan.

III. CONCLUDING REFLECTIONS

Acknowledgment of Jesus as the Christ, the Son of the living God, is the very foundation of the Gospel. As such, it is requisite for admission into the body of Christ and, therefore, is requisite for membership in the local church.

Unfortunately, too many churches are guilty of rushing people into the water and extending to them the "right hand of fellowship" without making a diligent effort to ascertain whether they have a correct conception of Jesus as Savior and Lord. Neglecting this, we have pews filled with unregenerate people, some of whom become entrenched in the church's hierarchy, only to become stumbling blocks, hindering the church's mission and ministry. Indeed, this is only one of the many reasons why we must take great care to insist that the first person that every member gets to know is Jesus Christ.

PRAYER

Dear God, our everlasting heavenly Father, we thank You for the gift of Your Son, who died that we might have peace with You and with one another. Grant us, we pray, the grace that we might walk in a manner worthy of this high calling and privilege. In Jesus' name, we pray. Amen.

WORD POWER

Disciple *(mathetes* [Greek: ma~the~tis])—A learner; one who accepts the views of the teacher, and practices them with a view to leading others as well. Jesus' disciples not only accepted the teachings of Jesus, but they carried out His mandate to spread His Word. Disciples today are baptized believers who rest upon Jesus' sacrifice, believe in the work of the Holy Spirit, and imitate Christ.

HOME DAILY BIBLE READINGS
(July 21-27, 2008)
Christ as Messiah

MONDAY, July 21: "The Promise of a Savior" (Isaiah 43:1-7)
TUESDAY, July 22: "Who Am I?" (Matthew 16:13-16)
WEDNESDAY, July 23: "Tell No One" (Matthew 16:17-20)
THURSDAY, July 24: "Get behind Me" (Matthew 16:21-23)
FRIDAY, July 25: "Transfigured" (Matthew 17:1-4)
SATURDAY, July 26: "Acclaimed" (Matthew 17:5-8)
SUNDAY, July 27: "Elijah Has Already Come" (Matthew 17:9-13)

LESSON 10   August 3, 2008

DOERS OF THE WORD

DEVOTIONAL READING: **Psalm 92:1-8**
PRINT PASSAGE: **James 1:17-27**

BACKGROUND SCRIPTURE: **James 1**
KEY VERSE: **James 1:22**

James 1:17-27—KJV

17 Every good gift and every perfect gift is from above, and cometh down from the Father of lights, with whom is no variableness, neither shadow of turning.
18 Of his own will begat he us with the word of truth, that we should be a kind of firstfruits of his creatures.
19 Wherefore, my beloved brethren, let every man be swift to hear, slow to speak, slow to wrath:
20 For the wrath of man worketh not the righteousness of God.
21 Wherefore lay apart all filthiness and superfluity of naughtiness, and receive with meekness the engrafted word, which is able to save your souls.
22 But be ye doers of the word, and not hearers only, deceiving your own selves.
23 For if any be a hearer of the word, and not a doer, he is like unto a man beholding his natural face in a glass:
24 For he beholdeth himself, and goeth his way, and straightway forgetteth what manner of man he was.
25 But whoso looketh into the perfect law of liberty, and continueth therein, he being not a forgetful hearer, but a doer of the work, this man shall be blessed in his deed.
26 If any man among you seem to be religious, and bridleth not his tongue, but deceiveth his own heart, this man's religion is vain.
27 Pure religion and undefiled before God and the Father is this, To visit the fatherless and widows in their affliction, and to keep himself unspotted from the world.

James 1:17-27—NRSV

17 Every generous act of giving, with every perfect gift, is from above, coming down from the Father of lights, with whom there is no variation or shadow due to change.
18 In fulfillment of his own purpose he gave us birth by the word of truth, so that we would become a kind of first fruits of his creatures.
19 You must understand this, my beloved: let everyone be quick to listen, slow to speak, slow to anger;
20 for your anger does not produce God's righteousness.
21 Therefore rid yourselves of all sordidness and rank growth of wickedness, and welcome with meekness the implanted word that has the power to save your souls.
22 But be doers of the word, and not merely hearers who deceive themselves.
23 For if any are hearers of the word and not doers, they are like those who look at themselves in a mirror;
24 for they look at themselves and, on going away, immediately forget what they were like.
25 But those who look into the perfect law, the law of liberty, and persevere, being not hearers who forget but doers who act--they will be blessed in their doing.
26 If any think they are religious, and do not bridle their tongues but deceive their hearts, their religion is worthless.
27 Religion that is pure and undefiled before God, the Father, is this: to care for orphans and widows in their distress, and to keep oneself unstained by the world.

BIBLE FACT
Hearing and reading the Word of God is essential for every Christian. Thus, if we are not to be nominal Christians; it is critical to do exactly what the Word says. We must be teachable and receive the Word and then apply it to our daily lives.

UNIFYING LESSON PRINCIPLE

Some people have abundant knowledge, but it does not necessarily motivate their behavior. What is the appropriate relationship between knowing what to do and acting on that knowledge? James tells us that as God's people, we must not only hear the Word of God but we must also respond to it with transforming action.

TOPICAL OUTLINE OF THE LESSON

I. Introduction
A. Hypocrisy
B. Biblical Background

II. Exposition and Application of the Scripture
A. God Gives Good Gifts (James 1:17-18)
B. Qualities of a Christian (James 1:19-20)
C. Doers and Hearers of the Word (James 1:21-25)
D. Getting a Firm Grip on the Tongue (James 1:26-27)

III. Concluding Reflections

LESSON OBJECTIVES

At the completion of this lesson, the students are expected to:

1. Understand the meaning and danger of hypocrisy;
2. Understand what it means to deceive oneself;
3. Recognize the importance of leading consistent lives; and,
4. Recognize the power of Christian behavior to draw unbelievers to Christ.

POINTS TO BE EMPHASIZED

ADULT/YOUTH

Adult Topic: **Committed Living**
Youth Topic: **Right on Living**
Adult/Youth Key Verse: **James 1:22**
Print Passage: **James 1:17-27**

—James wrote this letter to Jewish Christians who had been scattered due to persecution.
—Every good and perfect gift comes from God the Father, whose love never changes.
—James demonstrates the struggle of the early church to learn to live as Christians.
—James mentions a "perfect law," not based on human passions, through which believers may obtain freedom.
—"The perfect law" is a Jewish description of Mosaic Law.
—Religion consists of more than devotional exercises. These compare with Matthew 25:35-36.
—The word *blessed* is used in verse 25 similar to the way it is used in Matthew 5:3-11.

CHILDREN

Children Topic: **Obey God's Word**
Key Verse: **James 1:22**
Print Passage: **James 1:19-25**

—Jesus teaches that it is better to listen and learn before we talk.
—When we become angry as we communicate with one another, we displease God.
—When God's truth is firmly planted in us, we have the power to obey God.
—God blesses those who obey His Word.

I. INTRODUCTION

A. Hypocrisy

Hypocrisy, in classical Greek, was used without any evil connotation. The verb behind the noun meant simply "to answer." The interpretation of dreams, the public recitation of poetry, and acting in a play could all be designated as hypocrisy. This term, however, represented a component of acting in a Greek drama that influenced its subsequent development.

In the drama, the actor often wore a mask that concealed his true identity. This background in Greek drama was totally unparalleled in the thought and the culture of the Hebrew people. Because of this absence of correspondence of thought and situation, the RSV eliminates both "hypocrisy" and "hypocrite" from its translation of the Old Testament, even though the KJV employs both.

By the time the Old Testament was translated into Greek, the word *hypokrisis* had an actively evil connotation. In the LXX (Septuagint), the Greek translation of the Old Testament, the term became synonymous with "impiety," "transgression," and "lawlessness."

In the New Testament, the word was used to signify human conduct that was externally religious but insincerely motivated, simulating goodness. The Pharisees were especially prone to this. They were actors of the first order. They sacrificed truth for appearance. They were more concerned about reputation than they were about reality. They lost sight of reality in their deception of others to such a degree that they deceived only themselves.

The Lord Jesus was particularly harsh in His criticism, giving perhaps the most graphic representation of hypocrisy in His description of the Pharisees as "whitewashed tombs, which outwardly appear beautiful, but within they are full of dead men's bones and all uncleanness" (see Matthew 23:27-28, NKJV).

The Pharisees were intensely religious in their outward actions, but their hearts were full of sin and wickedness. Their true motives were concealed under a cloak of pretense.

B. Biblical Background

The book of James is a practical book that seeks to address the relationship of faith to works. Genuine faith, James explained, will be manifested in good works. What are good works? A good work, theologically speaking, is any activity of a moral agent which proceeds from a right motive—love. According to Christian theology, "we love him, because he first loved us" (1 John 4:19). In other words, God is the source of love.

The essence of Jesus' teaching is love in action. "By their fruits you shall know them" (Matthew 7:20) means that you can tell what a person really believes to be true by her or his actions. If one behaves wickedly, that is because one believes in wickedness.

Truth, according to Christianity, is determined by revelation; and deeds are then judged by their correspondence to the revealed standard of truth. Good works are, therefore, commanded to be done by the believer, as ordained of God (Ephesians 2:10), and are useful to those who benefit from them (Titus 3:8-9).

II. EXPOSITION AND APPLICATION OF THE SCRIPTURE

A. God Gives Good Gifts
(James 1:17-18)

Every good gift and every perfect gift is from above, and cometh down from the Father of lights, with whom is no variableness, neither shadow of turning. Of his own will begat he us with the word of truth, that we should be a kind of firstfruits of his creatures.

Verse 17 emphasizes two attributes of God: first, His goodness; and second, His unchangeableness. Inasmuch as God is the Creator of all things and He is good, then it follows logically that everything that is good comes from this good God. Such a good God cannot be the source of evil inasmuch as this good God is also unchangeable.

To illustrate the unchangeableness of God, James employs two astronomical terms. The term he uses for "unchangeableness" is *parallage,* and the word for the turn of the shadow is *trope.* Both of these words have to do with the variation which the heavenly bodies show—the variation in the length of the day and the night, the apparent variation in the course of the sun, the phases of waxing and waning, and the different brilliance at different times of the stars and the planets.

Variability, or change, is characteristic of all created things. As the Creator of light, God is referred to as the "Father of lights," the Creator of the lights of heaven—the sun, the moon, and the stars. The lights change, but in Him who created them, there is no variation or shadow of turning.

The line in a popular song affirms, "Everything must change; nothing stays the same." This is true of everything living, but God is the exception. He does not change. He is the same today, tomorrow, and forevermore. What a blessed assurance this is for those of us who trust Him!

A demonstration of the goodness of God is shown in His decree to create humankind. For it was "of His own will He brought us forth." It was not something that He needed to do. The creation of humankind did not add anything to His person nor would it have subtracted anything from Him had He chosen not to create humans. How could it be otherwise? If His decree to create would make Him better, then He would not be unchangeable!

Of course, this reference to creation here is not physical, but spiritual, indicated by the instrument that He used to effect this creation—the word of truth, the Gospel. The reference to believers as a kind of first fruits is drawn from such Old Testament passages as Exodus 34:22 and Leviticus 23:10, which referred to the first portion of the harvest given to God, a foretaste of that which was to come. James refers to those early Christians to whom he wrote as the first fruits of subsequent generations of God's creatures.

B. Qualities of a Christian
(James 1:19-20)

Wherefore, my beloved brethren, let every man be swift to hear, slow to speak, slow to wrath: For the wrath of man worketh not the righteousness of God.

James was speaking, first, about the reception of the Word and then, second, to our communication in life in general. "Be swift to hear" (verse 19)—that is, be ready and willing to listen. Then, James says to be slow to speak; that is, to take precautions, and to consider and weigh your response before you speak. A person who continually talks cannot hear what anyone else is saying, thus, by the same token, will not hear God when He speaks.

It has been aptly said that "God gave us one mouth, but two ears, to indicate that we are to listen twice as much as we are to speak." The book of Proverbs is full of the perils of speaking too hastily: "In the multitude of words there wanteth not sin: but he that refraineth his lips is wise (Proverbs 10:19). Or, "He that keepeth his mouth keepeth his life: but he that openeth wide his lips shall have destruction" (Proverbs 13:3).

Finally, the restraint of anger is demanded. Anger will close the mind to God's truth and cause others to reject any words of counsel. The connective "for" in verse 20 gives the reasoning that lies behind the last exhortation. Anger did and does not produce the righteous life that God desires. An angry attitude cannot create an environment in which righteousness flourishes. Love always has more power than anger.

C. Doers and Hearers of the Word
(James 1:21-25)

Wherefore lay apart all filthiness and superfluity of naughtiness, and receive with meekness the engrafted word, which is able to save your souls. But be ye doers of the word, and not hearers only, deceiving your own selves. For if any be a hearer of the word, and not a doer, he is like unto a man beholding his natural face in a glass: For he beholdeth himself, and goeth his way, and straightway forgetteth what manner of man he was. But whoso looketh into the perfect law of liberty, and continueth therein, he being not a forgetful hearer, but a doer of the work, this man shall be blessed in his deed.

James uses a series of vivid words and pictures to convey to his readers the necessity of ridding themselves of sin. The term "lay aside" was used for stripping off one's clothing. The hearers were to get rid of all defilement in the same manner that one strips off soiled garments.

Both of the words James uses for defilement are vivid. The word we have translated "filthiness" is *ruparia*—and it can be used for the filth which soils clothes or soils the body. It is a derivative of *rupos,* and when that word is used in a medical sense, it means "wax in the ear." So, in a sense, James may have been telling his readers to remove the wax from their ears so they could hear, with meekness, the Word of God. Describing God's Word as the "implanted Word that has the power to save your souls" (verse 21, NRSV) suggests that the readers were believers who already possessed the truth. Thus, James was not calling for an initial response to the Gospel message, but rather, was challenging believers to a full and intelligent appropriation of the truth as they grew in spiritual understanding.

We cannot hope to grow in spiritual maturity simply by attending church and listening to the Word proclaimed. We must apply the Word to our lives by laying aside the sins with which we so easily become entangled. This can only be done, however, when we develop meekness and gentleness. This is a state of mind and an attitude which the Greeks described as the mean between excessive anger and a total lack of anger. It is the quality of a person whose feelings and emotions are under control.

To emphasize the necessity of putting one's belief into action in order to become doers of the Word and not hearers only, James used the illustration of a man looking at his face in a mirror. The look would not be a casual glance, but rather, would refer to one who had made a careful observation. It is also illustrative of a woman who has looked at herself in the mirror, intently checking her makeup to see if anything is out of place, then who leaves without making the needed corrections to the flaws she observed.

It is analogous to individuals who not only attend worship services regularly, but also listen attentively to the Word, even taking detailed and lengthy notes. Yet, when the person leaves the service, he or she fails to pick up the notes again, or to make the changes which the Word has called for. Yet, they will return week after week with notebook in hand. It is as if the person goes away and immediately forgets what he or she has written. Listening to the Word, even intently, will not produce the changes needed for spiritual maturity. We must become doers. Put into practice what you profess to believe. Walk your talk!

In contrast to the person who simply hears the Word but fails to do what it teaches is the person who both listens and puts what he or she hears into practice. This practice is listed as comprising four activities. First, a person looks intently into God's truth. That is to say, he or she both observes and absorbs. It is the phrase used to describe John's act of stooping and looking into the sepulcher of Jesus (John 5:20). Second, this person continues in God's truth. She or he is the one whom the psalmist (Psalm 1) describes as "meditating on His word day and night." Third, this person is not a forgetful hearer, practicing the discipline of Scripture memorization, and committing the Word to memory. Fourth, and most important, that one is a *doer* of the Word. This one will be blessed in what he or she does. Blessings flow not simply from hearing the Word; true blessings are the result of doing the Word.

D. Getting a Firm Grip on the Tongue (James 1:26-27)

If any man among you seem to be religious, and bridleth not his tongue, but deceiveth his own heart, this man's religion is vain. Pure religion and undefiled before God and the Father is this, To visit the fatherless and widows in their affliction, and to keep himself unspotted from the world.

The word translated "religion" here is *threskeia,* and its meaning is not so much religion as worship, in the sense of the ceremony. The adjectival use of this term describes a person who performs the external acts of religion, such as public worship, fasting, and even tithing, but neglects to bridle his or her tongue. The uncontrolled tongue reveals that this person's religion is worthless.

Bridling one's tongue means "to restrain or curb what one says." A horse is restrained with a bridle. A Christian who has no control over his or her tongue is engaging in self-deception. (For more details, see the section on Word Power.) In essence, James is saying, "The finest ritual and the finest liturgy you can offer to God is serving the poor and exercising personal purity." To God, real worship does not lie in wearing the right colors on special days or even in magnificent musical renditions; rather, it lies in the practical service of humankind and in the purity of one's personal life.

Just as the tongue is small and causes a lot of damage to our Christian witnessing, so does any sin. If there is any one sin which the Christian faith does not control, it is the evidence of a vain encounter with Jesus Christ. This is why Isaiah cried, "Woe is me! for I am undone…and I dwell in the midst of a people of unclean lips" (Isaiah 6:5).

III. CONCLUDING REFLECTIONS

The use of the word "law" reveals James's Jewish orientation and that of his readers. But James qualifies the word to make sure his readers do not misunderstand. He describes this law as "perfect," and as being characterized by "liberty." It is not merely Old Testament law, nor is it Mosaic Law perverted to become a legalistic system for earning salvation by good works. When James calls it the "perfect law," he has in mind the sum total of God's revealed truth. It is not merely the preliminary portion found in the Old Testament, but also the final revelation made through Christ. Furthermore, it is the "law of liberty," which means that it does not enslave. It is not enforced by external compulsion. Rather, it is freely accepted and fulfilled with glad devotion under the enablement of the Spirit of God (Galatians 5:22-23).

This is of supreme importance to God's people in the church age. We do not live under the sacrificial law, which requires us to maintain certain dietary regulations. Nor do we live under the kind of civil law which regulated behavior between persons, as did God's people of old. However, we do live under the moral law, the Decalogue—or the Ten Commandments. We are still obligated to abide by God's law in our behavior as well as in our beliefs. Though we do not have pharisaic, religious police observing our every move, we do have the indwelling Spirit of God, prompting us to submit to the perfect law of liberty.

PRAYER

Dear God, our heavenly Father, we praise You for Your unchanging faithfulness toward us. We confess that we are not worthy of Your manifold blessings. We, like others, have sinned and come short of Your standards. We ask You to forgive us for our shortcomings and to renew in us a right spirit, that we might walk worthy of Your high calling. In Jesus' name, we pray. Amen.

WORD POWER

Bridle *(chalinagoogeo* [kali~na~goo~geo])—this word means "to lead or guide by bridle, to hold in check, restrain, and to not allow the tongue to run amuck." Plato said, "I think that the argument ought to be pulled from time to time and not to be allowed to run away." Christians need to declare a fast on the tongue not to talk about anybody in the church.

HOME DAILY BIBLE READINGS
(July 28–August 3, 2008)

Doers of the Word

MONDAY, July 28: "The Full Effect of Endurance" (James 1:1-4)

TUESDAY, July 29: "Ask in Faith" (James 1:5-8)

WEDNESDAY, July 30: "How to Boast" (James 1:9-11)

THURSDAY, July 31: "Endure Temptation" (James 1:12-15)

FRIDAY, August 1: "Everything Is from God" (James 1:16-21)

SATURDAY, August 2: "Blessed in Doing" (James 1:22-27)

SUNDAY, August 3: "How Great Are Your Works" (Psalm 92:1-8)

IMPARTIAL DISCIPLES

DEVOTIONAL READING: **Matthew 25:31-46**
PRINT PASSAGE: **James 2:1-13**

BACKGROUND SCRIPTURE: **James 2**
KEY VERSE: **James 2:5**

James 2:1-13—KJV

MY BRETHREN, have not the faith of our Lord Jesus Christ, the Lord of glory, with respect of persons.

2 For if there come unto your assembly a man with a gold ring, in goodly apparel, and there come in also a poor man in vile raiment;

3 And ye have respect to him that weareth the gay clothing, and say unto him, Sit thou here in a good place; and say to the poor, Stand thou there, or sit here under my footstool:

4 Are ye not then partial in yourselves, and are become judges of evil thoughts?

5 Hearken, my beloved brethren, Hath not God chosen the poor of this world rich in faith, and heirs of the kingdom which he hath promised to them that love him?

6 But ye have despised the poor. Do not rich men oppress you, and draw you before the judgment seats?

7 Do not they blaspheme that worthy name by the which ye are called?

8 If ye fulfil the royal law according to the scripture, Thou shalt love thy neighbour as thyself, ye do well:

9 But if ye have respect to persons, ye commit sin, and are convinced of the law as transgressors.

10 For whosoever shall keep the whole law, and yet offend in one point, he is guilty of all.

11 For he that said, Do not commit adultery, said also, Do not kill. Now if thou commit no adultery, yet if thou kill, thou art become a transgressor of the law.

12 So speak ye, and so do, as they that shall be judged by the law of liberty.

13 For he shall have judgment without mercy, that hath shewed no mercy; and mercy rejoiceth against judgment.

James 2:1-13—NRSV

MY BROTHERS and sisters, do you with your acts of favoritism really believe in our glorious Lord Jesus Christ?

2 For if a person with gold rings and in fine clothes comes into your assembly, and if a poor person in dirty clothes also comes in,

3 and if you take notice of the one wearing the fine clothes and say, "Have a seat here, please," while to the one who is poor you say, "Stand there," or, "Sit at my feet,"

4 have you not made distinctions among yourselves, and become judges with evil thoughts?

5 Listen, my beloved brothers and sisters. Has not God chosen the poor in the world to be rich in faith and to be heirs of the kingdom that he has promised to those who love him?

6 But you have dishonored the poor. Is it not the rich who oppress you? Is it not they who drag you into court?

7 Is it not they who blaspheme the excellent name that was invoked over you?

8 You do well if you really fulfill the royal law according to the scripture, "You shall love your neighbor as yourself."

9 But if you show partiality, you commit sin and are convicted by the law as transgressors.

10 For whoever keeps the whole law but fails in one point has become accountable for all of it.

11 For the one who said, "You shall not commit adultery," also said, "You shall not murder." Now if you do not commit adultery but if you murder, you have become a transgressor of the law.

12 So speak and so act as those who are to be judged by the law of liberty.

13 For judgment will be without mercy to anyone who has shown no mercy; mercy triumphs over judgment.

UNIFYING LESSON PRINCIPLE

People often value other people in relation to their material wealth. By what criteria do we determine our values? James teaches that Christians should make no distinctions in their treatment of people based on material wealth.

TOPICAL OUTLINE OF THE LESSON

I. Introduction
 A. Respecter of Persons
 B. Biblical Background

II. Exposition and Application of the Scripture
 A. True Faith Requires Impartiality (James 2:1-4)
 B. A Call for Impartiality (James 2:5-7)
 C. The Royal Law: Love Your Neighbor (James 2:8-13)

III. Concluding Reflections

LESSON OBJECTIVES

At the completion of this lesson, the students will know that:

1. God did not deal with us on the basis of our social class, but on the basis of our human needs;
2. God is no respecter of persons; and,
3. Respect for all persons, especially those who are less fortunate, is important to God.

POINTS TO BE EMPHASIZED

ADULT/YOUTH

ADULT TOPIC: **Honoring All People**
YOUTH TOPIC: **No Bench? Don't Judge!**
Adult Key Verse: **James 2:5**
Youth Key Verse: **James 2:4**
Print Passage: **James 2:1-13**

—James warned Christians against "favoritism."
—James taught that if a person broke one law, he or she broke them all. He reasoned that each law was part of the whole—the covenant (James 2:10).
—The Roman world in which James wrote and lived was an extremely hierarchical world full of class-consciousness and slavery.
—James continues to undermine the teachings and practices of that hierarchy by insisting that all are equal before God.
—Mercy is central to the teaching of James.
—The themes in this passage are similar to themes found in the writings of Hebrew prophets such as Micah and Amos.
—Verse 11 quotes the Decalogue from Exodus.
—James 2:8 and 2:13 are similar to Matthew 6:14-15 and 18:21-35.

CHILDREN

Children Topic: **Don't Play Favorites**
Key Verse: **James 2:8**
Print Passage: **James 2:1-9**

—Favoritism is inconsistent with the teachings of Jesus.
—All persons were created in God's image and deserve kind and fair treatment.
—When we learn to love God, we will also be able to love all kinds of people.
—Showing favoritism results from evil thoughts and selfish motives.

I. INTRODUCTION

A. Respecter of Persons

In the previous lesson, James showed us the importance of putting spiritual truth into practice. In this lesson, he demonstrates how showing partiality, or discrimination, violates the standard of God's truth. The concept of partiality is expressed in the *King James Version* by use of the term *respecter of persons*. The literal meaning of the Greek term is, "receive the face" and is derived from the Hebrew idea, "to raise the face" or "to accept favorably." It is a term mainly confined to biblical and Christian writers. A typical instance of the idea appears in Deuteronomy 10:17. God could not and cannot be bribed to accept favorably those who should be rejected.

In the Old Testament, the idea may be used in a good sense (for example, 1 Samuel 25:35; Malachi 1:8, 9) but it frequently means "showing partiality," as in Leviticus 19:15, where a guilty man's poverty was no grounds for his being accepted favorably.

In the New Testament, the positive connotation disappears and it invariably means "to show partiality to a person because of his or her external possessions, position, or privilege, without regard to true worth." "God is no respecter of persons" (Acts 10:34), neither accepting the Jews because of their privileges nor rejecting the Gentiles because of their lack of them.

But while God was and is no respecter of persons, we also discover in Romans 2:11 and Galatians 2:6 that respect must be given where it is due (Luke 20:21-25; Romans 13:7).

B. Biblical Background

The commandment to believers to match their behavior with their beliefs is given in light of the fact that each believer will be judged in accordance with his or her deeds at the judgment seat of Christ (2 Corinthians 5:10). In the Scriptures, this "judgment seat" is seen as a judicial bench where court decisions are made (Matthew 27:19; Acts 18:16).

However, this appraisal should not be regarded as a judicial examination that will bring upon us divine condemnation for our sins. The atoning work of the Lord has adequately taken care of this for all who trust Him for their salvation (Romans 8:1, 30-34). But we will answer for the total output of our Christian lifetimes while we are on earth, for we are responsible for our actions.

This means that we will be required to explain the reasons for our conscious earthly behavior since the time of our salvation (Luke 19:12-15). Because it is our duty to do the Lord's will and to carry out His commission for our lives in working with Him in building the church, we are answerable to Him for the use of our bodies, time, energy, abilities, opportunities, material goods, spiritual possessions, and the like. The works that do not meet the Lord's approval will bring us unprofitable results, or wages.

The works that meet His approval will be rewarded by His granting us a suitable position of administration in His earthly kingdom, and we will have some capacity for intimate fellowship with Him. Christians look to that day with expectant joy.

II. EXPOSITION AND APPLICATION OF THE SCRIPTURE

A. True Faith Requires Impartiality
(James 2:1-4)

MY BRETHREN, have not the faith of our Lord Jesus Christ, the Lord of glory, with respect of persons. For if there come unto your assembly a man with a gold ring, in goodly apparel, and there come in also a poor man in vile raiment; And ye have respect to him that weareth the gay clothing, and say unto him, Sit thou here in a good place; and say to the poor, Stand thou there, or sit here under my footstool: Are ye not then partial in yourselves, and are become judges of evil thoughts?

James begins his discussion of partiality with a prohibition: "…have not the faith of our Lord Jesus Christ, the Lord of glory, with respect of persons" (James 2:1). The Greek sentence construction is used of prohibiting a practice already in progress. The evidence of this sinful practice had already been uncovered (see verse 6 later, under the "B." section). Thus, the prohibition means "to stop showing favoritism, and let this practice proceed no further."

This prohibition is consistent with the former exhortation to believers to be careful that our actions are consistent with our profession of faith. The point here is that the practice of favoritism, or discrimination, is inconsistent with the faith of our Lord Jesus Christ. Also, the faith of our Lord includes the fact that God loves the world and that Christ died for it. If God and Christ showed mercy without favoritism, so should believers.

To illustrate this point, James uses a hypothetical situation: "For if there come unto your assembly with a gold ring, in goodly apparel, and there come in also a poor man in vile raiment; And ye have respect to him that weareth the gay clothing, and say unto him, Sit thou here in a good place; and say to the poor, Stand thou there, or sit here under my footstool: Are ye not then partial in yourselves…" (James 2:2-4). One would have welcomed the well-dressed individual over the poor one, and thereby played favorites.

In the Roman world, the rich wore togas that clearly identified their social class. The Jewish Christians of that day were guilty of giving preferential treatment to the rich by escorting them down to the choice seats in the synagogue, while restricting the poor to the seats in the rear or balcony. The term "sit at my footstool" heightened the unequal treatment of the speaker, who had a stool for his feet, versus the beggar, who was relegated to sitting on the floor.

The condemnation of this practice is expressed in a question. However, the Greek construction leaves no doubt as to James's opinion, "Are ye not then partial in yourselves, and are become judges of evil thoughts?" (verse 4). The answer being apparent, James's issued the indictment that they would have become judges with evil thoughts. The meaning of this play on words is, "In so judging between men, the readers had become unjust judges." When we as believers discriminate between individuals based upon their social and economic status, we become unjust judges. We are not exemplifying the Spirit of Christ.

B. A Call for Impartiality
(James 2:5-7)

Hearken, my beloved brethren, Hath not God chosen the poor of this world rich in faith, and heirs of the kingdom which he hath promised to them that love him? But ye have despised the poor. Do not rich men oppress you, and draw you before the judgment seats? Do not they blaspheme that worthy name by the which ye are called?

The early church was, as is the church today, made up primarily of those from the economically poor or lower classes. While poverty is generally not a desired state, God has special regard for the poor who become rich in faith and, thus, heirs to the kingdom. The aspect of the kingdom that James had in mind was in the future. It was the eternal kingdom that Christ equated with eternal life (Matthew 25:34, 46). This inheritance meant more than entering the kingdom; it also involved ruling with Christ (see 1 Corinthians 6:9; Galatians 5:21; 2 Timothy 2:12).

The rich oppressed the poor and as a result blasphemed against God. James pointed out how the behavior of those early Christians contrasted with the behavior of God by asking three pointed questions: First, "Do not rich men oppress you?" (verse 6). The term "oppress" is translated by some as "exploit" and is a strong term describing the brutal and tyrannical deprivation of a person's rights.

The second question he posed, also in verse 6, was whether the rich would "...draw you before the judgment seats?" The implication of the word "draw" is the act of issuing a subpoena and forcing a person to come to court (cf. Acts 16:19).

The third question asked, "Do not they blaspheme that worthy name by which ye are called?" (verse 7). To *blaspheme* is to speak irreverently and disrespectfully. The *worthy* name referred to here is the name of Christ, by which believers are identified as Christians.

To show favoritism to those who blaspheme the name of God is the greatest contradiction of all. To discriminate against those for whom God has shown preference and then to show preference to those who blaspheme His name is highly disrespectful of God. Believers are to regard all people with impartiality, regardless of economic or any other earthly considerations.

C. The Royal Law: Love Your Neighbor
(James 2:8-13)

If ye fulfil the royal law according to the scripture, Thou shalt love thy neighbour as thyself, ye do well: But if ye have respect to persons, ye commit sin, and are convinced of the law as transgressors. For whosoever shall keep the whole law, and yet offend in one point, he is guilty of all. For he that said, Do not commit adultery, said also, Do not kill. Now if thou commit no adultery, yet if thou kill, thou art become a transgressor of the law. So speak ye, and so do, as they that shall be judged by the law of liberty. For he shall have judgment without mercy, that hath shewed no mercy; and mercy rejoiceth against judgment.

The commandment to love one's neighbor is called the "royal law," but not simply because of its lofty character. Rather, it is so called because it is a part of the supreme law to which all other human relationships are subordinate. It is the summation of all laws (Matthew 22:36-40). The persons who keep this supreme law "do well" (verse 8).

The right course of action for believers toward those who enter the sanctuary is to show favor to everyone, whether rich or poor. Loving one's neighbor means overlooking superficial distinctions such as wealth and quality of clothing. It means showing kindness to a person in spite of any perceived distasteful qualities that the person may have.

In the sight of God and human beings, partiality violates the whole law. James elevates the practice of showing partiality from simply being un-Christian or discourteous to an act of sin. This conclusion is based upon sound legal ground, "But if you show partiality, you commit sin and are convicted by the law as transgressors" (verse 9, NRSV). This is a transgression of the "royal law."

Anyone who shows favoritism breaks the supreme law of love. James underscores the importance of not breaking even a single law: "For whoever shall keep the whole law and yet offend in one point, he is guilty of all" (verse 10). The suggestion that anyone could keep the whole law is, of course, hypothetical, but is used to illustrate the point that favoritism is against the law. For even if one could keep all the commandments of God but violate this one, that person is condemned as though having violated each and every one.

God did not and does not allow selective obedience. We cannot choose to obey the parts of the law that are to our liking and disregard the rest. The Pharisees obeyed the Sabbath law but ignored others, such as honoring their parents (see Matthew 15:1-7).

Verse 11 opens with the explanatory "For," showing that the author is continuing the explanation from verse 10. He does so with a simple illustration based on the unity of God's law.

Although God's law has many facets, it is essentially one, being the expression of the character of God Himself. To violate the law at any one point is to violate the will of God and to contradict the character of God. The same God who said "Do not commit adultery" also said "Do not commit murder." It is also the same God who gave the royal law of love for one's neighbor. The person who breaks just one of these laws has "become a transgressor of the law." Although but one commandment is broken, the entire law of God has been broken.

The command, "So speak ye and so do" (verse 12) is stronger in the Greek text than in the English translation. James says, "So speak and so act!" By employing the present tense in both verbs, he is calling for continuing action. James would have his readers speak and act in light of the fact that they "will be judged" at the judgment seat of Christ (2 Corinthians 5:10). The standard of judgment will be "the law of liberty," rather than the enslaving legalistic system developed by the scribes and Pharisees.

God's mercy always triumphs over judgment. Nevertheless, judgment without mercy will be the lot of the unmerciful—those who refuse to show mercy when it is within their ability to do so. No doubt mercy is singled out because James has the poor man of verse 2 in mind. Instead of receiving the mercy that he needed, the man received cruel discrimination at the hands of professing Christians. The basic principle that underlies verse 12a was stated by Christ Himself (Matthew 18:33). The recipient of mercy should likewise be merciful. In fact, mercy should be the mark of the regenerated person.

The practice of love (or mercy) shows that God has performed a work of grace in the believer's heart, making one like Christ. The believer will be judged by the law of liberty, which is the law of love. Believers who do not practice partiality, but instead practice love, will triumph at the judgment seat.

III. CONCLUDING REFLECTIONS

This matter of showing partiality is one that believers are apt to treat as nominal or inconsequential. It does not receive the attention as do the commandments against adultery or murder. We are more inclined to think of this commandment as compliance-optional, as those who are offended by it are not members of our local congregations; and as such, we are not likely to suffer because of it or even become aware of it.

It is a common practice among our churches to have special seats, that though they do not have the word "reserved" on them, they are in fact reserved. Proof of this is seen when some unsuspecting visitor sits in "our" seat or comes to church dressed shabbily. At best, we may respond by giving that person a long, condemning look; or worse, we might ask him or her to move, or disregard the person's presence.

This lesson teaches us that partiality is not simply looked upon by God with a mere glance of disapproval; rather, it is looked upon by Him as rebellion and lawlessness. The slightest infringement of God's law indicates self-will and lack of subjection of the heart. It ultimately means that we have not submitted ourselves to Him and His commandments for our lives.

PRAYER

Most merciful, gracious Father, we ask Your forgiveness for our attitudes and actions of favoritism toward those made in Your image. We praise and thank You today for being a God who is no respecter of persons. We thank You for looking beyond our human frailties and faults and seeing our need for salvation. Help us, we pray, to look beyond the outward appearances of those we encounter, and to see within their hearts their need to know You. In Jesus' name, we pray. Amen.

WORD POWER

Poor (Greek: *ptochos* [to-kos])—the word means "the poor, with respect to the world." They are the ones who have fallen through the cracks of government bureaucracy. They are the ones reduced to begging, and not of their own will. They are those asking for alms; however, they have faith in God and trust Him for His mercy. They are among us and we must help them and regard them without partiality.

HOME DAILY BIBLE READINGS
(August 4-10, 2008)
Impartial Disciples

MONDAY, August 4: "Sheep or Goats?" (Matthew 25:31-46)

TUESDAY, August 5: "Acts of Favoritism?" (James 2:1-4)

WEDNESDAY, August 6: "God's Favored" (James 2:5-7)

THURSDAY, August 7: "The Royal Law" (James 2:8-11)

FRIDAY, August 8: "The Law of Liberty" (James 2:12-17)

SATURDAY, August 9: "Faith and Works" (James 2:18-20)

SUNDAY, August 10: "An Active Faith" (James 2:21-26)

LESSON 12   **August 17, 2008**

WISE SPEAKERS

DEVOTIONAL READING: **Proverbs 15:1-4; 16:21-24**   BACKGROUND SCRIPTURE: **James 3**
PRINT PASSAGE: **James 3:1-10, 13-18**   KEY VERSE: **James 3:10**

James 3:1-10, 13-18—KJV

MY BRETHREN, be not many masters, knowing that we shall receive the greater condemnation.

2 For in many things we offend all. If any man offend not in word, the same is a perfect man, and able also to bridle the whole body.

3 Behold, we put bits in the horses' mouths, that they may obey us; and we turn about their whole body.

4 Behold also the ships, which though they be so great, and are driven of fierce winds, yet are they turned about with a very small helm, whithersoever the governor listeth.

5 Even so the tongue is a little member, and boasteth great things. Behold, how great a matter a little fire kindleth!

6 And the tongue is a fire, a world of iniquity: so is the tongue among our members, that it defileth the whole body, and setteth on fire the course of nature; and it is set on fire of hell.

7 For every kind of beasts, and of birds, and of serpents, and of things in the sea, is tamed, and hath been tamed of mankind:

8 But the tongue can no man tame; it is an unruly evil, full of deadly poison.

9 Therewith bless we God, even the Father; and therewith curse we men, which are made after the similitude of God.

10 Out of the same mouth proceedeth blessing and cursing. My brethren, these things ought not so to be.

.....

13 Who is a wise man and endued with knowledge among you? let him shew out of a good conversation his works with meekness of wisdom.

14 But if ye have bitter envying and strife in your hearts, glory not, and lie not against the truth.

15 This wisdom descendeth not from above, but is earthly, sensual, devilish.

16 For where envying and strife is, there is confusion and every evil work.

James 3:1-10, 13-18—NRSV

NOT MANY of you should become teachers, my brothers and sisters, for you know that we who teach will be judged with greater strictness.

2 For all of us make many mistakes. Anyone who makes no mistakes in speaking is perfect, able to keep the whole body in check with a bridle.

3 If we put bits into the mouths of horses to make them obey us, we guide their whole bodies.

4 Or look at ships: though they are so large that it takes strong winds to drive them, yet they are guided by a very small rudder wherever the will of the pilot directs.

5 So also the tongue is a small member, yet it boasts of great exploits. How great a forest is set ablaze by a small fire!

6 And the tongue is a fire. The tongue is placed among our members as a world of iniquity; it stains the whole body, sets on fire the cycle of nature, and is itself set on fire by hell.

7 For every species of beast and bird, of reptile and sea creature, can be tamed and has been tamed by the human species,

8 but no one can tame the tongue--a restless evil, full of deadly poison.

9 With it we bless the Lord and Father, and with it we curse those who are made in the likeness of God.

10 From the same mouth come blessing and cursing. My brothers and sisters, this ought not to be so.

.....

13 Who is wise and understanding among you? Show by your good life that your works are done with gentleness born of wisdom.

14 But if you have bitter envy and selfish ambition in your hearts, do not be boastful and false to the truth.

15 Such wisdom does not come down from above, but is earthly, unspiritual, devilish.

16 For where there is envy and selfish ambition, there will also be disorder and wickedness of every kind.

People often say unwise and harmful things to and about others. How can people become kinder in their speech? James exhorts people to discipline their tongues by accepting the wisdom and peace that come from above.

17 But the wisdom that is from above is first pure, then peaceable, gentle, and easy to be intreated, full of mercy and good fruits, without partiality, and without hypocrisy.
18 And the fruit of righteousness is sown in peace of them that make peace.

17 But the wisdom from above is first pure, then peaceable, gentle, willing to yield, full of mercy and good fruits, without a trace of partiality or hypocrisy.
18 And a harvest of righteousness is sown in peace for those who make peace.

TOPICAL OUTLINE OF THE LESSON

I. Introduction
A. Meekness and Wisdom
B. Biblical Background: Blessings and Curses

II. Exposition and Application of the Scripture
A. Warning against Becoming a Religious Teacher (James 3:1-5)
B. Taming the Tongue (Hebrews 3:6-10)
C. Heavenly Wisdom Versus Demonic Wisdom (James 3:13-18)

III. Concluding Reflections

LESSON OBJECTIVES

At the completion of this lesson, the students are expected to:

1. Have a greater understanding of the power of the tongue;
2. Gain insight into the challenge of controlling the tongue;
3. Have a greater understanding of the relationship of the tongue to godliness; and,
4. Have a greater desire to control their tongues.

POINTS TO BE EMPHASIZED

ADULT/YOUTH
Adult Topic: **Thoughtful Speech**
Youth Topic: **Put a Sock in It!**
Adult Key Verse: **James 3:10**
Youth Key Verse: **James 3:13**
Print Passage: **James 3:1-10, 13-18**

—James wrote of the dangers of uncontrolled speech.
—We can control our speech only through the wisdom of the Holy Spirit.
—James uses colorful metaphors such as bridles, ships, and fire.
—James makes the distinction between human wisdom and true wisdom which comes from God.

CHILDREN
Children Topic: **Speak Wisely**
Key Verse: **James 3:9**
Print Passage: **James 3:1-12**

—Teaching is a spiritual gift with the responsibilities of speaking and doing what positively affects the lives of others.
—Proper speech involves saying the right words at the right time and controlling one's desire to say what should not be said.
—The Holy Spirit can purify our hearts and give us power to control our tongues.
—We were made in the image of God, but the tongue reminds us that we have fallen into sin.

I. INTRODUCTION

A. Meekness and Wisdom

If an individual is to become a wise speaker who practices thoughtful speech, his or her conduct must be governed by two qualities: wisdom and meekness.

Wisdom is an attribute of God; it is the revelation of the divine will to humankind (1 Corinthians 2:4-7). Wisdom involves a spiritual understanding of the will of God (Matthew 13:54). A distinctive element in the New Testament is its identification of Jesus Christ as the wisdom of God, who is of course the ultimate source of the Christian's wisdom (1 Corinthians 1:24).

Meekness closely resembles gentleness and moderation. In its original usage, meekness signified distress and helplessness, but acquired a moral significance which denoted contrition of spirit before God, becoming synonymous with humility (Psalms 22:24-26; 147:6).

Meekness in the Old Testament is primarily God-focused. Also in the New Testament, meekness is humility born of trustful submission to God, but it results in gentle, forgiving unselfishness toward others. The meek are mighty for God's purposes (consider Moses) (Numbers 12:3).

B. Biblical Background: Blessings and Curses

James contrasts two forms of speech (verse 9)—"blessings" and "curses"—which may come out of one's mouth. The primary meaning is "to convey a gift by a potent utterance" (Genesis 1:22, 28). When human beings are said to bless God, the reference was and is to praising and giving thanks. In blessing human beings in the Old Testament, God bestowed temporal and spiritual well-being on them (Genesis 26:12-13). However, this is more particularly associated with spiritual benefits in the New Testament (Acts 3:26; Ephesians 1:3).

Cursing is the opposite of blessing. When the term is so employed, there are no sacred associations, and the word runs the gamut from divine to satanic. In general usage, a curse is an imprecation or an expressed wish for evil. Directed against God, a curse is blasphemy (Job 1:5, 11). It may be a desire uttered to God against another person or thing. A curse was believed to have innate power to carry itself into effect. We see this in Zechariah 5:1-3, where the curse inevitably found its victim. Curses among the heathen were supposed to be rooted in the power of self-realization (see Numbers 22:24 on Balaam).

II. EXPOSITION AND APPLICATION OF THE SCRIPTURE

A. Warning against Becoming a Religious Teacher (James 3:1-5)

MY BRETHREN, be not many masters, knowing that we shall receive the greater condemnation. For in many things we offend all. If any man offend not in word, the same is a perfect man, and able also to bridle the whole body. Behold, we put bits in the horses' mouths, that they may obey us; and we turn about their whole body.

Behold also the ships, which though they be so great, and are driven of fierce winds, yet are they turned about with a very small helm, whithersoever the governor listeth. Even so the tongue is a little member, and boasteth great things. Behold, how great a matter a little fire kindleth!

James's first concern in this passage has to do with those who desired to be "teachers" in the scattered Jewish Christian congregations. A somewhat similar situation is reflected in 1 Timothy 1:7. The translation "masters" (KJV) is an Old English term for teachers (for example, schoolmaster). The grammatical construction of the sentence indicates that there were many individuals who were coveting the prestige of teaching, some of whom were not qualified by either natural ability or spiritual gifts. James, therefore, warned that they should not presume to be able to teach because teachers would be judged more strictly than others.

The *King James Version* translation, "we shall receive the greater condemnation" (James 3:1), calls for sober reflection on the part of teachers and pastors. The Greek term *krina* refers to the decision of a judge, whether favorable or unfavorable. James says that the judgment of teachers will be especially strict because greater responsibility rests on teachers. The reason for this is that the teacher's essential instrument is the tongue, which is so easily misused.

Verse 2 begins with "for," indicating an explanation for the previous statement. The teacher's responsibility is weighty because the tongue is the most difficult member of the body to control. The literal meaning of the phrase "to stumble" figuratively refers to acts of sin (cf. 2:10). Thus, the author declares the universality of sin, even among believers. The person who "does not stumble" in his speech—that is, who never commits sins of speech—is a "perfect man." James explains in

the next sentence that anyone who can control his or her tongue surely will be able to *bridle* or control the whole body.

The author illustrates the powerful influence of the tongue by citing two examples: First, he refers to horses that are controlled by placing small pieces of metal in their mouths, called bits. Even though the horse's weight and size far exceed that of the bit, and his strength far exceed that of the human rider, yet the horse is controlled by the bit. James then refers to three factors which made ships of that day difficult to control: they were large; they were driven by fierce winds; and they were steered by a very small rudder.

The term "even so" makes application of the preceding two verses. Like bits and rudders, the tongue is a small instrument, yet it boasts of great things. By making this comparison, James is expressing the possible negative effects of an unbridled tongue. A person's entire life and testimony can be destroyed by an uncontrolled tongue.

B. Taming the Tongue (James 3:6-10)

And the tongue is a fire, a world of iniquity: so is the tongue among our members, that it defileth the whole body, and setteth on fire the course of nature; and it is set on fire of hell. For every kind of beasts, and of birds, and of serpents, and of things in the sea, is tamed, and hath been tamed of mankind: But the tongue can no man tame; it is an unruly evil, full of deadly poison. Therewith bless we God, even the Father; and therewith curse we men, which are made after the similitude of God. Out of the same mouth proceedeth blessing and cursing. My brethren, these things ought not so to be.

James said, "The tongue is a fire, a world of iniquity" (verse 6). Indeed, throughout the history of the church, we have seen how seemingly small and inconsequential rumors and lies have turned brother against brother, husband against wife, neighbor against neighbor, and even nations against nations. The corrupting influence of the tongue reaches out and "setteth on fire the course of nature" (verse 6), and is able to exert influence upon every sphere of life. It is, James says, "set on fire of hell" (verse 6). The destruction which the tongue causes has its origins in hell.

To further illustrate the influence and power of the tongue, James said, "Every kind of beasts, and of birds, and of serpents, and of things in the sea, is tamed, and hath been tamed of mankind" (verse 7). We can visit the circus and other places of entertainment and observe how man has been able to tame and control all kinds of animals by the use of his tongue. He can tell them to "Sit, speak, lie down," and even to "dance," and they all do so in response to his verbal command. Yet, the tongue is untamable. In verse 10, James rebukes believers for allowing their tongues to become instruments for blessing God and cursing the human beings who have been made in His likeness.

C. Heavenly Wisdom Versus Demonic Wisdom (James 3:13-18)

Who is a wise man and endued with knowledge among you? let him shew out of a good conversation his works with meekness of wisdom. But if ye have bitter envying and strife in your hearts, glory not, and lie not against the truth. This wisdom descendeth not from above, but is earthly, sensual, devilish. For where envying and strife is, there is confusion and every evil work. But the wisdom that is from above is first pure, then peaceable, gentle, and easy to be intreated, full of mercy and good fruits, without partiality, and without hypocrisy. And the fruit of righteousness is sown in peace of them that make peace.

The phrase "wise and understanding" is a technical term among the Jews for teachers, scribes, and rabbis. James's concern here is not for what they say, but rather, for how they li[ve]. Thus, anyone who claims to be a teacher or scribe must demonstrate his or her credentials by good conduct. Apparently, there were some individuals among James's readers who professed to be wise, but who harbored attitudes of "bitter envy and self-seeking." He rebuked those who were behaving in such a manner. An individual harboring bitter envy and strife in his or her heart was an indication that the person's will had not been submitted to God. James cautioned believers not to boast or lie against the truth.

Though James referred to the attitude described in the previous verse as *this wisdom,* it was the wisdom claimed by the would-be teachers to which he had previously referred. God was and is the source of genuine wisdom; the pseudo-wisdom claimed by the teachers was not from Him. It was *earthly, sensual,* and *devilish.* Wherever this kind of envy and self-seeking exists, there also could and can be found confusion and every "evil thing." The evil to which he referred is selfish zeal, which did and does destroy spiritual life and work.

In contrast to the wisdom spoken of in verse 15, James described the heavenly wisdom in verse 17.

The one who possesses this wisdom is enabled to control his or her tongue. Such an individual sows not the seeds of dissension, but rather the seeds which produce the fruit of righteousness. Such a person sows in peace, and reaps peace. A true child of God is a peacemaker.

When the tongue is surrendered to Christ and dominated by the Spirit, it becomes one of our most useful members; when it falls under the control of the enemy it works untold grief and damage.

III. CONCLUDING REFLECTIONS

If ever there was a time when we as a people need to exercise the power of the tongue to become peacemakers, that time is now. Consider how much conflict today is caused by wrong use of the tongue.

Christ acted as a peacemaker between God and human beings, reconciling us to God in offering Himself as a sacrifice to satisfy God's divine justice. As a result of such, we now have peace with God (Romans 5:1). This ministry of reconciliation, or serving as peacemakers, was committed to us by our Lord. We now can use our tongues to proclaim the Gospel of reconciliation and become peacemakers.

Not only does the Gospel enable us to be peacemakers between God and humankind, but we also can become peacemakers among the nations of the world. Under the empowering influence of the Holy Spirit, we can use our tongues to make peace in our homes between husbands and wives, acting as counselors. We can use our tongues to make peace between parents and children by serving as mentors and mediators. We can use our tongues in church conflicts as instruments of sober conversation and prayer. We can use our tongues in schools to encourage administrators, teachers, and students alike to stay the course.

PRAYER

Almighty, everlasting God, we thank You for the privilege of prayer, wherein we may use our tongues to confess our sins, being assured of Your forgiveness. We confess that we have not always used our tongues for Your glory. We confess that we have allowed our tongues to become instruments of conflict rather than instruments of peace. Forgive our sins, cleanse us from unrighteousness, and strengthen us so that we might become peacemakers. In Jesus' name, we pray. Amen.

WORD POWER

Fountain (*pege* [pay-gay])—it means "a fount, source, or supply of water and blood." Naturally, a fountain does not gush out two types of water—both sweet and bitter. A Christian who has encountered Christ in the true sense has no double tongue. If a Christian has a double tongue, James said that the source is not right.

HOME DAILY BIBLE READINGS

(August 11-17, 2008)

Wise Speakers

MONDAY, August 11: "The Tongue of the Wise" (Proverbs 15:1-4)
TUESDAY, August 12: "With Greater Strictness" (James 3:1-4)
WEDNESDAY, August 13: "Corralling the Tongue" (James 3:5-9)
THURSDAY, August 14: "Purity of One's Words" (James 3:10-12)
FRIDAY, August 15: "Born of Wisdom" (James 3:13-16)
SATURDAY, August 16: "Sown in Peace" (James 3:17-18)
SUNDAY, August 17: "Wise and Pleasant Speech" (Proverbs 16:21-24)

LESSON 13   August 24, 2008

PEOPLE OF GODLY BEHAVIOR

DEVOTIONAL READING: **Proverbs 3:13-18**
PRINT PASSAGE: **James 4:1-12**

BACKGROUND SCRIPTURE: **James 4**
KEY VERSE: **James 4:8**

James 4:1-12—KJV

FROM WHENCE come wars and fightings among you? come they not hence, even of your lusts that war in your members?

2 Ye lust, and have not: ye kill, and desire to have, and cannot obtain: ye fight and war, yet ye have not, because ye ask not.

3 Ye ask, and receive not, because ye ask amiss, that ye may consume it upon your lusts.

4 Ye adulterers and adulteresses, know ye not that the friendship of the world is enmity with God? whosoever therefore will be a friend of the world is the enemy of God.

5 Do ye think that the scripture saith in vain, The spirit that dwelleth in us lusteth to envy?

6 But he giveth more grace. Wherefore he saith, God resisteth the proud, but giveth grace unto the humble.

7 Submit yourselves therefore to God. Resist the devil, and he will flee from you.

8 Draw nigh to God, and he will draw nigh to you. Cleanse your hands, ye sinners; and purify your hearts, ye double minded.

9 Be afflicted, and mourn, and weep: let your laughter be turned to mourning, and your joy to heaviness.

10 Humble yourselves in the sight of the Lord, and he shall lift you up.

11 Speak not evil one of another, brethren. He that speaketh evil of his brother, and judgeth his brother, speaketh evil of the law, and judgeth the law: but if thou judge the law, thou art not a doer of the law, but a judge.

12 There is one lawgiver, who is able to save and to destroy: who art thou that judgest another?

James 4:1-12—NRSV

THOSE CONFLICTS and disputes among you, where do they come from? Do they not come from your cravings that are at war within you?

2 You want something and do not have it; so you commit murder. And you covet something and cannot obtain it; so you engage in disputes and conflicts. You do not have, because you do not ask.

3 You ask and do not receive, because you ask wrongly, in order to spend what you get on your pleasures.

4 Adulterers! Do you not know that friendship with the world is enmity with God? Therefore whoever wishes to be a friend of the world becomes an enemy of God.

5 Or do you suppose that it is for nothing that the scripture says, "God yearns jealously for the spirit that he has made to dwell in us"?

6 But he gives all the more grace; therefore it says, "God opposes the proud, but gives grace to the humble."

7 Submit yourselves therefore to God. Resist the devil, and he will flee from you.

8 Draw near to God, and he will draw near to you. Cleanse your hands, you sinners, and purify your hearts, you double-minded.

9 Lament and mourn and weep. Let your laughter be turned into mourning and your joy into dejection.

10 Humble yourselves before the Lord, and he will exalt you.

11 Do not speak evil against one another, brothers and sisters. Whoever speaks evil against another or judges another, speaks evil against the law and judges the law; but if you judge the law, you are not a doer of the law but a judge.

12 There is one lawgiver and judge who is able to save and to destroy. So who, then, are you to judge your neighbor?

UNIFYING LESSON PRINCIPLE

Many people act greedily, engage in disputes, or judge others in order to obtain something they want. What alternatives exist to such behavior? James says that people must submit themselves to God, who frees them from behaving in ungodly ways.

TOPICAL OUTLINE OF THE LESSON

I. **Introduction**
   A. Godliness and Worldliness
   B. Biblical Background

II. **Exposition and Application of the Scripture**
   A. Consequences of Pride (James 4:1-6)
   B. The Blessing of Humility (James 4:7-10)
   C. Avoid Judging Others (James 4:11-12)

III. **Concluding Reflections**

LESSON OBJECTIVES

At the completion of this lesson, the students are expected to:

1. Understand the concept of godliness and the blessings that flow from godly living.
2. Understand the concept of worldliness, and the evil results it produces; and,
3. Develop a desire to live responsibly before God and human beings.

POINTS TO BE EMPHASIZED

ADULT/YOUTH

Adult Topic: **Living Responsibly**
Youth Topic: **Greed Is Out!**
Adult Key Verse: **James 4:8**
Youth Key Verse: **James 4:7**
Print Passage: **James 4:1-12**

—James, like Paul, wrote that we cannot change our behavior through human will, but only through submitting ourselves by faith to God.

—James wrote that we have mixed feelings within ourselves when we try to follow Christ and at the same time try to be accepted by the world. We think God will give us what we need to live in a worldly style, yet we cannot serve two masters, for we will displease both.

—Instead, we need to commit ourselves fully and completely to God. If we seek to please and follow God, He will grant us His joy and laughter.

—The Bible teaches us to make an honest assessment of our spiritual flaws with full confidence that God will forgive and heal us (for example, Psalm 51; 2 Chronicles 7:13-15; 1 John 1:9).

—There are many examples of other warnings in the Bible about judging others.

CHILDREN

Children Topic: **Let God Be the Judge**
Key Verse: **Matthew 7:1**
Print Passage: **James 4:7-8, 11-12; Matthew 7:1-5**

—Because God has already defeated Satan, believers who submit to God are empowered to resist the devil.

—When believers yield the control of their lives to God, God's Spirit purifies them.

—God, the only Lawgiver and Judge, is the final Judge.

—God calls us to judge ourselves first and then help others by constructively criticizing and lovingly forgiving them.

I. INTRODUCTION

A. Godliness and Worldliness

In general, the term "godliness" means piety or reverence, whether toward human beings or God; but Christian godliness is restricted to reverence toward God. On the other hand, the term can be used to refer to the idea of "holiness" and therein refer to behavior among human beings. The true concept of godliness includes both elements—right attitudes toward God and right conduct that arises from a right relationship with God. Godliness is devotion and right action springing from that devotion, generated by the power of the Holy Spirit (2 Timothy 3:5; 2 Peter 1:3).

B. Biblical Background

The idea of judgment appears in various contexts in the New Testament, usually in the ethical sphere. The verb *krino*, "to judge," is used in three contexts: 1) to give a verdict (Luke 7:43; Acts 15:19); 2) to distinguish, to discriminate (1 Corinthians 11:31; 14:29); and 3) to investigate, to scrutinize (1 Corinthians 4:3). The Christian conscience makes ethical judgments unavoidable and imperative. "He that is spiritual, judgeth all things" (1 Corinthians 2:15). But how can this statement be reconciled with Jesus' imperative, "Judge not," in Matthew 7:1? Or, with Paul's declaration that one who is spiritual is judged by no human being (1 Corinthians 2:15)?

An examination of the contexts of these passages reveals that Jesus had in mind that one should not judge another without first judging oneself. Furthermore, Paul determined that a spiritual person cannot be judged by any human being regarding spiritual things.

II. EXPOSITION AND APPLICATION OF THE SCRIPTURE

A. Consequences of Pride
(James 4:1-6)

FROM WHENCE come wars and fightings among you? come they not hence, even of your lusts that war in your members? Ye lust, and have not: ye kill, and desire to have, and cannot obtain: ye fight and war, yet ye have not, because ye ask not. Ye ask, and receive not, because ye ask amiss, that ye may consume it upon your lusts. Ye adulterers and adulteresses, know ye not that the friendship of the world is enmity with God? whosoever therefore will be a friend of the world is the enemy of God. Do ye think that the scripture saith in vain, The spirit that dwelleth in us lusteth to envy? But he giveth more grace. Wherefore he saith, God resisteth the proud, but giveth grace unto the humble.

James begins by asking his readers, "Where do wars and fights come from among you?" These two words were generally used to refer to national warfare, but they also had become common, forceful expressions of any kind of open antagonism. He adds to the first question, "Do they not come from your desires for pleasure…?"

The word for "pleasure" is drawn from the prevalent philosophy of that day, "hedonism," which viewed pleasure as the chief goal of life. These desires reside and *war in your members*. James pictures the believer's body as a battle-ground where the flesh carries on a campaign to gain satisfaction against the promptings of their spirit.

The thought of verses 2-3 employs strong terminology—*lust, covet, war, fight*, and *murder*—to express the intense degree of desiring something so badly that one is willing to do anything to obtain it. Yet, in spite of the consuming intensity of their desire, they cannot obtain it. Their failure to receive what they desire is rooted, first of all, in their failure to ask for those things that they truly need and for the things that are pleasing to God.

Christians behave like children when they pray to God for things that are based solely upon their lusts for pleasure. Children ask for things with no regard for the potential danger. God, our heavenly Father, does not honor such prayer requests.

The rebuke of this verse is about spiritual unfaithfulness. The noun translated "adulterous people" is feminine, meaning "adulteresses." It is reasonable, therefore, to understand "adulteress" as a figure of speech for spiritual unfaithfulness.

As Christians we must contend with satanic forces that compete for our affection. James uses the term *world* to refer to the system of evil controlled by Satan. James is speaking specifically here of the pleasures that lure our hearts from God. By its very nature, then, *friendship with the world is enmity with God.* The word *enmity* means "hatred, hostility." For the believer to have a warm, familiar attitude toward this evil world is to be on good terms with God's enemy. It is to adopt the world's set of values and want what the world wants instead of choosing according to divine standards. The person, therefore, who chooses to be a friend of the world becomes an enemy of God.

B. The Blessing of Humility (James 4:7-10)

Submit yourselves therefore to God. Resist the devil, and he will flee from you. Draw nigh to God, and he will draw nigh to you. Cleanse your hands, ye sinners; and purify your hearts, ye double minded. Be afflicted, and mourn, and weep: let your laughter be turned to mourning, and your joy to heaviness. Humble yourselves in the sight of the Lord, and he shall lift you up.

The idea expressed in this verse, coupled with the previous one, is that God does indeed set a high standard for wholehearted love and devotion for His people; however, He gives grace that is greater than the demand for faithfulness. The gift of grace points back to God's demand for loyalty. God, in grace, gives His people the help they need to resist the appeal of the world and to remain loyal to him. The humble are the people who willingly submit to God's desire for them rather than proudly insisting on satisfying their own desires for pleasure.

This verse begins with the term *Therefore*, to indicate that the logical response to Proverbs 3:34 is that since God opposes the proud but helps the humble, believers should submit to Him. Submission is not the same as obedience. It is the surrender of one's will, which leads to obedience. In this and the next three verses, James issues a series of commands: *submit, resist, come near, wash, purify, humble,* and *speak no evil.* These are not words of advice; rather, they are commands, demanding action. The immediate response of the believer toward God is to submit, while the immediate response toward the devil is to resist him at all cost.

The series of commands continues with "Draw near to God...." In focusing their hearts on pleasure, James's readers had drifted away from God. Though still His people, they had become estranged from Him. But the assurance that God would welcome them back accompanied the command to return: "He will draw near to you." The idea of drawing near refers not simply to space, but also to an attitude and a behavior. The believer draws near to God in worship, in prayer, and in setting one's heart on the things of God. The command to "cleanse your hands" is an admonition to make one's conduct pure. Similarly, the command "purify your hearts" insists upon purity of thought and motive. *Double-minded* indicates a state of inconsistency and instability.

James saw the deplorable state of believers and said *Lament*—a strong word meaning "to repent in misery." They also are commanded to *mourn*. Their lives had been marked by laughter and joy, but they were to change their "laughter to mourning and their joy to gloom."

With the words, *humble yourselves,* James returned to the text quoted from the Old Testament (verse 6). God graciously gives aid to the humble; therefore, *humble yourselves.* Here, the specific form of humbling is that of repentance for the sin of transferring one's affection from God to the pleasures of the world.

C. Avoid Judging Others
(James 4:11-12)

Speak not evil one of another, brethren. He that speaketh evil of his brother, and judgeth his brother, speaketh evil of the law, and judgeth the law: but if thou judge the law, thou art not a doer of the law, but a judge. There is one lawgiver, who is able to save and to destroy: who art thou that judgest another?

The prohibition introducing this verse is that against slander, or speaking evil of another. It goes further than the term "slander," however, which is a broad term that refers to the act of making false charges or misrepresentations that damage a person's reputation. Rather, it refers to any form of speaking against another person. Even if what is said is true, James prohibits it being said in a harsh and unkind manner.

The reason for the prohibition that James gives is that the one who criticizes or judges another brother or sister "speaks against the law and judges it." The law referred to here is "love your neighbor as yourself." To speak against your neighbor is to violate the Law. The person who does so places himself or herself above the Law and, by his or her action, declares the Law to be a bad or unnecessary statute. Rather than submitting or "keeping it," such persons pass judgment on its validity and set it aside.

In passing judgment, these critics have usurped a position of authority that is reserved for God alone. God is the one lawgiver. Since He gave the law, He alone is qualified to judge those who are responsible for keeping it. The one who judges is setting up a standard of personal conduct as a rule of life.

Only God has the correct view of life. That He is "able to save and destroy" is proof that He is in a position to enforce the law, rewarding those who keep it, and punishing those who violate it. He knows whether a sinner will repent or not. God stands supreme as giver of the law and as its judge.

The injunction in our text is designed to root out the harsh, unkind, critical spirit that continually finds fault with others. Churches need to conduct healing services, whereby members may confess their sin of judging others among others.

III. CONCLUDING REFLECTIONS

One of the greatest deceptions being perpetrated in the church today is that of a "prosperity" gospel. It purports to teach that God wants all of His people to prosper in health and wealth. Either unknowingly or consciously, such teachings are rooted not in Christianity, but rather in secular humanism, where the human being is the measure of all things. It may be traced historically to the philosophy known as "hedonism," which is that all actions can be measured on the basis of how much pleasure and how little pain they produce. It also can be traced to the nineteenth-century British philosopher John Stuart Mill, who pioneered the theory of Utilitarianism. A utilitarianist believes that all action should be directed toward achieving the greatest amount of happiness.

This philosophy recommends pursuing one's own happiness in God as the ultimate in human pleasure. It deceives us into believing that if we would but attend church regularly, worship ecstatically, and pray fervently, God will, in turn, lavish His love on us by giving us the materialistic desires of our hearts.

The teachings of this lesson are diametrically opposed to such a view. As believers, we are to recognize that to follow Christ means to live a life here on earth with heaven in view. It means to view this world and all it holds as temporal and heaven and its promises as permanent and eternal.

PRAYER

Dear God, our heavenly Father, we praise You for not only sending Your Son to die in our stead, but also for sending Your Holy Spirit to dwell in us, leading, guiding, and empowering us to live godly lives. Forgive us, we pray, for behaving in ways that are not pleasing in Your sight. Help us now to put aside all malice and evil thinking and help us that we might do what is good, acceptable, and perfect in Your sight. In Jesus' name, we pray. Amen.

WORD POWER

Speak Against *(katalaleite* [ka~ta~lale~ite]) **to speak against; reduce to nothingness. The grammatical structure of this word is a prohibition of ongoing attitude. It is a command to quit speaking against a brother or sister in Christ. James encourages us not to speak against the image of God.**

HOME DAILY BIBLE READINGS
(August 18-24, 2008)
People of Godly Behavior

MONDAY, August 18: "Understanding and Peace" (Proverbs 3:13-18)
TUESDAY, August 19: "Ask Rightly" (James 4:1-3)
WEDNESDAY, August 20: "Yearn for God's Spirit" (James 4:4-7)
THURSDAY, August 21: "Humble Yourselves" (James 4:8-10)
FRIDAY, August 22: "Do Not Judge" (James 4:11-14)
SATURDAY, August 23: "Seek God's Wishes" (James 4:15-17)
SUNDAY, August 24: "Living in the Light of God" (Ephesians 5:8-11)

LESSON 14   August 31, 2008

PRAYERFUL COMMUNITY

DEVOTIONAL READING: **1 Thessalonians 5:16–22**   BACKGROUND SCRIPTURE: **James 5**
PRINT PASSAGE: **James 5:13–18**   KEY VERSE: **James 5:13**

James 5:13-18 —KJV

13 Is any among you afflicted? let him pray. Is any merry? let him sing psalms.
14 Is any sick among you? let him call for the elders of the church; and let them pray over him, anointing him with oil in the name of the Lord:
15 And the prayer of faith shall save the sick, and the Lord shall raise him up; and if he have committed sins, they shall be forgiven him.
16 Confess your faults one to another, and pray one for another, that ye may be healed. The effectual fervent prayer of a righteous man availeth much.
17 Elias was a man subject to like passions as we are, and he prayed earnestly that it might not rain: and it rained not on the earth by the space of three years and six months.
18 And he prayed again, and the heaven gave rain, and the earth brought forth her fruit.

James 5:13-18 —NRSV

13 Are any among you suffering? They should pray. Are any cheerful? They should sing songs of praise.
14 Are any among you sick? They should call for the elders of the church and have them pray over them, anointing them with oil in the name of the Lord.
15 The prayer of faith will save the sick, and the Lord will raise them up; and anyone who has committed sins will be forgiven.
16 Therefore confess your sins to one another, and pray for one another, so that you may be healed. The prayer of the righteous is powerful and effective.
17 Elijah was a human being like us, and he prayed fervently that it might not rain, and for three years and six months it did not rain on the earth.
18 Then he prayed again, and the heaven gave rain and the earth yielded its harvest.

BIBLE FACT

The work of ministry is demanding and difficult because it deals with the human heart. The human heart is the most difficult destination to reach on earth. It cannot be reached by education or the minister's effort. God is the only one who can reach the heart of human beings. Therefore, one must know how to move God through prayer so that He will reach the human heart.

Powerful and effective prayer cannot come when there is only a shallow knowledge of God. Romans 10:14 says, "How then shall they call on him in whom they have not believed?" Knowing God through a personal relationship with Him gives confidence in the time of prayer.

Elijah prayed and stayed the course of nature. He called the worshipers of Baal to contest. He knew that God would take the glory, and He did. Feeble prayer secures no result and neither brings glory to God or good to humanity. Elijah's fervent prayer was his offense and defense, yielding results to the glory of God. This is the heritage and right of every child of God.

UNIFYING LESSON PRINCIPLE

People's attitudes toward life shape the way they respond with joy or concern to circumstances and events. How can we achieve a positive attitude that leads to powerful and effective living? James teaches that our lifestyle is to be shaped by an attitude of prayer.

TOPICAL OUTLINE OF THE LESSON

I. **Introduction**
   A. Prayer
   B. Biblical Background: Faith Healing

II. **Exposition and Application of the Scripture**
   A. An Injunction to Church Members (James 5:13-14)
   B. Prayer of Faith and Its Effect (James 5:15-16)
   C. The Exemplary Prayer Life of Elijah (James 5:17-18)

III. **Concluding Reflections**

LESSON OBJECTIVES

At the completion of this lesson, the students are expected to:

1. Gain a greater appreciation for the role of prayer in the life of the church community;
2. Gain insight into the power of prayer; and,
3. Understand how prayer can affect one's health and wholeness.

POINTS TO BE EMPHASIZED

ADULT/YOUTH

Adult Topic: Powerful and Effective Living

Youth Topic: Knee Theology Works!

Adult Key Verse: James 5:13

Youth Key Verse: James 5:16

Print Passage: James 5:13-18

—Prayer is talking to God and waiting to hear what God speaks to us.

—Churches that make a practice of anointing the sick cite this passage.

—The letter closes (verses 19-20) with a practical comment that God's truth leads to righteousness.

—In many places in the Scriptures and in this passage, communal prayer is very powerful.

—James ended his letter with appeals to God's people to pray.

—He warned the rich that their wealth would be useless in the last days and they would suffer because of their injustices and greed.

—He appealed to the faithful to be patient until the second coming of Jesus. The time was short, so they needed to endure rather than place their salvation in jeopardy by complaining against others or swearing an oath.

—We are to pray, sing songs of praise, anoint the sick, and confess to one another.

—This is the summation of James's letter; it is a letter about community—how important it is, what it is, and how to live in one.

—Prayer is at the heart of the believer's life and at the core of community life.

CHILDREN

Children Topic: Pray Always

Key Verse: James 5:16

Print Passage: James 5:13–18

—James teaches that personal prayer is a right response for one who is in trouble and the use of songs of praise is a good way to express one's joy.

—The prayers of faithful church leaders are often part of God's healing process.

—When we have mistreated persons, we need to ask God for forgiveness and ask them to forgive us.

—If our sin has affected the congregation, it is necessary to confess our faults publicly.

I. INTRODUCTION

A. Prayer

The doctrine of prayer is not an appendix to be added after one has completed the basic doctrines of the Christian faith. A view of prayer is essential to one's view of God's relation to the world and humanity's relation to God. Therefore, as we begin this lesson on prayer, it is instructional for us to take note of Jesus' teaching on the subject.

Christ's doctrine of prayer is dominated by His insistence upon the fatherhood of God. God is essentially our Holy Father. God acts in a fatherly manner to all human beings. But He acts on a different level to those who are His children through His grace. God takes into account their repentance and faith in Him.

B. Biblical Background: Faith Healing

This term describes healings that occur contrary to normal medical expectation, wrought by virtue of a special spiritual gift (1 Corinthians 12:28). Biblical miracles of this kind are regarded as having come through direct divine action in response to the faith of the sick person (Matthew 9:2; Mark 9:24).

Jesus Christ miraculously healed all types of disease and cast out demons. During His earthly ministry He gave His disciples power to heal diseases and cast out demons (Matthew 10:1). This power was also exercised after Pentecost, when again the need for faith is mentioned (Acts 14:9), and, more specifically, faith in Christ (Acts 3:16).

II. EXPOSITION AND APPLICATION OF THE SCRIPTURE

A. An Injunction to Church Members
(James 5:13-14)

Is any among you afflicted? let him pray. Is any merry? let him sing psalms. Is any sick among you? let him call for the elders of the church; and let them pray over him, anointing him with oil in the name of the Lord.

This passage addresses how the believer should respond to various circumstances of life. The first circumstance addressed is that of suffering. Herein, we are instructed, "If anyone is suffering, let him pray." The phrase used here is not a reference to any particular kind of suffering; rather, it includes physical sickness, undergoing economic hardship, emotional turmoil, and all kinds of unpleasantness. When the Christians encounter trouble of any sort, they are not to respond with either anger or frustration; rather, they are to pray.

James next addresses the Christian's proper attitude and behavior in times of plenty: "If there be among you anyone cheerful, let him sing psalms." The word *let*, in its original grammatical structure, means "to cultivate an inner attitude of singing." Psalms were the praise language of God's people, and therefore were to be used for singing praises to God. This passage teaches us to recognize, remember, and respond to God as the giver of all perfect gifts with songs of praise.

B. Prayer of Faith and Its Effect (James 5:15-16)

And the prayer of faith shall save the sick, and the Lord shall raise him up; and if he have committed sins, they shall be forgiven him. Confess your faults one to another, and pray one for another, that ye may be healed. The effectual fervent prayer of a righteous man availeth much.

Sickness is another circumstance that calls for prayer, and James gives us instructions about this. This passage has been the subject of much controversy and is, admittedly, difficult to understand. It is helpful, however, to keep in mind that this epistle was written to the Jews during the transitional period from Judaism to Christianity. As such, it will be recalled that when the twelve apostles were sent out by the Lord Jesus to the house of Israel, they were told and empowered to heal the sick by anointing them with oil (Mark 6:13). This is the only other instance in the New Testament where this method is known to have been employed.

This anointing is significant because of its definite connection to the testimony of Israel. There may be some truth in the view some have held that the oil itself was a healing ointment, and that God blessed the means used in connection with the recovery of the sick. But James specifically declares, "The prayer of faith will save the sick," though this would not necessarily mean that any virtue residing in the oil itself was ignored. When God answers prayer, He often blesses the means used.

The instructions here involve both oil and prayer; and both are to be done in an obedient exercise of faith (see the concluding remarks of this lesson for further discussion). Furthermore, if the sick person has committed sins, there will be forgiveness. There is much to commend to the idea that physical illness was a disciplinary agent sent by God to bring spiritual healing as a means to wholeness. In other words, God permits illnesses in the body to bring sinners to the point of recognition of their need for Him as healer. This recognition results in twofold blessings—spiritual and physical healing.

From the promise of verse 15 an inference is drawn. Since confession of sin and prayers of faith bring healing, Christians should confess their sins to one another and pray for one another. It is not merely the elders who are told to pray, but Christians in general. If a person has sinned against another, that person should confess the sin to the one who was offended. Then, the two of them should pray for one another in the confidence that the effective, fervent prayer of the righteous avail much. Believers are declared to be righteous because they have been accounted as such through the blood of Jesus. As such, their prayers are fully able to secure results.

When this verse is coupled with the teachings of the previous verse, there emerges the twin concept of confession before both God and human beings. Sin separates; it separates us from God. Therefore, the confession of sin to both is given here as a means of restoration. If persons are to be right with one another, they first must be right with God. On the other hand, fellowship with God cannot be claimed to exist where there is no fellowship with others.

C. The Exemplary Prayer Life of Elijah (James 5:17-18)

Elias was a man subject to like passions as we are, and he prayed earnestly that it might not rain: and it rained not on the earth by the space of three years and six months. And he prayed again, and the heaven gave rain, and the earth brought forth her fruit.

James closes this lesson on prayer by giving us an example of a praying man who achieved miraculous results. Elijah was a man with a nature like ours. He did not possess any superhuman powers; he was by nature a human being and nothing more. Elijah possessed a weaker nature, as do we. Elijah prayed that it would not rain; it did not rain and when he prayed again, the heaven gave abundance of rain (1 Kings 17:1; 18:42-45).

Two things characterized Elijah's prayer. First, Elijah was a righteous man. Second, he prayed fervently. His righteousness as an Old Testament figure was so declared because of his faith in God. However, to his faith he added *earnest* prayer. The idea here should be coupled with that of *fervent*. The former means "specific" and the latter means "with energy." Thus, the type of prayer to which James refers and exhorts is prayer that is characterized first by enthusiasm and perseverance, and secondly with specificity.

Elijah was on a mission for God. He was sent to King Ahab, who led the Israelites away from the path of God. Elijah did not fear the king and his false prophets. He called for a contest to determine whether Yahweh or Baal is God. We too are called to challenge the people in authority if they are leading us astray. When we stand for God He will stand up for us.

We who have been in church for long periods of time and have been given the privilege of praying in the public assembly and offering up prayers for the sick must be ever mindful of these two ideas. Fervent and earnest prayer is neither dead nor repetitious; it is not general, but specific. We must avoid the temptation to simply repeat memorized prayers that we have heard uttered by our forebears—for such prayer is vain.

We must also keep in mind the specific thing for which we are praying; in this instance, it refers to healing. There are times for general prayers, but most often, our prayers call for specificity.

III. CONCLUDING REFLECTIONS

The widespread practice of anointing with oil has been the subject of much discussion and deserves a comment as we reflect upon the teachings of this lesson. First, it must be remembered that the practice of anointing with oil is attested throughout all periods of Hebrew history. As such, it was used for religious, medicinal, and cosmetic purposes. The earliest usage in pre-monarchy times seems to be recorded in Genesis 28:18, where Jacob anointed the pillar he had erected in Bethel.

During the time of the Judges, it was assumed that a king was inducted into office by anointing (see Judges 9:8, 15). Since persons ritually anointed were believed to have received the holiness and virtue of the deity in whose name they were anointed, it was also believed that they received a special endowment of the Spirit of Jehovah (1 Samuel 10:10; 16:13). There was a transfer of divine powers and authority. By extension, "to anoint" became a metaphor for the bestowal of God's favor (Psalms 23:5; 92:10) for the designation of someone to a particular place or office.

The practice of anointing with oil continued into the New Testament period (Acts 10:38; 1 John 2:20, 27). In our lesson, James is addressing a Jewish audience, and as such, he refers to practices with which the Jews would have familiarity—thus the reference to the anointing with oil. The significant idea to be remembered is that the oil, though it may have had medicinal value, was used as a vehicle for the believers to demonstrate their faith. Therefore, for us, the practice of anointing with oil may be done if it is done in both obedience and faith.

Anointing should not be used as a substitute for prescribed medications. Conversely, if it is used as a demonstration of the church's obedience and faith in the God of the Bible, then its usage may be termed biblical. God can and does use anything to heal, if it is done in obedience and in faith. On the other hand, if it is not done in faith and obedience but, rather, as some kind of demonstration of spiritual power by those administering it, then it is cultic, unbiblical, and sinful.

PRAYER

Dear God, our heavenly Father, how thankful we are for the privilege of prayer. We are grateful that You have extended to us the privilege of entering into Your presence with the confidence that You hear us and that You care for us. Thank You for allowing us to cast all of our cares upon You. Strengthen us to develop more resolve to develop our prayer lives and to spend more time with You in prayer. It is in Jesus' name that we pray. Amen.

WORD POWER

Effectual, Fervent *(energoumene* [ener-gou-mene])—this is the root word for "energy." Here it means "to be active, efficient, putting energy into a task in order to complete it. This is the type of prayer Jesus prayed in Luke 22:44. Jesus prayed and the sweat from His face fell like drops of blood. That is praying with energy (effectual, fervent).

HOME DAILY BIBLE READINGS
(August 25-31, 2008)
Prayerful Community
> MONDAY, August 25: "Pray without Ceasing" (1 Thessalonians 5:16-22)
> TUESDAY, August 26: "The Plight of the Rich" (James 5:1-6)
> WEDNESDAY, August 27: "Patience and Endurance" (James 5:7-12)
> THURSDAY, August 28: "Pray for One Another" (James 5:13-15)
> FRIDAY, August 29: "The Prayer of the Righteous" (James 5:16-18)
> SATURDAY, August 30: "Stay with the Truth" (James 5:19-20)
> SUNDAY, August 31: "Prayer for Community Power" (Ephesians 3:14-21)

GLOSSARY OF TERMS

These words are from the lessons in this Commentary. They are carefully chosen to enable the superintendents, teachers, and pastors to lead in the in-depth study of the Word of God. The insight gleaned from them will deepen the spiritual life of the participants.

Authority (Greek: *exousia* [ek-sou-sia])—means privilege, force, or control. It also means delegating power to someone or something on behalf of another superior.

Beguile (Hebrew: *rahmah* [raw-maw])—to delude with persuasive words or covert actions; to deceive or betray someone.

Beguile (Greek: *exapatao* [eksa-pa-tao])—means to cheat without remorse. It is to deceive in order to accept falsehood for truth.

Bondswoman (Hebrew: `*amah* [aw-maw])—this word refers to a female slave, maid, or servant. It also means concubine.

Called (Hebrew: *qara* [kaw-raw])—to call someone out of obscurity and send the individual out on a mission. It also connotes the idea of encounter.

Christ (Greek: *Christ, Christos*)—anointed one, the official name of our Lord and Savior.

Cross (Greek: *starous* [stow-ros])—a stake or post set upright with a crossbeam. A cross was an instrument of capital punishment devised by the Romans.

Disciple (Greek: *mathetes*)—means pupil, or learner. The word describes one who professes to have learned certain principles from a leader and maintains them on that leader's authority.

Dominion (Hebrew: *radah* [raw-daw])—means to have supreme authority; to tread down under one's feet, to overpower, put under servitude, or crumble.

Dream (Hebrew: *chalom* [kha-lome])—a dream is a type of experience having moral, spiritual, and intellectual significance. It is a state of mind in which images, thoughts, and impressions pass through the mind during sleep (see Job 33:15-18).

Dumb (Greek: *siopao* [see-o pao])— to lack the power of speech; to become involuntarily silent for a period of time.

Dwell (Hebrew: *yashab*)—to sit down, loaf around, be at ease, settle down, and be less active, particularly in the things of God.

Fever (Greek: *puresso* [pu-res-so])—to burn. This type of fever refers to a high fever. The high temperature causes the body to suffer from dehydration.

Fornication (Greek: *porneia*)—means sexual immorality.

Hate (Hebrew: *sane;* Greek: *miseo*)—to detest, persecute, love less; a feeling contrary to love. Hatred begins from nursing a grudge against a brother or sister (see Genesis 27:41).

Heaven (Hebrew: *shamayim* [shaw-mah-yim])— It is the dwelling place of God (see Psalm 2:4; Deuteronomy 26:15).

Image (Hebrew: *tselem* [`se-lem])—a representative figure or likeness. Something cut out of wood, stone, or any concrete material.

Importunity (Greek: *anaideia* [annah-ee-die-ah])— persistence in making a request or demand.

Intreated (Hebrew: *arthar* [aw-thar])—to intercede and stand in the gap on behalf of someone who is under attack from an enemy.

Kindred (Hebrew: *mishpachal* [mis-paw-khaw])—a family, circle of relatives, or clan.

Lust (Greek: *epithumeo* [epi-thoo-meo])—to set the heart upon, to long for a forbidden object whether rightfully or wrongfully; an obsessive sexual craving.

Marriage (Greek: *gamos* [ga-mos])—the word *gamos* comes from the root *gam*, which is "to bind or to unite."

Mediator (Greek: *mesites* [me-see-tace])—a go-between, a reconciler, an intercessor, an arbitrator, or one who mends fences between two parties.

Oath (Hebrew: *horkomosia*)—a solemn statement to validate a promise.

Obeisance (Hebrew: *shachah*)—to bow, bend, or defer to a superior.

Patience (Greek: *hupomone*)—steadfastness despite opposition; to remain under, to maintain an unruffled temper, to have endurance under extreme circumstances.

Posterity (Hebrew: *she`eriyth* [she-ay-reeth])—means offspring, residual or surviving family members who keep a generation alive.

Recompense (Greek: *antapodoma* [anta-podo-ma])—a return of a favor, a payback, or an invitation to those who have invited you.

Scribe (Hebrew: *caphar* [saw-far]; Greek: *grammateis*)—a record keeper or transcriber. In religious connotations, it means a student of the Scriptures.

Soul (Hebrew: *nephesh*; Greek: *psuche*)—the vital existence of a human being. When God created the first human being (Adam), God breathed on him and he became a living soul. Our souls are an invisible element in our body, and only God knows where they are kept.

Sundry (Greek: *polumeroos* [polu-me-roos])—means many portions, or uncountable ways. The Old Testament messages came from different sources, times, and stages to the people of old. God revealed Himself in a progressive manner.

Throne (Hebrew: *kicce*; Greek: thronos)—a royal seat. A throne symbolizes kingly power, authority, and dignity. It is an exalted position of earthly kings, rulers, and judges.

Tongue (Hebrew: *lashon*; Greek: *glossa*)—the organ of taste and speech, it is used variously in the Bible. The tongue can be sharpened like a sword (Psalm 64:3) or behave like a serpent (Psalm 140:3). This means that the tongue can utter poisonous words (Psalm 5:9).

Transgression (Hebrew: *pesha*; Greek: *parabasis*)—means to revolt morally, nationally, or religiously. It is a rebellious act inwardly or outwardly against the law or duty.

Treasure (Greek: *thesauros*)—wealth, literally or figuratively. In the New Testament, treasure has two meanings: (1) material treasure—money or other valuable goods; and (2) spiritual treasure (see Luke 12:33).

Witness (Greek: *maturios*)—one who is mindful, heeds instructions, or one who has seen, heard, or knows a matter with certainty (see Matthew 18:16; Hebrews 12:1).

Worship (Hebrew: *shachah* [shaw-kaw])—prostration in terms of paying homage to royalty or God. It also refers to bowing down in reverence to a higher power. In the religious context, it is paying reverence to God almighty.